Campaigns of
The 146th Regiment
New York State Volunteers

Also known as Halleck's Infantry, the Fifth Oneida,
and Garrard's Tigers

Compiled by
Mary Genevie Green Brainard

Preface and New Material
By Patrick A. Schroeder

Patrick A. Schroed

Foreword by
Brian C. Pohanka

SCHROEDER PUBLICATIONS
2000

ISBN: 1-889246-08-5

Printed by Sheridan Books
Fredericksburg, Virginia

SCHROEDER PUBLICATIONS
12 Camellia Drive
Daleville, VA 24083
www.civilwar-books.com

NEW MATERIAL
TABLE OF CONTENTS

NEW PHOTOGRAPHS

a

ACKNOWLEDGEMENTS

One of the most fascinating aspects of this project was getting in touch with so many descendants of the soldiers that served with the 146th New York. These people generously came forward with photographs and reference materials for this work. In at least one incident long lost relations were put in touch with each other through a shared interest in the book. Everyone I can think of that contributed in any way to this project are listed here in alphabetical order. Without their kind assistance this project would not have been possible.

There are several who deserve special mention for their contributions. The undertaking seemed possible after viewing the 30 or more photos of 146th New York soldiers in the collection of Donald Wisnoski. He continuously informed me of new images that came to light, as well as assisted with some research aspects, and put me in touch with numerous descendants. The acquisition of Alfred H. Palmer's (Co. C, 146th New York) scrapbook added immeasurably to the excitement of this project. Palmer's granddaughter, Cornelia Needham, contributed supplementary photos. The images from the collection of Michael J. McAfee illustrate some of the best examples of men in Zouave uniform, as well as several unique views of officers and early war subjects. The photographs of unit members at the Rome Historical Society proved a veritable treasure that has contributed significantly to the book. Brian C. Pohanka's images, editorial, and historical insight have added immensely to the completion of the project. A special thanks to thanks to David Plass, Daniel Miller, and the Hendrick Hudson Chapter of the Daughters of the American Revolution, for their contributions, especially the photograph that enhances the dust jacket and adds to the attractiveness of the book, and to my wife Maria, who expertly designed the dust jacket and checked after my grammar and formatting using her meticulous editing skills. Also, my heartfelt thanks to, Debbie Trieber, a granddaughter of Mary Genevie Green Brainard, who lent her encouragement and shared Mrs. Brainard's scrapbook with me.

Adriance Memorial Library, Poughkeepsie, NY; Harold Akers, Schuyler Lake, NY; Brian Bennett, Scottsville, NY; Michael F. Bremer, Colts Neck, NJ; Dave Bruinix, Macedon, NY; John P. Burdick, Clinton, NY; Thomas A. Canfield, Freeville, NY; Mary Cleary, Waterville, NY; Edmund D. Cocks, Petersburg, VA; Joel Craig, Germantown, NY; Russ Davis, Utica, NY; Melissa Delcour, Fredericksburg, VA; Guy DeMasi, Stamford, CT; Edward L. DeSanctis, Albany, NY; David Dudajek, Whitesboro, NY; Edward Entwhistle, Utica, NY; Edwina Allen Essex, Lebanon, OH; Ann H. Ford, Skaneateles, NY; Geoff Gorsuch, Franklin, OH; Randy Hackenburg, Boiling Springs, PA; Scott Harrington, Placentia, CA; Millicent Rader-Harris, Utica, NY; Keith L. Hendricks, Harwood,

MD; James J. Hennessey, Baltimore, MD; Roger Hunt, Rockville, MD; Hendrick Hudson Chapter of the Daughters of the American Revolution, Huson, NY; Gordon E. Johnson, Houston, TX; Monica Knight, Thendara, NY; Charles Brandegee Livingstone, Calais, ME; Thomas & Beverly Lowry, Woodbridge, VA; Micheal J. McAfee, Newburgh, NY; Al McGeehan, Holland, MI; Jean McGurk, Cassville, NY; John L. McGurk, Frankfort, NY; Daniel Miller, Caro, MI; Zoe Anne Miller, New York Mills, NY; Eric Mink, Fredericksburg, VA; Robert L. Mould, Utica, NY; Cornelia Needham, Lakeland, FL; Elmer Niles, Sauquoit, NY; Oneida County Historical Society, Utica, NY; Seward R. Osborne, Oliverbridge, NY; Town of Paris Historical Society, Paris, NY; Gene M. Parsons, Penn Yan, NY; Laura Perkins, Vernon, NY; Anna Pierce, Chadwicks, NY; David Plass, Poughkeepsie, NY; Brian C. Pohanka, Alexandria, VA; Charlotte Powell, Forest Grove, OR; Betty J. Quibell, Safety Harbor, FL; Harry Roach, Henryville, PA; Rome Historical Society, Rome, NY; Mark Schultz, Utica, NY; Ronald Schultz, Rome, NY; Leo G. Seaton, Camden, NY; Guy Smith, Halesite, NY; Diane E. Stebbins, Utica, NY; Jeanne Szatko, Utica, NY; Richard K. Tibbals, Berwyn, IL; Mildred Timmerman, Utica, NY; Debbie Treiber, Port St. John, FL; United States Army Military History Institute, Carlisle, PA; William C. Weber, Rome, NY; Michael Welch, Atlanta, GA; Matthew Williamson, Bear, DE; Michael Winey, Mechanicsburg, PA; Donald Wisnoski, Chadwicks, NY.

FOREWORD

No Northern state provided more men for the Union war effort than New York. And in the early autumn of 1862, with the Federal armies hard-pressed by a determined foe, and with ranks depleted by battle and disease, the Empire State answered the call for volunteers willing to support the Republic for a three-year term of service.

The citizens of Oneida County were not to be found wanting amidst the crisis, and the "Fifth Oneida" regiment or "Halleck Infantry" as the unit was also known, was conceived with a sense of patriotic obligation that scarcely needed the added inducement of the bounty money local businessmen had contributed to lure recruits to the colors. The war had long since been recognized as a grim business—casualty lists from the recent bloodbath at Antietam attested to that. Thus with the unfamiliar heft of knapsack and musket, and clad in uniforms of Federal blue, the men of the 146th New York Volunteer Infantry departed for the front as so many thousands had before them.

These New Yorkers were fortunate to learn the profession of arms under the stern tutelage of a veteran Regular Army officer. Colonel Kenner Garrard had graduated from West Point in the Class of 1851, and served his military apprenticeship as a dragoon and cavalryman on the Western frontier. He expected his volunteers to live up to the standards of the "Old Army," and while they occasionally bridled at their commander's discipline, the men from Oneida were likewise proud to call themselves "Garrard's Tigers."

These fledgling soldiers had much to prove—to their neighbors and their county, to their colonel and to themselves. Their determination to acquit themselves with honor was given added impetus by their regiment's assignment to General George Sykes's Second Division of the Army of the Potomac, a division that was largely comprised of U.S. Regulars—men who were looked upon as something of an "Old Guard" amidst the tens of thousands of state volunteers that made up the bulk of Major General Ambrose Burnside's army.

Upon their arrival at Warrenton, Virginia, on November 13, 1862, Colonel Garrard's 146th was attached to the lone volunteer brigade in Sykes's division—a force commanded by another Military Academy alumnus, Colonel Gouverneur Kemble Warren. Some two weeks earlier the newly organized 140th New York had likewise joined Warren's brigade. Largely recruited in the Rochester area, that unit was led by the brilliant Irish-born Colonel Patrick O'Rorke—first in the West Point Class of June 1861—and like Garrard and Warren a devoted proponent of military professionalism.

The third unit in the brigade was Colonel Warren's former outfit, the 5th New York Volunteer Infantry—better known as "Duryée's Zouaves." Garbed in the exotic red and blue uniform of the famed French colonial troops, the worn regalia and sun-browned faces of these American Zouaves attested, like their depleted ranks and bullet-torn banners, to hard and unremitting service.

f

Considered by many observers to be the best-drilled and disciplined volunteer regiment in the Army of the Potomac, these "Red Devils" were veterans, and they made sure the "fresh fish" of the 140th and 146th knew it.

What many of the new arrivals did not know was that their assignment to Warren's brigade was due not only to the West Point backgrounds of their respective commanders, but to the fact that they, too, were intended to receive the colorful Zouave attire made famous by the hard-fighting 5th New York.

On September 22, five days after the battle of Antietam, the charismatic and controversial commander of the Army of the Potomac, Major General George B. McClellan, had ordered Colonel Warren to proceed to New York to select three of the new regiments for assignment to his brigade. "These regiments are to be organized, armed, equipped, and uniformed in the same manner as the 5th Regiment of New York Volunteers," McClellan informed Warren, "and with that regiment are designed to form a brigade to be commanded by yourself." Apparently McClellan had assured Warren of a brigadier's star, for on September 26, the latter wrote Lieutenant Colonel Hiram Duryea of the 5th New York: "I am promised promotion so that yours is certain too."

On October 6, Warren, who was visiting his family home at Cold Spring, informed division commander Sykes that Colonel Garrard's 146th New York was nearly ready to start for the front. "He wishes to come in the Brigade," Warren wrote, "and we cannot do better than take him." Charles G. Bartlett, son of a West Point professor, a former captain in the 5th New York and now Lieutenant Colonel of the 150th New York, was also anxious that his unit—organizing at Poughkeepsie—be assigned to Warren's brigade. The third regiment that Gouverneur Warren desired for his command was the 165th New York, a natural choice as unlike the 146th and 150th, the 165th had already been issued the Duryée Zouave uniform, and was officered in large part by veterans of the "Old Fifth."

As fate would have it both the 150th and 165th were assigned elsewhere; but Warren gladly accepted the services of the 140th, having been favorably impressed with Patrick O'Rorke, whom he had known at West Point during his pre-war tenure as an instructor at the Military Academy. Warren was disappointed, however, to find that the requisite number of Zouave uniforms needed to outfit the new regiments was for the time being unavailable. Both the 140th and 146th marched to war in more traditional garb, though as late as November 30, Lieutenant Henry H. Curran of the 146th noted: "The regiment as well as our whole brigade, is to be furnished with the Zouave dress, thus forming what will be known as the Zouave Brigade."

Plans for a Zouave Brigade fell by the wayside when its most significant advocate, General McClellan, was relieved of command of the Army of the Potomac. Seven months passed, and the 146th New York earned the status of veterans through hard campaigning and combat experience in the battles of Fredericksburg and Chancellorsville, before the concept was revived through an interesting turn of events.

Like a number of other Federal units recruited at the outset of the war, the 5th New York Infantry had been mustered in for a two-year term of service. Immediately following the Union defeat at Chancellorsville, those Duryée Zouaves who had signed up in the spring of 1861 received the welcome and long anticipated orders to return to Manhattan for muster out. However, the 5th New

York also had on its rolls 325 soldiers who had enlisted, subsequent to the unit's initial organization, for a three-year term of service. Much to their chagrin, these three-year men learned that rather than return home with their comrades they would be required to serve out their time—in the ranks of the 146th New York.

Some of those 325 Zouaves were absent sick in northern hospitals, or on detached duty. Others risked punishment for desertion by going back to New York with the two-year men come what may. In the end 234 veterans of the 5th New York were transferred into the 146th, and for a while their sullen and occasionally disobedient behavior contrasted sharply with the famed discipline of the "Red Devils." But over time they settled back into military routine, made friends with the Oneida volunteers, and imparted their traditions of valor and skill to their new comrades. In the battles to come 106 of the former 5th New Yorkers became casualties, 32 dying on the field of battle, of wounds, or as prisoners of war.

A result of this influx of Zouave soldiers into the ranks of the blue clad 146th New York was the resurrection of plans to uniform the regiment in Zouave attire. The long deferred metamorphosis occurred in the first week of June 1863, and for the remainder of the war "Garrard's Tigers" would march, fight and die wearing short jackets, tasseled fezzes and baggy trousers— à la Zouave.

While the dark blue, red-trimmed jackets and scarlet pantaloons of the 5th New York had closely resembled the clothing worn by French Zouave regiments, the uniform that was issued to the 146th New York in June of 1863— light blue in color, with yellow trim—was in fact inspired by the garb of the French Army's Tirailleurs Algériens (Algerian Sharpshooters), or "Turcos" as they were popularly known. Like the Zouaves, the Turcos traced their origins to French North African campaigns of the 1840s, and the exotic, loose-cut clothing worn by tribes indigenous to that region. But while Zouave units were by the mid 1850s composed entirely of French-born personnel, the three Turco battalions in French service consisted of native North Africans whose officers and senior non-commissioned officers were mostly Frenchmen. Zouave and Turco alike shared a reputation for dash and devil-may-care bravado that seized the public's imagination as the epitome of what elite light infantry units were expected to be.

Sporting their Turco uniforms, the 146th New York took part in the defense of Gettysburg's Little Round Top, where their newly appointed brigadier, Stephen H. Weed, fell with a fatal wound. Their garb made them conspicuous on that strategic, boulder-strewn summit, though the unit's casualties were far less than those suffered by their comrades in the 140th New York, whose gallant Colonel Patrick O'Rorke was numbered with the slain.

In January of 1864, as the contending armies rested in their respective winter encampments, both the 140th New York and 155th Pennsylvania were in turn issued their own distinctive variations of the Zouave uniform. A year and four months after the idea had first been proposed, the Fifth Corps finally had its Zouave Brigade. Later reinforced by the 5th New York Veteran Zouaves, the colorful brigade would endure the trials and tribulations of the Army of the Potomac through to the bitter end at Appomattox—their presence an obvious refutation of the popular but historically invalid notion that fancy uniforms were somehow impractical, and disappeared after the first few months of the conflict.

With the regimental pride and expectations of battlefield glory that the Zouave uniform evoked, there came a price to be paid in blood. For the Fifth

Corps's Zouave Brigade that grim reckoning came on May 5, 1864, as Grant began his relentless effort to vanquish Lee's Army of Northern Virginia in the battle of the Wilderness.

No survivor could ever forget the fury and desperation of their doomed charge across Saunders Field, one of the few open parcels of ground amidst the scrub and underbrush of that hellish battlefield. The 146th New York was particularly hard hit; their loss of 312 men—65 of them fatally injured—was the second highest toll of any Federal regiment in the battle. The dead included Colonel David T. Jenkins and Major Henry H. Curran—the latter awaiting his promotion to lieutenant colonel. The bodies of those talented, articulate and brave young officers were never recovered; like so many others they simply vanished in the holocaust of smoke and flame.

The subsequent engagements at Spotsylvania, North Anna and Cold Harbor; the Siege of Petersburg with its series of fights for control of the Weldon Railroad, and the final climactic battles at White Oak Road and Five Forks claimed the lives of 53 more men of the 146th, with many others crippled by wounds or illness. The Zouaves, like that grand Army of the Potomac, passed through their ordeal with dignity and honor—often thwarted, but ultimately victorious.

* *

Despite the regiment's unique uniform and gallant record, it is unlikely that the deeds of the 146th New York would have been chronicled while its veterans still lived were it not for the dedication and commitment of a remarkable woman named Mary Genevie Green Brainard.

A near contemporary of the young men who had marched off to fight for their country in the autumn of 1862, and like them a native of Oneida County, Mrs. Brainard was 65 years old when the regiment's fiftieth anniversary commemoration fired her determination to undertake a detailed history of the 146th. Recognizing her obvious devotion and considerable vigor, former Captain Alonzo I. King and 50 comrades who attended that October 1912 reunion welcomed the idea and lent Mrs. Brainard their wholehearted cooperation. Brainard zealously set about her task, incorporating wartime letters and diaries, and drawing from the personal recollections of Captain King and the other old soldiers. Adopting the personal pronoun "we," she wrote as if the voice of the regiment—which indeed she was.

Born at Hubbardsville, New York, on August 21, 1847, Mary Genevie Green was the daughter of a prominent banker and could trace her lineage to John and Priscilla Alden of Mayflower fame. Educated at a district school and three local seminaries, she cherished a life-long interest in poetry and literature, and became an accomplished writer. At 23 she married Ira DeWane Brainard, a successful businessman in the town of Waterville, which became her home. By the time of her death in 1931, Mary Brainard had outlived her husband and two of their three children; but her outgoing personality ensured that the last decades of her long life were neither lonely nor sedentary.

A big woman, forceful and energetic, Mrs. Brainard zealously undertook a variety of philanthropic causes for the betterment of her community. She financed a local chapter of the YMCA and construction of the Waterville Public

Library, as well as the rebuilding of the Methodist Church to which she donated a Tiffany stained glass window. A true social activist, she was a fervent supporter of Black education in the deep South, and of overseas missionary work. She sponsored a local Rescue Mission and personally saw to it that migrant workers and homeless "tramps" were fed, housed and given a healthy dose of religious inspiration. By authoring a history of the 146th New York, Mary Brainard sought to honor the service and sacrifice of her fellow citizens in the cause of the Union.

Nearly two years in the making, the regimental did the unit proud, and was hailed by the aging veterans as a worthy tribute to the earnest patriotism of their youth. Moreover, despite the plethora of war-related volumes published in the half century since Appomattox, press views were uniformly favorable. Reflecting the conventions of the time, most newspaper critics professed some astonishment that the history was the product of a woman's research and writing skills.

"It is a very unusual thing for a woman to undertake such a task," noted the Worcester Massachusetts *Gazette*, "and that she has performed it unusually well is greatly to her credit and equally to the satisfaction of the veterans themselves." Acknowledging the importance of regimental histories for "historians of the future," the *Boston Transcript* remarked, "The One Hundred Forty-Sixth Regiment is fortunate in having so devoted a friend and talented historian."

In a typically magnanimous gesture, Mrs. Brainard presented a copy of her book, free of charge, to every survivor of the regiment who was a member of the veterans' organization. "It has been a great pleasure to prepare this work," she wrote in an April 28, 1915, letter to 146th veteran William L. Snyder, "I trust you will overlook the errors that perhaps appear and accept the volume as the most that I could do to perpetuate the record of your valiant service in behalf of our beloved country." The veterans themselves were effusive in their praise. "I can not find words to express my thanks," wrote Gilbert E. Martin, a former private in Company B: "I prize it very highly & so will my children & grandchildren after I am gone; it is the most complete work of the kind I ever saw. It tells it just as I remember it."

At least one old soldier floated a tentative marriage proposal to his regimental chronicler, whose husband Ira Brainard had passed away shortly before she finished her book. Writing from Oklahoma City on May 15, 1915, John H. Yourdan reported, "I am a widower of nearly two years & desirous of becoming acquainted with an ex-soldier widow with a view to matrimony.... I sincerely hope you will take no offence from the above." Mary Brainard's response has not survived, and while she remained a widow the affection of her soldiers was manifested by their gift of a beautiful engraved silver pitcher as a token of their undying esteem.

I trust that this heavily illustrated reprint of Mary Genevie Green Brainard's regimental history will serve as a memorial not only to the fighting Zouaves of the 146th New York, but to the care and devotion of the woman who so ably told their story.

Brian C. Pohanka
Alexandria, Virginia

PREFACE

The 146th New York has long been my favorite Civil War regiment. Having been raised, like the regiment, in Oneida County, I felt a close connection to those soldiers. The 146th had a solid fighting reputation, and for the last two years of its service wore exotic Zouave uniforms. Oneida County sent four other regiments to the war prior to the formation of the 146th. The 14th, 26th, 97th, and 117th all proved to be reliable combat units. But when all is said and done, beyond a doubt, the 146th was the most famous regiment raised in the county.

While still a teenager, I purchased a copy of Mary Geneive Green Brainard's book, *Campaigns of the 146th Regiment New York State Volunteers*, and read it with enthusiasm. I was fascinated with the rigors of their service, intrigued by their battles, and saddened by the loss of brave commanders David T. Jenkins and Henry H. Curran—their bodies never recovered, their fate a mystery. The book's numerous photographs, small as they were, helped me identify with those soldiers.

My fascination with the 146th has never waned, and I wondered whether or not to undertake a retelling of their story. But a competent regimental history had already been written. Interest in the regiment appears to be on the rise—partly due to their Zouave uniform. Was there anything that could be done to honor the brave soldiers of the 146th New York to insure that they are not forgotten? Today it is difficult to obtain a copy of Mrs. Brainard's book. Over the years, the demand and price continued to increase. Not long ago, I acquired a scrapbook of a drummer of the 146th with numerous images of individuals belonging to the regiment; the unit seems to be a highly photographed group. For two years, I collected photographs to use in this reprint of Mrs. Brainard's regimental history.

The principal additions to the reprint are a photographic section, complete with biographical sketches of the soldiers depicted, and an index that makes the book a much more efficient reference source. Initially, I expected that perhaps 75 photographs might be incorporated into the new work. However, with several newspaper articles written about the project, a little advertising, and word of mouth, over 150 photographs have been assembled. The generous contributions of descendants, collectors, and research institutions, have added considerably to the magnitude of this project.

Putting a picture of a soldier with a name, in a sense brings them to life once more. Mrs. Brainard's book already had numerous photos, but there evidently are plenty more out there. For the most part I have not reused photographs already printed in the original volume unless there was more to the photo than revealed in the book, the clarity is considerably improved, or it is a different view of the subject. I was primarily interested in discovering new images, and many of the photographs are published here for the first time. I've chosen to include as many different portraits of a soldier that could be found. In some cases, I have incorporated both pre and post war images. This may assist to identify previously anonymous photos in the future. In several instances I used newspaper pictures that may not reproduce too well, but I deemed it better to include them rather than not having an image of the soldier. Accompanying each photograph is a biographical profile, derived from service and pension records at the National Archives, as well as newspaper accounts and information provided by descendants. Sometimes the photographs depict the soldier in civilian attire or in the uniform of another unit. Representatives from the 5th New York (Duryée's Zouaves), the 17th New York (Westchester Chasseurs), and the 44th New York (Ellsworth's Avengers) also appear in the photographic section. These men were later consolidated with the 146th, each man to serve out his unexpired term of service.

Between the new material at the beginning and the photographic section at the end, Mrs. Brainard's book is reproduced in fidelity—with the exception of new photographs added to the blank side of the photographic pages in the first printing. The original book also included two fold out maps—one of troop positions at the Battle of the Wilderness, the second showing the territory covered by the 146th New York during the war. The Wilderness map has been inserted on the page facing 181. The second map, large and unwieldy, has not been included as it traces the movements of the 146th, which mirror that of the Army of the Potomac. Maps with this information are abundant and relatively easy to locate.

Above all, I wished to reprint and enhance Mrs. Brainard's book as a worthy tribute to the men who served in the gallant 146th, to ensure that they are not forgotten. They were volunteers, who willingly left their parents, wives, children, and occupations, to do their part to save the Union. I sincerely hope that this volume will ensure that these men are remembered, and that their heroic deeds and sacrifices will live on for present and future generations.

Patrick A. Schroeder
Daleville, Virginia

MARY GENEVIE GREEN BRAINARD
Mrs. Mary Genevie Green Brainard 1847 – 1931. (Donald Wisnoski Collection)

Campaigns of
The One Hundred and Forty-Sixth Regiment

New York State Volunteers

Also known as Halleck's Infantry, the Fifth Oneida, and Garrard's Tigers

Compiled by

Mary Genevie Green Brainard

With 56 Illustrations and Maps

G. P. Putnam's Sons
New York and London
The Knickerbocker Press
1915

The Knickerbocker Press, New York

INTRODUCTION

THE groups of girls sewing and knitting for the war refugees across the water remind me of my girlhood days. The church in a little country village of Central New York, where I lived, formed a "Ladies' Aid Society" to work for the soldiers. All the old linen that had been saved for years by our mothers, was brought out and the girls scraped the lint from it for use in the hospitals. We made quilts, knit mittens, and packed boxes that were distributed through the Christian Commission. That was fifty years ago, but it is still fresh in memory.

It was war, dreadful war then as it is now, but in our own beloved land. When the call came for men in the early sixties, many of my friends and acquaintances answered promptly and marched to the front. It is the experiences of one of the regiments that went from my own neighborhood that I have tried to relate in this volume. What a pity that Curran was not spared to relate in his own graceful language the story of his regiment! The Fifth Oneida has no historian of its own. It has been my pleasure to know many of the officers and men of this valiant regiment, and I have often heard them recount their adventures. As a labor of love, therefore, and not for gain, I have endeavored, during the past few years, to gather together their fragments of stories and crystallize them into this narrative. Many have aided in the work. To give credit to all, whose kindly suggestion or bit of evidence has been of help, would be impossible in this short space. Major A. I. King has been a constant help.

Horace B. Sweet, whose father was Captain of Company F, prepared the maps and aided us in other ways. My son, C. G. Brainard, has worked with me in gathering data and in writing. Mr. C. C. Cunningham passed two summers in interviewing survivors of the regiment, in consulting authorities, and in writing. Chas. L. King, secretary of the 146th Regiment Volunteers' Association, has also aided materially in many ways.

The survivors of the regiment, one and all, have been most gracious to me, freely placing at my disposal old letters, photographs, diaries, scrapbooks, and old newspaper clippings. Captain Pitcher's letters and diary, Lieutenant William Wright's diary, and others have been freely used. One of my greatest helps was the letters of Lieut.-Colonel Curran. These letters were published in book form for private distribution in 1867, entitled *Memorial of H. H. Curran by Edw. North*. A list of the principal authorities consulted may be found in the appendix. I have endeavored, in footnotes through the text, to give the authority in each case, but may perhaps have neglected to do this in every case; if so, I wish to say that I have used all sources of information freely and desire to give full credit here.

I tried to follow a style that would indicate the narrative was a composite, and therefore in referring to the regiment used the personal pronoun "we," and also tried to weave in the story or history of the regiment so it would make a connected narrative of one unit of the army of which it was a part. In other words, to fit the regiment into its place in the Brigade, Division, Corps, and Army respectively. Not a history of the war, but of this regiment in the war.

There are necessarily many errors, although I have tried to eliminate error and inaccuracy as much as possible, but such as it is I offer it as my contribution to keep fresh in the minds of those who may chance to read the glorious deeds and valiant service to our country of the men of Oneida

County, many of whom have gone Beyond and some of whom are still our friends and neighbors.

MARY GENEVIE GREEN BRAINARD.

WATERVILLE, N. Y.,
December, 1914.

This chapel made of logs, poles, and mud was erected by the men of the 146th New York State Volunteers, with the aid of other men of their brigade, near Beverly Ford, Va., 1863. Many of the noted generals of the Civil War attended services here

CONTENTS

Contents

ILLUSTRATIONS

History of the 146th Regiment

CHAPTER I

FROM ROME TO ARLINGTON HEIGHTS

THE War of the Rebellion had been in progress for fifteen months, and the people of the North had come to know something of the cost, misery, and sacrifice it entailed. Half a million men already had been sent to the front by the States that remained loyal to the Union. It was evident, however, that to continue the war with any prospect of success would require a much larger contribution of men. The governors of eighteen of the loyal States, therefore, suggested to President Lincoln, in a joint letter dated June 28, 1862, that he extend through them another call for three hundred thousand men to be enlisted for three years, and accordingly, a few days later, the President issued his third call for volunteers.

To this appeal, New York State, which had already furnished over a hundred and forty thousand men, now prepared to answer by contributing twenty thousand men more than its quota of 59,705. On July second, the day following the President's call, Governor Morgan issued the following proclamation, which was in full harmony with the rising spirit of patriotism in the State:

This appeal is to the State of New York; it is to each citizen. Let it come to every fireside. Let the glorious example of the

I

Revolutionary period be our emulation. Let each feel that the commonwealth now counts upon his individual strength and influence to meet the demands of the government. The period has come when all must aid. New York has not thus far stood back. Ready, and more than willing, she has met every summons to duty. Let not her history be falsified, nor her position lowered.

This sentiment met a hearty response throughout the State, which was divided into districts for the purpose of systematically raising the required number of men. Oneida County, known as the Nineteenth District in this apportionment, had already furnished three regiments of infantry which were rendering good service at the front, besides sending considerably more than its quota of men for the cavalry, artillery, and engineers' corps. The committee appointed for the Nineteenth District, of which Honorable Horatio Seymour, a short time later elected Democratic Governor of New York, was chairman, felt that they would be doing all that could be expected of them if they were able to enroll one regiment. The first meeting of the committee was held at Bagg's Hotel in Utica on July 14, 1862, and by the twentieth of August, scarcely a month from the time actual enrollment began, nearly eleven hundred men had enlisted. One thousand of these were enrolled as the One Hundred and Seventeenth New York Volunteers, known as the Fourth Oneida. On August 22, 1862, they left Rome and served subsequently in the Department of Virginia, the Department of the South, and the Army of the James.

Even after the full enrollment for the One Hundred and Seventeenth Regiment had been completed, the applications for enlistment continued to come in. The committee determined therefore to use as a nucleus for the formation of another regiment the men who had been left when the full quota of the One Hundred and Seventeenth Regiment was filled. On Tuesday, August 19, 1862, the State authorities gave formal permission to complete the organization of an additional regiment, the Fifth Oneida, and Mr. David T.

Colonel David T. Jenkins

Killed at the Wilderness

Colonel James G. Grindlay

Brevet Brigadier-General

Colonel Kenner Garrard

Later Brig.-Gen. and Brevet Maj.-Gen.

Lt.-Col. Henry H. Curran

Killed at the Wilderness

Lt.-Col. Peter C. Claesgens

JESSE J. ARMSTRONG

Armstrong was 32 years old when he enrolled on Sept. 3, 1862, at Rome, and mustered in as captain of Co. B on Oct. 10, 1862. Sick with "Bilious Inflammatory Rheumatism" in Mar. and Apr. 1863, he rejoined the regiment before the Battle of Chancellorsville and was slightly wounded at Gettysburg on July 2, 1863. Promoted lieutenant colonel on Oct. 23, 1863, and in temporary command of the regiment at the end of Dec. 1863, his military ability could not sustain him in such as position. Upon the request of Col. David T. Jenkins, a board of officers was appointed "to examine the capacity, qualifications and efficiency" of Armstrong. With an unfavorable finding looming, "for the good of the service" he resigned his commission on Apr. 1, 1864. Armstrong died Feb. 21, 1880, at Rome. This photo of Armstrong has a Brady back mark. (Donald Wisnoski Collection)

Jenkins, of Vernon, was appointed adjutant to superintend the enrollment and to take charge of the regiment until a regular commander was chosen. The military committee immediately invited applications from proper persons in the various towns in the county to recruit for the new regiment, and at the same time authorized the payment of the full bounties, including national, state, and county—$200.00 in all,—to every volunteer.

The recruiting offices in the cities and villages were re-opened, and a wave of patriotic enthusiasm swept over the county which bade fair to complete the enrollment within an unusually short period of time. Those were indeed stirring days. Each town vied with its neighbor, each ward with the adjacent ward, and every man and woman con-stituted himself and herself a committee of one to secure volunteers for this, the latest Oneida regiment. Bonfires, torchlight processions, brass bands, and the like usually associated with political campaigns were everywhere in evidence. War meetings were held in churches, school-houses, and other public buildings in towns and at the coun-try crossroads. Soldiers on leave of absence from the front encouraged the work by their appearance at these meetings in full regimental regalia, or traveled through the country districts in wagons, accompanied by a band and a speaker whose persuasive powers were calculated to fire the most dimly smoldering spark of patriotism in the heart of man or boy.

Early in August, President Lincoln issued a fourth call for volunteers, and efforts to enroll men were redoubled. By order of the mayor of Utica, all business in that city was suspended after four o'clock each day. Bells were rung at that time, and the remainder of the day devoted to the work of recruiting. The newspapers throughout the county per-formed their part by publishing stirring appeals, calling every man to come to the aid of the Union.

It was during this period of unparalleled enthusiasm and

patriotic zeal, accompanied by the sound of martial music and the sight of thousands of gay banners streaming from every house and public building, that the recruiting of the Fifth Oneida was carried on. The number of enrollments increased daily. Recruits were gathered from every walk of life. The pulpit and college contributed their share, and likewise the workshop, the loom, and the harvest-field. The men and boys of Oneida County cheerfully volunteered their services and, if need be, their lives, for the work of preserving the unity of the Nation.

On August twenty-sixth, by order of Adjutant Jenkins, the recruits were commanded to report at Camp Huntington, in Rome, as fast as they were enrolled.[1] Camp Huntington, which had been so named as a tribute to Honorable B. N. Huntington, a member of the military committee who resided in Rome, was ideally located. The camp, which originally had been chosen by Colonel Pease as the rendezvous of the One Hundred and Seventeenth Regiment, the first of the Oneida County regiments to leave from Rome, was beautifully situated on dry and elevated ground in the extreme western part of the village, about three quarters of a mile from the Courthouse on James Street. The lot, comprising about twenty acres, was owned by Mr. Enoch Armstrong. It was surrounded by a high rail fence, and was bordered on the south by Dominick Street and on the north by Liberty Street. The regimental buildings, consisting of barracks, kitchen, and mess-houses, were the only ones on the ground. The quartermaster's department was placed within convenient distance of the main entrance to the camp, which

---

[1] The companies were recruited principally: A at Utica; B at Vérnon, Rome, and Annsville; C at Utica, Rome, and Marcy; D at Boonville, Hawkinsville, Rome, and Whitestown; E at Camden, Augusta, Rome, Utica, and Marshall; F at Utica, Lee, Rome, Florence, Annsville, Ava, Marcy, and Whitestown; G at Clinton, Kirkland, Bridgewater, and Plainfield; H at Utica, Rome, and Sangerfield; I at Trenton, Remsen, Western, Westmoreland, Steuben, Lowell, Rome, Vernon, and Verona; K at Paris, Sangerfield, Clayville, Utica, Marcy, Clinton, Deansville, Marshall, and Whitesboro.

The Historic Camp Huntington at Rome, N. Y., as it Appeared in 1862

From a pen sketch by F. S. Honsinger

Here the One Hundred and Forty-sixth Regiment drilled, preparing for war

UNIDENTIFIED

This unidentified member of the 146th New York appears here in the first uniform issued the regiment before leaving for the seat of war. The top of his hat apparently has the numeral "146" enclosed in a wreath. The dark blue pants, breast pocket and shoulder tabs—trademarks of "The New York State Jacket"—distinguish this first issue to the "Fifth Oneida." (Michael J. McAfee Collection)

was in the southeast corner of what is now the intersection of Dominick Street and Dockstater Avenue. The recruits were quartered in low, one-storied shacks which were constructed long enough to accommodate a company in a single shack. A level portion of the ground near the center of the camp was used as a parade- and drill-ground, and on the bright September days squads of men could be seen practicing the facings and marchings under the direction of the officers. The manual of arms and target practice were advanced lessons which the recruits did not learn until in camp near Washington, as there were only enough guns at Rome for use on guard duty.

The regiment received its numerical designation as the One Hundred and Forty-sixth New York Volunteers on September ninth and at that time there were nearly seven hundred and fifty men enrolled, the majority of whom were in camp at Rome. Colonel Henry S. Armstrong, of the State militia, now took charge of the camp, and under his supervision the work of organizing and drilling was continued.

Life in the camp at Rome was by no means irksome for us. Furloughs were freely granted and there were frequent diversions from the routine of drill and guard duty. Friends and relatives formed a constant stream of visitors. On Wednesday, September sixteenth, the Oneida County Fair opened at Rome, and Camp Huntington soon became one of its most attractive "side-shows." A custom was begun which at once met with our hearty approval. The ladies from each village in the county came to Rome on different days and treated the men from their village to a home-cooked dinner served on the camp-ground. Frequently, these functions were made the occasion of presenting a sword to one of the officers, or pistols to some of the men, so that by the time we left camp there was hardly a member of the regiment who did not have some weapon specially designed for the slaying of "Jeff" Davis, "Bobby" Lee, or "Stonewall" Jackson.

When the regiment received its numerical designation, Major De Lancey Floyd Jones, of the Eleventh United States Infantry, was commissioned as Colonel, but he was compelled to decline the position. As the time was drawing near for the regiment to leave for the front, it was essential that some-one be procured as soon as possible. Prominent Oneida County officials corresponded with the authorities at Washington and as a result the command of the regiment was offered to Lieutenant-Colonel Kenner Garrard, the commandant at West Point. A telegram was received from Colonel Garrard on September twenty-sixth, accepting the position and stating that he expected to arrive in Rome the following day, Saturday. Plans were immediately formulated for tendering him a fitting reception. A platform was hastily constructed at the entrance of the camp, speakers were secured, and preparations made for a hearty demonstration in his honor. Colonel Garrard arrived at Rome on the 3.10 P.M. train, Saturday, September twenty-seventh. The regiment was drawn up in two lines on Dominick Street, and then, preceded by the Rome and Utica bands, marched to Camp Huntington, where the principal features of the reception took place. Judge Bacon, of Rome, in welcoming our Colonel made a happy suggestion.

To more than any other man [said Judge Bacon], our thanks are due to Major-General Halleck for his service and attention in providing this regiment with an efficient commander. General Halleck is a native of Oneida County. This camp is almost within sight of his birthplace. Let us call this regiment the "Halleck Infantry."

Judge Bacon's proposal was received with cheers, which signified the hearty approval of the men, and our regiment thus received a name which brought us a signal honor after we arrived at Washington.

Even before we left Rome we were given an opportunity of ascertaining something of the character of our new commander. Colonel Garrard, being a regular officer and a graduate of West Point Academy, was a strict disciplinarian and conducted all regimental affairs with the highest degree of military precision. He was a well-built man of more than average height, with sandy hair and complexion, was slightly bald, and wore a heavy beard. His piercing gray eyes were capable of striking terror in the heart of anyone who incurred his displeasure. At first, we were all inclined to believe that he was a martinet, and it was not until we had had an opportunity of witnessing his sterling courage on the field of battle, and associating with him during miles of heavy marching, that we came to love and respect him. We soon found that he always had uppermost in his mind the welfare of the men under his command, a preoccupation which later manifested itself in many little incidents. Immediately on taking charge of the camp at Rome, Colonel Garrard ordered a thorough cleaning-up; more rigid rules were made relative to absences from camp, and the officers were required to lodge themselves at houses in the immediate vicinity of the camp instead of in hotels and boarding-houses in the center of the village. As the time drew near for us to proceed to the front, Colonel Garrard was more liberal in granting furloughs to those who wished another opportunity for visiting their families before we had to leave.

One very pleasant feature of our stay at Camp Huntington took place shortly before we left. This was a dinner for the entire regiment given by the ladies of Rome on October first. The mess-hall was decorated for the occasion and we were served with a banquet that was frequently recalled during months of hard campaigning.

Marching orders at last were received for Wednesday, October eighth, but the vast amount of work necessary to be done delayed our leaving until the succeeding Saturday, October eleventh. The men on furlough were recalled by means of notices published in the various newspapers, and for a few days Camp Huntington was the scene of great activity. The regiment was officially mustered into the service of the United States on October tenth, and on the following day we left for the front.

At noon on Saturday, October eleventh, the order to "fall in" was responded to with greater celerity than ever before. Our knapsacks, formed by wrapping clothing and other articles in a rubber blanket, were strapped on our shoulders. Ham and bread to last three days were put in our haversacks, which were carried at the left side by means of a strap over the shoulder. The regimental line was formed and we marched to the cars which had been run on a siding west of the railroad station and not far from the camp. Only a few friends were at the camp to bid us good-bye, and so quietly and unostentatiously was the march made to the train that numbers of people who had assembled along Dominick Street, expecting that we would march through the village to the railroad station, were not aware that the regiment had gone until it was almost too late to wave a last farewell.

As the train, consisting of some twenty-odd coaches, approached Utica, many of us anticipated receiving some token of remembrance or having one more interview with relatives and friends, but in this we were disappointed. The train reached Utica at three o'clock and a crowd of more than a thousand people had assembled there to bid us adieu. Sisters, wives, and mothers who had prepared delicacies and keepsakes as parting gifts ran along the platform as the train passed slowly through the station, in their eagerness to reach us. Some of the officers, who were in a car by themselves, jumped off the train, expecting it would stop. When the men attempted to follow suit, they found that the doors of the cars had been locked, to prevent just such an occurrence. Slowly the train rolled past the station, and left behind those who had been so eager to greet us. Hurriedly hands waved the adieus we had no time to speak, and familiar scenes and faces were soon lost in the distance. Such a leave-taking from our native county was not what we had expected, and many were the outspoken reproaches for what was then considered a great injustice.

We arrived in Albany at nine o'clock that evening and immediately marched to the Delavan House, where we were given sandwiches and coffee prepared by the ladies of Albany for the regiments passing through the city. As soon as the wants of the "inner man" had been satisfied, we were ferried across the Hudson and boarded a train on the Hudson River Railroad, which was waiting to convey us to New York. The night that followed was by no means a restful one. We slept as well as we could on the floors of the cars or on the seats, which were none too comfortable.

For some reason the train was delayed at Tivoli for three hours, so that it was ten o'clock Sunday morning before we arrived in New York City. From the railroad terminal we marched through Tenth Avenue, Houston Street, and Broadway to the "Park Barracks" in City Hall Park, where we were served with a "government dinner," which was palatable only because of the sauce of appetite with which our fast of the night had abundantly provided us. The day passed quietly, and at half-past five in the afternoon, not being able to obtain cars, we boarded two steamers for South Amboy, N. J. As we sailed down New York Bay, the setting sun lighted up the wonderful city which we were leaving behind, and a hush came over all who witnessed the beautiful scene. The two great rivers dotted with vessels flowed on either side of the narrow strip of land, teeming with life, which lay between. To the north could be seen the undulating hills of Harlem interspersed here and there with houses. To the east the city of Brooklyn scrambled up its steep heights, with the tree-clad hills of Long Island stretching southward and displaying a fast-disappearing mass of variegated foliage. To the west, the rugged highlands and palisades of New Jersey stood like sentinels over the bivouac of the great city.

We were not given much time for reflections, however, for the wind, which at first had gently fanned us, gradually increased in force. By the time the Narrows were reached our small vessels rolled and tossed to such a degree as to persuade many brave soldier boys to unpack their "natural haversacks." The night was extremely dark and after South Amboy was reached two hours were consumed in a contest with wind and wave in effecting a landing. Finally, the steamers were made fast to a skeleton wharf and the work of debarkation began. The beams composing the dock were some distance apart and great difficulty was experienced in getting from the boats to the shore. One man[1] slipped through the trestle and was drowned before any one could go to his rescue in the pitchy darkness.

The regiment was ashore, however, by midnight and immediately boarded a train for Philadelphia. We arrived at the Delaware River about half-past five the next morning and crossed on the ferry into Philadelphia. On arrival we were invited to breakfast at the "Cooper Shop Volunteer Refreshment Saloon," on Otsego Street. This was an enterprise conducted by the citizens of Philadelphia for feeding the men of all regiments passing through that place on their way to Washington. It was an undertaking of considerable magnitude, an entire regiment being accommodated at a time. The ladies of the city had charge of the service, and so well was it conducted that, although another regiment had breakfasted just previous to ours, the tables were neatly and tastefully arranged. The fare consisted of sliced bologna, cold ham, bread, butter, cheese, and hot coffee, all well prepared and heartily appreciated. The great hall was appropriately decorated with the national colors, and there was an atmosphere of hospitality and good cheer about the place. Before leaving, we joined in giving three cheers for the "City of Brotherly Love," which had not belied its name.

After breakfast, we marched about a mile and a half

[1] William H. Smith, private, Co. B.

to the Philadelphia, Wilmington and Baltimore Railroad Station, and waited there in a cold, drizzling rain until noon. A car containing several cases of whiskey was standing on a siding. The exploring instinct, which some of the boys had, was rewarded, while we were waiting for our train, by the discovery of this "extract of corn," as they facetiously called it. It was, as one of them remarked, "miserable in the superlative degree," but was, nevertheless, consumed within a short time after its discovery.

Our train for Baltimore was at last ready, and we were soon on our way to that city. Within an hour we passed through the beautiful country lying between Philadelphia and Wilmington. Many of the houses along the route were large and beautiful, and there was an air of prosperity about the neat farms.[1] The vegetables in the garden seemed as green as they are in New York in June. At Perryville our train was ferried over the Susquehanna River to Havre de Grace on a large boat accommodating twenty cars. After entering Maryland we saw the same evidence of prosperity and cultivation; even the negroes' huts were white-washed and looked neat and tidy. As we approached Baltimore, however, the land became more barren and uncultivated. The guards stationed along the railroad were posted at more frequent intervals as we neared the city. We entered Baltimore at about five o'clock in the evening and were received in a warm and enthusiastic manner. As the train drew in, a crowd of Union enthusiasts, waving flags and cheering lustily, surrounded the cars and escorted the train into the station. This reception upon our entrance was quite different from the one we received as we passed through the city to take the train for Washington. It was a silent march in the dusky twilight, with only now and then a handkerchief waved or a flag thrown out to greet us.

Before our departure for Washington we took supper at a "Volunteer Saloon" and then again boarded a train for the

[1] Letter of Lieutenant H. H. Curran.

Capital City, which we reached at six o'clock the following morning. We marched along Pennsylvania Avenue, past the Treasury Building, and then proceeded across the famous Long Bridge into Virginia. On both sides of the road leading from Long Bridge to Arlington Heights, which was our destination, were thousands of cattle, sheep, and hogs, the well-guarded treasures of the commissary department. Ambulances that passed us, carrying sick soldiers to the hospitals in Washington, were another evidence that we had finally come within close proximity to the army.

We were by this time considerably fatigued from three days and nights of travel. Near Fort Albany we filed to the right and reached Camp Seward at half-past three Monday afternoon, October the thirteenth. This was to be our camping-ground for a few weeks. Camp Seward was beautifully situated on an eminence known as Arlington Heights, about equally distant from Forts Albany and Richardson. We were some four miles from the new capitol, which in its magnificent proportions loomed in full view of our camp. While we lay at Arlington Heights, the present dome of the building was being built, and we were able to witness the daily progress of its construction. At our feet the tortuous Potomac crept along towards the ocean, as though loath to part with the attractive features of its lovely valley. To the westward, we could see miles upon miles of the land of "Old Dominion," the theatre of the gigantic conflict which was being waged between the two great sections of the Nation. Throughout our entire experience as a regiment we never had another camp-site which quite equaled this one in the charm of its location.

Immediately after our arrival at camp, rations were given out and rifles distributed to us, with ten rounds of ammunition for each man. General Casey, who commanded the defenses of Washington, soon came riding by with his staff and informed Colonel Garrard that an attack by the enemy that very night was within the range of possibilities.

We took seriously the order to be prepared to "fall in" immediately if the signal were given, and bivouacked on the ground with our rifles at our sides. Nothing occurred, however, and we enjoyed a pleasant slumber beneath the open sky, and woke up very much refreshed. We soon learned that it was the custom to inform new regiments on their arrival that an attack was imminent, in order to impress upon them the necessity for vigilance and precaution.

The next day tents arrived, and our regiment soon formed a small section of the great white city stretched along the west bank of the river opposite Washington. These tents were quite spacious, fifteen of them being sufficient to accommodate an entire company. Two large wall tents served as quarters for the officers. Various ingenious contrivances were fitted up within the tents by both officers and men, and we were soon quite comfortable.

CHAPTER II

FROM ARLINGTON HEIGHTS TO FALMOUTH

THE process of transforming the "Halleck Infantry" from civilians into soldiers now began in earnest. After days of arduous drilling under the expert tutelage of Colonel Garrard we soon achieved quite a degree of perfection in military tactics. The weather, during our stay at Arlington Heights, was ideal for such work. The days, except for an occasional haze that pervaded the atmosphere, were clear and cloudless. The nights gradually became warmer than when we first arrived, and it seemed like early September weather.

The men were freely granted furloughs and it was not long before most of us had thoroughly explored the vicinity of our camp. Excursions to Washington were frequent, and we contributed our share to the large numbers of soldiers in uniform who gave the city its decidedly military appearance. Washington in 1862 was, indeed, a strange sight. Wealth, magnificence, poverty, and squalor mingled together indiscriminately. Hundreds of soldiers pushed their way through crowds that thronged the streets from morning till night. On all sides were seen the evidences of war. Long trains of wagons slowly wound their way in every direction; artillery thundered up and down the streets; cavalry galloped here and there; and long solid lines of infantry made their way slowly through the city.

A number of us visited the abandoned residence of General Lee. It was a stately building of the Southern colonial type, surrounded by spacious gardens which contained traces of many rare and beautiful flowers. It was located not far from Camp Seward and within view of the Potomac and the national capital.

On October eighteenth, General Casey reviewed the troops under his command, consisting of five thousand infantry and a battery of artillery, which constituted his division for the defense of Washington. This review, which took place on East Capitol Hill, was really a great spectacle, and the fact that we were forming a part of it particularly impressed us. Two weeks later, on Sunday, November second, a special honor was conferred upon us when General Halleck and his staff visited our regimental camp. It was understood to be the first unofficial visit which the General-in-Chief had conferred upon any regiment. Before leaving, he informed Colonel Garrard that the regiment had been assigned to the Fifth Corps, Army of the Potomac, and would be in Warren's brigade of Sykes's division.

The very next day, while the regiment was being mustered for pay at noon, we received orders to leave immediately for Harpers Ferry to join our corps. All was bustle and hurry. Rations for three days were prepared, and by four o'clock we were ready to start. These plans were suddenly changed, however, as a courier arrived with an order countermanding the one previously received. The reason for this change in orders was that the Army of the Potomac had left Harpers Ferry and was marching southward. This was somewhat vexatious to us, for we really were anxious to start for the front, but during the week that followed we grew accustomed to such experiences, for the giving and countermanding of marching orders followed each other almost as regularly as the alternations of day and night.

To add to the irritation of this uncertainty, the weather, which had been uniformly agreeable, suddenly became so cold that a general scramble for blankets and warmer clothing ensued. A severe snowstorm made it somewhat uncomfortable for a time, but the warm sun melted the snow the next day and put an end to the premature winter.

During this last week at Camp Seward we were instructed in target shooting. We had to use the clumsy Austrian rifles, with which we were first equipped, and at practice fired away as though the object were the very bitterest of "Johnny Rebs." A poor shot never failed to bring forth a cry of derision, and if a man did make a strike in or near the "bull's-eye," it was invariably ascribed to good fortune rather than to skill in marksmanship.

Changes in the force at Arlington Heights had been taking place nearly every day since our arrival. Regiments were coming and going continually, sometimes four or five leaving or arriving in a single day. As a result of this shifting process, we were soon the oldest regiment of the many to be seen from our camp.

On November eighth, we again received marching orders and passed the day preparing for our departure. Our knapsacks and haversacks were packed and rubber blankets and shelter tents were drawn from the quartermaster's department. These shelter tents consisted of two pieces of cotton cloth, each about four feet square. One piece was given to each man and at night the pieces were buttoned together and stretched over a pole, furnishing shelter for two men in each tent. The tents thus pitched were open at both ends and were about two feet high at the ridge. They had, however, this one disadvantage—rain ran through them like a sieve.

It had been planned that we should leave on Saturday, but something always seemed to happen to prevent our leaving on schedule time. On this occasion it was a delay in the arrival of a supply train, which did not reach us until the following day. Sunday morning dawned crisp and cold and we were ready to start at nine o'clock. Another slight delay prevented our getting away in the morning, but finally, at two o'clock Sunday afternoon, we were at last on the move. We marched to the westward over the Centerville turnpike,

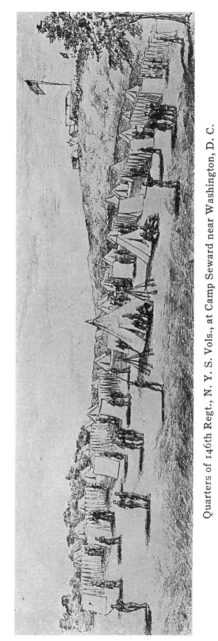

Quarters of 146th Regt., N. Y. S. Vols., at Camp Seward near Washington, D. C.

Taken from the back of an old envelope

UNIDENTIFIED OFFICER
Wearing pinstripe pants, and officer's sack coat, with a vest and a dangling watch fob, this unidentified officer of the 146th New York has the numbers "146" enclosed in a wreath on the front of his kepi. The photo was taken by W. C. North in Utica, and has a three cent tax stamp cancelled in Aug., either 1864 or 1865. (Donald Wisnoski Collection)

the "great war path" leading into the heart of the Confederacy. After proceeding about four miles we went into camp for the night. The place selected was on a side hill, with a stream of pure, cold water at the foot and an oak wood at the top. At five o'clock we ate a supper of ham, bread, and coffee, and "taps" was sounded early in order that we might have a good rest in preparation for the succeeding day's march. At half-past four the next morning we were awakened when the bugle sounded reveille. Breakfast was finished by six o'clock, then our goods were repacked, and within two hours we were on the road again.

It was on this march that we began to realize some of Colonel Garrard's sterling qualities. He did not urge us forward unwarrantably, but, realizing we were new troops, granted us a ten or fifteen minutes' rest after every four miles of marching. Colonel Garrard was always careful to select a good camping-ground and our march for the day was usually finished an hour or so past noon. The first duty was to pitch tents and get the camp in order, and the remainder of the afternoon was given over to recreation. The favorite pastime was to hunt the rabbits which were numerous along the roads and in the nearby fields and woods, and which varied our rations.

The country through which we passed was woody and uneven, but the road was broad and easy to travel. The land was dreary and desolate and bore the plainest evidences of the ravages of the war. Its uninviting aspect, however, was not due to the war alone, for the soil itself is very poor and thin.

On Monday we passed through Fairfax Court House, a squalid little hamlet of twenty or thirty dwellings, entirely deserted save by aged negroes. The old Court House itself excited no little comment. It was a smoky-looking building and was being used for army stores. We camped about a mile beyond the hamlet in a pleasant grove, where the abundance of wood and water enabled us to make a comfortable resting-place for the night. We reached Centerville Heights before noon the next morning. Here the road passed at right angles over three parallel ridges of hills, which were separated by broad level plains. At the summit of the third ridge, on the western side of which lies the village of Center-ville, were five small earthworks, surrounded by abatis and connected by rifle-pits. They had been thrown up by the Confederates, and from them fire could be concentrated upon an approaching force on any part of the broad plain. The works were at least a mile in length and the extremities were about equally distant from the highway. We rested for a few minutes at the summit of this ridge, and soon after we resumed the march reached Centerville. This village was much like Fairfax Court House, but perhaps dirtier and more uninviting, if that were possible.

After passing through Centerville, the road turned to the left and ran across low woodlands for three or four miles. The soil was what the negroes call "persimmon color," a sort of brownish-red shale. About three miles from Centerville we came to Cub Run, around which were large numbers of log huts, which had been occupied the winter before by the Confederate troops.

A march of two miles from this place brought us to the famous Stone Bridge over Bull Run. Just across it we went into camp, on a strip of lowland which bore evidence that it had been frequently used as a camp-ground by regiments on their way from Washington. Bull Run is a shallow stream about twenty-five feet wide, running over a bed of shale. The eastern bank is of solid rock about twenty feet high and nearly perpendicular. The other bank is low and marshy. The bridge, as its name indicates, was built of stone, with three arches and two piers. A portion of the bridge which had been blown up by the Confederates was replaced by logs. On the flat on the western side of the Run trees had been felled for a space of about six acres, behind which the Con-federates had concealed themselves to fire on the Union troops as the latter crossed the bridge in the course of the two battles fought here.

In the afternoon nearly everyone took a stroll over the historic ground in the vicinity. All around, the roads and fields were strewn with cartridge-boxes, canteens, bayonet sheaths, bullets, shells, fragments of clothing and similar articles. In the stream itself unexploded shells were so numerous that a dozen or so could be seen at one time. Farther on, about a mile or two from camp, in a woods bordering the Manassas road, the marks of the battle were even more numerous. Just in front of these woods a regimental line of battle was distinctly marked by innumerable pieces of paper which had been torn from cartridges. In the wood itself large trees had been twisted from their bases and hundreds of saplings broken and bent in one direction by the terrific force of the hurtling shells. Here, too, was the saddest sight of all—hundreds of dead men lying as they had fallen, with a slight covering of dirt tossed carelessly over their bodies.[1] Such sights were not calculated to inspire pleasant thoughts in the minds of new soldiers like ourselves. In fact, they produced a sense of depression that many of us found it difficult to cast off.

Early the next morning we were off again. The country, as we advanced, became much richer in appearance, and we saw many stately mansions and large, well-cultivated farms. The villages, too, were neat and attractive. We were making only easy marches and before noon encamped about four miles from Warrenton. The next day, Thursday, November thirteenth, we joined the Army of the Potomac at

[1] Lieutenant H. H. Curran, from whose letter this description is adapted, continues the description as follows: "In some cases the bleached skeletons or rotting and blackened bodies stared us in the face. In nearly every case the legs and arms, only partially covered, were upturned to view. In every direction the carcasses of horses lay putrefying, completing the horror of the awful scene. These bodies, thus neglected, were all those of Union soldiers, for the Confederates had buried their dead in graves in small plots surrounded by fences and, wherever possible, had placed a small board on each grave, bearing the name of the soldier lying therein."

Warrenton, and were brigaded with the Fifth New York, famous as the Duryea Zouaves, and the One Hundred and Fortieth New York, from Monroe County.

We had passed the preliminary stages of our life as soldiers and the movements of our regiment as a separate unit were ended. Henceforth, our fortunes were to be merged with the other regiments of the Army of the Potomac, and we were to participate in all future campaigns of that organization against the Confederate Army of Northern Virginia. The commander of the Army of the Potomac, when we joined it, was General Burnside, who had succeeded General McClellan only a short time before, and the army was on its march from Harpers Ferry, where it had been encamped since the battle of Antietam, in September, to occupy the heights at Falmouth, opposite the city of Fredericksburg on the Rappahannock River. The Fifth Corps, to which we were attached, was then under the command of General Butterfield.[1] The brigade to which our regiment was assigned was commanded by General Warren and was the Third Brigade of the Second Division, Fifth Corps, this division being commanded by General Sykes. The other two brigades of the division were composed of regiments of the Regular Army. Our assignment to membership in such a body of men gave promise of hard fighting ahead for the regiment, and we were ready and eager for it.

The Army of the Potomac lay at Warrenton for three days after our arrival. We soon became accustomed to our new surroundings and the usual routine of camp life. Our regimental camp was situated about a mile north of the village and about a mile and a half from the road, the tents being pitched on a hillside at the edge of a dense cedar grove. Close by were the camps of the Fifth New York and the One Hundred and Fortieth New York, our comrades in Warren's brigade, and not far away were the camps of the two brigades of Regulars attached to our division.

[1] Major-General Daniel Butterfield was a native of Utica, N. Y.

In the early '60's Warrenton was a pretty little village about half the size of Rome, New York, of that date. In the parlance of the South, Warrenton was a "right smart place," containing many handsome private residences of brick and stone. It was, of course, deserted by most of its inhabitants, and the soldiers made free use of all the property. Several churches in the town were being used as Confederate hospitals in which the sick and wounded, who had been left behind when the Army of Northern Virginia had evacuated the village, were being taken care of.

On November seventeenth, the Army of the Potomac resumed its march towards Falmouth. Reveille sounded in our regimental quarters at four o'clock that morning and we were on the move in an hour or two. Soon after setting out, we reached the top of a small hill, from which point we could see some fifty or sixty different regiments in motion. The waving flags and glistening bayonets presented an inspiring spectacle. Soon a fine, drizzling rain began to fall and the marching was heavy and tedious. We trudged on until the middle of the afternoon and then halted for a rest of an hour or two. At five o'clock the march was resumed across lots and through woods and swamps. We had no idea where we were going, but plodded on behind the regiment in front of us. Darkness enveloped us and the route we were taking was very hard to travel over. Soon we saw lights in the distance and about eight o'clock we halted for the night at a small cluster of houses known as Warrenton Junction, on the Orange & Alexandria Railroad. We pitched our tents as well as we could in the rain and darkness, and after a supper of hard-tack and ham turned in and slept soundly.

Another hard day's march was in store for us, over the fields and through the woods in the direction of Falmouth. Many fell out of the ranks and strayed by the road over night. Late in the afternoon we came to a halt, having made nineteen miles in the mud and rain. We passed an extremely disagreeable night, during which it rained steadily. With water dropping in our faces through the roofs of the so-called shelter tents, and lying on stones and pieces of wood, none of us rested very well. At nine o'clock we started off again, our brigade leading the march of the corps. As the brigade moved to the front to take the lead, we passed the Fourteenth New York, or First Oneida Regiment, and some of us waved hasty greetings to friends and acquaintances in that regiment as we marched by. Through the rain that fell steadily, and in the midst of the deepening mud, the column literally ploughed along for a distance of six or seven miles. Then a halt was called and we went into camp, remaining there three days. We were about eight miles northwest of Fredericksburg on the opposite, or eastern side of the Rappahannock River. Near our camp was Hartwood Church, but we christened the place "Camp Misery," and that name aptly describes it. We were having our first experience in the Virginia mud and we were made to realize that we had never really known what mud was while we were in the North. It seemed as if there was no bottom to this soil, no "hardpan" or stones at the base, nothing but mud, mud, mud, as far as it was possible to go down. The entire army was at a standstill, for the roads were so muddy that satisfactory marching was impossible and it was out of the question to move the artillery and wagon trains. Decidedly low spirits prevailed throughout the whole army. Many of the older regiments around us were tired of the service and anxious to return home, and the infection spread among the new regiments through their intercourse with the old.

After three days of such experiences, the roads were deemed by General Burnside to be in good enough condition to resume the march, and the army was put in motion on Saturday, November twenty-second. We had expected to start out early in the morning, but it was the middle of the afternoon before we left our camp to resume our journey southward. We proceeded about six miles and then the brigade got off on the wrong road, but managed to find a good camping-ground at dark.   The next morning we started out again at daylight and after frequent delays, due to the great number of troops that were marching, reached our destination at Falmouth that night.   Taking no note of our surroundings, we hastily prepared for rest as best we could. The weather had become clear and dry and except for a rather chilly breeze was all that could be desired.   The next morning we began the work of setting up our camp.   The site selected for the camp was a part of the Henry farm, the birthplace of Patrick Henry.   We encamped to the left of the house and near Potomac Creek.   We were within an eighth of a mile from the headquarters of General Hooker, the commander of the Center Grand Division.   General Burnside's headquarters, too, were not far distant, for we could witness the balloon ascensions which were frequently made for the purpose of ascertaining the position of the Confederates on the heights back of Fredericksburg, just across the river to the south.   The site of our camp had evidently been previously occupied by the Confederates, for among the trees evergreens had been tastefully entwined and worked into festoons, arches, and entrances, probably to mark a reception to some of their generals.[1]

As it was probable that we should be encamped here for some time, we proceeded to make ourselves as comfortable as possible.   Our shelter tents were fixed up in good shape. By joining tents together and using logs as foundations we were able to make residences that afforded us a fair degree of comfort.   We, were however, a very homesick set of men, and the feelings of many were best expressed by the slang phrase which was heard on every side: "Why did I leave my three square meals a day to be a soldier?"   Sickness became quite prevalent.   The surgeon reported at one time over a hundred of the regiment in the camp who were unfit for duty.   Besides these, many had been sent to the hospital in Washington.

[1] Letter of Lieutenant Curran and Diary of James P. Pitcher.

At Camp Henry we celebrated our first Thanksgiving Day in the field. Only a few of the boys were favored with boxes from home, so that the day could hardly be said to have been one of much feasting. Most of us had to be content with crackers pounded up in syrup, but it required a great deal of imagination to consider it anywhere near as palatable as the roast turkey or other delicacies which we would have had at home.

As regards lack of comforts, however, our lot was the same as that of all the hundred and fifty thousand men composing the Army of the Potomac, whose camps were dotted over the wide plateau from the Rappahannock to the Potomac. Here the entire army lay comparatively idle, from the latter part of November until the middle of December. During this time the commanders reviewed the army by divisions. These reviews, full of life and action, furnished spectacles that were really most brilliant. Our turn came on November twenty-ninth, when Sykes's division of the Fifth Corps was reviewed by General Hooker. The three brigades of the division, nearly five thousand strong, were first drawn up in line of battle in two solid ranks, six paces apart, with the colors and officers in front. The ranks were then opened, making the front of each brigade line nearly half a mile in length. General Hooker and his staff rode down the front to the end of the line, each regiment as he passed saluting with presented arms, drooping colors, and the roll of drums. When the procession had passed down the entire line, the front rank was faced about. General Hooker then rode up between the ranks. This finished, each brigade was wheeled into column by company and marched past the General and his staff, after which the regiments returned to their own quarters. These reviews were the only feature out of the ordinary during our stay at Falmouth that fall. The daily duties were, of course, ever present, and we were being prepared by drills and target practice for what might be in store when active campaigning was resumed.

CHAPTER III

THE BATTLE OF FREDERICKSBURG

THE city of Fredericksburg, which is situated on the south bank of the Rappahannock River opposite the place where the Army of the Potomac was encamped at Falmouth, was one of the most important strategic points in northern Virginia. Almost exactly equidistant from Washington and Richmond, about fifty miles from each city, Fredericksburg was on a direct line of communication between the two capitals. The army that held it was in a position to advance with comparative ease against the capital of the enemy when opportunity offered, or to hasten to the protection of its own chief city when occasion required. Its position was one of great natural strength, as it was located directly on the river and was surrounded on all sides by an encircling amphitheater of bluffs and hills.

When General Burnside assumed command of the Army of the Potomac on November 9, 1862, he had been urged by President Lincoln and General Halleck to occupy the heights in rear of Fredericksburg, and to push on if possible from that point toward Richmond.[1] Contrary to the wish of the authorities at Washington and with only their half-hearted assent, he moved his army instead on the north side of the Rappahannock and brought it to Falmouth, opposite Fredericksburg.[2] A policy of delay on Burnside's part enabled the Confederates to reinforce the small garrison

[1] Letter of November 5, 1862.
[2] Report of General Halleck, W. R., 31, p. 46.

that was holding Fredericksburg by Longstreet's corps and a portion of Stonewall Jackson's corps, so that by the time Burnside decided to assume the offensive and endeavor to capture the city, it was held by about twenty-five thousand Confederates. They had greatly strengthened their position on the hills surrounding the city by the erection of rifle-pits and earthworks, and were well prepared to dispute the occupation of the town.

This ridge on which the Confederates had posted themselves extends from near the junction of the Massaponax and the Rappahannock, about five miles south of the town, to a point opposite Falmouth, about two miles north of Fredericksburg. Directly back of Fredericksburg the hills are somewhat lower than the average height of the ridge,[1] and here, on a plain that slopes gently toward the river, a railroad from Richmond enters the city; as do likewise two highways, one from Orange Court House to the west and the other from Richmond to the south. A third road ran parallel to the river about three quarters of a mile from the outskirts of the town and connected the two main roads. This road is the one that has become famous as the "sunken road."[2] The plain on which the town of Fredericksburg is situated extends between the range of hills and the Rappahannock. It is about a half mile broad at its northern end and stretches out to a breadth of over two miles near its southern extremity along the Massaponax.

Despite the natural strength of such a position and the further fact that his army would have to cross a swiftly flowing river before attacking, General Burnside resolved to attempt to carry the heights by an assault. The attack was to be made at two points, the first directly back of the town, where the railroad and highways crossed the depression in

---

[1] These hills directly back of Fredericksburg are known as Marye's Heights.

[2] At the present time the city is built up toward the hill considerably farther than in 1862, so that the distance from the city to the famous "sunken road" is much less than it was at the time of the battle.

the hills, and the second some distance below at a point known as Hamilton's Crossing. In order to protect the crossing of his troops on the pontoon bridges, the Union commander stationed a heavy force of artillery, numbering a hundred and forty-seven guns, along the north bank of the Rappahannock, covering the entire length of the Confederate batteries on the other side.

Preparations were made to cross the river at Fredericksburg and about four miles below. Three pontoon bridges were to be thrown across at the former, and two at the latter point. At a conference held in General Burnside's headquarters on December ninth, he outlined the plan of operations to his three Grand Division commanders. General Sumner, with the Right Grand Division, was to concentrate his forces at the upper and middle bridges, and crossing these, to proceed directly through the city and attack the Confederate position on Marye's Heights. General Franklin, with the Left Grand Division, was to take his troops across the bridge below the town and march along the river road, attacking the Confederate position just below Fredericksburg. General Hooker, with the Center Grand Division, was to cross the upper bridges in rear of Sumner, and hold his command in readiness to support either the Right or Left Division in their attack on the enemy's position. These instructions were given with the view to placing the bridges across the river on the morning of December eleventh.[1]

In carrying out the orders outlined above, the various corps of the Army of the Potomac broke camp early on the morning of Thursday, December eleventh, and marched

[1] It is well to bear in mind that at this time the Right Grand Division consisted of the Second Corps, under Major-General Darius N. Couch, and the Ninth Corps, under Brigadier-General Orlando B. Willcox; the Center Grand Division of the Third Corps, under Brigadier-General George Stoneman and the Fifth Corps, under Brigadier-General Daniel Butterfield; and the Left Grand Division of the First Corps, under Major-General John F. Reynolds, and the Sixth Corps, under Major-General William F. Smith.

to the respective positions assigned them, preparatory to crossing the Rappahannock.

This move against the Confederate position at Fredericksburg was the occasion of our regiment leaving camp near Falmouth. On the evening of December ninth we had received orders to cook three days' rations and be prepared to start the next day. Contrary to expectations, however, we remained quiet in our camp throughout the tenth. About three o'clock the next morning, the notes of the bugle awoke us from a sound slumber. Breakfast was soon dispatched, and by five we were ready to start. All of us felt sure that before many hours had passed we were going to have our first experience of actual warfare, but we were, nevertheless, in excellent spirits, eager to do our part. At half-past five a low, booming sound reached our ears, the report of the first gun that opened the engagement. This was immediately followed by loud, cracking, thunder-like reports, that seemed to shake the earth beneath our feet, as the heavy guns began the cannonade in earnest. Deafening cheers rose from our own camp and the camps of those about us as thousands of men gave voice to their feelings of impatience and anxiety. About six o'clock in the morning we filed into line and started for the banks of the Rappahannock. With the other regiments of General Sykes's division, we marched on the right of the corps line, along the Stafford road. General Griffin's division, the first, proceeded along a road farther to the left; and between our division and his line of march moved the third division of the corps, under General Humphreys. It was a pleasant morning, clear, cold, and frosty; and soon after starting the sun rose in unwonted splendor, promising a beautiful day for the beginning of the enterprise. About half-past seven our division turned aside into the woods, and remained there for over an hour and a half. Again we started, and marched on rapidly, the sound of the cannon becoming louder and louder as we approached the place where the batteries were stationed. When we had gone about

Capt. King—Capt. Guthrie—Lieut.
Buckingham
Servant—Capt. Cushman—Capt.
Jenkins, Petersburg, 1864

Corporal J. Conrad Neuschler

James Shaw, Alfred H. Palmer

Drummer Boys

James Pitts—Geo. Wheeler—Fred
White—Lieut. King ——

Beverly Ford, Va.—Summer, 1863

UNIDENTIFIED SERGEANT

A gaunt unarmed 146th New York sergeant spends some of his meager soldiers' wages to have his picture taken in the field—probably at the 1863-64 winter encampment at Brandy Station, VA, or during the siege of Petersburg. He wears a striped shirt, and his jacket appears somewhat rumpled. Note that the photo was taken outdoors with a painted canvas backdrop that can also be seen in several pictures with soldiers of the 146th. The unusual shape of the sergeant's head is because he is wearing a large white turban wrapped around his fez, but owing to the white canvas background, the turban is washed out and nearly invisible in this image. (Donald Wisnoski Collection)

five miles from our camp, we emerged from the woods and after ascending a gentle slope obtained a good view of the whole gigantic spectacle. Only a glimpse, however, was granted us, for we soon turned to the left into a muddy ravine, sheltered from the enemy's batteries on the other side of the river by a low rise of ground and a beautiful grove of large oak trees. On this hill were breastworks in which were stationed several Parrott rifled guns, which continually threw shells far onto the opposite heights. Our regiment soon stacked arms and prepared to await an order which should command us to move across the river.

The promise of a beautiful day which we had received in the early morning had been fulfilled; the sun came out warm and it seemed more like a May day in the North than like a winter day. A number of us climbed the hill which overlooks the river, and from this vantage point the whole battleground of the center and right was spread out before us. The entire river bank on the Union side seemed to be lined with flame. Once in a while we could hear the cracking of the guns of the enemy's sharpshooters, who were on the opposite bank. The sight was truly magnificent. With the noise of artillery was mingled the crash of buildings, the bursting of shells, and the crackle of flames, that were breaking forth from many places in the city. Sometimes the noise of the shells was like that of deep thunder; again it would be sharper; some gave forth the sound of a dismal howl, very much like the yelping of a hound; others screamed in a high shrill tone; then again, nothing could be distinguished but a rushing, vibrating sound.[1]

All day the Union batteries continued the cannonading but received practically no response from those of the enemy. The Confederate sharpshooters, however, were busy, and by their effective work from the windows of houses along the river bank they prevented the engineers from laying the pontoons. Several regiments of infantry crossed the river

[1] From description by Captain Henry H. Curran, in letter written home.

in boats and succeeded in driving the sharpshooters out of the city. When this was accomplished, the pontoons were completed, and the advance of the Right Grand Division, under General Howard, crossed the river and camped in the streets of Fredericksburg. As it was nearly dark when General Howard crossed, the greater part of the Right Division remained on the north bank of the river over night. In the meantime, General Franklin, with the Left Grand Division, had been able to lay his bridges with but slight opposition, showing that the enemy invited attack, and he had taken the majority of his troops to the Fredericksburg side of the river by the evening of the eleventh.

On the following day the bombardment was continued by the Union batteries, and the Confederates replied with equal vigor. Masses of shells and cannon-balls were thrown from one side of the river to the other. Those of the Union batteries were designed to check the fire of the Confederate artillery on the opposite heights, but many fell short of their mark and crashed into the city, demolishing and setting fire to many houses. The Confederates, on the other hand, directed their fire at the troops crossing on the pontoon bridges or already stationed in the city. While the artillery belched forth its deadly volleys, the main body of the Army of the Potomac moved slowly over the river and took position in the city preparatory to an assault on the Confederate line the following day.

When the fire of the artillery ceased at dark on Thursday, it was followed by a weird and uncanny silence. Throughout the night all was quiet, so terribly quiet that the stillness seemed oppressive. The fires in the city continued, and threw over the whole countryside a lurid light. Many of us found it impossible to sleep, so great was the sense of anxiety and expectancy that haunted us. On the afternoon of Friday we listened with a curious thrill to the sharp cracking of rifles that told us fighting was going on in the outskirts of the city. Clouds of smoke rose continually and hovered above the houses, lit here and there by bursts of yellow flame. Friday night was a repetition of the preceding one, although we were now more accustomed to our position and were able to snatch a few hours' rest. The morning of the thirteenth dawned bright and warm, the sun continuing his good offices of providing May weather in the middle of December. For a few hours after daylight all remained quiet, but sometime between nine and ten o'clock, as we judged, both artillery and musketry fire began with great fury. As many as possible secured positions of vantage from which we could watch the battle on the other side of the river. The spectacle that met our eyes was one of great splendor and well calculated to inspire awe in the minds of all who witnessed it. The Union troops were hurling themselves against the fortifications on the hill immediately back of Fredericksburg. As they advanced across the plain, a distance of three quarters of a mile, traveling through mud almost knee deep, the Confederate infantry at the base of the hill, concealed from view behind stone walls and breastworks, swept them with murderous broadsides, and at the same time the artillery on the ridges higher up poured round after round of grape and canister into the advancing columns. Brigade after brigade advanced in face of the awful fire and melted away before the sheet of flame that greeted it. We could see the lines move forward steadily until they met the fire of the enemy's guns, which swept them aside with irresistible force. We could hear the cheers of the gallant men as they recovered somewhat and charged again in vain on those impregnable batteries. All day long we watched the progress of the slaughter. Fighting against a foe located in a position that was naturally one of great strength and which had been fortified by a triple tier of batteries, the Union troops never had the least semblance of a chance to gain the victory. Yet with a courage seldom, if ever, equaled they charged undaunted over the rough ground directly at the batteries, until stopped by a torrent of fire it was beyond the scope of human possibilities to pass. Three times the troops of the Right Grand Division assaulted the Confederate position in front of Marye's Heights, but they were as often compelled to retire to their position in the streets of Fredericksburg.[1] Meanwhile, four miles farther south the Left Grand Division twice charged the Confederate position at Hamilton's Crossing, but were twice repulsed. While the battle was raging, the Third Corps, of the Center Grand Division, was sent to the aid of the Union forces on the Fredericksburg side of the river.

Finally, about three o'clock in the afternoon, our rôle as spectators was ended and we were called upon to participate in the battle. Led by Generals Hooker and Butterfield, the Fifth Corps started to cross the river between three and four o'clock. Our regiment fell into line promptly when the command was given and we awaited with anxiety our entry into Fredericksburg. Lieutenant-Colonel Jenkins, at the suggestion of Colonel Garrard, rode down the line at this time, and in a few words spoken firmly and clearly called upon the regiment to respond to this, our first call to active duty, in a manner that would bring honor to ourselves, our corps, and our native country. His words called forth a hearty cheer. After a few minutes' further delay, we filed out with the other regiments of the corps and marched down the hill behind which we had lain for two days.[2] We

---

[1] It was in these assaults that General Meagher's Irish Brigade, consisting of the Twenty-eighth Massachusetts, the Sixty-third, Sixty-ninth, and Eighty-eighth New York, and the One Hundred and Sixteenth Pennsylvania Regiments, rendered such gallant service. Out of over 1200 men whom their gallant commander led into the fight in the morning only 280 reported for duty at the close of the day.

[2] The majority of the men kept their nerve well, but the prospects of this first battle were too much for some of the weak-hearted ones. Two men, as the regiment started out, fell to the rear with the intention of deserting. They, were captured, however, by the provost guard and after our return from Fredericksburg were tried by court-martial. One was sentenced to be shot, the other to lose his pay for a period of time. The condemned man, before the sentence could be carried out, made his escape in a clever manner. He was

proceeded slowly across a muddy flat and then through a deep gorge, which brought us to the river bank, where the pontoon bridges had been laid over which we were to cross. All about us on our march we passed many evidences of the presence of an army: dead horses and mules lying where they had fallen, broken caissons, gun-carriages, and articles of clothing of every description. Some delay was experienced in getting over the river, owing to the narrowness of the bridges, and we were compelled to wait our turn. The corps crossed over the three bridges by divisions, our division, under General Sykes, on the right or northernmost bridge, Griffin's division on the left, and Humphreys's in the center. While crossing the bridge, we loaded and capped our guns, and on reaching the other side clambered rapidly up the steep bank and ran through the streets of the city at a rapid double-quick. It was quite warm and our exertions in running caused us to perspire freely. The spectacle which the city afforded as we passed through it was one that beggars description. The ravages made by fire were visible on every side, and many of the buildings on the streets we passed through were still burning. It seemed as if nearly every house was torn and rent by shells. Bricks, stones, and lumber were strewn about the streets. Hundreds of knapsacks were there, thrown away by the men in their haste to reach the battlefield. As we ran on, we met hundreds of men returning exhausted from the scene of conflict. Many were bringing in the wounded in litters or in their arms. It was anything but an encouraging sight for us, as we were advancing to the attack, to see those mangled and bleeding bodies borne past us. When we came near the outskirts of the city, we were halted to allow several pieces of artillery to file past us. Darkness was now rapidly coming on. Near by, it seemed as though it were within a few hundred feet, the rattle of musketry was plainly heard, telling us that the

---

given clothing by a Southern sympathizer in the neighborhood and after many adventures reached Canada in safety.

battle was still raging. Again we started and continued our advance until we reached the edge of the city.

While we had been making the crossing of the river, General Hooker was ordered to send a division of the Fifth Corps to the support of General Sturgis's division of the Ninth Corps. Griffin's division was assigned to this duty, leaving only Sykes's and Humphreys's divisions in the Fifth Corps, or, as it would be designated by orders issued from headquarters, the "Center Grand Division." When these two divisions had reached the outskirts of the city, that of General Humphreys filed off to the left of the road which runs out of Fredericksburg toward the west and formed by brigade front, Sykes's division, in which our regiment was included, forming in a similar manner on the right of the road. Lying as we were on a gentle slope we were exposed to the fire of the enemy's artillery, but fortunately darkness was almost at hand and our presence was not discovered by the Confederates.

While the remnant of the Center Grand Division had been taking the position described above, General Hooker had received orders from Burnside to attack the enemy's position on Marye's Heights. General Hooker carefully surveyed the point of attack and, after conversation with several of the officers of the Right Grand Division and his own command, was convinced that it would be a useless waste of life to attack with the force at his disposal. He sent an aide to General Burnside to inform him that it was not wise to attack, but the reply came that the attack should be made. General Hooker thereupon visited Burnside in person and sought to have him revoke the order, but without avail. The two small divisions of the Fifth Corps were ordered to assault a position against which the columns of the Second and Ninth Corps had hurled themselves time after time throughout the earlier part of the day without making any visible impression. It was sheer madness to suppose that they could be successful where the others had failed, but General Hooker had no alternative but to obey the command of his superior officer and order the assault. He brought up every available battery of artillery, for the purpose of supporting the attacking column.

When the order for attack was given, Humphreys's division, on the left, led the assault, and with fixed bayonets made a most gallant charge on the enemy's works. With the other regiments of Sykes's division, we stood in readiness to support Humphreys's men and to follow them forward if they gained any success. We were not called upon, however, to advance, for as General Hooker had anticipated, the assault by Humphreys's division was met with such an awful fire from the Confederate musketry and artillery that the lines literally melted away before it. The superb gallantry of the men, many of them engaged in their first battle, rivaled that of the Irish Brigade in their assault on the same position earlier in the day. When, as General Hooker expressed it, he had "lost about as many men as he was ordered to sacrifice," he commanded Humphreys's division to fall back, and brought up the First and Second brigades of Sykes's division to cover this retrograde movement. It was necessary to do this for the repulse that the attacking columns had sustained was so complete and their losses so heavy that, had the enemy followed up their advantage, without this precaution the result might have been most disastrous. During this time, our regiment, and the others of Warren's brigade, had been held awaiting orders, on the edge of the city limits on the extreme right of the Fifth Corps line.

After this unsuccessful attempt to storm the batteries on Marye's Heights, the Fifth Corps remained in their position on the outskirts of the city throughout the night. The two brigades of Regulars in Sykes's division were in an extremely precarious situation, being commanded to hold the advanced position they had attained when supporting Humphreys's retreat, and later in the night they were ordered by General Burnside to advance still farther and relieve some of the men of the Second Corps who were lying in the very face of the enemy's batteries.[1]

Our regiment was indeed fortunate in not having to endure the rain of fire to which so many of our corps had been exposed. We lay, as has been said, on the slope of a gentle rise of ground and the snow and rain of the early part of the month, followed by several warm days, had converted the ground into a veritable bog of mud, nearly a foot deep. Comfortable sleep in such circumstances was out of the question. Some of us went a short way into the city and found boards or fence rails which we used for beds.[2] It was like sleeping on rafts on the water.

The groans of the wounded on the field not far from us, and the rattle of the ambulances bearing them into the city, made the night most miserable. Some of the cries which we heard were most sad; others, despite the agony they revealed, seemed almost ludicrous. The voice of one unfortunate soldier, seemingly that of a mere boy, called out over and over again, "Charlie! Charlie!" in an appeal for aid to a brother or comrade whom death, perhaps, had claimed, and the cry remained unanswered. In broken English a badly wounded young German loudly called, "Somebodies dake me to dot

---

[1] General Sykes in his report comments on the conduct of these troops as follows: "At 11.00 P.M. these two brigades moved to the front, relieved the troops in advance, and held their ground until the same hour the following night. The position was one of extreme peril—in an open field, within a hundred yards of the enemy, who was securely sheltered behind stone walls and rifle-pits. They remained under constant fire for twelve hours, and could offer in resistance only the moral effect of that hardihood and bravery which would not yield one foot of the line they were required to protect. No better test of the quality of troops could be shown than that displayed by these brigades. Patience, endurance, discipline, and courage were conspicuous."

[2] Some comments made by Captain Henry H. Curran, in a letter to his mother, are interesting in this respect: "You would have been surprised to see with what avidity the soldiers seize on boards for a sleeping-place. One reason is that it keeps one from coming in contact with the ground, but this is not the only one. You have often heard, no doubt, of the soft side of a board. Well, boards are really soft. Oftentimes, when the ground made my bones ache I have mounted a board, and it seemed like jumping into a feather bed."

hospidal!" Again and again he shrieked, half in German, and half in English, but his cries grew fainter and finally ceased, as he, too, passed Beyond.

Towards morning, these sounds grew less frequent, but other things disturbed our rest. We had no blankets and became so cold that we shivered involuntarily; so much so that it was with great difficulty we could retain our places on our "beds." We realized that when morning came our position would be discerned by the Confederates, and knew that the fact of its being the Sabbath would not deter them from opening a destructive fire upon us.

Just before dawn, the order was passed silently along the entire brigade line to fall back into the city as quietly as possible. This was accomplished without confusion, and with the other regiments of the brigade we took position in the outermost street of Fredericksburg on the western side of the town. We did not remain there long, for the enemy soon discovered our position and began to drop shells unpleasantly close to the place where our regiment was stationed. One shell struck a pump in the street within a few feet of where several members of Company "D" were standing. It killed an artillery horse near by and then bounded to one side and struck a member of that company on the leg, wounding him severely.[1] When this accident occurred, the regiment hurriedly moved into the next street, farther away from the enemy's batteries.

Shortly after we had taken our place with the other regiments of the brigade in this second street we heard rumors that another assault was to be made on the Confederate position that day and that our division was to have the very questionable "honor" of leading it. If the order had been given we should have been obliged to advance over an open space for about half a mile, exposed to the fire of a hundred hostile cannon, and charge almost impregnable

[1] This man was Chester Hall, of Boonville, a private. He died from the effects of his wound, in the hospital at Washington, on December 30, 1862.

intrenchments from behind which thousands of muskets could have concentrated their fire upon us and numerous field batteries raked our advancing ranks with murderous grape and canister. In fact, we were in line awaiting the order to make the charge, but fortunately, at about two o'clock in the afternoon, the order was countermanded.

A council of war had been held, at which Generals Hooker, Sykes, and Warren, men whose reputation for fighting was above suspicion, had protested that such an assault would be a useless waste of life, and they had finally persuaded General Burnside to rescind his order for another attack.

Sunday was, accordingly, spent in idleness. It was, however, not entirely devoid of excitement, for the enemy's batteries dropped shells into the city at frequent intervals and many of them struck so near as to be decidedly uncomfortable. Many of us were not content to remain quietly in the streets of Fredericksburg, but roamed about that portion of the town in which we were stationed and broke into the gardens and houses in search of "adventures." It must be acknowledged, too, that we did not refrain from taking some of the things we found in these places and appropriating them to our own use. Many and varied were the articles we came upon, and a number of our experiences while "prowling around" were rather amusing. A barrel of molasses was found in the cellar of one of the houses. The news quickly spread, and a "raid" was made on the cellar. The first-comers filled their small tin cups in the ordinary manner but in a few minutes so large a crowd had gathered that the "sticky sweetness" came forth far too slowly to supply the increased demand, so the barrel was dragged out into the street and the head split open. Even this did not suffice, as the many hands reaching in their cups completely clogged the wide opening and none could be withdrawn. To make sure that all might have a taste, a compromise was reached, and each took his place in line for half a cupful. In the scramble to fill all cups, much smearing of hands, heads, and clothing resulted. In another cellar a large stove was kept busy all day, on which we fried flapjacks, meat, fish, etc., all of which we found in the adjacent houses. One of the members of Company "C"[1] discovered in a nearby house what he thought was an unusually fine quality of pancake flour. He brought some to the cellar and, mixing it with water, started to cook some cakes for himself. Not securing the expected result, he gave the stuff a closer examination and discovered that what he had thought to be flour was in reality plaster of Paris.

Another group from our regiment climbed through the second-story window in the rear of a pretentious-looking house and came upon a ladies' wardrobe filled with expensive dresses, cloaks, and other articles of feminine apparel. Some of us dressed up in these clothes and slid down a rope into the rear garden, where we held an impromptu cotillion. The house, however, proved to be the one that Colonel Garrard had chosen for his headquarters, and our "festive gathering" was rudely interrupted by the appearance of our commander at one of the first-floor windows, from which, fairly bristling with rage at our unsoldierly conduct in the very face of the enemy, he commanded that we return the garments to the room from which we had taken them and leave the garden immediately. As he added to this injunction a threat to shoot the first man he found attempting to enter the house by the window or rear door, we were glad enough to obey, and in our further escapades were careful to leave the Colonel's headquarters religiously alone.

The happiest discovery we made in Fredericksburg, from many standpoints, was that of a large quantity of plug tobacco which had been stored away in an upper room of what was evidently a much-used warehouse. This tobacco was distributed to the men of the regiment and proved an unexpected luxury while we remained in Fredericksburg and for several days after our return to Falmouth.

[1] Sergeant J. Albert Jennison.

Despite these diversions in the line of marauding expeditions, the day passed slowly. Our position was really one of great danger. We did not know when the Confederates might begin to fire into the city in earnest. The shells which they did throw into the city occasionally had but little effect. Some came whizzing down the streets, frequently wounding or killing those who did not dodge quickly enough; others crashed into the sides of the houses; while still others fell harmlessly into the gardens in front or rear of the houses. We soon became accustomed to them, and took no notice except when they fell unusually close. One place was as safe as another, for there was as much danger behind the brick walls as in the open fields, and we simply had to take our chances of being hit.

Towards evening, Sunday, our regiment marched into two or three quite extensive gardens surrounded by brick walls a short distance nearer the outskirts of the city and the batteries on the hill. Here we prepared for our night's rest, lying in a position to protect ourselves as much as possible from stray bullets and shells. The night was clear and quite warm, so that we were able to obtain a good night's rest.

Monday morning broke clear and pleasant and the hours until noon passed wearily, for we lay in position expecting to be ordered to the front to attack the enemy's batteries. Towards noon it became quite hot, and uncomfortable to stand for a long time in the sun. Many were not satisfied with the usual hardtack and salt pork when the dinner hour arrived, and remembering their good fortune of the preceding day, went again in search of something better than the regular army fare. The experience of three of the officers[1] on such an exploring expedition as related by one of them is rather interesting:

Entering the cellar of a very fine mansion, we passed through several dark rooms and passageways, finding nothing that could

[1] These officers were Lieutenant-Colonel Jenkins, Captain Durkee, and Captain Curran, as told by the latter.

Private James B. Fiske

Sergt. Orlo Jones and brother, from
97th New York

Standing: Capt Wright—Lieut. Fowler
Lieut. Buckingham—Capt. Walker
Sitting: Servant—Lieut. Brownell
Capt. James Jenkins

Corporal Frederick Ernst

Showing uniform worn by 146th Regt. from
Spring of 1863 to expiration of service

UNIDENTIFIED
A dark hair and mustached 146th New York private holds a Springfield rifle, which in this case is most likely a photographer's prop. He is in complete Zouave regalia. (Rome Historical Society Collection)

minister to our bodily wants. Finally we found ourselves in a basement kitchen, with a huge fireplace, and numerous articles of food around us. The occupants of this apartment were three old negroes, two women and a man. After some parleying, they were induced to go to work and prepare a dinner for us. The meal when completed consisted of very good boiled pork, very good, extraordinarily good corn-bread, and superb hot corn-cakes. I never relished anything so much in my life. For dessert we had rich peach turnovers, and topped off with some Havana cigars. We departed very much refreshed. They charged us $2.50 for the meal, but reflecting that nothing they gave us was their own we thought a dollar would suffice them.

Monday afternoon we passed the time as we had the day before. One of the men[1] expressed it, "Roaming about the streets, lounging in the gardens, and dodging shells." About eight o'clock in the evening we received orders to fall in, and soon marched in the direction of the Confederate works, turning to the right into a lane, just at the outside of the city. From this point we sent out working parties to dig rifle-pits and breastworks. This movement was part of a plan formulated at a council of war held in the afternoon at which it had been determined to abandon the city during the night and recross the Rappahannock. Barricades and rifle-pits were ordered constructed along the outskirts of the city, connecting with the brick walls and houses which were loop-holed. This work was assigned to General Warren, in command of our brigade. When completed, the barricades extended from a plateau to the right of the Gordon house west of Amelia Street, to the street to the east of Hanover Street. Those to the right of Amelia Street were built by General Humphreys's division; those extending from Amelia Street to Hanover Street by the Regulars of Sykes's division; and the barricade of Hanover Street and the rifle-pits to the left of it by a detachment from our regiment, under the supervision of Colonel Garrard.[2]

[1] James P. Pitcher, Company "D."

[2] General Warren says in his report: "I cannot omit to praise the energy

As soon as the work of building the barricades and rifle-pits was completed, pickets were sent out from our regiment and the Fifth New York in front of our brigade line, and from other regiments of the Fifth Corps in front of the lines of their respective brigades.[1] While this was being done, the rest of the Army of the Potomac began to withdraw as silently as possible and under cover of the darkness, made more intense by a drizzling rain that fell throughout the night, moved slowly across the pontoon bridges to the north bank of the Rappahannock. The Fifth Corps was left in the city to act as rear guard and cover the movement in case the enemy became aware of it and sought to attack the flanks of the retreating army.

The position of our regiment and the others of the Fifth Corps left in Fredericksburg for this purpose was a peculiarly precarious one, but those who remained with the main body of the regiment reposed themselves as comfortably as possible for the night. We stretched out in the mud or on the sidewalks and cobblestones and endeavored to get a few hours' rest. One of our officers[2] describes an incident that took place at this time on his portion of the line as follows:

Just as I was almost asleep, I heard a familiar noise in front of me. I looked up, and sure enough, a poor old cow was standing not far from where I was "reposing." One man held her by the horns, another by the tail, while several others took turns milking her. She must have been a very meek cow, for they milked and milked until I thought the poor cow would die, and yet she stood

---

exhibited by the working details as shown by the work accomplished with a great deficiency of tools, and must mention particularly Colonel Garrard and Captain Locke (Fourteenth U. S.)."

[1] General Warren, in his report, refers only to the Fifth New York as performing picket duty in front of the brigade line, but Captain (then Sergeant) A. I. King, Adjutant (then Corporal) William Wright, and O. J. Barker, of Co. "G," living at the time this account was written, were themselves members of one of the details from the One Hundred and Forty-sixth assigned to this duty.

[2] Captain Henry H. Curran.

and made no sign. It seemed so utterly ridiculous to see men in such a position of danger so intent on milking that cow, that I laughed until the perspiration poured off of me.

For the men who were out on picket duty the night was a long and weary one, and all did not go well with the detail from our regiment. The campfires within the Union lines were to be kept burning brightly throughout the night to cover all appearances of retreat while portions of the corps, in their turn, moved out to recross the river. As the last detachment crossed, the pickets were to be drawn in, and it was hoped this would be effected before dawn. The officers in command of the pickets were given orders accordingly and were explicitly instructed not to bring in their men until they received definite word to do so. Through some confusion, the order for the pickets to fall back did not reach the officer in command of the detachment from our regiment,[1] and he relates what took place on his post that night as follows:

It began to rain early in the evening and the storm increased in violence, so that by the time we had our sentries posted the rain was coming down in torrents. The men walking back and forth over their beats were soon plastered with mud. In our front we could occasionally hear calls from the enemy's sentinels. From the rear in the direction of our own camp came the sound of an army at work throwing up intrenchments. By midnight, however, every sound but that of the rain and the wind had ceased. At regular intervals during the night the sentries on the extreme right and left would meet the sentries posted on either side of us. Just before daybreak a picket came in and reported to the corporal of the guard[2] that the sentries on our left must have been withdrawn, as no sentry had come out to meet him for some time. The corporal at first thought that the man had conjured up this story as an excuse for leaving his post and was on the point of reprimanding him and sending him back when a

[1] Captain (then Sergeant) A. I. King, Co. "K."
[2] William Wright, Co. "K."

sentry from the other end of the line came and reported that he had not met a sentry from the pickets adjoining on his side lately and was fearful that something might be wrong. The corporal immediately reported the circumstance to me, and we began an investigation. We walked out some distance from either end of the line and also to the rear, but not a soul could be found in any direction, and the stillness was so intense that it seemed as though my little squad of men were the only living beings on the earth. The sentries on both sides of us had certainly been withdrawn and our camp in the rear deserted, unknown to us and without our having been informed. We were very much alarmed of course, and could not understand why we had been left after the army had made their retreat. The Colonel's orders to me had been positive, "Do not bring in your men until ordered to do so," and here we were out on the plain, a small group of men within a few rods of the enemy's pickets, and certain to be discovered before long. There was only one thing for me to do under the circumstances and that was to try to withdraw my men as quietly as possible and strike out for the river, hoping to reach it before daybreak. The distance was not great, but on account of the darkness, the mud, and the uneven ground we could not make very rapid headway. It, however, was not long before we struck the main street leading down to the river front. By this time it was beginning to grow light and we redoubled our efforts to reach the river. We did not have far to go, and if we could only reach the river before the pontoons were pulled up we felt that we should be safe from possible capture. The city was entirely deserted save for the broken caissons, dead artillery horses, and the débris left by the retreating army. We ran down the street on the double-quick.

The Confederates, who had discovered that the Union forces were retreating across the river, unlimbered their batteries and began to send shells flying into Fredericksburg. The very first shell that was fired came whizzing over our heads. Down we went, flat on our faces, not knowing where the shell might burst. Fortunately, it exploded a considerable distance down the street ahead of us. We got up and hurried on towards the river. When we reached the water front, the pontoon that we expected to find there was gone. It looked for a while as though every means of crossing had been destroyed, and it was with difficulty that I succeeded in keeping some of my men from plunging into the river. Our only hope of crossing safely was in finding still intact one of the other pontoons located farther up the river. The fog was very thick and we could not see a great distance ahead of us. A few minutes' run, however, brought us within sound of men at work. We hurried on and reached the last pontoon just as it was being broken from its fastenings. The engineers quickly stretched planks from the boats to the river bank and we ran across them in single file. When we reached the other side of the river, everything was in confusion and it was several hours before we finally came up with our regiment.[1]

As may be gathered from the account of the adventures of the pickets given above, our regiment had, with the others of the corps, passed safely over the pontoon bridge in the retreat from Fredericksburg. We were the last regiment to recross the lower bridge[2] and one of the very last regiments to leave the Fredericksburg side. We splashed on through mud, up nearly to our knees, until we reached the hill whence we had started three days before to enter the battle. We stayed there one night, and the next morning came back to our old camp on the Henry farm near Potomac Creek.

[1] The detail had been reported as missing and Colonel Garrard immediately summoned the sergeant and told him that he had been reduced to the ranks. Explanations followed which showed that the orders sent out just before daylight to withdraw for some reason had not been delivered. The Colonel revoked his order reducing the sergeant to the ranks and instead promoted him to the position of Second Lieutenant, at the same time promoting the corporal to sergeant.

[2] Letter of Captain H. H. Curran, December 18, 1862.

CHAPTER IV

THE WINTER AT FALMOUTH

AFTER Fredericksburg we settled down to camp routine in the same quarters we had occupied before the battle. Although we had taken no part in the actual fighting, we at least had passed through an exciting experience. To be exposed to the fire of an enemy's batteries is certainly a most uncomfortable and dangerous position to be placed in, and extremely trying to raw troops, as we were at the time. The regiment as a whole had stood the test unflinchingly and we had reason to be proud of our behavior when under fire for the first time. While few admitted it, most of us, deep down in our hearts, had felt uneasy. Those qualms and nervous shivers that many of us experienced could not be called, perhaps, exactly cowardice; nevertheless it was a great relief to feel that we had come out of the ordeal with such a small loss.

The weather for the first two weeks after our return from Fredericksburg was clear and delightful. The health of the camp during this time was fairly good. The scourges of disease that had so harassed us before the battle and had caused the camp to be known to the soldiers as "Camp Dysentery," fortunately did not reappear immediately. It was not surprising, however, that as the days passed sickness should overcome the less hardy among us. In spite of the precepts and precautions of our Colonel, unsanitary conditions necessarily prevailed to a considerable extent. The great majority of us were young men or mere boys who had never been away from home before, and we had not yet had sufficient military experience to know how to conduct ourselves properly in camp.

The camp life of a soldier was not a continuous round of uninterrupted pleasure. There was a monotony to the routine of duties, there was exposure to cold and inclement weather, and a decided lack of the comforts which we had enjoyed at home. These features of a soldier's life had been very carefully omitted by the orators and recruiting officers who had urged us to enlist.

Certain of our regimental officers chafed under this hardship and discipline. It was in fact so distasteful to some that they tendered their resignations. Colonel Garrard willingly approved such applications for dismissal, telling the officers who made them that they had missed their vocation. The enlisted men who might have wished to return to their homes, not having, of course, the privilege of resigning, were compelled, unless they were physically disabled, to make the best of the situation, no matter how unpleasant it might be. The great majority were true soldiers in spirit and only a very few resorted to desertion to avoid these necessary hardships.

During the winter at Falmouth, Colonel Garrard was urged by General Halleck and General Casey to take command of a brigade. He, however, declined this honor. He seemed to feel, as one man expressed it,[1] "that he could better serve his country by making a raw regiment into a good one than by taking a brigade."

Not a very large proportion of the regimental officers in the Union army had had any military experience before the war broke out. Our Colonel on the contrary was a graduate of West Point and also a veteran of the Mexican War, and, therefore, well-equipped to make us an effective, well-drilled regiment. His care and oversight extended to every man and animal under his command. The power which he

[1] A. P. Case.

used was, no doubt, arbitrary, but it was legitimate, and was used solely with the intention of benefiting the regiment. Withal, he was a very modest, tender-hearted man, generous to a fault, lavish of everything he possessed, willing to divide his last crust with the meanest private in the regiment, making no provision for his own personal benefit or comfort. For several weeks after the winter began in real earnest he lacked what most of the men and officers had—a fire in his tent. Never, even in the severest weather, had he any straw between his blanket and the ground; and for many weeks his only shelter at night was an old wedge tent, with which he was contented until it grew so dilapidated that it would hold together no longer. As an illustration of Colonel Garrard's personality the fact may be cited that he knew the name of every man in the regiment, and it was no unusual thing to have him call out of the ranks by name some man who had been delinquent, or, on the other hand, to commend someone who might be worthy of praise.

His supervision extended even over so commonplace a matter as our cooking. In this art we were at first sadly unsophisticated, and the health of the men began to be affected thereby. To remedy this Colonel Garrard established the system of company cooking, by which the work for an entire company was done by two or three men. Gradually the novices were pressed into service and taught by those who were more skilled, so that by the end of the winter almost all of us had become fairly proficient cooks.

Colonel Garrard was a strict disciplinarian, and demanded of his company officers intelligent coöperation in all his plans, and he did not hesitate to punish those who were indolent or lax in their duties. If an orderly sergeant was careless or indifferent, he was promptly relegated to the ranks and a worthy private often substituted in his place, much to the disgust of those who expected promotion in the order of their enlistment, without regard to merit. More than one captaincy which became vacant by reason of promotion or dismissal was filled by a Second Lieutenant whom the Colonel deemed more worthy of the promotion than a superior officer. Schools for the company commissioned officers and for the orderly sergeants were conducted by our Colonel, in which the pupils were instructed by him in the mysteries of military tactics; and they were compelled to put what they learned to immediate use in company and battalion drills.

It took some time to instill into the volunteer soldier, used to the democracy of civil life, the realization that a system of "caste" existed in the army, conformity to which was one of the first essentials of military life. Colonel Garrard early began to instruct the men in this phase of discipline and conduct. He insisted that the privates should not loaf about their officers' tents and fires. Every private and officer was compelled to salute his superior, who, in turn, must return the courtesy. When on guard duty, the men were taught to salute the officers with their guns, as in the Regular Army. He made the captains and lieutenants responsible for the conduct of the men in their respective companies, and censured them severely if they failed to take proper care of their men, both as regards cleanliness of person, surroundings, and military conduct. Of course, such regulations as the foregoing soon became a part of our everyday life, and required no very strict enforcement. The fact that Colonel Garrard, from the very beginning, insisted upon all the niceties of military discipline and distinction soon characterized our regiment as being different from a great many of the volunteer regiments in which army regulations were not rigidly enforced.

The Colonel's methods in bringing about such discipline were simple, yet very effective. If any of the men became boisterous and noisy or started to quarrel among themselves they were compelled to walk around in a large circle every other hour for twenty-four hours. The penalty for some offenses consisted of being compelled to carry heavy logs strapped to the shoulders for a period of eight or ten hours. Often the punishment was milder, and might consist in being compelled to wear a placard fastened to the back, setting forth the nature of the offense for which it had been placed there. At roll call, on parade, or drill the men were required to turn out promptly, right to the mark; and quite frequently entire companies were sent back to their tents to come out a second time if they did not do so properly when the first call sounded, or they were often sentenced to an extra hour of drill for being slow.

The daily routine of our camp life was as follows: reveille was sounded at daybreak and all turned out for roll call; as soon as that was over the tents were swept and scrubbed thoroughly and the blankets hung out in the sun; at half after seven, the whole regiment was turned out armed with brooms and spades and charged up and down the camp ground, until the white earth was fairly made to shine, the dirt thus collected being carried to Potomac Creek each day in wagons and dumped into the river; at nine o'clock, breakfast; then an hour and a quarter drill in movements and manual of arms; at twelve o'clock came dinner; at two o'clock, another hour and a quarter drill; at half after four an hour on dress parade or battalion drill; then supper; at eight o'clock roll call again; this was followed by an hour of leisure, and when "taps" was sounded at nine o'clock it usually found us ready to "turn in" for the night. Sunday, especially for the officers, was often a busier day than the others, for at that time attempts were made to bring up the odd jobs of the week. The regiment was not drilled on that day, but instead was paraded for inspection of arms, clothing, and persons. Each regiment was required to do twenty-four hours of guard duty each week. There were also irregular duties as brigade and division guards, which were equally proportioned among the troops of the brigade and division. Extra details of men for repairing roads and bridges, unloading cars, etc., completed the round of duties while in camp, and almost completely crowded out all thoughts of leisure.

During the little time that we were not employed actively we sought recreation in the few diversions which the camp afforded. Reading was a favorite pastime of many, and card-playing was indulged in by nearly all, "Old Sledge" or "Seven-up" being one of the favorite games. On clear, cold days a few went skating on Potomac Creek. Snowball fights among the men of the different companies took place occasionally when the snow was just right for "packing," and these affairs sometimes assumed the proportions of miniature battles in which the entire regiment participated. Such conflicts usually started from the camp of Company "A," who were the most belligerent, and would begin by the men of that company bombarding the "street" of another company at the other side of the camp. Soon the whole regiment would be involved, the officers taking part as well as the men and leading their commands in charges and countercharges. Often missiles harder than snow were used in the thick of the fight, and the battles were almost as bloody as some in which we participated during active campaigning. The fight was ended, usually, by the interference of the Colonel or other field officer, or by one battalion of the regiment driving the other into their tents.

The camp of our brigade covered eight acres and was situated on level ground on the top of a high bluff. The tents were connected by artificial evergreen hedges, forming picturesque company "courts" or "streets," ten in number. These streets were still further beautified by placing holly trees in the center of each. When we became more inured to our life and better satisfied with our situation, rivalry ran high among the different companies as to the neatness and cleanliness of their several "streets."

Our tents were the "wall" type, about nine feet square on the ground and about four feet high at the eaves. The sides were constructed of rough logs, and the canvas stretched over a ridge pole which was elevated in the center of the "tent." The cracks between the logs were filled with mud. Floors of rough-hewn boards were laid, and loose hay or straw scattered thereon. Each tent accommodated four or five, and sometimes six, men. The beds were like onion beds in a garden, the sleeping space being fenced in with narrow boards. Pine boughs or leaves on the bottom completed the bed, which was two and a half feet wide. A few nights' sleep in such a bed destroyed effectively all the "effeminacy" supposed to be contained in the leaves, and we soon learned to "bone down to it," as we described habituating ourselves to such sleeping quarters. The only furniture in the tents were rude chairs and tables constructed from boxes and rough-hewn wood, but each tent contained a fireplace built of mud and stones, the chimney of which was formed by a barrel from which both heads had been removed. Frequently one of these wooden chimneys caught fire during the night, and the frantic efforts of the men to extinguish the blaze reminded one vividly of an Indian war dance.

When we first arrived at Falmouth, the country round about was dotted with woods, but these rapidly disappeared as the trees and bushes were chopped down for use as firewood and in tent and furniture construction. The landscape soon began to look as desolate as Arabia, being scarred and seamed by the removal of sods and earth and the building of numerous narrow roads leading through the woods connecting the various sections of the vast army camp. This scarcity of wood was one of the greatest aggravations of our life at Falmouth, for it necessitated our going long distances from camp each day in order to procure sufficient fuel for our use. The so-called roads were so rough that it was impossible to traverse them with teams and wagons, and the men were forced to carry the wood on their shoulders a distance of over a mile, and later two and even three miles each day.

A diversion from camp life which was highly pleasing to a great many was the picket duty that devolved upon us in

Lieut. Henry G. Taylor

Henry Everleth

Sutler's Clerk

Private Edward Morris

Captured at Weldon R. R.
Died in hands of Confederates

Private Francis A. England

UNIDENTIFIED CORPORAL

This full-standing view of an unidentified 146th New York corporal was taken by photographer C. M. Tuttle in Lyons, NY. The soldier's vest and the chair cover are tinted red. (Guy Smith Collection)

our turn. The Army of the Potomac held the north side of the Rappahannock River for a considerable distance north and south of Fredericksburg, and each regiment was called upon at regular intervals to furnish its quota of pickets for guarding the line. Some sixty-odd men, under command of a captain, formed the usual detail for such work, and this duty was looked forward to as the time for such assignment drew near. A member of Company "D"[1] wrote home of his first experience of picket duty, as follows:

We were ordered out on picket duty with fifteen minutes to prepare our rations and bed-clothing. We tramped about four miles and swore until 3.00 F.M. Then we were marched into a pine thicket (half of us), where we found brush shanties, made a rousing fire, cooked coffee, pork, and hardtack and ate heartily, it being the first meal since morning. This picketing, as it is for us to-night, is a "gay" experience. Imagine you see a brush shanty with a large fire in front of it, and seated on the windward side of it E. P.[2] leaning against the center-pole, feet to the fire, and almost asleep; next, on the corner of the tent, sits or reclines Joe[3] with his "sweet-briar"; next is Eg.[4] with a copy of *Frank Leslie*, which came after we had formed in line; then come Cook[5] and Jones,[6] each smoking and talking about the soundness of old Horace Greeley; then comes "last but not least" your soldier friend, who, bended on his knee with knapsack on a rail and a letter on that, is writing to you. The sky is filled with stars and the moon is in "full bloom," the cold wintry wind whistles through the pine tops and makes one think of a northern winter in earnest, but here in our little camp we heed it not. I wish you were here to see for yourself one of the luxuries in the life of a soldier. I would give five dollars for a correct sketch of this, our first night at picketing. Long shall it be remembered. I used to think what fun it would be to camp out, stand guard, travel, etc., and my wishes are being gratified now.

Although we had at Falmouth practically none of the

[1] Letter of James P. Pitcher.
[2] Elijah P. Fisk.
[3] Joseph S. Lowery.
[4] Marvin Egleston.
[5] Sylvester O. Cook.
[6] Orlo H. Jones.

comforts of civilization, we were not entirely cut off from the world at large. Except in severe weather, mail reached us at regular intervals and was always most welcome, bringing, as it did, news of our home and loved ones. The mail for each company was left with the orderly sergeant and for a few minutes after the arrival of each mail his tent was the center of a group of anxious and expectant men, while the mail was being sorted and distributed in alphabetical order. As a further means of keeping in touch with current events, we were supplied with newspapers at ten cents a copy by boys who rode into camp on horseback with the papers which they got from the nearest point on the railroad.

Visitors to camp came at rare intervals and were always the source of much curiosity and admiration, especially if they were of the kind described by one of our officers[1] as follows:

We had in camp to-day a "green-back" of unknown denomination, immensely above par in value, and looked at covetously by all. It was a beautiful young lady in green riding dress, soldier's cap with veil, prancing horse, and showy retinue of officers. Whence or whither we knew not, we only gazed and admired. It was a real apparition.

Occasionally we saw a civilian with a glossy "stove-pipe" hat and an umbrella under his arm, and perhaps overshoes on. Needless to say, we looked upon such evidences of civilization with hearty contempt.

The very brightest moments in our life at Falmouth were the times when we received boxes from our friends at home, containing all manner of comforts, and "good things" in the line of edibles. Various articles of clothing and home-made delicacies of every description were the usual contents of such boxes, and the fortunate recipients were glad enough to share the good things with their less favored companions. Needless to say, such gifts elicited the warmest appreciation

[1] Letter of Quartermaster A. Pierson Case, Jan. 4, 1863.

from those who received them, in the form of expressions of gratitude, which were best worded by a simple description of the reception accorded the box on its arrival. A characteristic letter is one written by an officer[1] to his wife and parents:

Hurrah! The box has come! We had just finished a meal of soup and hardtack, and felt indignant that we must wait for hunger to come again to our assistance. (The following day.) We had a fine time with the box yesterday. Were determined to have another dinner if it killed us. About 6.00 P.M. we had the turkey, apple sauce, and cookies on the table, and had a grand time. This morning I opened a roll of sausage marked "From Mother" and had some for breakfast. It almost took me back to Vernon. The Colonel said when the box came and we dove into it that we acted like a parcel of children, but he soon became a child with us, being completely converted through the instrumentality of one of mother's good doughnuts. He now thinks "boxes" are nice affairs. Wishes he had a wife or sweetheart to send him a box occasionally. The senders are all remembered gratefully.

Most of the boxes from home were sent so as to arrive on or about a holiday, but delays sometimes occurred to prevent their arrival for several days, and sometimes even weeks. The holidays, therefore, Christmas and New Year's, were celebrated as best we could with the limited means at our command. The officers dressed themselves in their finest uniforms and visited their friends in the various brigades and divisions. The regimental bands of the Regulars, who were camped not far from us, furnished most delightful music throughout the day, and the entire camp took on a gala appearance. New Year's Day, especially, was looked upon by many as an excuse and occasion to celebrate.

After the excitement of the holiday season had passed, the early part of January dragged slowly along, with but few diversions. The most important of these was a review

[1] A. P. Case.

of the entire army held by General Burnside during the second week of the month. Our corps, the Fifth, was reviewed by the General on January eighth. Most of the regiments had been in the service long enough to have acquired a soldierly bearing. The martial music of the bands, the torn and tattered banners waving in the breeze, and the serried ranks, fifteen thousand strong, presented a magnificent spectacle. We were told by the older men of the brigade that a review was usually the precursor of a movement by the army, and we looked forward to it from that day.[1]

About ten days later the prediction of our older comrades was fulfilled. Pontoons and artillery were assembled; hospital tents erected; arms and accouterments of every variety repaired and replenished. Orders were received to march on January seventeenth, but they were later countermanded. Again the order came to move early on the morning of the eighteenth; then to start at noon; then an order to wait till nine that evening; and later all orders to march were countermanded for that day. This delay in starting was due to the fact that the weather suddenly became intensely cold and the commanding general was fearful that it might interfere seriously with the movements of the troops. The weather moderated somewhat on the twentieth, and on the evening of that day we received orders to move which were not countermanded. We started out at daylight on the following morning in the midst of a driving rain which soon made the mud very deep.

The Second Corps, under General Couch, was left on the east bank of the Rappahannock below Fredericksburg for the purpose of deceiving General Lee as to the real nature of the movement, and the Eleventh Corps, under General Sigel, remained in position near Falmouth. The rest of the Army of the Potomac moved northward in the direction of Banks's

[1] January fifteenth new Springfield rifles were distributed to the regiment, replacing the Austrian rifles with which we had been equipped.

Ford, with the intention of crossing at that point and meeting the Confederates in the open plains north of Fredericksburg, in the vicinity where General Hooker was to fight the disastrous battle of Chancellorsville the following spring.

The plans had been well-laid and all might have gone well if the weather had continued favorable to the project. The rain, however, which had begun during the night of the twentieth, continued with unabated fury throughout the succeeding day; by the morning of the twenty-first the earth was soaked and the river banks had the appearance of a quagmire.

With the rest of the Fifth Corps, our regiment plodded on through the mud as well as we could all day on the twenty-first, but it was beyond the scope of human possibilities to make much progress in the deepening mud. Pieces of artillery which were ordinarily drawn by four or six horses found difficulty in making progress with ten and twelve, and finally the horses and mules were unhitched entirely and long ropes were attached to the gun-carriages on which the men, sometimes almost an entire regiment on a single rope, pulled valiantly in an effort to extricate them from the mud that covered them almost to the mouths of the cannon. On no march in which we participated were the "necessities" of war more terrible than on this one. If a horse or mule dropped in its harness, it was quickly cut loose and the wagons which followed passed over the body, crushing out the little remnant of its life. The men who were compelled to drop out, and there were a great number, were left either to die or to crawl along as best they could. It was impossible to do otherwise. Every wagon was loaded, and the ambulances were filled with the sick who could not walk at all. These were some of the "necessities" of that unnecessary march. Even a semblance of order was out of the question and each man made his way as well as he could, in or out of the road.

The delay on the part of the Union army due to the

difficulty of marching had given the Confederate commander time to become cognizant of the movement, and he hastened to place his army on the western bank of the Rappahannock in such a position as to guard the fords. When the Union forces, therefore, reached Banks's Ford on the evening of the twenty-first they found that not only had the river risen so as to make a crossing extremely precarious, but also that the Confederates on the opposite side were prepared to vigorously oppose a crossing. General Burnside made an effort to bring up his artillery on the morning of the twenty-second, but it was utterly impossible on account of the mud. The men struggled heroically, but to no avail. The Union commander was compelled to bow to the inevitable and to give up the enterprise entirely.

Despite the utter futility of the movement, our regiment, in common with all the others that participated in the unfortunate expedition, was compelled to remain in the vicinity of Banks's Ford from Wednesday noon until Saturday morning. The days were spent floundering about in the mud, and the nights in the utmost misery, the depth of the mud precluding any possibility of lying down to secure much-needed rest. We had no shelter whatever, and only the protection of clothing and blankets which soon became saturated by the rain and almost useless. Attempts to build fires to warm ourselves and dry our clothes were worse than futile, for the dampness of the wood and the pelting rain converted them into vast "smudges" which almost blinded the men. Some were so badly affected as to require several weeks to recover from the effects of the smoke. Huddled together in the mud exposed to the fury of the elements or seeking refuge in the doubtful shelter of small trees and scrub bushes, our plight was indeed a pitiful one. To make our condition still more miserable, hunger was added to our hardships. The rain had spoiled the hardtack, sugar, and coffee which we had carried in our knapsacks, and we had nothing left but rancid salt pork. We rescued this from the conglomerate mass into which the water had converted the food in our haversacks and fried it as well as we could on the ends of sticks over the smoky fires, nearly blinding ourselves in the process. On Friday some hardtack was at last obtained and distributed, and a little whiskey was given to each man. We were thus able to ward off utter starvation.

In the meantime, the enemy on the opposite bank of the river had amused themselves by taunting the Union pickets, and went so far as to erect signboards, bearing the legends, "Stuck in the mud," "This way to Richmond," "Come on over and whip us," and similar inscriptions.

Even the most unfortunate expeditions, however, end at last, and relief from the misery of the celebrated "Mud March" came to us in time. On Saturday, January twenty-fourth, we started with the other regiments of our corps for Falmouth. The return march was made in fairly good order. We arrived in camp again late that same afternoon. Strange to say, this spot that we had been so glad to leave a few days before now looked like a haven of rest, but it took several days to recuperate after this fruitless expedition and resume our daily routine of work and drills.

The disastrous results of the "Mud March" brought about another change in the command and organization of the Army of the Potomac. While the army was still in the vicinity of Banks's Ford, General Burnside prepared and submitted to the President a most astounding order removing many of his most prominent subordinates from their commands and dismissing others from the service of the United States. This unusual order was not approved by President Lincoln, and General Burnside immediately requested to be relieved from the command of the Army of the Potomac. This was done and General Joseph Hooker was assigned to his place. Besides his service with the Army of the Potomac, Hooker had been for a number of years on the Pacific Coast and was a most efficient organizer. His selection as commander of the army was well received by both officers and men, so that the salute fired on January twenty-seventh telling of his appointment was greeted with cheers and a renewed spirit of confidence and hope on the part of the rank and file.

Shortly after he assumed command, General Hooker made several changes in the organization of the army, the most important being the abolition of the system of "Grand Divisions," which had originated with Burnside. The corps was made the unit of organization, and the order bringing this about, which was issued on February fifth, assigned General Reynolds to the command of the First Corps; General Couch to the Second; General Sickles to the Third; General Meade to the Fifth; General Sedgwick to the Sixth; General Sigel[1] to the Eleventh; and General Slocum to the Twelfth.

Throughout the Fifth Corps several changes also took place. Many of the regular regiments were broken up on account of their reduced numbers and the men were assigned to other commands. A little later General Warren, the commander of the brigade of which our regiment formed a part, was assigned to the staff of General Hooker, and he was succeeded by Colonel Patrick H. O'Rorke, of the One Hundred and Fortieth New York Volunteers.

These changes in the general organization of the army did not affect our regiment in any way. It was midwinter and we could not expect an active campaign again until spring. February brought alternate snow and rain, with just enough cold weather to make it extremely disagreeable, and March was ushered in by a snowstorm of great severity. During these two months there seemed to be no place where we could find relief from the fitful elements, and much suffering resulted.

Picket duty in such inclement weather was far from pleasant and like every other duty became extremely weari-

[1] Relieved soon after and Major-General O. O. Howard appointed in his place.

some. We welcomed anything that tended to relieve its monotony; even so trivial an incident as that which one of our officers[1] relates:

Tuesday morning[2] we started for the picket line. The snow was over a foot deep, and the thermometer marked not much above zero. I had no active duty during the day, except superintending about half a mile of the line, and the guarding of a "secesh" house, a little outside of the lines. I stayed at a negro hut, attached to a house just inside the lines. The house was a very comfortable place, with its large fireplace and pile of blazing logs. An aged horse; a weazen-faced, sanctimonious little old man, with a long chin, and a much longer nose, and two sleek locks of hair darting from behind two enormous ears; a very demure-looking cat, that seemed to take delight in lying on its back in the snow and pawing the air vigorously—these three gave the only signs of life about this quaint old Virginia house, hidden among the trees. About dusk, Pat Thomas[3] told me that he had scraped the old man's acquaintance and was invited in to spend the evening. He also told me that there were young ladies there, so I went with him, and had a very pleasant time. The owner of the house was an Episcopal clergyman, rector of the Aquia church at Stafford Court House, a church which had been standing, as he said, with a smile of pleasure not slightly tempered with pride, a hundred and ten years. His wife, a very calm, statue-like old lady, was entertained by Lieutenant Lowery. She was very deaf, but the Lieutenant made a vigorous onslaught and by dint of loud shouts and using his hands as a trumpet, probably passed a very happy evening. Pat Thomas palmed himself off for a surgeon, and indulged in a very learned discussion with the old gentleman, who was quite inquisitive and desired to learn much on various difficult operations and unusual diseases. I, being thus thrown into the company of the young lady, who proved to be very agreeable and refined—a niece of Surgeon-General Hammond—of course, passed a pleasant evening. It was the first time I had talked to a female in six months, and it seemed odd enough. . . . The next day at noon the enemy's cavalry

---

[1] Captain Curran.   [2] February fourteenth.
[3] At that time Hospital Steward.

feigned an attack on our lines of cavalry, drove them in upon us, and then retired. It was quite a pleasant bit of excitement, after so long a lazy spell. I wish they had attacked us. I had my fifty men posted where they could have cleared away five times their number, the best spot for defense in the line. They did not come upon us, though, and we lost the chance of fun. . . . The next morning I awoke about 8.00 o'clock, and thought it was summer. The snow was nearly gone, and the sun was shining very warm. Squirrels came from their hiding-places and chattered merrily. Robins and jays and numerous other birds sang merrily. Buzzards and crows were flying lazily overhead, quails and pigeons whirred and rushed by our camp-fires. . . . Cold rain two days later, however, admonished us that it was not quite summer yet.

About the first of April the weather became much pleasanter and continued growing more and more balmy and clear every day. With the coming of the spring days, the health of the regiment improved rapidly and we soon had more than five hundred men on duty. Regular drilling, which it had been necessary to abandon during the unpleasant weather of early March, was resumed. The entire camp was drained, the streets graded and lined on either side with evergreens, making our abode look quite cheerful. Target shooting was begun again, which aroused a friendly rivalry. The firing was by company at a target two feet square and the members of Company "D" excelled at this, establishing themselves as champions.

During the first week in April, Colonel Garrard spent a few days in Washington, to supervise the making of new uniforms for the regiment. They were to be of the "zouave" type, similar to those worn by the Fifth New York, and we looked forward to receiving them with a great deal of interest. In the meantime, we were taught the zouave bayonet drill, in preparation for the arrival of our uniforms.

As the days grew warmer and brighter, we knew that a spring campaign would soon begin, and many speculations were made as to its objectives. Various rumors were circulated, but we, as members of the rank and file, could only wait until those in authority determined upon the move that should be made.

The last event of importance that occurred while we lay at Falmouth was the gigantic review of the Army of the Potomac by President Lincoln. The cavalry were reviewed on April sixth, and the President passed the next day visiting the infantry camps. When he arrived at our brigade camp, the Fifth New York was, at his request, called upon to give an exhibition drill. Its camp was just a short distance from ours on a rise of ground on the same side of the road, so that we could see the drill plainly from the place where we were drawn up in line. On April eighth, our regiment was called out to participate in the review itself, which was held in an open plain opposite Fredericksburg and in full view of the Confederates encamped on their heights on the other side of the river. The number of troops participating was estimated at over a hundred thousand men and the magnificence of the display surpassed that of any similar event from the beginning of the war until the Grand Review in Washington at the close. The column occupied the entire day in passing the point where President Lincoln and General Hooker had stationed themselves and the men who took part were compelled to wander about for that length of time, hungry and out of sorts. Although a review was always a very beautiful and impressive spectacle, it was decidedly unpopular with the reviewed.

Thus ended our first winter in camp, spent on the heights at Falmouth. The rigorous life had been, on the whole, of much benefit to the regiment. Death had claimed a number of our comrades; sickness had disqualified others from further service; a few had been transferred to the ambulance corps or wagon trains as drivers and helpers. The personnel of the regiment was made up now of efficient soldiers, and in discipline, drill, and all-round military proficiency we were pronounced by our commanding generals as fully equal to the regiments of the Regular Army.

CHAPTER V

THE CHANCELLORSVILLE CAMPAIGN

A S the spring of 1863 advanced the time appeared opportune to General Hooker for an aggressive movement
against the enemy. General Lee was weakened by the
absence of General Longstreet and a portion of his corps,
who were marching against Suffolk; and the Army of the
Potomac would soon lose twenty thousand effective soldiers
through the expiration of service of that number of nine
months' and two years' men.

The plan of campaign as outlined by General Hooker
and submitted to President Lincoln on the eleventh of April
was a threefold one. The plan provided that the cavalry,
under General Stoneman, should cross the Rappahannock
and Rapidan by the fords above the junction of these rivers,
and, sweeping down between Fredericksburg and Richmond,
cut off the communications between these cities by destroying the railroad and holding the highways connecting them.
The infantry and artillery were to be divided. A large
force under General Sedgwick was to be thrown across the
Rappahannock River below Fredericksburg, and the remaining corps of the army were to follow General Stoneman across the upper Rappahannock and make a detour
back of the river for the purpose of striking the Confederates, encamped on the heights back of Fredericksburg, in the rear, or of drawing them out for a battle in
the open in the vicinity of Chancellorsville, where they

would not have the protection of intrenchments and breastworks.

The plan of campaign was a comprehensive one, and skillfully worked out. General Hooker, furthermore, was able to keep his prospective operations against Lee more secret than McClellan and Burnside had been able to do. The Federal corps commanders did not know what the plans were to be until they received orders to march; and General Lee, although informed of the operations of the Union cavalry, apparently did not comprehend the full significance of the movements of his opponent.

The campaign began on April twelfth, when Stoneman's cavalry were sent to make a crossing of the Rappahannock at the fords above Falmouth. The movement, however, was executed so slowly, due to heavy rains rendering the fords impassable, that it proved a failure so far as cutting off Lee's communications with Richmond was concerned. The cavalry were obliged to remain on the north bank of the river until April twenty-ninth, when they crossed on the pontoon bridges laid for the passage of the infantry.

General Hooker, even though Stoneman's operations had been delayed, determined to continue the campaign as planned. He accordingly ordered forward the Fifth Corps, under General Meade, together with the Eleventh Corps, under General Howard, and the Twelfth, under General Slocum. These troops moved over the road the cavalry had taken leading to the fords north of Falmouth. The Second Corps, under General Couch, was dispatched to gain possession of the United States and Banks' Fords on the Rappahannock between Fredericksburg and the junction with the Rapidan. The First, Third, and Sixth Corps, under command of General Sedgwick, prepared to cross the Rappahannock south of Fredericksburg.

Sunday evening, April twenty-sixth, we had retired with no expectation of having to start out on a campaign the next morning. At five o'clock, however, the following

Capt. Joseph S. Lowery
Wounded at Cold Harbor

Sergt. Sylvester O. Cook
Trans. to 16th N. Y. Heavy Artillery

Lieut. Peter D. Froeligh
Killed at the Wilderness

Capt. Joseph B. Cushman

Lieut. J. Albert Jennison

JOSEPH B. CUSHMAN

Cushman, shown wearing a Zouave officer's uniform, was 26 years old when he enrolled on Oct. 7, 1862, at Rome and mustered in as first lieutenant of Co. K on Oct. 10, 1862. He was absent with leave starting Jan. 21, 1863, to recover from remittent fever. Cushman was present and commanding the company from Mar. to Aug. 1863. He was absent sick with chronic diarrhea and stomach irritation starting on Sept. 28, 1863. On the day of his return to regiment, he was promoted captain and transferred to Co. C on Oct. 28, 1863. Cushman was absent commencing Apr. 19, 1864, convalescing from chronic diarrhea. He was honorably discharged on June 1, 1864, having tendered his resignation on account of physical disability (chronic diarrhea and remittent fever). Cushman died Mar. 29, 1914, at Vernon. (Patrick A. Schroeder Collection)

morning we received orders to be ready to march at ten. The numerous things to be done preparatory to a departure filled the early hours of the morning with activity, but at half after nine our regiment was in line with the rest of Sykes's division. Every man was loaded as if he were a beast of burden, with eight days' rations, ammunition, coat, blanket, knapsack, and gun. "Hooker's Pack Mules" was a term applied to the men by some wit as they started out, and its aptness caused it to pass rapidly through the ranks of the entire army. At ten o'clock the Fifth Corps began the march, our division in the lead and the brigades marching in numerical order. Artillery and pack mules brought up the rear, and the ambulances and wagons were left behind. It was a delightful day, although warm, and as we proceeded overcoats were discarded and were strewed along the road on both sides. While on the march General Meade rode by us with his staff, and was greeted with lusty cheers as he passed along the line. After going about eight miles the corps went into camp on the side of the road in the vicinity of Hartwood Church. We recognized the place as the "Camp Misery" of our march from Warrenton the preceding fall. Shortly after our arrival some of the men conceived the idea of appropriating the boards of which the church was built for beds and this plan proved so popular that the entire church was torn down and used as sleeping-quarters. Having brought no shelter tents we wrapped ourselves in our blankets and with the sky for a canopy passed a comfortable night bivouacking along the roadside.

The next day we remained idle in camp until two o'clock in the afternoon, waiting for the Eleventh and Twelfth Corps to pass us. A cold rain began to fall soon after we started, making the roads very soggy and the going heavy and disagreeable. Night set in, but still we waded on through the deepening mud. At last we halted in the vicinity of Crittenden's Mills and "turned in" about eleven o'clock. We slept uncomfortably on the wet ground, and were on the march at seven o'clock the next morning. Towards noon we came to the high hills overlooking Kelly's Ford, where the troops which had preceded us were crossing on pontoon bridges stretched over the river. Below us we could see dense masses of cavalry, artillery, and pack mules, while farther on, across the river, the long converging lines of the Eleventh and Twelfth Corps stretched away in the dim background. It was a beautiful view. The turf was bright and fresh, the foliage was just opening in the vast forests on either side, while many orchards of peach and apple touched the landscape here and there with white and rosy patches.

At Kelly's Ford, the Third Division of our corps, under General Humphreys, was left behind to protect the crossing, but with the other two divisions of the corps our regiment followed the long column that had gone before us across the pontoon bridges. Having crossed the Rappahannock north of its junction with the Rapidan, the latter river was below us, towards the south. The plan of campaign called for crossing this river and entering the forest in the vicinity of Chancellorsville. The Eleventh and Twelfth Corps were to cross at Germanna Ford and we, with the Fifth Corps, about six miles farther east at Ely's Ford.

After an all day's march through the mud and rain we reached Ely's Ford on the Rapidan about six o'clock in the evening. We halted for only a few minutes, when the order was given to ford the stream, as there were no pontoons ready for crossing. We stripped off our lower garments and each man tied his belongings into a large bundle which he carried above his head. The water of the river, which still retained the temperature of the winter snow and ice, was doubly cold to us, heated as we were by our exertions on the march. Each man, as he stepped into the swiftly flowing stream, shuddered involuntarily and gave a grunt of disapproval. The water in the middle of the river was more than waist deep and it was no easy matter to wade across it with our burdens above our heads. Some tried to float over on logs or hastily improvised rafts, but the great majority of these came to grief and were precipitated headlong into the icy stream. Guns, cartridge-boxes, and various articles of clothing were frequently dropped into the water and the scramble which ensued in an effort to recover them added to the confusion. The men of small stature and the drummer boys especially found this fording of the Rapidan rather perilous. One of the latter,[1] a diminutive lad about thirteen or fourteen years old, nearly lost his life in his heroic effort to get across the stream. He started out holding onto two men, but unable to keep his hold was carried quickly down the stream, struggling bravely and calling for help. Several of the men tried to catch him, but he slipped out of their grasp. Fortunately, the boy held fast to his drum, and that kept him up. Colonel Garrard, who saw the accident, came to his assistance and, placing the boy on his horse in front of him, carried him safely to the other shore.

The entire regiment was at last across the stream in safety, and with the rest of the division marched a short distance and then bivouacked along the road and in the woods on either side. Some sought refuge from the rain beneath the sheltering limbs of the trees, but most of us were too tired to take any note of our surroundings and, wrapping ourselves in our blankets, lay down to sleep.

We were aroused early on the following day, and by seven o'clock the two divisions of the corps, Sykes's and Griffin's, were on the march in the order named. After going about a mile, our division turned off into the woods to the left and a short distance through the trees brought us to a road leading to United States Ford. Griffin's division continued its march on the road to Chancellorsville. Although the rain continued unabated the march now became an exciting one, for we were told that we should

[1] James Shaw, Co. "C."

find two brigades of the enemy at the ford. Weary and footsore though we were, the news cheered us up and we trudged merrily along, hoping to attack and overwhelm them before they could make good their escape. The mud grew deeper and more slippery every hour, but we pressed rapidly on, almost at a dog-trot. Suddenly we saw a clearing ahead, dotted with tents, the camping-ground of the enemy. We reached the place but found it deserted. The tents still standing, and numerous articles of food and clothing scattered about, bore evidence of the haste with which the Confederates had departed. After a few minutes' rest we were off again, returning to the main road that Griffin's division had taken. We reached it and pushed on to Chancellorsville, arriving there in rear of Griffin. Here we rested for two hours and those of us who were not completely fatigued from the rapid marches had an opportunity to try to remove some of the mud and dirt with which our clothes were covered. We lay right beside the one large house of which Chancellorsville consisted. It was a very large straggling building, constructed entirely of brick. The distinguishing characteristic of nearly all Southern houses, the large colonial pillars, was present on its front, but it lacked the beauty of the average Virginia plantation house, being situated on low level ground on which there were but ten or twelve trees within a radius of perhaps an eighth of a mile. As we saw it on this dreary, rainy spring day, it presented anything but a cheerful appearance.

While we lay at Chancellorsville, Griffin's division continued its march towards the Rappahannock on the road leading to Banks's Ford. Shortly afterwards, our division started out on the road leading to Fredericksburg. We passed several rifle-pits that had been constructed by the enemy, and when we had journeyed about a mile down the road, turned off to the right and, after sending out pickets, encamped for the night in a dense oak wood. As we were thus situated, our regiment formed part of a line extending from Chancellorsville in a northeasterly direction toward the Rappahannock composed of Griffin's and Sykes's divisions of the Fifth Corps. The other division of the corps, Humphreys's, was still in the rear, camping that night on Hunting Run.

While the Fifth Corps had thus moved from the camp at Falmouth to its position in the vicinity of Chancellorsville, the other corps of the Union army had been carrying out their part in the campaign. The Eleventh and Twelfth Corps had crossed the Rapidan at Germanna Ford, meeting only slight opposition from a few of the enemy's cavalry, and proceeded along the Orange turnpike to Chancellorsville. They arrived there on the afternoon of the thirtieth a little after we did and went into camp on the west of the hamlet. The Twelfth Corps was posted in the woods on a line nearly parallel to the plank road, with the left resting near Chancellorsville and the right near a church about a mile and a half distant. The Eleventh Corps joined the right of the Twelfth, with its right bending northward so as to rest on Hunting Run. General Sedgwick, on the morning of the twenty-ninth, crossed the river below Fredericksburg with the First, Third, and Sixth Corps and took position in front of the Confederate line of works. On the thirtieth the Third Corps under General Sickles was detached from this command and ordered to United States Ford to cooperate with the Second Corps at that place. Thus, by the evening of April thirtieth, the Army of the Potomac was in a position to meet the Confederate forces if they should leave their camp on the heights at Fredericksburg, or, if the latter held their ground, to attack them from both front and rear. The directness of the plan, the rapidity with which it had been thus far carried out, and the confidence of both commanders and men gave good promise of the ultimate success of the campaign.

These movements of the Army of the Potomac placed the Confederate Army of Northern Virginia in a precarious situation. General Lee found himself threatened from both front and rear by a force considerably stronger than his own, and he must have realized that the problem of extricating himself from the position was not an easy one. From the fact that General Sedgwick, who was stationed in front of the Confederate position at Fredericksburg, remained inactive, General Lee came to the conclusion that the main attack was to be made on his flank and rear. He therefore determined to leave a force sufficient to hold his lines at Fredericksburg, and with the greater part of his army to meet the attack which was threatened from the direction of Chancellorsville. At midnight on April thirtieth General McLaws with his division marched toward Chancellorsville, and he was followed at dawn by General "Stonewall" Jackson with the greater part of his corps.

Thus it will be seen that by the morning of Friday, May first, the two hostile armies lay between Fredericksburg and Chancellorsville within a few miles of each other, spread out in two semicircles, the axis of that formed by the Confederate army at the former and that of the Union army at the latter point. Any attempt on the part of either of these forces to advance from its position would necessarily bring about a conflict along some portion of the opposing lines. The situation was favorable for the beginning of a severe engagement.

General Hooker had arrived at Chancellorsville during the night. He took the initiative in the battle, when he moved out the left of his line, consisting of the Fifth and Twelfth Corps, to take a position to uncover Banks's Ford, the left resting on the river. General Sykes's division, in which our regiment was stationed, formed the center of the advance and moved along the turnpike. To the right was the Twelfth Corps, under General Slocum, and to the left Griffin's division of the Fifth Corps; while Humphreys's division was held in reserve in the rear. These movements were begun on Friday, May first, about eleven o'clock in the morning.   The Twelfth Corps moved on the plank road and when about two miles from Chancellorsville met the enemy's skirmishers, who slowly fell back.   General Griffin moved down the road towards Banks's Ford without opposition, and when within about two miles of that place was ordered to return, as General Hooker had received word that the enemy's line was not located as he had expected it to be.

Simultaneously with the others, Sykes's division moved out of the woods on the right and advanced along the turnpike towards Fredericksburg.   Directly in front of our regiment in the line of march was a battery of artillery, which we had received orders to support and protect.   About a mile and a half from Chancellorsville the head of the column encountered some Union cavalry sharply engaged with the enemy's skirmishers and gradually falling back before them.   The division line was immediately thrown out in the open fields along both sides of the road, forming by brigades in three parallel lines with skirmishers in front. Our brigade was on the right and our regiment on the end of the line on that side.   The firing soon became sharp and as we advanced the bullets sang all about us and an occasional shell from a battery which was in range burst over our heads or in our midst.   Here, while charging the enemy at the opening of the battle of Chancellorsville, the first member of our regiment to die on the battlefield fell, pierced by a bullet through his breast.[1] He was killed instantly.   A few of his comrades stopped long enough to dig a hurried grave under an oak tree and, after wrapping a blanket about his body, placed it in the grave and hastily threw over it a few shovelfuls of earth.   The firing grew hotter and hotter, but the line pressed on and charged up a low ridge, driving the enemy from its summit after some heavy fighting. Here we were ordered to lie down, for the musketry fire from the woods in front was very deadly.   A battery of

[1] Sergeant W. P. Burnham, Co. "E."

artillery to the left seemed to have caught just the right "bead" and kept dropping its shells all about us. The deadly missiles sang through the air and exploded with a crash over our heads or plunged harmlessly into a hill just to one side. The rattle of the musketry was incessant and the balls fell in our midst with deadly accuracy. The officers, in particular, were in a dangerous position, for their uniforms made them targets for the enemy's sharpshooters. Our Lieutenant-Colonel continued to expose himself unnecessarily and was counseled by Colonel Garrard not to do so. The Colonel also advised all our officers to keep themselves under cover as much as possible and to tear off their shoulder-straps until the fight was over, in order to make themselves less conspicuous.

While Sykes's command had been able to drive the Confederates before it and assume the position assigned to it, the other Union forces to the right and left had not carried out the plans as anticipated. As we have said, Griffin's division on the left was recalled, and the Twelfth Corps on the right had met unexpected obstacles in the form of heavy underbrush and impassable forests. As a result, Sykes's division found itself isolated from the rest of the army and in a position to be flanked by the enemy on both left and right. This the Confederate General McLaws, whose troops were engaging those of Sykes, proceeded to do, sending men to both sides of Sykes's position and furiously attacking it. A suspicious and unexpected fire from the right of the line was the first intimation we had that the enemy were on our flanks. Soon we could hear the noise of a similar fire from the left as well and we realized that we were exposed to the cross-fire of the enemy. To meet the situation, General Sykes threw his First Brigade, the Regulars under General Ayres, rapidly to the left, and six companies of our regiment, under command of Lieutenant-Colonel Jenkins, to the right. The detachment from our regiment moved out on the double-quick, spreading out as skirmishers and meeting the enemy's fire from behind trees, rocks, and fences.

Separated from the rest of the army and in danger of being surrounded by the enemy, the position of Sykes's division was a critical one; still, he determined to hold it as long as possible. At this time, General Warren, who had accompanied Sykes, rode to General Hooker's headquarters at Chancellorsville to explain the state of affairs. The commanding general directed Sykes to fall back, as the whole advance in the direction of Fredericksburg had been recalled. The order to retire was conveyed by staff officers to the various brigades and regiments of Sykes's command and was promptly obeyed. Hancock's division of the Second Corps assisted in the retrograde movement and the main part of the command marched toward Chancellorsville along the turnpike as slowly and coolly as if on parade.

While the order to retire was being transmitted to General Sykes, the six companies of our regiment who were holding the right of the line were engaged in desperate and exciting conflict. They had found the enemy in the woods just across some open fields and were exchanging shots with them as fast as they could load and fire. When the order to fall back was given four of the companies retired in good order and reached the line of the division in safety. Companies "A" and "G," however, who were farthest to the right, did not hear the bugle sounding the recall, and kept pressing forward long after their comrades had fallen back. Soon they found themselves surrounded by the enemy and entirely cut off from the rest of the regiment. The Confederates came upon them from all sides, firing rapidly and closing in with shouts of triumph. Our comrades were taken completely by surprise and were compelled to retreat, as the enemy outnumbered them ten to one. Company "G" was crossing a cornfield when it was surrounded and commanded to halt and surrender. Captain Powell rallied his men as well as he could and they furiously attacked the

Confederates, fighting them hand to hand and running in the direction the main body of the regiment had taken. The Captain and the greater part of his men were able to fight their way through to the Union line. Meanwhile, Captain Durkee of Company "A," who with his men had been caught in a similar trap, was not meeting such good fortune. The company had just climbed over a rail fence when the Confederates came upon them in force, and in their hasty retreat, several of the members of Company "A" were killed or wounded as they attempted to climb the fence in face of the enemy's fire, or were captured or lost their guns and haversacks as they tried to scramble through or under it. Captain Durkee was severely wounded by a bullet striking him in his arm near the shoulder blade, but he led those of his men who escaped to a small clearing in the center of which was a log cabin, and in this they took refuge. The Captain's wound was a severe one and he was in danger of bleeding to death. He expressed a wish for a doctor, and a private[1] in his company volunteered to go and bring a surgeon, if possible, to take care of the wound. As the man darted out of the cabin he was fired at repeatedly by the Confederates but, by good fortune, escaped being struck by any of the shots. His heroic attempt, however, to procure medical aid for his Captain was unavailing, for only a few moments after he had started the enemy closed about the cabin and captured Captain Durkee and the men who remained with him.[2] Only a

---

[1] William J. Bright, Co. "A."

[2] An interesting story is told in connection with Captain Durkee's experience in the hands of the Confederates. He was carried through the lines and laid on the ground with a number of other wounded prisoners. While there a group of Confederate officers rode by, one of whom was a surgeon. Captain Durkee recognized him as such by his sash and, thinking that he might possibly be a brother Mason, gave the Masonic sign of distress. It was recognized, and the surgeon, who proved to be Dr. Todd, brother of the wife of President Lincoln, dismounted and examined the Captain's wound. He saw that it was a serious one and that it would be necessary to amputate the arm. He immediately ordered a rude table constructed from such material as lay about,

few of the members of Company "A" escaped, and these, when they reached the regiment, were minus a good proportion of their belongings, which they had dropped in their hurried retreat before the advancing Confederates.

The retrograde movement on the part of the Union forces placed Sykes's division in approximately the same position it had occupied in the morning. Hancock's division of the Second Corps lay farther out on the road toward Fredericksburg, connecting with our brigade of Sykes's division, under command of Colonel O'Rorke. By five o'clock in the afternoon the Fifth Corps occupied a line from Chancellorsville to the river, consisting of Sykes's, Griffin's, and Humphreys's divisions, in the order named. About six o'clock the same evening the enemy advanced along the turnpike in Sykes's front; and General Hancock, who, we have seen, was stationed in that position, fell back before them.

Our entire brigade had stacked arms and we were lounging about after supper, smoking and resting, when firing began in our front, and a few minutes later the men of the Second Corps filed along the road in orderly manner. As the last brigade passed, General Hancock sent word to Colonel O'Rorke that the enemy were following him in force and advised our brigade commander also to retire. Although the suggestion, coming from such a source, was worthy of some consideration, Colonel O'Rorke, as he states in his report, determined to hold his position, if possible, as he had received no word from General Sykes to leave the ground. He immediately threw his brigade into line of battle. The Duryea Zouaves on the left nearest the road, the One Hundred and Fortieth New York in the center, and our regiment on the right, wheeled rapidly into position

and there, in the open air, the distinguished surgeon skillfully amputated the Captain's arm. He saw that the Captain was given as good attendance as possible and a few days later Captain Durkee was carried on a stretcher by Confederate soldiers to the Union picket lines under a flag of truce.

with machine-like precision. The movement was not finished before the pickets came running in and the enemy were seen advancing over the crest of the ridge on the opposite side of a ravine which lay in front of us. They showed two lines, each about equal to a regimental front. The right of their line could not be seen as it was concealed by a grove of young pines. The Confederates paused for a moment on the top of the ridge and then, as if to nerve themselves for the onslaught, gave their battle yell and came down on the double-quick, shooting, capturing, and literally running over the unfortunate pickets, who scrambled behind all sorts of obstructions.

As our regiment and the One Hundred and Fortieth New York were not yet seasoned veterans, Colonel O'Rorke thought it prudent to open fire before the enemy got very close. When their second line, therefore, appeared he gave the command to begin firing. The enemy had been blazing away quite rapidly for some time before a gun was fired by our brigade, and our sensations as we saw for the first time a force approaching us in line of battle are indescribable. Our nerves tingled with excitement, but when the word to fire was given, all was changed. We rose up by files and gave them volley after volley. Still they came at us. We began to laugh and cheer; not a man flinched; some who were without arms begged their comrades to let them have theirs for a moment that they might join in the fight. We stood up in the ranks, loaded and fired with as much precision as if on battalion drill. We silenced the fire of the Confederates for a moment but again they came at us. Once more they were repulsed and this time disappeared slowly over the crest of the hill in our front, when we ceased firing. We were not again attacked. At dark, the pioneers of the brigade were set to work felling trees in our front to form an abatis and digging a rifle-pit across the road on the left flank.

In the hours of quiet succeeding the noise of battle,

while we lay in our position with the other regiments of the brigade, we talked about the exciting events of the day. Here, on the opening day of the battle of Chancellorsville, we had received our introduction to active fighting both on the skirmish line and in line of battle. Speaking of his feelings during the conflict, one of our officers[1] wrote in a letter composed a few days later:

Of all the delightful sensations that of a battle is the most pleasant I ever experienced. Every nerve in the body thrills with excitement. Every sense is so wide awake and keen. I laughed at others to see them so excited, and then would find myself rather excited also, and immediately become quiet. It is useless to attempt to tell how you feel. It is indescribably delightful, and I do not wonder that old soldiers love the battle-field. Its dangers you never think of. The hope and desir of success absorb your whole attention.

The engagement in which Sykes's division participated on the turnpike was the only active fighting of importance that took place on May first. General Sedgwick, stationed in front of Fredericksburg, had placed his command in a position to make a demonstration in force against the enemy's fortifications on Marye's Heights, but the order calling for this movement was countermanded before it was fully carried out. The Second and Third Corps, which had crossed the Rappahannock at United States Ford, took up position in the vicinity of Chancellorsville, to the left or east of the Fifth Corps.

General Hooker now considered two general plans of operations. One was to remain in position and intrench, awaiting an attack by the Confederates; the other was to choose a point of attack, and advance with his whole force of five corps upon it.[2] General Warren was in favor of the latter plan, and urged upon his superior the advisability of adopting it. General Hooker, however, decided upon

---

[1] Captain Curran.   [2] W. R., 39, p. 199.

the other course, believing that the enemy would attack him and that he could assume the offensive after repulsing them. This he was encouraged to do by the fact that his position was a most advantageous one from which to meet an attack. It is described as "a position of great natural strength, surrounded on all sides by a dense forest filled with a tangled undergrowth, in the midst of which breastworks of logs had been constructed, with trees felled in front, so as to form almost an impenetrable abatis."[1] The left of the Union line extended from Chancellorsville to the Rappahannock, the right stretched westward along the Germanna Ford road more than two miles. The weakest part of this line was the right wing, composed of the Eleventh Corps, which was "in the air," but General Hooker was assured by General Howard, commanding this corps, that he would, by the nature of the ground, be able to hold his position in spite of whatever force the Confederates could bring against him.

After General Hooker decided to await attack, some slight readjustments of the Union line were made for the purpose of strengthening it. The Fifth Corps line was contracted by withdrawing Sykes's division from the turnpike and placing it on the Mineral Spring road behind Chancellorsville. We were aroused a little after midnight and silently moved out on the road and marched to this new position, which we reached about daybreak. Although the main body of the troops left its position during the night the picket line remained in its original position until morning in order to conceal the movement from the enemy. Lieutenant-Colonel Jenkins was general officer of the division pickets that night, and the account he gives of their withdrawal is illustrative of many similar experiences on outpost duty:

The enemy were massing their troops so close to our picket line that we could distinctly hear their commands and some of

[1] Report of General Lee, War Records, 39.

their conversation. We frequently heard the whiz of their bullets, also, as they kept up a fire on our pickets, which we returned. It was bright moonlight. Our line was in the woods and I had the men stationed in the shadows behind the trunks of large trees. Visiting the sentinels to give them orders at midnight that night was somewhat exciting. As I approached a sentinel, he remained motionless as a statue without turning his eyes from the direction of the enemy. I whispered the orders to him and went on in this way to each in succession. It took about three hours to get around. With the regulars I had about six or seven hundred men scattered over a line of about two miles. At two o'clock in the morning I went around again and gave the orders about falling back to the place of rendezvous at the signal. I then took my position with the two pieces of artillery and waited anxiously the going down of the moon, which was just about daybreak. Our pioneers had been busy during the night chopping trees to form an abatis, and after they were withdrawn I had men beating on trees with clubs to keep up the illusion, for we could hear the voices of the concealed foe, so near that any change in the noises on our side would have excited their suspicion. At last I gave the signal to fall back. It would take twenty minutes to get the command together ready to move out, and if any of the detachments failed to get the order, or if they were too slow in forming, it would throw us into daylight. Soon a shot was fired and loud groans of a wounded man followed. I thought we were discovered, but I learned later that it was a Rebel picket who was shot. Then one of the officers I had sent out with the order to fall back came running in all out of breath and said he had missed his way and could not find his detachment. I at once set out with him in all haste, and put him on his track. As good luck would have it, all of the detachments arrived within five minutes of each other and I moved them to their new position without losing a man.[1]

In the meantime, the Confederates had not been idle. Lee had established his line of battle in front of Chancellors-

---

[1] Lieutenant-Colonel Jenkins was highly complimented by General Sykes for his work in successfully bringing in these pickets.

6

ville, at right angles to the plank road, extending on the right to the Mine Road and on the left in the direction of Catharpin Furnace. It, however, was evident to General Lee that a direct attack upon the Union position would be attended with great difficulty and loss, and it was therefore resolved to endeavor to turn Hooker's right flank and gain his rear, leaving a force in front to hold him in check and conceal the movement. The execution of this plan was intrusted to "Stonewall" Jackson, Lieutenant-General of the Army of North Virginia, with his three divisions, under command of Generals Rodes, Colston, and A. P. Hill. Only the commands of McLaws and Anderson remained in front of the Union line. Early on the morning of May second, General Jackson marched by the Furnace and Brock roads, his movement being covered by the cavalry under General Stuart.

General Birney, in command of a division of the Third Corps, who had been sent to occupy an interval between the Eleventh and Twelfth Corps with his troops, noticed a large body of troops moving to the right across his front on the morning of the second and reported the circumstance to his corps commander, General Sickles. The movement indicated to the latter a retreat toward Gordonsville or an attack upon the Union right and he hastened to report it to General Hooker. He expected to be ordered to follow the Confederates in force but, instead, after several hours had elapsed, was commanded to advance cautiously and harass them as much as possible. By the time the Union forces moved out, the main body of Jackson's column had passed and Sickles's advance met only the rear-guard of the Confederates, who fled before them after losing a number of prisoners.

After a long and fatiguing march, Jackson's troops reached the old turnpike about three miles west of Chancellorsville, and about sundown Jackson struck the right wing of the Union army with his entire force. The Eleventh

Capt. William A. Walker

Wounded and captured at the Wilderness

Capt. Henry E. Jones

Wounded at the Wilderness

Capt. A. I. King

Wounded at the Wilderness

Lieut. Charles L. Buckingham

Killed between lines at Weldon R.R.

Capt. Charles K. Dutton

CHARLES L. BUCKINGHAM

The 22-year-old Utican was appointed second lieutenant of Co. I on Oct. 17, 1863, and joined the regiment at New Baltimore, VA. At the Battle of the Wilderness on May 5, 1864, Buckingham suffered a bullet wound in the upper third of his right thigh. The wound and an ulcer that formed as a result of it, kept him from rejoining the army until July 23, 1864, having been promoted first lieutenant July 1, 1864. Buckingham transferred to Co. B, on Sept. 2, 1864, and met with an unfortunate fate that same day. Buckingham, along with Capt. Robert Green from Co. C of the 5th New York Veteran Infantry, met Confederate officers between the lines at Petersburg during an arranged cease fire. The officers chatted and traded newspapers. But as the Federals started back, some South Carolina soldiers fired a volley. Buckingham sustained a mortal wound to his side and died that afternoon. Green was wounded in the leg, but recovered. A picture of a clean-shaven Buckingham appears on the previous page. (Donald Wisnoski Collection)

Corps, which occupied this position, was overwhelmed by the suddenness of the attack. Position after position was carried by the onrushing Confederates, the guns captured, and every effort of the Union troops to rally was defeated by the impetuosity of the charge. The advance of Jackson's corps continued until arrested by the abatis in front of the line of works near the center of the Union line. Here they were stopped by the artillery of the Twelfth Corps and the battle raged with great fury. The success, however, won by the Confederates in this brilliant movement was more than counterbalanced by the loss of their great commander. General Jackson was mortally wounded toward the close of the day by some of his own men, who, as he was riding in the darkness, mistook his staff for the Union cavalry and fired upon them.

While these events had been transpiring on the right, our regiment lay in position with the rest of Sykes's division on the Mineral Spring road back of Chancellorsville. During the day details were sent out to chop down trees, and an abatis nearly two hundred feet in width was constructed in front of our line. Heavy firing to the west of the Chancellor house told us that the battle had begun in earnest. The Confederate artillery to the left had begun a heavy cannonading as a diversion and we could hear the battle raging with the utmost fury. We waited in suspense until evening, when the tidings reached us of the disaster to the Eleventh Corps. We were ordered out to the front at a double-quick with the other regiments of the division, and formed in line of battle in front of the batteries, seeking to stay the tide of stragglers that came running from the front. The refugees were a veritable mob, rushing backward without the slightest semblance of order, seeking only to escape the bullets and bayonets of the enemy. It was impossible to stop them and they were permitted to pass through to the rear. As we marched toward Chancellorsville, the scene was one of the utmost confusion, troops advancing to the front to meet the enemy, and the stragglers running past them on every side.   Horses and mules ran in all directions, some of them with clattering wagons at their heels, rushing wildly hither and thither in an extremity of terror.   As night came on, the scene changed from one of confusion to one of splendor.   Long lines of sparkling brightness marked the places where infantry fought desperately.   The thunder of heavy guns almost deafened us, with its terrible reverberations.   Shells crashed and tore along through the forest, or burst high over our heads.   The shouts of the victors were mingled with the groans of the dying.   Huge fires lighted up the vast woods in every direction, enabling us to see the silent stretcher-bearers gliding past us with mangled and bleeding forms.

Throughout the early hours of the night the battle raged, the bright moonlight permitting movements with as great facility as if it were day.   The Third Corps was in the thickest of the fight, having been thrown to the right of the line when the Eleventh Corps broke.   Through its good work much of the ground lost by the latter corps was regained, together with many pieces of artillery and hundreds of prisoners.   The moon went down shortly after midnight and brought a lull in the bloody conflict.   The din of battle was succeeded by an unearthly stillness, broken only by the groans of the wounded, the rustle of the wind through the leaves of the trees, and the calls of the whip-poor-wills and other night birds.   Although it was imperative that we get as much rest as possible, many a man in our regiment found it impossible to go to sleep after the command had been given to bivouac on the field, but lay awake for hours listening with awe to the strange noises of the night.

Finally day broke—the morning of Sunday, May third— and in the dim light of early dawn we were ordered into line and passed down the road a short distance to the right, where our brigade took position in rear of the second brigade, which was in line of battle.   Here our regiment remained for two days, taking no further part in the battle but nevertheless busily engaged in throwing up breastworks of fallen trees and constructing abatis.

The battle was renewed on Sunday, when the Confederates attacked the position occupied by the Third and Twelfth Corps. No attempt was made to send either the First, Fifth, or Eleventh Corps to their assistance. Three times the works occupied by the Third Corps were carried by the Confederates, and as often the latter were compelled to abandon them. It was during this time that General Hooker was incapacitated at the Chancellor house, as the result of a contusion which he sustained when a shell struck a pillar of the house against which he was leaning.

From the position our regiment occupied the noise of the battle was terrific. The roll of musketry sounded like the whir of machinery. Occasional reports received from the front told us at times that the conflict was in favor of our comrades, at others, that they were being hard pressed by the Confederates. Our hopes fluctuated with the receipt of each new bit of intelligence, now buoyed up by the promise of victory, now sunk by tidings of defeat. Long lines of prisoners were brought along the road in front of us; hundreds of stretcher-bearers passed, carrying the badly wounded, while many others who had been slightly injured limped painfully to the rear in search of the hospitals, with arms dangling in hastily improvised slings or leaning on crutches or canes made from limbs of trees which they had cut on their way.

On Sunday afternoon, General Hooker recovered sufficient self-control to give directions, and by his order the whole Union line withdrew to a new position north of the Chancellor house, the right of which was already occupied by the First and Fifth Corps. When the movement to accomplish this change of position began, the Third Corps filed along the road near our regimental camp. The men looked worn and fatigued from their severe fighting. Some of them dragged cannon which they had captured from the enemy, along the hot, dusty road, kissing and hugging them as if they were old friends.[1] The withdrawal of the Union forces ended the battle of Sunday, May third.

Throughout the fourth, both armies lay idle, the Confederates being completely exhausted and General Hooker not deeming it advisable to take the initiative by attacking them. At a council of war held at Hooker's headquarters that evening, General Meade expressed the opinion that the enemy should be attacked and that a retrograde movement should not be thought of.[2] His counsel, however, did not prevail, for General Hooker had resolved to move his army across the Rappahannock.

General Sedgwick, who had been engaging the Confederates at Fredericksburg with varying success, received orders at two o'clock on the fifth to withdraw across the river and take up the bridge, which he did promptly and successfully.

The order to withdraw called our regiment from a position which had grown extremely unpleasant. We had lain quietly in the woods for three days, growing poor on hardtack and raw beef. Since we had crossed the Rappahannock nearly a week before we had had only infrequent opportunities to build fires to cook our food, and the cattle from the commissary department were simply shot down, divided among the men, and usually eaten raw, the only sauce to

[1] Related by Captain Curran in letter, in which he also described how the officers of the One Hundred and Forty-Sixth went out to the front where the batteries were stationed and saw a number of the Union generals, whom he comments on as follows: "Hooker was greeted with loud cheers as he passed down the line. There was Sickles, as neat and elegant as if he were promenading Broadway. He wore a proud, triumphant look as his corps passed him, and well he might, for they had done noble fighting. Griffin came yawning along and flung himself under the shade of a tree, so lazily that it seemed hard to believe him the lion he is in battle. Meade was there, looking as calm and keen and scholarly as ever. Sykes was stern and eagle-eyed, changing not a muscle of his face as he conversed eagerly with his associates."

[2] The details of this council are given in the book, *The Fifth Army Corps*, pp. 473–481.

make the meat at all palatable being the tasteless hardtack. Tuesday afternoon it rained long and hard. The ground was covered to a depth of three or four inches with water. We were wet to the skin and our plight was a miserable one. We received orders at eight o'clock on the morning of Wednesday, May sixth, to recross the river, and started out at two in the afternoon. All the troops that had been stationed around Chancellorsville, about the same time, began to make their way slowly to the Rappahannock, where they crossed on pontoons laid for the purpose. The Fifth Corps brought up the rear, covering the retreat, and we trudged through seas of mud, knee deep and sticky as mucilage. Fortunately, the crossing of the river was made unmolested. Lieutenant-Colonel Jenkins, who had charge of the pickets of our division, which was the last to cross, remained at the pontoon bridges until the last man had gone over and reported that there were no signs whatever of the enemy.

After crossing the Rappahannock, we continued our march until we arrived once more at our camp on Potomac Creek, tired, wet, and disappointed. In this latter respect, however, we were no exception, for a feeling of dissatisfaction prevailed throughout the entire army at the outcome of the Chancellorsville campaign, which, begun with such promise of success, had proved nothing more than a miserable failure.

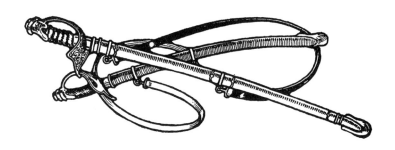

CHAPTER VI

FROM FALMOUTH TO FREDERICK

THE activity of the Chancellorsville campaign was followed by a cessation of hostilities between the Army of the Potomac and the Army of Northern Virginia that lasted throughout the remainder of the month of May, 1863. It was a period during which both armies were recuperating from the effects of the severe fighting in which they had participated on the first few days of the month. The ranks of the Union forces had been sadly depleted, both by the heavy losses in the battle and by the expiration of service of a large number of men. Moreover, the morale of the army was shattered by the disastrous results of the campaign. It was eminently fitting that some time be given to recuperation in numbers and spirit. Although the losses on the part of the Confederates were considerably less than those of the Federals, the close of the Chancellorsville campaign found them, also, quite exhausted. The Confederates, therefore, were evidently as well satisfied as their opponents to remain inactive for a time while undergoing a process of rejuvenation and reinforcement.

As far as our regiment was concerned, we had to congratulate ourselves upon the fact that the losses sustained were very slight. Although the only real fighting we had seen during the battle of Chancellorsville was on the first day, when we were out on the Orange turnpike, it was, nevertheless, the first time we had actually engaged an enemy. Many of us had narrow escapes from wounds and death, as was evidenced by torn trousers, coats, knapsacks, and hats, through which musket balls had passed. Our brigade commander, O'Rorke, testified that we had stood the test as soldiers, for in his report he commented on the coolness and attention to duty of the officers and men of the two new regiments of the brigade, the One Hundred and Fortieth and the One Hundred and Forty-sixth.[1]

After the Chancellorsville campaign, the location of our regimental camp was changed from the Henry farm to a site just west of our former camp, on the road from Stoneman's Station to the Falmouth and Stafford Court House turnpike, formerly occupied by the Fifth New York.[2] We were situated on a grassy mound and had an extensive view in all directions. On the east the Potomac River was visible at Belle Plain, and to the west we could see far beyond the picket lines. We had very little drilling, but found quite enough to do in policing the camp and picketing. The weather was uniformly pleasant and at times very warm, so that on some days we had all we could do to devise ways and means to avoid liquefaction. Bowers of evergreen twelve feet high and about twelve wide were constructed in front of the officers' tents and they found the shade very acceptable, as there was hardly a tree within a mile of our camp.

On the whole, our first impressions of a Virginia summer, gained at this time, were not pleasant ones. Intense heat prevailed. Numerous reptiles and insects which inhabited the meadows and woods all about us frequently invaded

[1] General Sykes, in his report of the part taken by his division in the campaign, wrote as follows: "In these ten days' operations my troops were patient, enduring, and gallant. Long, harassing, and wearisome marches were performed with alacrity and cheerfulness. When the hour of battle came they were successful and confident. Probably in no campaign of the war were the energies of troops taxed more than in this."

[2] On May fourth, while in the vicinity of Chancellorsville, about two hundred men of the Fifth New York were transferred to the One Hundred and Forty-sixth. They were the three years' men whose term of service did not expire at the same time as the majority of the regiment.

the precincts of our camp. All the realm of nature seemed fairly teeming with life. Snakes of all kinds abounded—green, black, yellow, blue, spotted, and striped; long and short; rattlers, moccasins, copperheads, and many others less deadly. Numerous lizards basked in the sun or crept noiselessly about. All sorts of bugs, beetles, and ants crawled everywhere. As an offset to this disagreeable throng there were many beautiful birds—great lazy buzzards circling through the air, hawks shrieking, cardinal-grosbeaks flitting about on trees and bushes, thrushes and catbirds, beautiful specimens of woodpecker, tiny birds of dazzling blue color; in short, hundreds of species. We were entertained with most delightful melodies from the soft-singing thrush, the Virginia mocking bird, and many minor songsters. At night the ominous whip-poor-will piped his melancholy song, which had seemed so strangely sad and lonesome when we heard it that night in the woods at Chancellorsville. In marshy hollows and dismal places "peepers" and other insects kept up an incessant din, and the deep-throated frogs added their booming notes to the doleful chorus.

This section of Virginia in which we were located, just east of the Rappahannock, is one of the poorest in the whole State and had been rendered doubly barren by the ravages of war. But few houses met our view and these were for the most part small and dilapidated. Only here and there did we see a plantation house of any considerable size. One such place, however, a number of our officers passed on their way to and from the corps hospital, which they visited frequently to call upon the sick and wounded. One of them[1] describes an incident which took place on the plantation as follows:

On my return from the hospital one day I fell in with a good specimen of a Virginia family. I was lying on a grassy bank, by one of the most beautiful springs of water I ever saw, watching

[1] Captain Curran.

the fish at play in its cool depths. The farm on a little hill just above bore marks of prosperity and thrift. Neat out-houses and barns, fields just green with the young crops, and fine orchards of pear, peach, and apple trees. Soon a tall, lank young man came down to the spring accompanied by a smaller youth, who bore the name of Pomp. If I had not seen the face of the older one I should have been sure he was a negro, for he spoke the peculiar dialect of the Americanized negro exactly. He displayed great ignorance and no breeding. He said the farm consisted of six hundred acres, that they formerly owned ten or fifteen negroes, who had all left them, and he, moreover, thought it no great loss as they would never work unless they were forced to. He showed me two neglected graves where two Virginia gentlemen were buried who had killed each other in a duel. Soon the brothers left and the more interesting part of the family appeared. First a lad seven years old, then one of five years, then a girl four, and then a little, toddling girl two years old. They were decidedly bright youngsters. The boys brought each a large pail, the four-year-old a pitcher, the babe a cup. I engaged them in conversation. They told me they went to school to an old gentleman who had been a colonel in the Revolution, but who had now become a country pedagogue and taught at a little school half a mile away. The seven-year-old said there was a "right smart" lot of children in the family, seven alive and six dead. The five-year-old remarked, "Wouldn't there be a heap if they was all here." Soon the two eldest mounted the pails full of water on their heads, Dutch fashion; the four-year-old took the pitcher on hers, and the two-year-old the cup, and away they marched for the house.

Nearly a month passed in comparative idleness in our location on Potomac Creek. Bathing in the creek, which ran a short distance from our camp, reading, playing cards, receiving visitors from near-by regiments or going to visit them ourselves, constituted our only diversions. On May twentieth, the Ninety-first and One Hundred and Fifty-fifth Pennsylvania regiments were transferred from Allabach's brigade of the Third Division to our brigade; and a short time later Captain Stephen H. Weed, of the Regular Army, who had commanded the artillery of the Fifth Corps, was commissioned Brigadier-General of Volunteers and assigned to the command of our brigade, which now consisted of four regiments.

On June third occurred an event of great importance in the history of our regiment. That day we received the new zouave uniforms, which we had been expecting for some time. The One Hundred and Fortieth New York were likewise accorded the honor of wearing this style of uniform, which had been so notably distinguished by the famous Duryea Zouaves, a large number of whom were now in our regiment. The new uniform greatly pleased us all, not only because of its greater beauty but also because of its advantages in comfort and utility over the regulation infantry uniform. The zouave uniform consisted of large baggy trousers, blue in color, which were fastened at the knees; a fez cap, bright red in color, with red tassel; a long white turban which was wound around the hat, but worn only for dress parade; a red sash about ten feet long which was wound about the body and afforded great comfort and warmth; and white cloth leggins extending almost to the knees. The first dress parade succeeding the receipt of our new uniforms was a most brilliant affair. We had no end of fun in dressing ourselves preparatory to it, for there were many things about our new costumes which some of us did not understand. It required laborious work and considerable time to adjust them properly. The turbans, especially, caused us no end of trouble, until we found that the best way to wind them about our heads was to have a comrade circle round and round with the sash in his hands until it was properly draped about the fez cap. Finally, after much perspiring and considerable profanity, the entire regiment was arrayed and swung into line. With our Turkish trousers and our turbans, we looked not unlike the soldiers of Mahomet.

On the evening of the very day our new uniforms arrived, orders were received by Colonel Garrard, who was acting as commander of the brigade, to move as soon as possible. We were aroused at one o'clock the next morning and commanded to pack up preparatory to starting out on the march. By four, everything had been pulled down or ripped up; the officers' valises and mess chests packed and with their clothing and camp equipage shipped to Alexandria to be stored until the close of the campaign. As the first rays of the dawn appeared, our brigade, in light marching order, moved out on the Falmouth road which runs roughly parallel with the Rappahannock. We crossed several small creeks bordered by low-lying swamp-lands until we reached a fork in the road, one branch of which led to United States Ford[1] and the other to Richards's Ford, the former below the junction of the Rappahannock and Rapidan Rivers and the latter just north of it. Here the regiments of the brigade separated, our regiment and a battery of rifled guns continuing on the way to Richards's Ford, under command of Lieutenant-Colonel Jenkins, and the other three regiments, with artillery, journeying to United States Ford, with Colonel Garrard in temporary command. We reached Richards's Ford before noon, after a rapid march of fifteen miles, and pitched our shelter tents along the bank of the Rappahannock, fastening them up over slender limbs of trees bent to form an arc, in much the same way that bamboo tents of the Orient are built. Pickets were immediately sent out along the river bank north and south of the ford, extending over a distance of five miles. The other regiments of the brigade south of us were deployed in a similar manner, patrolling the east bank of the Rappahannock.

This sudden move on the part of our brigade from its camp near Falmouth was part of a simultaneous movement

---

[1] So named because a mine in the vicinity had formerly been operated by the United States Government. The mine was at that time deserted, and at the present time the ford, mine, and road are almost forgotten.

by a considerable portion of the Army of the Potomac, for the purpose of guarding more effectively the fords along the Rappahannock River. General Hooker, on June third, received word that the Confederate forces were being drawn away from the vicinity of Fredericksburg and were moving northward. The exact nature of the movement could not be determined; but, fearing that General Lee might endeavor to cross the Rappahannock and advance on Washington, the Union commander threw a large part of his forces in the direction taken by the Confederates, but on the eastern side of the river, and stationed them in such a way as to guard the approaches to the capital. The line thus guarded extended from Beverly Ford on the north to Fredericksburg on the south.

The camp of our regiment at Richards's Ford was comfortably situated in a dense pine and cedar woods. We had not brought our large tents, mess chests, or baggage, as it was thought possible that we might be called upon to move at any moment and we were accordingly kept in readiness to start out at once. When we first went on picket duty along the river the Confederate pickets on the opposite side came out and watched us, evidencing the greatest apparent astonishment at our new zouave uniforms. Some of them disappeared into the bushes and soon returned with a party of officers who watched us a long time with field glasses. We were on friendly terms with the pickets of the enemy and held communication with them almost daily. Rafts were floated across the river and newspapers, coffee, and tobacco exchanged in this way. The river was only a little over a hundred feet in width, so that conversation was an easy matter, and good-natured banter was passed back and forth. This was the first opportunity we had had to become acquainted with the Confederates in a friendly manner at close range and it was a surprise, to some of us at least, to find these men quite like ourselves in a great many ways and not at all the "barbarians" some of our

Northern journalists and orators had pictured them to be. They were clad in either butternut or grey clothes and were generally well dressed so far as comfort was concerned, but they did not present a very military appearance. Some wore hats of black, some of grey, and some wore caps which we recognized as having been intended originally for use in the Union army but which had been pressed into the service of the Confederacy by right of conquest.

Although we had no arduous labor to perform, our life at Richards's Ford was extremely wearing. While we were in camp we were kept busy building redoubts, rifle-pits, and abatis, and were ready, at five minutes' notice, to repel any attack against the ford or to march to any point on the river. Each man was compelled to be out on picket duty every other day because of the great distance our regiment was patrolling. The pickets would lie back in the woods the greater part of the day, coming down to the river front at night. It rained frequently, rendering picket work doubly discomforting, but the majority of us had now become so used to rain, cold, and exposure that we did not mind the vagaries of the elements in the least.

While our regiment was thus employed at Richards's Ford, great movements had been taking place which were destined soon to involve us. The force of Confederates left by General Lee along the Rappahannock and in Fredericksburg was for the purpose of deceiving General Hooker as to the Confederate commander's real intentions. With the main body of his army, General Lee had marched from Fredericksburg on June third; had entered the Shenandoah Valley at Chester Gap, and was proceeding northward on the west of the Blue Ridge Mountains, General Ewell's corps leading the advance.

That General Lee had no definite objective point in view when he began this campaign is evidenced by the fact that he states in his report that the movement was made simply for the purpose of transferring the scene of hostilities north of the Potomac. He felt that the time had come for him to take the offensive, but as to just what point he should strike in his invasion of the North he was undecided.

General Hooker learned that the main body of Lee's army had left Fredericksburg on the very day the Confederates began their march and, as we have seen, had hastened to guard the east bank of the Rappahannock. He then spent several days in corresponding with the authorities at Washington, in an effort to gain their assent to a plan whereby he would place his army between Lee and the city of Richmond, and engage separately the two parts into which the Confederate forces had thus divided themselves. This plan, however, was not approved.[1] General Hooker, consequently, in accordance with suggestions from Washington, began a general advance northward eight days after the Confederate forces had started in that direction. The Army of the Potomac moved on the eastern side of the Blue Ridge, on the other side of which the Army of Northern Virginia had proceeded.

The Third Corps, under General Sickles, was the first body of troops to leave Falmouth in the endeavor to locate the Confederates. The following day, June twelfth, the First Corps, under General Reynolds, the Eleventh Corps, under General Howard, and the Twelfth Corps, under General Slocum, were put in motion. On June thirteenth, the Fifth Corps, under General Meade, the Sixth Corps, under General Sedgwick, and the Artillery Reserve started northward, and on June fifteenth, the Second Corps, under General Hancock, brought up the rear.

The Fifth Corps was engaged in guarding the Rappahan-

---

[1] During this correspondence, General Hooker received the following characteristic letter from President Lincoln: "In one word, I would not take any risk of being entangled upon the river, like an ox jumped half over a fence and liable to be torn by dogs front and rear, without a fair chance to gore one way or kick the other. If Lee would come to my side of the river, I would keep on the same side and fight him or act on the defense, according as might be my estimate of his strength relatively to my own."

nock from Beverly Ford to Fredericksburg, when the orders were transmitted to march Saturday, the thirteenth. With the orders to move came also the startling news that nearly all of Lee's army was marching into Pennsylvania, which was the first intimation that the rank and file had received that the Confederates were moving northward. The detachment of our regiment that was out on picket duty when the order to move was received was instructed to remain in position along the river until the entire corps was in motion, and a similar order was issued to the pickets of the other regiments of the corps, in order to conceal as long as possible the departure from the Confederates who were guarding the opposite side of the river. Captain Curran, of Company "I," who was in command of our regimental pickets, was also left in charge of the brigade pickets. The rest of the regiment left camp that evening and marched to the Falmouth road, where we fell in behind the other regiments of the brigade moving up from United States Ford.[1] It had

---

[1] Captain Curran describes his experiences on the picket line after the regiment had left and their efforts to catch up with the rest of the corps as follows: "I was to stay until relieved by cavalry; if they did not come, to wait until my rations gave out, and then get to Washington the best way I could. Rather a dubious prospect, as it seemed then, especially as my spirits were not improved by a tremendous rain-storm which lasted until midnight, wetting us thoroughly. Morning broke very pleasantly and I soon perceived that the enemy on the other bank had no suspicion that our forces had gone. About 9.00 A.M. our pickets at Richards's Ford were relieved by the cavalry, but I had to wait until 4.30 P.M. for the pickets at United States Ford. Meanwhile, I ate cherries, drank copious draughts of fresh milk, and visited some of the inhabitants, who subsisted principally by gold digging. There is a large quartz mine here, which is said to yield a very fair profit. . . . Finally, a little before 5.00 we started, made Hartwood Church, and there met an orderly from General Sykes, who left me orders to follow on as soon as possible as I was outside the picket lines. Just then, I heard artillery firing in the rear, but it was dark, so I camped on the Briggs farm, a little west of Hartwood Church. At 5.00 the next morning we were jogging along at a racking pace on the Warrenton turnpike. A little later, at 8.00 A.M., we reached White Ridge, twelve miles from Hartwood Church. Here, a short distance ahead, we saw a few stragglers from the army, who mistook us for Rebs and started off at a double-quick. I was in no condition and had no inclination to pursue. It began to get in-

begun to rain before we left our camp and continued with increasing severity throughout the greater part of the night. The storm was accompanied by thunder which seemed to shake the ground with its deafening reverberations and by vivid lightning which pierced the pitchy darkness of the night with weird, swiftly darting beams. We plowed

tensely hot, and the men labored very hard. At 11.00 A.M. we reached Brister-burg, seventeen miles from Hartwood. Here I met another orderly, who showed me the road to Catlett's Station. It was now terribly hot, and the men began to lag. After three miles' marching, I got within the lines, and then we rested beneath the shade trees of a Virginia planter's house. We slept, enjoying a little breeze which sprung up. About 2.00 o'clock a long cloud of dust appeared over the road leading back to Hartwood. As it approached we saw that it was a detachment of the enemy's cavalry who must have crossed at the ford we left the night before. In the vale below us, squadrons of cavalry were wheeling, their bright sabers glistening in the dazzling sunlight. We got up and moved on slowly, for the sun was melting hot. A detachment of Regulars joined us, thirteen or fourteen left behind on duty the same as ours. We made Weaver-ville, thousands of cavalry on every side threatening us. The heat was intense; four of the men fell prostrate; seven or eight more were completely tired out; but we were compelled to push on. We passed Catlett's and rested by the side of a small muddy pool, with twelve miles still before us. It was now four o'clock. The cavalry in long, sinuous lines were moving up, on both sides of the Orange and Alexandria Railroad. We were forced to move on, or go to Rich-mond as captives. Leaving ten or fifteen sick in charge of Lieutenant Jones, with orders to urge them on as fast as possible, we resumed our march at 5.00 o'clock. Soon we came upon thousands of stragglers, lining the road on either side. The army had passed and left half its number to follow. Cavalrymen were driving them in like cattle, and urging them forward. After frequent halting, we at last reached Bristoe's Station and camped, having made nine miles in seven hours. Getting a few crackers from stores that had been left to be destroyed, we ate supper and 'retired.' At dawn we were up, made coffee, and prepared to move on. The sick had come up during the night, and the news that the Fifth Corps was at Manassas Junction, only four miles off, inspired us all to renewed efforts. At 11.00 o'clock we reached the regi-ment, and had a good long rest until the next morning. It was surprising how many 'contrabands' followed the army, aiming for Washington. I remember one little darkey, not more than five years old, who was coming up the railroad just at dusk. A fatigue cap almost concealed his face, and something that looked very much like the southeast part of a shirt swept the ground behind. I halted him and asked, 'Where are you going, incipient nig?' He looked up, showing a very handsome, roguish face, grinned and laughed, 'Oh! I'se boun' fo' freedom.' He walked faster than I could, and soon disappeared, still bound for freedom."

through the mud and rain until one o'clock the next morning, and then bivouacked for the few hours of the night that were left at our old camping-ground in the vicinity of Hartwood Church. Despite the condition of our camping-place, we slept well for about three hours, when we were aroused and after a hasty breakfast resumed our march in the direction of Warrenton Junction. We covered a distance of twenty-five miles that day before bivouacking on Cedar Run, which we reached at eight o'clock Sunday evening. Up again at sunrise, we broke camp before six and continued our march in a northeasterly direction along the railroad. As we proceeded the rays of the sun beat down upon us with an intensity that was almost unbearable. The heat was terrific, and many dropped by the way, completely exhausted. Throughout the entire corps, men broke down by the hundreds. Those who fainted from exhaustion and fell in the ranks were carried to one side and left in the shade of trees to recover. Only a hundred men of our regiment reached Manassas Junction with the main body of the corps, which arrived at that place by nine o'clock Monday morning, and the other regiments suffered proportionately. After resting for a few minutes at the Junction, our regiment marched about a mile farther and then went into camp, well satisfied to rest in quiet for the remainder of the day. Our halt near Manassas lasted for another day, and the stragglers who had dropped out on the march overtook us, as did also the men who had been left on the Rappahannock as pickets. From our camp we could see the light and smoke of many fires along the railroad track, where stores were being burned to prevent them from falling into the hands of the Confederate cavalry who were scouring the country along the flanks of the Union army.

The march of the corps was resumed on the seventeenth, when we were aroused at one A.M. and at three started out along the road which runs almost due north from Manassas to Centerville. It was another day of intense heat and we experienced much suffering on the march. The country through which we passed was quite attractive, but the roads were dry and dusty and our throats became parched and raw as we plodded along under the unclouded sun. The streams and springs were nearly dried up and we were compelled to drink water so thick with mud that it was only after long waiting that the horses would touch it. We marched slowly, with frequent halts, passed through Centerville, and went into camp at a place called Gum Springs on Broad Run in the middle of the afternoon, having covered a distance of twenty miles. When we reached the camping-place our regiment had dwindled to about fifty men, three captains, and less than half of the lieutenants. We, however, were no exception, in this respect, as all the regiments of the corps had been sadly depleted by men dropping out along the line of march. Most of the missing came in during the night. We had a good night's rest and remained in camp all the next day. We could hear firing to the north, in the direction of Leesburg, but it was imperative that we have some rest before pursuing the march farther. Our feet were so covered with blisters that under ordinary circumstances we would not have been fit for duty for at least two weeks, but stern necessity demanded that we shortly resume the march. In the afternoon a thunderstorm brought us rain which was very welcome and cleared the atmosphere to some extent. With the rest of the Fifth Corps, our regiment remained in the vicinity of Broad Run until five o'clock on the afternoon of June nineteenth, when we started out and marched in a roundabout way until we struck the Leesburg turnpike, along which we moved toward the mountains. We covered only six miles in all, and then went into camp.

We were now in the pleasant mountain country of western Virginia, a short distance from the little village of Aldie, located in a gap of the Bull Run Mountains. It was a pretty hamlet, nestling among the surrounding hills, and possessed a quiet charm which had been noticeably lacking in the towns and villages we had seen in the portion of Virginia we had just left. It was the sincere hope of all of us that we had seen the last of the miserable country along the line of the Rappahannock.

For a week our regiment lay near Aldie. The position of the regimental camp was changed from time to time, each successive location affording some advantage over the previous one. We were called upon frequently to leave our camp and prepare to move out to the support of the cavalry, who were fighting almost daily a short distance to the west of us in the numerous gaps of the Blue Ridge. On none of these occasions did we take part in any real fighting. During the time we were not on picket duty or policing the camp we strolled over the surrounding country and helped ourselves as we pleased of the fruit, especially cherries, which grew in the vicinity. Short walks from our camp brought us to several splendid vantage points along the Bull Run Mountains and as we looked over the Loudon Valley, which lay between those mountains and the Blue Ridge, we all admitted that we had never looked down on a scene of greater beauty.

Our week of comparative leisure at Aldie was brought to a sudden termination on the morning of June twenty-sixth, when we were roused from our slumbers at one o'clock and started off at three along the turnpike to Leesburg. We marched the twelve miles from Aldie to that place as rapidly as possible, and then, after waiting about an hour, turned off on a road running almost due east and crossed the Potomac River at Edwards Ferry, continuing our march about eight miles beyond the river. We passed many fertile farm lands and comfortable houses and the country on every side seemed extremely prosperous. We bivouacked late that night, having covered a distance of twenty-five miles during the day. Only a few hours of rest were granted us, for we resumed the march at daybreak the next morning and continued northward in the direction of Frederick City. We forded the Monocacy River and rested an hour at noon along the roadside. We now saw many other troops, as the roads leading northward were crowded with them, all pushing northward as rapidly as possible and congregating in and around Frederick. Finally, we came to a halt about four miles from the city, having marched another twenty-five miles.

While our regiment, with the others of the Fifth Corps, had been making its way northward as rapidly as possible by forced marching, all the other corps of the Army of the Potomac had been likewise moving rapidly in that direction. Thus, by the evening of June 27, 1863, the entire Union army was concentrated in the vicinity of Frederick City, Maryland. The line extended from Harpers Ferry to the mouth of the Monocacy River, and from Middletown to Frederick. The most recent returns showed an aggregate of a little over a hundred thousand men in effective service.

At the same time, the Army of Northern Viriginia had been making its way northward, west of the Blue Ridge Mountains, and had penetrated into Pennsylvania for a considerable distance. Its strength at this time was estimated as about the same as the Union forces. Reliable information placed its advance, Ewell's corps, on the Susquehanna River between Columbia and Harrisburg; another corps, Longstreet's, at Chambersburg; and the third corps, Hill's, between that place and Cashtown, about five miles due north of the village of Gettysburg.

It was while the two great armies were thus situated, when the rear of one was distant only about thirty-five miles from the advance of the other, that General Hooker, the Union commander, was at his own request removed from the command of the Army of the Potomac and General George G. Meade appointed in his stead. The order from Washington notifying Meade of his appointment reached him during the night of June twenty-seventh.

The appointment of General Meade to the position as commander of the Army of the Potomac necessitated several important changes throughout the Fifth Corps. General George Sykes, our division commander, was assigned to the command of the corps; and General Romeyn B. Ayres, of the First Brigade of Regulars, took command of our division.

CHAPTER VII

GETTYSBURG

WHEN General Meade assumed command of the hundred thousand men composing the Army of the Potomac, he faced a task as great as any that ever confronted a military genius in actual warfare. Northern territory was being invaded by an army fully as large as his own, composed of veteran soldiers flushed with the confidence inspired by a succession of victories and under the command of a general who had surpassed in energy and skill all who had so far opposed him. The rich cities of Pennsylvania were panic-stricken, for the only semblance of a Union force between Lee's invading army and the country north and east of the Susquehanna River was about sixteen thousand men under General Couch at Harrisburg. These were mostly State militia, and entirely inadequate for an effective defense of the threatened territory. The Army of the Potomac had, in pursuit of the invaders, reached only as far as Frederick City, Maryland, and was more than fifty miles in rear and to the southwest of the advance of Lee's columns. The feeling throughout the North was that if Meade could not strike Lee's army before the Confederates should succeed in crossing the Susquehanna, an irreparable blow would be given to the Union. General Meade's problem consequently was to maneuver so as to cause the Confederate commander to abandon his march on Harrisburg, and to meet him in battle before the Confederates could threaten any other important city or evacuate Pennsylvania entirely. The responsibility that was thus placed upon the new commander of the Army of the Potomac in the midst of a crucial campaign was not a light one. It was a situation the turn of which the nation watched anxiously.

The new Union commander spent the twenty-eighth of June familiarizing himself as far as was practicable with the position of his own army and the movements of the Confederates. On the following day, he resumed active pursuit of the enemy by putting in motion his entire army on four roads leading out of Frederick City to the northward, bearing slightly to the east. By the evening of the thirtieth, therefore, the Union line extended from Emmitsburg on the west to Manchester on the east. The First, Third, and Eleventh Corps, under command of General John F. Reynolds, were collected about the former place; the Sixth Corps was at the latter place; and between them were the Twelfth Corps at Taneytown, the Second at Frizellburg, and the Fifth at Union Mills. All of the places named are small villages in Maryland, lying just south of the Pennsylvania line.

General Lee had completed plans for a general advance on the city of Harrisburg, Pennsylvania, when these movements of the Army of the Potomac became known to him. As the rear of the Confederate army was thus menaced Lee resolved to prevent, if possible, the further progress northward of the Union forces. To accomplish this purpose he ordered Generals Longstreet, Hill, and Ewell, commanding the three corps composing his army, to concentrate their forces near the village of Gettysburg, Pennsylvania, as rapidly as possible. Generals Longstreet and Hill, who were in the vicinity of Chambersburg when this order was received, moved in a southeasterly direction toward Gettysburg; and General Ewell proceeded toward the same point from Carlisle, marching in a southerly direction.[1]

In the meantime, the cavalry of the two armies had met

[1] See Report of General Lee, W. R., 44, p. 307.

in many skirmishes and in several severe engagements, indicating that the main bodies of the hostile armies were rapidly converging. On the evening of the thirtieth, General Buford, commanding a divison of Union cavalry, reported to General Meade that the enemy were approaching Gettysburg from the west on the Chambersburg road. General Reynolds was immediately directed to occupy Gettysburg, and hastened from Emmitsburg with his own corps, the First, for the purpose of doing so.

The little village of Gettysburg, toward which the two great armies were moving on the night of June 30, 1863, is located in southern Pennsylvania, slightly to the east, about eight miles north of the Maryland line, and almost in the very center of Adams County, of which it is the county-seat. It is, moreover, the center of a network of roads converging at this point, which lead on the north to Harrisburg, Carlisle, Newville, and Mummasburg; on the east to York and Hanover; on the south to Baltimore, Taneytown, and Emmitsburg; and on the west to Hagerstown and Chambersburg. Harrisburg is forty-six miles distant, almost due north, and Baltimore is fifty-two miles to the southeast. The village is surrounded, at varying distances from its center, on the east, south, and west by low-lying hills, which are the northern extremities of the Blue Ridge. The single narrow hill to the east of Gettysburg is known as Benners Hill. The hills to the south of the village form an elevation which is roughly in the form of a fishhook,[1] the barb of which lies to the eastward and is formed by Culps Hill; Cemetery Hill constitutes the bend of the hook, Cemetery Ridge the straight side, which is terminated on the south by two roughly conical-shaped hills, known as Little Round Top and Round Top, in the order named. The hills on the west are in the form of a narrow ridge, which extends from a few miles north of the village to a point opposite the Round

[1] General Howard employs the simile of a fishhook in a description of Gettysburg battlefield.

Tops. The northern extremity of this ridge is known as Oak Hill, but the chain as a whole is called Seminary Ridge, deriving its name from a Lutheran seminary situated thereon just west of Gettysburg. The valley between Seminary and Cemetery Ridges, south of the village, is approximately two miles wide, varying, of course, at different points along the line. This valley is pierced by the road leading from Gettysburg to Emmitsburg. The roads from Taneytown and Baltimore, however, enter Gettysburg from the eastern side of Cemetery Ridge. Two small streams take their rise a few miles north of Gettysburg, both flowing in a southerly direction, one on the east and one on the west of the town. Rock Creek, on the east, is close to the village and passes to the east of Culps Hill, crossing the Baltimore turnpike back of the Round Tops. Willoughby Run, the stream on the west, is separated from the village by Seminary Ridge, in back of which it flows, crossing the Hagerstown and Chambersburg roads. Such is, in brief, the topography of the country which was to become the scene of a great and decisive battle.

When General Reynolds, leading the advance of the Union army, reached Gettysburg by way of the Emmitsburg road, early on the morning of July first, he found the cavalry under Buford warmly engaged with the Confederate infantry, which had debouched through the hills on the Chambersburg road northwest of Gettysburg. He immediately moved around the town, and without a moment's hesitation hurled his troops as they arrived on the field against those of the enemy. The battle soon raged with the utmost fury, regiment striking regiment and brigade meeting brigade, the men engaging in hand-to-hand conflict and fighting like demons. Here it was that General Reynolds fell, mortally wounded. Here, too, the "Iron Brigade"[1] and the Pennsyl-

---

[1] The Twenty-fourth Michigan, Nineteenth Indiana, and Second, Sixth, and Seventh Wisconsin Regiments.

vania "Bucktails"[1] earned unending glory, the former brigade fighting until four fifths of the men were killed or wounded and the latter until nearly three fourths were lost. Urged on by General Howard, the Eleventh Corps came on to the field to the support of the First, and their commander took temporary command of the Union forces that were engaged. The battle continued fiercely until two o'clock in the afternoon, about which time General Ewell's corps of Confederates began to arrive on the roads from the north, outflanking the Union line. For nearly two hours the men in blue held out against superior numbers, but at last General Howard gave the command to fall back through the village to Cemetery Hill, on which he had already posted artillery and a force of infantry. Slowly the Union troops withdrew, not in precipitate flight, but making stand after stand and fighting heroically all the way to the village. Seven times the Twenty-fourth Michigan, of the Iron Brigade, rallied and fought desperately until the field was strewn with their dead. The movement was successfully completed but many were taken prisoners, due to the confusion incident to passing through the streets of the town.

While the First and Eleventh Corps were withdrawing from their position west of Gettysburg, General Hancock arrived on the field, with an order from General Meade for him to assume command. He immediately posted his troops to repel an attack which the enemy made on the right flank. It was not a very vigorous one and the Confederates desisted from further offensive movements for the remainder of the day, content with having gained possession of the village and Seminary Ridge. In the evening, the Twelfth and part of the Third Corps reached the ground and took position on the right and left, respectively, of the troops previously posted.

[1] So-called because they wore strips of deerskin attached to their caps. The brigade consisted of the One Hundred and Forty-Third, One Hundred and Forty-Ninth, and One Hundred and Fiftieth Pennsylvania Regiments.

General Meade now determined to give battle at Gettysburg, being satisfied that it was the intention of the Confederates to continue their offensive tactics, and being assured by Hancock and Howard that the position was strong and could be readily defended.[1] He, therefore, issued orders that evening to all the corps commanders to concentrate their troops at Gettysburg, and directed all trains to be sent to the rear. He broke up his headquarters at Taneytown at ten o'clock the same night and proceeded to the field, arriving there at one o'clock on the morning of the second.

While the First and Eleventh Corps had been opening the battle of Gettysburg by the engagement on July first, referred to frequently as the "battle of Oak Hill," our regiment, with the other regiments of the Fifth Corps, had been pressing forward by forced marches to reach the scene of conflict.

When the order was issued by General Meade for the entire Army of the Potomac to move northward from Frederick City on June twenty-ninth, we started out from our camp in the vicinity of that town shortly before noon, and after a rapid march of fifteen miles camped for the night near Liberty, Maryland. On Tuesday, the thirtieth, we resumed the march at three o'clock in the morning. Corps headquarters were established that night at Union Mills, Maryland, and our regiment camped near by, having made twenty-three miles from Liberty, by way of Johnstown Junction and Frizellburg. On the following morning we were awakened at daybreak and resumed the march, plodding along the hot, dusty roads at a rate of speed that only the hardiest could endure and that caused many to fall out of the ranks completely exhausted.

On this day's march, as on the several preceding it, a heavy cloud of dust rose from the feet of the thousands of marching men, blinding our eyes, parching our throats, and stifling our attempts to breathe. The air seemed as hot as

[1] Report of General Meade, War Records.

the breath of a furnace, and we panted and gasped every time we inhaled its dust-laden fumes. Our feet were so badly blistered that every step was extremely painful and many of us took off our shoes and stockings and carried them on the ends of our bayonets. Our discomforts, however, were somewhat mitigated by the kindly treatment we received from the inhabitants of the country though which we passed, which formed a striking contrast to the sullen looks and often outspoken imprecations which greeted us on our marches in Virginia. From the time we crossed into Maryland, people came frequently to the doors of their houses and waved a greeting or spoke a word of cheer. Often, too, their sympathy was expressed in a more tangible manner, by the distribution of fruit, pies, bread, cakes, and cups of rich milk or cold water. These favors were frequently given by the children, who stood at the gates or along the roadside, and many a smiling little lass or robust young lad of "My Maryland" wished us success in the coming engagement.

All along the route, we saw many evidences of the presence of the Confederate cavalry a day or two before. Here and there were places where they had fought skirmishes with the Union cavalry, and at many of the farmhouses where we stopped for food we were told that the enemy had taken provisions, horses, or anything they chose, leaving the people almost destitute.

We crossed the celebrated Mason and Dixon's line before noon, and as we left "Dixie land" behind us we heard the noise of firing in the direction of Gettysburg that told us the battle had already begun. We reached Hanover in the afternoon and halted for a time to partake of food which had been prepared for us by the citizens of the town. While resting here a strong guard was placed over the men, but the officers were permitted to go about the town at will and procure refreshments. As one of the men [1] expressed it in

[1] James P. Pitcher, Co. "D."

Capt. Thomas A. Wilson
Mortally wounded at Five Forks

Lieut. John McGeehan
Captured at the Wilderness

Capt. W. H. S. Sweet
Captured at the Wilderness

Capt. James E. Jenkins
Wounded at Gettysburg

Capt. Lawrence Fitzpatrick
Captured at the Wilderness

UNIDENTIFIED SERGEANT
A dapper, well-mustached, seated sergeant of the 146th New York, complete with a checkered shirt and necktie. This crisp, clear, hard image well illustrates how the yellow trim of the uniform often photographed black. (Michael Welch Collection)

his diary, "Didn't we swear!" We had inspection and then fell into line quickly just as the sun was setting, one of those large, red, clouded sunsets, and at "quick-step march" we filed out of Hanover to the westward. As we marched along in the bright moonlight people came to the roadside and sang patriotic songs, and waved us forward with cheers that seemed to hail us as their deliverers. We traveled about fourteen miles from Hanover, and it was nearly midnight before we halted, near a village called Bonaughtown, about five miles from Gettysburg.

Only one or two hours' sleep were granted us despite our great fatigue, for at one o'clock the word was passed along the line to resume the march. There was a rustling along the road on the line which marked the bivouac of the Fifth Corps. Dusky forms arose one after another, and fires were quickly lighted. "Make your coffee and fall in," was the word passed along. At early dawn, while it was still almost dark, we were again jogging along the road at a rapid gait. We turned to the left and up the Baltimore pike. To the left from this again, we crossed Rock Creek, and at seven o'clock were massed in the woods a mile back from the Union front. At ten o'clock A.M., having heard no sounds of battle, we moved out in the direction of Cemetery Hill.

As we advanced, we beheld the marshaling of forces that ever portends a coming conflict: troops filing slowly through the woods to right and left, orderlies rushing here and there, artillery wagons lumbering noisily along the uneven roads. Again, with the other regiments of the division, we were halted in a beautiful wood of oak, and formed in mass, stacking arms. The booming of cannon in the direction of Cemetery Hill had been growing more and more frequent as the day advanced. Still, with that habitual stoicism with which the soldier ever regards the prospect of an encounter, after listening to a few discharges we dozed as calmly and chatted as carelessly as if assembled on a festive occasion. It was now three in the afternoon, and still we heard nothing but vague rumors. In the distance we could hear a hurrying and a rustling, but concluded that it was only another change in position, or a corps going into camp. Suddenly Colonel Garrard gave the command, "Fall in!" There seemed to be something about his tone that told us the hour had come for us to enter the battle. In rapid succession came the orders from each captain, "Shoulder arms!" "Left face!" "Forward, double-quick!" We were sure now that work was ahead. Our regiment led the brigade and division, and the road ahead was clear. Troops massed in the woods near by gazed at us inquiringly. "Give 'em hell, boys," some of them shouted as we passed. Ahead of us a red flag was flying, marking a hospital of the Third Corps. Surgeons stood about the tents, with hands in pockets, waiting for patients. Attendants and stewards, holding suspicious-looking parcels and instruments, looked very sober as they moved silently about. We passed several ammunition wagons, from which men were carrying cartridges to the front in the direction we were going. We met a crowd of wounded men coming in from the line of battle, some limping, some with dangling arms, others only slightly hurt. A few pallid faces looked painfully from bloody stretchers. These groups of men, too, shouted, "Give 'em hell," as they shook their fists in the direction of the enemy. We asked no questions, but kept running steadily on. The officers ran back and forth along the line, shouting, "Close up!" "Steady!" "Keep your places!" "Load as you go!" and various other injunctions. We were breathing heavily, and every nerve was tense. We could hear the artillery fight plainly now, and also a smothered, distant, ominous cracking that told of musketry fire at close range. Wooded hills were in front of us. A light battery came rushing from the rear at full speed. It was Battery "D" of the Fifth United States, under Lieutenant Hazlett. We opened our ranks to let them pass, and they disappeared in the distance. We skirted the woods at the foot of a rock-crowned eminence, Little Round Top, and emerging from the shelter of the trees, found ourselves on the field of Gettysburg, just in back of the Third Corps, which was fighting in the Peach Orchard and the Wheat Field.[1]

The advent of the Fifth Corps on the field of Gettysburg, described from the standpoint of our regiment in the foregoing paragraph, was at an extremely opportune moment. Events had taken place with such rapidity throughout the day that the hour when our corps was called from its position on reserve, where we had lain during the morning, marked one of the great crises in the battle, when the issue seemed to hang in the balance between victory or defeat for the Union arms.

The Confederates had abated to a considerable degree the vigor of their assault on the northern portion of the Union line at Culps and Cemetery Hills and had been concentrating their efforts on the left of the Union position. Here, the Second Corps, under General Hancock, had formed along Cemetery Ridge and the Third Corps, under General Sickles, had extended the Union line outward to the Emmitsburg road. The most advanced position of this corps was at Sherly's Peach Orchard and from this point the line bent backward to the foot of Little Round Top, forming an acute angle.[2] The extreme weakness of such a formation had been readily perceived by the Confederate commanders, and to Longstreet's corps, stationed on Seminary Ridge opposite, was assigned the duty of attacking it.

In this corps were regiments unsurpassed throughout all the Confederate armies. A typical one was the Second Georgia of Toombs's brigade. A year before, in one of the Seven Days' fights, this regiment, numbering then 271

---

[1] The foregoing is adapted from a description written in a letter by Captain Henry H. Curran, Co. "I."

[2] There has been considerable controversy concerning the responsibility for assuming this position, but it is generally conceded that Sickles misinterpreted or misunderstood orders received from Mead and took up the position indicated contrary to the latter's wishes.

men, "fought about half or three quarters of an hour against overwhelming numbers, said to have been nine regiments of the enemy. When the fight ceased, but two men were able to fire their pieces. All were either killed, wounded, or unable to fire, not being able to hold their pieces. Others were out of ammunition. A few, that were not hurt, went off with the wounded."[1] Two months later, at Antietam, this same regiment with the Twentieth Georgia held a bridge for several hours against an army corps, repulsing five successive attempts of the Union troops to cross the bridge. Such was the caliber of the men chosen to assault the Union line in front of Round Top on the afternoon of July second.

It was several hours past noon when the attack was made. Under cover of a heavy fire from the batteries on Seminary Ridge the gray line advanced. They struck the men of the Third Corps in the Peach Orchard and one of the most desperate fights in the annals of warfare took place at that point. They hurled themselves upon the center of the Union line defended by the Second Corps at Cemetery Ridge. They charged unflinchingly the regiments of the Third Corps who had occupied the "Devil's Den," a rocky chasm at the foot of Big Round Top. Still others, a brigade of Texans, skirted the foot of Little Round Top on the south and sought to gain possession of the eminence.

It was sometime during the terrific conflict that was taking place on the left of the Union position that orders had been given to the Fifth Corps to go to the aid of this portion of the Union line. The wearers of the Maltese Cross had responded promptly, as we have seen, rushing toward the threatened point on the double-quick.

In the meantime, other developments had transpired with lightning-like rapidity to influence the tide of battle. They emanated from a single man, a Union general, serving as a member of Meade's staff. Standing on Little Round

[1] From the report of the Lieutenant-Colonel commanding the regiment.

Top, in company with a group of signal officers and two or three orderlies, Gouverneur K. Warren looked out from this vantage point upon the progress of the fight.[1] He saw the rush of the Confederate advance against Cemetery Ridge checked for a moment by the sacrifice of a line of artillery, which held its ground until the enemy came up over its guns, and the First Minnesota Infantry, who hurled themselves on the Confederates and fought until 225 men out of 262 were killed or wounded—the highest mortality of the whole war. He saw Hancock rally his men and slowly drive the enemy back, fighting hand to hand at every step. He saw the men of the Third Corps stationed in the Peach Orchard overwhelmed by the attack on front and flank and melt away before the onrushing Confederates. He saw a brigade of Georgians take possession of Devil's Den, despite the heroic efforts of its defenders. He saw also—and the sight filled him with desperation—that the Texans were slowly winding around toward Little Round Top, on which he stood, and that they would gain it unless something was done immediately. Little Round Top in the hands of the Confederates and the battle was lost to the Union! With their artillery stationed thereon, they might have swept the entire line from Culps Hill on the right to Cemetery Ridge on the left! It was a supreme moment in the battle! Warren hastily sent a dispatch to Meade requesting that troops be sent to this point at once. The order was passed on to Sykes, in command of the Fifth Corps, and Vincent's brigade of the First Division was assigned to this duty. But the Confederates were drawing nearer and nearer, and Warren's anxiety for the fate of Little Round Top grew more and more intense. Soon the musket balls began to fly around him and the signal-men were about to fold up their flags and withdraw, but Warren requested them to continue waving in defiance. Springing on his horse, Warren,

[1] A statue of General Warren marks the point from which he viewed the battle through his field-glasses on the afternoon of July second.

accompanied by another mounted officer, now rode hastily down the side of the hill to the road on which he could see troops moving out in the direction of the Peach Orchard.

The troops that Warren had observed moving rapidly to the front and the sight of which had given him an inspiration for the defense of Little Round Top were those of the Fifth Corps, who were going to occupy the line at the left which Sickles should have taken and to support the troops of the latter who were fighting in the Peach Orchard and Wheat Field. The First Division, with the exception of Vincent's brigade, which had been detached to occupy Little Round Top from the rear, had already passed the foot of the hill when Warren reached the road. The Third Brigade of the Second Division, of which we were a part, was just passing, and Warren encountered the head of the One Hundred and Fortieth New York, which was bringing up the rear. It was Warren's old brigade, which he had commanded at Fredericksburg and Chancellorsville, and the men of the One Hundred and Fortieth recognized him and greeted him with a cheer. Warren came straight toward the head of the regiment, where Colonel Patrick H. O'Rorke, the commander, was riding with several other officers. He called out to O'Rorke, beginning to speak when at a considerable distance in an excited and impulsive manner, and said that the enemy were advancing unopposed up the opposite side of the hill down which he had just come and that he wanted the regiment to go up to meet them. O'Rorke answered, "General Weed is ahead and expects me to follow him." "Never mind that," Warren hastily replied, "bring your regiment up here and I will take the responsibility."

It was a perplexing situation, but without hesitating O'Rorke turned to the left and with his regiment followed the officer who had been riding with Warren, while Warren himself rode rapidly on toward the head of the brigade line, to consult with General Weed.[1] He found that Weed had ridden ahead in company with Lieutenant Warren, a brother of the General, but for what reason is not definitely known. General Warren immediately halted the brigade to await Weed's return. Weed soon came back with an order from General Sykes to take his brigade on to Little Round Top, and the regiments immediately hurried up the hill by a countermarch.[2]

As we have seen, our regiment with the other regiments of the brigade, the One Hundred and Fifty-fifth and Ninety-first Pennsylvania, marching in the order named, continued on the double-quick in the direction of the Peach Orchard after we had passed the north end of Little Round Top. While the events described in the foregoing paragraph were taking place, we were rapidly advancing across an open plain. Here we were exposed to a raking fire of musketry coming from the left, where the troops of the enemy had outflanked the Third Corps and were advancing toward Little Round Top. We had gone only a short distance from the woods when a shot struck one of our men,[3] severing the arteries of the neck. He expired a few minutes afterward in the arms of his brother,[4] being the first member of the regiment killed at Gettysburg.

[1] Foregoing adapted from historical sketch by Captain Porter Farley, of the One Hundred and Fortieth New York, who accompanied Colonel O'Rorke.

[2] It seems evident from the report of General Sykes, commanding the Fifth Corps, that it was his intention to have General Weed's brigade occupy Little Round Top when he sent it to the left in rear of the First Division. General Weed however was responding to the urgent calls for help from General Sickles when Warren overtook his brigade and halted it. The report of General Sykes reads as follows: "On my return with the remaining troops of the corps I found the greater part of Weed's brigade moving away from the height where its presence was vital. I dispatched a staff officer to know of the General why he had vacated the ground assigned to him. His reply was, 'By order of General Sickles.' I at once directed him to occupy it, which was done at the double-quick step." The fact remains however that Warren saved the day by sending the One Hundred and Fortieth up the hill prior to this. [3] Robert W. England, Orderly Sergeant, Co. "K."

[4] Francis A. England, Co. "K."

We soon reached another strip of woods, where we were halted in line of battle for a few minutes. Then it was that Warren rode to the head of the line and waited for General Weed. Soon the order to countermarch was given, and on the return our regiment brought up the rear. We passed over the same open plain and then began the difficult scramble up the side of Little Round Top. We ascended the hill from the northern and most gently sloping side, but even at this point the climb was not an easy one. All semblance of order was soon lost, each man taking care of himself as best he could. The men of the three regiments mingled indiscriminately, now and then lending each other a hand over the more difficult places. A section of Hazlett's battery was ascending the hill at the same time and the horses were being lashed to their utmost efforts. Some of the men grasped the wheels of the gun carriages and sought to aid the poor animals. With much straining, pushing, and hauling, the guns were slowly brought up the hill.

As the heights were gained, the confusion of the ascent was added to, if anything, for as each man came up he rushed pell-mell into the mêlée that was taking place at the top and on the southern slope of the hill. The men of the One Hundred and Fortieth New York, who had preceded us, had reached the summit at just the right moment, for the brigade of Texans was panting up the southern slope and had almost gained the heights. The right of its line had encountered Vincent's brigade on the side of the hill, but had outflanked the Union troops and was pressing upward. Springing from his horse, Colonel O'Rorke shouted, "Down this way, men!" Loading muskets and fixing bayonets as they ran, they rushed down the rocky slope with the impetus of a charge. As he led his men, Colonel O'Rorke was struck in the neck by a bullet and died almost instantly. The One Hundred and Fortieth struck the line of Confederates, and was soon engaged with them in hand-to-hand conflict. This regiment was being outflanked and outfought by superior numbers, when the rest of Weed's brigade came to its support. The tables were now turned, and the Confederates were forced to fall back, although they fought desperately at every step.

The scene on the slopes of Little Round Top, in which the men of our regiment were taking so active a part, was one of the wildest confusion. The bitter conflict was carried on tenaciously, butts of guns, bayonets, and even stones, with which the ground was plentifully sprinkled, being used as weapons. We fought in silence, but as the Confederates were slowly driven back, a cheer rose from the Union ranks and we pressed the enemy with vigor.[1]

As the enemy retired, General Weed began to assemble his command by regiments and to restore order out of the confusion that existed. The flag of each regiment was placed at a certain spot and the buglers sounded the "assembly." While this order was being executed, General Weed was struck by a bullet, evidently fired by a sharpshooter stationed in Devil's Den. A number of officers were grouped about the General when he was struck, and Captain Hazlett was bending over him when he, too, was shot, and fell by Weed's side. Captain Hazlett was carried to the hospital, but died about eight o'clock that night. General Weed expired without regaining consciousness, except that Lieutenant-Colonel Jenkins, of our regiment, who was kneeling at his side, thought he heard him murmur something in which he spoke the words, "my sister."

On General Weed's death, Colonel Garrard, our regimental commander, being senior colonel, assumed command of the brigade and under his direction the work of establishing it firmly on the hill was continued. The One Hundred and Fortieth New York was stationed on the southern slope toward the left, its line connecting with that of Vincent's brigade, now under command of Colonel Rice, its commander having, like ours, been killed during

[1] This fight took place between 4.00 and 5.00 o'clock P.M.

the terrific conflict. The Ninety-first Pennsylvania was placed next in order, on the southwestern side of the hill. Then came Hazlett's battery of artillery, and on its right our regiment, continuing the line along the western crest, while the One Hundred and Fifty-fifth Pennsylvania formed on our right, the end of its line resting on a deep gorge.

As soon as the regiments took their positions, men from each went down the slope to the front and stationed themselves behind the rocks which thickly strewed the side of the hill. They were also instructed by Colonel Garrard to erect a rough stone wall to afford better protection for themselves. Soon after this disposition was made, the Confederates attacked vigorously, advancing for a considerable distance up the slope in a final effort to take the hill. They came on unflinchingly, firing as they advanced. Shooting uphill they found it difficult to get the range. They struck the skirmish line in front of the One Hundred and Fortieth New York and Ninety-first Pennsylvania first, but soon reached the point where our regiment and the One Hundred and Fifty-fifth Pennsylvania were stationed. We greeted them with round after around of musketry, and it was impossible for them to make headway. They slowly fell back, after suffering great loss.

This encounter ended our active fighting for the day, but the conflict continued until some time after dark in the vicinity of Round Top, a daring charge being made by the United States Regulars of the Fifth Corps in the fields to the right, where they were later supported by the Pennsylvania Reserves. The Twentieth Maine, under Colonel Chamberlain, also gained possession of Big Round Top after heavy fighting.

When darkness had precluded the possibility of the enemy making another attack against our position on Little Round Top, we made ourselves as comfortable as possible for the night. The ground, covered with bowlders of varying sizes and many small stones and pebbles, made about as poor a bivouac as one could very well conceive of, but so worn out were we by the strenuous work we had undergone that it required more than a few stones to spoil our slumbers. After marching more than twenty miles the night before and then spending a day in anxious waiting and several hours in active fighting, we sought rest on the rough and stony ground with as much avidity as if it were a feather bed.

Throughout the night no firing took place, but the cries and groans of the wounded could be plainly heard, and the men of the ambulance corps were busy carrying off these unfortunates under cover of the darkness.

On the morning of July third reveille was not sounded, but the officers quietly visited their various commands and told the men to be on the alert to repel any attack that the enemy might make on their position. No assault, however, was made against Little Round Top and we passed the morning listening to the firing in other parts of the field and dodging the bullets of the sharpshooters in Devil's Den. These men kept up their deadly work, "picking off" with unerring aim all who had the temerity or rashness to expose themselves. General Warren was wounded later in the day by the fire of one of these sharpshooters, the bullet striking him in the neck. The wound was not a severe one, and after binding his handkerchief about it, he continued his survey of the field, at which he had been engaged when the ball struck him, despite the appeals of some of his fellow-officers to leave the dangerous place. Sometime during the day two companies of Berdan's United States Sharpshooters were sent to Little Round Top, and as they were on an elevation overlooking Devil's Den, they were able to check the enemy's fire very effectively. As the day wore on, therefore, it became possible for those who occupied Little Round Top to venture out with impunity from behind the bowlders and stone fences.

The spectacle that greeted us from our position on the eminence of Little Round Top was a magnificent one. We had a complete and uninterrupted view of the great battle-field which covered nearly twenty-five thousand acres of ground. To the south, Big Round Top reared its head some hundred and fifty feet above us, and its crest was occupied by the men of the Twentieth Maine and some of the Pennsylvania Reserves. At the foot of this hill and at an angle to the southwest were the cavernous rocks so appropriately named Devil's Den. In front and below us stretched the level ground of the Wheat Field and, still farther out, to the northwest, the ill-fated Peach Orchard. Back of these gleamed the guns of the Confederate artillery, stretched along Seminary Ridge. North of us, the Union line was formed by the remainder of the Fifth Corps, and portions of the Sixth, Third, Second, and First, stretching northward in the order named. Cemetery Ridge, which these troops occupied, ceased almost entirely as an elevation a few hundred yards from the foot of Round Top, but it gradually ascended until it achieved the dignity of a hill at its northern end. Here it was that the Eleventh Corps was posted, the men camping on and among the tombstones in the Cemetery. Farthest to the right, on the barb of what we have termed this fishhook-shaped formation, was Culps Hill, ranking in height second to Big Round Top among the hills included in the battlefield, but with more sloping sides. The men of Ewell's corps of Confederates had climbed this hill on the afternoon of the second and had driven off the few troops of the Twelfth Corps who had been left to hold it. At dawn on the third, however, the Union forces regained the hill, thereby rendering the Union line once more intact. Thus far, the only success achieved by the Confederates was the victory north of the town on the first day, and the occupation of Devil's Den and the overwhelming of the Third Corps' advanced position on the second day.

Another day, however, was to be required, before the result of the battle could be definitely determined. General

Meade very wisely decided to remain on the defensive, for from information he had received he was led to believe that the Confederate commander was concentrating his forces for another desperate attack. That such was the case was shown by the developments later in the day. General Lee, after a careful study of the Union position, resolved to endeavor to pierce the center of the line. Contrary to the advice of Longstreet, he determined to hurl Pickett's division of fifteen Virginia regiments, supported on the left and right by other troops, against this, the weakest portion of his opponent's line.

The musketry fire that had started before sunrise on the right of the Union line, where the Twelfth Corps was retaking Culps Hill, was followed for a time by artillery fire from the Confederates on Benners Hill against this position. Suddenly, at about ten o'clock, the firing ceased entirely along the whole line and an ominous silence prevailed, broken only by the subdued voices of the men as they moved about preparing their food, or sat around in little groups talking earnestly. The majority, however, lay idly in the sun, seeking to gain a few hours' rest before the battle was renewed.

While the Union army was thus occupied, the Confederates moved nearly a hundred and fifty guns to the heights of Seminary Ridge and prepared to open fire on the line of blue stretched opposite them. Three hours wore slowly on, but still no move was made by either of the gigantic armies.

It was sometime between one and two o'clock, nearer the former hour, when two puffs of smoke and flame shot out from the Washington Artillery of the Confederate army, stationed just opposite the point where our regiment had emerged from the woods at the foot of Little Round Top on the previous afternoon. Instantly, every eye was turned toward the position from which the sound came. The first flash was immediately followed by the roar of over a hundred guns, as the entire force of the enemy's artillery opened fire on the Union position. Nearly a hundred guns stationed on Cemetery Ridge began to reply to the fire of the Confederates and soon the noise was deafening,—"the heaviest cannonading ever heard on the American continent."

Many of the enemy's shells came screaming in the direction of Little Round Top and burst on the side of the hill among the rocks or flew high over our heads, emitting a shrill shriek as they passed. Hazlett's battery, stationed just in back of our regiment, replied in like manner and the roar of the guns fired only a few yards back of us and above our heads made it seem, as one man[1] expressed it, as if the end of the world had come. The sensations we experienced at this time are almost impossible to describe. One of our officers,[2] writing a few months later, speaks of the scene as follows:

I have often thought I would give anything for an oil painting by a good artist of that scene which I shall never forget while life lasts. There was that high bluff, covered with rocky crags, among and on which our brave zouaves were disposed in every possible position. On the central rock was the signal flag telling the story of the battle. And there was Warren, the master mind, it seemed, of the field, with his neck patched up from the wounds received on that spot. There were Sykes and Bartlett and Garrard, as cool as if witnessing a review, while those rifled guns of Hazlett's were within fifteen yards of the same place, and firing directly over their heads at the Rebel lines, which broke into confusion every time a shell was thrown. And then if the group of Meade and his staff, who came there later, were added, it seems to me it would make an excellent position to locate an historic picture of the battle.

Although the Confederates devoted some of their fire to the entire Union line, they concentrated the greater part of it on that portion of the line along the low ground on Cemetery Ridge, working havoc among the batteries of

---

[1] Lieutenant A. P. Case.   [2] Colonel David T. Jenkins.

artillery stationed there, but doing comparatively little harm to the infantry, who were sheltered behind stone walls, breastworks, and trenches. By direction of General Meade, the Union gunners ceased firing at the end of two hours and the Confederate commander, believing perhaps that his artillery fire had silenced these batteries, now ordered the infantry of Pickett's division to prepare for the charge.

Under cover of the heavy smoke which had settled over the field like a gray pall, Pickett formed the three brigades of his division which were on the field, while troops of Hill's corps prepared to support him on right and left. Then, as the Confederate artillery ceased firing and the smoke slowly lifted, the greatest military spectacle of the war burst into view from our position on Round Top. Pickett's fifteen Virginia regiments moved forward across the field in perfect alignment, as though on dress parade, the brigade commanders in front. The line crossed an open plain nearly a mile in width, and from the time they started the men in gray were directly in range of the Union guns. They were greeted by a fire of shell, grape, and canister which mowed them down like grass before a scythe, but still they pressed onward, steadily, silently, marching as though on review. As they neared the Union line their charge grew more impetuous, and they came unflinchingly right up to the very muzzles of the Union guns. They charged up and over the batteries, bayoneting all who came within their reach. For a moment the men in blue wavered, and it seemed as though the desperate charge of the Confederates would be successful. Reserve batteries were brought into play and a brigade of the First Corps, under General Stannard, swept around the flank of the Virginians and struck the line with telling force. The fight raged desperately for a few minutes, but the Confederates gradually gave way and retreated, leaving in killed and wounded a percentage of their number hitherto unprecedented in warfare.

When it became certain that the Confederates had **been**

repelled and that the Union position was safe, a great shout arose again and again from the four miles of Union soldiers. A dozen generals, heroes of many battles, shouted and clapped their hands, and even wept for joy.   We who were stationed on Little Round Top contributed our share to the great jubilation, throwing our caps, guns, and canteens into the air and hugging each other in our joy.

CHAPTER VIII

AFTER GETTYSBURG

AS the sun went down on the night of July 3, 1863, there was not a man in our regiment who did not realize that the three days' battle in which we had taken so active a part and the closing scenes of which we had witnessed from our excellent vantage point on Little Round Top, had been one of the greatest and most decisive of the war. General Lee had brought his magnificent army of veterans through the Shenandoah Valley into Pennsylvania in the hope that his invasion would be so successful as to cause the North to sue for peace, at terms which the Confederacy would dictate; but his fondest ambitions had been frustrated in the three days' fight on the field of Gettysburg. He had been checked at every crucial point, and his problem now was not as to how he should pursue his invasion, but as to how he should escape with his shattered army to the country south of the Potomac.

The night of the third was dark and stormy. The terrific cannonading during the battle had caused a downpour of rain that fell in torrents throughout the night, and an intense darkness settled down over the great battlefield, as though to blot out the scene of carnage. Despite the rain and darkness, however, great activity prevailed. There were thousands of wounded to be taken care of; the dead, still lying on the battlefield, were to be given as decent burial as circumstances permitted, and there were rations and ammunition to be thought of, in case the battle should be renewed the following day. During the night, also, the lines of the opposing armies were contracted and strengthened, each commander seeking to secure as strong a position as possible should the other endeavor to dislodge him on the morrow.

On the morning of the fourth, a reconnaissance in front of Little Round Top by the first brigade of our division and a similar move on the right by a brigade of the Twelfth Corps revealed the fact that the Confederates had withdrawn from in front of the wings of the Union army and had concentrated all their force in the center of their position on Seminary Ridge. General Lee had thus assumed a position on the defensive. The Union commander, likewise, remained within his defenses. The rain continued unabated throughout the day, which was passed in removing the wounded and burying the dead. This respite rejuvenated the men somewhat from the effects of the long marches and days of desperate fighting.

The night of the fourth of July the Confederate army began its retreat from Gettysburg, and on the next morning it was ascertained that it was moving southward on the Fairfield and Cashtown roads. The Sixth Corps, the strongest numerically of the seven composing the Army of the Potomac, and which had taken no active part in the battle, was sent in direct pursuit. The rest of the Union army was put in motion in the direction of Williamsport, Maryland, in an effort to head off the retreating Confederates.

General Lee marched through Hagerstown, Maryland, the head of his columns reaching Williamsport on the evening of the sixth and the rear on the morning of the seventh. Here he found the river swollen so much by the recent rains as to be impassable at the Williamsport and Falling Waters fords; and, unfortunately for him, all his pontoon bridges, by which he had crossed on the way north, had been destroyed by a detachment of Union cavalry. He was compelled to come to a halt on the north bank of the Potomac, and, accordingly, took up a strong position along the heights bordering Marsh Creek, with his right resting on the Potomac and his left on Conococheague Creek, near Hagerstown.

We left our position on Little Round Top in pursuit of the Confederates on the afternoon of Sunday, July fifth, with the entire Fifth Corps. It was an agreeable sensation in some respects to be ordered to pursue. The great majority of us, nevertheless, would have been more satisfied had we been given a few days longer to rest. We were still footsore and weary from our long march prior to Gettysburg, which had compelled many of the soldiers to go barefoot, when their feet had become so swollen that they could not put on their shoes. Those who were still in this unfortunate predicament were granted permission to remain with the ambulance corps and the field hospitals to help take care of the sick and wounded. The first day we marched only about six miles and went into camp on the banks of a small stream called Goose Creek. We hailed a stream as a camping-ground with many expressions of joy, as it offered us the first opportunity to bathe we had had in many a day, and we sported about in the water to our hearts' content before turning in for the night.

The next day the weather continued cloudy with frequent showers. We started out in the morning to resume our march, but had hardly fallen into line when word was received of the capture of Harpers Ferry by Union troops. With this news came instructions to remain in camp for another day, and we accordingly broke ranks and returned to our camping-ground by Goose Creek, glad of the day's respite thus granted us. We were awakened about two o'clock the next morning and started out immediately in the direction of Middletown. We traveled twenty miles that day and the order to turn into camp was a most welcome one. The next day we were up early and the corps starting out at six o'clock marched to Middletown and camped near this village of a dozen houses. From Middletown the march was continued by easy stages, and on the afternoon of July tenth

we reached a position in front of the Confederate intrenchments on the heights along Marsh Creek, where our corps
joined the rest of the Army of the Potomac.

The two armies lay confronting each other near Williamsport for two days, July eleventh and twelfth. As they were
thus stationed, the Confederates had a decided advantage
in position, located on a long rise of ground, made doubly
strong by many natural obstacles. General Meade considered the enemy's position too strong to attack without
first making a careful examination. He, therefore, ordered a
reconnaissance in force, supported by the entire army, for
the morning of the thirteenth. This proposed move was
deemed unwise by the corps commanders, and it was postponed until the next day. The Union generals in the meantime held a council of war to determine what would be the
best method to follow in order to dislodge the enemy. The
Confederate commander, however, decided the matter for
himself, for during the night he withdrew his army across
the Potomac and started down the western side of the Blue
Ridge Mountains into the Virginia valleys.

A reconnaissance having been finally determined upon,
the entire Union army, numbering eighty thousand men,
moved out on the morning of the fourteenth in battle array.
Each corps was in line, each brigade in columns of regimental
front. Advancing over wide, cultivated fields, the great
army swept forward majestically, with hundreds of flags
flying and tens of thousands of bayonets glistening in the
sun. In the center was the artillery in two parallel lines, the
sides were flanked with cavalry, and the whole force was
preceded by pioneers armed with axes and similar instruments for removing obstacles from in front of the marching
host. The fields had been covered with acre after acre of
waving grain, but when the host had passed the country
appeared as though a tornado had swept over and devastated
it.

The disappointment of the commanders and of the men

at finding that the Confederates had disappeared can more easily be hinted at than described. We had all advanced confident of victory, feeling sure that we would be able to crush the Confederates or, at least, administer a telling defeat. When it became certain that the "birds had flown," preparations were immediately made to follow them. General Meade, decided not to pursue the Confederates directly in their rear, but to cross the Potomac farther east and follow south on the eastern side of the Blue Ridge, thereby preventing the enemy from debouching suddenly into the fertile valleys on the eastern slope, and at the same time threaten the approaches to Richmond.

We bivouacked on the banks of the Potomac on the night of the fourteenth, and began marching southward at daybreak the next morning. Each day's march was a forced march; we had no rest until we reached the Rappahannock. The weather, except for two short days, was intensely hot. The extreme heat and long marches compelled many to drop out of the line from sheer exhaustion. The main body of the advancing army was followed by thousands of stragglers who toiled on behind, the provost guards not having the hardness of heart to compel them to hurry forward to their regiments. "Straggling" was a chapter in the life of a soldier that a large proportion of us were compelled to experience at some time or other during our period of service, and not a few took the occasion of this march from Gettysburg into Virginia to taste of its mingled joys and sorrows.

In the North at this time the draft was being enforced to replenish the diminished ranks of the Union regiments. On July twenty-second, three officers and six men[1] were sent from our regiment to Elmira, New York, to take charge of the conscripts who were assigned to duty with the One Hundred and Forty-sixth. Similar details from other regi-

---

[1] Officers: Captain Curran, Lieutenant Comstock, Lieutenant Wilson.

ments were sent to the various recruiting stations for the same purpose.

For a long time on our journey southward no mails reached us nor were we permitted to send any out, and, in fact, there was hardly any opportunity for letter writing. A small mail did reach us on July twenty-seventh, and among the letters it contained was one from Washington to Colonel Garrard, notifying him that he had been commissioned as Brigadier-General, in command of our brigade. In the evening an impromptu serenade was given him by the Twelfth Infantry Band, hired for the purpose by our regimental officers. The command of the regiment accordingly devolved upon Lieutenant-Colonel David T. Jenkins, who led us for the rest of this campaign and until his death in the Wilderness fight.

For weeks, now, beginning from the time we left Falmouth on the chase after Lee, we had been so constantly on the move that there had been no chance to groom ourselves. "I have not seen a change of clothing since we left Maryland," one of the officers[1] wrote home, "but I have the satisfaction of being just as healthy as I am dirty." When we reached the Rappahannock about the middle of August, it gave us the first opportunity we had had in a long time to clean up, and we boiled our clothes, underwear, shirts, and uniforms, in whatever utensils we could press into such service.

The occasion for the halt of the Army of the Potomac on the north bank of the Rappahannock was the receipt by General Meade of instructions from Washington not to attack General Lee in the position the latter had assumed at Culpeper Court House. The reluctance of the authorities at Washington to have Meade attack Lee in this position brought about a period of rest for both armies that was heartily welcomed.

During this time of waiting along the Rappahannock our

[1] Lieutenant-Colonel Jenkins.

camp, with those of the other regiments of the Fifth Corps, was established in the vicinity of Beverly Ford, about five miles from Warrenton. We were in a comfortable position, on rising ground, the camp being situated pleasantly in the midst of fragrant pine woods. Here we spent several days in uninterrupted ease, our only duties being the routine of camp work and occasional picketing.

Enforced idleness, however, was not conducive to the best military discipline, for if not employed the men were very apt to complain of various grievances, both real and fancied. To furnish employment for the men, therefore, one of our regimental officers suggested that they build a church in a clearing near the camp. The suggestion immediately found favor with the men themselves, and they took up the work with great earnestness. The construction was begun by the men of our own regiment. As the work progressed others offered their services and soon the entire brigade took a hand. Logs were carried from the near-by woods and placed upright in the ground. A fairly good mortar was made by mixing the tough Virginia clay with water, and this plaster was applied liberally in the openings between the logs. The work was carried on rapidly and in good spirit, and the church, when completed, was a pretentious affair considering the fact that we had so few tools with which to build it. From the time the church was finished until we left Beverly Ford, the building was crowded at the services held there by the regimental chaplains each Sunday. Officers of corps other than the Fifth as well as officers of brigades other than our own frequently attended services in the church, and on clear Sundays the railing built around the outside of the building was crowded with horses hitched to it while the officers who owned the animals were inside the church lending their voices to the chorus that made the surrounding woods resound with many a familiar hymn.

At Beverly Ford, we were in direct touch with the rail-road, and our mail arrived and was sent out at regular intervals. The newspapers from the North that we received were of particular interest to us, for they contained accounts of the campaign we had just gone through, which enabled us to realize for the first time the great drama in which we had taken a part. The papers of a later date expressed the great dissatisfaction which prevailed in the North at Lee's escape without another battle, a dissatisfaction that, no doubt, was increased by the fact that the draft had been instituted. Referring to the army having gone into camp on the Rappahannock one disgruntled journalist said sarcastically, "The Army of the Potomac is now luxuriating in its summer bowers," as though envying us our situation. This was but typical of many similar comments made by the press in criticism of the conduct of the war, and they were well calculated to arouse the ire of the men in the army who read them. These criticisms seemed unreasonable to us, and the subject was one that was frequently discussed by the men in camp, especially after the arrival of a mail containing the latest editions, giving us the views of some of the "fireside" patriots in the North.

On the morning of August eighth, our brigade was sent with a detachment of engineers to Beverly Ford, and crossed on pontoons laid for the purpose to make a reconnaissance to the westward. About a hundred and fifty men from our regiment crossed the river in boats ahead of the others, and held the opposite heights while the bridge was being laid by the engineers. When the entire brigade had crossed we remained at the bridge while the other regiments reconnoitered the ground for a considerable distance, searching for signs of the enemy. None were found, and the brigade returned to camp at evening but was almost immediately ordered back to the ford to protect the pontoon bridge which had been left in place. The brigade camped at the ford over night, and on the following day, Sunday, made a similar excursion across the river but with the same results as on the previous day. In the evening the pontoon was taken up and the brigade returned to its position with the rest of the corps.

The following day we were given another opportunity to celebrate, as we had done when Colonel Garrard was commissioned Brigadier-General, for Lieutenant-Colonel Jenkins, who had succeeded the former as commander of the regiment, received his commission as Colonel, accompanied by a congratulatory letter from Governor Seymour of New York. At evening a serenade was given Colonel Jenkins by the Eleventh Infantry Band. General Garrard and his staff came to the camp of the regiment as soon as they heard the music and spent the evening with our officers. The "Royal Tiger," as the men admiringly called the General, was urged to sing and responded by rendering the following song:

"Green grow the leaves on the hawthorn tree,
   Green grow the leaves on the hawthorn tree,
   With a rangle and a jangle, for they never could agree.
     Chorus—And the subject of my song is har-mo-nee."

The other verses of the song were the same as the first, and on the second and succeeding choruses the whole regiment joined in, "making the welkin ring." General Garrard presented Colonel Jenkins with two pairs of shoulder straps, one which he had worn while in the field and another pair given him at West Point when he accepted the command of the regiment.

For the first time since we left Falmouth, we were in camp long enough to institute drills and dress parades. They were again held at regular intervals and with our new zouave uniforms we felt we were making a splendid appearance.

On August thirteenth, two brigades of United States Regulars in the division with us were sent to New York City under command of General Ayres, to aid in quelling the memorable draft riots in that city. The order was first issued to General Ayres and called for the taking of his entire division, but this was corrected at the last moment, so that the anticipation we had felt of a visit North at the first receipt of the news was unfulfilled.

While in camp at Beverly Ford one of the most impressive though not one of the pleasantest incidents of our whole career as a regiment occurred. Five men who belonged to that despicable class known as "bounty-jumpers," who had deserted from the One Hundred and Eighteenth Pennsylvania as soon as they received their bounties, had been sentenced by General Meade to be executed in sight of the entire Fifth Corps. The execution took place on August twentieth in a large meadow which formed a sort of amphitheater, through which ran a small stream of water. A bridge was thrown across the stream and on the other side, to the right, five graves were dug and coffins placed beside them. In the afternoon all the regiments of the corps that could be spared from other duties were marched to the ground and formed in line of battle on three sides of the meadow. Our regiment was stationed in front of the very center of the line, so that we were nearest to the scene of the solemn affair. When everything was in readiness, the prisoners were brought in an open army ambulance escorted by the provost guard of the First Division and a regimental band that played a funeral march as the solemn procession advanced. The five men were of different religious faiths, two Protestants, two Catholics, and a Jew, and were accompanied by ministers of their respective faiths. The men alighted from the wagon and, attended by the clergymen, walked to the place where the graves had been dug, and were placed in a sitting position on the coffins. The firing party, consisting of sixteen files of men from the provost guard, was drawn up about sixty feet from the prisoners. When the clergymen had spoken with them for a short time the bugle sounded "Attention!" and the ministers withdrew. Then the eyes of the condemned men were blindfolded and they were left alone. Four were cool and seemed unconcerned, but the

Execution of Deserters from 5th Corps on August 20, 1863. A few privates of 146th Regt. were members of firing squad and the regiment itself is seen directly back of firing squad, with their drum corps on the left and the officers on the right

Redrawn from a war-time print in *Harper's Weekly*.

UNIDENTIFIED

This incredibly well tinted tintype was taken in the field—at Brandy Station or Petersburg. See the back cover of the dust jacket for the actual tinted color. This mustached Zouave private wears his turban, leggings and jambiéres. He holds his Springfield rifle with the bayonet affixed, and has on his belt with the cap box and bayonet scabbard visible. To the right can be seen the leg of another soldier waiting to have his "likeness" made. (Daniel Miller Collection)

fifth, the Jew, appeared to be overcome with terror. The firing detail was marched to within ten paces of the prisoners seated on the coffins while a breathless silence pervaded the audience of more than ten thousand troops. Suddenly the command of the provost marshal rang out, "Ready, aim, fire!" With the last word the guns were discharged and the five men fell back upon their coffins. While the bodies were being placed in the coffins for burial the bugle sounded the "Recall!" and the troops who had witnessed the execution headed by their regimental bands playing lively airs marched back to camp.

The last incident in our life at Beverly which was in any way out of the ordinary routine took place on September ninth. At that time a brigadier's sword with sash and belt was presented to General Garrard by the officers of the One Hundred and Forty-sixth and the presentation was made the occasion of an all-round "good time" by the officers and men of the regiment. The band of the Fourteenth Infantry furnished music. Refreshments had been purchased in Utica, New York, and sent to our camp in preparation for the event, to which all the brigade officers had been invited. A large space was cleared in the midst of the woods and that evening the officers, even though no ladies were present to grace the occasion, danced a cotillion on the floor of pine needles. The soldiers gathered round in a large semicircle lighted with innumerable small campfires, and were interested spectators of the gay scene. The band played familiar airs, the men sang, and, all in all, it was a night long remembered by all who in any way participated.

CHAPTER IX

BRISTOE AND MINE RUN

IN the early part of September, the authorities at Washington began to urge upon General Meade the desirability of his attempting to make some telling move against the Confederates before winter put a stop to hostilities. Both armies had lain at rest opposite each other for two or three weeks, until September 15, 1863, when General Meade finally began a series of maneuvers against the Confederate position which were met with similar maneuvers on the part of the Confederate commander. For several weeks both armies were again almost constantly on the move, passing and repassing over the roads in this section of Virginia and visiting and revisiting the few small villages and hamlets which dotted the country. Frequent skirmishing took place between small detachments of the hostile armies, but no battle of importance was fought.[1]

The campaign, futile though it was, brought many days of arduous marching and countermarching for our regiment. We were not permitted to remain in any one place for more than a day or two at a time and orders to move seemed always to come just as we had begun to make ourselves comfortable in camp. One day we received orders to raise our tents from the ground by the use of logs or planks, preparatory to remaining in them for some length of time, but we had no sooner started the work than other orders were received calling for an immediate movement. At another time a

[1] Known as the Bristoe campaign.

large number of us had completed arranging our tents as though to go into winter quarters when the bugle once more called us to take up the march.

The movements on the part of the Union army were so bewildering that the men themselves had no conception whatever of their design, and in many cases even the corps and division commanders were at a loss to know just what was expected of them. One of the simpler of the movements was the attack on Rappahannock Station on November sixth and seventh. The Fifth and Sixth Corps led the advance, and were preceded by nine hundred skirmishers under General Garrard, our former well-loved regimental commander. None of the One Hundred and Forty-sixth were in this detail of skirmishers, but the regiment was held in readiness on the field. Very largely through the excellent work of General Garrard the attack on the Confederate position was successful and the Union army proceeded to occupy the enemy's quarters at Rappahannock Station, which had already been fitted up as winter quarters for the Confederate army. Hundreds of long huts had been built. They were covered with split shingles and each hut had a door, chimney, and fireplace. In that part of the quarters assigned to our regiment an order from General Lee was found, instructing the men to erect these huts for winter quarters. We picked up also some pieces of letters and other scraps of paper which showed us that the Confederates were evidently in very reduced circumstances. One of our officers[1] found a letter from a girl in Georgia to her brother in the army, in which she said: "Mother went all over town yesterday to get some cloth for your uniform. She found some at only one store, and they wanted $250 for it." Another letter from South Carolina said: "The Yankees have attacked Charleston and I guess they will take it, for they seem to be getting most everything nowadays."

During the many weeks of continual marching the rigid

[1] Colonel Jenkins.

discipline which usually prevailed throughout the whole army was considerably relaxed, especially in so far as forbidding the men from roaming over the country outside of the picket lines was concerned. It became the custom for small bands of soldiers to prowl around in search of edibles in the form of live stock or vegetables and fruit. It was quite a simple matter to induce a friend who might be on guard at night to let one or two men go outside the camp limits and it was no unusual thing to hear in the middle of the night the scurrying of feet accompanied once in a while by the squawk of a chicken or the squeal of a pig. The sound of a rooster's crowing during the night was the signal for a raid by the men, a race to the place sometimes taking place between the marauders of several different regiments who had heard the noise. General Sykes, the commander of the Fifth Corps, finally issued orders to the officers of the regiments to keep a strict watch on their men to prevent this roaming about the country, and also ordered the company officers to inspect the food which was prepared for the men. If any meat, poultry, or vegetables not a part of the army ration was found, the man having it in his possession was required to give a strict account as to how he had acquired it. If the account was not satisfactory the offender was liable to be brought before a field officer's court for trial. While it would be exaggerating to a slight degree to say that the men of the One Hundred and Forty-sixth were never guilty of participation in these depredations, none of them, after the order spoken of was issued, were ever caught in the offense and brought to trial for it.

An event of special importance to us took place about this time. It was the receipt of a new regimental flag that was presented to us to replace our old flag which had been given by the citizens of Oneida County and which had now become so worn as to be unserviceable.[1] A circular dated

---

[1] The flag of the One Hundred and Forty-Sixth Regiment from Oneida County is now preserved at the State Capitol, Albany, and the flag that was

November 1, 1863, issued by Colonel Jenkins, while we were in camp near Three Mile Station, reads as follows:

The regiment has just received with proper solemnities a new stand of colors, and it has now to transmit to the Governor of the State of New York the old flag whose tattered folds will speak more eloquently than words of the work which the sons of New York are performing in behalf of the country. It will recall the hard-fought fields of Fredericksburg, Chancellorsville, and Gettysburg. To some it may bring a tear of remembrance for the brave dead who have fallen in its defense. It will never cause a cheek to blush with shame.

Fight under the new flag as gallantly as you have done under the old, and you may hope ere another year passes to carry it back to your homes, to receive the thanks of a grateful country.

By order of Col. DAVID T. JENKINS.

WILLIAM WRIGHT, Lieut., Acting Adj.,
146th N. Y. Volunteers.

The order was read together with other orders to the regiment on dress parade in the afternoon. Colonel Jenkins stood at some distance from the regiment, facing it. Adjutant Wright stood midway between the Colonel and the first rank, directly in front of the former. He read the order in a clear voice, then turned toward the Colonel and saluted. The Colonel acknowledged the salute and the Adjutant turned toward the regiment to deliver the next order. This process was continued until all the orders of the day had been read, when the Adjutant took his place in line with the Colonel, ten paces from him, after which the Colonel conducted a regimental drill.

During the temporary lull in hostilities after the capture of Rappahannock Station, Longstreet's corps of the Confederate army was sent to the west to participate in the campaign in Tennessee. Three corps from the Army of the

_____

presented to it at Three Mile Station is preserved in the building of the Oneida County Historical Society at Utica, New York.

Potomac were likewise dispatched by General Meade to participate in the same campaign on the Union side. With his army thus depleted, General Meade was loath to begin another campaign, but the pressure from Washington was so strong that he decided to make another invasion of Lee's territory, despite the fast-approaching winter. This movement, known as the Mine Run campaign, began during the latter part of November and lasted about ten days.

When the Union forces had so successfully driven the Confederates before them at Rappahannock Station on November sixth and seventh General Lee had retreated south of the Rapidan and had intrenched himself in the great Wilderness in that part of northern Virginia, his line extending for a short distance along the Rapidan and then bending southward for a distance of about four miles, with the right resting on Mine Run. General Meade planned to cross the Rapidan at the fords to the east of the Confederate position and advance on the roads leading south from these fords until he reached the Orange and Fredericksburg turnpike and the Orange plank road, when, moving westward along these roads, he hoped to turn the right flank of the Confederate army. Lee's position was well-chosen, for the Union army, in order to attack him, would have to pass through the tangle of trees and bushes which covered the entire area of the Wilderness and would thus be greatly hindered by natural obstacles.

The movement of the Army of the Potomac across the Rapidan had been set for November twenty-fourth, a circular order being issued to the corps commanders the preceding evening informing them as to the part each corps was expected to play. During the night of the twenty-third the rain fell heavily and the next day, when the army started to move, the roads were found to be in such a condition as to preclude all operations for a day or two. It was not until November twenty-sixth, therefore, that the Union forces got under way preparatory to crossing the Rapidan. Promptly at six in the morning the various corps of the Army of the Potomac started out. General Warren, with the Second Corps, was to cross the river at Germanna Ford and march along the turnpike in the direction of Robertson's Tavern. The Third Corps, under General French, and the Sixth Corps, under General Sedgwick, were to cross at Jacob's Mill and continue on a road from that point toward the Tavern, connecting with the Second Corps. The Fifth Corps, under General Sykes, followed by two divisions of the First Corps, under General Newton, was to cross at Culpeper Ford and turn up the plank road to Parker's Store, and, if possible, to Robertson's Tavern. Thus it will be seen that it was Meade's purpose for the first day to concentrate his forces in the vicinity of the Tavern, where they would be within striking distance of the Confederate position.

As the Fifth Corps left its camp near Rappahannock Station on the morning of the twenty-sixth our regiment was thrown out as flankers for our brigade. The weather, which had been pleasant for over a month, had become very cold following the storm of the twenty-third, and the frozen roads, filled with deep ruts, made the going very difficult. The corps proceeded slowly to the banks of the Rapidan at Culpeper Ford, where a regiment was sent over in boats to protect the crossing of the main body of troops. The entire corps was over by noon and continued on its march along the road leading from Culpeper Ford on the south side of the river, until the Orange plank road, the southernmost of the two parallel roads running west, was reached, when the corps turned up this road to the westward. As the other column of Union troops, farther to the right, had experienced some difficulty and opposition in crossing the Rapidan, the Fifth Corps was ordered to delay its march westward, and bivouacked for the night in the Wilderness near the intersection of the Germanna and Orange plank roads.

The following day the march was continued along the Orange plank road. At nine o'clock Parker's Store was reached, and here the Union cavalry under General Gregg were met. The cavalry continued ahead of the column and soon encountered the enemy's cavalry, but gradually drove them backward. The country bordering the road was so densely wooded that the cavalry were compelled to fight on foot, and it was impossible to send skirmishers along the flanks to assist them. When New Hope Church was reached, the Fifth Corps troops were deployed as much as possible and a spirited encounter with the enemy ensued during the afternoon. The enemy, however, gradually retired, and everything was quiet by evening. General Sykes reported matters to the commanding general and was instructed not to advance farther, as the Third and Sixth Corps had been delayed and had not effected a junction with the Second Corps, as had been planned. Another uncomfortable night was spent in the heart of the Wilderness, the intense cold piercing to the very marrow of the unfortunate men who were exposed to its rigors.

On the following day the Fifth Corps proceeded to Robertson's Tavern, and in the afternoon relieved the Second Corps, taking position across the Orange turnpike in front of Mine Run. The opposite bank of the creek at this point had an elevation of over one hundred feet, with a gentle, smooth slope to the creek of about a thousand yards. The Confederate line was established on the crest of this slope, in an extremely advantageous position. During the day the Third and Sixth Corps were slowly brought up with the rest of the army and a general assault was planned for the following day. The Union forces were formed in two columns about equal in size, that on the right commanded by General Warren, and the one on the left by General Sedgwick.

The artillery opened fire at eight o'clock on the morning of the thirtieth, and skirmishers were sent over the creek in front of General Sedgwick's column. No movement, however, was made by General Warren, and at about a quarter to nine o'clock he sent word to General Meade that he considered the position in his front too strong to attack with any reasonable hope of success. General Sedgwick delayed his advance while Meade visited Warren, and after a careful investigation concurred in the opinion of the latter. The assault was abandoned and the various corps returned to the positions they had occupied the previous night. It was ascertained the next morning that the Confederates had spent the night in further strengthening their position, and Meade, after due deliberation, decided to withdraw his army entirely and return to his position north of the Rapidan.[1]

This decision to return was received with rejoicing by the men of our own regiment and, in fact, by the men of every other regiment as well. The Mine Run campaign was a hard campaign for all who participated in it. The weather was intensely cold and the nights, spent as they were in the open with only blankets as covering, were full of suffering. Many of us had been assigned to picket duty on at least one of the nights spent in the Wilderness and this work was well-nigh unbearable. The ground was full of creeks and swamps which were covered with a thin layer of ice which broke

[1] Although harshly criticized by many in the North for not attacking the Confederate position at Mine Run, the action of General Meade in withdrawing was heartily approved by officers and men throughout the whole of his army. Colonel Talley, of the First Pennsylvania Reserves, in speaking of the campaign says: "The army, perhaps the Union cause, was saved, due to the clear judgment and military skill of those grand officers, Meade and Warren. . . . If officers less cautious and less able had been in command, the battle, likely, would have been fought there and then. It is very tempting to a commanding officer—after marching far and maneuvering much, with the people at home so anxious and so urgent, though so ignorant of the surroundings, for forward movements and dashing fights—when he has reached the enemy to attack him, however strong his position. Had the two armies fought at Mine Run the result would have been the greatest slaughter in the history of the United States." One of our own officers, Major Curran, in writing home a few weeks later, reiterates this opinion in the following words: "Meade's victory at Mine Run was even greater than at Gettysburg. It was a great moral victory, for he must have believed, judging from the past, that unless he fought, he would be removed and disgraced."

through as the men walked over it, wetting them up to their knees. Skirmishers frozen stiff and dead were frequently brought to the rear during those two days of maneuvering. In camp many were afraid to sleep for fear of freezing and spent the night walking and running back and forth, the ground often being spattered with blood from their swollen and bleeding feet. Added to all this, rations were not issued regularly, and for over a day we were forced to face these hardships on empty stomachs, which rendered them doubly acute.

Relief could not come to us immediately, as it was no simple matter for the Union army to extricate itself from the position it occupied in the treacherous undergrowth of the Wilderness. With the rest of the Fifth Corps, our regiment lay in the woods until nightfall of December first, while the corps which lay in our rear began the retrograde movement. Our turn came at last. We marched all night, moving silently through the woods until we reached the Orange turnpike, along which we proceeded for about three miles, when we struck into the woods again and made a short cut to the Germanna Ford road. Resting at the ford only long enough to cook our coffee and partake of a hasty breakfast, we crossed the Rapidan and marched to Stevensburg, where we remained over night. The next day the march was continued to Rappahannock Station, and on December fourth, we reached Warrenton Junction. Here we remained in camp two days. While at this place, General Sykes received orders to distribute the Fifth Corps along the Orange and Alexandria Railroad[1] for the purpose of guarding the railroad, which formed the base of supplies for the Army of the Potomac, from any attacks which might be made upon it by the Confederate cavalry or by the numerous guerrilla bands which infested the vicinity. The corps was disposed by brigades at intervals along the road from Brandy Station to Fairfax.

[1] Now the Virginia Midland Division of the Richmond & Danville R. R.

Group of Officers of 146th Regt. at Warrenton Junction, Spring of 1864

IDENTIFICATION CHART
OF OFFICERS OF 146TH NEW YORK REGIMENT

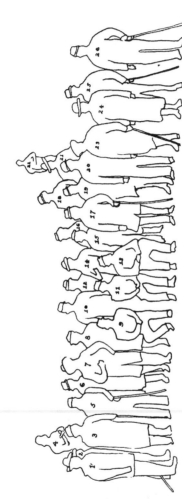

RANK · GIVEN · AS · OF · APRIL · 15 · 1864

1. CAPT · B · F · WRIGHT ·
2. 2ND LIEUT · A · E · BROWNELL ·
3. 1ST LIEUT · A · I · KING ·
4. ASSIST · SURGEON · ROBT · FENWICK ·
5. 1ST LIEUT · LEVI · A · YORK ·
6. 1ST LIEUT · QT · MR · MARVIN · EGGLESTON ·
7. CAPT · THOMAS · WILSON ·
8. CAPT · HENRY · E · JONES ·
9. LIEUT · COL · HENRY · H · CURRAN ·
10. CAPT · JAMES · E · JENKINS ·
11. COL · DAVID · T · JENKINS ·
12. CAPT · JAMES · GRINDLEY ·
13. SURGEON · THOMAS · M · FLANDRAU ·

14. CAPT · JOS · H · DURKEE ·
15. 1ST LIEUT · JOS · S · LOWERY ·
16. 2ND LIEUT · DAVID · IMMERMAN ·
17. REGIMENTAL · ADJUTANT · WILLIAM · WRIGHT ·
18. CAPT · JOS · B · CUSHMAN ·
19. 1ST LIEUT · PETER · D · FROLEIGH ·
20. 1ST LIEUT · W · H · SEWARD · SWEET ·
21. 2ND LIEUT · CHAS · L · BUCKINGHAM ·
22. PRIVATE · FROM · CO · "I" · (NAME · LOST) ·
23. 2ND LIEUT · LAWRENCE · FITZPATRICK ·
24. 2ND LIEUT · ARTHUR · V · COAN ·
25. 1ST LIEUT · WILLIAM · FOWLER ·
26. 2ND LIEUT · HUGH · CHALMERS ·

Our regiment, with the other regiments of the brigade and a battery of artillery, all under command of General Garrard, marched to Bealeton Station on December sixth and relieved a portion of the First Corps which had been stationed there. The following day we began work on the erection of a camp for our winter quarters and during the time we were not on picket duty or busy with other details of camp routine worked steadily at this task for over a week.

CHAPTER X

WINTER OF '63-'64

WHEN our camp at Bealeton was at last completed, we voted unanimously that it was the best we had ever had and the peer at least of any in the army. Our lodgings were little huts built of logs to a height of about five feet with roofs of canvas. Company streets had been laid out in regular order. The camp was kept neat and tidy. The streets were swept each day and many of the little huts were decorated with boughs of evergreen gathered in the near-by forest. Everything had been arranged so conveniently that we looked forward to passing a comfortable winter in these quarters.

The vicinity in which we were encamped was infested by guerrillas and it was not safe to stray far beyond the lines. These bands of guerrilla marauders were a daring lot and it was necessary for us to be constantly on the alert, in anticipation of any raid or attack they might make. Their method of warfare was that of stealth rather than that of bravery. Groups of them quite frequently dressed in Federal uniform and in this fashion were often able to get within the Union lines unobserved, and before detected tear up a portion of the railroad, steal a few wagons, and sometimes get away with several prisoners. Usually, however, if a Union soldier was made a prisoner by a guerrilla band it was because he had strayed too far outside of his own line.

One of the officers of the brigade, a member of one of the United States Regular regiments, lost his life while we were camped at Bealeton by allowing his affections to overbalance his judgment, causing him to fall into a guerrilla ambush. He was a brilliant young fellow, a graduate of West Point. One day while out on scout duty beyond the picket line he made a chance acquaintance with a young woman living on a near-by plantation. She was a charming Southern girl and after their first meeting, whenever a favorable opportunity offered, he would stroll out to her house for a friendly visit in spite of the warnings she gave him of the danger he was running. He made the trip once too often and the last time, as he was passing along the narrow bridle path through the woods toward camp, he was instantly killed by a volley from an ambushed band of guerrillas. The marauders took what valuables were found on the body and left it hidden in the bushes. The guerrillas had become so bold in their operations that the killing of this officer caused General Ayres, our division commander, to attempt to rid the section of these bands, or, at least, deal them a severe punishment. Cavalry videttes were accordingly posted at strategic points without the lines. We soon had our revenge, for on the body of one of the guerrillas, shot by a vidette in a midnight encounter a short time after, were found the watch and other belongings of the young officer. His body was found a few days later and buried with military honors.

Such an incident as the above well illustrates the precaution that was necessary for all of us to exercise in the matter of going beyond the lines while we lay at Bealeton Station, and, in fact, during all the time we were encamped in the vicinity of the Orange and Alexandria Railroad. The guerrillas roamed about the country in bands numbering from ten or a dozen to over a hundred men, and their presence made it imperative that we should keep constantly on the alert in anticipation of a raid or attack.

The days in camp at Bealeton passed pleasantly enough, for winter had not yet begun in earnest and the weather was mild and pleasant, about like that which we were accustomed to have in April in our native county. While we lay there a number of us were at some time or other on a detail which worked on a corduroy road constructed for the purpose of bringing the wagon trains more easily from the railroad to the various camps. Christmas Day was passed at Bealeton. A number of the boys received boxes of sweetmeats from home that day and the good things which they contained were freely shared with their comrades who had received none.

Our expectation of passing the winter in these comfortable quarters was not fulfilled. The day after Christmas, December twenty-sixth, our brigade received orders to move at nine the next morning. When we were ready to start a cold, miserable rain set in. Following the railroad we jogged along through the mud for eight miles, arriving near Warrenton Junction[1] at one o'clock in the afternoon. Here we found very good huts erected and, in the shelter they provided from the driving rain, thought ourselves very fortunate. The next morning the true state of affairs came to light. We found that we were surrounded on two sides by stumps and on two sides by mud holes. The huts, although well constructed, were arranged without any regard to uniformity or symmetry. Our disgust was expressed by one of our officers[2] who wrote home, "It is very shocking to the taste of those accustomed to well-arranged camps."

The duty which now devolved upon our brigade was the guarding of the railroad from Catlett's Station to Licking Run, a distance of about four miles. Located as we were our brigade was somewhat isolated from the rest of the army and was in what was probably the worst guerrilla country in Virginia.

Upon our arrival our officers did not suppose that we should remain at Warrenton Junction for any great length of time and consequently did not require us to fit up the camp. Colonel Jenkins assumed command of the brigade on Decem-

[1] Now Calverton. [2] Major Curran.

ber thirtieth, General Garrard having been called to Washington, and the command of the regiment devolved upon Lieutenant-Colonel Armstrong. During the fall campaign a large number of conscripts had been assigned to our regiment, so that at the beginning of the winter we numbered about nine hundred and fifty men, more by a hundred than when we left Rome. Not all, of course, were with the regiment, a large percentage being away on furlough, in the hospital, or on detached service in the provost guard or ambulance corps. We, therefore, numbered on our arrival at Warrenton Junction about five hundred officers and men.

As the days passed without orders for a further move we came to the conclusion that we were destined to spend the remainder of the winter in our camp at this place, and, in view of this fact, prepared to make ourselves more comfortable. The huts were placed in better order, a camp drill-ground was cleared, and we soon assumed the high standard of military efficiency which characterized our regiment throughout its service, whether in the camp or field.

New Year's Day of 1864 was a typical "army holiday" with us, spent in feasting upon the dainties furnished by our friends at home or purchased from the sutler, who had laid in a special store in anticipation of a rush of business during the holiday season. In the evening Colonel Jenkins and Major Curran had as their guests at a dinner, consisting of roast turkey, stewed oysters, and pie, Colonel Gregory and Lieutenant-Colonel Sinex of the Ninety-first Pennsylvania, Lieutenant-Colonel Pearson of the One Hundred and Fifty-fifth Pennsylvania, Colonel Ryan of the One Hundred and Fortieth New York, and Captain Gibbs of the First Ohio Battery of Artillery.[1]

Those who had had the foresight to repair their huts on our arrival at Warrenton Junction were given cause to congratulate themselves. About a week after we reached the place the weather suddenly became much colder and for

[1] Told in letter from Major Curran.

several weeks thereafter we experienced all the hardships of a rigorous winter. The weather moderated considerably during the latter part of January and the first two weeks in February, but winter renewed its grip during the middle of the latter month and continued its undisputed sway until late in March. While the cold was not quite as severe as in the climate we were accustomed to, it penetrated our cotton shelters with the greatest ease. More than once several horses froze to death during the night, and it was no unusual thing in the morning to find men lying senseless from the effects of the cold.

Despite the rigors of the winter, however, the health of the regiment was uniformly good. Four fifths of the sickness that prevailed was among the conscripts, who, like ourselves a year previous, were finding it difficult to accustom themselves to life in the open, exposed to the mercies of a none too gentle climate. That sickness which did exist was very largely chronic diarrhœa, malaria, severe colds, with a few cases of typhoid pneumonia. As evidence of the improved conditions under which we lived and the fact that we had become accustomed to camp life it is only necessary to point out that only one member of our regiment died of disease during the entire winter season at Warrenton Junction, whereas nearly fifty had succumbed to its effects during the winter of 1862–63 spent at Falmouth.

The good health which characterized the regiment and prevailed generally throughout the entire army was due in large measure to the fact that the quality of the rations furnished by the commissary department was the best that we received during our entire service. As usual, hardtack, bacon, and the "nutritious bean" composed the regular diet, and this was varied occasionally by rice and a form of condensed vegetables. The latter, however, proved unsatisfactory, and was not at all popular with the men. Besides the food furnished by the government, once in a while we received boxes of delicacies from the Christian Commission

This Valentine was drawn and sent by Surgeon Thomas M. Flandrau from Warrenton Junction, Va., Winter of 1864, to his wife at Rome, N. Y. At bottom of sketch the headquarters of the Third Brigade, Second Division, Fifth Corps are shown; to the left the Zouave uniform worn by the regiment, to the right the flag of the Fifth Corps, etc.

THOMAS M. FLANDRAU

This 36-year-old Rome native, who mustered in as surgeon on Aug. 25, 1862, spent much of his time as surgeon in chief of the brigade, and in June of 1865, was in charge of the 2nd Division of the 5th Corps. In Dec. of 1863, Flandrau suffered a severe contusion of the left leg, and recovered while at home in Oneida County. In Jan. 1864 his wife became sick and later that Sept., his daughter fell dangerously ill, and he procured leave of absence on both occasions. He mustered out with the regiment on July 16, 1865. On July 16, 1867, the War Department brevetted Flandrau lieutenant colonel for faithful and meritorious services to date from Mar. 13, 1865. He died in Rome in 1898. (Donald Wisnoski Collection)

of the Young Men's Christian Association, that during the war rendered a most noble service by this and other methods.

That section of the Orange and Alexandria Railroad which our brigade had been assigned to guard was one of the most important along the entire route. Warrenton Junction was used as a wood depot between Alexandria and Brandy Station, at which the wheezy little wood-burner locomotives stopped to replenish their fuel. During the winter the government erected large repair shops and storehouses here for rations and ammunition. While these were in process of construction some six hundred truckmen, blacksmiths, machinists, and carpenters were busily engaged. About three hundred more workmen were constantly kept at work cutting firewood and hauling it to the station with the assistance of the patient "ox brigade." Ten or twelve immense frame buildings were built for the use of various departments of the army service, so that the Junction became a miniature metropolis, of which we, as its guardians, were both citizens and policemen.

In order better to protect the railroad at the Junction and also to assist the workmen, a battalion of the regiment was sent to the Junction itself on January twenty-fifth, under command of Major Curran. Here two redoubts were thrown up and the men camped in the vicinity of the depot. The five companies of infantry which composed the battalion and a section of artillery were stationed on each side of the railroad track and during the time they were not working on the fortifications erected a very comfortable camp. The location was much pleasanter than the regimental camp and the men assigned to the duty of protecting this section of the road soon felt at home in their new quarters. Near the depot were located a bakery, barber shop, news room, "dogertype"[1] studio, and telegraph office. These places, particularly the news room and studio, became favorite loafing places for the men during the hours of leisure.

[1] Daguerreotype, pronounced by the soldiers as though spelled "dogertype."

The thing we had to fear most during this winter of '64 was attack from the guerrillas or the Confederate cavalry under General "Jeb" Stuart. Rumors were constantly being received that the latter was preparing for a raid on a large scale, while the presence of the former in the vicinity was a constant menace. Whenever the report was received that Stuart was anywhere in the neighborhood preparations were made to give him a warm reception. Abatis was placed in front of the fortifications, and the men were called from their work and stationed behind the redoubts. This occurred quite frequently, but we were always disappointed, for the Confederate cavalry never made an attempt to destroy the railroad or the Union warehouses during our stay there.

The long winter days passed slowly. Many of us took advantage of the winter recess to visit our homes in the North, and, in common with the rest of the army, were very grateful for the liberality with which furloughs were granted. While we were in camp we amused ourselves as best we could after our day's work was over, singing, playing ball, boxing, pitching quoits, etc. It must be acknowledged, too, that there was considerable gambling among the men at this time, particularly after each pay-day when no small proportion of the money received changed hands with the run of the cards. Those of us who did not enjoy recreation of this kind spent our leisure, to a very large extent, in reading novels or periodicals. These were procured either from the Christian Commission or from our friends at home. The Christian Commission did a fine work in furnishing the men with good literature. There was a wide variety of taste in reading displayed. The military novels of Charles Lever were great favorites, Thackeray was read to some extent, and one officer[1] speaks of the pleasure he had reading Palgrave's *Golden Treasury of English Verse*. Of current literature the *Atlantic Monthly* and *Harper's Weekly* were by far the most popular periodicals.

[1] Major Curran.

For those of us who were on duty near the railroad station the greatest source of interest was the daily arrival of the passenger trains, one each way. They stopped for about half an hour, while wood was being loaded on the engine, and almost always some of us were sure to find some old acquaintances from other parts of the army. The frequent visitors to the regimental camp were most welcome. The wives, daughters, sisters, and sweethearts of the officers visited camp occasionally during the first few weeks of the winter, but the danger from guerrilla raids became so great that the ladies were prohibited from venturing so near to the enemy's country. Natives from the country round about came into the camp almost every day for the purpose of selling or buying, for the inhabitants were obliged to depend almost entirely upon the commissaries of the army for some of the staple food-stuffs. Milk, butter, fresh eggs, pies, and vegetables were bartered for sugar, salt, pork, or coffee. The appearance of some of these natives caused us great amusement. One day a very peculiar "rig" came into camp, consisting of a lumber wagon drawn by cows, on one of which a young darkey was mounted, performing the office of driver with the aid of a whip. Inside the wagon were a woman and two small children, who came for something to eat. They were given an order to buy from the commissary and started off, feeling very happy. Before such an order on the commissary was granted the recipients were required to take the oath of allegiance to the United States Government.

We received a call one day [writes Major Curran] from two old ladies, who wore old-fashioned calico hoods with pasteboard stiffenings, two girls about fifteen carrying large pillowcases of butter, one small girl with a long and very dirty nose, one lame boy with white hair, and another boy with white hair and big boots. We invited them to come into the tent and gave them seats. "We've cum to see ef we could maybe get some groceries of com'sary," one of the old ladies said. "Yes, I think so, but sit down, you must have had a long walk." "Yaas, sir, and a right smart aggerawatin' one, too." The Colonel asked them if they were willing to take the oath of allegiance, stating that they could not buy unless they did. The lame boy immediately rose, "I'm dog-goned ef I will; let's go home." The other youngster chimed in and all declared that they would not take the oath. Finally one of the old ladies agreed to swear "to bear true faith, etc.," and, having sold a little butter and procured some sugar, they disappeared.

Although the majority of those who came in were willing to undergo the formality of taking the oath, we knew that they were bitterly rebellious and entirely unreliable. The women quite frequently asked for a little "sperit," for the "rheumy" or some other complaint. "These Fairest of the Fair Virginians are great horsewomen, and ride anything from an ox to a sled stake, 'I reckon,' and they are 'right smart' at a bargain, too."[1]

Something decidedly out of the usual run of our life as soldiers took place while at Warrenton Junction in the form of a great religious revival held under the auspices of the Christian Commission. The meetings were held in a large tent or, on pleasant days, in the open air in the woods, and were conducted by the regimental chaplains and evangelists in the employ of the Commission. Notices of the meetings were read on dress parade and the men responded in surprisingly large numbers. At the meetings hymn-books were distributed to the men and the best singers in the various regiments led the singing, in which all present took part enthusiastically. Nearly two hundred were converted by these evangelistic meetings in our brigade alone and the work was attended by equally good results throughout the entire army. That this wave of religious enthusiasm did not vitally affect all the members of our regiment is attested by an entry which occurs in the diary kept by a member of Company "D."[2] The entry reads, "Some of the boys off on a big

---

[1] From letter written by James Pitcher, Co. "D."   [2] James Pitcher.

drunk last night." Curiously enough an entry in the diary kept by a member of Company "G"[1] for the same day states, "Attended a prayer meeting in Lieutenant York's[2] tent."

One of the saddest incidents, from many standpoints, of the winter at Warrenton Junction was the death and funeral of Captain Joseph B. Sackett of the One Hundred and Fifty-fifth Pennsylvania Volunteers of our brigade. The Captain and another officer were visiting the camp of the Regulars which was situated on the other side of a small stream called Kettle Run. While there a heavy rainstorm arose, causing the waters of the stream to rise suddenly. That evening, when the Captain and his companion returned and endeavored to cross the stream, the Captain's horse became alarmed at the depth of the water and threw the Captain off, and kicked him as he fell, rendering him insensible. The Captain was drowned. His companion, however, reached the opposite shore in safety. The body of the Captain was recovered later by a detachment of Regulars.

Captain Sackett had been granted fifteen days' leave of absence at the time of the accident, and intended to leave the next morning for Pittsburg. General Garrard issued orders to pay Captain Sackett the honors of a military funeral from the camp of the regiment to the railroad station, a mile distant. The entire brigade was massed for the solemn occasion. The command of the funeral column was assigned by General Garrard to Colonel D. T. Jenkins of the One Hundred and Forty-sixth New York Volunteers. The body of Captain Sackett, enclosed in a handsome coffin, was borne upon an artillery caisson. The thirty-two musicians, with their instruments, composing the brass band of the United States Regulars, headed the cortège, and in compliment of the companionship, a regiment of the United States Regulars occupied a position in the funeral column.

[1] Orville J. Barker.

[2] Lieutenant York, when the war broke out, was pastor of the Methodist Church at Bridgewater, New York, and a large percentage of his company ("G") was recruited from among the young men of his church and Sunday school.

General Garrard, and all of his staff, with colors draped in mourning, participated in the procession. The sight was most impressive, the plain where the funeral procession was formed and paraded to the station affording a fine view of the troops composing the funeral cortège.[1]

It was during this winter that our regiment bade farewell to our former commander, General Garrard. During the latter part of January he was assigned to duty in Washington, but a few weeks later word was received that he had been given an important cavalry command in the Army of the Cumberland. General Garrard subsequently distinguished himself by his work under Sherman and at the close of the war was one of the most popular and efficient commanders in the army.

Through General Garrard's influence at Washington new zouave uniforms were procured for all the regiments of our brigade.[2] They reached us in January and from that time forth the "Zou Zou" brigade made a dashing appearance on parade or in line of battle. Under General Garrard's expert tutelage all the regiments of the brigade had reached a high degree of efficiency in drill, and General Sykes expressed it as his opinion that we were the best volunteer brigade in the army. Our uniform made us more or less conspicuous and it behooved us to perfect ourselves in all the duties and excellencies of military life so that our prominence should serve to spread abroad only a good reputation. Even after General Garrard left us, therefore, the same strict military discipline which had characterized his administration of our regimental affairs was continued under the commanders who succeeded him.

On February ninth the brigade was reviewed by General Ayres and his staff.

[1] From *Under the Maltese Cross*, a history of the One Hundred and Fifty-fifth Pennsylvania Volunteers.

[2] Up to this time only the One Hundred and Fortieth and the One Hundred and Forty-sixth had worn the zouave uniform.

Colonel David T. Jenkins and Staff, when Col. Jenkins was in Command of Third Brigade, Second Division, Fifth Corps, Warrenton Junction, Va., Winter of 1864

UNIDENTIFIED

This dark-eyed, dark-haired, pipe-toting unidentified 146th New York Zouave wears a white collared checker shirt. He apparently wears a fez or an unusual leisure cap. The original image is a gem size tintype—smaller than a postage stamp. (Michael F. Bremer Collection)

It was a very brilliant affair, and the new uniforms of the brigade presented a very gay spectacle indeed. The day was fine and there was a large number of visitors, ladies included, to witness the affair. Afterward the General inspected the fort at the Junction and expressed himself much pleased with it.[1]

The last event of importance that occurred during the winter of 1864 was the reorganization of the Army of the Potomac, which took place early in March. This reorganization was the result of an entirely new plan adopted by Congress and the President for the conduct of the war.

Although the reverses which the Union arms had suffered at the beginning of the great conflict had been somewhat mitigated by the victories during the summer of 1863 in both East and West, there was still a feeling prevalent in the North that a great deal more should have been accomplished. The lack of concerted action had come to be regarded as the chief fault in the conduct of the various separate armies comprising the Union forces. In order to bring about this unanimity of purpose it was decided to give some one man charge of the active operations of all these armies, and to that end the grade of Lieutenant-General was revived by Act of Congress on February 29, 1864. Major-General Ulysses S. Grant, who had been so successful in his operations in the West, crowning his good work there by the siege and capture of Vicksburg, was called to Washington to accept this new commission as Lieutenant-General and received it from the hands of President Lincoln on March ninth.

It now became Grant's purpose so to work with the seventeen distinct commanders of the various armies that there should be a decided concert of action and unanimity of purpose.[2] He regarded the Army of the Potomac as the center; the Union line from this army to Memphis as the right wing; the Army of the James as the left wing; and all the troops in the South as a force in rear of the enemy. Offi-

[1] From letter written by Major Curran.   [2] *Memoirs*, vol. ii., p. 56.

cers and soldiers on furlough, of whom there were many thousands, were ordered to their proper commands; concentration was the order of the day, and it was hurried forward as rapidly as circumstances would permit, in preparation for the spring campaign.

The Army of the Potomac was strengthened by the return of the Ninth Corps, under General Burnside, which had been operating in Tennessee, but for a considerable time this corps remained independent of the Army of the Potomac so far as its organization and command was concerned. At the same time a reorganization took place within the Army of the Potomac itself. General Meade became convinced that better results could be achieved by reducing the number of corps and placing a larger number of men in each corps, thereby effecting an organization similar to that which had prevailed throughout the war in the Army of Northern Virginia. He accordingly dissolved the First and Third Corps and consolidated them with the Second, Fifth, and Sixth Corps. A change was also made in the commanders of these three corps. General Gouverneur K. Warren replaced General Sykes in command of our corps, the Fifth; General Winfield S. Hancock was placed in command of the Second Corps; and General John Sedgwick retained command of the Sixth Corps. Such drastic changes necessitated the shifting of many officers throughout the whole army. Many commanders of divisions and brigades were relegated to the commands of brigades and regiments, respectively; and hundreds who had confidently looked forward to promotion as staff officers were retained in their various companies. While the reorganization caused no small amount of dissatisfaction and discontent for a time, both officers and men, with but few exceptions, soon became accustomed to and were pleased with the new organization, particularly as its greater efficacy soon became apparent during the subsequent campaign.

Under the new organization the changes made in the

Fifth Corps itself placed our regiment in the first brigade of the First Division, the position of honor. Here we were brigaded with the One Hundred and Fortieth New York, the Ninety-first Pennsylvania Veteran Volunteers, the One Hundred and Fifty-fifth Pennsylvania Volunteers, and five regiments of United States Regulars. Brigadier-General Charles Griffin, a most efficient officer, was placed in command of the division; and Brigadier-General Ayres, our former division commander, was assigned to the command of the brigade. As now constituted, the Fifth Corps consisted of four divisions commanded by Generals Griffin, Robinson, Crawford, and Wadsworth, respectively, with an artillery brigade under command of Colonel C. S. Wainwright.

With the appointment of General Ayres as commander of our brigade Colonel Jenkins resumed command of our regiment. Lieutenant-Colonel Armstrong having tendered his resignation, his position was taken by Major Curran,[1] who was, in turn, succeeded by James Grindlay, the senior Captain.

For the first time during our career the members of the One Hundred and Forty-sixth wore the *red* maltese cross as members of the First Division of the Fifth Corps.[2] Although we little dreamed it at the time, we were destined to see our hardest service under this emblem during the few months that we wore it, before we were returned, shattered and diminished in numbers, to membership in the Second Division, under the white cross.

On March tenth, the day after General Grant received his commission, he visited the Army of the Potomac en-

[1] The commission confirming the appointment of Major Curran as Lieutenant-Colonel was not issued until after his death in the Wilderness, and Captain Grindlay's commission as Major did not reach him until after the command of the regiment had devolved upon him.

[2] The various corps of the Union army were designated by different symbols, such as Fifth Corps—Maltese Cross; Second—Three-leaf Clover; Twelfth—Five-pointed Star, etc. These symbols were colored red, white, and blue for First, Second, and Third Divisions, respectively.

camped in the vicinity of the Orange and Alexandria Railroad. In some way the fact of his visit was noised about
several hours before his arrival, so that when his special train
stopped for a half-hour or so at Warrenton Junction there
were thousands of soldiers at that point waiting to receive
him, all eager to catch a glimpse of their new commander.
One of the officers of our regiment[1] chanced to be on guard
duty with his company that day and as the men crowded
about the car, at one window of which the General was
sitting, the officer tried to hold them in check, but the task
proved one almost impossible of accomplishment. The men
could not be restrained, but pushed and crowded about the
car, some even climbing upon and over it, shouting and
cheering. In the midst of the excitement Colonel Jenkins
came upon the scene and ordered the men to disperse. General Grant had been an interested spectator of the whole
affair and as Colonel Jenkins attempted to force the men back
he raised the car window and said, good-naturedly, "Never
mind, Colonel, the boys won't hurt me." Colonel Jenkins
smiled at the General, and, acknowledging the command,
retired and permitted the "boys" to continue their demonstrations unmolested.

General Grant went as far as Brandy Station, where he
visited the headquarters of the Army of the Potomac and
spent a few hours in conversation with General Meade, who
had been retained by the former as commander of this
army. On his return an incident took place the particulars
of which were widely circulated and caused the men to feel
great admiration and enthusiasm for General Grant. As
the special train was leaving the station at Brandy a young
private soldier who had just received a leave of absence to
visit his mother, who was very ill in New York City, attempted to climb upon the rear platform of the train, thinking it was the regular passenger train which left each day.
The guard was on the point of compelling him to get off

[1] Lieutenant King, Co. "C."

Col. David T. Jenkins (left), General Spaulding (50th N. Y. Engineers), and Capt. James E. Jenkins (right) at Headquarters of Gen. Spaulding, Warrenton Junction, Va., Spring of 1864

UNIDENTIFIED
Apparently wearing a shirt vest of the old 5th New York, Duryée's Zouaves, that were consolidated with the 146th New York on May 4, 1863, this sash-less veteran still has a saucy look about him. He wears a shortened tassel on his fez, and sports a thick mustache and goatee. There are indications that this soldier was killed during the war, possibly in 1864. (Gordon E. Johnson Collection)

when Grant opened the door and commanded the guard to let the boy remain. He took the lad into the coach with him and in a conversation learned the particulars of the case. He permitted the boy to stay on the train until it reached the end of the line and then bade him good-bye with the wish that he might find his mother improved in health. As the story was repeated about the campfires of the army, with the many embellishments which are bound to creep into such a narrative, the men conceived a deep affection for their new commander. "It was worth ten thousand men for the Army of the Potomac," as one of our officers[1] expressed it.

Winter slowly melted into spring, which brought with it days of peculiarly disagreeable weather, of which mud and rain were the chief components. Early in April it rained steadily and heavily for thirty-six hours, making a large river of every creek, floating our tents, carrying away bridges, and doing all manner of damage. Fortunately, the mud was not particularly bad at Warrenton Junction, but at Brandy Station and Culpeper it was said to be unfathomable. The few days of rain, however, were followed by several weeks of warm and pleasant weather and with each succeeding sunny day our spirits rose higher in anticipation of the active work of the spring campaign. The grass grew fresh and green, the trees became luxuriant with great variety of blossoms. Multitudes of birds made music in the morning and hundreds of frogs made melody throughout the night. To the superficial observer everything seemed quiet and peaceful, but behind the scenes there was much work going on. Each army was striving to the utmost to put itself in a state of thorough preparation, for there was a feeling on both sides that the first few battles of the year would be the most sanguinary of the war.

As preparations for the campaign were completed the great question in the minds of all became, "When will the army move?" That Lee would wait for his opponent, Grant,

[1] Major King.

to make the first move, there was hardly a shadow of doubt. General Lee's offensive campaign of the previous year had proved so disastrous that it was practically certain he would not attempt a similar move in opening the campaign of 1864. General Grant's intentions, therefore, would determine the nature of the campaign in which we would soon be actively involved.

CHAPTER XI

THE WILDERNESS

THE engagement known as the Battle of the Wilderness was the first that was fought between the Army of the Potomac and the Army of Northern Virginia after Grant had been placed in command of all the Union armies. This battle, therefore, was the first engagement of the war in which Lee had Grant as his opponent. The occasion of the battle was when Lee contested the advance of Grant after the latter, with the Army of the Potomac and Burnside's corps, crossed the Rapidan and began his march southward. The opposing armies had been separated by this river for several months. The Union army, with headquarters at Culpeper, north of the Rapidan, had been encamped during the preceding winter on the peninsula formed by the junction of the Rapidan and Rappahannock rivers and also at points along the Orange and Alexandria Railroad, guarding the approaches toward Washington. The Confederate army had passed the same winter in camp south of the Rapidan, with headquarters near Orange Court House.

General Grant took the initiative in the campaign and his movement southward brought our camp life at Warrenton to a sudden close. The orders for the regiment to move came at an extremely inopportune moment so far as our camp recreations were concerned. One of the ways in which we often helped to pass the time during the warm spring days in camp at Warrenton was in a series of ball games.

This, in fact, was the most popular sport the men engaged in to break the monotony of camp life. Teams chosen mostly from the enlisted men selected by their company officers would be made up whenever the season of the year was favorable for the sport and a long enough stay in camp at any one place permitted. But often one regiment would challenge another from the brigade to a game of ball, and this always furnished an afternoon of good sport. The last days at Warrenton were enlivened by the interest taken in an advertised game between two teams within our own regiment and the spare money of many of the boys was wagered on the outcome.[1] The orders, however, that came for us to break camp at Warrenton necessitated postponing this game.

These orders to move were not entirely unexpected as we all knew, of course, that spring would bring a campaign in some direction. The rank and file of the army, while they never knew until orders were given when they were to move or what was to be in store for them, nevertheless always had an intuitive feeling of movements about to be begun and battles that would be fought. Often also just prior to a campaign cases were frequent of men foreseeing their own death. The day before we broke camp at Warrenton the Second Lieutenant[2] of Company "H" accosted a private,[3] who often acted as regimental barber, with the cheerful news that inasmuch as he expected to be hit in the head by a bullet in the next battle, he wanted his hair cut so that it would be easy for the surgeon to get at the wound. Seated upon a log with his head against a tree his hair was cut close, and four days later he fell in the charge through the clearing at the battle of the Wilderness, pierced by a bullet through his forehead as he had predicted.

[1] Robert T. Warren, brother of General Warren, and familiarly known as "Bob," was captain of one of these teams, and "Pete" Froeligh, Second Lieutenant of Company "H," who had (recently) been transferred to the One Hundred and Forty-sixth Regiment from the Fifth New York, was captain of the other.

[2] Peter Froeligh.   [3] Fletcher Dimblely.

Group of Officers of 146th Regiment at Headquarters of Third Brigade, Second Div., Fifth Corps, four days before the Battle of the Wilderness. The majority of these Officers were killed or wounded in the charge at the Battle of the Wilderness on May 5, 1864

Standing, left to right—Lt. Chalmers, Lt. Loomis, Lt. York, Capt. Wilson, Capt. Stewart, Capt. Jenkins, Lt. Walker, Capt. Cushman, Lt. Timmerman, Quartermaster Egleston, Capt. B. F. Wright, Lt. King, Lt. Coan (with hat), Lt. Lowery, Lt. Fowler, Lt. Sweet (with cloak), Lt. Fitzpatrick, Capt. Durkee

Sitting, left to right—Asst. Surgeon Fenwick, Capt. Henry Jones, Surgeon Flandrau, Col. David T. Jenkins, Major Grindlay, Lt.-Col. Curran, Adjutant Wright, Chaplain Payson

Saturday, April 30, 1864, was a pleasant spring morning. For us it was a busy morning, as we had received orders to march that day. Before noon the brigade had struck tents and was on the way to Brandy Station in accordance with orders that had been issued to concentrate at this point before midnight of May 3d all the various divisions and brigades of the Fifth Corps preparatory to crossing the Rapidan. The first night out from Warrenton we camped in the woods near the Fiftieth New York Regiment of Engineers about a mile east of the Rappahannock River. The next morning at sunrise we started down the railroad again towards Rappahannock Station. The pontoon over which we were to cross the river was not finished when the head of the column reached the river and consequently many forded it. After the crossing was made we proceeded west along the railroad as far as Brandy Station, a march of about six miles, and went into camp early in the afternoon within sight of the place.

We stayed here Sunday night, all day Monday, and part of Tuesday.[1] The scene about us, excepting for the life that moving troops put into it, was one of desolation. Clustered about the railroad station were a few unpretentious houses. The village housed before the war a few white families. Now it served as a base for army supplies; it was a strategic point on the Orange and Alexandria Railroad, and none inhabited it but soldiery. Along this railroad and over all the surrounding country the armies of the North and South had marched and fought. Here and there on the landscape could be seen the ruins of plantation houses. A huge fireplace and tall chimney standing alone in the center of a clearing told the story of war more vividly than words. Near our camp at Brandy stood one of these solitary chimneys. Sunday afternoon a few of the soldiers strolled over to the ruined house. Inquisitive as they always were, they craned

---

[1] During the stay of the regiment at Brandy eight men left the regiment to join the navy.—From Pitcher's diary.

their necks up inside the fireplace to get a view of the sky above, and hidden there was an old white-haired negro who, perhaps, remembering the cavalry fight that had taken place near this same spot the prevous autumn, had sought a safe refuge on the appearance of the soldiers.[1]   They pulled him out and the old fellow, trembling at first with fear, soon began to take courage when he saw that no harm was meant to him.   He was very eloquent in his way and told the soldiers gathered about him, with gesture and grimace, of the fighting he had seen before and which he had expected was going to be renewed when our regiment had camped so near his domicile.

These few days of May were busy ones for all who had in charge the movements of the troops.   For the first time since the war began all the armies of the North, wherever located, were carrying out their separate programs in accordance with the comprehensive scheme for united action that had been prepared by General Grant.   The part that had been assigned to the Army of the Potomac, of which our regiment was but a single unit, was to turn the right flank of the Army of Northern Virginia and continue southward towards Richmond.

The Army of the Potomac, at this time technically under the command of General Meade, was composed of three army corps of infantry, namely, the Second, Fifth, and Sixth Corps, and one cavalry corps under the command of Major-General Sheridan, together with artillery under the command of General Hunt, an engineers' brigade, and a large park of supply wagons.   Acting also in conjunction with the Army of the Potomac in this movement southward was the Ninth Corps under the command of General Burnside.

To provision such an army and to control the movements of the various units composing it preparatory to their advance across the Rapidan was no small task.   From the twenty-seventh of April until the third of May the time was

---

[1] Probably the engagement of October 11, 1863.

occupied in bringing together near Culpeper the various units of this vast army. At Brandy Station our regiment was near the appointed rendezvous and as the schedule did not call for general movements to be begun until midnight of May third we passed part of the day, Monday, May second, in camp waiting for the appointed time.

The day opened bright and warm. Mail was distributed in the morning and we ourselves had leisure to write. The wind was from the south and towards noon the horizon began to blacken with evidences of a storm. The wind increased in violence. To some the storm was an ominous sign, coming as it did out of the south. It was a beautiful sight. A cloud of red dust rose before the shower and, coming towards us from the distance, resembled the smoke of a burning city. In a few minutes it struck the camp with terrific force. First a wind and sand storm, then a downpour of rain. The storm had broken upon us so suddenly and with such intensity that it nearly wrecked our camp. The contents of the mess chests were blown in every direction. The rain came down in torrents and though it soon spent its force and quickly cleared away, the damage it had done left the camp a sorry spectacle.

Thinking, perhaps, that we should have another day of waiting here in camp, the game of ball that had been necessarily postponed by our hurried departure from Warrenton and on which so many had staked a large portion of their available cash was arranged to be played. It was hardly started, however, when the bugle sounded the "general" and by noon we had again broken camp and marched on about six miles farther west, paralleling the railroad to near Culpeper. Here we halted, as the men supposed, for the night and went into camp preparing for an all-night rest. Our officers, however, knew differently, as orders had been issued to brigade commanders for every man to be in line and on the march southward by midnight. Reveille sounded at 11 P.M. and soon after we started on our way, every man

loaded with fifty rounds of ammunition and three full days'
rations in his haversack. No body of troops was ever better
equipped in morale, arms, and clothing than was this army
when it started out that night, and the address of General
Meade to the Army of the Potomac read before each regiment
calling upon each man to do his full duty met with warm
response.

Almost at the same time that we began our march at
midnight on the third of May, 1864, all the troops of the
three corps comprising the Army of the Potomac that had
been collected in this vicinity from their previous scattered
positions were on the move. Their objectives were to be the
destruction of Lee's army and the capture of Richmond, the
Confederate capital. Before another day had passed this army,
if all went well, would be south of the Rapidan, on the right
of Lee's encampment and ready to fight in the Wilderness or
to march farther south as the destiny of war might determine.

Every precaution was taken by those responsible for our
movements to see to it that the enemy should get no inkling
of them. The cavalry had been ordered on ahead, accompanied by pontoon trains and engineers' corps, and the day
before guards had been placed in all the occupied houses on
or in the vicinity of the route the army was to take for the
purpose of preventing any communication with the enemy by
the inhabitants. The fords by which the Army of the
Potomac was to cross the Rapidan were southeast of Culpeper, which for so long had been the headquarters of the
commanding general, and were several miles to the right of
Lee's encampment. The Fifth and Sixth Corps, commanded
by Generals Warren and Sedgwick, respectively, were to
cross the Rapidan at Germanna Ford, while General Hancock with the Second Corps was to cross a few miles farther
east at Ely's Ford.

The little village of Stevensburg, "a hamlet of a half
dozen age-worn houses sitting at the foot of a bare hill,"[1]

[1] Schaff, *Battle of the Wilderness.*

was on our line of march. In this village two roads meet, one coming from Brandy off to the northwest and one from Culpeper nearly due west. We came down the Culpeper road into Stevensburg along with the rest of the Fifth Corps. Down the other road and following us through Stevensburg came the Sixth Corps. Burnside with the Ninth Corps was back near Warrenton to protect the rear in the event of an unsuccessful or delayed crossing of the Rapidan as planned. From the high ground near Stevensburg where it had been camped, the rear of Hancock's Second Corps was moving out on its way to Ely's Ford as we came into the village. Leaving Stevensburg the Fifth Corps passed out on the narrow main highway, that was built in Washington's time, leading to Fredericksburg. Our regiment was near the head of the column; the first division of the corps was leading and the brigades were marching in their numerical order. The Second Corps ahead of us kept straight on their road to Ely's Ford. The Fifth Corps with the Sixth Corps behind us soon branched off from this road and stumbled along over crossroads until we reached the plank road leading direct to Germanna Ford. The night was dark and these crossroads unfamiliar to our commanders. Here and there, however, along the route squads of cavalry were placed to guide us in the darkness. The detachment of cavalry that had preceded the column was already on the other side of the river when we, the infantry, arrived at the ford. A few Confederate pickets had been found on the opposite side of the river but the cavalry soon cleared the way for us so that our crossing was unmolested. We filed off to one side of the road after crossing the pontoon and stacked our arms about sunrise. Orders had been given not to build campfires. A few twigs and sticks, however, that each man was able to collect for himself sufficed to furnish fuel for small fires over which we made our coffee.

In putting into execution the orders that would bring our regiment to its appointed camping-place and to make way for the troops that were surging over the pontoon behind us only a short respite was allowed for breakfast. As soon as we had finished our coffee, we filed out onto the Germanna plank road towards Wilderness Tavern, which was some six or seven miles south of the river. The road was uneven and narrow with thick woods on either side. We marched on until we reached the Orange and Fredericksburg turnpike, where we filed off to the right about sundown past Wilderness Tavern and went into camp on the edge of the road a mile farther westward.

Our camping-ground was a familiar one, for we recognized the road as the route over which we had journeyed the preceding November during the futile Mine Run campaign. There was no complaint whatever as to scarcity of firewood and we were soon busy cooking our meal over many tiny fires which we tried to make as smokeless as possible in an effort to conceal our presence from an ever-watchful enemy.

The portion of northern Virginia south of the Rapidan into which General Grant had pushed his army was appropriately called "the Wilderness." This forest is a belt about thirty miles in length paralleling the course of the Rapidan and extending from near Orange Court House on the west almost to Fredericksburg on the east. Its width is somewhat irregular, varying from ten miles at its widest point to narrow broken belts of trees in the vicinity of Fredericksburg.

This forest area is aptly described as "a maze of trees, underbrush, and ragged foliage,"[1] "thickets of stunted pine, sweet-gum, scrub oak, and cedar,"[2] and "a jungle of switch, ten or twenty feet high."[3]

General Grant established his headquarters on the morning of the fourth of May at Wilderness Tavern, a clearing and hostelry at the intersection of the Germanna Ford

[1] *Photographic History of the Civil War*, Review of Reviews Company.
[2] *Battles and Leaders of the Civil War*, General E. M. Law.
[3] "Notes and Recollections of the Opening of the Campaign of 1864," *Massachusetts Military Historical Society Papers.*

plank road and the Orange and Fredericksburg turnpike, two roads that traversed north and south and east and west, respectively, this "vast no-man's land"—the Wilderness. In accordance with the plans which had been carefully worked out by General Grant for bringing his troops through the Wilderness, Warren with the Fifth Corps had been ordered to move to the vicinity of Old Wilderness Tavern on the Orange Court House pike,[1] Sedgwick with the Sixth Corps, who had crossed the Rapidan in the rear of Warren, was ordered to bivouac on Warren's right between the turnpike and the river, while Hancock, with the Second Corps, was to march down from Ely's Ford where he had crossed the river, paralleling the route we took, and bivouac in the vicinity of Chancellorsville, about six miles east of us.

In these respective positions the fighting force of the Army of the Potomac slept on their arms in the midst of the forest the night of the fourth of May, 1864, fatigued by their twenty-mile march, uncertain as to what the morrow would bring forth, but nevertheless confident that their commander had planned well and that they would not be likely to turn back until they had accomplished that for which they had set forth. By sundown all three corps of the Army of the Potomac were safely over the Rapidan and at or near their places of encampment. During the night Burnside's corps was hurrying southward from the Rappahannock to overtake Meade and Grant in the Wilderness while the supply trains, nearly 4000 wagons in all, filled with rations and ammunition, were rumbling across the pontoon over the Rapidan in our rear.[2] In the message notifying the Washington government that his army had been safely transported across the Rapidan, General Grant said, "Forty-eight hours will demonstrate whether the enemy intends giving battle

[1] Another name for the Orange and Fredericksburg pike.

[2] On the evening of May fourth, Adjutant Wright made his last report to army headquarters, showing the strength of the regiment to be twenty-four officers and five hundred and fifty-six men present for duty.

this side of Richmond." In less time than Grant names, events developed that showed the progress of his army southward was to be stubbornly contested by the enemy and that, in fact, the first test of strength was only a few hours distant.

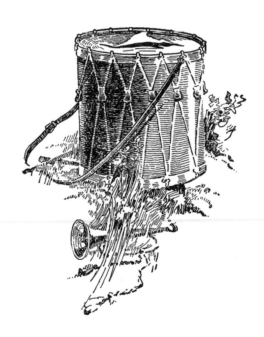

CHAPTER XII

BATTLE OF THE WILDERNESS

IT was reckoning without due appreciation of General
Lee's military intuition to presume that the Union army
would be allowed to invade this territory without decided opposition. The Confederate commander had so maneuvered
on former occasions whenever the Union forces had ventured
into the meshes of the Wilderness as to cause their speedy
retreat. He had anticipated some movement on the part
of General Grant, and, ever on the alert, was ready to act
as circumstances might demand. As soon, therefore, as
he was assured that the Union forces were crossing the
Rapidan by the fords on his right, he left his intrenchments
around Orange Court House and moved rapidly to the eastward. His troops, in fact, were all in motion before the
Army of the Potomac had finished its crossing. Lee's
soldiers, who by count were much fewer in number than the
men at Grant's command and poorly equipped in compari-
son with the Northern troops, had, nevertheless, the confident spirit of seasoned veterans. General Lee planned to
hurl these troops of his, tried and found true on so many
similar occasions, upon the advancing columns of General
Grant, and perhaps once more the invading forces would
be compelled to retire, as both Hooker and Meade had been
forced to do, at Chancellorsville and Mine Run.

There were two main roads by which the Confederates
could move forward to the attack—the southernmost road,

called the Orange and Fredericksburg plank road, and the Orange turnpike, which paralleled the former, running east and west between it and the Rapidan. General Ewell's corps was sent forward by General Lee to the east on the turnpike road on the afternoon of the fourth while we were marching to our camping-ground located on the same road. General Hill's corps was also marched to the east at the same time by way of the Orange plank road; and Long-street's corps, which had been guarding the river to the west of Lee's encampment, was hurried along behind Hill on the plank road. These movements of the Confederates were, of course, unknown to us at the time, although Ewell's soldiers were actually turning into camp only a few miles west of us.

As the ashes of our campfires burned low we prepared to make ourselves as comfortable as possible for the night. A small stream[1] found its way through the forest, and in this we bathed our tired feet. As night enveloped us, we sought rest. The bivouac of an army in an enemy's country, in the midst of such surroundings, makes a vivid picture in every soldier's mind that is never blotted out, and a picture, also, that defies description in words. Songs and hilarity peculiar to youth are often the accompanying features of a soldier's campfire. In the Wilderness jungle, however, this night before the battle, no songs or revelry were heard. An unusual solemnity pervaded the camp. The wildness of our surroundings, the consciousness that we were in an enemy's country, unfamiliar both to ourselves and to our commanders, produced a sense of ominous dread which many of us found it almost impossible to shake off. The flutterings and calls of the night birds and the stir of insect life in the densely populated underbrush of the Wilderness mingled with the subdued voices of the men, seeming to forebode evil to those who had invaded this solitude, and many a man that night committed his soul to God in earnest prayer.

[1] Wilderness Run.

While we slept, Colonel Jenkins, who had been detailed as general officer of outposts, stationed the corps pickets a distance out to the west of the corps encampment. The closeness of the enemy was not suspected, but the pickets intrenched themselves as a matter of precaution. Here they passed a weary vigil, with outposts thrown out at intervals in their front.

Unmolested thus far, Grant's army had moved forward through this maze of wilderness underbrush and along the narrow roads, in outstretched fan-like shape. For nearly a week the orders for each day had been carried out as planned, each unit fulfilling its assigned part with almost clock-like precision. The program for another day was arranged for while the army rested, which would call for the various corps, divisions, brigades, and regiments to be moved forward like the pieces in a game of chess. This program provided that Warren, with the Fifth Corps, should start at five o'clock the next morning and take his corps by the farm road to Parker's Store, and, having reached it, extend his right to meet Sedgwick's Sixth Corps, which was to take the position that Warren held on the turnpike. Hancock, making a long sweep from where his corps, the Second, was encamped at Chancellorsville, was to take position on Warren's left. General Burnside's command, the Ninth Corps, was to take the place of reserve at Germanna Ford. These orders, had they been executed as given, would have pushed the army, in an inverted wedge-shaped mass, another day's journey through the Wilderness, its front an uneven line six or seven miles in width, the cavalry ahead and on the flanks.[1]

These movements planned for the fifth of May necessitated an early rising, for the Fifth Corps was to be ready to march by five o'clock in the morning. The order of

[1] General Meade had ordered the Union cavalry to remain out on the turnpike to the westward, but through some error they failed to do so.—War Records, 67, p. 290.

march as planned was for the Third Division of the corps to lead, next to them the Fourth Division, followed by the Second, with the First Division in the rear. Our regiment being in the First Division was, therefore, to be one of the last to leave camp. The circular containing these orders is interesting to read inasmuch as it shows how carefully Headquarters wished to have the army feel its way along through the Wilderness forest and be ready at a moment's notice for attack. Flankers were to be thrown well out to the right from each division, and passing every crossroad each division was to have a detachment in good covering position well out on the right flank, from which direction the enemy might be expected, to hold the road while the remainder of the division passed. "The troops," the circular continued, "must be kept well closed and held well in hand. The head of the column will move slowly to enable the divisions to keep well closed up on each other. The necessity for this is paramount and must be kept constantly in mind."

As a further precaution against surprise General Warren, our corps commander, sent an officer with a written order to Colonel Jenkins, commanding the corps outposts, instructing him, if he had not already withdrawn his pickets before the order reached him, to keep them out until the four divisions of the corps were well on the road on the line of march toward Parker's Store.

It was nearly six o'clock[1] when Crawford's division (the Third) took up the line of march over a farm road connecting the turnpike with the Orange plank road on its way to Parker's Store, with cavalry in advance.[2] Wadsworth's division (the Fourth), getting under way about seven o'clock[3]

[1] From letter of General Crawford, dated May fifth, at 8.00 A.M.

[2] The Orange turnpike and the Orange plank road, it should be remembered, run almost parallel due east and west. The farm road connecting them leaves the turnpike about one half of a mile west of Old Wilderness Tavern and runs diagonally, striking the plank road at Parker's Store.

[3] From report of Colonel J. W. Hoffman, commanding second brigade, Fourth Division.

followed Crawford along the same road. These two divisions, therefore, were the only portions of the Fifth Corps that started out for the day's march, as planned. Before the remaining divisions of the corps could get under way to carry out the program for the day's march as laid down by General Grant, events were happening on the picket line that disarranged all their marching plans.

At the first break of day our Colonel, while still on duty with the outposts, was standing near the picket line in the center of the turnpike which led from Orange Court House, where Lee had been encamped, to Wilderness Tavern, around which the Union forces had passed the preceding night. The road lay like a gently undulating ribbon stretched out in a straight line due east and west, and he could look several miles to the westward through this avenue in the forest. Peering down this open lane, he saw at some distance off a body of troops advancing down the road and filing off into the woods on either side. Skirmishers and scouts were immediately sent out by him through the woods to learn, if possible, the strength and position of the enemy that had just appeared.

The officer whom General Warren had dispatched with instructions to Colonel Jenkins not to bring in the pickets until the entire corps was in motion reached the commander of outposts shortly after the latter had discovered the enemy in the distance. Colonel Jenkins read the order from General Warren, and taking a pencil, wrote on the back of it as follows:

The rebel infantry have appeared on the Orange Court House turnpike and are forming a line of battle, three quarters of a mile in front of General Griffin's line of battle. I have my skirmishers out, and preparations are being made to meet them. There is a large cloud of dust in that direction.

This report of Colonel Jenkins that the enemy had appeared to the west of his line on the turnpike was quickly forwarded by Warren to General Meade, who in turn sent word to General Grant in a dispatch that was received at headquarters at seven-thirty A.M. This was the first official information that General Grant received that Lee's troops had arrived and were about to give battle in the Wilderness. The dispatch from General Meade conveying this information to General Grant read as follows:

The enemy have appeared in force on the Orange pike, and are now reported forming line of battle in front of Griffin's division, Fifth Corps. I have directed General Warren to attack them at once with his whole force. Until this movement of the enemy is developed, the march of the corps must be suspended. I have, therefore, sent word to Hancock not to advance beyond Todd's Tavern for the present. I think the enemy is trying to delay our movement, and will not give battle, but of this we shall soon see. For the present I will stop here, and have stopped our trains.[1]

The dispatch that General Grant forwarded to General Meade in reply has in it one phrase characteristic of the

[1] The dispatch that General Warren sent to Colonel Jenkins requesting him to keep his pickets out until the four divisions of the corps were well on their line of march was dated but, unfortunately, did not have the time at which it was sent noted thereon. Neither does Colonel Jenkins, in the indorsement on this dispatch which he sent back to General Warren, note the time. We, however, have assumed that previous to the arrival of this officer from General Warren with the dispatch referred to, Colonel Jenkins had advised his superior, General Ayres, who in turn had advised General Griffin, the division commander, of the appearance of the enemy in his front. The basis for this assumption is a dispatch dated May fifth at 6.00 A.M. that Warren sent to Meade, which reads as follows: "General Griffin has just sent in word that a force of the enemy has been reported to him coming down the turnpike. The foundation of the report is not given. Until it is more definitely ascertained no change will take place in the movements ordered. Such demonstrations are to be expected, and show the necessity for keeping well closed and prepared to face toward Mine Run and meet an attack at a moment's notice." We assume that General Meade not only had in his possession the message we have just quoted above, but also that General Warren had forwarded to him the substance of Colonel Jenkins's indorsement, when Meade sent the message to Grant that arrived at 7.30 A.M. which we have quoted in the text, and which we have assumed also is the first knowledge that Grant had of the appearance of the enemy that morning.

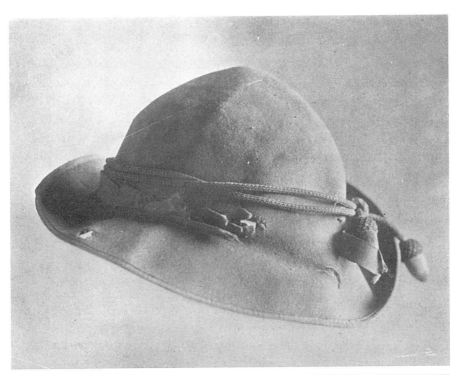

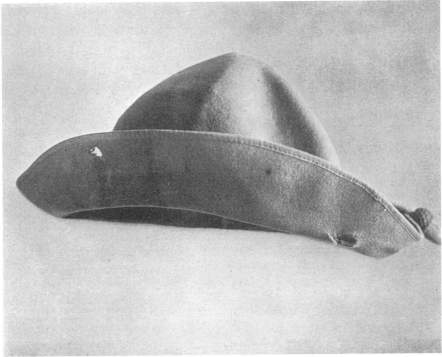

Hat worn by Captain A. I. King at the Battle of White Oak Road, Va., showing bullet holes

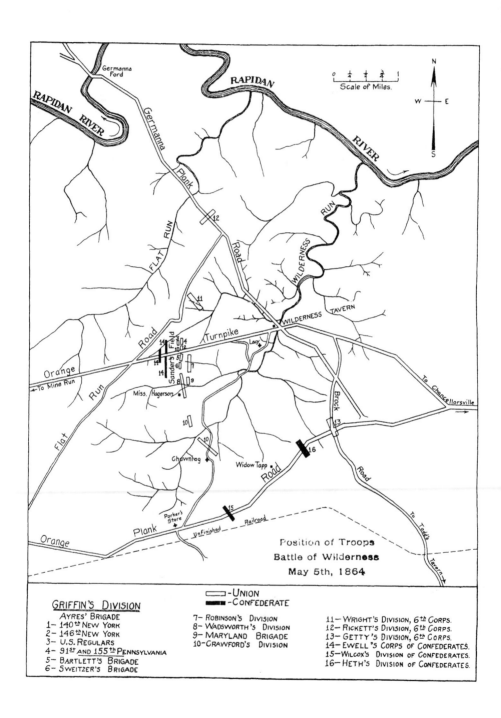

Germanna
Ford

RAPIDAN

RAPIDAN RIVER

RIVER

0   ¼   ½   ¾   1
Scale of Miles.

N
W   E
S

Germanna

Plank

FLAT RUN

Road

WILDERNESS RUN

WILDERNESS TAVERN

WILDERNESS

Road

Turnpike

Lacy

To Chancellorsville

Orange

←To Mine Run

Flat

Run

14
Sander's Field
14
4
2
5
7
8   9
Miss. Hagerson

Brock

Road

11

10
10

Chawning

Widow Tapp

Road

16

To Tedly's

Parker's
Store

15

Unfinished   Railroad

Orange   Plank

Road

Tavern

Position of Troops
Battle of Wilderness
May 5th, 1864

▭ –UNION
▬ –CONFEDERATE

GRIFFIN'S DIVISION

AYRES' BRIGADE
1– 140th NEW YORK
2– 146th NEW YORK
3– U.S. REGULARS
4– 91st AND 155th PENNSYLVANIA
5– BARTLETT'S BRIGADE
6– SWEITZER'S BRIGADE

7– ROBINSON'S DIVISION
8– WADSWORTH'S DIVISION
9– MARYLAND BRIGADE
10– CRAWFORD'S DIVISION

11– WRIGHT'S DIVISION, 6th CORPS.
12– RICKETT'S DIVISION, 6th CORPS.
13– GETTY'S DIVISION, 6th CORPS.
14– EWELL'S CORPS OF CONFEDERATES.
15– WILCOX'S DIVISION OF CONFEDERATES.
16– HETH'S DIVISION OF CONFEDERATES.

tactics of the former, and the spirit of which shows no in-clination on the part of the Union commander to hesitate or turn back even though he was apparently surprised to find General Lee so near at hand. "If any opportunity presents itself," said Grant, "for pitching into a part of Lee's army, do so without giving time for disposition."

The officer who had delivered General Warren's dis-patch to Colonel Jenkins on the picket line, in returning from this duty down the turnpike on his way to Warren's headquarters at Old Wilderness Tavern, drew up his horse in front of our regimental camp and called for the command-ing officer. Lieutenant-Colonel Curran promptly responded. We had just bestirred ourselves and were boiling our coffee when the officer appeared. His horse was covered with foam from hard riding, and the news he brought that the enemy had appeared out on the turnpike was quickly passed from mouth to mouth. The verbal order to Lieutenant-Colonel Curran from Colonel Jenkins was to send immedi-ately two companies of our regiment to the picket line as a support. The men from the two companies[1] that were chosen for this duty fell in promptly, without waiting to finish breakfast, and filed out to the west down the turn-pike. Keeping near the woods on each side of the road, the men proceeded as rapidly as possible with bent bodies and arms at trail to the position designated by Colonel Jenkins. Here one company[2] deployed to the left of the road, and the other[3] to the right, both taking position just behind the picket line.

They were sheltered in the forest, but through trees a short distance in their front could be seen a clearing of some size, and beyond that some three or four hundred yards distance, on a little rise of ground, the forest began again. An occasional musket shot was heard from a scout in front,

[1] Co. "C," under command of Lieutenant King; Co. "F," under command of Lieutenant Sweet.

[2] Co. "F."　　　　　　　　　　　　　　　　　　　[3] Co. "C."

indicating an enemy sheltered securely in the woods like themselves but, of course, giving no sign of their numbers or purpose.

General Meade who, as we have seen, had been promptly notified that a force of some character was in our front, did not deem it to be a force of any size or one that would interfere greatly with the marching orders that had been issued for the day. As a matter of precaution, nevertheless, he ordered the Army of the Potomac to halt immediately and await further developments before proceeding farther through the Wilderness.[1]

Even before these orders from his superior reached him, General Warren, as early as half-past six, had sent word to General Griffin directing him to push out a reconnaissance in force at once, in order to learn how large a force it was that Colonel Jenkins had reported on his front.[2]   General Griffin selected General Bartlett, commander of the third brigade

[1] "May 5, 1864—7.30 A.M., to Commanding Officer Second Corps: The enemy are on the Orange pike about two miles in front of Wilderness Tavern in some force. Until the matter develops the Major-General commanding desires you to halt at Todd's Tavern. (Signed) A. A. Humphreys, Maj.-Gen. and Chief of Staff." The message to General Warren does not appear in the Records, but some such message as that referred to is spoken of in Meade's communication to Grant, received by the latter at 7.30, quoted in the text on page 180.

[2] That Colonel Jenkins, likewise, felt his responsibility fully and was anxious not to be taken unawares is shown both by his sending to our Lieutenant-Colonel Curran for two companies to support him on the picket line and by the dispatch he sent to General Griffin, our division commander, in which he points out to Griffin that if General Crawford's division should move out too far there would be an interval in the corps line and the left should be reinforced. The entire message read as follows: "I hear firing on the left of our line. I think it is Sweitzer's line. If General Crawford has moved out we have no connection on the left; in that case the left should be reinforced. General Warren orders me to keep the skirmish line out until the corps is well under way. The enemy's infantry are forming line of battle on the right and left of the Orange pike. There is a heavy dust in the direction of Robertson's farm, about one mile out. I would like a field officer of division to assist me, as I may have to go to some other part of the line.

"(Signed) D. T. Jenkins,
"Colonel and General Officer of Outposts."

of the First Division, which had camped near us, to execute this order.[1]

An hour or two, perhaps, passed by; idly to the enlisted men waiting in the woods, but anxious hours to our commanders. It might have been about half-past eight or nine o'clock when the officers of the One Hundred and Forty-sixth on the picket line were standing in the road, endeavoring to locate with a glass the movements of the enemy. While they were thus employed, Generals Warren, Griffin, and Ayres rode up.[2] General Warren, taking the field-glasses offered him by one of our officers,[3] looked out down the road, and turning towards Generals Griffin and Ayres, exclaimed, "They have discovered our movements. Send for some of the most available troops at once."

What General Warren saw was a stream of men, which Colonel Jenkins had noticed some hours before, moving in his direction. As they filed silently into the woods on each side of the road the rays of the sun glistened for a moment on their bayonets and were reflected through the cloud of dust that rose from the feet of the marching men. It was Ewell's corps of Confederates, numbering between fifteen and twenty thousand men, taking their positions, although this fact was not recognized at the time.

[1] Two regiments of this brigade, the Eighteenth Massachusetts and Eighty-third Pennsylvania, both under command of Colonel Hays, were directed by General Bartlett to move out at once to the picket line. As soon as they reached the pickets two companies from each regiment were detailed to move forward as skirmishers. It was quickly ascertained that the enemy was present with strong infantry force, and that he was busily engaged throwing up breastworks. Upon making this report to the brigade commander the regiments were ordered to retire. Later, the two regiments were moved to the left of the first line on detail south of the road.

[2] As proof of General Warren's presence on the picket line we submit the following notation on a message from General Crawford, forwarded by Warren's headquarters to General Meade: "Major-General Humphreys, Chief of Staff. The above [the message from Crawford] just received, 9.00 A.M. General Warren is examining Griffin's front. (Signed) Fred T. Locke, Asst. Adj. Gen."

[3] Lieutenant Walker.

Hurried orders were issued by General Warren for the disposition of his command. The various divisions and brigades of the Fifth Corps were placed in such a manner as to make a general assault upon the position which the enemy were establishing in the woods to the right and left of the Orange turnpike. General Crawford with the Third Division, who, as we have seen, had been halted in his march toward Parker's Store, was directed to establish a line of battle facing westward, his right connecting with Wadsworth's division. This latter division, the Fourth, was lined up in similar manner, with Robinson's division, the Second, in support. The Maryland brigade of Robinson's division joined on the right of Wadsworth's division, the other brigades being held in the rear as reserves. The right of the Maryland brigade connected, in turn, with the left of Griffin's division, the First. Two brigades of this division, under command of Colonel Sweitzer and General Bartlett, respectively, continued the corps line to the Orange turnpike, and the remaining brigade of the division, the one in which our regiment was stationed, under command of General Ayres, took position on the north or right side of the pike.

The ground on which the Fifth Corps was thus drawn up in battle array was that of the Lacy estate, a worn-out farm lying between the Orange turnpike and the Fredericksburg plank road. On a few fields which had been cultivated the year before were to be seen the stubble and remains of the crops they had borne, but the greater part of the area was covered with young trees and many species of bushes and vines. Across this open space zigzagged the farm road along which Crawford and Wadsworth had marched during the early morning hours. This road left the turnpike a short distance west of Old Wilderness Tavern and running diagonally to the southwest connected with the Fredericksburg plank road at Parker's Store. On the right side of this farm road about a quarter of a mile from the turnpike stood the Lacy house, surmounting the crest of a small hill and overlooking this barren domain. The worn and somewhat dilapidated house and outbuildings and the acres of wild, sparsely cultivated land stretching westward and terminating in dense woodlands, formed a break in the stretch of the Wilderness, but one that was fully as dismal as the forest itself.

As rapidly as possible the regiments of the Fifth Corps took the positions assigned to them in carrying out their commander's orders. With the other regiments of Ayres's brigade, the eight companies of our regiment that had remained at our camping-place of the night before now moved out on the turnpike and marched to the westward. The One Hundred and Fortieth New York was in the lead, followed immediately by the remaining companies of our regiment, the Regulars of the brigade next in order, while the two Pennsylvania regiments brought up the rear. We covered the quarter mile from our camping-ground to the picket line in a few minutes, and the regiments of the brigade rapidly took position in the woods north of the road, forming in two lines of battle. In the first line, the left of the One Hundred and Fortieth New York rested on the turnpike and the right of the line was continued by the Regulars. Directly in rear of the One Hundred and Fortieth our regiment took up its position, the One Hundred and Fifty-fifth and Ninety-first Pennsylvania Regiments prolonging our line on the right.

Sometime while these dispositions were being made, General Ayres turned to Colonel Jenkins and told him that his Lieutenant-Colonel could take our regiment into the charge, and that as the brigade advanced ahead of the pickets he could take the latter, including two companies of the One Hundred and Forty-sixth, to the rear and form them there. Colonel Jenkins, however, replied that he preferred to lead his regiment if there was any fighting to be done. Upon gaining his commander's consent to participate in the charge, he ordered the two companies to take their proper places in the regimental line.[1]

Although all was now ready for the attack, so far as the Fifth Corps was concerned, still the order to advance was not given. General Warren realized that a force of considerable size confronted him and was anxious to carry out both the spirit and letter of General Grant's injunction to "pitch into a part of Lee's army if an opportunity presents itself." His usual caution and good judgment, however, told him that it would be unwise to attack without waiting to make proper connections on his left and right. In a notation on Grant's message ordering an attack, General Meade had informed Warren that Wright's division of the Sixth Corps was making its way through the woods from the Germanna plank road to connect with the right of Warren's line. It was for these troops, therefore, that the latter was waiting before ordering an assault on the enemy's position.

Orderlies were riding rapidly from one general to another with dispatches, scouts were making their way through the woods to the right of Griffin's line of battle to meet and hurry forward the troops of the Sixth Corps who were expected at that point, and a rattling fire of musketry was taking place between the pickets of the hostile forces as they lay opposite each other.

All of the available forces under Grant's command were preparing to meet the attack of Lee's entire army, in case later developments should prove that it was the whole Confederate Army of Northern Virginia which had appeared so suddenly and unexpectedly on the right flank of the Union forces as they wound their way slowly through the Wilderness. Besides the preparations made by the Fifth Corps,

[1] In describing this incident in a letter written to General Grindlay in 1887, Captain Sweet says, "The cool, brave, and determined manner of Colonel Jenkins when making this request impressed me so vividly that nearly a quarter of a century has not impaired the sharp outline of the picture."

which we have noted, the Second Corps was halted at Todd's Tavern, farther to the southward; the Sixth Corps, with the exception of the one division that was endeavoring to connect with the Fifth Corps line, was being massed in the vicinity of Old Wilderness Tavern; and the Ninth Corps was crossing the Rapidan at Germanna Ford, to support the Army of the Potomac at whatever point its presence might be needed. Thus, spread out in the form of an irregular arc, extending from Todd's Tavern on the south to the Rapidan on the north, the Union line, facing west and southwest, awaited the engagement which the commanders by this time began to realize was likely to take place, but the magnitude of which none could guess.

For about three hours our regiment lay in the woods awaiting the order to charge. We were free from the anxiety that harassed our commanders and the buoyant spirit of youth asserted itself despite the nature of our surroundings. Had it not been for the bullets that tore through the branches of the trees at frequent intervals, sending showers of leaves or pine needles upon those below, one might have supposed we were awaiting the start of some pleasure excursion rather than the beginning of a furious battle. We passed the time lying about in small groups, talking and loafing in the shade of the trees, even engaging in the boyish sports of mumble-the-peg and throwing dice. Jokes and stories were exchanged, but some spoke seriously with one another, committing some keepsake to a comrade's care. The regimental officers, too, were similarly employed, or rather unemployed. They grouped together as closely as possible without losing sight of their commands. Occasionally one crawled along the ground on hands and knees and pricked a comrade with the point of his sword, the ejaculation of surprise and anger which this action elicited being greeted with hearty laughter.

In direct contrast with the spirit that prevailed among us was the serious concern that filled the mind of General Warren, our corps commander. Every moment was precious, as it gave the enemy time to strengthen their position further and be better prepared to meet an attack. So close were the lines at some points that the noise of felling trees for building breastworks was plainly audible, and Warren's subordinates sent in frequent messages informing him that, from all appearances, the Confederates were manning their line of works in ever-increasing numbers. Meanwhile the troops of the Sixth Corps were meeting many obstacles in their attempt to penetrate the thick forests.

It was now nearly noon and General Warren determined to make an attack without waiting for the support of the Sixth Corps on the right. The order was transmitted to the division and brigade commanders and the Fifth Corps moved promptly to the attack. The advancing line swept westward across the fields, through bushes and stunted woodlands, toward the heavier forests where the enemy were known to be concealed. From where Crawford's division was located at Chewning's farm, a mile or so southwest of the Lacy house, the line extended northward across the Orange turnpike. Along the southern edge of the pike moved Bartlett's brigade, while Ayres's brigade on the other side of the road formed the northernmost extremity on the line of attack.

The first line of this latter brigade, composed of the One Hundred and Fortieth New York and the United States Regular troops, advanced across a clearing in their front,[1] on the edge of which they had lain for some time. The second line of the brigade, composed of our regiment and the Ninety-first and One Hundred and Fifty-fifth Pennsylvania, moved up immediately and occupied the position the others had vacated at the edge of the clearing. Here we unslung our knapsacks and threw ourselves down among the bushes and trees to avoid unnecessary danger, preparatory to following the first line into the charge whenever the command might be given.

[1] Sanders's field.

As we lay in the underbrush we had our first view of that portion of the ground between the two armies which was to be our battlefield. It was a narrow, deserted clearing, oval in shape, extending about eight hundred yards north and south and four hundred yards east and west, and lay between two irregular ridges in the forest. The turnpike crossed it a little diagonally just south of its center. The field sloped gently between its eastern and western sides, and in the middle was a gully through which had once run a small stream, but which now lay bare and dry. The clearing had evidently been planted with corn the season before, for much of the stubble remained. At the north end of the field there was an irregular intrusion of stunted pines and cedars, intermingled with bushes and vines of every description. Surrounded on every side by the somber forests, the clearing was the only open, sunny spot visible as far as the eye could see.

Within a few moments after our arrival on its border this open space became the scene of great activity and furious conflict. The One Hundred and Fortieth advanced rapidly across it under a heavy fire from Steuart's brigade of Virginia and North Carolina troops,[1] who were concealed in the woods on the opposite side. The Regulars advancing on the right struggled with the tangle of vines at the northern end of the field and, impeded in this way, could not keep their line even with that of the One Hundred and Fortieth. The interval was rapidly increased as the latter bore off diagonally to the left, following the turnpike. Despite the deadly fire that greeted them, the One Hundred and Fortieth pressed on undauntedly, crossed the gully in the center of the field, and engaged in a hand-to-hand conflict in the woods on the other side. The interval between their line and the Regulars, however, gave the Confederates an opportunity of which they were not slow to take advantage, and they came down upon the flank of the One Hundred and

[1] W. R., Serial 67. Report of General Ewell, p. 1070.

Fortieth, completely overwhelming the gallant New Yorkers.

Two guns of Battery D, First New York Artillery, dashed up the road, the horses galloping furiously as the drivers lashed them with their whips. The battery, if it could reach a point on the pike from which it could rake the Confederate line with its fire, would counterbalance the effect of the flank attack. The gray-coated sharpshooters, however, lodged in tops of trees that skirted the western edge of the clearing, picked off many of the valiant troopers and killed or wounded their plunging horses. The men of the battery hastily unlimbered their guns and sent two volleys of grape and canister up the road on which they had been compelled to halt. The result, however, was more disastrous to the Union troops than to the Confederates, for the left of the One Hundred and Fortieth had crossed the road in its charge and received the brunt of the artillery fire from the rear. [1]

A shrill blast of the bugle gave the order for us to advance to the support of the One Hundred and Fortieth. The commands from Colonel Jenkins, "Attention!" "Take arms!" "Fix bayonets!" "Forward march!" followed each other in rapid succession, and the regiment marched forward in line of battle, officers in front and the men in close ranks.

The trees extending farther out on the northern or right-hand side, as we have seen, enabled the companies on the left of the line to reach the clearing first. Two or three companies had thus emerged from the woods when our Colonel gave the command, "Forward, double-quick!" The order was repeated by the company officers and those on the right spurred forward. Away we charged over the field, preserving our alignment as well as we could under the circumstances. Over the plowed ground, doubly rough by reason of the stubble, we dashed, our muscles tense, our nerves steeled for the approaching conflict.

[1] *Reminiscences* of Captain Porter Farley, One Hundred and Fortieth New York.

Just as we reached the gully, a withering volley of musketry was poured into our line, followed a moment later by another. Many threw their arms wildly into the air as they fell backward, the death-rattle in their throats. Others, wounded more or less severely, reeled in their tracks and collapsed upon the field or staggered to the rear in search of aid. Paying but slight heed to our stricken comrades, the rest kept on, with clenched teeth, breathing in quick gasps from the exertion of running and the excitement of battle.

With the rattle of the musketry was interspersed the booming of the cannon stationed on the road. Their fire obliqued across the front of our line, and some of us were so close that we could feel the strong wind of the discharges.[1]

Down one side of the gully and up the other we ran, our line somewhat broken now by the fire. We rushed into the woods a short distance farther on, firing as we ran, holding our guns in readiness for a fight at close quarters. The Confederates, receiving this impetuous charge, fell back but continued to keep up a deadly fire upon us from behind trees and breastworks.

The companies to the left had entered the woods first, but as each successive company to the right crossed the field they, too, plunged into the underbrush, which was so dense in some places that we could scarcely make our way through it. Closing with the enemy, we fought them fiercely with bayonet as well as bullet. Up through the trees rolled dense clouds of battle smoke, circling about the green of the pines and mingling its fleecy billows with the white of the flowering dogwoods. Underneath, men ran to and fro, firing, shouting, stabbing with bayonets, beating each other with the butts of their guns. Each man fought on his own resources, grimly and desperately.

As rapidly as possible the companies to the right hastened to enter the furious conflict. Nearly all had crossed the

[1] Letter of Captain W. H. S. Sweet.

gully and were making their way into the woods when a new element was added to the already sanguinary contest. Through an interval between our line and the troops to the right of us appeared suddenly almost an entire brigade of the enemy. They signaled their approach by one of their demoniac battle-yells and at the same time poured a volley into our flank. The fire of the artillery on the road had been silenced by this time, and from that direction also another force ran down the turnpike and struck us upon the left flank.

The result was a complete rout, and escape to the rear became the only alternative to being killed or captured. So dense was the smoke and so confusing the noise and excitement of the battle that men lost their heads completely, rushing directly into the enemy's fire in the belief that they were going to the rear. Some of the officers lost all trace of their companies and, utterly bewildered, ran hither and thither looking for their men.[1]

The enemy covering the field, those of us who were in the woods ran a gauntlet of fire on the way to the rear. Holding our canteens to our heads to procure the slight protection they afforded, we dashed blindly in the direction from which we had made our charge. Many stumbled and fell on the rough ground and were taken prisoners before they could resume their flight. Others took refuge in the gully, but only delayed their capture for a few moments by doing so. Several ran down the turnpike and threw

[1] This portion of the conflict is vividly described, from the standpoint of those companies already in the woods, by Captain W. H. S. Sweet in a letter written several years later: "We ceased firing when not a rebel opposed us and we seemed to be successful. I knew of the danger of being flanked, as by charging over the open field we broke the continuity of our general line of battle and the rebels were adepts in finding gaps. Twenty paces to the rear, enabled me to look over the open field we had just crossed. We were not only flanked, but doubly flanked. Rebel troops covered the open field. We were in a bag and the string was tied. Those of our regiment who escaped were principally from the right where the flanking movement of the rebels seems to have been discovered just in time to make escape possible."

themselves behind the bodies of the artillery horses, thus avoiding the flying bullets as they regained their breath and strength to continue the mad dash. The wounded limped painfully along or crawled over the ground on hands and knees. Many fell an easy prey to the Virginians and North Carolinians, whose appearance in such overwhelming numbers had wrought havoc with our regiment. The bright red of our zouave uniforms mingled with the sober gray and butternut of the Southerners, creating a fantastic spectacle as the wearers ran to and fro over the field, firing and shouting.

In such a place one cannot measure time very accurately. It may not have been more than five or ten minutes from the moment we charged across the field until we were forced to fall back, but during that brief time we inflicted and suffered a terrible loss. It would be impossible to recount all the deeds of individual daring and bravery that transpired during those few minutes of terrific fighting. Many of the most heroic of our number perished in the conflict, and others fell into the hands of the enemy to undergo long months of hardship in Southern prisons, only to succumb at last to the extremity of misery and privation they were compelled to endure.

Some few incidents, however, are vividly recalled. Chief among these is the account of the saving of the regimental flag, that bit of cloth held so dear by all of us, and to have lost which would have been a dark blot upon the record of our regiment.

In the center of the line, the color guard had just crossed the gully when the Confederates came down upon the right flank. At the first volley the color-bearer[1] fell severely wounded, struck by three of the whizzing bullets. The flag was grasped by another member of the guard and carried by him until he fell dead upon the field. The corporal,[2] the only member of the guard who remained unharmed,

---

[1] George F. Williams, Co. "B."   [2] Conrad Neuschler, Co. "I."

13

picked up the colors as they dropped from his comrade's hand, and started for the rear. In his haste he failed to notice the gully across his path and stumbled headlong into it, carrying the colors with him. There he remained until wounded and captured. The colors as well would have fallen into the hands of the victorious Confederates, had not a sergeant,[1] almost at the moment his comrade fell, picked up the flag and continued the flight. Unheeding the demands of the gray-clad soldiers to stop and surrender, and dodging the bullets they fired at him by bounding from side to side like a rabbit, he reached the woods in safety. The flag, torn and soiled, was preserved to the regiment.

The conduct of our Chaplain[2] furnished one of the most memorable incidents of the charge. He had been with the regiment only a few months and it was his first experience of actual fighting. While we lay in the woods awaiting the order to advance many of the officers and men gave him their money, watches, and other trinkets, telling him what to do with them in case the owners did not return. The Chaplain would be reasonably secure from danger in the rear, and our valuables safe in his care. We had reckoned without a knowledge of our Chaplain's character in supposing he would stay in the rear for as the line of battle advanced he followed close behind to lend his aid in taking care of the wounded. Absorbed in his work and forgetting alike his own safety and the safety of the valuables that had been given him, he was among those who reached the woods and took part in the fight at close quarters. When we were flanked on right and left, he fought his way to the rear by the side of one of the captains[3] and escaped without a scratch, and, fortunately, without losing any of the things intrusted to him. When he was laughingly reprimanded by some of the officers whose possessions he had so rashly

[1] J. Albert Jennison, Co. " C. "   [2] Edward P. Payson.
[3] Joseph H. Durkee.

risked, he smiled sheepishly and promised not to forget his "stewardship" again.

Soon after we were repulsed and while the wounded were being removed from the field, a new horror was added to the awful holocaust. The day was unusually hot and the leaves and grass lay dry and blistered under the rays of the sun. The woods took fire at many points and, carried by a strong wind, the flames swept across the open field. Friend and foe joined in fighting the common enemy, for the dead and wounded of both sides lay upon the ground between the lines. As the fire advanced it ignited the powder in the cartridge-boxes of the men and blew great holes in their sides. The almost cheerful sounding "Pop! Pop!" of the cartridges gave no hint of the dreadful horror their noise bespoke. The wounded tried desperately to crawl to the road or the bare gully, but many were overtaken by the flames and perished miserably, some when safety seemed almost within their reach. Swept by the flames, the trees, bushes, and logs which the Confederates had thrown up as breastworks now took fire and dense clouds of smoke rolled across the clearing, choking the unfortunates who were exposed to it and greatly hindering the work of the rescuers. The clearing now became a raging inferno, in which many of the wounded perished and the bodies of the dead were blackened and burned beyond all possibility of recognition, a tragic conclusion to this day of horror.

As the lengthening shadows of the forest fell about us, the saddest roll call in the history of the regiment took place. Major Grindlay, the senior officer, assumed command, and by his order the shattered ranks were drawn up in line, slowly and silently. There was lacking the alertness and cheerfulness which had prevailed before the battle. The sad and discouraged faces of the men, their worn and tattered uniforms, and the bullet-riddled flag drooping in the center of the line, formed a mournful contrast with our jaunty appearance of only a few days before. The voice of the officer who called the roll did not ring with its accustomed clearness, and the echo of its sound among the trees was the only response to the majority of the names that were read.

A remnant of our regiment remained. Only ten commissioned officers out of twenty-four who had entered the battle responded to their names, and this was the case with 254 out of 556 enlisted men. In one company only ten survived, in another all but fifteen had been swept away by the fortunes of war, while here a lieutenant, himself the only surviving officer, mourned the loss of all but a handful of his men.[1]

The fate of many of our gallant comrades was never ascertained. This was true of many of the officers as well as of the men. In the thickest of the fight, Colonel Jenkins had been observed by a brother officer, leaning for a moment on his sword wiping the perspiration and blood from his face with his handkerchief. He had reached within a few feet of the enemy's works, cheering his men by his presence and inspiring them by his wonderful courage. This momentary glimpse in the midst of conflict was the last time our Colonel was ever seen. It was many months before we definitely knew whether he had been killed or only wounded and captured.[2]

---

[1] With a single exception (the Second Vermont, of Getty's division, Sixth Corps) our regiment suffered a greater loss than any other regiment engaged in the battle of the Wilderness on the Union side.

[2] The fate of Colonel Jenkins forms one of the saddest, yet most interesting chapters in the history of our regiment. For several months conflicting rumors and reports were received at frequent intervals and it was not until the early part of September that we learned beyond the shadow of a doubt that he had been killed in the charge and his body buried on the field of battle, from which it was never recovered.

Some correspondence of his brother, Captain James E. Jenkins, in regard to the matter is very interesting.

Under date of May seventh, Captain Jenkins wrote to his cousin as follows: " I write to you that you may break the sad news that I have to write as gently as possible to mother. My dear, brave brother David is wounded and in the hands of the enemy. I have made every exertion to learn the extent of his injuries, but can learn nothing. I have every reason to think, however, that

Regarding Lieutenant-Colonel Curran more was known. He was observed as the battle waged fiercest making his way through the underbrush in front of the enemy's works.

it was nothing further than a wound in the lower part of the leg, but which prevented him from getting off the field. . . . General Griffin assures me that David cannot be worse than a prisoner wounded and no doubt he will be paroled soon. I am nearly crazy with excitement and want of rest. . . . For God's sake be careful how you break this news to mother. Give her every hope for the best."

On May fourteenth a portion of a letter to his mother reads as follows: "I have some cheering news to give from David. A prisoner who has just been taken saw him a few days ago, and says he has only one slight wound in the head and that he was walking around. He described David perfectly, saying that he wore a red cap trimmed with gold lace, the only one of the kind in the army except in our brigade. And there was no other field officer taken from this brigade. . . . It has cheered me up wonderfully. . . . No doubt there will be an exchange soon."

On June twenty-eighth a portion of another states: "I do not think that David is among the officers exposed to our fire at Charleston. A list of their names was published and David's did not appear among them, though I almost wish it might have in order to relieve our anxiety. I cannot but think that the Colonel mentioned as passing through Lynchburg referred to him, but cannot account for our not hearing from him before this in some way or another."

Sometime in July a private, Griffith Williams, who had been taken prisoner and escaped, stated that he saw Colonel Jenkins in a squad of prisoners in which he had also been placed. While being marched to the rear the Colonel with one or two others attempted to escape, but he was shot and instantly killed, and was buried where he fell.

This report was later contradicted by a letter written to Captain Jenkins by the color sergeant, George F. Williams, in which he says that he heard members of the Confederate provost guard say that they had found the body of Colonel Jenkins on the field and had buried it there.

This report was substantiated by the testimony of three Confederate prisoners confined at Fort Delaware, one of them an officer. An item in the Utica *Morning Herald* speaks of this as follows: "Colonel Jenkins was shot on the battlefield of the Wilderness and died there during the battle. One of the men claims to have placed the Colonel's coat under his head, and states that he died soon after. He has given up a pocket-knife which he took from the Colonel's pocket. This man belongs to the same company and regiment (the Forty-fourth Virginia) as the man who had in his possession the articles taken from the body of Major Curran. None of them know of his burial, but a member of General Ewell's provost guard, who was on duty at the Locust Grove Hospital, said that a detail from that guard, himself one of them, was sent over the field to gather up the arms and bury the dead and that they buried the body of Colonel Jenkins."

He was seen to hesitate for a moment, and look about him in an endeavor to locate the direction among the maze of trees. Another officer stood near by, and Curran placed his hand on the officer's shoulder, exclaiming, "This is awful!" The officer turned to him and asked, "Where are all our men?" "Dead," replied Curran, and at that instant, without another word, plunged forward himself, killed by a bullet through his head.[1]

This contest would furnish many stories of desperate gallantry and heroic endurance. Despite the confusion of the wild dash to the rear, some had paused for a moment to lend their aid to those who were too severely wounded to take care of themselves. In not every case was such an offer accepted. The First Lieutenant of Company "C"[2] was observed by a brother officer making an effort to crawl to safety. He was wounded three times, one bullet passing through his neck below his ears, another shattering his forearm, and the third passing through his leg at the thigh. The officer, though wounded himself, stopped and attempted

[1] Lt.-Col. Curran, who was a thorough gentleman in every respect, was somewhat fastidious in his dress. On the morning of the battle, for some reason, he prepared his toilette with even more than his usual care. He put on his full uniform, resplendent with gold lace, and wore his gold watch and college fraternity pin. His body, as it lay on the field, was robbed by a Confederate soldier, a member of the Forty-fourth Virginia Regiment, who took his money, watch, and gold pin. A few months later the Virginian was taken prisoner and sent to the Union prison at Elmira, New York. Captain Claesgens, of our regiment, was on duty at Elmira at the time and one day he noticed a commotion among a group of the Confederate prisoners. On investigation, he found them disputing over a gold watch and some other articles. He ordered the things turned over to him and at once recognized them as belonging to Lt.-Col. Curran. Through Captain Claesgens, the articles were forwarded to Curran's relatives.

In connection with Lt.-Col. Curran's death, an item from a Richmond paper of May seventh is interesting: "A dead Yankee General with the initials H. H. C., supposed to be Couch or Casey, was found in front of Ewell's corps." The elaborate manner in which Curran was dressed no doubt led the Confederates to believe that his rank was higher than it really was. Major A. I. King was the officer to whom Curran spoke as told in the text.

[2] William A. Walker.

to assist the Lieutenant from the field. The latter, however, insisted that his comrade leave him and make good his own escape.[1] These individual instances of gallantry could be recounted again and again.

It was some time before we could estimate what our actual loss was. Here we were at the beginning of a crucial campaign and in the first battle our regiment had been reduced in numbers more than half. Furthermore the high *esprit de corps* which had characterized the regiment was seriously weakened by the loss, through death, wounds, and capture, of fourteen of our officers[2] and a large percentage of the men who had been with us from the time we were mustered into service.

Although we had suffered somewhat more heavily than the average, we were no exception as regards depleted ranks and lessened morale. The first day's fighting in the Wilderness had been on the whole disastrous to the Union forces. The troops near us had been repulsed with considerable loss. On our right, the Regulars and the two Pennsylvania regiments of our brigade had not encountered the enemy in the open, but had engaged them heavily in the forest, their contest being more characteristic than ours of the peculiar method of combat used in the Wilderness, which has been referred to as a "scientific bushwhack of 200,000 men."[3] Like ourselves the line to the right of us had been repelled by superior numbers.[4] On our left,

[1] Lieutenant Walker was taken prisoner by the Confederates and confined in Lynchburg, Virginia, prison for several months. He was exchanged in January, 1865, and after spending a few weeks in the hospital at Washington, returned to the regiment and served as brigade ambulance master until the end of the war.

[2] Killed: Colonel Jenkins, Lieutenant-Colonel Curran, Lieutenant Froeligh. Wounded: Captains Jones and B. F. Wright, Adjutant Wm. Wright, Lieutenants Walker, King, Buckingham. Captured: Captain Powell, Lieutenants Sweet, Fitzpatrick, and McGeehan.

[3] *Wadsworth of Geneseo*, p. 255.

[4] *Under the Maltese Cross*, a history of the One Hundred and Fifty-fifth Pennsylvania Regiment.

Bartlett's brigade and Wadsworth's division had driven the Confederates for some distance on the south side of the turnpike, but in the end they had been outflanked and forced back with great loss. Crawford's division, too, farther south, had become involved in the meshes of the forest and had met with similar disaster. Getty's division of the Sixth Corps, which had been sent along the road in our rear past Old Wilderness Tavern, had seen heavy fighting. Wright's division of this corps, for which Warren had waited to come up on his right, had not become engaged until late in the afternoon, and kept up a lively skirmish fire throughout the night. Another corps of the Army of the Potomac, the Second, under Hancock, had come into contact with Hill's corps on the plank road and Brock road, and had fought fiercely in what was practically a drawn contest.

The next morning the battle was renewed along the entire line, but at the end of the day's fighting, the outcome was still uncertain. The contest of the sixth of May virtually ended the battle of the Wilderness, for, although the two armies lay confronting each other during the entire day on the seventh, the only action was that which took place along the skirmish line.

For our regiment, the first day's fight ended the active conflict. We remained with the other regiments of the brigade on picket duty on the left of the turnpike throughout the morning of the sixth and late in the afternoon took up a position behind intrenchments.[1]

[1] The Confederate historian General E. M. Law, in his book *Battles and Leaders of the Civil War*, in the chapter "From the Wilderness to Cold Harbor," makes the following statement: "The lines were in such proximity at one point in the woods that when the Federal troops gave way, the One Hundred and Forty-sixth New York Regiment threw down its arms and surrendered in a body." This statement is, of course, untrue. The regimental organization of the One Hundred and Forty-sixth was as complete at the close of the battle as at the beginning. No further refutation of the assertion is needed than the record of the regiment from the Wilderness to the close of the war. It is true that an entire Union regiment did surrender in the Wilderness on May fifth, but it was the Seventh Pennsylvania Reserves of the first brigade of Craw-

The battle of the Wilderness had been fought, the victory was uncertain, and months of hard service were still before us.

---

ford's (Third) division. "This regiment was captured by a stray company or two of the Sixty-first Georgia of Gordon's brigade. Both commands were wandering about lost when they suddenly encountered each other, and the quick wit of the Confederate commander enabled him to capture a force greatly outnumbering his own."—Footnote in *Wadsworth of Geneseo*, p. 266, confirmed by *A Soldier's Story of His Regiment* (Sixty-first Georgia), p. 144, and *History of the Pennsylvania Volunteers*, i., 729.

CHAPTER XIII

SPOTTSYLVANIA TO COLD HARBOR

GENERAL GRANT, in his *Memoirs*, summarizes the result of the battle of the Wilderness as follows: "Our victory consisted in having successfully crossed a formidable stream, almost in the face of an enemy, and in getting the army together as a unit." There is no doubt that the cost in lives had been far greater than Grant had anticipated. This fact, however, did not deter him from his original intention of making a general movement around the right flank of Lee's forces and pressing on toward Richmond.

On the seventh of May the Union commander moved his army by way of the Brock road and the road leading through Chancellorsville and Piney Branch Church to the vicinity of Spottsylvania Court House. Here the army was again, on the following day, spread out in a roughly fan-shaped position, the Fifth Corps occupying the right on the Brock road, the Sixth Corps the center, and the Ninth Corps the extreme left. Hancock, with the Second Corps, remained for a time at Todd's Tavern in the rear, but during the morning of the ninth of May was brought up on the right of the Fifth Corps. Lee, in the meantime, had advanced along the Catharpin road, south of the Fredericksburg plank road, and had taken up a position enclosing Spottsylvania in a semicircle, prepared to oppose Grant's advance to the southward.

The remnant of our regiment, now under the command of Major James Grindlay, started with the rest of the Fifth Corps on the evening of the seventh along the Brock road toward Spottsylvania. It had rained intermittently all day, as it continued to do for several days to come, so that the roads were very heavy. The march was further impeded by the enemy's cavalry, who resisted stubbornly the advance of Robinson's division, which was in the lead. An engagement of considerable extent was fought at Piney Branch Church and our regiment was brought upon the field but did not become actively engaged.

The next morning, when a few miles from Spottsylvania, the resistance of the enemy became so determined that General Warren realized their main line had been encountered. Accordingly, in pursuance of orders from Grant, he proceeded to spread out his line to cover the Confederate position. This was not accomplished without a great deal of difficulty, many sharp skirmishes and numerous small encounters taking place before Warren was able to carry out his purpose.

The portion of the line assigned to our division was a rise of ground to the left of the Brock road known as Laurel Hill, and the encounter at this point assumed the proportions of a small battle before the Confederates were dislodged. At one time in the conflict the Confederates charged the line of the brigade in front of ours with great impetuosity and the Union troops fell back before them. General Ayres, however, rallied our brigade and we checked the Confederate advance and finally drove them from the hill.[1]

During the night of the eighth we were kept busy throwing up breastworks in order to strengthen our position, to hold it in case the enemy tried to regain the ground they had lost. The Confederates kept up an almost constant firing with both musketry and artillery. Their sharp-

[1] The One Hundred and Forty-sixth Regiment was first mentioned in General Orders for gallantry on this occasion.

shooters also did effective work whenever opportunity offered, and the shells from their heavy guns fell frequently near our line.

By the evening of the eighth the Union line was in position from the east bank of the Po River to the west bank of the Ny River, just north of Spottsylvania, but their front was completely covered by the Confederate line, stretching in a similar arc just south. On the morning of the ninth the Second Corps attempted to cross the Po and flank the enemy, but a double bend in the stream made it inadvisable to do so as they would have been isolated from the rest of the Union army.

For two days a series of sorties and skirmishes took place between the opposing armies, an assault of considerable proportions being made on the eleventh, but without definite advantage to either side. On the twelfth a general assault was made by the Union forces all along the line and a terrific battle ensued, one of the bloodiest of the war. The Sixth and Ninth Corps on the left were able to force the Confederate line and captured all the enemy's outer works for a considerable distance. The ground over which the Fifth Corps was compelled to charge was cut by a deep ravine and the assault at this point was unsuccessful, although the corps was able to repulse a counter-assault on its works later in the day.

Our regiment participated in this engagement on the twelfth, advancing from our breastworks and driving the enemy's pickets for a considerable distance. The fighting continued for three hours and for a time was very severe. During the battle a heavy rain fell. We were drenched to the skin and part of the time fought in water and mud nearly waist deep. On the evening of the same day our brigade was hurried to the left to aid the column from the Second Corps under Colonel Upton, which had made a most heroic effort to take the enemy's line, but which had been compelled to fall back when victory seemed within its grasp because it was not supported as planned. With the assistance of our brigade Upton was able to re-form his line and repulse the attack made upon him by the enemy. We lay that night in the vicinity of the Second Corps, and at daybreak returned to our own lines in the midst of a driving rain, and once more threw up breastworks.

The result of this battle of Spottsylvania was, like that of the Wilderness, an indecisive one on the whole. The Union forces, however, broke through the Confederate line on the right, and gained thereby an advantage which compelled General Lee to retire to an inner and shorter line and also permitted Grant to pass to the east of Spottsylvania Court House. To accomplish this maneuver Warren and Wright were sent around to the left of Burnside during the night of the thirteenth.

This movement necessitated renewed activity for our regiment. On the morning of the thirteenth, with the rest of the brigade, we marched about one mile to the right and, as usual, threw up intrenchments, in which we remained throughout the day. We were recalled from this position at nine o'clock in the evening. At nine-thirty the regiment was on the march. The pickets were left out and fires kept burning to cover up our movement as much as possible. We marched out on the Fredericksburg Road, leading to Spottsylvania, and were soon involved in one of the most difficult night marches we had yet experienced. The mud was nearly knee deep the greater part of the way and in some places even deeper still. We accomplished only about six miles during the entire night, as the mud rendered the road well-nigh impassable. The rain which fell heavily throughout the night and the intense darkness which prevailed resulted in all manner of difficulties and confusion. Many were forced to drop out through sheer weariness and exhaustion. With a view of obviating the difficulty mounted men had been posted along the route, but it was impossible, through the swamps, dense forest, and pitchy darkness, to make connections. As a result, when General Warren reached the appointed place near Spottsylvania Court House the next morning he had with him only about one thousand men. Our brigade, minus the somewhat large proportion of its men who had dropped out during the night, was among the first to arrive.

We found the enemy's cavalry occupying a small hill in front, and by General Warren's orders, a portion of the brigade (the One Hundred and Fortieth New York and Ninety-first Pennsylvania) was directed to drive them from their position, as the hill afforded a good lookout over the surrounding country and Warren desired to use it for that purpose. The attack was successful, the enemy were driven off, and the whole brigade took up position on the hill. We remained here until the middle of the afternoon, when we were relieved by a brigade of the Sixth Corps. They, however, occupied the hill for only a few hours, as the enemy in a gallant charge regained the hill a short time afterward. Our brigade commander, General Ayres, was again ordered to take the hill and in this assault all the regiments of our brigade participated and the enemy were once more displaced. At night we were again relieved by a portion of the Sixth Corps, but bivouacked near the base of the hill.

By evening the Fifth and Sixth Corps were in position, bringing the Union line east of the Court House, facing west and running north and south. During the night General Lee shifted his position to cover this new front, and the two armies faced each other as before.

For two days the relative position of the combatants remained the same, Grant seeking by reconnoitering and skirmishing to draw the Confederates out for a battle in the open. From our position on a small rise of ground, the enemy could be plainly seen. They were opposite us about a mile distant and had covered their line by breastworks, from behind which no amount of maneuvering could induce them to come.

At evening on the seventeenth the Fifth Corps was ordered to throw up rifle-pits, and our brigade labored all night at this uninteresting and back-breaking task. While we were thus engaged, the Second and Sixth Corps were withdrawn and moved to the right for the purpose, as we later ascertained, of making another grand assault. Twenty pieces of artillery were brought to the support of the Fifth Corps and on the morning of the eighteenth, the assault was made, the artillery beginning a heavy cannonading as a diversion. The guns were within fourteen hundred yards of each other and our brigade lay in rifle-pits to be ready to support the artillery in case of an assault by the enemy. The Union guns opened at sunrise and continued shelling the enemy for about an hour without response. Then our guns ceased firing and the Confederates began a cannonade with great fierceness. Their firing was very accurate and in some cases went through our rifle-pits. The bursting shells and flying sticks and clay were far from pleasant, but none of the men of our regiment were injured. It was one of the most fearful artillery duels we ever witnessed and our precarious position prevented us from deriving any pleasure from the spectacle. The assault by the rest of the Union forces proved unsuccessful; the men became entangled in a deep morass and were compelled to retreat after suffering heavy losses.

General Grant now realized that attacking Lee while the latter remained in his strongly entrenched position near Spottsylvania Court House would mean only a useless sacrifice of men. The maneuvers from May thirteenth to eighteenth had evidently convinced Grant that General Lee could not be drawn out of his works for an engagement in the open, and the Union General, therefore, determined to continue his move by the enemy's right flank toward the North Anna River, and, crossing that stream, march directly on toward Richmond.

Accordingly, on the nineteenth, Hancock, with the Second

Corps, started in that direction along the line of the Fredericksburg Railroad with instructions to get as far toward Richmond as he could. Lee was not slow to divine this movement. He hesitated to pursue directly in Hancock's rear because of the three remaining corps of the Union army which would then be in his own rear. He, however, started Longstreet's corps, now commanded by Anderson, after Hancock on the turnpike parallel to the latter's route.

On the same day a portion of Ewell's corps attempted to turn the right of our corps line, but they were repulsed, although with considerable loss of life. This fighting did not involve our brigade.

Orders were received on the twenty-first for Warren to follow Hancock. These orders brought relief to us. We had lain for several days in shallow rifle-pits, which, to say the least, is an unpleasant position when exposed, as we had been, to bursting shells and whizzing bullets. The movement to the south on the part of the Fifth Corps began at ten o'clock in the morning, Crawford's division and the cavalry taking the lead. It was nearly two P.M. before our brigade got under way. We marched twelve miles to Guiney's Station, arriving at ten o'clock, and bivouacked there for the night. The head of the Fifth Corps line, in the meantime, had gone on as far as Milford, making connection at that place with the Second Corps.

When Lee perceived that Warren had followed Hancock on the twenty-first Ewell was dispatched to the support of Anderson; and when Wright and Burnside brought up the rear of the Union army, leaving their position on the evening of the same day, Early, who had succeeded Hill in command of the remaining corps of Confederates, marched parallel to them in the rear of Anderson and Ewell. Consequently, the roads being somewhat shorter for the Confederates, when the Army of the Potomac reached the North Anna River, it found the Army of Northern Virginia drawn up to welcome it on the other side.

The country through which we marched on our way to the North Anna presented an entirely different aspect from any we had seen so far during our "sojourn" in northern Virginia. The road on either side was lined with fertile farm lands, dotted here and there by large, well-kept houses, exhibiting every outward mark of comfort and prosperity. The rain had ceased, the sun shone forth warm and bright, and our spirits rose higher and higher as we were given the first opportunity we had had of forgetting the many hardships we had suffered in the dreary Wilderness.

At that portion of the North Anna River to which the scene of activities had been transferred the river makes a bend to the southward for about a mile and then, after running in its general direction (northwest) for the same distance, turns abruptly northward, thereby forming a narrow neck of land in the form of a horseshoe between these bends of the river. The advance of the Union forces reached the river at this point on the evening of the twenty-second; the Second Corps on the eastern side of the "horseshoe" and the Fifth Corps on the western side. As it was desired to cross the river as soon as possible, no delay was permitted and at daylight on the twenty-third the two corps moved forward to make the crossing. The head of the Fifth Corps line, General Cutler's division, soon reached a fork in the road from which one road leads to the railroad bridge to the eastward and the other to the ford at Jericho Mills to the west. General Warren chose the former and marched toward the railroad bridge, skirmishing with the enemy's cavalry. He was soon recalled from this road as it had been planned that the Second Corps should cross the North Anna at the railroad bridge. An about-face, therefore, placed the division in which we were stationed in the lead, with Cutler bringing up the rear, and in this order the corps marched back to the forks and from that point took the road to Jericho Ford, the head of the line reaching there about one o'clock that afternoon. The artillery was placed

14

in position to protect the crossing and the corps was pushed over the river as rapidly as possible.

The North Anna at Jericho Ford was a swift-flowing stream and was almost waist deep. As there was no bridge it was necessary to ford the stream. Each regiment as it reached the bank halted for a few minutes while the men were given time to take off their shoes and stockings. These were hastily fastened to the end of the bayonets and, suspended thereon, were carried above the head while wading through the water. Not everyone reached the other side with dry clothing; some slipped on stones or on the muddy bottom and landed with a loud "splash" in the water, while others were given "encouragement" in such a performance by some of their comrades. We had been warned that the enemy might appear and attack us at any time and as soon as the other side was reached each regiment hurried into line and moved off in the direction of the woods to the position which had been assigned it. So hastily was this movement made that in some cases the men were not given time to put on their shoes, and the march through woods and across the stubble of the fields in bare feet elicited many grunts from those in this unfortunate predicament.

By the time our regiment, which was among the first to cross, had reached the other side we could hear firing accompanied by shouts and cheers in the woods ahead of us. We could see hogs running about in the woods and we first thought the firing and cheering meant extra rations for us. We, however, soon discovered that the firing was of a more serious nature. Our skirmishers had encountered the enemy's pickets and were driving them away from the river.

The engineers had preceded us and had blazed trees for the men to fell in such a way as to form a hastily-improvised breastworks. We had just completed this work on the edge of a wood bordering a large open field when the skirmishers from our division came running in saying that the

Corporal James P. Pitcher, Co. D
Showing uniform of 146th from time of enlistment until Spring of 1863

JAMES P. PITCHER

This photo shows Pitcher after his promotion to first lieutenant on Jan. 29, 1865. He wears a Zouave officer's jacket, an officer's vest, a black velvet collar, and a 5th Corps badge. Pitcher was only 18 when he enrolled as a corporal in Co. D at Boonville on Aug. 29, 1862, and then advanced to sergeant before mustering in on Oct. 10 at Rome. A clerk by trade, Pitcher had been born in Leyden, was 5'6", with a light complexion, black eyes, and brown hair. Made first sergeant in July/Aug. 1863, Pitcher was absent for a time being wounded by a bullet in the shoulder at Gettysburg on July 2 (though a notation on his records says July 3). He was admitted to Harewood Hospital on July 24. The missile was not extracted until Sept. 28. Pitcher returned to duty on Dec. 10, 1863. Though entirely healed, he had "not the full use of his left shoulder." Promoted to quartermaster sergeant on Jan. 1, 1864, he was again promoted to second lieutenant of Co. D, on Oct. 19, 1864, and began duty as the regimental adjutant to date from Dec. 1, 1864. After promotion to first lieutenant of Co. I, Pitcher applied for a furlough on Feb., 28, 1865, to visit his sick father. While home, an attack of cholemia (jaundice) and soreness of spinal muscles from his wound kept him home until rejoining the regiment on Apr. 19, 1865. He mustered out with the regiment on July 16, 1865, near Washington, DC. Pitcher was brevetted a captain by the War Department Oct. 14, 1865, to date Mar. 13, 1865. (Donald Wisnoski Collection)

enemy were advancing in considerable numbers. Their statement was soon confirmed, for a long line of gray-clad soldiers emerged from the other side of the field and charged our works. By command of our officers, we reserved our fire until the enemy were half-way across the field and then, at a given signal, rose up from behind our breastworks and gave them volley after volley. They came on unflinchingly, and for a time it looked as though we might be compelled to give way. Our officers ran to and fro encouraging us to keep the line and above all could be heard the voice of our regimental commander, Major Grindlay, shouting, "Give 'em h—l, boys; give 'em h—l!" Our position at the Wilderness was just reversed, for we were now on the defensive behind breastworks, and we responded to these injunctions with right good will, pumping charge after charge into the advancing Confederates. The firing had, in the meantime, broken out along the whole division line and for a few minutes as pretty a fight as we had ever participated in took place. The enemy could not withstand this heavy fire and gradually gave way. Every man in the regiment cheered and yelled at the top of his voice as the Confederates began to give way and rushing out from behind our breastworks charged them across the field. The retreat, at first orderly, soon became a hasty one, and the enemy was, in fact, routed at all points along the line of battle. After returning to our position behind the breastworks, pickets were thrown out and the line of works strengthened. We then had an opportunity to rest awhile in an improvised camp.

While the Fifth Corps had been engaged in establishing itself on the south side of the North Anna, the Second Corps had reached the river at the railroad bridge and had met with stubborn opposition from a large force of the enemy, entrenched on the south bank of the river. During the night this force withdrew and the Second Corps accordingly crossed the river the next day and occupied the works which the enemy had vacated.   Meanwhile, the Sixth Corps had followed the Fifth Corps across the river at Jericho Ford during the night of the twenty-third, and the Ninth Corps had remained on the north side, at about the center of the narrow neck of land.

On the morning of the twenty-fourth General Warren ascertained that the enemy had retired from in front of the Fifth Corps and during the day he located them three or four miles farther down the river.   Late at night orders were received for the Fifth Corps to follow the Confederates and develop a position in their front.

These orders to advance relieved us from our position in the intrenchments and on picket duty which was rendered extremely dangerous by reason of the sharpshooters who were lurking in the woods.   Early on the morning of the twenty-fifth our brigade, with the entire Fifth Corps, moved about two miles forward and went into position in front of the enemy at Little River, near the Virginia Central Railroad.   General Wright with the Sixth Corps was stationed on the extreme right, so that the evening found the two armies once more drawn up facing each other.

The Confederates, however, had a decided advantage in position.   Lee had stationed his forces in masterly manner. His center was thrown forward and held the river.   The wings formed an obtuse angle with their flanks well supported on difficult natural obstacles.   Burnside, in the Union center, had attempted to force a crossing on the twenty-fourth but had been repulsed by Early with considerable loss.   Hancock was on the left of the Union line, with Warren and Wright, as previously stated, holding the other side.   The wings of the Union troops were thus separated from the center by the North Anna River and from each other by the Confederate army.

It was utterly impossible for the Union troops to attack with even the slightest chance of success.   The Union forces, in fact, were in a dangerous, if not critical position,

Grant soon realized this and prepared to withdraw his forces to the north side of the river as rapidly as possible.

The Fifth and Sixth Corps were accordingly ordered to retire from their position, which they both did on the night of the twenty-sixth. As the latter corps crossed farther to the north it had the right of way on the one road leading to the eastward and the Fifth Corps was compelled to halt until daybreak before following it. During the night rations were issued and preparations made for a long march on the succeeding day. As soon as the first gray light of dawn began to appear the Fifth Corps started forward and at nine o'clock the ambulances and wagon train followed.

The rain which fell the day before was followed by extreme heat and on the march the moisture-laden atmosphere was most oppressive. We, nevertheless, were obliged to keep going and it was not until late at night that we halted and bivouacked in the vicinity of Mangohick Church. At daylight on the twenty-eighth the march was continued and at eleven o'clock our brigade crossed the Pamunkey River near Hanover Town. A halt for the remainder of the day gave us a little rest, but early on the twenty-ninth the corps resumed its march toward the Totopotomoy River. Griffin's division, of which we were a part, led the march, crossed the Totopotomoy, and advanced a distance of about a mile and a half in the direction of Shady Grove, skirmishing with the enemy, who harassed us on either side, attempting to check our progress.

In the meantime, the remainder of the Union army had been brought as far as the Totopotomoy and stretched in unbroken line along the north bank of the stream. General Lee had made no attempt to obstruct the withdrawal of the Union troops from his front, but he had put his army in motion even before all the Union forces had left the river. He was thus able, because he moved along an inner and shorter route, to take position on the southwest bank of the Totopotomoy before the Union troops reached the other side.

On the thirtieth a reconnaissance was made in force with the three corps of the Union army to determine the nature of Lee's position, the Sixth Corps going toward Hanover Court House, the Second Corps along the Totopotomoy, the Fifth Corps on the Shady Grove Road, the Ninth Corps being held in reserve.

Our division, which was leading the line of march of the Fifth Corps, continued in the direction of Shady Grove, toward which we had started on the preceding day. The resistance of the enemy grew stronger and stronger, a severe attack being made from the left on the road leading to Mechanicsville. General Crawford's division was dispatched to drive them away and take possession of the road. Crawford met with decided opposition in the vicinity of Bethesda Church but finally drove the enemy off. Our brigade, with Sweitzer's brigade of the same division, steadily drove the enemy back along the Shady Grove Road until a clearing was reached. Here the Confederates made a determined stand and our regiment actively participated in the hot skirmish that took place. Neither side gained any particular advantage and when it grew dark both contestants bivouacked in the positions they had been occupying.

The movements of the day had revealed the fact that Lee was strongly posted on all three roads which led directly from Hanover Town to Richmond. It was evident that he could be dislodged only by a hard struggle or by clever tactics. As was previously the case at the North Anna, Grant resolved upon the latter course and ordered a general move in the direction of Cold Harbor. Sheridan's cavalry were hurried there in advance and occupied a portion of the ground. The rest of the army prepared to follow, but owing to an error in transmission of orders a slight delay was occasioned. This gave the wily Lee an opportunity to anticipate the movement on the part of the Union forces and when the latter reached Cold Harbor they found the Confederates once again occupying a commanding position in front of them.

When the Sixth Corps, which had formed our rear, arrived at Cold Harbor, the Confederates contracted their line and began to occupy inner and stronger intrenchments. While this movement was taking place, General Grant supposed it to be an advance of Anderson's corps of Confederates directly across Warren's front from left to right and therefore ordered Warren to advance and attack. Warren opened with the artillery and our division and the Fourth division advanced against the enemy. Soon firing began all along the line. Our regiment, with the rest of the brigade, was soon engaged in active skirmishing with the enemy. The ground over which we were advancing was swampy and rapid progress was very difficult. From behind trees the enemy took hurried shots at our line as it advanced and then rapidly retreated behind the shelter of other trees or lines of breastworks. For an hour the skirmishing was very heavy, but by this time the enemy had all retired behind their inner line of works and General Warren recalled his men, as the intrenchments behind which the enemy had retreated were too formidable to be attacked with promise of success.

The line of the Fifth Corps was now, the morning of June second, spread out to cover so much territory that it was necessarily weak, and Grant therefore ordered Burnside to mass the Ninth Corps in the rear and to the right of the Fifth, to support the latter in case of attack. When Burnside began to execute this order, on the afternoon of the second, he was attacked and a part of his forces driven through a swamp, the enemy capturing many prisoners. At the same time the front of the Fifth Corps was assaulted. Our division, commanded by General Griffin, was ordered forward to the assistance of the Ninth Corps. The brigade in which we were stationed was hastily formed on the left of the line, with Bartlett in the center and Sweitzer on the right, and the three brigades of Griffin's division advanced on the double-quick to meet the enemy. A dense cloud of dust indicated that a heavy force was approaching. As our brigade was on the extreme left of the line it was the first to encounter the Confederates and we soon became hotly engaged with them. We strung out in skirmish order and advanced as rapidly as possible with our bodies bent to the ground to avoid the musket balls that whizzed over our heads. Keeping our knapsacks up close to our heads we crawled along, stopping occasionally just long enough to take aim and fire.

Two or three of the regiment were killed and several were wounded during this advance. Our knapsacks were a real protection. We used them as shields and as a result bullet-holes were torn in many a precious article which had long been treasured as a memento of some friend or sweetheart, but, sad as such a calamity undoubtedly was, the owner was much better satisfied than if it had been his head which the bullet found. A member of Company "K"[1] raised his head just a little too high above his knapsack and was hit in the mouth by a bullet, which passed through his cheek, knocking out some of his teeth and breaking others. It didn't seem to hurt him much, though, for he calmly turned to the man next to him and said rather dryly, "Well, I guess I'll have a pretty looking mug now," thereby evincing a regard for his personal appearance which was, to say the least, highly commendable. Not everyone, however, could find any element of humor in the exciting skirmish in which we were taking part. A little spatter of rain which fell as we started out soon turned into a heavy shower and we found great difficulty in reloading our guns as we crawled along the ground and through the underbrush, which was dripping with water. We were able to hold our own, notwithstanding this fact, until a new turn was given to affairs in a decidedly unexpected manner.

[1] "Dad" Young.

So impetuous was the attack made by the Confederates that a portion of the Ninth Corps gave way before it and in a few moments the enemy were in the rear of the skirmish line of our brigade. The first intimation we had that this was the case was when the bullets commenced pinging at us from behind and our brigade commander came hurrying up shouting that the "Rebs" were in our rear and every man was ordered to look out for himself. For a time all was confusion. The first thought of each man was to escape from the trap in which we had been so neatly caught. We took to our heels and most of our regiment succeeded in breaking through and reaching the main line in the rear, but a large number of the brigade were captured.

After the first panic was over the officers re-formed and rallied the brigade behind an inner line of works from behind which we met the enemy's attack with round after round of musket fire. Although outnumbered five to one the brigade held its position until a brigade from General Cutler's division came to our assistance. Simultaneously, the Confederate advance was repelled all along the line. It was nearly dark by this time and no further demonstrations were made, the Union forces being unable to follow up their advantage. As a result of the day's work our regiment was for the second time mentioned in general orders for distinguished gallantry. In the engagement we lost sixty-eight men killed, wounded, and captured.

On the evening of June second the Union line as formed at Cold Harbor from left to right was—Hancock, Wright, Smith, Warren, and Burnside. Despite the fact that Grant knew Lee to be in an exceedingly strong position he resolved to make one more effort to dislodge him by sheer force from his intrenchments. At half-past four on the morning of June third, Hancock, Wright, and Smith assaulted the Confederate position. From the time they left their intrenchments the Union troops were exposed to the fire of the enemy, who poured musketry, canister, and shell into the advancing line.   In less than an hour from the time the eighty thousand men had rushed forward upon the enemy over eight thousand dead and wounded had been left on the field.   Cold Harbor is usually referred to by historians as the one great mistake in the career of General Grant.   He himself speaks of it in his memoirs in the following terms: "I have always regretted that the last assault at Cold Harbor was ever made. . . . No advantage was gained to compensate for the heavy loss we sustained."

While the assault at Cold Harbor was taking place our regiment was actively engaged in fighting at the north end of the line.   Burnside, with his own corps and the First and Fourth Divisions of the Fifth Corps, had been ordered to attack for the purpose of creating a diversion.   The assaulting column, of which we were a part, was successful in carrying an advanced line and repulsed several subsequent attempts on the part of the enemy to retake it.

During the night of the third the Confederates abandoned the northern part of their line at Cold Harbor and the next day the Ninth Corps was withdrawn and posted between Warren and Smith.   Two days later the Fifth Corps also was withdrawn from the right of the Union line and massed in the rear.

Several days of inactivity followed while the command was located in position at Bethesda Church and Warren took advantage of the opportunity to effect a reorganization in the corps.   After the battle of the Wilderness the Second Division had been broken up and the Maryland brigade of that division had remained independent, under the orders of the corps commander.   This, however, was only a temporary arrangement, but no previous opportunity had been given to bring about a permanent one.   General Ayres, who had been our brigade commander in the First Division, was now placed in command of a newly organized Second Division.   Our brigade itself was broken up, our regiment, the One Hundred and Forty-sixth, together with the One Hundred and Fortieth New York and the Regulars, being transferred to the first brigade of this newly organized Second Division. A short time later the brigade was further augmented by the addition of two more regiments of United States troops, transferred from the Ninth Corps, and the new regiment of Fifth New York Veteran Volunteers. Brigadier-General Joseph Hayes was placed in command of the new brigade, which contained eight regiments, more than any other brigade in the corps, but which was in numerical strength hardly as large as our regiment alone had been when we started for the front. Some changes were also made at about this time in the personnel of the other divisions and brigades of the corps, and at the end of June the Fifth Corps as organized consisted of four divisions of three brigades each. The division commanders were:— First, Brigadier-General Charles Griffin; Second, Brigadier-General Romeyn B. Ayres; Third, Brigadier-General Samuel W. Crawford; Fourth, Brigadier-General Lysander Cutler.

The few days' rest that we secured while encamped near Bethesda Church were extremely welcome.

CHAPTER XIV

PETERSBURG

GENERAL GRANT had failed to deal any telling blow during the forty days of campaigning from the Rapidan to the James. His plan of turning the flank of Lee's army and marching directly on Richmond had been repeatedly frustrated. In the Wilderness, at Spottsylvania Court House, the North Anna River, and Cold Harbor, the Army of Northern Virginia had either been hurled upon Grant's forces in such a way as to inflict severe losses or had been successfully interposed between Grant's army and the Confederate capital. For Grant to have acknowledged defeat by turning back would have cast a heavy gloom throughout the entire North and might have resulted in a decision to sue for peace. The sentiment at the North in favor of ending the war even at the cost of dividing the nation was growing rapidly and any such move on the part of the Army of the Potomac would no doubt have resulted in a triumph for the "peace" party and an outcome of the war favorable to the Confederacy.

In view of these facts, Grant resolved on the bold move of taking his army across the Chickahominy and James rivers, hoping to capture the city of Petersburg, which lay about sixteen miles due south of the Confederate capital, and thus cut off communications between the latter city and the rest of the South. Thus the immediate objective of the Union forces operating in this section of the country became the

"Cockade City,"[1] as Petersburg was called, instead of Richmond.

Grant had been holding his army as closely as possible to the Confederate lines in the vicinity of Cold Harbor in order to prevent Lee from sending reinforcements into the Shenandoah Valley. To withdraw his army from so close contact with the enemy, march it fifty miles, cross two rivers, and bring it into a new position was an extremely hazardous task, but Grant proceeded to carry it out with masterful skill. All possible precautions were taken before the movement was begun. Boats were collected at points along the James for ferrying the army across; scows loaded with stone were sunk in the channel of the river as near as possible to Richmond to prevent the Confederate gunboats from interfering with the crossing; cavalry were sent to make a demonstration on the James above Richmond and destroy portions of Lee's line of supplies from the Shenandoah; and intrenchments were constructed along the north bank of the Chickahominy River, from the position of the army at Cold Harbor to the point of crossing. With these preliminary arrangements completed, the march of the Army of the Potomac across the Chickahominy and James rivers began on the evening of June twelfth.

As the Fifth Corps took the lead in the first stage of the movement, our regiment was among the first to leave the intrenchments near Cold Harbor and start southward. In anticipation of the general change of position the corps moved out of the intrenchments on the afternoon of the eleventh, and shortly after dark on the twelfth began the march on the road leading to Long Bridge on the Chickahominy, by way of Tunstall's Station on the Richmond and York River Railroad and St. Peter's Church. In

[1] During the War of 1812 Petersburg sent a company of volunteers to Canada. In passing through Washington on their return they were publicly thanked by President Madison and told that thenceforth Petersburg would be known as "The Cockade City of the Union."

common with all the bridges in the vicinity of Richmond, Long Bridge had been destroyed, so that its name was merely that of a geographical point. The crossing was, therefore, to be made on pontoon bridges constructed as the head of the column reached the river.

We passed in the rear of the main Union intrenchments at Cold Harbor, at some points so closely as to be able to discern their outline through the flickering light shed by the campfires of the troops occupying them. The men seated about the fires or moving to and fro lent a fantastic appearance to the scene as we hurried by through the darkness of the night.

After an all-night march, broken by frequent halts, we reached the Chickahominy at Long Bridge and crossed over the river on the pontoons that had been laid by the engineers' corps. The detachment of cavalry which, as usual, preceded the infantry column, had encountered the enemy in considerable force on the other side of the river and were briskly engaged with them when we made our crossing. Our division was immediately sent to the support of the cavalry, and we turned in a northwesterly direction along an old plantation road leading into a heavy bog land, known as White Oak Swamp. Soon we spread out as well as we could in line of battle, moving with great difficulty over the muddy ground. The swamp was typical of the many found along the low-lying Virginia and North Carolina coasts, of which the Great Dismal Swamp is the best known. Our advance was a struggle through a dense undergrowth of twining vines and swamp-grasses. The inhabitants of the bog, including snakes and birds, scurried here and there as we proceeded or started up from our feet with a cry and a whir on the part of the birds and a sharp, venomous hiss from some of the reptiles. The Confederates fell back as our division advanced, firing a few scattering volleys without doing us any harm. Soon the roads across the swamp were cleared, and with the rest of the division we returned to the road leading from Long Bridge to Riddell's Shop, where we remained until evening.

While Ayres's division was thus engaged in clearing the White Oak Swamp roads, the other divisions of the Fifth Corps went farther westward to cover the roads leading to Richmond and to give Lee the impression that the Army of the Potomac was advancing upon that city. Meanwhile, the other corps crossed the Chickahominy and marched to Wilcox's Landing on the James River. The Second Corps reached this place on the afternoon of the thirteenth and the Sixth and Ninth on the following day.

As soon as the rest of the army had crossed the Chickahominy and were well on their way to the James, the Fifth Corps relinquished its position guarding the roads to Richmond and followed the route taken by the others. Rations had been issued on the afternoon of the thirteenth, and about eight o'clock that evening the march was resumed, our regiment moving with the rest of the corps in the direction of Charles City Court House. Progress was slow as a large body of cavalry and numerous wagon trains preceded us. Although we travelled nearly all night we got only as far as St. Mary's Church, a distance of about ten miles from where we had started. The frequent halts and unusual delays had tried our patience severely, so that by the time we reached the church we were completely worn out, and were glad enough to lie down on the road and fall asleep when the order to halt was given. Only a short time was allowed us for rest, for early on the morning of the fourteenth we started out again and marched to Charles City Court House, which we reached in the afternoon. Here we erected our tents in a field about two miles from the village and took up our position preparatory to crossing the James.

While we were going into camp at Charles City the Second Corps was being ferried across the river, for the purpose of hurrying on towards Petersburg, and the pontoon bridge was being constructed for the passage of the artillery and wagon trains. The site of this pontoon bridge was between Wilcox's Landing and Windmill Point, where the river was over two thousand feet wide, with an unusually strong tidal current. Despite the many difficulties of such an operation the pontoon was laid between four o'clock and midnight on the fifteenth and the crossing of the main body of the army began.

The delay occasioned by the passage of the troops ahead of the Fifth Corps gave us a day's rest at Charles City Court House, which proved very welcome. We lounged about our tents, enjoying the luxury of idleness that came only at rare intervals. In the afternoon, four days' rations were issued and we knew that considerable work was in store for us. About two o'clock on the morning of the sixteenth the sound of the bugle roused us from our heavy slumbers, and we began the march to Wilcox's Landing. We stumbled on through the darkness and reached the bank of the James at that point about daybreak. After some delay we were ferried over the river on a steamboat, landing at Windmill Point about ten o'clock. As we were crossing on the boat, the wagons and artillery were slowly wending their way over the pontoon bridge, the activity of the moving trains making it appear like some gigantic serpent stretching from one bank of the river to the other.

The Fifth Corps finished the crossing by one P.M. and the rear-guard of the army, composed of the Sixth Corps, reached the south bank of the James by midnight. As each successive corps crossed the river it hurried southward by divisions to invest the city of Petersburg.

General W. F. Smith, with his corps, belonging to the Army of the James, had been sent on ahead to make immediate advance on the city while the Army of the Potomac was crossing the James. It was for the purpose of supporting Smith that the Second Corps had been hurried over the river on June fourteenth. Through frequent delays and a lack of impetuosity,[1] Smith carried only an outer line of

---

[1] See Grant's *Memoirs*, vol. ii., p. 186.

works, and, when the Second Corps came to his support on the evening of the fifteenth, he contented himself with replacing his troops in the captured intrenchments with those of this latter corps. On the morning of the sixteenth the Second Corps captured a small additional portion of the Confederate works and later in the day General Meade arrived on the ground and ordered another assault, with less satisfactory results.

By this time General Beauregard, in command of the Confederate forces in Petersburg, had been reinforced and the fighting was stubborn and bloody. Thus these preliminary assaults on the Confederate works at Petersburg, made by the Eighteenth[1] and Second Corps while the Fifth, Ninth, and Sixth Corps were crossing the James, were without definite result. General Meade, who during a temporary absence of Grant at City Point was directing operations, now determined to bring up his entire army and endeavor to carry the Confederate works by a general assault.

There was hardly a man with the regiment who was not impressed by the animated beauty of the scene as we stood on the south bank of the James on the afternoon of June sixteenth waiting for a few hours for the rest of the division to cross before starting southward. Both banks of the river were swarming with activity as the boats plied back and forth carrying their loads of soldiers, and the pontoon bridge seemed alive with the moving trains and artillery wagons. The river flowed serenely between banks of green verdure, crowned here and there with large trees throwing their shade upon the grass and moving water. The setting of this scene was more appropriate for peace and harmony than war and strife. All thoughts of the weary days of marching in store for us were forgotten. One sad thought, however, crept into the minds of many, and that was the remembrance of the brave comrades we had left lying on the bloody fields all the way from the Rapidan to the James.

[1] General Smith's corps.

15

While the afternoon sun shown down upon this scene we left the south bank of the river and with the rest of the division moved southward in rear of the Ninth Corps, the other division of the Fifth Corps following ours. All night the march was continued along roads the names of which we did not know, until, early in the morning, we reached the line which was being rapidly thrown around the east and south sides of the city of Petersburg. After many delays and frequent changes from place to place the regiment took position, with the rest of the Fifth Corps, in the works to the left of the Ninth Corps, which had been taken from the enemy the day before.

Throughout the entire day on the seventeenth fighting continued on the front of the Second and Ninth Corps with heavy losses on both sides and with no apparent gain to either. During this time our regiment lay in reserve, sheltered behind breastworks at a considerable distance from the enemy.

On the night of the seventeenth the Confederate General Beauregard withdrew from the position he had been holding, moving his forces across a ravine and taking position on the other side of the Norfolk Railroad cut. His new line was from five hundred to one thousand yards in rear of his former one, and was shorter and more advantageous. In the meantime, General Meade, having learned from scouts and Confederate deserters that only a portion of Lee's army had arrived to support Beauregard, resolved to make a simultaneous assault with all his forces early on the morning of the eighteenth.

Orders for the attack were transmitted to the corps commanders on the evening of the seventeenth, and at dawn the following morning the Union troops came out from behind the intrenchments they had been occupying and advanced against the Confederate works in their front. The line of attack extended from a point about a quarter of a mile south of the City Point Railroad on the north to the Norfolk Railroad on the south, and was formed by the Second, Ninth, and Fifth corps in the order named. Ayres's division of the Fifth Corps, in which was our regiment formed the extreme left of the Union line.

As the Union forces advanced only a scattering fire of artillery greeted their approach and it was soon ascertained that the Confederates had, during the night, retired to an inner line of works. Several hours' delay resulted, while the new line of works was being reconnoitered, and then orders were issued to resume the attack at twelve noon.

During the morning our regiment was moved two or three times, and we were employed in throwing up breast-works. At noon, when the signal to attack was again given, we moved out once more. Over rough ground, cut by many ravines and covered with stones and bowlders of various sizes, we ran, obliquing to the right. The Confederates fired upon us with their artillery, but withheld their infantry fire for a fight at close quarters. When we had gone a short distance and had suffered somewhat from the enemy's artillery fire the order to halt was given. We were now in an open cornfield, fully exposed to any fire that the Confederates might see fit to direct against us. We began at once to throw up small ridges of dirt with our cups and bayonets and soon each man had a miniature breast-work in front of him, behind which he made himself as small as possible to avoid the Confederate fire. The enemy, when they perceived that we were not going to advance farther, opened with their musketry as well as artillery and for a few minutes our position was as uncomfortable as any in which the regiment had ever been placed. Musket balls fell all around us, while shells dropped among us occasionally, killing and wounding a large proportion of our already sadly depleted number. Despite the danger of the position, the regiment held its ground, but was not called upon to advance farther. Assaults were made by various portions of the Union forces at intervals during the rest of the afternoon, it being impossible because of the roughness of the ground to make a concerted attack. During the day Lee had reinforced Beauregard with practically his entire army and the Confederates fought desperately along the whole line of attack. Some of the Fifth Corps reached within twenty feet of the Confederate line before being forced back. The Second and Ninth Corps met unexpected obstacles in attempting to cross the many ravines and the Norfolk Railroad cut, and were driven back with heavy losses. The assault had not met with the success anticipated. The positions gained by the several corps were intrenched. The tedious work of investing the city of Petersburg had begun.

Several changes in position were made, at the conclusion of which the Union line was as follows: on the right, the Ninth Corps; next in order, the Fifth; then the Second and Sixth in the order named, the latter corps bending its line slightly to the westward. Our division remained on the left of the corps and the regiment was stationed near the Jerusalem plank road in the vicinity of Fort Sedgwick.

For the first week during which we lay in front of Petersburg our life was almost unbearable. The Confederates, who were located on ground considerably higher than ours, kept up a constant fire, and it was dangerous to show one's head above the breastworks. There was a piece of woods about a hundred yards back of our regiment, from which we got our firewood. While running from our works to these woods we were in full view of the Confederates and they were given all the chance they wanted to "pepper" us as we ran. To escape the danger of such work we hit upon the scheme of getting our wood before the fog lifted in the morning, and some of us took our coffee with us and cooked it in the woods before daybreak.

The long hot days passed slowly in the trenches. The water that we procured in our canteens during the night or early morning hardly ever lasted throughout the day and we suffered greatly from thirst under the warm rays of the sun. Many risked their lives in making the journey to the woods and back for the purpose of filling their canteens with the precious fluid. A member of Company "C"[1] describes such a trip for water as follows:

One day when the sun was blistering hot I got so thirsty that I couldn't stand it any longer and resolved to go to the woods for some water. I tried to induce someone to go with me, but could not do so, so decided to try it alone. Many of the boys asked me to fill their canteens for them, but I took only a few belonging to my best friends. I went down the ditch as far as I could go and then took a long breath for the hundred yard dash across the open space. Bending as low as possible, I started out. As soon as I emerged from the shelter of our breastworks the Confederates began to fire at me. Men from my regiment and the one next to us (the Fifteenth New York Heavy Artillery) were watching me and they shouted after me words of encouragement and sarcastic advice. I reached the woods without getting clipped and had a good drink of water and filled my canteens. With the water they contained they made quite a load and I knew I should be very lucky if I got to the line in safety. I realized I should have to take my chances, so started back over the field, legging it as hard as I could go. The Confederates had been expecting me, I guess, and did their best to hit me as I ran. The bullets struck all around me, some of them so close that I could hear the whistle. The fact that they were up higher than I was, saved me, I guess, for I reached the line in safety. It was the last time I tried the experiment however.

The men of the Heavy Artillery regiment, nearly all of whom were Germans, had seen me, and one of them decided that he would try it. He made the trip to the woods all right and filled his canteens and cooked some coffee. On the way back, however, he was not so fortunate as I had been. When within a few yards of the intrenchments he was struck by a bullet in the forehead and was killed instantly. A member of our regiment immediately ran out and appropriated the canteens and coffee the unfortunate fellow had been carrying. The man's companions took exception

[1] Frederick Ernst.

to this action and threatened to come to our part of the line and whip us. They swore at us in German for some time, but before the matter came to blows some officers interfered and put an end to the trouble.

As rapidly as possible the intrenchments behind which we were sheltered were added to and improved, and in a short time we had an elaborate network of redoubts, trenches, and field works constructed. Some of them were high enough to conceal the approach of an army wagon, through which means our supplies and ammunition were brought us. The breastworks in front were from ten to twelve feet in thickness, and under them bombproofs were built for shelter in case of shelling from the mortar batteries of the enemy. Bombproofs were also made for the officers, whose quarters were not so close to the breastworks, and who were in danger of being blown into the air at any moment the Confederates should see fit to drop a bombshell into their midst. These bombproofs were constructed as follows: A hole was dug in the ground in the shape of a cellar, perhaps four feet deep and eight or ten feet square. Blocks, cut from pine trees, a foot in thickness, were placed as uprights at the corners of the excavations, and upon these pine logs were laid, completely covering the cellar. Dirt was then thrown upon the logs and packed down until there was a covering of several feet of solid earth. In this manner thousands of bombproofs were built along the whole line of both armies. They were much cooler than tents, and sheltered the occupants from the hot sun as well as from the shells of the enemy.

As the days of the siege progressed the firing of the sharp-shooters and the occasional artillery duels grew less frequent and after the first week or so it was safe to show one's self above the breastworks. Gradually there came to be much fraternizing of the Confederate and Union pickets, and a considerable trade between the men of the two armies was carried on in a small way. The "Johnnies" were always glad to exchange tobacco for anything for personal use, as coffee, sugar, needles, thread, etc. It became no unusual sight to see the men of both armies sitting on top of their redoubts in the evening holding animated conversations and gayly bantering each other. In this intercourse with the enemy, our regiment bore its part and we had many conversations with the Confederates in the trenches opposite us. Commenting on this relationship one of our officers[1] writes: "The other day two men of our regiment engaged with a couple of the 'Johnnies' in a game of cards, the stakes being the fate of the country. Of course, our side was victorious."

Unexpected relief came to us when we had been in the intrenchments about ten days, for on June twenty-eighth the brigade was relieved from this duty, and we moved back a short distance and camped near the Norfolk Railroad cut. Here inspection was held and the regimental returns of casualties and requisitions for pay were made out by the acting adjutant and forwarded to Washington. Working parties from the regiment were sent out each night to assist in building breastworks and rifle-pits, but this was the only work required of us aside from the daily routine. We had now become so used to working at night that we could see almost as well in the darkness as in the light, and were able to accomplish nearly as much as though we had been working during the day. We had reason to congratulate ourselves every day as the time wore on and we were not called upon to return to the intrenchments.

The weather during this period was oppressively hot. No rain fell from the third of June to the nineteenth of July, a period of forty-seven days. There was no surface water; the springs, the marshes, the ponds, and even the streams of considerable size were dry. The dust was several inches thick upon the roads and bare plains, and the passage of

[1] Captain James E. Jenkins, July 7, 1864.

troops or trains over them raised great clouds of fine dust. The surface soil was porous, and at no great depth below it were strata of clay in which there was an abundance of cool water.   Many wells were sunk and the necessary water obtained in this way.

A diversion from the monotony of the siege was furnished on the thirtieth of July.   Near the center of the Ninth Corps line a regiment of Pennsylvania miners had dug a tunnel under the nearest point of the Confederate works only a hundred yards distant.   The Confederates had learned that mining was being carried on but had been unable to strike the tunnel by counter-mining.   They came to have vague and exaggerated fears and many people in Petersburg believed that the whole city was undermined.[1]   The work had been going on for nearly a month and when completed consisted of a straight tunnel five hundred feet long, ending in a lateral gallery seventy feet in length.   In this gallery had been placed eight thousand pounds of powder, with slow matches.   To distract the enemy's attention from its explosion on the thirtieth and to diminish, if possible, the force that held the lines immediately around Petersburg, a portion of the Army of the Potomac under General Hancock was sent across the James at Deep Bottom to threaten Richmond.   This had the desired effect, as Lee sent a large force to confront Hancock, leaving his intrenchments but lightly manned.

It was realized by General Grant that the explosion of the mine itself would do but little good; but it was expected to make such a breach in the enemy's line that a strong column could be thrust through to take the works on either side in reverse.   For this task Ledlie's division of the Ninth Corps was chosen—a most unfortunate choice, as it developed later.   The other divisions of the Ninth Corps were ordered to hold themselves in reserve to follow Ledlie's division, and the Eighteenth Corps,[2] of the Army of the James, and

[1] *History of the War of Secession*, p. 447.
[2] Formerly General W. F. Smith's corps, now under command of General Ord.

the Fifth Corps, under Warren, were brought into position to support the Ninth Corps in its assault.

In carrying out these plans, our regiment, with the rest of the Fifth Corps,[1] moved to the right. From our position we were witnesses of a great deal that occurred on the eventful day, July thirtieth.

A few minutes before five o'clock in the morning the mine was exploded. A vast mass of earth, surrounded by smoke, with the flames of burning powder playing through it, rose two hundred feet into the air, seemed to poise there for a moment, and then fell. The Confederate fort with its guns and garrison, a portion of the Twenty-second South Carolina Regiment, was completely destroyed and a huge crater about thirty feet deep and nearly two hundred feet long was opened. Immediately the artillery along the Union lines opened fire, to protect the assaulting column. Ledlie's division pushed forth into the crater and, instead of gaining the crests immediately, stopped there. General Ledlie did not accompany his men and there was no one to direct them. Over half an hour passed, during which the Confederates, who had left the neighboring intrenchments in terror, had time to rally. Soon they began to fire upon the men gathered in the crater. General Burnside tried to remedy the difficulty by sending in more men, and at length sent his colored division, under General Ferrero. They attempted to charge up the side of the crater but were met with a heavy fire and broke in great confusion. Their wild retreat created disorder among all the troops in the crater, who were now huddled together in a mass without definite purpose. The Confederates soon concentrated both musketry and artillery upon them, while shells were lighted and rolled down the sides, creating a veritable slaughter. The effort had proved a stupendous failure.[2]

[1] Except one division left in the trenches.

[2] Grant, in his *Memoirs*, commenting thereon, says: "It was due to inefficiency on the part of the corps commander and incompetency of the division commander who was sent to lead the assault."

Sometime during the occupation of the crater by the Ninth Corps, General Ayres, of our division, requested the privilege of leading his command forward in an attempt to secure the desired point. General Warren, however, declined to let him go, deeming it too late. When we heard of this later there was considerable speculation among us as to what might have been the result had our commander's request been granted. The division might have achieved an undying fame and hastened the end of the war by several months, or we might have met the fate of the hundreds of brave men who were sent into the awful pit of death.

As it was, our regiment took no part in the actual fighting on the thirtieth, remaining on reserve until the middle of the afternoon, when we returned to our camp near the railroad cut. During the time, however, some of the boys found an opportunity to raid a sutler's tent that had been deserted by its occupant when a Confederate shell burst uncomfortably near.

For two weeks after the catastrophe of the crater, the regiment remained in a state of inactivity. The warm rays of the August sun poured down upon our heads without mercy. When we were not on active duty on picket or building and repairing intrenchments, our time was largely spent in endeavoring to find places where the temperature was not quite so high as that of the lower regions is reported to be. This was by no means an easy task. General Sherman's definition of war applied very aptly to our life during the siege of Petersburg.

The summer was, everywhere, a season of comparative inactivity. We received reports through the newspapers that reached us with a fair degree of regularity of the operations in other parts of the country. Sheridan's campaign against Early in the Shenandoah Valley was attracting the greatest attention at this time, and he was gradually driving his opponent out of the valley and

First Lieutenant and Adjutant
Edward Comstock

Lieutenant and Quartermaster
Marvin Egleston

Regimental Adjutant
William Wright

Surgeon Thomas M. Flandrau

Lieutenant and Adjutant
James P. Pitcher

Chaplain Albert Erdman

UNIDENTIFIED
A unique charcoal sketch of a 146th New York Zouave private. The drawing was probably made after the war, based on a wartime photograph. (Harold Akers Collection)

cutting off the Confederate source of supplies in that direction.

For the purpose of further embarrassing Lee, General Grant now determined to conduct similar operations in the vicinity of Petersburg.

CHAPTER XV

WELDON RAILROAD

ONE of the important lines of supplies between Petersburg and the south was the Weldon and Petersburg Railroad, running due south out of Petersburg. This line was carefully guarded by the Confederates, and an attempt to capture it made in June two or three days after the unsuccessful assaults referred to in the previous chapter was repulsed with heavy loss. During the month of July and until the middle of August, therefore, the Confederate communications were cut off only on the eastern and southeastern sides of the city.

The second week in August Grant received information from various sources that led him to believe that Lee had detached a large portion of his forces from Petersburg to reinforce Early in the Shenandoah Valley. Deeming such a condition a good opportunity for him to continue his offensive tactics, Grant sent General Hancock with a considerable force to threaten Richmond from the north side of the James River. Hancock gained nothing, however, for Lee threw a strong force into the intrenchments and repelled his attacks.

At the other, or left, end of the Union line, much was gained, for Grant took advantage of the weakening of Lee's right to seize the Weldon Railroad. The Fifth Corps was chosen for this work. The night of August fourteenth the corps left the trenches and camped near by. Its place in the trenches was taken by the Ninth Corps extending its line.

General Warren was instructed to move as secretly as possible by going south for a considerable distance before turning toward the west to strike the railroad. The intention was to make a lodgment upon the Weldon Railroad as near the enemy's lines as practicable and destroy the road as far south as possible. A brigade of cavalry accompanied the Fifth Corps in the movement and the Ninth Corps was held in readiness to support Warren in any success he might gain.

At four o'clock on the morning of August eighteenth, our regiment, with the rest of the Fifth Corps, broke camp and marched south along the Jerusalem plank road a distance of about two miles, when the column turned off on to a road running westward. The weather was extremely warm and an oppressive tropical rain fell, making the roads and fields through which we were compelled to march very muddy and sticky. Many men fell out by reason of the excessive heat and heavy marching and great difficulty was experienced in moving the wagons and gun carriages.

Griffin's division was leading the march of the corps, our division under General Ayres second in line. Soon after turning off from the plank road the Confederate cavalry was encountered about seven o'clock. General Griffin immediately formed line of battle by brigade, with skirmishers deployed, and the enemy's cavalry was soon dispersed. The corps reached the railroad between nine and ten o'clock, and Griffin's division was disposed in such a way as to cover the road toward the south and west from Globe Tavern.

The country into which the Union forces had thus advanced was covered, on both sides of the railroad, by heavy timber lands, interspersed here and there by open fields and small farms. Parallel to the railroad and only a short distance from it ran the Halifax road leading into Petersburg.   Beyond this road, a mile to the west, the Vaughan road ran in the same general direction, merging with the Halifax road about a mile and a half from Globe Tavern.

As soon as Griffin's division had been secured in its position, Ayres's division marched to the northward along the railroad.   Our brigade, commanded by General Hayes, was in the lead and our regiment and the One Hundred and Fortieth New York were deployed as skirmishers, preceding the line of march.   As we were going directly toward Petersburg, which was only four miles distant, we expected to encounter the Confederates at any moment.   In this we were not disappointed, for we soon came upon their skirmishers, who fell back as our lines advanced.   When we had driven them for about a mile we came suddenly upon their line of battle, drawn up on the edge of the woods bordering an extensive cornfield.   A detachment of our regiment, under command of Captain Stewart, passed through a gap in the Confederate line unwittingly, and before it could extricate itself was surrounded and captured.   The main body of the regiment continued to crawl through the cornfield as skirmishers, with arms at trail.   The Confederates had opened fire at our approach and the bullets sang over our heads, clipping off the tops of the corn.   Soon the artillery as well as musketry began to play upon the advancing line of our division.   Simultaneously, the enemy's line of battle charged.   Our regiment on the skirmish line promptly fell back, firing as we ran.   Ayres's division, however, was completely outflanked, and the order to fall back was transmitted by the brigade commanders and was executed in some confusion.   General Ayres brought up his artillery as rapidly as possible, and under its protection the line was reformed.   Meanwhile, Crawford's division had got into position on the right.   The entire Union line now advanced and a hard struggle ensued.   The Confederates were finally repulsed and retreated, leaving their dead and wounded on the field.

That ended the fighting for the day, but we were not given an opportunity to rest that night, despite the fact that we had been on the move since early morning. Rifle-pits were constructed along the front of the Union position, and our brigade was disposed in the works bordering the railroad on the right. The line in this direction was continued by the Fifteenth New York Heavy Artillery, a brigade of Cutler's division that had been sent to reinforce Ayres, and the Maryland brigade of Ayres's division curving to the rear. Our division remained quietly in this position until about four o'clock in the afternoon of the following day.

The next day, August nineteenth, General Warren endeavored to connect his position on the Weldon Railroad with the left of the main Union line near Jerusalem plank road. For this purpose, Bragg's brigade of Cutler's division was sent to establish a connection on the shortest line. The brigade took the wrong road, and became confused in the woods. The Confederates took the offensive and cut off a portion of Bragg's command and at the same time came down and attacked the position occupied by our division on both front and right flank. Our brigade repulsed the attack in front, but the Confederates broke through on the right and swept down upon the rifle-pits occupied by our regiment and the rest of Hayes's brigade. As they swung around they cut off a portion of our brigade and took over two hundred prisoners, among them General Hayes, our brigade commander. The remainder of the brigade now fell back, fighting at every step, and formed about seven hundred yards in the rear, the command devolving upon Colonel Frederick Winthrop, of the Fifth New York (Veteran). General Ayres now waited for a few minutes and then made a counter attack to regain his former position. The fighting for a time was very severe but the impetuosity of the Union advance finally drove the Confederates from the works. Ten minutes later the enemy attacked the front of our division line again, but this time we were able to repulse them. Once more shortly after dark, they charged against our works making a desperate effort to drive us from them. But General Ayres summoned help from Griffin and was able to repel the attack.

Realizing that the position he had gained was an important one, from which the Confederates might make further efforts to dislodge him, Warren determined to strengthen himself in it. This was done on the night of the twentieth by throwing up breastworks and digging trenches. Just in the rear of the position our division was occupying was a bit of rising ground, and General Ayres decided to occupy that. Our regiment with the others of the division was engaged during the night in throwing down the works we had occupied and building a new line on the crest of the rising ground in the rear. Abatis was hurriedly erected in front of these works and wires were stretched across the ground in such a way as to interfere with any charge that might be made against the position. At two o'clock on the morning of the twenty-first our division was drawn back to this new line. The men of the regiment had been fighting and building breastworks for three days with only short intervals for rest and we were completely worn out. Despite this fact, a large detail was called upon to go out on picket duty in front, to give the signal in case the Confederates should make an attack on the morrow. Very reluctantly the men called upon for this work obeyed, and they filed slowly out to fight fatigue and keep a watchful vigil over the camp of their sleeping comrades.

About six hours later three of these pickets from our regiment were sitting on an abandoned rifle-pit, smoking and talking. One of them remarked that he didn't care very much whether he was captured or not, but another,[1] who had been taken prisoner at Chancellorsville, replied that unless the "Johnnies" had their hands on him he was going to try to get away as long as he could keep running.

[1] Frederick Ernst, Co. "C."

At that moment the sound of firing reached them from the right, where the pickets were farther out. Soon the pickets came running in from this direction, saying that the Confederates were approaching in heavy force. The three men sprang up and joined in the flight to the Union lines. The firing had given warning to the men in the trenches and they were rapidly getting into position. We, of the One Hundred and Forty-sixth, could see the pickets running towards us and recognized several of our comrades among them. Suddenly a number of the men fell flat on their faces and we thought that they had been hit by the enemy's fire. To our surprise, they hurriedly scrambled to their feet again and continued toward us. A few steps more and again they plunged to the ground. It dawned upon us then what was the cause of their strange behavior. They had tripped over the telegraph wires stretched about a foot high along the ground. The men, too, realized what was the matter and they carefully picked their way the rest of the distance, being greeted with laughter as they approached. They, however, were in no mood to enjoy this merriment.

The advance on the part of the Confederates which this coming-in of the pickets heralded was the beginning of another day of hard work. The attack on the Union position was made by a heavy force of infantry, cavalry, and artillery. A scattering fire was kept up for some time, and then, about ten o'clock, the Confederates made an assault all along the north and west of the Union position. The enemy struck the line of our division directly in front of our brigade and for a few minutes every man of the regiment was busily engaged in loading and firing. For a moment it seemed as though the enemy were going to capture our works, but Colonel Winthrop rallied his brigade and repelled the attack. General Ayres now ordered a counter charge, and our regiment with the rest of the division came out from behind the intrenchments and in a few minutes our advance struck the Confederates and captured a large number of prisoners and several colors. All along the corps line the fighting was very heavy, but in a few hours the Confederates were completely repulsed and retired in some confusion. A skirmish fire was kept up throughout the remainder of the day, but no further attack was made by the Confederates in force. The intrenchments were now extended by the Ninth Corps from the Jerusalem plank road to unite with the Fifth Corps on the Weldon Railroad.

This capture of the Weldon Railroad played an important part in the capture of Petersburg and the overthrow of the Confederacy, for the ground won by Warren was never recovered by the enemy.

A day or two after the success of the Fifth Corps, General Hancock, who had returned from the north side of the James, was sent with two divisions of the Second Corps to destroy the road as far south as Rowanty Creek. This expedition was by no means an unqualified success, for although the road was torn up for a considerable distance, the Confederates met Hancock at Ream's Station and a heavy engagement followed which ended disastrously for the Union forces. They were compelled to return to Petersburg after suffering a heavy loss.

A period of quiet now ensued on the south side of the James in the vicinity of Petersburg. During the remainder of August until the last week of September our regiment remained with the Fifth Corps camped near the Weldon Railroad. The picket lines of the Union forces were close to those of the Confederates and after a week or two a spirit of good fellowship prevailed among the outposts of the two armies. It was as a result of this intimacy that the only incident of importance in connection with the history of our regiment during this period took place. The incident was the death of Lieutenant Buckingham of Company "B." The treachery that caused his death was quite in contrast to the good feeling that often prevailed between the soldiers of the contending armies when on picket duty.

On the morning of September second a cessation of firing had been agreed upon and the men exposed themselves in perfect confidence that the truce would be rigidly observed. Some Confederate officers sent word to our line that they would like to exchange newspapers and Lieutenant Buckingham and an officer of the Fifth New York went out between the lines, met the Confederate officers, and after talking with them a few minutes and exchanging papers, started back to our line. They had almost reached it when some Confederates, South Carolinians, we learned later, who were posted on the right of where the interview had taken place, fired a volley, wounding Lieutenant Buckingham in the side and the other officer slightly in the leg. A few of us ran out immediately and carried the Lieutenant to the surgeon's tent. Here he was given every attention possible, but the wound proved to be a mortal one and he died during the afternoon. The treachery of the Confederates caused much indignation not only in our regiment but throughout the entire brigade and it was some time before friendly relations were resumed between the pickets in the vicinity where the incident had taken place.

Exchanging newspapers furnished one of our comrades [1] with a few moments' diversion of an entirely different type and also afforded considerable amusement as he related it to others in the regiment. We were always particularly desirous of obtaining possession of Confederate newspapers, particularly those published in Richmond, and the Confederates on their part were equally anxious to procure Northern papers from Washington, Philadelphia, or New York. This particular member of our regiment was on picket duty one day and was reading a copy of the Richmond *Inquirer* some weeks old, which had gone down the line in his company. He noticed a Confederate picket not far away who was also reading a newspaper. Finally he hailed the other, "Hey, Johnny, what ye got?" "Richmond *Inquirer*," the

[1] Lieutenant J. Albert Jennison.

Confederate promptly responded, "what's yours, Yank?" "New York *Herald*. Let's swap." The Confederate assented and they met each other half-way and exchanged papers and then went back to their posts. When Lieutenant Jennison looked at the paper he saw that it was a copy of a New York paper about a month old and that the Confederate had fooled him. He, nevertheless, took it good naturedly, and called to the other, "Well, Johnny, you didn't get much the better of me." The Southerner simply grinned in response.

This inactivity which was so welcome to the rank and file was extremely distasteful to General Grant. Acting on the advice of Halleck at Washington, who counseled him, in view of the approaching election and spirit of opposition to the draft, to "go slow," Grant had consented to a temporary cessation of hostilities. In the later part of September, however, he decided to resume his offensive operations against Petersburg and Richmond.

Two corps of the Army of the James were sent against Richmond, and were able to capture a considerable portion of the Confederate intrenchments in that direction. In coöperation with this movement against Richmond, General Meade directed Warren, commanding the Fifth Corps, and Parke, now in command of the Ninth Corps, to leave one division in the intrenchments and with the other two divisions from each corps move to the west to attack the Confederate line of works in that direction and, if deemed practicable, to attempt to capture the South Side Railroad leading into Petersburg.

The movement was begun on the morning of September thirtieth, and once more our regiment left the intrenchments to take part in active operations. Our brigade, under command of Lieutenant-Colonel Otis, of the One Hundred and Fortieth New York, moved out of the intrenchments at seven o'clock on the morning of the thirtieth, and with the rest of Ayres's division followed Griffin's division over the roads and across fields to the westward. When the Vaughan road was reached, Warren halted his command for two hours, during which time our regiment was detached from the rest of the brigade and sent north on the Vaughan road to support a cavalry detachment. We remained here throughout the day, without becoming engaged with the enemy. In the evening the regiment returned to the brigade, which was then occupying a line of works that had been captured by the division.

The contest had ended favorably for the Union forces, Warren gaining possession of a redoubt at the junction of the Poplar Spring and Squirrel Level roads, known as Fort McRae. The two divisions of the Ninth Corps had also been brought up on the left after some heavy fighting, and Warren and Parke were prepared to resume the contest on the following day.

Our brigade was disposed on the evening of the thirtieth in the following order: Twelfth and Fourteenth United States on the right of the captured redoubt; our regiment and the Fifteenth New York Heavy Artillery on the left; while the Tenth and Seventeenth United States and the One Hundred and Fortieth New York were held in reserve in the rear. We spent some time in throwing up breastworks and repairing the damage done to the fort during the day's conflict. In the evening the Tenth and Twelfth United States regiments were advanced as pickets and the other regiments disposed themselves for the night. At eight o'clock the next morning, October first, while the two regiments on the picket line were being relieved by the Seventeenth United States and the One Hundred and Fortieth New York the Confederates advanced in considerable force in an effort to regain the fort. The pickets were quickly driven in and the enemy charged our brigade line. They were repulsed by a well directed fire and fell back after suffering a heavy loss. Lieutenant-Colonel Otis was severely wounded during this engagement and was carried from the field, Major Grindlay, of our regiment, succeeding him as commander of the brigade. Command of the regiment now devolved upon Captain Wilson, the senior officer.

A sharp picket fire was kept up during the day, and late in the afternoon skirmishers went out from the brigade under command of Lieutenant Thieman, a Regular officer, and drove the Confederate sharpshooters from the woods and houses in front. Our regiment did not take a very active part in these maneuvers, known as the battle of Poplar Spring Church, except during the time our works were charged by the enemy, when three of our men were wounded.

On the second of October our regiment was withdrawn from the fort and with the Fifteenth New York Artillery was sent to a new position about four hundred yards in the rear of the old line, where we threw up breastworks. The rest of our brigade was now replaced in the redoubt by a brigade from Griffin's division, and for two days we were engaged in constructing a line of works to connect with the left of the Union position on the Weldon Railroad. Several houses in front that served as refuges for Confederate sharpshooters were burned down and the ground was cleared of bushes, trees, and other objects that might aid the enemy in case of attack.

When these operations were completed the regiment took position with the rest of the brigade in the breastworks near the Vaughan road. Here we remained for a few weeks, during which the only notable event that took place was the transfer to our regiment on October eleventh of nearly two hundred men from the Forty-fourth New York. This regiment, originally called the "Ellsworth Avengers," had been composed of picked men from every county in New York State and during its three years of service had performed gallant work and seen heavy fighting on many occasions. The men transferred to our regiment to complete their term of service were seasoned veterans and added great strength to our sadly depleted ranks.

CHAPTER XVI

OPERATIONS ON HATCHER'S RUN AND RAID ON WELDON RAILROAD

THE four months of heavy fighting and constant maneuvering from the middle of June to the middle of October had given the Union forces a line of works extending east and south of Petersburg from the Appomattox River to a point about two miles west of the Weldon Railroad. The Confederates still retained possession of the country on the west of the city and of the South Side Railroad, which paralleled the course of the Appomattox River for some distance westward.

Two routes remained open by which the Confederates received supplies. One was by way of the South Side Railroad, and the other by wagon trains from the Weldon Railroad by way of Hatcher's Run and the Boydton plank road. General Grant resolved to make a great effort to capture these lines of communication, and for that purpose dispatched a heavy force against the Confederate intrenchments at Hatcher's Run. This force was expected to break through the Confederate line at this point and push on against the South Side Railroad. Generals Grant and Meade accompanied the expedition, which consisted of the greater part of the Second, Fifth, and Ninth Corps.

The movement began on October twenty-seventh and was continued throughout the following day. It, however, proved a stupendous failure, the Union forces failing to penetrate the Hatcher's Run line and getting only within six miles of the railroad. Our regiment was one of those selected to take part in this expedition, but we did not become engaged with the enemy at any time during the two days, remaining on reserve throughout the entire operation.

Following the unsuccessful two days' campaign the regiment returned to its former position near the Weldon Railroad. From this time until the first week in December was another period of inactivity which was passed in camp. The site which our camp occupied at this time was one that had been determined by military necessity rather than a desire for comfort. It was upon a thin, sandy soil, underlaid with clay, holding moisture and giving it forth readily under the rays of the sun. The general surface was flat and but poorly drained. Water was obtained from springs and shallow wells and hardly fit for drinking purposes. Wood, however, was sufficiently abundant and we did not have to travel far to get it, as we had been obliged to in some of our other encampments. The region was noted for its malarious character and quinine formed an article of daily "diet." We began, in fact, to think that our commissary department considered that delectable article as taking the place of something more substantial, for our food at this time was of a grade even lower than that to which we were usually accustomed.

We were fatigued, worn, and exhausted by the hardest campaign of the war—that from the Rapidan, through the Wilderness, Spottsylvania, the North Anna, Bethesda Church, Petersburg, to the Weldon Railroad. The constant labor in the trenches, on forts, and in the building of roads, together with daily and nightly exposure in rifle-pits and sleepless vigilance on picket duty, kept up a constant strain upon the physique as well as the morale of the men. The miserable location of our camp was hardly conducive to an immediate recovery from the effect of such work, and malarious diseases were common among us. Early in the fall we had begun building our log "tents," and before cold weather set in we were all well sheltered. Despite this fact we looked forward with dread to a winter in such quarters.

On November first a change was made in the personnel of our corps, when the United States Infantry regiments which had been connected with the corps since its organization were ordered to New York to report to General Dix. Our regiment had been in the division with these troops since we joined the corps, and in the brigade with them since the beginning of the campaign of 1864. Their losses had not been replenished, as ours had been by men from other volunteer regiments, and at the time of their dismissal they were, in the words of General Warren, "reduced to mere skeletons." We were sorry to bid them good-bye, for they had always proved good comrades. The Regulars often said of the volunteers that "they never knew when they were beaten," and we could with equal sincerity say of them that they were most gallant soldiers.

Preparations were made early in December for an important movement by the entire Fifth Corps. The aversion to passing a winter in camp on the Weldon Railroad was very strong. We therefore were quite pleased to learn that our corps was to be relieved by the Sixth Corps, which had just returned from its successful work in the Shenandoah Valley. On December sixth four days' rations and sixty rounds of ammunition were issued to each man, and two days' rations and forty rounds were placed in the wagons. This was an indication of hard work and we were all curious to know what it was going to be.

Our questions were soon answered, and we found that the object of the expedition was once more the long-suffering Weldon Railroad. It was now planned to destroy the road as far south as possible, in order to prevent supplies being brought north on it and transferred to wagons for transportation into Petersburg. General Warren was chosen to lead the Union forces, and his command consisted of his own corps, the Fifth, Mott's division of the Second Corps, a division of cavalry under General Gregg, four batteries of artillery, and three companies of engineers.

The whole force was on the move at six o'clock on the morning of December seventh, notification having been given beforehand of the time of starting so that preparations might be complete and the start simultaneous. Moving south, the cavalry proceeded along the railroad, destroying it as they went, while the infantry and artillery took the Halifax plank road. Our division, Ayres's, was the third in line, preceded by Crawford's and Griffin's of the Fifth Corps and followed by Mott's division of the Second Corps. The plank road bridge across Warwick Swamp, a few miles south, was found to be destroyed and this caused some delay. Fifteen minutes sufficed to make a passage alongside for the infantry, but a bridge with crib-work pier about forty feet long had to be constructed before the artillery and wagons could pass. It began raining about half-past eight o'clock and continued through the greater part of the day, clearing about dark but clouding up again at midnight.

The head of the column reached the Nottoway River about noon and Crawford's and Griffin's divisions crossed on pontoons and camped on the other side. Our division and the division of the Second Corps remained on the north bank of the river and also went into camp. Early the next morning the line of march was taken up to strike the railroad at Jarratt's Station. The regiment crossed the bridge with the rest of the division about two o'clock in the morning. It was raining heavily at this time, so that we were almost as wet as if we had swum the river instead of crossing over by way of the bridge. The entire command was on the move by four-thirty, and the bridge was taken up soon after daylight.

The rain soon ceased, and we proceeded at a good rate of speed. The country through which we passed had been entirely free from the ravages of war and presented a pleasing appearance, when contrasted with the desolate, almost desert, land in which we had been accustomed to operate. Fertile fields extended as far as the eye could see on every side, farmhouses bordered the road, and there were cattle and livestock of every description. These latter were too great a temptation for many of the men and they fell out of line upon some pretext or other and scouted around, killing hogs, sheep, turkeys, geese, chickens, or other bird or animal whose meat promised a welcome change from the fare provided by the commissary. The noise of this firing led many to suppose that the men were skirmishing with the enemy.

While the infantry were marching along the road the cavalry were destroying the railroad, for General Warren delayed setting the former to this task, fearing that the enemy might appear suddenly in large force. The march towards Jarratt's Station was continued throughout the day and about the middle of the afternoon our regiment reached the railroad at this point. Here we halted and were given an opportunity to cook dinner, rest, and sleep for a few hours. About six o'clock the three divisions of the Fifth Corps went out upon the railroad and began to tear up the track, the troops of the Second Corps remaining with the wagon train to give the signal in case of attack. The work of demolishing the railroad was accomplished in the following manner: Men lined up along each rail and then, at a given signal, all stooped down and lifted the rail, tearing it from the ties. The ties were piled along the side of the road and the rails laid over them. The pile was then ignited and the ties burned. This caused the rails to bend and while the iron was still hot the rails were twined around the trunks of trees. Needless to say, this process effectively destroyed the railroad. By the light of the moon and the fires along the track the work was continued until midnight and then the troops bivouacked until daybreak.

Early on the morning of the ninth the work of destruction was renewed. One division was kept in readiness to meet any attack the Confederates might make, while the others, after tearing up the rails in their front, moved to the left, or southward, alternatively. In this manner rapid progress along the road was made until the north bank of the Meherrin River was reached at a point known as Hicksford. Here the bridge was found to be destroyed and General Warren ascertained that the Confederates were strongly posted on the southern bank. After a personal examination of the enemy's position Warren came to the conclusion that it would take at least two days to dislodge them and make the crossing. As the men were worn out and not provisioned for this length of time and as the weather threatened a heavy storm, he determined to abandon the enterprise and be content with what he had accomplished.

Preparations accordingly were made for returning northward. After the work of destroying the railroad was completed, our regiment camped with the rest of the command on the north bank of the Meherrin River. Some of us resumed our foraging expeditions over the surrounding country, but the great majority were well satisfied to remain quiet in camp. In the evening half a day's ration of bread and a full ration of beef were issued, the first beef we had received since the expedition started.

About eight o'clock in the evening a storm of cold sleet began and lasted through the night, causing much suffering to both men and horses. The storm still continued at daybreak, and the roads were rapidly becoming impassable. This determined General Warren to hasten his return. He sent the main column on the road direct to Sussex Court House, with the brigade of cavalry ahead to clear the way and watch the side roads. Griffin's division, in the lead, guarded the trains, and was followed by Mott's, Ayres's, and Crawford's divisions in the order named.

Most of the houses along the route were deserted or contained only helpless women and children, there being scarcely a man to be found. We, however, learned later that the cavalry, scouting on the flanks, came upon evidence that the enemy were lurking in the woods, for a number of Union soldiers who had strayed out of the ranks on the outward march were found dead, more than one having been murdered unawares as he slept. In retaliation, almost every house along the way was burned and much property was destroyed.

The head of the column reached Sussex Court House at dark, and here more evidence of the temper of the inhabitants of the country was discovered. The bodies of several Union soldiers were found lying in front of the Court House itself, and the cavalry, who made the discovery, immediately set fire to the town, burning a portion of it to the ground before General Warren arrived and stopped the work of destruction.

Our regiment bivouacked along the road near Sussex, but a cold mist fell during the night, so that we got little sleep or rest. In the morning, with the rest of Warren's command, we moved on towards the Nottoway River. Here Warren met Potter's division of the Ninth Corps, which had been sent to his assistance, in anticipation of an attack. Bridges were rapidly laid across the river and the entire command crossed before dark and camped near Belcher's Mill. The weather cleared during the night and was very cold. The mud in the morning was frozen stiff, so that the artillery and trains passed along easily, but the men suffered very much from their feet, which were now quite sore and blistered from the long marches. Many removed their shoes and walked barefoot over the frozen ground.

Warren's troops reached the Union line on the afternoon of December eleventh, having traveled a distance of more than one hundred miles, besides performing the heavy labor of destroying the railroad. General Warren states in his report, "The men marched and behaved most praiseworthily during this tiring expedition in most disagreeable weather — weather which almost precluded rest and sleep."

CHAPTER XVII

PRISON EXPERIENCES

ON the return the Fifth Corps took up a position at a point about halfway between the Halifax road and the Jerusalem plank road, where a camp was established and preparations made for passing the winter. The ground at this point was higher than that of our former camp and offered more advantages as an army camp site.

Perhaps the disastrous effects of the raid were better realized after we had returned to camp than they were during the period of active work, for more than one severe case of throat and lung trouble resulted among the men of the regiment as a result of the little "excursion" we had taken part in during the bleak December rain and cold.

The winter which followed (1864–65) was an unusually severe one. At times the Potomac River was closed to navigation, on account of the ice, a condition which exists but very infrequently during the winter seasons. Weather, however, which otherwise would have been almost unbearable caused us comparatively little distress, for by this time we had become quite inured to the cold. We compared our condition at this time with what it was during our first winter at the front when we were in camp at Falmouth. We had believed, most of us, that we were hale and hearty specimens of manhood when we enlisted, but we felt now that even our closest friends would have had difficulty in recognizing in the hardened, tanned, and bearded *men* the boys who had left the old county on that memorable eleventh of October, 1862. It was not without a feeling of sadness that we recalled that time, for the proud Fifth Oneida, nearly a thousand strong, seemed now but a mere handful. Despite the fact that our ranks had been augmented by men from other regiments, principally the Fifth, Seventeenth, and Forty-fourth New York, we now numbered barely three hundred. Many of our comrades slept their long last sleep on the fields of battle, others suffered unspeakable hardships in Southern prisons, and still others lay on beds of pain in Federal hospitals, while some had been sent home to fight the battle of life as best they could handicapped by the loss of a limb, the effects of a wound, or the ravages of disease. Those of us who remained were among the hardiest, for only men of iron with nerves of steel could have endured what we had endured, suffered what we had suffered.

Although all of us had grown old in appearance, we were still boys at heart and many were the tricks we played on one another, while friendly rivalry ran high among the various companies, or rather the remnants thereof, in the few contests our limited means would permit us to improvise. It was during these long winter days that we found our chief diversion in recounting tales of experiences, long to be remembered, through which we had gone during our two years of service. Seated around our campfires and avoiding as best we could the wintry air we lived over again our lives as soldiers, and there was hardly a man who did not contribute his quota of adventuresome "yarns." The remark that the "history of the Civil War will never be known until each man has told his story" was well illustrated at this time. In this general exchange of stories many of us learned for the first time the part the other men had played in the battles in which our regiment as a whole had figured so prominently. Not all the stories, however, were about familiar events in which all had had a part, for during this winter on the Weldon Railroad many comrades returned to the regiment after long periods

of absence in which a great variety of adventures had be-
fallen them. Some told of bitter months of suffering in the
prisons of the enemy and of their escape from this condition
of "living death." It was stories of this kind which always
evoked the greatest degree of interest on the part of the
listeners and the narrators were called upon to recount them
many times, each repetition seeming but to add to their zest.
The story told by a member of Company "H"[1] was a
typical one. He had been one of those captured at the
Wilderness after that fateful charge on the never-to-be-
forgotten fifth of May, 1864. Like many another he had not
heard the order to retreat, and, as he expressed it, when he
looked up from where he was hugging the ground and pepper-
ing away at anything that looked like a "Reb" he was
amazed to find that all his comrades had disappeared. Jumping up hastily, he had dashed wildly toward the place where
the Union forces had been. He had encountered two sergeants who were dragging back the wounded Lieutenant-
Colonel Curran and, stopping to exchange a word with them,
had heard a vicious bullet whiz through the air and strike
down one of the men.[2] Doubly alarmed at this evidence of
the closeness of the enemy he had continued his flight but
before going far was stopped by five Rebs who, in a gruff
manner, demanded instant surrender. He clutched his gun
and snapped at one of them, but as fate would have it, the
gun did not go off. Realizing that it was folly to attempt to
resist he signified his compliance with their command and
was ordered to drop his gun. Very reluctantly he obeyed,
and accompanied by two of the men started towards the
enemy's lines. Within a quarter of a mile they came across
two men who were carrying the color sergeant of our regiment who had been badly wounded. Another half mile and
familiar ground was reached—a small brook on the banks of
which the regiment had camped the fall before. Here there
were about twenty-five men of the regiment who had been

[1] George Mould of Sauquoit, New York.   [2] Orderly Sergeant Dugan.

captured, together with many more from other regiments, and, misery loving company, things seemed a little more cheerful. Later in the day the Confederates took all their prisoners to a place called Robertson's Tavern and there a halt was made. One by one the captives kept straggling in until there were several hundred in the same unfortunate predicament, quite a good proportion of whom were from the One Hundred and Forty-sixth. About dusk, the Confederates had formed their captives in line and marched them to Orange Court House.

On the way they had passed Longstreet's corps in the woods. Several men ran jubilantly into the road and inquired whether the whole Yankee army had been captured. All about Orange Court House, which had been the headquarters of the Army of Northern Virginia during the preceding winter, were seen evidences of the haste with which the Confederates had left their encampment to start in pursuit of the invading Union troops.

A stop for the night had been made at Orange Court House, and on the following day the prisoners had been marched to Gordonsville. From Gordonsville the Confederates had sent the prisoners along a regular route, through Lynchburg and Danville, where halts of several days' duration had been made, until finally the captives had reached Andersonville.

In Andersonville prison the second chapter of the adventures of those who were taken captive at the Wilderness began. Over one hundred men of the One Hundred and Forty-sixth endured the awful sufferings of confinement in this prison, and about seventy of them went through the gates of the foul den never to return alive.

The prison itself, as our comrades saw it, was an enclosure containing about sixteen acres, surrounded by pine logs set upright in the ground, projecting about twenty-five feet above the surface and extending five or six feet into the earth, hewn so as to fit closely together. Through the center, running east and west, was a small sluggish stream of per-

17

haps three feet in width and five or six inches deep, bordered on either side by a marsh or bog varying in width from one hundred to two hundred feet, which was entirely uninhabitable. From this bog the ground rose gradually to the stockade, thus affording to some extent drainage for the higher ground into the swamp below. On top of the stockade sentryboxes were located at regular intervals, from which the sentinels could easily view the entire enclosure. On each slope were massive gates, which were surrounded by a second or outer stockade, and these gates afforded the only avenue of communication with the outer world.

As our comrades reached the fatal place where they were to be confined for they knew not how long, they were halted with the rest of the prisoners in a small enclosure; the gates behind were then closed before those in front were opened, great care being exercised that both sets of gates should not be open at the same time.

The scenes which had been revealed to them as they passed into the enclosures caused even the bravest of the men to shudder. As one[1] of them said:

I had often visited field hospitals after a great battle and had become accustomed to scenes of suffering resulting from such casualties, and had seen my nearest and best friends shot down at my side, but I was quite unprepared for the phases of human misery which were here disclosed. Stand anywhere you would, and you could not escape the sight of the dying and the dead. Many of the men had been transferred from other prisons and were terribly emaciated from their long sufferings. Their blackened skin, their long hair, their sunburnt and smoke grimed faces, and their half-naked condition, served to give them the appearance of inhabitants of some other world, rather than of flesh and blood human beings like ourselves.

But the newcomers were soon to realize that it would require only a few months to reduce them all to the same

[1] John Goff, Co. "G."

pitiable state. Their existence in the prison was a veritable "living death." The number of men in the enclosure varied from eighteen thousand to thirty-three thousand, and huddled together so closely as scarcely to be able to move, with many of the men so emaciated as to be unable to stand upon their feet, the conditions were unspeakable. The small stream described above afforded the only means of obtaining water for this large multitude. To aggravate the matter, the quarters of the guards were located up the stream from the prison and it furnished a dumping ground for the filth and refuse of their encampment. As a result, along the edges of the stream a thick, greasy scum had accumulated, which rendered the water still more offensive. Around the inside of the entire stockade at a distance of about twenty feet from the wall, posts had been driven and narrow strips of board nailed across them. This was known as the "dead line," and was established by reason of an attempt of the earlier prisoners to scale the stockade and escape. The guards were instructed to shoot any man crossing or even touching this line, and many a poor fellow in his desire to get a drink of water which was less impure than that in the stream within the center of the stockade, who reached his cup under the dead line for this purpose, was shot down like a wild beast. So frequent were the casualties among new prisoners that a watchman had been stationed at the place to warn them, but even this did not altogether stop the practice, for men would risk their lives for a drink of decent water.

Meager though the fare had sometimes been during the hurried marches of active campaigning, our comrades testified that it was an overwhelming bounty compared to that which they received in the prison. A small handful of meal and a thin strip of worm-eaten bacon was the day's allowance, and quite frequently even the latter was missing. It was possible, for those who were fortunate enough to have retained some money with them, to buy sundry articles of food from traders who were permitted by the authorities to come into the prison. At one time a sutler, duly authorized by the officials in charge of the prison, plied his trade in vegetables and tobacco. The small dealers established themselves along what was called Market Street. Their stock consisted, perhaps, of a peck of beans, about the same quantity of flour, sweet potatoes, and tobacco, and certain well-to-do merchants might have a dozen or half-dozen onions. The prices in greenbacks were exorbitant and ranged somewhat as follows: beans, per pint, $1.00; flour, per pint, $1.50; sweet potatoes, from ten cents to twenty cents each; tobacco, $1.00 an ounce; onions an inch in diameter $1.00, and larger ones proportionately more.

Besides the rations, each man was allowed a stick of wood about the size of his arm, which was expected to last as fuel for cooking for three days. By clubbing together and splitting the wood into small pieces it was possible for the men to scald their food. About once a week a teaspoon of salt was given them, which was usually consumed at one meal. There were, of course, almost no cooking utensils in the prison, and the ingenuity displayed to supply their place was astonishing. Pieces of tin, old cans, tin plates, and half canteens were all pressed into service. Some built ovens or arches of the clay which underlaid the soil, a small hole about the size of the cup or plate being left in the top over which to heat the food. In this way it was possible to economize on fuel and utilize much of the heat which would escape from an open fire.

No shelter whatever was provided for the prisoners despite the fact that they were kept there throughout the entire year. The first prisoners who had been admitted had found the ground covered with stumps and brush and from these many of them had constructed rude huts which protected them in some degree from the wind and rain, but as they had no tools except clubs, wooden wedges, and pocket knives, their houses looked more like the handiwork of Hottentots

General Butterfield
Commander of Fifth Corps at
Fredericksburg

Maj.-Gen. Gouverneur K. Warren

Maj.-Gen. George G. Meade

Brig.-Gen. George Winthrop
Killed at Five Forks

Brig.-Gen. Romeyn B. Ayres

UNIDENTIFIED
An unidentified private of the 146th New York is adorned with his long yellow-tasseled red fez. (Michael J. McAfee Collection)

than that of skillful workmen, as many of them were. At the time however the men from our regiment who were captured at the Wilderness entered, this material was exhausted and even the roots had been dug up and used. Many men had burrowed into the ground like animals and others had built rude mud huts to protect themselves from the cool of the nights. As summer was fast approaching when our comrades came to the prison they were comparatively fortunate in thus avoiding the cold weather and regretted their lack of shelter only when a downpour of rain made outdoor life without sufficient clothing extremely disagreeable.

Among so great a number of men existing under such conditions the death rate was necessarily extremely high. During the summer months when the heat was severe, hundreds died each day and were carried by their emaciated comrades to the gate through which they were to be taken and laid at rest. Sickness and disease of every description were rampant. Speaking of these conditions one of our comrades said:

Accustomed as I was to mingle daily among men suffering from the most loathsome forms of disease, a visit to the south gate during a sick call was more than I could endure, and I visited the place only to help carry some comrade too weak to walk. The sight at such times beggars description. As we approached the gate the way became obstructed by dozens of poor wretches crawling along painfully on their hands and knees, in the vain hope of getting some relief from their intense suffering. Many of them would become exhausted and fall over on the blistering sand, writhing and screaming in pain until death came to their relief; many more had wounds which had broken out afresh or were covered with ulcers; some were reduced to mere skeletons; others with limbs swollen to twice their natural size. The details of their condition were too revolting for description, and I can hardly recall them now without a shudder.

After the long months of exposure to the rain with the ground for a bed the prisoners' clothes became so rotten that

it was with difficulty they could be kept together. Nearly
all sold their buttons or traded them for some delicacy, and
their place was supplied with strings, roots dug from the
ground, or wooden pins. Sometimes in returning the meal
sacks in which the rations were received, by skillful manipula-
tion five could be made to count as six and the one could be
retained from which to ravel thread to mend enough holes
to keep the clothes from falling off. Their only supply of
clothing was from the dead, and the dying were therefore
closely watched, sometimes as many as a dozen anxiously
waiting to claim everything which would afford the slightest
protection.

A short time after our comrades had been installed in the
prison a band of desperadoes was organized among the men,
who preyed upon the "fresh fish," as the new prisoners were
called, stealing clothing and money from them and sometimes
killing them and leaving their bodies to be taken out with
those unfortunates who had died from disease or exposure
during the night. Finally these desperadoes carried things
with such a high hand that some of the other prisoners formed
a body called the "Regulators." They hunted the desperadoes for three days and captured about a hundred of
them. They were taken out of the prison and given a jury
trial before the Confederate authorities, the proceedings of
which were kept and sent to Washington by the prison
officials. Six of the ringleaders were sentenced to be hung,
which was done on gallows erected in the prison in full view
of all the prisoners. At the suggestion of the "Regulators"
the authorities organized three companies of police among
the prisoners, and these companies, numbering a hundred
each, took turns policing the prison each day. Two or three
of the men of the One Hundred and Forty-sixth were members of this prison police force.

Those of us to whom life in our camp that winter had
grown extremely irksome were put to shame as our comrades
endeavored to give us some conception of the awful mo-

notony of the life they had endured in Andersonville. To
them in their unfortunate plight the days had indeed seemed
to fly on "leaden wings." Each month had seemed like a
year. The only news of the outer world which they had
received came from the new prisoners, who arrived at frequent intervals, and from the few newspapers which it was
occasionally possible to procure. Each day the heroism of
quiet endurance and heroic patience to bear suffering was
exhibited. A member of Company "G" who had survived
the awful life at Andersonville tells the story of such heroism
on the part of another member of the company, a lad[1] barely
eighteen years old. He was a diffident and retiring fellow
who had, during his service with the regiment, made no
enemies and but few friends. He had been always ready to
respond to the call of duty, often volunteering to take the
place on guard or picket of a comrade who was worn out by a
long and tiresome march. Such traits had earned the respect
of his associates, but he had seemed to care but little for their
companionship. He had been taken prisoner at the Wilderness and soon after reaching Andersonville had contracted a
contagious disease. Lying on the ground in the blistering
sun and the pitiless rain, his companions could do but little
to alleviate his sufferings, but what little they could do was
done cheerfully. More than once did they spread their
coats over him in the driving rain, hoping thereby to keep
him warm, though realizing that no amount of clothing
could keep him dry. He had finally become too weak to
stand upon his feet and those who had aided him realized
that the end of his suffering was not far distant. One day
a discussion arose among the men surrounding him as to the
responsibility for the policy of non-exchange of prisoners.
Various views were expressed and the discussion gradually
became more and more animated, until some of the men de-
nounced the Administration for its treatment of the whole
question. The young lad had been an interested listener,

[1] George Lewis.

and at this outburst of temper signified his desire to speak. Slowly and painfully rising to his knees, he scored the angry disputants unmercifully, calling them "dress-parade" soldiers and advising them to apply for umbrellas and feather-beds without delay. As his voice began to fail he raised his right hand and exclaimed, "Rather than have the government sacrifice one iota of principle I would rot here a hundred times!" Those whose sentiments had called forth this reproof from the dying lad were put to shame, and every man unconsciously raised his hand to salute as the boy toppled back upon his bed of rags. Not long thereafter our young comrade, like Nathan Hale, gave up his life for his country, no doubt regretting, with the great patriot, that it was the only one he had to offer.

Relief came to the prisoners in Andersonville rather unexpectedly, when the prison authorities received news of the capture of Atlanta by the army under General Sherman. This was the signal for the distribution of many of the prisoners to various other points in the Confederacy where they would be less likely to be retaken by "Kilpatrick's Cossacks," as one of the Confederate officers termed the Union cavalry.

While in Andersonville the men of our regiment had consorted together as much as possible, lending each other aid in various ways and sharing the meager means of shelter they had been able to procure. When word came to leave the prison they kept together as much as possible and nearly all the men from the One Hundred and Forty-sixth in the prison were among the number taken to Florence, South Carolina. This place had been reached before preparations were completed to receive the prisoners and they were accordingly placed in an open field and surrounded by two lines of sentries, while workmen were engaged in constructing a stockade for their reception. The opportunity to escape at this time was too good to be neglected. Escape in large bodies was impossible so that each man decided to "take care of himself," and the men from the One Hundred and Forty-sixth who had been close comrades in misery for so long consequently became separated. Some were too ill to muster strength enough to elude the vigilance of the guards and the more fortunate of the survivors were given the difficult choice between the duty of attending their sick comrades and the opportunity of escaping. Those who could not go were most urgent in their desire that the others should endeavor to get away. One in particular[1] pointed out the fact that he had only a few days to live and insisted that his comrades should try to rejoin the regiment as soon as possible and "get in a whack" for him the first time they had a chance.

[1] Thomas G. Sayer, Co. "G."

CHAPTER XVIII

PRISON EXPERIENCES (*Continued*)

A S the men from the One Hundred and Forty-sixth separated at this time they began a series of adventures,
each unique in some respects, but all, as we heard them from
their lips, equally interesting and absorbing. Three members of Company "H"[1] made good their escape when they,
with many others, had been sent out one day by the Confederates in search of firewood. They had concealed themselves in the underbrush until nightfall and had traveled all
night. One of them had made a rough copy of a map of the
country which had been shown him by another prisoner
while in Andersonville and by its aid they had been able to
reach the Great Peedee River the next day. They had struck
the river on the grounds of a large and fertile plantation
but on the opposite side were low-lying lands and swamps.
As these latter promised better shelter from the enemy's
cavalry whom they felt sure would be sent in pursuit the
three men had crossed the river on a hastily improvised raft
and started down on the other side. Before going far they
discovered a boat caught against a snag. Their rejoicing
at the discovery prevented them from realizing that such
fortune was "almost too good to be true," for as they learned
later, the boat was one of a considerable number placed in
the river by the Confederates for the use of escaping prisoners
in order to facilitate their capture as they came down the

[1] George Mould, Isaac Foster, and Joseph Whalen.

river. They remained in hiding with the boat until dark and then started to drift downstream. About twelve o'clock they heard the report of a gun, and, fearing that it was a picket of the enemy, had hauled the boat into the swamp and remained there until the next morning. At daylight two of them decided to go in search of something to eat, and, leaving the other in charge of the boat, started out, blazing the trees on the way so as to be able to find their way back. Some wild fruits and edible leaves were found and these constituted their fare for the day. Some half-decayed boards were also discovered and the men took them back and made paddles of them. At night the journey down the river was resumed and with the aid of the paddles they were able to keep well within the channel and to make fairly good progress with the current of the stream. At one place the boat was nearly dashed to pieces against a low-lying railroad bridge, but a quick push by one of them as he lay sprawled in the bottom of the boat sent them safely through the middle archway. There was another boat under the bridge and as they passed someone in it called out, "Whar you goin'?" Our comrades thought it was some negroes fishing and answered, "Down de ribber." Keeping as much as possible in the shadow of the trees, they came to a large bar, which glistened white through the darkness of the night. As they drew near the bar, someone commanded them to halt and fired a gun, striking within five feet of the boat. Our comrades decided that "discretion was the better part of valor" and obeyed the command, pulling their boat upon the sand bar. They were taken to the bank of the river and were told sarcastically to "make themselves as comfortable as possible," while their captors prepared to receive some more expected guests. About an hour later another boat came down the river and, upon being stopped in the same way, was found to contain four more refugees. Six more were captured that night, making a total of thirteen. At daybreak the Confederates took their prisoners to a planter's shed, where they remained until about nine o'clock, when the planter called them into his house and gave them a square meal which served as breakfast and dinner combined. As one of them remarked in relating his story, "It was the only good meal I ever had under the Confederacy."

Fortunately, the prisoners made the best of their opportunity to eat, for it proved to be forty-eight hours before they were given anything more by their captors. The march back to Florence was a tedious one, rendered so by the fact that the men were unable to walk rapidly because of their great physical weakness. While passing along the roads, men, women, and children were frequently met, all of whom evidenced a great deal of curiosity and but few any degree of sympathy, however slight. The sight of Florence prison was almost a welcome one, for it promised rest from a journey which had been full of suffering on the part of the prisoners.

Florence, being comparatively new ground, was much more comfortable as an abode than Andersonville had been, but even so, as one of the men said, he wouldn't recommend it as a place to live for the rest of one's life. They had been confined here until February, when the news of Sherman's further operations decided the Confederates to move their prisoners once more. The men from Florence, over a thousand in number, were accordingly marched under guard to Wilmington, North Carolina. Our comrades testified that this journey was the most trying march they ever experienced. Many of the men were so emaciated that they were compelled to often crawl along on hands and knees. A large number died by the way. As the grim column passed through the streets of Wilmington children ran from them screaming with fright, women were seen to cover their faces and weep, and even the men could hardly endure the sight of the awful spectacle this company of starving, ragged men exhibited. The stay in Wilmington was not a long one for the Union forces were rapidly approaching and the Confederates were compelled to take their prisoners out of the city. Three of the men from our regiment,[1] were with a party which started for Goldsboro, but they were able to make good their escape before they had gone far, and, after wandering for a few days in the woods, met an old negro who told them that "Lincoln men" were in Wilmington and took them in a rickety wagon to the Union camp. "The old flag never looked so good to us as it did at that time," said one of the men when telling his story, and "we gave three cheers as we saw it floating over the city where the stars and bars had been such a short time before."

Equally interesting to us who listened was the story told by one of the members of Company "G."[2] Like the others he managed to escape while the prisoners from Andersonville were at Florence awaiting the construction of the stockade. On the second or third day after their arrival he bade his comrades good-bye towards evening and after sauntering leisurely around the camp for a few minutes lay down near the guard line, watching an opportunity to escape when the guard was not looking. The chance soon came and springing to his feet he dashed through the line. The guard whirled and fired at him, but, as he had anticipated, in such haste that he did not take steady aim, the bullet merely tearing a buckle from the legging of the escaping prisoner and leaving a stinging sensation which, as he said, led him at first to think he had been seriously hit. In a short time he reached a near-by swamp and was soon joined by another, and younger lad, from a Michigan regiment, whose experience had been similar to his own. They soon started together into the swamp, but in the darkness progress was slow and the refugees were uncertain as to the direction in which they were traveling. About midnight they reached a railroad embankment and after climbing it walked along the railroad for some distance until a trestle was reached. They soon found that the trestle terminated in a bridge which

[1] George Mould, Isaac Foster, C. King.   [2] John Goff.

spanned a fairly broad river. They decided to cross on the bridge and did so by crawling along on hands and knees. When within a few feet of the northern bank they were challenged and told to surrender. Clinging to a plank suspended over a river, with a rifle leveled at their heads, the two lads were in no position to argue the proposition. Their captors laughed at their discomfiture, but gave them some sweet potatoes, and lighting a large pile of chips and shavings, told them to eat all they wanted. After this unexpected good fortune in the matter of edibles the recaptured prisoners fell asleep and upon awakening next morning found that several other prisoners had been captured in crossing the river. which they also learned, for the first time, was the Great Peedee.

While the Confederates were discussing what disposition to make of their prisoners, the latter were interviewed by a party of women, whom our comrade described somewhat picturesquely as

a variety of the genus homo with which we were not familiar. The older ones wore immense cotton sunbonnets and on their arrival were smoking black clay pipes, and when these were extinguished one of them produced a bar of "nailrod" tobacco from which each took a chew. They were sallow, angular, "divinely tall," but could hardly be described as "divinely fair." One of the younger ones, however, was rather good looking in spite of her frowsy head, her bare feet, her coarse cotton dress, and protruding,pantalets. We complimented her unsparingly on her beauty. She seemed anxious to show her appreciation of our good opinions, and replied, "I'm doggoned if you-all ain't ther perlitest outfit I've ever saw!"

The prisoners captured in crossing the Peedee were confined in a large warehouse on the banks of the river, and within a day or two after our comrade was captured they numbered over thirty. With the aid of an old case knife the prisoners removed a lock from the rear door of the shed and one day, while the guards were being diverted by two or three of the more proficient story-tellers in the front of the building, the prisoners went out of the rear door and bolted for the swamp. Our comrade with one other prisoner traveled all night and the next morning hid in a small clump of timber near an extensive plantation. Just as they were about to lie down to sleep during the day they were startled by the sound of horses' hoofs, and threw themselves hurriedly to the ground. From their position they could hear about half a dozen horsemen go clattering past, cursing the escaping prisoners. This proximity to the road decided them to cross the road and endeavor to reach a more secluded wood not far distant. Soon after reaching this place another party of horsemen appeared, who thoroughly "scoured" the woods they had just left and caused the refugees to congratulate themselves on their good judgment.

For several days the two men continued their journey northward, sleeping in the woods during the day and traveling as far as possible at night. Their food was obtained, as our comrade told us, by the "catch-as-catch-can" method. Some days they could get nothing but acorns and wild grapes, and at other times they had an abundance of sweet potatoes, green corn, and watermelons, all of which were, of course, eaten raw. They had with them a small piece of canvas and by using a section of a grapevine for a rope made a dip-net with which they caught fish from the creeks and small ponds. These were taken into the cane brakes a long distance, a fire was lighted with matches obtained from an old negro, and the fish were baked. "They were," as our comrade said, "so nearly all bone that it was almost impossible to eat them, but the odor was no doubt very nourishing and remained with us for several days." As a last resort, the refugees sometimes applied for food at the negro quarters on the plantations through which they passed. Their requests were usually granted, and sometimes they were told by the negroes to remain in hiding until night, when food was sent out to them.

One day, after having barely escaped being betrayed into the hands of Confederate cavalry by a treacherous old negro, the two lads were sleeping in a strip of woods on a large plantation when they were awakened by shouts and curses and springing to their feet saw an old planter pointing a revolver at them. He was accompanied by about a dozen negroes, who, when the planter demanded their surrender, advised them to do so, "else Massa 'll shoot yer, suah." The refugees told the planter a pitiful story of the hardships they had endured, which seemed to touch a warm spot in his heart, for he invited them to take dinner with him. On the way to the house he drew a long, black bottle from his pocket and after offering it to his guests, took a very persistent "pull" at it himself. He was extremely "mellow" in his conversation, but at no time forgot that he was a "gentleman, sah." Our comrade told of their experience with the planter in the following words:

He seemed very proud of his family and could doubtless trace his ancestry back to William the Conqueror. Indeed, he made several attempts to do this and only failed because of stopping to take a drink, after which he would commence at the beginning. His lineage was too long for his thirst. His name, as he assured us perhaps twenty times, was G—— B——, Esq., a graduate of —— Hill. He conducted us into the house, ordered the servants to get us a dinner, and sent his field hands back into the cotton fields. In a short time a good-looking mulatto girl came in and announced dinner, led the way into the dining-room, and having seated us took her station behind us armed with a large bundle of peacock feathers which she slowly waved over the food in order that there might be no flies on it. The dinner consisted of sweet potatoes, corn bread, and ham, and plenty of molasses and buttermilk, a regular picnic for boys of our abstemious habits. Having finished our meal we started back to the room where we had left our host, but before entering caught sight of him leaning back against the wall, apparently fast asleep. Telling the servant that we would be back in a minute, we stepped out of the rear door and ran for the woods, traveling the remainder of the day and nearly all night in a southerly direction, hoping thus to escape pursuit.

Another amusing adventure which the "travelers" had was their meeting with another man from the prison who had escaped in a manner similar to theirs. One morning they discovered a man watching them and supposed they were to be again taken into custody, but after looking awhile concluded that he was either a refugee like themselves or a Confederate deserter, in either case likely to be friendly. They beckoned to him and after some hesitation he came and met them. He proved to be a German from one of the Wisconsin regiments, who had crossed the Peedee by swimming, and was headed northwesterly, "to go by Scherman's men," as he said. They told him that Sherman was at Atlanta, farther south, and that he could not possibly reach his forces, in the direction he was taking, to which he replied, "I peen von der Vest, Scherman was all ofer dot gountry." Our comrade, who told of the meeting in a most amusing manner, said he should like to be able to describe him but thought himself unequal to the task. His dress was a mixture of Federal and Confederate uniforms in about equal parts, with a seasoning of articles which he had confiscated from clothes lines as being "contraband of war," and taken altogether, constituted a work of art which only women initiated into the mysteries of a crazy quilt could appreciate. He remained in hiding with our comrade and his companion, and at night the three started forward again. They soon found themselves confronted by a stream of considerable width and the two latter proposed to rest until morning, when they could take a survey of the situation. The German, however, would not listen to this. He said he could "svim dot river schoost like falling a log ouf." Accordingly he stepped off the bank and went down with a loud splash. In a few seconds he came up with a remark "dere vas more vasser as I tink." He was satisfied, thereafter, to remain with the other two until morning, when the body of water was found to be only a pond or lagoon which they easily circled. As usual, they remained in hiding during the day, and at night the German bade them good-bye, and started in his favorite direction.

The story of his adventures as related by our comrade was in many ways amusing, but, as he said, it must not be supposed that this trip was a pleasure excursion only, filled with a succession of amusing incidents and adventures. The days of vigilant watching and nights of weary marching were such as could not be soon forgotten. To be hunted night and day, tramping barefooted through brakes and brambles in the darkness, ignorant much of the time of their direction and always of their location, hungry and footsore, continually in dread and danger of arrest, with nerves strung to such a tension that the breaking of a twig or the falling of a leaf would startle them from their sleep, and with every white inhabitant an enemy, was not an experience of un-alloyed pleasure, and needed a preparation at Andersonville to be moderately enjoyable. The obstacles to be overcome were of such proportions and the chances of success so remote that they were at times tempted to surrender, but the re-membrance of the stockade and the hope that perhaps, after all, they might possibly reach the Union lines, stimulated them to renewed efforts. The several escapes they had made and the constantly increasing distance from the prison encouraged them more and more to believe success possible and with increased caution they pushed on. They had crossed the State line and were well up in North Carolina, it being their purpose to reach New Bern, which they knew was in possession of the Union forces. Finally, one night they came upon what they thought was a reserve picket post. A squad of soldiers were seated around a blazing fire and the fugitives watched them some hours, thinking they would post sentries and thus disclose their line. Instead of this, however, they lay down to sleep and the refugees concluded that they were simply stopping for the night and decided to flank them. In doing so the horses became alarmed, and the uproar they set up speedily brought out the men to search for the cause of their fright. The first impulse of the two lads was to run, but it was an impulse only. Their feet had become so poisoned in the swamps and were so swollen that walking was very painful and running out of the question, so they crawled under some bushes in the hope of being over-looked. Their hope was vain, however, for the horses continued their symptoms of fright and the soldiers lighted pine knots and soon dragged the unfortunate refugees out.

The next day they were taken to a small station, placed on the cars, and shipped to Marion Court House, where they were held in jail a few days, when they were taken back to Florence and turned into the stockade. Their final delivery did not come, therefore, until the prisoners were taken to Wilmington, when they made their escape in a manner similar to that of the three members of Company "H," whose story is related above.

The adventures of the officers of our regiment who fell into the hands of the enemy at the Wilderness were by no means less interesting to us than those of the privates. A Captain[1] of one of the companies which went to the support of the picket line on that memorable morning, in a letter written to one of the Utica papers, tells the story of his capture and prison experiences as follows:

Those of our regiment who discovered the movements of the enemy in time made good their escape to the rear, but about 125, including the slightly wounded, unaware that the enemy were flanking them, delayed their retrograde movement until it was too late. When they emerged from the woods they found the open field over which they had charged covered with the enemy. They were entirely surrounded and in ten minutes were marched to Robertson's Tavern, one mile in rear of the enemy's position, as prisoners of war. While our orderly sergeant, who had been

[1] W. H. S. Sweet.

severely wounded, was being borne to the rear on a stretcher his zouave uniform attracted the attention of a group of Rebel officers, one of whom was General Ewell. He was placed upon the ground and the officers surrounded him. General Ewell remarked, "What makes your boys fight so? Your regiment fought like hell!"

By 4 P.M. the Rebels had collected at Robertson's Tavern all the captures of the day, amounting, as I found later, to forty-six officers and nine hundred eighty-one men. They then put the column of prisoners in motion for Orange Court House. We marched all night with very infrequent rests until 2 A.M. the next morning, at which time we reached Orange Court House. On the 6th day of May they marched us to Gordonsville, where we received our first ration from the Rebel government. It consisted of a few hardtack and a small piece of corn beef. We were put on board a train of cars for Lynchburg, Va., on the following morning, and we reached that place at 2 P.M. the same day. The officers were confined in the old Norville House, a filthy place, with all the stenches that inhabit an old jail. Our number was increased in a few days by two squads, and among them were Generals Seymour and Shaler. We left Lynchburg for Macon, Ga., on the 17th of May and arrived at our destination on the 24th, having been among the first to pass from Danville, Va., to Greensboro, N. C., over Jeff Davis's Military Railroad. At Augusta, Ga., we were turned over to the Provost Marshal, Captain Bradford, a son of Ex-Governor Bradford of Maryland.

We were then put into the stockade, where we found the Libby officers, numbering some nine hundred. Squads of fresh captures were continually arriving until the number was increased to nearly sixteen hundred. During the night of July 27th six hundred were sent to Charleston, S. C., to be put under the fire of the Union batteries at Morris Island. On the following day six hundred were sent to Savannah, Ga. We remained there until the 13th of September, when we were transported to Charleston and put under fire. For two weeks we were crammed into the small yard of the Charleston jail. Most of us were without any protection from the inclemency of the weather. A portion of our Savannah party, with Colonel Miller of the One

Hundred and Forty-seventh, N. Y., at the head and numbering eighty-six (I being one of them) were assigned to the Broad Street House, the nearest point to our batteries at which our officers were confined. It was a first-class private residence abandoned by its owner, Mr. Conor, a lawyer, on account of the frequency with which Union shells struck in its vicinity. It was one of the few buildings in that portion of Charleston which had not been destroyed by the terrible conflagration of 1861. Sitting under the porch of the house, we spent many an evening pleasantly watching the flight of the large shells from the Union batteries. Soon after hearing the report of the gun, five miles distant, we could discover in the direction of the fire what appeared to be a large star, majestically climbing into the heavens until it reached its greatest altitude, when it would descend, with constantly increasing velocity, and finally explode with a report as loud as that of an ordinary piece of field artillery. The fragments would sometimes fall among us, but, strange to say, no prisoner was killed or wounded. Some of the missiles would strike half a mile above us in the city. At least one half of the shells would strike the buildings and crash through with terrific noise.

Our authorities having retaliated for the placing of the prisoners under the fire of the batteries, the Rebels found a plausible reason for our removal in the breaking out of yellow fever. We arrived at Columbia, S. C., on the morning of the 6th of October and on the following day were marched across the Congaree River into an open field, two miles from town. Here we were herded like a drove of cattle with no other protection than such as small evergreen trees afforded, and were exposed to the inclemency of the October and November weather. A few axes were owned by officers in camp and permission was obtained to go out under guard into the woods to cut timber for huts. The number of axes, however, was so insufficient that eight weeks elapsed before most of the officers had made themselves comparatively comfortable. This was the only camp where we were not surrounded by a stockade. We have never failed, however, to have that other appendage, to wit, an interior line ominously styled the "dead line" some ten paces inside the line of sentinels. The absence of the stockade afforded our officers an excellent opportunity to escape. There were probably five hundred escaped from this camp, but most were recaptured at distances varying from a few rods to 150 miles.

On the 12th of December we were removed to the yard of the State Lunatic Asylum at Columbia. Here, again, we were without protection. The Rebel authorities promised to furnish lumber for buildings, but it came so slowly that during our eight weeks' residence there only twelve barracks were erected. These, built by the officers, would accommodate only one third of us. The others finally obtained a variety of old tents.

On the 15th of February we were hurried away from Columbia to make room for General Sherman. After spending two weeks at Charlotte, Raleigh, and Goldsboro, we were taken on a railroad to within nine miles of Wilmington and paroled prisoners of war.

CHAPTER XIX

BATTLE OF HATCHER'S RUN

THE winter we passed on the Weldon Railroad was fairly full of activity for us. Despite the several attempts of the Union forces to cut off the route of communication by way of Hatcher's Run, it was reported that the Confederates were still receiving supplies in this direction. The route of the wagon trains was from Hicksford, the point to which the Fifth Corps had torn up the Weldon Railroad, up the Meherrin River to the Boydton plank road and thence through Dinwiddie Court House to Petersburg. Although the winter was rapidly passing, General Grant planned to make one more attempt to break up this line of supply.

Accordingly on February fifth, a cavalry division under General Gregg was sent to the Boydton plank road to intercept the Confederate supply trains moving thereon. Two days later, a heavy force of infantry and artillery was dispatched to coöperate with the cavalry in breaking up the route of supplies. General Meade accompanied the infantry as commander of the expedition. In this movement, as in all similar movements in the vicinity of Hatcher's Run and the Weldon Railroad, the main activity was to center around the Fifth Corps, under General Warren. He was directed to move by the shortest route to Dinwiddie Court House and join forces with the cavalry at that point. General Humphreys, who had succeeded General Hancock in command of the Second Corps, was ordered to follow the Fifth Corps and keep up communication with Warren, holding his command in readiness to support the latter.

Those of our regiment who were out on picket were recalled on the evening of February fourth. Four days' rations were issued to us and the next morning at seven o'clock we set out with the rest of the Fifth Corps, moving south on the Halifax plank road. The column was preceded by three squadrons of cavalry. Our division led the infantry, followed by Griffin's and Crawford's divisions, with the artillery and baggage trains in our rear. The crossing of Rowanty Creek was reached about ten o'clock and the bridge was found to be destroyed. About a hundred Confederates were stationed on the southern bank, prepared to dispute the crossing. A squadron of dismounted cavalry kept down the enemy's fire while Gwyn's brigade of our division crossed the creek to dislodge the small Confederate force. The order then came for us to cross. The stream was about sixty feet wide and of too great a depth to be forded. A thin coating of ice enabled a few to cross dry-shod before the ice gave way. Some of the taller men waded over but most of us had to strike out and swim although trees were cut down and thrown into the stream to assist those in crossing who could not swim. This order to plunge into the ice-cold water in the middle of winter was promptly obeyed, but not particularly relished by any of us. While the infantry was crossing in the manner described a bridge was constructed for the cavalry, artillery, and trains and the entire command was safely over the stream shortly after four o'clock. Each regiment as it crossed the creek moved out on the Vaughan road towards Dinwiddie Court House and took up position along the Boydton plank road without further opposition from the Confederates. Our brigade, under General Winthrop, lay in line of battle at the intersection of a military pike road with the Vaughan road. When it became apparent that the enemy were not present in the vicinity in any force, we speedily built up roaring fires over which we dried our clothes and prepared a hasty meal. The small comfort of hot coffee and dry clothes was indeed most heartily welcomed.

At nine o'clock that evening as we were about to bivouac for the night, the order to "fall in" was given. Warren had been instructed to move up the Vaughan road and join his forces with those of Humphreys at the crossing of Hatcher's Run to be prepared for any concentration of the enemy in the morning. It was a cold winter's night and past midnight before we were fairly on the march. The roads were frozen hard and we keenly felt the cold. The next morning we were about exhausted, as we had had no sleep and had been almost constantly on the march a day and a night. Despite this fact, we hardly had time to prepare a hasty pot of coffee before we were ordered forward to the attack. At eight o'clock Warren had received instructions to feel out the Confederates along his front and fight them, if possible, outside their works. For some reason the order given us to advance was countermanded. Humphrey's corps advanced but the Fifth Corps remained inactive throughout the morning. At one o'clock in the afternoon, our brigade moved out to support the cavalry, who were skirmishing heavily with the enemy some distance down the Vaughan road. The brigade arrived at the contested point during a lull in the fighting and the cavalry outposts were immediately relieved by our regiment and the Fifth New York. The One Hundred and Fortieth New York and the Fifteenth New York Heavy Artillery were deployed in an open field, the former on the right and the latter on the left side of the road. These dispositions had hardly been made when the Union cavalry advanced to the attack in heavy columns. They soon became engaged with the Confederate infantry and for a few minutes we could hear rapid firing in front of the place where our regiment was stationed. Soon the cavalry, having been roughly handled, retired in some confusion, the Confederates following them closely. General Winthrop now ordered up the regiments of his brigade on the double-quick. Our brigade charged along the road and across the open field, firing as we ran. Before we could close with the Confederates they fell back to the shelter of the woods and General Winthrop did not attempt to follow them. Once or twice again the Confederates attempted to advance over the open, but our brigade, which in the meantime had been reinforced by a brigade from Griffin's division, repulsed them handsomely each time. Finally, about five o'clock, our ammunition having become exhausted, we were relieved from our position on the Vaughan road by another brigade of the First Division. Then, having replenished our cartridge boxes, the brigade was ordered out on picket, covering the road leading to Dabney's Mill, where we remained until the afternoon of the seventh.[1]

The other troops under Warren and Humphreys had not fared so well as had our brigade. They had advanced against the Confederate position, and, after a spirited contest, had driven them back for some distance, but the Confederates receiving reinforcements soon regained the lost ground. On the morning of the seventh Warren and Humphreys renewed the attack and took a considerable portion of the Confederate works.

The line of Union intrenchments was now extended to Hatcher's Run at the Vaughan road crossing, the Second Corps occupying the works and the Fifth Corps being massed in rear of the Second. Our regiment went into camp

[1] General Winthrop, in his report of this engagement, says: "It is but simple justice to say that I have rarely seen troops fight with more animation or maintain their ground more stubbornly against such superior numbers as confronted them in the earlier part of the engagement. With such troops I shall always feel confident of success."

First Lieutenant Robert P. Warren, of the One Hundred and Forty-sixth, acting as aide-de-camp to General Ayres, was given special mention by the latter for zeal, intelligence, and good conduct during the operations of the day. The One Hundred and Forty-sixth Regiment as a result was for the third time mentioned in General Orders for distinguished service.

in the vicinity of the operations of February fifth and sixth on a high rolling surface where there was good water and plenty of wood. Once more we erected log huts covered with canvas and made ourselves as comfortable as possible. The benefit of the improved site of our camp was immediately visible in the prompt disappearance of all sickness. A period of rest under favorable sanitary conditions soon prepared us for that short, snappy, and decisive campaign which was to close the war.

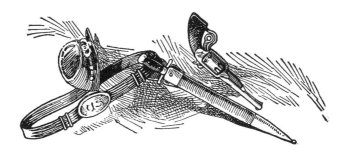

CHAPTER XX

APPOMATTOX CAMPAIGN

A T the opening of the spring campaign of 1865 the Army of Northern Virginia, despite the heroic efforts of the Union forces to dislodge it, still held Richmond, the capital of the Confederacy, and the city of Petersburg, which was the key to the former place. The Confederate commander, however, found that his position was growing more and more untenable as the days passed. The toils of a stronger opponent were drawing closer and tighter, the Confederates were being slowly overcome by superior force despite their desperate resistance. The plans outlined by General Grant a year before had met with almost unvarying success. Sherman, with the Army of the West, by his march through Georgia and the Carolinas had effectually destroyed all lines of communication between Virginia and the far South. Sheridan had finally driven Early from the Shenandoah Valley. One by one the Southern ports had been closed to blockade runners and Wilmington, N. C., the last which remained open, had been occupied by a Northern army on February twenty-second. Thomas had almost completely annihilated Hood in Tennessee. Grant, with the Army of the Potomac and the Army of the James, drew the bonds more closely about Lee and his sadly depleted army, who were tenaciously holding on to Richmond and Petersburg. The Confederate government desired to hold their capital at all hazards, if possible, fearing the moral effect it would have to abandon it in view of the already fast-growing spirit of despondency that prevailed throughout the South. It, therefore, was a most desperate situation in which the Confederate commander found himself. It was utterly impossible for him to secure reinforcements. The few men in the South who were still available did not respond to the frequent calls in the way they had at first, for there was a general dissatisfaction and depression felt throughout the South over the recent conduct of the war. A condition bordering on utter desolation prevailed in the greater portion of the Southland and thousands were on the verge of starvation. The sufferings of wife and children at home called from his duty under the stars and bars many a brave Confederate soldier who had for four years risked his life for the cause which he now saw it was beyond human power to save. As a consequence, Lee not only was unable to secure new men, but the army he had was fast dwindling by reason of desertions. His commissariat also had become almost entirely depleted. Cut off from its sources of supplies in the Shenandoah Valley and from the south, the condition of the once-glorious Army of Northern Virginia was indeed pitiful. Only the despairing courage of the leaders remained. The Great Rebellion bid fair soon to become the great Lost Cause. Their only hope of success lay in their being able to prolong the war until the people of the North grew tired of the struggle or until recognition from some powerful European nation was granted them. General Lee urged the consent of the officials of his government to a plan whereby he should hastily abandon Richmond and Petersburg, and, uniting his army with that of Johnston, who was in the Carolinas, retire to the fastnesses of the Alleghanies and there wage a sort of guerrilla warfare until satisfactory terms of peace could be agreed upon. Reluctantly this consent was given and Lee prepared to carry out this plan. The campaign which began with the assault on Fort Stedman on March twenty-fifth and ended with the surrender at Appomattox on April ninth resulted from this effort on the part of Lee to extricate himself from his perilous position and to retreat to the western part of Virginia.

In order to veil his attempt to withdraw from his intrenchments Lee created a diversion by an attack on the center of the Union lines at Fort Stedman on March twenty-fifth. Although at first successful, he was later repulsed by a counter attack on the part of the Union troops and, losing an outer line of pickets, found himself still more closely pressed.

Undeceived as to Lee's purpose and anticipating a retreat from Petersburg, Grant now ordered a great movement to the left to intercept the Confederates. Only a small force was kept in front of Petersburg and the turning force was made solid and strong. On the morning of March twenty-ninth nearly the whole of the Armies of the Potomac and the James were put in motion westward. Soon the Union line extended from the Appomattox on the east to Dinwiddie on the west. A heavy storm on the thirtieth of March arrested operations momentarily but the next day the two forces clashed at several points. The Second Corps encountered the Confederates at Dabney's and Burgess's Mills, the Fifth Corps at the White Oak road, and Sheridan with his cavalry fought desperately at Dinwiddie Court House and Five Forks. The fortunes of the day were about evenly divided. Sheridan, however, was hard-pressed and Warren with the Fifth Corps was sent to his assistance during the night of the thirty-first and the morning of April first. The Confederates made a desperate stand at Five Forks and the battle at that place on the afternoon of April first was one of the sharpest of the war. The Confederates, however, were finally routed and the pursuit to the westward continued.

Movements now followed each other with lightning-like rapidity. The Confederate works before Petersburg were assaulted on the morning of April second and one by one fell before the victorious Union army. On the third Richmond was evacuated, the retreating Southerners setting fire to the city. The fleeing Army of Northern Virginia was hard pressed from all sides. Lee dared not halt, for Union columns were upon his right, his left, and his rear. A running fight was kept up between the two armies all the way. On April sixth Ewell's division, numbering some eight thousand men, was cut off at Sailor's Creek, surrounded, and captured. The Confederates, disappointed in not receiving supplies on their arrival at Amelia Court House, were literally starving. Those who were best off had but a few handfuls of corn and even the buds of trees were put to use for food. Thousands deserted daily, or straggled by the way, too weak in spirit or in body to proceed farther. At last all way of escape was cut off save over the narrow neck of land between the James and Appomattox rivers to the west of Farmville. Lee strove to reach it in time, but Sheridan's cavalry intercepted him at Appomattox Court House. Lee was trapped, but he made one more effort to break through by attacking the cavalry. Reinforcements of infantry, however, arrived in time to prevent him from doing it and he was left no alternative but to surrender. After a short correspondence, Grant and Lee met at the house of a Mr. McLean on the outskirts of the village and terms were agreed upon.

Such was the so-called Appomattox campaign which terminated the great war and at last crowned the Union arms with complete victory. The part which our regiment played in these movements was as important as that of any single regiment on the Union side. Upon the Fifth Corps fell the chief burden of the pursuit, so far as the infantry was concerned, and our membership in that corps guaranteed us active participation in the work of the campaign.

From our camp near Hatcher's Run the sounds of the firing at Fort Stedman on March twenty-fifth were quite audible, and as usual at such times there were many rumors as to the extent and magnitude of the Confederate attack. The next morning we were aroused early and with the entire Fifth Corps started off toward the east, arriving at the

Gurley house about six o'clock. Here the corps halted for a short time and then our Division (the Second) and the Third Division were sent to the lines of the Ninth Corps to support them in an attempt to regain the works lost to the enemy the day before. At the same time the First Division was sent to the aid of the Second Corps where it was hotly engaged during the day. We reached the lines of the Ninth Corps and were held in reserve while that corps, under General Parke, vigorously attacked the Confederates and without our assistance recaptured Fort Stedman and an outer line of works as well. In the evening the regiment returned to camp without having been engaged with the enemy.

For two days more we lay in camp and then, on the morning of March twenty-ninth, the great movement to the westward, which was destined to involve us in days of hard fighting and tiresome marching, began. We broke camp at three A.M. and with the entire corps marched south through Arthur's Swamp. Our division was in the lead, as it had been on the occasion of the first great movement of the Army of the Potomac a year before, opening the campaign of 1864. Griffin's division followed us, while Crawford brought up the rear. The marching was very difficult for spring was fast coming on and added greatly to the marshy character of the ground over which we were moving. The country was of the forest kind common to Virginia and was well watered by swampy streams. The surface was level and the soil of clay, which, mixed with the abundant water, formed a sort of quicksand in which the hoofs of the horses and the wheels of the wagons and artillery found but little support. We crossed Hatcher's Run by fording and then proceeded to Rowanty Creek, where a few of the enemy's pickets were encountered but quickly dispersed. Crossing over the creek on Monk's Neck Bridge the column proceeded along the Old Stage and Vaughan roads until the Chapple house was reached, where we were about two miles from Dinwiddie Court House. With the head of the column, our regiment reached the latter place at about eight o'clock in the morning. Here we halted until noon, when General Warren was directed to return by the Vaughan road to the Quaker road, and thence by it to the Boydton plank road, to connect with the left of the Second Corps. When the corps started out this time the First Division led the march with our division following immediately after, and our brigade heading the division. The head of the column encountered a force of Confederates about a mile and a half from the junction of the Quaker and Boydton roads and a sharp engagement ensued. Our brigade was hurried to the assistance of the First Division and the enemy's line was speedily forced back to the intrenchments on the White Oak road.

We bivouacked in this vicinity on the night of the thirtieth, our division camping some distance down the Quaker road while the First and Third Divisions were near the junction of that road with the Boydton plank road. A heavy storm arose during the night, the rain falling in sheets and the wind howling through the trees and occasionally bringing one or two to earth with a crash due to the splintering of limbs and branches. We, however, were so fatigued by the day's marching that even this great "war of the elements" did not prevent our sleeping soundly despite the fact that we were exposed to its full force.

We were awakened early the next morning and hastily partook of a meager breakfast of coffee and hardtack. Our division received orders to reconnoiter the country lying between the Boydton plank road on the east, the White Oak road on the north, and a road running from Dinwiddie northward to the White Oak road, on the west. In doing this our brigade (the first) was sent out on a picket line connecting with the main line on the right and extending westward to the vicinity of the Dabney house on the White Oak road. General Ayres's reconnaissance and that of Bartlett's brigade of the First Division, which was made at the same time to the eastward, revealed the fact that the

19

Confederates had intrenched themselves in a line of works along the north side of the White Oak road. All operations that day were greatly hindered by the heavy rain which fell and by the swampy condition of the ground. Our division bivouacked in the vicinity of the Dabney house and our regiment was on picket duty during the afternoon and throughout the night of the thirtieth.

While on this picket line a peculiar incident took place, the true solution of which we were never able to find. Toward dusk a young lieutenant emerged from the woods in front of the enemy's works with quite a large company of men. They crossed the road with their guns trailing and came directly toward us. When about an eighth of a mile from our line the party halted and the officer, who was a handsome, well-built fellow, came forward. When within speaking distance of our line he stopped and asked whether we were Confederates or Yanks. The officer in command of our line at this point,[1] replied that we were Union men and just then a member of Company "A"[2] stepped out and leveling his gun at the officer said, "You're my prisoner." The lieutenant surrendered without a word and was taken to corps headquarters. As soon as his men saw that he was captured they turned and ran back into the woods. Not a shot had been fired during this time and we were at a loss to understand the meaning of the strange action on the part of the officer and his men. We, however, concluded that it had very likely been their intention to surrender the entire company, as such incidents were not infrequent during the closing days of the war.

The following morning General Ayres received orders to concentrate his command near the Dabney house, which he did, posting his men in a field lying just east of the house. The second brigade lay nearest the house, then the third brigade, and to the right the first brigade. Our regiment was recalled from the picket line and the One Hundred and Forti-

[1] Captain King.   [2] Thomas Wheeler.

eth New York took our place in front of the brigade. Our position was on a slight elevation commanding the White Oak road, on the other side of which, across an open field and about a half-mile distant, we could see the enemy and judged them to be in considerable force. As this White Oak road was the shortest route to Five Forks, an important strategic point, it was desirable to gain possession of it, and Warren accordingly commanded General Ayres to take the road and intrench a brigade upon it.

We were building our fires and spreading out our blankets preparatory to passing some time in this position when orders to fall in line were given. To our surprise, only our brigade, under Brevet Brigadier-General Winthrop, was ordered to advance, the other brigades of our division and a brigade of the Third Division being held in the rear as supports. We knew that we were outnumbered by the enemy, nevertheless had no alternative but to obey. We started out on the double-quick in line of battle. The Fifth New York was on the left, the Fifteenth New York Heavy Artillery (acting as infantry) in the center, and our regiment on the right. We passed through the pickets of the One Hundred and Fortieth New York and they fell back to let our line go ahead. The enemy outnumbered us ten to one and they gave it to us hot and heavy as we advanced. Through the heavy fire our brigade charged with unwavering and unbroken front. The enemy's fire wrought havoc with our line; men were falling on every side, but still we pressed forward. General Winthrop and our Colonel seemed to be everywhere leading and encouraging. On reaching within ten or fifteen yards of the enemy's position, two lines of battle, rising from their ambush, were hurled upon the thin and already weakened line of our brigade. The Fifth New York, which had struck the works on the left first, was hurled back by force of numbers, then the Fifteenth New York gave way, and finally our line on the right was struck and we retired in some confusion. General Winthrop worked gallantly in whipping the line into shape and although we were retreating it was done in good order. When we reached the line of our support, a brigade of the Third Division, this brigade merely fired one volley and then retired. The enemy had emerged from a strip of woods and had flanked the other brigades of Ayres's division so that his entire command was driven before the exulting Confederates. When the lines of the First Division were reached the corps reformed, and led by the First Division and supported by a portion of the Second Corps to the east, drove the enemy from their intrenchments on the White Oak road. [1]

Following this engagement at the White Oak Road the Fifth Corps remained massed near the Boydton plank road and prepared to pass the night there. During the night our division was ordered to go to the support of General Sheridan at Five Forks. Tired out as we were we reluctantly fell in line and midnight found us making another difficult night march, down the Boydton plank road toward Dinwiddie Court House.

If there ever was a dark night it was that night of March 31, 1865. It seemed literally impossible to see one's hand before one's face and we stumbled along in the darkness in a manner by no means calculated to raise our spirits. The enemy's cavalry were facing Sheridan at Dinwiddie Court House, so before we arrived there a staff officer from General Sheridan met our commander with instructions to turn off on a road leading west into a road leading from Dinwiddie to the White Oak road, and thus come upon the left and rear of the Confederates. As our division approached, just after daylight, the enemy hastily decamped. General Ayres did not deem it wise to follow, so ordered a halt and we secured several hours of much-needed rest.

At Sheridan's request the remainder of the Fifth Corps

---

[1] General Winthrop said in his report of this engagement: "The regiments of the brigade on this occasion distinguished themselves by their valor and discipline under circumstances peculiarly trying."

was brought down to his aid during the morning of April first and at noon he decided to attack, with the view of isolating the Confederates at this point from the main body of Lee's army, and either capturing the forces or driving them westward. General Warren was ordered to take position in such a manner as best to support the cavalry. Crawford's division took position on the right of the Gravelly Run Church road in such a manner that the center of his line would strike what was supposed to be the angle of the Confederate line and thus be the first to encounter their works. Griffin's division took position in the rear of Crawford, while Ayres's division (which was the smallest in the corps) was placed on the left of the road to engage the enemy in their front and prevent reinforcements being sent to the angle, which it was believed Crawford and Griffin were in a position to assault and carry. The line was to move forward as formed until it reached the White Oak road, when it was to swing around to the left until at right angles to that road. The country on which the operations were to be made was a rough wooded ground, cut by numerous ravines. By four o'clock in the afternoon the divisions were in position and the order to advance and attack was given. Meeting only a slight resistance from a thin skirmish line in his front on crossing the White Oak road, Warren came to the conclusion that the enemy's line of battle was in the edge of a dense wood some three hundred yards north of the road, and so continued his advance in the direction the line had started.

Our division, under Ayres, after crossing the road received a heavy musketry and artillery fire on our left, which at once showed that the enemy's intrenchments did not, as had been supposed, extend to anywhere near the Gravelly Run Church road, but were, in fact, about eight hundred yards west of it. Ayres's division had been advancing with the second and third brigades in two lines, our brigade in support, but as soon as General Ayres perceived the direction of the enemy's fire, he changed front to the left by facing the second brigade to the left and filing it in that direction. In order to save time, our brigade was thrown into the front line on the left of the second, bringing the third brigade up in support. After this change of front we pushed forward. Pressing down a hill to the edge of a swamp the enemy's intrenchments were discovered through a dense underbrush. Our brigade, which was leading, was met by a hot fire from the enemy. An abatis and slashings which the enemy had placed in their front further impeded our progress. Undismayed, however, by the hot fire, and unchecked by the obstacles in the way, we rushed upon the works and carried them. Our color-bearer[1] placed the regimental flag on the Confederate intrenchments and the regiment swarmed over after him. After a few moments the brigade quickly wheeled to the left upon the enemy's exposed flank and their utter and complete rout was effected. Deeds of real heroism were being performed on every side during the sharp hand-to-hand fighting. Here five or six men would crawl through some small opening in the brush and leap upon the Confederate works only to meet men equally brave and desperate in a life and death struggle. There a Union soldier sprang unaided on the breastworks and wrested a battle flag from its position or from the very hands of the color-bearer. Our men fought bravely, even ferociously, and pursued the flying enemy relentlessly. Just as we had reached the enemy's breastworks the brave General Winthrop, who had been leading the brigade, fell mortally wounded, his last words as they bore him from the field being full of cheer and encouragement to his men. But the battle was by no means over, for soon after we gained the works of the Confederates and had dislodged them an attack suddenly developed on our flank. For a moment we were bewildered and it seemed as though in the confusion the battle might be lost. The sweeping fire of the enemy struck many a brave fellow to earth. In our regiment Captain Thomas Wilson of Company "B" was

[1] Harvey Gifford, Sergeant Co. "K."

among those who fell. He was mortally wounded and was borne from the field. Defeat was averted largely through the efforts of Colonel Grindlay of the One Hundred and Forty-sixth, who assumed command of the brigade when Winthrop fell and who rallied the men for another attack against the unexpected force of the enemy. Again victory was on our side and again we drove the enemy from their position. Our brigade alone captured more than one thousand prisoners and four stands of colors.[1]

The Union forces were successful on all parts of the field. The error in regard to the position of the Confederate line had been fortunately discovered in time. To General Warren was due a large share of the credit for retrieving this error. He visited Crawford's and Griffin's division on the field of battle and turned them around in time to complete the destruction of the enemy's works which our division had so successfully begun. While leading the final charge which drove the enemy from their position Warren's horse was shot under him within a few paces from where the Confederates were making a last stand; an orderly by his side was killed, and Colonel Richardson of the Seventh Wisconsin who sprang between Warren and the enemy was severely wounded. In his *History of the Fifth Army Corps*, Colonel William H. Powell says, "Warren was now afoot, and had the bullet which pierced his noble horse pierced the heart of the man it would have been a trifle to the missile which pierced his brain an hour later." At the very close of the battle and with no reason apparent other than the excitement of conflict and the passion of the moment, General Sheridan in person directed General Griffin to take command

[1] Of these latter two were secured by men in our regiment, Corporal Thomas J. Murphy of Company "G" capturing one and Private David Edwards, Company "H," another. On recommendation of Colonel Grindlay and General Hayes these men later received medals of honor. Colonel Grindlay also was awarded a medal of honor for his conspicuous bravery in this engagement, thus bringing the total of such medals of honor up to three for our regiment out of sixteen which were awarded to the entire Fifth Corps throughout its service.

of the Fifth Corps and push the enemy down the White Oak road.

Thus the joy of victory was considerably dampened for the men of our corps by reason of the removal of their commander. Warren had endeared himself to the entire Union army by his great work at Gettysburg when he snatched Little Round Top from the hands of the triumphing Confederates and prevented what would almost certainly have been a Union defeat. As our corps commander, all his men had learned to love and respect him, for, although his bravery and gallantry were beyond all question, he was never impetuous to the point of rashness nor was he ever guilty of needlessly sacrificing his men to gain glory for himself.

After the rout of the enemy was found to be complete the entire corps and the cavalry followed them for some distance, cutting off and capturing many of them, until darkness put an end to the pursuit.

The Union victory at Five Forks was a crushing blow to General Lee. He had counted upon holding that position in order to cover his retreat westward. There was now nothing for him to do but to endeavor to escape by precipitous flight in the direction of the Alleghanies.

With the rest of the Fifth Corps our regiment remained on the battlefield of Five Forks during the morning of April second. We were engaged in caring for the wounded, burying the dead, and destroying the old arms which had been captured with the prisoners. Orders were then received by General Griffin to move northward and westward to assist in cutting off the retreating Army of Northern Virginia. The order to fall in line was given and shortly after the noon hour the entire corps was in motion. The First Division, now under command of General Bartlett, led the line of march and the other divisions followed in numerical order. We proceeded up the Ford's road, across Hatcher's Run to Cox's Station on the South Side Railroad, which is the junction with the Cox road running in the direction of Petersburg.

At this point the column was halted for a short time while Chamberlain's and Gregory's brigades of the First Division drove back a considerable force of the enemy which disputed the progress of the corps, also capturing a train of cars which happened to be at the station. At half-past three the march was resumed and we proceeded up the Cox road and the railroad for some distance, finally turning into the Namozine road, along which the command bivouacked for the night near Sutherland Station.

On the morning of the third the cavalry began a vigorous pursuit of the fleeing Confederates and the Fifth Corps immediately followed. The corps marched westward along the Namozine road, crossing Namozine Creek on a bridge which was improvised by the engineers. The skirmish line of the First Division which preceded the corps picked up many straggling Confederates who were concealed in the woods. As our regiment proceeded, we saw many evidences of the haste with which the enemy were moving, in abandoned wagons and pieces of artillery, while all along the road were scattered knapsacks, blankets, and even side arms which had been discarded in the flight. Most of the stragglers whom we picked up were in a pitiful condition from lack of food and the months of suffering and exposure they had endured. They were only too willing to give themselves up for the sake of something substantial to eat, in many cases the first they had had for days. When the head of the column reached Deep Creek a halt for the night was made, the corps stretching out along the sides of the creek and on the road. We were footsore and weary from our long day's march of about twenty-five miles and while some took advantage of the opportunity to bathe in the creek the great majority were content to "drop in their tracks" and sleep.

Another day of gruelling work was ahead of us. Between four and five o'clock on the morning of the fourth the corps resumed its march, going by way of Dennisville and arriving at Jetersville on the Danville Railroad at half after five in the afternoon. We had marched over twenty-five miles and were now in front of Lee's army, which was at Amelia Court House foraging for supplies. After a hasty supper we were set to work, as were all the men of the corps, throwing up breastworks and intrenchments in anticipation of an advance by the enemy along the railroad and with a view of holding them until the remainder of the Union army could come to the assistance of our corps. We worked far into the night and were then granted a few hours of much-needed sleep.

Early the next day (April fifth) the work of strengthening our position was resumed and the line was completed before noon. We remained quietly in position throughout the rest of the day and had an opportunity to recuperate somewhat from the strenuous work which we had just gone through. As the Second Corps did not begin to arrive at Jetersville until half after two that afternoon, it will be seen that our corps, supported only by the cavalry, held that position from the afternoon of the fourth until the afternoon of the fifth in face of the entire Confederate army. There is no doubt but that Lee missed a golden opportunity in not attacking the comparatively small force which opposed him and pursuing his march to Burkeville Junction, where he would have had two or three roads over which to escape.

General Lee, however, did not dare remain at Amelia Court House more than a day, for he was being hard pressed from every side. The presence of the Fifth and Second Corps at Jetersville determined him to strike due westward, toward Farmville. Accordingly, our corps received orders to go in pursuit and at six o'clock on the morning of the sixth our regiment, with the others of the Fifth Corps, was on the road running from Jetersville toward Amelia Court House. We turned off, after going a short distance, on to the Prideville road and thence by way of Paineville to the vicinity of Ligintown. During the entire day we were pushed to the utmost extent and the march was long and tiresome, covering in all thirty-two miles and being the longest march we made during our years of campaigning. All along the route we saw more and more evidences of the precipitate retreat of the enemy, and many prisoners were captured.

We were aroused by the sound of reveille at five-thirty the next morning and reluctantly started off again. This day's march, however, was comparatively light, being only eighteen miles, and, after crossing Bush Creek, we camped for the night near Prince Edward Court House. But still another day of hard marching was ahead of us. We started off early on the morning of the eighth and moving up the Lynchburg Railroad by way of Prospect Station in the rear of the Twenty-fourth Corps, continued on the march until two in the morning of the following day, finally bivouacking within three miles of Appomattox Court House, having covered a distance of over twenty-nine miles. Despite our extreme fatigue, we were given only two hours' sleep. At four in the morning the bugles sounded and the order to fall in line was given. The Confederates had attacked the cavalry which stood in their way between Appomattox Court House and their route westward and were driving the Union troops before them. The Twenty-fourth Corps was moving out to the support of the cavalry, when General Ayres, with our division of the Fifth Corps, moved rapidly on a parallel line toward the firing. The First Division came up promptly on the right and all immediately moved forward on the double-quick and attacked the enemy. Slowly but surely the Confederates were driven from the hills and through the town.

Our regiment, with the others of our division, was charging down a side hill and over a level field with the intention of dislodging the enemy from his position. Our skirmishers were in front of us, and as our line advanced, the skirmishers advanced. Finally the enemy was so strong that we passed over the line of skirmishers. There were two lines in the rear of us. We started with trailing arms when a white flag was seen approaching. We were waiting for the command to charge the batteries on the hill. On a portion of this hill was an apple orchard since become famous for its associations. We had gotten only halfway up the slope when the officer with the white flag rode down toward us. The command was then given to halt and we waited there in line of battle for perhaps an hour, when the command came to stack arms. Soon the command, "In place rest," was given, and the soldiers, still in battle line formation, stretched themselves at full length upon the ground, glad of a chance to rest. After a time, aides passed down the line giving the word that the Confederates had surrendered. The brave General Lee had at last realized that further resistance was futile and, not wishing to sacrifice more of his men, had intimated his willingness to accede to Grant's terms. When this became known, the bugles all along the line were blown, the drums rolled, and the men sprang to their feet. Discipline for the moment was forgotten. A general jubilee took place. Some of us gave expression to our feelings by running to an orchard near by and throwing our canteens, haversacks, and coats into the trees, grabbing each other and rolling over and over on the ground; some laughed, some cried, all were overjoyed.

This demonstration lasted for some time. At last after giving vent to our feelings and as evening came on, quiet was finally restored. In two hours half the men were sound asleep, lying where our line of battle extended; most of us so tired we fell asleep without waiting for supper or even to make a cup of coffee.

CHAPTER XXI

THE RETURN HOME

LEE'S surrender was a cause of great rejoicing throughout the army as well as throughout all the North. This meant that we would probably soon be sent home to our families and friends. For a time immediately after the surrender it seemed as though all things conspired to make life miserable for the troops in the field. The condition of the wagon roads prevented the transportation of more than the meagerest quantity of supplies, and for a few days none could come by train as the bridges had been destroyed. So for two days in spite of the foraging expeditions that sought to fill our larders, we existed upon scant rations, and on top of it all, it rained for a day and a night.

About noon on April fifteenth the corps began its homeward march. The roads were knee deep with mud and our bedraggled appearance must have resembled the retreat of a defeated army, rather than an army that had participated in a great victory. We were half famished when the march began but were hopeful of meeting a train carrying provisions. but none came our way that first day. Many were the imprecations heaped upon the commissary department, the condition of the roads, and any and every thing which seemed to us to contribute in any way to our plight. Soon after dark the order was given to stack arms and break ranks for the night. Throughout the night it rained incessantly and the next day was cold and raw. It, however, brought relief in the form of a train-load of food for the corps which satisfied for a time the appetites of these thousands of hungry men. About noon we crossed the Appomattox River on a temporary bridge and soon reached the village of Farmville. While waiting here a dispatch was received at four o'clock in the afternoon announcing the assassination of President Lincoln.

On Monday, the seventeenth, the march was resumed by way of Burkeville and thence to Little Sandy Run. At this point, with the entire corps, we remained in camp until seven o'clock on the morning of the twentieth, when the march was continued to Nottoway Court House. Headquarters were established at this place and the corps relieved the Ninth Corps in guarding the railroad from Burkeville to Petersburg. All round about us the country gave every evidence of the ravages of war, and it seemed as though everything edible, whether in the form of plant or animal, had been taken by the Confederates.

With the other regiments of our corps we remained on this duty until May first, when the corps proceeded in the direction of Petersburg. After marches varying from eighteen to twenty-three miles per day we reached that city. Our former corps commander, General Warren, was acting as Governor of the "Cockade City" under orders from General Grant, and General Griffin, who had succeeded him, invited Warren to extend to his late corps the honor of a public review. General Warren accepted the suggestion and preparations were made accordingly. Each regiment was at its best for this occasion and as it passed the reviewing stand in front of the Bolingbroke House, gave cheer after cheer for our gallant former commander.

After passing through Petersburg the corps moved up toward Richmond, reaching there on May sixth. Here the entire Army of the Potomac had been assembled and a review was held through the streets of the city, at which General Halleck presided. The march was then continued and on the afternoon of the twelfth the white dome of the Capitol at

Washington was sighted. We went into camp about one mile from Falls Station on the Alexandria Railroad as members of the Fifth Corps for the last time. Here, also, for the first time, we saw General Sherman's army, which arrived a few days later and encamped on the heights above Alexandria.

On May twenty-fourth we took part in the Grand Review of the armies of Sherman and Meade which was held in the city of Washington. The two magnificent bodies of men passed through the streets, which were gorgeously decorated, and amidst the wildest enthusiasm were reviewed by President Johnson and his Cabinet, by the representatives of foreign governments, and by hundreds of thousands of people who had come to witness the imposing spectacle. Our brigade, clad entirely in zouave uniforms, was highly complimented from all sides, and our regiment, now numbering barely two hundred men, with our torn and tattered battle flag, was the subject of much comment. From our places in the ranks some of us could hear remarks by the bystanders as to how small the regiment was and how torn the flag, and our hearts swelled with enthusiasm and pride. Many friends and a few former comrades greeted us as we passed by in the great pageant. Now and then one of the boys would be attracted by a shout from someone among the crowds that lined the streets and would turn to recognize a relative, a friend, or perhaps a former brother-in-arms who had been compelled by wounds or sickness to retire from active service, but who had come to see the gallant "Boys in Blue" go by. In that moment of our supreme triumph those who had been with us when we marched to the front but who had been lost to us forever during the rigors of the long war were not forgotten. Mingled with the great joy which the occasion inspired was the great sorrow and regret that they could not be with us to share it. That we had survived while they had perished we had come to regard as one of those great mysteries which it was never given for man to understand.

That evening we returned to our camp on the other side

of the Potomac, rejoicing in the expectation of a speedy muster-out and a return to our homes. In this we were greatly disappointed, for many weeks passed before the army was finally disbanded. On June twenty-eighth, General Meade took leave of the Army of the Potomac, which he had commanded for two years. At the same time the regiments still to be mustered out were divided into three provisional corps, numbered First, Second, and Third and composed of the men of the Sixth, Second, and Fifth Army Corps, respectively.

This delay seemed unnecessary to us as we were all anxious to leave for home. One night during this period a great illumination and torchlight procession was organized and the men marched to each of the commanders' headquarters in succession and called upon them for speeches. Candles were lighted and stuck on the ends of bayonets, and the spectacle of some eighty thousand men thus equipped was indeed a most imposing one.

Finally the men grew so impatient that the discontent throughout the army alarmed the authorities at Washington and they took precautions against a possible invasion of the city by posting guards around the camp and covering the Long Bridge by a battery of artillery. On July fourth our regiment, with several others, was called upon to do guard duty at the Virginia side of the bridge in anticipation of a possible attempt on the part of the men of one of the other provisional corps to cross it. We, however, made it known to our officers that if any such attempt did take place we would not fire a single shot to prevent it. Fortunately, quiet was restored by the assurance that deliverance from the tiresome wait was near at hand.

On July sixteenth, the welcome news of our dismissal came at last, and the regiment was mustered out of the service of the United States. Three more days passed before it was possible to procure a train on which to take the regiment homeward, but on July nineteenth we at last set out.

Mirth and hilarity ran high and were manifested in various ways as each puff of the little engine brought us so much nearer our destination. We arrived at Syracuse by way of Elmira and Binghamton at noon, Thursday, July twentieth, and immediately went into camp on the ground which had been used by the Onondaga County regiments as a recruiting camp before leaving for the front.

We were soon to see our home county once more, for soon after our arrival at Syracuse we received word that a reception in our honor was to be held in Utica on Saturday, the twenty-second. We, therefore, spent the next day in cleaning up our uniforms and guns and in making our personal appearance as neat as possible. To our intense gratification, the day set for the occasion was a bright and beautiful one. We boarded the train at Syracuse in the morning and just a few minutes before ten o'clock arrived at Utica. An immense crowd greeted us at the station and followed us to Baggs's Square, where the regimental line was soon formed. The Forty-fifth Regiment of State Militia had been drawn up in line on both sides of Genesee Street and our regiment, having formed, passed it in review until the head of the column was reached. Then halting, the escort in turn passed before us. The procession was then made up in the following order:

Marshal F. X. Meyers, Lieutenant-Colonel of One Hundred and Seventeenth Regiment, and Aides.
Utica Brass Band
Colonel I. J. Gray and Staff,
Forty-fifth Regiment National Guards
Utica Fire Department
Reception Committee in Carriages
Veterans of other Oneida County Regiments
Drum Corps of the One Hundred and Forty-sixth Regiment, led by Wm. B. Chandler
Colonel James Grindlay and Staff
One Hundred and Forty-sixth Regiment
Horses of Colonel D. T. Jenkins and Lieut.-Colonel H. H. Curran

The city, which we were so glad to see again, presented a holiday appearance. Flags and pennants floated in the breeze, while the people turned out in force and throughout the day made the streets lively with their presence. The triumphal arch at Genesee Street Bridge bore inscriptions to the war-worn and weary Oneida County soldiers, and a new phrase, "Welcome Home," was painted thereon in our honor.

Our regiment turned out about 120 strong and clad in our gay zouave uniforms we were proudly conscious of ourselves as the heroes of the day. As the procession moved, the City Hall bell was rung constantly and this together with the crowds of people made the scene a lively one. The route taken was up Genesee Street to Fayette, to Varick, to Rutger, to John, to Chancellor Square. At this latter place what many considered the best treat of all awaited us, in the form of a score of tables fairly "groaning" with good things to eat which the ladies of the city had prepared for us. The women themselves were present and were busy making the final preparations as we drew in sight. Preceded by the carriage containing Judge Bacon, the orator of the day, we marched into the square. When we were properly drawn up in line fronting the carriage, Hon. Alrich Hubbell, Chairman of the Reception Committee, welcomed us home in a few well-chosen words and then introduced Judge Bacon. The latter's welcoming address was then delivered and was substantially as follows:

Colonel Grindlay, Officers, and you, my brave Fellow-soldiers: I esteem it a great honor that I have been permitted to address a word of welcome to you on your return home from your duty in the field. Never before have I felt able to command myself sufficiently to witness the return of any Oneida County regiment. Yet I have deeply sympathized with them all. I desired that the duty should fall upon some other one. I feel in respect to you almost the interest of a father in his children, for it fell to my duty in collusion with two other gentlemen who are here present to aid in organizing this Oneida County regiment *par excellence,* I may call it. Well do I remember that bright September day when it was my privilege to introduce to you your new Colonel and also your Lieutenant-Colonel and to give you a few words of counsel and encouragement, just as you were prepared to go to the front and endure the perils of war. I said to the Colonel, "Here are the stalwart men of Oneida, who have come from their farms and workshops and homes, and they are going to fight. Where you lead they will follow." Thank God! They did follow, to victory, and these few are permitted to return. I looked upon eight hundred men and I knew that many of them would go never to return as sad experience afterwards taught me.

You had the peculiar happiness of being commanded by one who had an honorable name, and he, now that the war is ended, stands high upon the roll of fame. I dare not ask myself how many who then heard me listen to me now. Of thirty-eight officers only five now return.

It is not necessary to recount your achievements; Oneida County knows them by heart. Your tattered ensign tells the story. Your other flag is covered all over with the names of your battles. Three months after you entered the service you were christened on the bloody field of Fredericksburg. Chancellorsville soon followed when our glories were dimmed, but how bright were they when Gettysburg burst upon the country. There you did valiant service. (Applause.) Subsequently you were enrolled in the army of that grand old soldier, Grant, and "fought it out on that line all summer," and through the winter. I need not recount those battles. Twenty-two are inscribed on the folds of that flag. You fought well and you had heavy losses.

I might call the roll of your dead heroes, your Jenkins, your Curran, your Wilson, your Buckingham, and the others who sealed their devotion to their country with their blood. Let me say it to his honor, that Colonel Jenkins, who, with his regiment, was on the skirmish line in too safe a place to suit him, sent forward for permission to lead his regiment into action. His request was granted and he went out and met the fatal bullet. He rests in an honored grave. I cannot speak of Curran and those other noble men. I regard them as brethren, and almost as children. And their devoted comrades, where are they? They lie in unknown graves. It is human to send up the aspiration, "Let me die among my kindred and be buried there." They lie on the battlefield. No human eye can see them, and only the Omniscient God knows their resting-place. His eye alone looks upon them. No hand of affection plants flowers on their graves, but their names will never be forgotten.

And now, my brave fellow-soldiers, you come back to us, and rejoice with us in a reunited country. You never lost faith in the perpetuity of our glorious government nor in your leaders, nor did we; but there were among us, and there are even now those who called the war a failure, "we couldn't conquer the South." The sequel shows that you and we were right. Those men may come in by a very late conversion, but not by the regeneration of a first birth.

Think of the contrast between this scene and those scenes you have so lately passed through. This is glorious old Oneida County and the grand old Empire State. They were never more beautiful than now. The Almighty has scattered blessing around us. The hills and vales and all nature are rejoicing, and freedom, prosperity, and unity remain. While we rejoice we should remember that many a household in Oneida County is clad in sackcloth because of their friends who are not, and you will find many places vacant on your return. The sod covers many a once familiar face. True it is

"There is no household without one vacant chair,
    No flock, however tended, but one is missing there."[1]

Those are sad thoughts but we must forget them and rejoice with you. We welcome you back to your firesides and the hearts of your countrymen. Your kind, your loyal countrywomen—blessing on them, they are loyal—have provided you a feast. Not raw pork and hardtack, either. They have a beautiful table. Go and devour its contents and show that while vailant in the field you are not wanting at the trencher.

I should like to speak of other things. My heart is full. I could go on by the hour telling what I know of you and your

[1] Judge Bacon's only son, a lieutenant in the Twenty-sixth New York Infantry, was killed while under a flag of truce between the lines at Fredericksburg.

achievements. Brave officers and men, let the unknown demi-gods who inhabit your Valhalla be ever freshly remembered. To you that survive I bid a hearty welcome. By your determination, endurance, fidelity, and perseverance you have acquired a new claim to our love and regard. Only last night a gentleman of this city, distinguished by his loyalty, said to me, "The men who come to us now are men who have grown up among the scenes of war to a sterling manhood. They will make good citizens." It is a majestic spectacle to see five hundred thousand discharged soldiers returning home. Their future is full of brightness, as is that of their disenthralled country. They and you have assisted in giving freedom to four millions of your race. God smiled upon the effort and sainted Abraham Lincoln was his instrument in accomplishing the grand result. In the coming days we shall rejoice in a united free republic, in all the broad borders of which the sun looks down upon no slave. Welcome to your native county, and the joys and privileges of citizenship. Welcome to a useful, happy life, and to a blessed life of immortality hereafter.

At the conclusion of the Judge's remarks our Colonel came forward and extended, in a fitting manner, the sincere thanks of himself and the regiment for the cordial welcome extended us. The band then struck up the national air, and one enthusiast immediately proposed three cheers and a tiger for "The Fighting Regiment—the One Hundred and Forty-sixth," in which the crowd joined heartily.

After the announcement by Chairman Hubbell that a zouave drill would take place in the park at three o'clock, we attacked the well-laden tables. Accustomed to getting the best of all contests, now, for once in our career, we were beaten. We struggled manfully, but the hospitality of the citizens of Utica was too great—we could not clear the tables. Many were the times recalled when we should have been overjoyed to have had but a small portion of the delectable good things which were now set before us, but it was a time for rejoicing rather than regrets and a jovial spirit of good-fellowship prevailed.

After a short rest, which was absolutely necessary for each and every one of us, we took part in a zouave drill before a large crowd of spectators who jammed the square to overflowing. Captain "Larry" Fitzpatrick led the bayonet exercises in capital style. Our years of exposure had hardened us and days of practice had made us proficient, and many compliments on our quickness and agility were given us.

At the conclusion of the drill three-day furloughs were granted by Colonel Grindlay to all who desired them, which was the same as announcing a furlough for the entire regiment. On Tuesday morning the boys returned to the camp at Syracuse and the next day we were paid off and mustered out of service. The great majority of us took advantage of the offer to keep our muskets and accouterments on paying $6.00, and we were also allowed to retain our knapsacks, haversacks, and canteens.

Thus was the career of the One Hundred and Forty-sixth New York Volunteers ended. It had been a career of which we had good reason to be proud, a career of gallant and arduous service in the hardest campaigns of the War of the Rebellion.

MEMBERS OF ONE HUNDRED AND FORTY-SIXTH REGIMENT, NEW YORK VOLUNTEERS

ORIGINAL

AGNE, FREDERICK J.—Age, 21 years. Enlisted, August 27, 1862, at Utica, to serve three years; mustered in as private, Co. F, October 10, 1862; promoted corporal, no date; killed in action, May 5, 1864, at the Wilderness, Va.

AITKEN, WILLIAM.—Age, 44 years. Enlisted, September 1, 1862, at Kirkland, to serve three years; mustered in as private, Co. G, October 10, 1862; mustered out with company, July 16, 1865, near Washington, D. C.

ALDEN, SPENCER B.—Age, 39 years. Enrolled, August 20, 1862, at Utica, to serve three years; mustered in as second lieutenant, Co. C, October 10, 1862; discharged, January 10, 1863, near Falmouth, Va.

Commissioned second lieutenant, November 3, 1862, with rank from September 3, 1862, original.

ALLEN, CHARLES F.—Age 21 years. Enlisted, August 26, 1862, at Augusta, to serve three years; mustered in as private, Co. E, October 10, 1862; discharged for disability, February 11, 1863.

ALLEN, CLIFFORD.—Age, 35 years. Enlisted, August 26, 1862, at Utica, to serve three years; mustered in as private, Co. C, October 10, 1862; mustered out, May 18, 1865, at Arlington Heights, Va.

ALLEN, GEORGE H.—Age, 20 years. Enlisted, August 29, 1862, at Augusta, to serve three years; mustered in as corporal, Co. G, October 10, 1862; promoted sergeant, March 9, 1863; captured in action, May 5, 1864, at the Wilderness, Va.; no further record.

ALLEN, OSCAR L.—Age, 21 years. Enlisted, September 4, 1862, at Vienna, to serve three years; mustered in as private, Co. I, October 10, 1862; mustered out, June 29, 1865, at Philadelphia, Pa.

AMIDON, OTHELLO H.—Age, 18 years. Enlisted, August 16, 1862, at Rome, to serve three years; mustered in as corporal, Co. B, October 10, 1862; returned to ranks, November 21, 1862; wounded in action, May 5, 1864, at the Wilderness, Va.; again promoted corporal, May 5, 1865; mustered out with company, July 16, 1865, near Washington, D. C.

AMIDON, SAMUEL.—Age, 26 years. Enlisted, August 26, 1862, at Paris, to serve three years; mustered in as private, Co. K, October 10, 1862; promoted corporal, no date; discharged, May 29, 1865. Died in 1895.

ANDERSON, JOHN M.—Age, 44 years. Enlisted, August 21, 1862, at Utica, to serve three years; mustered in as private, Co. C, October 10, 1862; transferred to Veteran Reserve Corps, September 2, 1863; mustered out therefrom as of Second Battalion, August 18, 1865, at Washington, D. C.

ARMSTRONG, JESSE J.—Age, 32 years. Enrolled, September 3, 1862, at Rome, to serve three years; mustered in as captain, Co. B, October 10, 1862; as lieutenant-colonel, October 23, 1863; discharged, April 1, 1864; commissioned captain, November 3, 1862, with rank from September 3, 1862, original; lieutenant-colonel, October 6, 1863, with rank from September 23, 1863, vice W. L. Corning, discharged.

ARNOLD, MARCUS J.—Age, 20 years. Enlisted, August 30, 1862, at Trenton, to serve three years; mustered in as private, Co. I, October 10, 1862; died of disease, December 14, 1862, at Falmouth, Va.

ASH, ROBERT.—Age 44 years. Enlisted, August 22, 1862, at Vernon, to serve three years; mustered in as private, Co. B, October 10, 1862; transferred to Veteran Reserve Corps, December 9, 1863.

ASHFORTH, G. ELIAS.—Age, 20 years. Enlisted, August 27, 1862, at Vernon, to serve three years; mustered in as private, Co. B, October 10, 1862; captured and paroled, no dates; absent, sick, since July 26, 1864; no further record.

ASHFORTH, GEORGE G.—Age, 23 years. Enlisted, August 27, 1862, at Vernon, to serve three years; mustered in as private, Co. B, October 10, 1862; killed in action, May 5, 1864, at the Wilderness, Va.

ASHLEY, CHARLES G.—Age, 18 years. Enlisted, September 1, 1862, at Kirkland, to serve three years; mustered in as private, Co. G, October 10, 1862; captured in action, November 27, 1863, at Mine Run, Va.; died of disease, June 3, 1865, at Andersonville, Ga.

ASHTNEW, ADAM.—Age, 20 years. Enlisted, August 30, 1862, at Vernon, to serve three years; mustered in as private, Co. B, October 10, 1862, discharged for disability, April 3, 1863, near Falmouth, Va.; also borne as Ashtenan.

AUBIN, FRANCIS.—Age, 44 years. Enlisted, August 21, 1862, at Boonville, to serve three years; mustered in as private, Co. D, October 10, 1862; transferred to Veteran Reserve Corps, September 3, 1863.

AVERY, GERRIT S.—Age, 19 years. Enlisted, August 29, 1862, at Boonville, to serve three years; mustered in as private, Co. D, October 10, 1862; discharged for disability, February 12, 1864, at hospital, Washington, D. C.

AVERY, JARED S.—Age, 22 years. Enlisted, September 6, 1862, at Paris, to serve three years; mustered in as private, Co. K, October 10, 1862; discharged for disability, June 20, 1863.

AVERY, JOHN.—Age, 27 years. Enlisted, August 30, 1862, at Boonville, to serve three years; mustered in as private, Co. D, October 10, 1862; captured in action, June 2, 1864, at Bethesda Church, Va.; paroled, no date; mustered out, June 24, 1865, at New York City.

BABCOCK, ELI A.—Age, 18 years. Enlisted, September 6, 1862, at Bridgewater, to serve three years; mustered in as private, Co. G, October 10, 1862; discharged for disability, May 28, 1865, at hospital. Died at Babcock Hill, N. Y., in 1911.

BAILEY, JOHN H.—Age, 21 years. Enlisted, October 8, 1862, at Rome, to serve three years; mustered in as private, Co. H, October 10, 1862; promoted sergeant, no date; mustered out with company, July 16, 1865, near Washington, D. C. Died April 16, 1912, at New York City.

BAKER, FREDERICK.—Age, 24 years. Enlisted, September 1, 1862, at Sangerfield, to serve three years; mustered in as private, Co. H, October 10, 1862; captured in action, November 28, 1863, at Mine Run, Va.; released, April 21, 1865, at Andersonville, Ga.; mustered out, June 22, 1865, at New York City.

BAKER, HENRY W.—Age, 28 years. Enlisted, August 27, 1862, at Utica, to serve three years; mustered in as private, Co. F, October 10, 1862; captured in action, May 5, 1864, at the Wilderness, Va.; died, no date, at Andersonville, Ga.

BAKER, JOHN.—Age, 21 years. Enlisted, October 2, 1862, at Rome, to serve three years; mustered in as private, Co. H, October 10, 1862; mustered out with company, July 16, 1865, near Washington, D. C.

BALIS, CHARLES R.—Age, 22 years. Enlisted, August 28, 1862, at Utica, to serve three years; mustered in as private, Co. A, October 10, 1862; promoted corporal and returned to ranks, no dates.

BALL, LYSANDER C.—Age, 30 years. Enlisted, September 6, 1862, at Western, to serve three years; mustered in as private, Co. I, October 10, 1862; mustered out with company, July 16, 1865, near Washington, D. C.

BALLOU, WALTER.—Age, 23 years. Enrolled, September 8, 1862, at Boonville, to serve three years; mustered in as first lieutenant, Co. D, October 7, 1862; discharged, December 28, 1862, near Potomac Creek, Va.; commissioned first lieutenant, November 3, 1862, with rank from September 8, 1862, original. Died, April 8, 1899.

BARBER, ORANGE.—Age, 33 years. Enlisted, August 22, 1862, at Paris, to serve three years; mustered in as private, Co. K, October 10, 1862.

BARDWELL ELIAS.—Age, 42 years. Enlisted, September 5, 1862, at Remsen, to serve three years; mustered in as private, Co. I, October 10, 1862; discharged, April 22, 1863.

BARKER, ORVILLE J.—Age, 18 years. Enlisted, August 29, 1862, at Augusta, to serve three years; mustered in as private, Co. G, October 10, 1862; promoted corporal, no date;

captured in action, May 5, 1864, at the Wilderness, Va.;
paroled, no date; discharged, June 14, 1865. Born at
Augusta, N. Y., Nov. 8, 1843; died at Clark's Mills, N. Y.,
May 28, 1913; killed by street car.

BARNES, ABIJAH W.—Age, 25 years. Enlisted, August 28,
1862, at Boonville, to serve three years; mustered in as
private, Co. D, October 10, 1862; promoted sergeant and
captured, no dates; died of disease, March 27, 1865, at
Salisbury, S. C.

BARNES, EZRA C.—Age, 33 years. Enlisted, August 29, 1862,
at Boonville, to serve three years; mustered in as wagoner,
Co. D, October 10, 1862; returned to company as a private,
no date.

BARNES, ISAAC W.—Age, 31 years. Enlisted, August 29, 1862,
at Boonville, to serve three years; mustered in as private,
Co. D, October 10, 1862; discharged for disability, January
16, 1863, at hospital, near Falmouth, Va.

BARNES, JAMES A.—Age, 33 years. Enlisted, September 6,
1862, at Bridgewater, to serve three years; mustered in as
private, Co. G, October 10, 1862; captured in action, March
31, 1865, at White Oak Ridge, Va.; no further record.

BARRETT, DANIEL S.—Age, 26 years. Enlisted, August 25,
1862, at Utica, to serve three years; mustered in as private,
Co. C, October 10, 1862; discharged for disability, July 10,
1863, at Alexandria, Va.

BASS, EDGAR C.—Age, — years. Enrolled at Rome to serve
three years, and mustered in as assistant surgeon, September
3, 1862; discharged, August 17, 1863.

Commissioned assistant surgeon, November 3, 1862,
with rank from September 1, 1862, original.

BATES, CHESTER.—Age, 18 years. Enlisted, August 29, 1862,
at Boonville, to serve three years; mustered in as private,
Co. D, October 10, 1862; promoted corporal, May 16, 1865;
mustered out with company, July 16, 1865, near Washington,
D. C., as Bales.

BATES, GEORGE W.—Age, 28 years. Enlisted, August 26, 1862,
at Paris, to serve three years; mustered in as private, Co.
K, October 10, 1862; promoted corporal and returned to
ranks, no dates; mustered out with company, July 16, 1865,
near Washington, D. C.

BATES, NORMAN.—Age, 20 years. Enlisted, August 29, 1862, at Boonville, to serve three years; mustered in as private, Co. D, October 10, 1862; mustered out with company, July 16, 1865, near Washington, D. C.

BECK, HEINRICH.—Age, 32 years. Enlisted, August 30, 1862, at Utica, to serve three years; mustered in as private, Co. F, October 10, 1862.

BECKER, VAN VRANKEN.—Age, 19 years. Enlisted, September 3, 1862, at Camden, to serve three years; mustered in as corporal, Co. E, October 10, 1862; returned to ranks, no date; discharged for disability, September 6, 1863, at Washington, D. C.

BECKWITH, ALMON.—Age, 36 years. Enlisted, August 28, 1862, at Annsville, to serve three years; mustered in as private, Co. B, October 10, 1862; discharged for disability, November 4, 1863, at Washington, D. C. Died at Rome, N. Y., in 1898.

BECKWITH, SAMUEL B.—Age, 40 years. Enlisted, August 29, 1862, at Annsville, to serve three years; mustered in as private, Co. B, October 10, 1862; discharged for disability, July 15, 1863.

BECKWITH, WILLIAM W.—Age, 23 years. Enlisted, August 29, 1862, at Annsville, to serve three years; mustered in as private, Co. B, October 10, 1862; transferred to Veteran Reserve Corps, February 28, 1865; mustered out as of Co. E, Fourteenth Regiment, Veteran Reserve Corps, July 31, 1865, at Washington, D. C.

BEDIMAH, HOSEA.—Age, 18 years. Enlisted, August 29, 1862, at Boonville, to serve three years; mustered in as private, Co. D, October 10, 1862; discharged for disability, November 27, 1862, at Washington, D. C.

BELL, RICHARD.—Age, 38 years. Enlisted, August 30, 1862, at Utica, to serve three years; mustered in as private, Co. A, October 10, 1862; mustered out with company, July 16, 1865, near Washington, D. C.

BELLINGER, GEORGE.—Age, 26 years. Enlisted, August 28, 1862, at Boonville, to serve three years; mustered in as corporal, Co. D, October 10, 1862; returned to ranks, no date; transferred to Veteran Reserve Corps, March 15, 1865. Died May 1, 1899.

BENEDICT, CHARLES G.—Age, 21 years. Enlisted, August 25, 1862, at Rome, to serve three years; mustered in as corporal, Co. B, October 10, 1862; returned to ranks, no date; discharged for disability, April 2, 1863, at Utica, N. Y.

BENEDICT, JAMES E.—Age, 29 years. Enlisted, August 25, 1862, at Rome, to serve three years; mustered in as private, Co. F, October 10, 1862.

BENNETT, ALEXANDER S.—Age, 19 years. Enlisted, August 28, 1862, at Boonville, to serve three years; mustered in as private, Co. D, October 10, 1862; transferred to Veteran Reserve Corps, January 23, 1864; mustered out therefrom as of One Hundred and Thirty-second Company, Second Battalion, July 8, 1865, at Harpers Ferry, Va.

BENNETT, SEYMOUR.—Age, 22 years. Enlisted, September 1, 1862, at Kirkland, to serve three years; mustered in as private, Co. G, October 10, 1862; absent, sick in hospital, since November 21, 1863; no further record.

BERGEE, ABRAM.—Age, 23 years. Enlisted, August 27, 1862, at Annsville, to serve three years; mustered in as private, Co. F, October 10, 1862; promoted corporal, October 1, 1864; sergeant, July 1, 1865; mustered out with company, July 16, 1865, near Washington, D. C.; also borne as Burgee.

BERNBECK, JOSEPH.—Age, 28 years. Enlisted, August 26, 1862, at Utica, to serve three years; mustered in as private, Co. C, October 10, 1862; also borne as Burnbeck.

BERRY, JR., JOHN H.—Age, 37 years. Enlisted, August 21, 1862, at Steuben, to serve three years; mustered in as private, Co. I, October 10, 1862; captured in action, May 5, 1864, at the Wilderness, Va.; paroled, no date; discharged for disability, May 31, 1865.

BESSEE, ROLLO.—Age, 18 years. Enlisted, August 30, 1862, at Westmoreland, to serve three years; mustered in as musician, Co. I, October 10, 1862; transferred to Veteran Reserve Corps, November 1, 1863; mustered out as of Co. E, Nineteenth Regiment, Veteran Reserve Corps, July 13, 1865, at Elmira, N. Y.

BIRDSELL, IRVING A.—Age, 23 years. Enlisted, September 1, 1862, at Trenton, to serve three years; mustered in as private, Co. I, October 10, 1862; promoted corporal, no date; died of disease, January 9, 1863, at hospital, Washington, D. C.

BISHOP, JOHN.—Age 24 years. Enlisted, August 28, 1862, at Boonville, to serve three years; mustered in as corporal, Co. D, October 10, 1862; returned to ranks, no date; also borne as Bischoff.

BLAKE, JAMES.—Age, 35 years. Enlisted, August 31, 1862, at Westmoreland, to serve three years; mustered in as private, Co. I, October 10, 1862; discharged for disability, January 16, 1863, at camp, near Potomac Creek, Va.

BLAKE, JR., PETER.—Age, 19 years. Enlisted, September 8, 1862, at Clinton, to serve three years; mustered in as private, Co. E, October 10, 1862; promoted corporal, January, 1863; sergeant, November 22, 1863; captured in action, May 5, 1864, at the Wilderness, Va.; paroled, December 16, 1864; promoted first sergeant, April 1, 1865; mustered out with company, July 16, 1865, near Washington, D. C.

Commissioned (not mustered) second lieutenant, June 17, 1865, with rank from February 1, 1865, vice T. Wheeler not mustered.

BLAKEMAN, GEORGE W.—Age, 25 years. Enlisted, August 21, 1862, at Utica, to serve three years; mustered in as private, Co. C, October 10, 1862; promoted corporal and returned to ranks, no dates; discharged, June 2, 1865, at Washington, D. C.

BLANCHARD, DANIEL.—Age, 21 years. Enlisted, August 27, 1862, at Kirkland, to serve three years; mustered in as private, Co. G, October 10, 1862; captured in action, May 5, 1864, at the Wilderness, Va.; paroled, no date; mustered out with company, July 16, 1865, near Washington, D. C. Died at Clinton, N. Y., in 1911.

BOLL, FREDERICK.—Age, 44 years. Enlisted, August 30, 1862, at Florence, to serve three years; mustered in as private, Co. F, October 10, 1862; discharged for disability, May 9, 1863, at Washington, D. C.

BONFOY, BENJAMIN F.—Age, 22 years. Enlisted, September 6, 1862, at Bridgewater, to serve three years; mustered in as private, Co. G, October 10, 1862; discharged for disability, March 12, 1863, near Falmouth, Va. Died in 1903.

BOTT, NICHOLAUS.—Age, 44 years. Enlisted, September 3, 1862, at Camden, to serve three years; mustered in as private, Co. E, October 10, 1862; discharged for disability, September 20, 1864, at Washington, D. C.

BOWERS, FRANCIS.—Age, 18 years. Enlisted, September 1, 1862, at Utica, to serve three years; mustered in as private, Co. C, October 10, 1862; mustered out with company, July 16, 1865, near Washington, D. C.

BREISH, JACOB.—Age, 22 years. Enlisted, August 22, 1862, at Utica, to serve three years; mustered in as private, Co. A, October 10, 1862; died of disease, June 2, 1863, in Regimental Hospital, near Falmouth, Va.; also borne as Brash.

BRIGHT, JOHN.—Age, 20 years. Enlisted, August 23, 1862, at Utica, to serve three years; mustered in as private, Co. A, October 10, 1862; wounded in action, May 3, 1863, at Chancellorsville, Va.; transferred to Veteran Reserve Corps, April 2, 1864; promoted corporal, January 18, 1865; mustered out as of Co. G, Ninth Regiment Veteran Reserve Corps, July 15, 1865, at Washington, D. C.

BRIGHT, WILLIAM.—Age, 18 years. Enlisted, August 23, 1862, at Utica, to serve three years; mustered in as private, Co. A, October 10, 1862; promoted corporal, no date; sergeant, March 1, 1865; mustered out with company, July 16, 1865, near Washington, D. C.

BROMILY, WILLIAM.—Age, 29 years. Enlisted, September 6, 1862, at Utica, to serve three years; mustered in as private, Co. H, October 10, 1862; promoted corporal, no date; sergeant, June 1, 1865; mustered out with company, July 16, 1865, near Washington, D. C.; also borne as Bromley.

BROOKS, JOHN.—Age, 30 years. Enlisted, August 27, 1862, at Boonville, to serve three years; mustered in as private, Co. D, October 10, 1862.

BROOKS, ROBERT P.—Age, 43 years. Enlisted, August 27, 1862, at Boonville, to serve three years; mustered in as sergeant, Co. D, October 10, 1862; returned to ranks, no date; discharged for disability, March 1, 1863, at hospital, Washington, D. C.

BROWER, LORENZO.—Age, 22 years. Enlisted, August 29, 1862, at Lee, to serve three years; mustered in as private, Co. F, October 10, 1862; captured in action, May 5, 1864. at the Wilderness, Va.; died of disease, November 26, 1864, at Florence, S. C.

BROWN, CHARLES E.—Age, 20 years. Enlisted, September 6, 1862, at Trenton, to serve three years; mustered in as corporal, Co. D, October 10, 1862; returned to ranks, no date; discharged for disability, March 12, 1863, near Falmouth, Va.

BROWN, HARVEY.—Age, 32 years. Enlisted, August 28, 1862, at Camden, to serve three years; mustered in as private, Co. E, October 10, 1862.

BROWN, THOMAS.—Age, 18 years. Enlisted, August 31, 1862, at Camden, to serve three years; mustered in as private, Co. E, October 10, 1862; promoted corporal, October 25, 1863; captured in action, May 5, 1864, at the Wilderness, Va.; paroled, December 16, 1864, at Andersonville, Ga.; promoted sergeant, April 1, 1865; mustered out with company, July 16, 1865, near Washington, D. C.; also borne as Thomas L. Brown.

BROWN, WILLIAM.—Age, 28 years. Enlisted, August 26, 1862, at Rome, to serve three years; mustered in as corporal, Co. F, October 10, 1862; returned to ranks, no date; transferred to Veteran Reserve Corps, September 1, 1863.

BROWNELL, ALBERT E.—Age, 22 years. Enrolled, September 3, 1862, at Paris, to serve three years; mustered in as private, Co. K, October 10, 1862; promoted sergeant-major, December 27, 1862; mustered in as second lieutenant, Co. A, January 30, 1863; discharged, November 25, 1864.

Commissioned second lieutenant, February 5, 1863, with rank from January 7, 1863, vice W. J. Stamford resigned; first lieutenant (not mustered), September 16, 1864, with rank from June 11, 1864, vice E. R. Matterson resigned.

BURBIDGE, EDWARD.—Age, 18 years. Enlisted, August 30, 1862, at Utica, to serve three years; mustered in as private,

Co. A, October 10, 1862; mustered out with company, July 16, 1865, near Washington, D. C. Died in 1902.

BURGETT, CHESTER E.—Age, 36 years. Enlisted, September 6, 1862, at Sangerfield, to serve three years; mustered in as private, Co. H, October 10, 1862; transferred to Veteran Reserve Corps, December 28, 1864. Died April 12, 1891, at Waterville, N. Y.

BURLINGAME, ANSON H.—Age, 20 years. Enlisted, August 29, 1862, at Augusta, to serve three years; mustered in as private, Co. G, October 10, 1862; captured and paroled, no date; promoted corporal, March 1, 1865; mustered out with company, July 16, 1865, near Washington, D. C.

BURLINGAME, ORIN.—Age, 18 years. Enlisted, August 29, 1862, at Boonville, to serve three years; mustered in as private, Co. D, October 10, 1862; discharged for disability, August 21, 1863, at Washington, D. C.

BURLINGAME, WILLIAM R.—Age, 22 years. Enlisted August 21, 1862, at Utica, to serve three years; mustered in as private, Co. A, October 10, 1862; died of disease, December 25, 1862, near Falmouth, Va.

BURNHAM, JOHN.—Age, 44 years. Enlisted, August 28, 1862, at Sangerfield, to serve three years; mustered in as private, Co. H, October 10, 1862; died, December 17, 1862, at Falmouth, Va.; also borne as Burnam.

BURNHAM, WILLIAM P.—Age, 33 years. Enlisted, August 23, 1862, at Whitestown, to serve three years; mustered in as sergeant, Co. E, October 10, 1862; killed in action, May 1, 1863, at Chancellorsville, Va.

BYAM, HARLOW.—Age, 44 years. Enlisted, August 30, 1862, at Lee, to serve three years; mustered in as private, Co. F, October 10, 1862; discharged for disability, April 27, 1863, at Lincoln Hospital, Washington, D. C.

CABEL, PETER.—Age, 38 years. Enlisted, August 30, 1862, at Rome, to serve three years; mustered in as private, Co. F, October 10, 1862; also borne as Cabal.

CADY, OSCAR L.—Age, 18 years. Enlisted, September 5, 1862, at Paris, to serve three years; mustered in as private, Co. K, October 10, 1862; mustered out with company, July 16, 1865, near Washington, D. C.

CALEN, CHARLES.—Age, 21 years. Enlisted, August 29, 1862, at Boonville, to serve three years; mustered in as corporal, Co. D, October 10, 1862; promoted sergeant and captured, no dates; died of disease, February 4, 1865, at Salisbury, N. C.

CAMPBELL, WILLIAM.—Age, 29 years. Enlisted, September 1, 1862, at Kirkland, to serve three years; mustered in as corporal, Co. G, October 10, 1862; promoted sergeant, March 9, 1863; transferred to Veteran Reserve Corps, September 2, 1863. Born September 23, 1832, at Blairgawnie, Scotland, and migrated to America in 1861; died May 22, 1911, at Westmoreland, N. Y.

CAPRON, WILLIAM.—Age, 24 years. Enlisted, August 25, 1862, at Trenton, to serve three years; mustered in as private, Co. I, October 10, 1862; captured in action, May 5, 1864, at the Wilderness, Va.; died of disease, September 18, 1864, at Florence, S. C.

CARPENTER, LEONARD W.—Age, 30 years. Enlisted, September 30, 1862, at Bridgewater, to serve three years; mustered in as private, Co. G, October 10, 1862; discharged for disability, December 19, 1863, near Warrenton, Va.

CARR, ARCHIBALD.—Age, 44 years. Enlisted, August 30, 1862, at Kirkland, to serve three years; mustered in as private, Co. G, October 10, 1862; discharged for disability, April 1, 1863.

CARR, WILLIAM.—Age, 45 years. Enlisted, August 30, 1862, at Kirkland, to serve three years; mustered in as private, Co. G, October 10, 1862.

CARY, PETER.—Age, 21 years. Enlisted, September 8, 1862, at Rome, to serve three years; mustered in as private, Co. B, October 10, 1862; captured in action, May 1, 1863, at Chancellorsville, Va.; paroled, March 14, 1865; killed in action, April 1, 1865, at Five Forks, Va.

CASE, A. PIERSON.—Age, 44 years. Enrolled at Rome, to serve three years, and mustered in as first lieutenant and quartermaster, August 30, 1862; discharged for disability, October 27, 1863.

Commissioned first lieutenant and quartermaster, November 3, 1862, with rank from August 30, 1862, original; brevet major by New York State Government. Born at Vernon, N. Y., March 22, 1818; married May 30, 1839, at Windsor, N. Y., to Miss Lovina W. Coburn, of Homer; appointed Cashier of Bank of Vernon in 1879; President in 1893; in 1852 served a term in New York State Legislature; died, September 15, 1900, at Vernon.

CASE, HORACE M.—Age, 38 years. Enlisted, September 5, 1862, at Verona, to serve three years; mustered in as sergeant, Co. E, October 10, 1862; mustered out with company, July 16, 1865, near Washington, D. C. Died in 1905.

CASSIDY, HUGH.—Age, 41 years. Enlisted, August 25, 1862, at Utica, to serve three years; mustered in as private, Co. C, October 10, 1862; transferred to Veteran Reserve Corps, December 1, 1863; mustered out therefrom, July 31, 1865, as of Co. C, Eleventh Regiment, at Rochester, N. Y.

CASSIDY, PATRICK.—Age, 33 years. Enlisted, August 20, 1862, at Rome, to serve three years; mustered in as private, Co. B, October 10, 1862; discharged for disability, February 11, 1864, at Camp Distribution, near Alexandria, Va.

CASWELL, HENRY E.—Age, 21 years. Enlisted, August 28, 1862, at Camden, to serve three years; mustered in as private, Co. I, October 10, 1862; discharged for disability, March 22, 1863, at Convalescent Camp, near Washington, D. C.

CATLIN, CHARLES M.—Age, 18 years. Enlisted, September 13, 1862, at Kirkland, to serve three years; mustered in as private, Co. G, October 10, 1862; promoted corporal, no date; discharged for disability, January 9, 1864, at Washington, D. C.

CAVANOUGH, OWEN.—Age, 18 years. Enlisted, September 2, 1862, at Boonville, to serve three years; mustered in as private, Co. D. October 10, 1862; killed in action, May 25, 1864, at North Anna River, Va.; also borne as Cavenaugh.

CHANDLER, W. BERIAH.—Age, 18 years. Enlisted, October 6, 1862, at Whitestown, to serve three years; mustered in as private, Co. D, October 10, 1862; appointed musician, no date; promoted principal musician, July 31, 1864; mustered out with company, July 16, 1865, near Washington, D. C., as William B. Chandler.

Commissioned (not mustered) second lieutenant, August 31, 1865, with rank from August 1, 1865, vice W. H. Luyster not mustered.

CHAPMAN, BENJAMIN G.—Age, 32 years. Enlisted, August 28, 1862, at Paris, to serve three years; mustered in as private, Co. K, October 10, 1862; promoted corporal, May, 1863; returned to ranks, no date; transferred to Veteran Reserve Corps, May 3, 1864. Died in 1902.

CHAPMAN, ISAAC.—Age, 31 years. Enlisted, August 30, 1862, at Kirkland, to serve three years; mustered in as private, Co. G, October 10, 1862; mustered out, June 15, 1865, at Philadelphia, Pa.

CHARLOT, THOMAS J.—Age, 44 years. Enlisted, September 24, 1862, at Lee, to serve three years; mustered in as private, Co. F, October 10, 1862; discharged for disability, January 15, 1863, near Potomac Creek, Va.; also borne as Charlotte.

CHARMVILLE, CLAUDE.—Age, 32 years. Enlisted, September 10, 1862, at Rome, to serve three years; mustered in as private, Co. B, October 10, 1862; wounded in action, June 18, 1864, near Petersburg, Va.; discharged for wounds, April 26, 1865, at Washington, D. C. Died May 10, 1899.

CHEESEBROUGH, ADAM.—Age, 28 years. Enlisted, August 28, 1862, at Sangerfield, to serve three years; mustered in as private, Co. H, October 10, 1862; wounded in action, March 31, 1865, at White Oak Road, Va.; died of his wounds, May 1, 1865.

CHISSON, JOHN.—Age, 25 years. Enlisted, August 27, 1862, at Camden, to serve three years; mustered in as private, Co. E, October 10, 1862; also borne as Chism.

CHRISTIAN, HENRY W.—Age, 37 years. Enlisted, August 28, 1862, at Utica, to serve three years; mustered in as private, Co. E, October 10, 1862; died of disease, December 22, 1862, at Henry House, Va.

CLAESGENS, PETER C.—Age, 36 years. Enrolled, September 10, 1862, at Rome, to serve three years; mustered in as captain, Co. F, October 10, 1862; as major, January 1, 1865; as lieutenant-colonel, April 1, 1865; mustered out with regiment, July 16, 1865, near Washington, D. C.

Commissioned captain, November 3, 1862, with rank from September 10, 1862, original; major, December 7, 1864, with rank from December 1, 1864, vice J. Grindlay, promoted; lieutenant-colonel, March 30, 1865, with rank from February 1, 1865, vice J. Grindlay promoted; bvt. colonel by U. S. from March 13, 1865.

CLAGHORN, EDWARD.—Age, 22 years. Enlisted, August 30, 1862, at Utica, to serve three years; mustered in as private, Co. H, October 10, 1862; captured in action, May 5, 1864, at the Wilderness, Va.; no further record; also borne as Cleghorn.

CLANCY, MICHAEL.—Age, 32 years. Enlisted, August 25, 1862, at Utica, to serve three years; mustered in as private, Co. C, October 10, 1862; absent, sick, since July 30, 1864; no further record.

CLARK, HENRY.—Age, 21 years. Enlisted, September 6, 1862, at Bridgewater, to serve three years; mustered in as private, Co. G, October 10, 1862; mustered out with company, July 16, 1865, near Washington, D. C.

CLARKE, F. ERWIN.—Age, 21 years. Enlisted, September 15, 1862, at Brookfield, to serve three years; mustered in as private, Co. G, October 10, 1862; died of disease, March 9, 1863, at Potomac Creek, Va.

COAN, ARTHUR V.—Age, 18 years. Enrolled, August 29, 1862, at Augusta, to serve three years; mustered in as corporal, Co. G, October 10, 1862; promoted first sergeant, March 9, 1863; mustered in as second lieutenant, Co. G, March 1, 1864; wounded in action, August 18, 1864, at Weldon Railroad, Va.; died of his wounds, September 30, 1864.

Commissioned second lieutenant, February 17, 1864, with rank from October 27, 1863, vice Wm. Wright promoted.

COLE, ABRAM.—Age, 44 years. Enlisted, September 6, 1862. at Bridgewater, to serve three years; mustered in as private, Co. G, October 10, 1862; transferred to Veteran Reserve Corps, September 10, 1863.

COLEMAN, JOHN.—Age, 44 years. Enlisted, August 26, 1862, at Westmoreland, to serve three years; mustered in as private, Co. I, October 10, 1862; transferred to Veteran Reserve Corps, December 25, 1864; mustered out therefrom as of Co. G, Twenty-second Regiment, August 7, 1865, at Camp Chase, Ohio.   Died in 1898.

COLLEGE, JAMES.—Age, 31 years.   Enlisted, August 30, 1862, at Utica, to serve three years; mustered in as private, Co. C, October 10, 1862; discharged for disability, May 30, 1865, at hospital.

COLWELL, WILLIAM.—Age, 25 years.   Enlisted, August 23, 1862, at Utica, to serve three years; mustered in as private, Co. A, October 10, 1862; wounded in action, May 3, 1863, at Chancellorsville, Va.; discharged for wounds, August 5, 1863, at Washington, D. C.; also borne as Colewell.

COMSTOCK, EDWARD.—Age, — years.   Enrolled at Rome, to serve three years, and mustered in as first lieutenant and adjutant, October 1, 1862; transferred as first lieutenant to Co. E, April 24, 1864; discharged, August 28, 1864.

Commissioned first lieutenant and adjutant, October 2, 1862, with rank from September 1, 1862, original; first lieutenant, October 6, 1863, with rank from September 28, 1863, vice T. A. Wilson promoted; bvt. major by U. S. Government, from March 13, 1865.

COMSTOCK, JULIUS.—Age, 32 years.   Enlisted, August 31, 1862, at Camden, to serve three years; mustered in as private, Co. E, October 10, 1862; discharged for disability, January 8, 1863, at Washington, D. C.

CONDON, JOHN.—Age, 42 years.   Enlisted, August 25, 1862, at Utica, to serve three years; mustered in as private, Co. C, October 10, 1862; died, November 28, 1862, near Falmouth, Va.

CONE, GEORGE W.—Age, — years.   Enrolled, September 2, 1862, at Rome, to serve three years; mustered in as captain, Co. A, October 10, 1862; discharged, November 29, 1862.

Commissioned captain, November 3, 1862, with rank from September 2, 1862, original.

CONGER, GEORGE W.—Age, 22 years.   Enlisted, August 20, 1862, at Utica, to serve three years; mustered in as private, Co. A, October 10, 1862; mustered out, July 2, 1865, at Washington, D. C.

CONLEY, JAMES.—Age, 35 years. Enlisted, August 27, 1862, at Florence, to serve three years; mustered in as private, Co. B, October 10, 1862; mustered out with company, July 16, 1865, near Washington, D. C.; also borne as Conly.

CONLEY, MARTIN.—Age, 45 years. Enlisted, September 3, 1862, at Trenton, to serve three years; mustered in as private, Co. I, October 10, 1862; transferred to Veteran Reserve Corps, September 1, 1863; retransferred to company, April 14, 1864; discharged for disability, March 9, 1865, in the field.

CONNAN, JOHN.—Age, 40 years. Enlisted, August 29, 1862, at Utica, to serve three years; mustered in as private, Co. C, October 10, 1862; mustered out with company, July 16, 1865, near Washington, D. C., as Connon.

COOGAN, JOHN.—Age, 23 years. Enlisted, September 18, 1862, at Marcy, to serve three years; mustered in as private, Co. G, October 10, 1862; promoted corporal, March 9, 1863; captured in action, May 5, 1864, at the Wilderness, Va.; paroled, no date; promoted sergeant, June 1, 1865, mustered out with company, July 16, 1865, near Washington, D. C. Died, April 1, 1909, at Whitesboro, N. Y.

COOK, GEORGE W.—Age, 19 years. Enlisted, August 21, 1862, at Utica, to serve three years; mustered in as private, Co. C, October 10, 1862; wounded in action, July 1–3, 1863, at Gettysburg, Pa.

COOK, GEORGE WASHINGTON.—Age, 25 years. Enlisted, August 31, 1862, at Camden, to serve three years; mustered in as private, Co. E, October 10, 1862; captured, no date; died of disease, August 31, 1864, at Andersonville, Ga.

COOK, JAMES E.—Age, 24 years. Enlisted, August 26, 1862, at Lee, to serve three years; mustered in as corporal, Co. F, October 10, 1862; returned to ranks, January 31, 1863; transferred to Veteran Reserve Corps, no date; mustered out thereof as of Third Company, Second Battalion, August 10, 1865, at Washington, D. C.

COOK, JOHN.—Age, 22 years. Enlisted, August 30, 1862, at Utica, to serve three years; mustered in as private, Co. F, October 10, 1862.

COOK, SYLVESTER O.—Age, 27 years. Enlisted, August 28, 1862, at Boonville, to serve three years; mustered in as private, Co. D, October 10, 1862; promoted first sergeant, no date; discharged, February 14, 1864, to accept promotion as second lieutenant, Co. D, Sixteenth New York Heavy Artillery. Died in 1900.

COOPER, ISAAC.—Age, 36 years. Enlisted, August 26, 1862, at Utica, to serve three years; mustered in as private, Co. H, October 10, 1862; transferred to Veteran Reserve Corps, no date; mustered out thereof as of Company H, Third Regiment, August 10, 1865, at Hartford, Conn.

COPPERSMITH, DANIEL.—Age, 21 years. Enlisted, August 25, 1862, at Rome, to serve three years; mustered in as private, Co. B, October 10, 1862; promoted corporal, January 9, 1863; sergeant, October 27, 1863; first sergeant, June 3, 1865; mustered out with company, July 16, 1865, near Washington, D. C. Died April 25, 1910, at Rome, N. Y.

COREY, JAMES.—Age, 18 years. Enlisted, September 6, 1862, at Augusta, to serve three years; mustered in as private, Co. E, October 10, 1862; captured in action, May 1–3, 1863, at Chancellorsville, Va.; died of disease while prisoner of war, December 7, 1864, at Charleston, S. C.

CORNING, WILLIAM S.—Enrolled, October 10, 1862, at Rome, to serve three years; mustered in as major, October 11, 1862; discharged, September 23, 1863.

Commissioned major, October 18, 1862, with rank from October 11, 1862, vice D. T. Jenkins promoted; lieutenant-colonel (not mustered), August 28, 1863, with rank from July 23, 1863, vice D. T. Jenkins promoted.

CORNWALL, JAY.—Age, 18 years. Enlisted, August 22, 1862, at Florence, to serve three years; mustered in as private, Co. F, October 10, 1862; wounded in action, March 31, 1865, at White Oak Road, Va.; died of his wounds, April 26, 1865, at Washington, D. C.; also borne as Cornell.

CORRAGAN, JOSEPH.—Age, 35 years. Enlisted, August 30, 1862, at Utica, to serve three years; mustered in as private, Co. A, October 10, 1862; captured in action, May 1–3, 1863, at Chancellorsville, Va.; paroled, July 26, 1863; mustered

out with company, July 16, 1865, near Washington, D. C.,
as Carrogon.

COSTER, ALONZO.—Age, 23 years. Enlisted, August 19, 1862,
at Utica, to serve three years; mustered in as private, Co.
A, October 10, 1862; captured and paroled, no dates; discharged, June 2, 1865, as Castor.

COSTER, ORLANDO.—Age, 21 years. Enlisted, August 19, 1862,
at Utica, to serve three years; mustered in as private, Co. A,
October 10, 1862; captured and paroled, no dates; mustered
out with company, July 16, 1865, near Washington, D. C.,
as Costor.

COUTEN, ISAAC.—Age, 22 years. Enlisted, September 2, 1862,
at Remsen, to serve three years; mustered in as private,
Co. K, October 10, 1862; also borne as Scouton; no record
subsequent to April 10, 1863.

CRANDALL, JOHN.—Age, 22 years. Enlisted, August 27, 1862,
at Camden, to serve three years; mustered in as private,
Co. E, October 10, 1862; no further record.

CRAWFORD, GEORGE F.—Age, 42 years. Enlisted, August 30,
1862, at Camden, to serve three years; mustered in as private, Co. E, October 10, 1862; mustered out with company,
July 16, 1865, near Washington, D. C. Died in 1896.

CRIPIS, SAMUEL.—Age, 42 years. Enlisted, August 29, 1862,
at Annsville, to serve three years; mustered in as private,
Co. F, October 10, 1862; discharged for disability, March
11, 1863, near Potomac Creek, Va.; also borne as Cripps.

CRONK, GEORGE E.—Age, 19 years. Enlisted, August 20,
1862, at Rome, to serve three years; mustered in as private,
Co. K, October 10, 1862.

CROOK, MOSES.—Age, 24 years. Enlisted, August 25, 1862, at
Paris, to serve three years; mustered in as private, Co. H,
October 10, 1862; died, January 17, 1863, at Aquia Creek,
Va.

CRUMB, WILLIAM S.—Age, 44 years. Enlisted, August 30,
1862, at Kirkland, to serve three years; mustered in as
wagoner, Co. G, October 10, 1862; died of disease, December
21, 1862, near Potomac Creek, Va.

CURRAN, HENRY H.—Age, 21 years. Enrolled, September 9,
1862, at Rome, to serve three years; mustered in as first

lieutenant, Co. E, October 10, 1862; as captain, Co. I, December 10, 1862; transferred to Co. B, November 1, 1863; mustered in as major, same date; killed in action, May 5, 1864, at the Wilderness, Va.

Commissioned first lieutenant, November 3, 1862, with rank from September 9, 1862, original; captain, November 24, 1862, with rank from November 6, 1862, vice E. Jones deceased; major, June 6, 1864, with rank from July 23, 1863, vice W. S. Corning promoted; lieutenant-colonel (not mustered), May 18, 1864, with rank from April 4, 1864, vice J. J. Armstrong resigned.

CURRAN, PHILIP C.—Age, 19 years. Enlisted, September 13, 1862, at Rome, to serve three years; mustered in as corporal, Co. B, October 10, 1862; returned to ranks, November 21, 1862; promoted sergeant, no date; discharged for disability, March 10, 1863, at Utica, N. Y.

Commissioned (declined) second lieutenant, September 16, 1864, with rank from August 30, 1864, vice H. Loomis promoted.

CURTIS, GEORGE.—Age, 40 years. Enlisted, September 6, 1862, at Utica, to serve three years; mustered in as private, Co. C, October 10, 1862; transferred to Veteran Reserve Corps, September 1, 1863. Died in 1897.

CURTISS, ELHANAN A.—Age, 21 years. Enlisted, August 30, 1862, at Camden, to serve three years; mustered in as private, Co. E, October 10, 1862; mustered out, June 15, 1865, at Whitehall Hospital, Philadelphia, Pa.

CUSHMAN, JOSEPH B.—Age, 26 years. Enrolled, October 7, 1862, at Rome, to serve three years; mustered in as first lieutenant, Co. K, October 10, 1862; as captain, Co. C, October 29, 1863; discharged for disability, June 1, 1864.

Commissioned first lieutenant, November 3, 1862, with rank from October 9, 1862, original; captain, October 6, 1863, with rank from September 23, 1863, vice E. V. Jewell discharged. Died March 29, 1914, at Vernon, N. Y.

DAGAN, JAMES H.—Age, 18 years. Enlisted, August 29, 1862, at Boonville, to serve three years; mustered in as private, Co. D, October 10, 1862; appointed musician, no date; transferred to Co. H, March 29, 1863; promoted corporal and returned to company as a musician, no dates; mustered out with company, July 16, 1865, near Washington, D. C.

DAILEY, JAMES.—Age, 25 years. Enlisted, September 6, 1862, at Lee, to serve three years; mustered in as private, Co. F, October 10, 1862; captured in action, May 5, 1864, at the Wilderness, Va.; paroled, February 28, 1865; discharged, June 17, 1865, at Annapolis, Md.

DAINAN, HEINDRICH.—Age, 44 years. Enlisted, August 29, 1862, at Camden, to serve three years; mustered in as private, Co. E, October 10, 1862; captured, no date; died, December 15, 1864, at Andersonville, Ga.; also borne as Fredrick Dimon.

DALTON, JAMES.—Age, 22 years. Enlisted, September 9, 1862, at Rome, to serve three years; mustered in as private, Co. I, October 10, 1862; transferred to Co. B, and wounded, no dates; died of his wounds, July 31, 1864, at Petersburg, Va.; also borne as James H. Dalton.

DANIELS, CEPHAS B.—Age, 20 years. Enlisted, August 20, 1862, at Utica, to serve three years; mustered in as private, Co. C, October 10, 1862; discharged for insanity, December 17, 1863.

DANIELS, JAMES A.—Age, 23 years. Enrolled, August 26, 1862, at Utica, to serve three years; mustered in as private, Co. A, October 10, 1862; promoted first sergeant, no date; mustered in as second lieutenant, Co. H, January 31, 1863.
Commissioned second lieutenant, January 22, 1863, with rank from December 28, 1862, vice W. M. Mott resigned.

DANN, WILLIAM J.—Age, 42 years. Enlisted, October 9, 1862, at Rome, to serve three years; mustered in as private, Co. K, October 10, 1862; transferred to Veteran Reserve Corps, September 30, 1863.

DAVIS, DAVID K.—Age, 35 years. Enlisted, September 15, 1862, at Plainfield, to serve three years; mustered in as private, Co. G, October 10, 1862; transferred to Veteran Reserve Corps, August 14, 1864. Died at Unadilla Forks, N. Y., in 1898.

DAVIS, EDGAR.—Age, 20 years. Enlisted, August 27, 1862, at Utica, to serve three years; mustered in as private, Co. A,

October 10, 1862; transferred to Co. B, Twelfth Regiment, Veteran Reserve Corps, no date; discharged, July 17, 1865, at Washington, D. C.

DAVIS, EDWARD J.—Age, 23 years. Enrolled, September 30, 1862, at Whitestown, to serve three years; mustered in as private, Co. D, October 10, 1862; promoted hospital steward, August 1, 1863; mustered in as first lieutenant, Co. E, March 3, 1865; wounded in action, March 31, 1865, at White Oak Ridge, Va.; mustered out with company, July 16, 1865, near Washington, D. C.

Commissioned first lieutenant, February 18, 1865, with rank from December 1, 1864, vice J. P. Pitcher promoted; brevet captain by U. S. Government, from March 13, 1865.

DAVIS, JAMES.—Age, 40 years. Enlisted, August 30, 1862, at Boonville, to serve three years; mustered in as private, Co. D, October 10, 1862; died, February 11, 1863, at Washington, D. C.

DAVIS, JOHN W.—Age, 21 years. Enlisted, August 30, 1862, at Remsen, to serve three years; mustered in as private, Co. I, October 10, 1862; died, March 20, 1863, in Division Hospital, near Potomac Creek, Va.

DAVIS, JOSEPH R.—Age, 21 years. Enlisted, August 20, 1862, at Utica, to serve three years; mustered in as private, Co. K, October 10, 1862; wounded in action and died of his wounds, June 18, 1864, at Petersburg, Va.

DEAN, JAMES.—Age, 37 years. Enlisted, August 25, 1862, at Kirkland, to serve three years; mustered in as private, Co. G, October 10, 1862; captured in action, May 3, 1863, at Chancellorsville, Va.; paroled, no date; mustered out with company, July 16, 1865, near Washington, D. C.

DEAN, MARTIN.—Age, 21 years. Enlisted, September 16, 1862, at Vernon, to serve three years; mustered in as private, Co. B, October 10, 1862; killed in action, August 18, 1864, at Weldon Railroad, Va.

DEDRICK, PETER.—Age, 19 years. Enlisted, August 28, 1862, at Boonville, to serve three years; mustered in as private, Co. D, October 10, 1862; died of disease, November 6, 1863, at Hawkinsville, N. Y.

DE FOREST, JAMES E.—Age, 24 years. Enlisted, August 19, 1862, at Utica, to serve three years; mustered in as private, Co. C, October 10, 1862; discharged for disability, December 24, 1862, at Washington, D. C.

DEMPSTER, JAMES.—Age, 30 years. Enlisted, August 29, 1862, at Utica, to serve three years; mustered in as private, Co. H, October 10, 1862; promoted corporal, captured in action, returned to ranks, and paroled, no dates; mustered out, June 9, 1865, at Washington, D. C.; also borne as Demster. Died in 1903.

DEVLIN, JAMES.—Age, 21 years. Enlisted, August 27, 1862, at Utica, to serve three years; mustered in as private, Co. H, October 10, 1862.

DILLENBECK, ADDISON.—Age, 27 years. Enlisted, August 27, 1862, at Steuben, to serve three years; mustered in as private, Co. I, October 10, 1862; captured in action, May 5, 1864, at the Wilderness, Va.; paroled, no date; mustered out, May 30, 1865, at Annapolis, Md.

DILLON, RICHARD.—Age, 24 years. Enlisted, August 30, 1862, at Kirkland, to serve three years; mustered in as private, Co. G, October 10, 1862.

DIMBLEBY, FLETCHER W.—Age, 22 years. Enlisted, August 21, 1862, at Utica, to serve three years; mustered in as private, Co. A, October 10, 1862; promoted sergeant, no date; captured in action, May 1, 1863, at Chancellorsville, Va.; paroled, July 26, 1863; returned to ranks, no date; transferred to Veteran Reserve Corps, April 1, 1865.

DIXON, THEODORE.—Age, 18 years. Enlisted, August 30, 1862, at Utica, to serve three years; mustered in as musician Co. C, October 10, 1862; returned to company as a private, no date; discharged for disability, August 15, 1863, at Washington, D. C.

DODGE, DON A.—Age, — years. Enrolled at Rome, to serve three years, and mustered in as captain, Co. K, October 10, 1862; discharged, January 7, 1863, near Falmouth, Va.; prior service as first lieutenant, Second Onondaga Infantry.

Commissioned captain, November 3, 1862, with rank from October 9, 1862, original.

DOHERTY, MICHAEL.—Age, 32 years. Enlisted, September 4, 1862, at Deansville, to [serve three years; mustered in as private, Co. K, October 10, 1862; promoted sergeant, January 31, 1863; mustered out with company, July 16, 1865, near Washington, D. C.

DONNELLY, JAMES.—Age, 40 years. Enlisted, August 30, 1862, at Westmoreland, to serve three years; mustered in as private, Co. I, October 10, 1862; discharged for disability, April 5, 1864, at Washington, D. C.

DOODY, PATRICK.—Age, 18 years. Enlisted, August 25, 1862, at Florence, to serve three years; mustered in as private, Co. F, October 10, 1862; discharged for disability, July 31, 1863, at Washington, D. C.

DORN, ANDREW.—Age, 19 years. Enlisted, September 1, 1862, at Boonville, to serve three years; mustered in as private, Co. D, October 10, 1862; captured, paroled, and promoted sergeant, no dates; mustered out, May 11, 1865, at West Buildings Hospital, Baltimore, Md.

DOWNING, ANDREW W.—Age, 28 years. Enlisted, September 2, 1862, at Lee, to serve three years; mustered in as musician, Co. F, October 10, 1862; transferred to Co. A, March 28, 1863, and to Veteran Reserve Corps, March 15, 1864; mustered out therefrom as of Co. H, Sixth Regiment, October 9, 1865, at Detroit, Mich. Died in 1906.

DRISKILL, WILLIAM.—Age, 39 years. Enlisted, September 3, 1862, at Camden, to serve three years; mustered in as private, Co. E, October 10, 1862.

DRUMMOND, WILLIAM.—Age, 44 years. Enlisted, August 31, 1862, at Vienna, to serve three years; mustered in as private, Co. I, October 10, 1862.

DUGAL, ALEXANDER—Age, 22 years. Enlisted, September 26, 1862, at Steuben, to serve three years; mustered in as private, Co. F, October 10, 1862; promoted corporal, October 1, 1863; transferred to U. S. Navy, May 2, 1864.

DUGAL, LOUIS.—Age, 25 years. Enlisted, August 29, 1862, at Ava, to serve three years; mustered in as corporal, Co. F, October 10, 1862; promoted sergeant, February 1, 1863; first sergeant, November 17, 1863; wounded and captured in action, May 5, 1864, at the Wilderness, Va.; paroled, no date; discharged for wounds, March 26, 1865, at Parole Camp, Annapolis, Md.

DUMONT, PETER L.—Age, 27 years. Enlisted, August 22, 1862, at Utica, to serve three years; mustered in as private, Co. A, October 10, 1862; promoted sergeant, no date; captured in action, May 1, 1863, at Chancellorsville, Va.; paroled, no date; killed in action, May 5, 1864, at the Wilderness, Va.

DUNBAR, ALVIN B.—Age, 24 years. Enlisted, August 26, 1862, at Lee, to serve three years; mustered in as private, Co. F, October 10, 1862; captured in action, May 5, 1864, at the Wilderness, Va.; paroled, no date; mustered out, June 27, 1865, at Jarvis Hospital, Baltimore, Md.

DUNN, ALBERT.—Age, 22 years. Enlisted, August 25, 1862, at Marshall, to serve three years; mustered in as private, Co. G, October 10, 1862; transferred to Veteran Reserve Corps, December 20, 1864. Of English parentage; married Margaret Winchester in 1866; moved to Saginaw, Mich., in 1873; died at that place, Feb. 24, 1902.

DUNN, GEORGE.—Age, 21 years. Enlisted in Co. A, August 25, 1862, at Utica, to serve three years, and mustered in as private, Co. K, October 10, 1862; captured and paroled, no dates; mustered out June 20, 1865, at Washington, D. C.

DUNNING, EDWARD S.—Age, 21 years. Enlisted, August 21, 1862, at Utica, to serve three years; mustered in as sergeant, Co. C, October 10, 1862; captured in action, May 5, 1864, at the Wilderness, Va.; paroled and returned to ranks, no dates; mustered out, June 30, 1865, at Annapolis, Md.

DURKEE, JOSEPH H.—Age, 25 years. Enrolled, September 9, 1862, at Rome, to serve three years; mustered in as second lieutenant, Co. E, October 2, 1862; as first lieutenant, December 10, 1862; promoted captain, Co. A, December 27, 1862; wounded in action, May 1, 1863, at Chancellorsville, Va.; discharged, May 12, 1864.

Commissioned second lieutenant, November 3, 1862, with rank from September 9, 1862, original; first lieutenant, November 24, 1862, with rank from November 6, 1862, vice H. H. Curran promoted; captain, December 10, 1862, with rank from November 29, 1862, vice G. W. Cone resigned. Died in 1909 at Stony Brook, N. Y.

DURRANT, GEORGE.—Age, 21 years. Enlisted, August 22, 1862, at Utica, to serve three years; mustered in as private, Co. H, October 10, 1862; transferred to Veteran Reserve Corps, no date; mustered out therefrom as of Co. F, Eighteenth Regiment, August 2, 1865, at Washington, D. C. Born in Norfolkshire, England, July 10, 1841; came to the United States when 12 years of age; married, November 9, 1864, to Sarah A. Jackson; died January 11, 1911, at New Hartford, N. Y.

DUTTON, CHARLES K.—Age, 21 years. Enrolled, October 6, 1862, at Rome, to serve three years; mustered in as second lieutenant, Co. H, November 1, 1862; as first lieutenant, December 26, 1862; as captain, September 20, 1864; discharged, March 13, 1865; subsequent service as captain, Co. M, Twenty-fourth Cavalry.

Commissioned second lieutenant, October 29, 1862, with rank from October 6, 1862, original; first lieutenant, December 10, 1862, with rank from November 29, 1862, vice J. H. Durkee promoted; captain, September 16, 1864, with rank from June 1, 1864, vice J. B. Cushman resigned; brevet major by U. S. Government, from March 13, 1865. Died, at New York City, in 1897.

DYER, HENRY M.—Age, 27 years. Enlisted, August 28, 1862, at Marcy, to serve three years; mustered in as private, Co. K, October 10, 1862; promoted sergeant, no date; died of disease, June 30, 1863, at Aquia Creek, Va.

DYER, HORACE S.—Age, 18 years. Enlisted, September 6, 1862, at Whitesboro, to serve three years; mustered in as private, Co. K, October 10, 1862; discharged for disability, March 5, 1863, at hospital, Washington, D. C.; also borne as Horace L. Dyer.

EAMES, JAMES C.—Age, 21 years. Enlisted, September 2, 1862, at Lee, to serve three years; mustered in as musician, Co. F, October 10, 1862; mustered out with company, July 16, 1865, near Washington, D. C. Born at Lee Center, N. Y., 1842; died at Stamford, N. Y., March 20, 1913.

EDIE, JAMES.—Age, 42 years. Enlisted, August 11, 1862, at Whitestown, to serve three years; mustered in as private, Co. F, October 10, 1862; mustered out with company, July 16, 1865, near Washington, D. C.

EDMONDS, JAMES O.—Age, 21 years. Enlisted, September 1, 1862, at Utica, to serve three years; mustered in as private, Co. C, October 10, 1862; discharged for disability, June 11, 1864, at Washington, D. C.

EDWARDS, DAVID.—Age, 22 years. Enlisted, September 3, 1862, at Sangerfield, to serve three years; mustered in as private, Co. H, October 10, 1862; promoted corporal, June 1, 1864; mustered out with company, July 16, 1865, near Washington, D. C.; awarded medal of honor for capture of flag at Five Forks, April 1, 1865. Born, in Wales in 1841; married November 13, 1873, to Eliza Ann Evans, who died January 27, 1880; in 1884 he married Sarah Hughes; died, at Waterville, N. Y., April 14, 1897.

EDWARDS, DAVID T.—Age, 43 years. Enlisted, August 23, 1862, at Utica, to serve three years; mustered in as private, Co. A, October 10, 1862; died of disease, December 19, 1862, in Division Hospital, at Falmouth, Va.

EDWARDS, IRA.—Age, 40 years. Enlisted, August 27, 1862, at Utica, to serve three years; mustered in as private, Co. C, October 10, 1862; died of disease, December 23, 1862, near Falmouth, Va.

EDWARDS, JOHN.—Age, 39 years. Enlisted, September 2, 1862, at Sangerfield, to serve three years; mustered in as private, Co. K, October 10, 1862; promoted corporal, March 1, 1865; mustered out with company, July 16, 1865, near Washington, D. C. Born in Wales, October 17, 1823; came to this country when quite young; he was married before entering the army; he died at Waterville, N. Y.

EGLESTON, MARVIN.—Age, 22 years. Enrolled, August 29, 1862, at Boonville, to serve three years; mustered in as first sergeant, Co. D, October 10, 1862; as second lieutenant, Co. B, January 1, 1863; as first lieutenant, Co. F, February 28, 1863; promoted quartermaster, November 19, 1863; mustered out with regiment, July 16, 1865, near Washington, D. C.

Commissioned second lieutenant, January 22, 1863, with rank from December 25, 1862, vice A. D. Townsley resigned; first lieutenant, February 23, 1863, with rank from January 10, 1863, vice G. H. Perry resigned; quartermaster, Novem-

22

ber 9, 1863, with rank from October 27, 1863, vice A. P. Case discharged; brevet captain by U. S. Government, from March 13, 1865.

EIPENCE, ADAM.—Age, 21 years. Enlisted, September 6, 1862, at Utica, to serve three years; mustered in as private, Co. H, October 10, 1862; captured in action, May 5, 1864, at the Wilderness, Va.; paroled, no date; mustered out, June 19, 1865, at York, Pa.

ELDEN, BRONSON.—Age, 37 years. Enlisted, August 31, 1862, at Camden, to serve three years; mustered in as private, Co. E, October 10, 1862; captured, no date; died of disease, September 1, 1864, at Andersonville, Ga.; also borne as Eldon.

ELGOR, JAMES C.—Age, 22 years. Enlisted, August 25, 1862, at Vernon, to serve three years; mustered in as private, Co. B, October 10, 1862; promoted corporal, November 22, 1862; died of disease, January 6, 1863, in camp, at Potomac Creek, Va.

ELLIS, ANSON D.—Age, 24 years. Enlisted, September 13, 1862, at Westmoreland, to serve three years; mustered in as private, Co. I, October 10, 1862; promoted sergeant and first sergeant, no dates; captured in action, May 5, 1864, at the Wilderness, Va.; died February 20, 1865, at Florence, N. C.

ELMER, HARRISON W.—Age, 22 years. Enlisted, September 6, 1862, at Bridgewater, to serve three years; mustered in as private, Co. G, October 10, 1862; captured in action May 1, 1863, at Chancellorsville, Va.; paroled, no date; discharged for disability, October 2, 1863, at Washington, D. C.

EMPEY, LA FAYETTE.—Age, 22 years. Enlisted, August 26, 1862, at Camden, to serve three years; mustered in as sergeant, Co. E, October 10, 1862; captured in action, June 2, 1864, at Gains Farm, Va.; paroled, February 25, 1865, at North East Bridge, N. C.; mustered in as second lieutenant to date, November 19, 1864; mustered out, June 20, 1865, at Annapolis, Md.

Commissioned second lieutenant, November 19, 1864, with rank from May 17, 1864, vice Peter C. Curran declined.

ENGLAND, FRANCIS A.—Age, 18 years. Enlisted, September 1, 1862, at Kirkland, to serve three years; mustered in as private, Co. K, October 10, 1862; promoted corporal and returned to ranks, no date; transferred to Veteran Reserve Corps, April 1, 1865; mustered out therefrom as of Co. I, Eighteenth Regiment, June 29, 1865, at Washington, D. C.

ENGLAND, ROBERT W.—Age, 18 years. Enlisted, September 1, 1862, at Kirkland, to serve three years; mustered in as private, Co. K, October 10, 1862; promoted sergeant, January 31, 1863; first sergeant, no date; killed in action, July 2, 1863, at Gettysburg, Pa.

ENTWISTLE, JOSEPH H.—Age, 18 years. Enlisted, August 25, 1862, at Utica, to serve three years; mustered in as private, Co. H, October 10, 1862; promoted sergeant, captured, and paroled, no dates; mustered out, June 1, 1865, at Annapolis, Md.

ERDMAN, ALBERT.—Age, — years. Enrolled at Rome, to serve three years, and mustered in as chaplain, October 10, 1862; discharged, August 3, 1863.

Commissioned chaplain, November 3, 1862, with rank from October 9, 1862, original.

ERNST, FREDERICK.—Age, 18 years. Enlisted, August 25, 1862, at Utica, to serve three years; mustered in as private, Co. C, October 10, 1862; captured in action, May 2, 1863, at Chancellorsville, Va.; paroled, no date; wounded at Gettysburg, July 3, 1863; promoted corporal, June 1, 1865; mustered out with company, July 16, 1865, near Washington, D. C.

ESMAY, ABRAM S.—Age, 22 years. Enlisted, August 22, 1862, at Utica, to serve three years; mustered in as private, Co. A, October 10, 1862; promoted quartermaster-sergeant, same date; discharged for disability, January 22, 1863.

ETHRIDGE, WILLIAM H.—Age, 21 years. Enlisted, August 25, 1862, at Vernon, to serve three years; mustered in as private, Co. B, October 10, 1862; transferred to Veteran Reserve Corps, September 1, 1863.

EVANS, DAVID.—Age, 40 years. Enlisted, August 27, 1862, at Utica, to serve three years; mustered in as private, Co. A, October 10, 1862; transferred to Veteran Reserve Corps, September 12, 1863.

EVANS, HENRY W.—Age, 44 years. Enlisted, September 3, 1862, at Rome, to serve three years; mustered in as private, Co. E, October 10, 1862; mustered out with company, July 16, 1865, near Washington, D. C.

EVANS, ROBERT.—Age, 35 years. Enlisted, August 30, 1862, at Remsen, to serve three years; mustered in as private, Co. I, October 10, 1862; transferred to Veteran Reserve Corps, October 21, 1863.

FALLON, PATRICK.—Age, 34 years. Enlisted, August 28, 1862, at Westmoreland, to serve three years; mustered in as private, Co. I, October 10, 1862; wounded, no date; discharged for wounds, May, 1864.

FANCY, JOSEPH.—Age, 39 years. Enlisted, August 19, 1862 at Utica, to serve three years; mustered in as private, Co. H, October 10, 1862.

FARNSWORTH, ERI Z.—Age, 19 years. Enlisted, August 21, 1862, at Augusta, to serve three years; mustered in as private, Co. E, October 10, 1862; wounded in action, June 2, 1864, at Cold Harbor, Va.; mustered out, August 15, 1865, at Elmira, N. Y.

FARRINGTON, SAMUEL.—Age, 44 years. Enlisted, September 2, 1862, at Kirkland, to serve three years; mustered in as private, Co. G, October 10, 1862; transferred to Veteran Reserve Corps, September 26, 1863; mustered out therefrom as of Thirty-third Company, Second Battalion, June 29, 1865, at Washington, D. C.; also borne as Samuel W. Farrington.

FAULKNER, WILLIAM R.—Age, 22 years. Enlisted, September 2, 1862, at Camden, to serve three years; mustered in as private, Co. E., October 10, 1862; promoted corporal, July 1, 1865; mustered out with company, July 16, 1865, near Washington, D. C.; also borne as Falkner.

FINIGAN, JOHN.—Age, 44 years. Enlisted, September 15, 1862, at Utica, to serve three years; mustered in as private, Co. H, October 10, 1862; discharged for disability, April 4, 1863, at Potomac Creek, Va.; also borne as Finnegan.

FISHER, JOHN.—Age, 22 years. Enlisted, August 25, 1862, at Utica, to serve three years; mustered in as private, Co. F, October 10, 1862; captured in action, May 5, 1864, at the

Wilderness, Va.; died of disease, December 5, 1864, at Charleston, S. C.

FISK, ELIJAH P.—Age, 39 years. Enlisted, August 29, 1862, at Boonville, to serve three years; mustered in as private, Co. D, October 10, 1862; promoted sergeant, and wounded, no dates; transferred to Veteran Reserve Corps, November 25, 1863.

FISK, LEANDER W.—Age, 26 years. Enlisted, August 29, 1862 at Boonville, to serve three years; mustered in as private, Co. D, October 10, 1862; discharged for disability, November 29, 1862, at Washington, D. C. Died in 1901.

FITCH, NATHANIEL.—Age, 23 years. Enlisted, September 4, 1862, at Western, to serve three years; mustered in as private, Co. K, October 10, 1862; discharged, May 3, 1865.

FLANDRAU, THOMAS M.—Age, 36 years. Enrolled at Rome, to serve three years, and mustered in as surgeon, August 25, 1862; mustered out with regiment, July 16, 1865, near Washington, D. C.

Commissioned surgeon, November 3, 1862, with rank from August 23, 1862, original; brevet lieutenant-colonel by U. S. Government, from March 13, 1865; brevet-colonel by N. Y. State Government. Died at Rome, N. Y., in 1898.

FLETCHER, JOHN A.—Age, 34 years. Enlisted, September 4, 1862, at Marshall, to serve three years; mustered in as private, Co. K, October 10, 1862.

FLYNN, MICHAEL.—Age, 22 years. Enlisted, August 30, 1862, at Florence, to serve three years; mustered in as private, Co. F, October 10, 1862; killed in action, June 18, 1864, at Petersburg, Va.

FORD, JOHN.—Age, 45 years. Enlisted, September 6, 1862, at Trenton, to serve three years; mustered in as private, Co. I, October 10, 1862; discharged for disability, September 6, 1863, at Washington, D. C.

FORT, ANDREW.—Age, 21 years. Enlisted, August 30, 1862, at Boonville, to serve three years; mustered in as private, Co. D, October 10, 1862; died, February 11, 1863, at Aquia Creek, Va.

FOSTER, BENJAMIN E.—Age, 21 years. Enlisted, August 19, 1862, at Utica, to serve three years; mustered in as private, Co. H, October 10, 1862; promoted corporal, March 28, 1863.

FOSTER, HARLAND M.—Age, 18 years. Enlisted, August 28, 1862, at Ava, to serve three years; mustered in as private, Co. F, October 10, 1862; died of typhoid fever, January 18, 1863, in Lincoln Hospital, at Washington, D. C.

FOSTER, ISAAC M.—Age, 18 years. Enlisted, September 3, 1862, at Utica, to serve three years; mustered in as private, Co. H, October 10, 1862; promoted corporal, no date; captured in action, May 5, 1864, at the Wilderness, Va; paroled, no date; mustered out, June 1, 1865, at Annapolis, Md.

FRANCISCO, FRANCIS E.—Age, 18 years. Enlisted, August 27, 1862, at Augusta, to serve three years; mustered in as private, Co. E, October 10, 1862.

FRANKLIN, JR., JOHN.—Age, 18 years. Enlisted, August 22, 1862, at Florence, to serve three years; mustered in as private, Co. F, October 10, 1862; wounded in action, May 27, 1864, at Totopotomay, Va.; died of his wounds, June 8, 1864, at Washington, D. C.

FREAS, PHILIP.—Age, 18 years. Enlisted, August 25, 1862, at Utica, to serve three years; mustered in as private, Co. C, October 10, 1862; appointed musician, no date; transferred to Co. A, August 20, 1863; mustered out with company, July 16, 1865, near Washington, D. C., as Frease.

FREDERICK, GODFREY.—Age, 22 years. Enlisted, August 25, 1862, at Kirkland, to serve three years; mustered in as private, Co. G, October 10, 1862; mustered out with company, July 16, 1865, near Washington, D. C. Died in 1895.

FRENCH, ANDREW J.—Age, 21 years. Enlisted, September 4, 1862, at Marshall, to serve three years; mustered in as private, Co. E, October 10, 1862; discharged for disability, February 14, 1863, at Washington, D. C.

FRENCH, EPHRAIM.—Age, 18 years. Enlisted, August 27, 1862, at Kirkland, to serve three years; mustered in as private, Co. G, October 10, 1862; captured in action, May 5, 1864, at the Wilderness, Va.; paroled, no date; mustered out, June 6, 1865, at York, Pa. Died, December 28, 1908.

FRITCHER, JOHN.—Age, 44 years. Enlisted, August 28, 1862, at Westmoreland, to serve three years; mustered in as private, Co. B, October 10, 1862; discharged for disability, March 11, 1863, at camp, near Falmouth, Va.

FULMER, JACOB P.—Age, 18 years. Enlisted, September 6, 1862, at Steuben, to serve three years; mustered in as private, Co. I, October 10, 1862; promoted corporal, no date; sergeant, July 1, 1865; mustered out with company, July 16, 1865, near Washington, D. C.

GARDNER, WILLARD D.—Age, 23 years. Enlisted, August 22, 1862, at Floyd, to serve three years; mustered in as corporal, Co. B, October 10, 1862; returned to ranks, no date.

GARIT, SAMUEL J.—Age, 32 years. Enlisted, August 28, 1862, at Boonville, to serve three years; mustered in as private, Co. D, October 10, 1862; captured, no date; died of disease, August 15, 1864, at Andersonville, Ga.

GARLOCK, ELIAS.—Age, 44 years. Enlisted, August 21, 1862, at Utica, to serve three years; mustered in as private, Co. K, October 10, 1862; discharged for disability, January 21, 1863, at Philadelphia, Pa.; also borne as Gorlock.

GARLOCK, JOHN.—Age, 28 years. Enlisted, August 26, 1862, at Vernon, to serve three years; mustered in as private, Co. B, October 10, 1862; killed in action, May 1, 1863, at Chancellorsville, Va.

GARRARD, KENNER.—Enrolled at Rome, to serve three years, and mustered in as colonel, October 10, 1862; discharged, July 25, 1863, for promotion to brigadier-general, U. S. Vols.

Commissioned colonel, September 23, 1862, with rank from same date, vice Delancey F. Jones declined; brevet major-general, by U. S. Government, from December 14, 1864.

GATES, REUBEN O.—Age, 18 years. Enlisted, August 19, 1862, at Utica, to serve three years; mustered in as private, Co. A, October 10, 1862; wounded and captured in action, May 5, 1864, at the Wilderness, Va.; died of his wounds, September 18, 1864, at Andersonville, Ga.

GAYLORD, DAVID B.—Age, 39 years. Enlisted, August 30, 1862, at Camden, to serve three years; mustered in as musician, Co. E, October 10, 1862; returned to company as a private, no date; discharged for disability, September 3, 1863.

GAYLORD, GEORGE M.—Age, 32 years. Enlisted, August 30, 1862, at Camden, to serve three years; mustered in as private, Co. E, October 10, 1862; captured, no date; died of disease, December 15, 1864, at Andersonville, Ga.

GEER, GEORGE A.—Age, 18 years. Enlisted, August 27, 1862, at Paris, to serve three years; mustered in as private, Co. H, October 10, 1862; transferred to Veteran Reserve Corps, July 23, 1864; also borne as Gear.

GERHARD, JOHN.—Age, 32 years. Enlisted, August 28, 1862, at Annsville, to serve three years; mustered in as private, Co. B, October 10, 1862; captured in action, May 5, 1864, at the Wilderness, Va.; died of chronic diarrhea, December 18, 1864, at Andersonville, Ga.

GIBBS, MENZO S.—Age, 20 years. Enlisted, August 20, 1862, at Utica, to serve three years; mustered in as private, Co. A, October 10, 1862; promoted corporal, no date; killed in action, May 3, 1863, at Chancellorsville, Va.

GIBBS, ORVILLE.—Age, 19 years. Enlisted, September 6, 1862, at Utica, to serve three years; mustered in as private, Co. H, October 10, 1862; captured in action, May 5, 1864; no further record.

GIBBS, SAMUEL.—Age, 22 years. Enlisted, August 28, 1862, at Boonville, to serve three years; mustered in as private, Co. D, October 10, 1862; wounded in action, July 3, 1863, at Gettysburg, Va.; discharged for wounds, January 15, 1864, at Washington, D. C.

GIBSON, ALONZO S.—Age, 20 years. Enlisted, August 26, 1862, at Camden, to serve three years; mustered in as corporal, Co. E, October 10, 1862; returned to ranks, November 3, 1862; captured, June 2, 1864, at Cold Harbor, Va.; paroled, November 20, 1864; promoted corporal, February 28, 1865; sergeant, June 3, 1865; mustered out with company, July 16, 1865, near Washington, D. C.

GIBSON, JAMES.—Age, 21 years. Enlisted, August 30, 1862, at Sangerfield, to serve three years; mustered in as private, Co. H, October 10, 1862; wounded in action, May 5, 1864, at the Wilderness, Va.; died of his wounds, June 18, 1864, at Washington, D. C.

GIBSON, MATHEW W.—Age, 28 years. Enlisted, August 25, 1862, at Vernon, to serve three years; mustered in as private, Co. B, October 10, 1862; discharged for disability, February 7, 1863, at Philadelphia, Pa.

GIBSON, ORSON B.—Age, 37 years. Enlisted, August 29, 1862, at Camden, to serve three years; mustered in as private, Co. E, October 10, 1862; commissary sergeant, same date; retransferred to Co. E, January 1, 1864, and returned to ranks; discharged for disability, January 16, ·1864, at Camden, N. Y.

GIFFORD, HARVEY.—Age, 32 years. Enlisted, September 4, 1862, at Marshall, to serve three years; mustered in as private, Co. K, October 10, 1862; promoted corporal, no date; sergeant, February 1, 1865; mustered out with company, July 16, 1865, near Washington, D. C.

Commissioned, not mustered, second lieutenant, June 17 1865, with rank from February 1, 1865, vice R. O. Jones not mustered. Died, February 14, 1887.

GILES, RICHARD S.—Age, 22 years. Enlisted, August 26, 1862, at Paris, to serve three years; mustered in as private, Co. K, October 10, 1862; promoted corporal and sergeant, no dates; discharged for disability, December 31, 1864, at Washington, D. C.

GILLMORE, JOHN.—Age, 40 years. Enlisted, September 1, 1862, at Kirkland, to serve three years; mustered in as private, Co. G, October 10, 1862; discharged for disability, March 15, 1863, near Falmouth, Va.; subsequent service in Co. C, Sixteenth Artillery.

GIVENS, WILLIAM W.—Age, 19 years. Enlisted, August 25, 1862, at Utica, to serve three years; mustered in as private, Co. A, October 10, 1862; wounded in action, May 3, 1863, at Chancellorsville, Va.; mustered out, May 19, 1865, at Albany, N. Y. Died in 1902.

GLOVER, EDWIN.—Age, 23 years. Enlisted, September 3, 1862, at Utica, to serve three years; mustered in as private, Co. C, October 10, 1862; captured in action, May 5, 1864, at the Wilderness, Va.; paroled, no date; promoted corporal, no date; sergeant, June 1, 1865; mustered out with company, July 16, 1865, near Washington, D. C. Died in 1901.

GLYNN, MARTIN.—Age, 27 years. Enlisted, at Rome, to serve three years, and mustered in as private, Co. A, October 10, 1862.

GODFREY, MAURICE.—Age, 21 years. Enlisted, August 28, 1862, at Utica, to serve three years; mustered in as private, Co. C, October 10, 1862; wounded in action, July, 1863, at Gettysburg, Pa.; mustered out with company, July 16, 1865, near Washington, D. C.; also borne as Morris Godfrey.

GOFF, JOHN W.—Age, 19 years. Enlisted, August 30, 1862, at Augusta, to serve three years; mustered in as private, Co. G, October 10, 1862; promoted sergeant, no date; captured in action, May 5, 1864, at the Wilderness, Va.; paroled, March 2, 1865, at Wilmington, N. C.; mustered out, July 22, 1865, at Rochester, N. Y.

GOODFELLOW, JOHN T.—Age, 22 years. Enlisted, August 30, 1862, at Kirkland, to serve three years; mustered in as private, Co. G, October 10, 1862; captured and paroled, no dates; mustered out with company, July 16, 1865, near Washington, D. C.

GOTTHILF, JACOB.—Age, 40 years. Enlisted, August 23, 1862, at Deerfield, to serve three years; mustered in as private, Co. F, October 10, 1862; transferred to Veteran Reserve Corps, September 30, 1863; mustered out as of Co. F, Ninth Regiment, Veteran Reserve Corps, July 18, 1865, at Washington, D. C.; also borne as Gothilf.

GOUGH, HUGH.—Age, 19 years. Enlisted, August 27, 1862, at Rome, to serve three years; mustered in as private, Co. B, October 10, 1862; wounded and captured in action, May 5, 1864, at the Wilderness, Va.; died of his wounds, November 10, 1864, at Andersonville, Ga.

GRAFF, JACOB.—Age, 22 years. Enlisted, August 21, 1862, at Utica, to serve three years, as private, Co. A.; died prior to muster-in of company.

GRAVES, FERDINAND V.—Age, 52 years. Enrolled, September 8, 1862, at Boonville, to serve three years; mustered in as second lieutenant, Co. D, October 10, 1862; discharged, January 10, 1863, near Falmouth, Va.

Commissioned second lieutenant, November 3, 1862, with rank from September 8, 1862, original. Died in 1896.

GREEN, HENRY W.—Age, 22 years. Enlisted, September 5, 1862, at Vienna, to serve three years; mustered in as private, Co. E, October 10, 1862; promoted sergeant, returned to ranks, and captured in action, no dates; died of disease, January 26, 1865, at Andersonville, Ga.

GREY, ALVAH.—Age, 20 years. Enlisted, August 28, 1862, at Boonville, to serve three years; mustered in as private, Co. D, October 10, 1862; promoted corporal and returned to ranks, no date; again promoted corporal, September 27, 1864; sergeant, May 11, 1865; mustered out with company, July 16, 1865, near Washington, D. C.

GRINDLAY, JAMES G.—Age, 25 years. Enrolled, at Boonville, to serve three years, and mustered in as captain, Co. D, September 8, 1862; as major, June 8, 1864; as lieutenant-colonel, January 1, 1865; as colonel, March 1, 1865; mustered out with regiment, July 16, 1865, near Washington, D. C.; awarded medal of honor.

Commissioned captain, November 3, 1862, with rank from September 8, 1862, original; major, May 18, 1864, with rank from April 4, 1864, vice H. H. Curran promoted; lieutenant-colonel (declined), December 7, 1864, with rank from December 1, 1864, vice H. H. Curran killed in action; again commissioned lieutenant-colonel, February 1, 1865, with rank from December 1, 1864, vice himself, declined; colonel, February 15, 1865, with rank from February 1, 1865, vice J. N. Potter commission revoked; brevet brigadier-general by U. S. Government from March 13, 1865. He was a member of the Loyal Legion and was three times elected president of the Fifth Corps Veteran Association; was twice married; his first wife was a Miss Anderson, of Boonville; his second, Miss Mary Peckham, of Utica. Died Oct. 19, 1907; killed by automobile at Troy, N. Y.

Born in Edinburgh, Scotland; came to this country when a young man and secured a position as bookkeeper in a tannery at Boonville; at close of war became a resident of Utica; prominent in political circles in the city and county; in 1892 he entered the State controller's office at Albany.

GUILLAUME, FREDERICK.—Age, 31 years. Enlisted, August 30, 1862, at Boonville, to serve three years; mustered in as private, Co. D, October 10, 1862; transferred to Veteran Reserve Corps, May 23, 1864; mustered out therefrom as of One Hundred and Sixty-sixth Company, Second Battalion, June 14, 1865, at Point Lookout, Md.; also borne as Guilliame and Guilleame. Died August 15, 1908, at Boonville, N. Y.

HACKETT, PATRICK.—Age, 37 years. Enlisted, August 21, 1862, at Utica, to serve three years; mustered in as private, Co. C, October 10, 1862; discharged for disability, August 17, 1863, at Washington, D. C.

HAHN, AGUSTUS.—Age, 36 years. Enlisted, August 29, 1862, at Deerfield, to serve three years; mustered in as private, Co. F, October 10, 1862; captured in action, May 5, 1864, at the Wilderness, Va.; released, May 1, 1865; mustered out with company, July 16, 1865, near Washington, D. C. Died, August 4, 1908, at Utica, N. Y.

HAIGH, MATTHEW B.—Age, 35 years. Enlisted, August 21, 1862, at Utica, to serve three years; mustered in as private, Co. H, October 10, 1862; absent, sick, since July 6, 1863, and at muster-out of company.

HALEY, CORNELIUS.—Age, 36 years. Enlisted, September 3, 1862, at Utica, to serve three years; mustered in as private, Co. C, October 10, 1862; mustered out with company, July 16, 1865, near Washington, D. C.

HALL, CHESTER.—Age, 22 years. Enlisted, September 1, 1862, at Boonville, to serve three years; mustered in as private, Co. D, October 10, 1862; wounded in action, December 15, 1862, at Fredericksburg, Va.; died of his wounds, December 30, 1862, at Washington, D. C.

HAMBERGER, SEBASTIAN.—Age, 21 years. Enlisted, August 26, 1862, at Utica, to serve three years; mustered in as private, Co. A, October 10, 1862; mustered out with company, July 16, 1865, near Washington, D. C., as Homberger. Died in 1905.

HAMBLIN, GEORGE.—Age, 35 years. Enlisted, August 22, 1862, at Utica, to serve three years; mustered in as private, Co. H, October 10, 1862; also borne as Hamlin.

HAMMOND, LE ROY.—Age, 22 years. Enlisted, September 4, 1862, at Bridgewater, to serve three years; mustered in as private, Co. G, October 10, 1862; captured in action, May 5, 1864, at the Wilderness, Va.; died, August 4, 1864, at Lynchburg, Va.

HANDWRIGHT, JR., JAMES.—Age, 21 years. Enrolled August 28, 1862, at Utica, to serve three years; mustered in as private, Co. A, October 10, 1862; promoted first sergeant, no date; captured in action, May 5, 1864, at the Wilderness, Va.; paroled, no date; mustered in as first lieutenant, Co. B, June 25, 1865; mustered out with company, July 16, 1865, near Washington, D. C.

Commissioned, revoked, second lieutenant, December 30, 1864, with rank from December 27, 1864, vice first lieutenant, June 17, 1865, with rank from February 1, 1865, vice H. G. Taylor not mustered; brevet captain by U. S. Government, from March 13, 1865.

HANNAY, THERON.—Age, 21 years. Enlisted, August 29, 1862, at Annsville, to serve three years; mustered in as private, Co. F, October 10, 1862; died of typhoid fever, July 2, 1863, at Frederick City, Md., as Hannah.

HARRINGTON, CARLOS.—Age, 29 years. Enlisted, August 27, 1862, at Utica, to serve three years; mustered in as private, Co. E, October 10, 1862; discharged for disability, April 29, 1865, in the field. Died at Utica, N. Y., in 1897.

HARRINGTON, MYRON.—Age, 18 years. Enlisted, September 5, 1862, at Camden, to serve three years; mustered in as musician, Co. E, October 10, 1862; returned to company as private, no date; discharged for disability, October 20, 1862.

HART, CHRISTIAN.—Age, 21 years. Enlisted, August 29, 1862, at Utica, to serve three years; mustered in as private, Co. F, October 10, 1862; promoted corporal and sergeant, no dates; killed in action, May 5, 1864, at the Wilderness, Va.

HART, HENRY.—Age, 21 years. Enlisted, October 2, 1862, at Rome, to serve three years; mustered in as private, Co. E, October 10, 1862.

HART, WILLIAM.—Age, 24 years. Enlisted, August 22, 1862, at Utica, to serve three years; mustered in as private, Co. C, October 10, 1862; discharged for disability, March 21, 1863.

HARTER, JOHN.—Age, 31 years. Enlisted, August 25, 1862, at Westmoreland, to serve three years; mustered in as private, Co. I, October 10, 1862; mustered out with company, July 16, 1865, near Washington, D. C.

HARTER, JOHN A.—Age, 38 years. Enlisted, September 6, 1862, at Bridgewater, to serve three years; mustered in as private, Co. G, October 10, 1862; appointed musician, no date; transferred to Co. E, March 28, 1863; killed in action, May 10, 1864, at Laurel Hill, Va.

HAYNES, WILLIAM.—Age, 27 years. Enlisted, August 30, 1862, at Utica, to serve three years; mustered in as private, Co. C, October 10, 1862; mustered out with company, July 16, 1865, near Washington, D. C.

HAYTHORPE, GEORGE.—Age, 35 years. Enlisted, September 29, 1862, at Rome, to serve three years; mustered in as private, Co. B, October 10, 1862; promoted corporal, June 12, 1863.

HECOX, CHARLES.—Age, 16 years. Enlisted, August 28, 1862, at Kirkland, to serve three years; mustered in as private, Co. B, October 10, 1862; appointed musician, no date; mustered out with company, July 16, 1865, near Washington, D. C.

HECOX, JOHN S.—Age, 22 years. Enlisted, September 13, 1862, at Kirkland, to serve three years; mustered in as private, Co. D, October 10, 1862.

HELMER, JOSIAH.—Age, 19 years. Enlisted, August 29, 1862, at Boonville, to serve three years; mustered in as private, Co. D, October 10, 1862; promoted corporal, no date; captured and paroled, no date; mustered out, May 30, 1865, at Annapolis, Md.

HEMSTREET, ALVA P.—Age, 30 years. Enlisted, August 31, 1862, at Russia, to serve three years; mustered in as private, Co. K, October 10, 1862; transferred to Co. I, no date; mustered out, June 24, 1865, at Washington, D. C.

HESS, JOHN.—Age, 21 years. Enlisted, October 2, 1862, at Rome, to serve three years; mustered in as private, Co. H, October 10, 1862; captured in action, May 5, 1864, at the Wilderness, Va.; paroled, no date; mustered out, June 22, 1865, at Hicks Hospital, Baltimore, Md.

HIBBARD, HIRAM F.—Age, 23 years. Enlisted, September 8, 1862, at Bridgewater, to serve three years; mustered in as private, Co. G, October 10, 1862; discharged for disability, February 7, 1863, at Philadelphia, Pa.

HILAND, PATRICK.—Age, 18 years. Enlisted, August 29, 1862, at Rome, to serve three years; mustered in as private, Co. B, October 10, 1862; wounded in action, May 1, 1863, at Chancellorsville, Va.; discharged for disability, September 15, 1863, at Washington, D. C.

HINKESTON, SR., WILLIAM.—Age, 41 years. Enlisted, August 13, 1862, at Utica, to serve three years; mustered in as private, Co. A, October 10, 1862; transferred to Veteran Reserve Corps, February 22, 1864; mustered out therefrom as of Co. C, First Regiment, July 31, 1865, at Rochester, N. Y.; also borne as Hinkstone.

HINKLEY, RALPH.—Age, 26 years. Enlisted, August 26, 1862, at Lee, to serve three years; mustered in as private, Co. F, October 10, 1862; promoted corporal, no date; captured in action, May 5, 1864, at the Wilderness, Va.; died, November 19, 1864, at Andersonville, Ga.

HINKSTONE, JR., WILLIAM.—Age, 18 years. Enlisted, August 30, 1862, at Utica, to serve three years; mustered in as private, Co. A, October 10, 1862; mustered out with company, July 16, 1865, near Washington, D. C.

HOAG, ALBERT.—Age, 21 years. Enlisted, August 30, 1862, at Westmoreland, to serve three years; mustered in as private, Co. I, October 10, 1862; died, March 7, 1863, in Regimental Hospital, near Henry House, Va.

HOAGLAND, ZADOCK P.—Age, 29 years. Enlisted, August 29, 1862, at Boonville, to serve three years; mustered in as private, Co. D, October 10, 1862; promoted sergeant, and returned to ranks, and promoted corporal, no dates; killed in action, June 2, 1864, at Bethesda Church, Va.

HOGAN, MICHAEL.—Age, 44 years. Enlisted, September 2, 1862, at Rome, to serve three years; mustered in as private, Co. B, October 10, 1862; discharged for disability, March 21, 1864, at Washington, D. C.

HOOK, HENRY B.—Age, 21 years. Enlisted, September 6, 1862, at Bridgewater, to serve three years; mustered in as private,

Co. G, October 10, 1862; wounded and captured, May 5, 1864, at the Wilderness, Va.; paroled, no date; mustered out with company, July 16, 1865, near Washington, D. C.

HOPKINS, WILLIAM H.—Age, 28 years. Enlisted, August 30, 1862, at Sangerfield, to serve three years; mustered in as private, Co. H, October 10, 1862; died of disease, December 19, 1862, at Falmouth, Va.

HOUGHTON, JOHN.—Age, 24 years. Enlisted, August 31, 1862, at Camden, to serve three years; mustered in as private, Co. E, October 10, 1862; discharged for disability, no date.

HOWARD, OSCAR.—Age, 25 years. Enlisted, August 29, 1862, at Rome, to serve three years; mustered in as private, Co. K, October 10, 1862; also borne as Oscar L. Howard.

HOWELL, DAVID E.—Age, 21 years. Enlisted, August 20, 1862, at Utica, to serve three years; mustered in as sergeant, Co. C, October 10, 1862; returned to ranks, no date.

HUFTAILING, STORM.—Age, 40 years. Enlisted, August 29, 1862, at Boonville, to serve three years; mustered in as private, Co. D, October 10, 1862.

HUFTALL, NELSON.—Age, 37 years. Enlisted, August 29, 1862, at Boonville, to serve three years; mustered in as private, Co. D, October 10, 1862.

HUGHES, EDWARD.—Age, 29 years. Enlisted, August 28, 1862, at Utica, to serve three years; mustered in as private, Co. E, October 10, 1862; captured in action, May 5, 1864, at the Wilderness, Va.; died of disease, December 11, 1864, at Florence, S. C.

HUGHES, JEHIAL.—Age, 18 years. Enlisted, August 29, 1862, at Boonville, to serve three years; mustered in as private, Co. D, October 10, 1862; died, January 2, 1863, at Washington, D. C.

HUGHES, JOHN J.—Age, 27 years. Enlisted, September 2, 1862, at Remsen, to serve three years; mustered in as private, Co. I, October 10, 1862; captured in action, May 5, 1864, at the Wilderness, Va.; died of disease, September 18, 1864, at Florence, S. C.

HUGHES, JOHN W.—Age, 23 years. Enlisted, August 30, 1862, at Remsen, to serve three years; mustered in as private, Co.

I, October 10, 1862; discharged for disability, March 11, 1863, near Potomac Creek, Va.

HUGHES, JOHN W.—Age, 21 years. Enlisted, August 26, 1862, at Rome, to serve three years; mustered in as private, Co. B, October 10, 1862.

HUGHES, WILLIAM.—Age, 30 years. Enlisted, September 1, 1862, at Remsen, to serve three years; mustered in as private, Co. I, October 10, 1862; mustered out, June 24, 1865, at Washington, D. C.

HUGHES, WILLIAM D.—Age, 29 years. Enlisted, September 2, 1862, at Rome, to serve three years; mustered in as corporal, Co. B, October 10, 1862; promoted sergeant, November 21, 1862; returned to ranks, June 25, 1863; mustered out, July 15, 1865, at Albany, N. Y. Born in Wales, and came to America in 1852; died, June 16, 1911, at Camroden, N. Y.

HYDE, ASA NILES.—Age, 23 years. Enlisted, August 29, 1862, at Annsville, to serve three years; mustered in as private, Co. B, October 10, 1862; promoted corporal, no date; returned to ranks, November 15, 1862; discharged, April 12, 1864, at Washington, D. C.

HYDE, EZRA J.—Age, 26 years. Enlisted, August 27, 1862, at Annsville, to serve three years; mustered in as private, Co. B, October 10, 1862; killed, July 3, 1863, at Gettysburg, Pa.

HYDE, SAMUEL.—Age, 36 years. Enlisted, August 27, 1862, at Kirkland, to serve three years; mustered in as private, Co. G, October 10, 1862; captured in action, June 2, 1864, at Cold Harbor, Va.; no further record.

JACKSON, CALEB L.—Age, 44 years. Enlisted, August 30, 1862, at Boonville, to serve three years; mustered in as private, Co. D, October 10, 1862.

JACKSON, FARRAR.—Age, 23 years. Enlisted, September 4, 1862, at Kirkland, to serve three years; mustered in as private, Co. G, October 10, 1862; promoted sergeant, March 3, 1863; captured in action, May 5, 1864, at the Wilderness, Va.; no further record.

JACKSON, JAMES H.—Age, 21 years. Enlisted, August 30, 1862, at Boonville, to serve three years; mustered in as private, Co. D, October 10, 1862.

JACKSON, JOHN.—Age, 28 years. Enlisted, August 30, 1862, at Kirkland, to serve three years; mustered in as corporal, Co. G, October 10, 1862; promoted sergeant, no date.

JAMES, JOHN.—Age, 20 years. Enlisted, August 29, 1862, at Steuben, to serve three years; mustered in as private, Co. I, October 10, 1862; discharged for disability, October 24, 1863, at Washington, D. C.

JAMES, JOHN.—Age, 19 years. Enlisted, August 30, 1862, at Rome, to serve three years; mustered in as private, Co. B, October 10, 1862; transferred, no date, and mustered out as of Co. G, Twenty-fourth Regiment, Veteran Reserve Corps, June 28, 1865, at Washington, D. C.

JAMES, JONATHAN.—Age, 21 years. Enlisted, October 8, 1862, at Frankfort, to serve three years; mustered in as private, Co. C, October 10, 1862; died, February 19, 1863, at Falmouth, Va.

JEFFERS, JOHN.—Age, 37 years. Enlisted, August 28, 1862, at Boonville, to serve three years; mustered in as corporal, Co. D, October 10, 1862; promoted sergeant, June 3, 1865; mustered out, July 26, 1865, at Syracuse, N. Y.

JENKINS, DAVID T.—Age, 26 years. Enrolled at Albany, to serve three years, and mustered in as first lieutenant and adjutant, August 26, 1862; as major, September 17, 1862; as lieutenant-colonel, October 11, 1862; as colonel, July 23, 1863; killed in action, May 5, 1864, at the Wilderness, Va.

Not commissioned first lieutenant and adjutant, commissioned major, October 2, 1862, with rank from September 17, 1862, original; lieutenant-colonel, October 11, 1862, with rank from same date, vice George Pomeroy not mustered; colonel, August 7, 1863, with rank from July 23, 1863, vice Kenner Garrard promoted brigadier-general, U. S. Vols.

JENKS, MARTIN S.—Age, 19 years. Enlisted, September 3, 1862, at Kirkland, to serve three years; mustered in as corporal, Co. E, October 10, 1862; returned to ranks, no date; discharged for disability, December 24, 1863, at Washington, D. C.

JENNISON, CHARLES E.—Age, 22 years. Enlisted, August 29, 1862, at Utica, to serve three years; mustered in as private,

Co. C, October 10, 1862; promoted corporal, no date; mustered out, July 7, 1865, at Washington, D. C.

JENNISON, HENRY J.—Age, 29 years. Enlisted, September 6, 1862, at Utica, to serve three years; mustered in as private, Co. C, October 10, 1862; killed in action, May 5, 1864, at the Wilderness, Va.

JENNISON, J. ALBERT.—Age, 21 years. Enrolled, August 21, 1862, at Utica, to serve three years; mustered in as private, Co. C, October 10, 1862; promoted sergeant and first sergeant, no dates; mustered in as second lieutenant, Co. K, January 17, 1863; as first lieutenant, February 1, 1865; mustered out with company, July 16, 1865, near Washington, D. C.

Commissioned second lieutenant, December 30, 1864, with rank from December 1, 1864, vice J. McGeehan promoted; first lieutenant, June 17, 1865, with rank from February 1, 1865, vice A. I. King promoted; brevet captain, by U. S. Government, from March 13, 1865.

JEPSON, THOMAS.—Age, 19 years. Enlisted, August 19, 1862, at Utica, to serve three years; mustered in as private, Co. K, October 10, 1862; transferred to Veteran Reserve Corps, May 31, 1864; also borne as Jepsom.

JEWELL, E. VERN.—Age, 23 years. Enrolled at Rome, to serve three years, and mustered in as first lieutenant, Co. B, September 3, 1862; promoted captain, Co. C, December 25, 1862; discharged, September 23, 1863.

Commissioned first lieutenant, November 3, 1862, with rank from September 3, 1862, original; captain, February 5, 1863, with rank from January 7, 1863, vice G. W. M. Lewis resigned.

JOHNSON, AMOS.—Age, 41 years. Enlisted, August 28, 1862, at Boonville, to serve three years; mustered in as corporal, Co. D, October 10, 1862; transferred to Veteran Reserve Corps, no date.

JOHNSON, CHARLES.—Age, 22 years. Enlisted, August 21, 1862, at Utica, to serve three years; mustered in as private, Co. K, October 10, 1862; promoted sergeant, no date; returned to ranks, January 3, 1863; promoted corporal and returned to ranks, no date; mustered out, June 6, 1865, at Washington, D. C.

JOHNSON, FREDERICK.—Age, 25 years. Enlisted, August 21, 1862, at Utica, to serve three years; mustered in as first sergeant, Co. C, October 10, 1862; discharged, December 23, 1863, for promotion to hospital steward, U. S. Army.

JOHNSON, GEORGE W.—Age, 22 years. Enlisted, August 30, 1862, at Rome, to serve three years; mustered in as corporal, Co. F, October 10, 1862; captured in action, May 5, 1864, at the Wilderness, Va.; paroled, March 4, 1865; mustered out, May 24, 1865, at New York City.

JOHNSON, THOMAS.—Age, 39 years. Enlisted, August 25, 1862, at Kirkland, to serve three years; mustered in as corporal, Co. G, October 10, 1862; returned to ranks, no date; discharged for disability, May 4, 1865. Died November 5, 1898.

JONES, DAVID.—Age, 30 years. Enlisted, September 10, 1862 at Remsen, to serve three years; mustered in as private, Co. I, October 10, 1862.

JONES, DAVID.—Age, 27 years. Enlisted, August 22, 1862, at Utica, to serve three years; mustered in as private, Co. C, October 10, 1862.

JONES, EDWARD.—Age, 19 years. Enlisted, August 22, 1862, at Utica, to serve three years; mustered in as private, Co. H, October 10, 1862; captured in action, August 19, 1864, at Weldon Railroad, Va.; paroled, March 5, 1865; mustered out with company, July 16, 1865, near Washington, D. C.

JONES, EDWARD O.—Age, 21 years. Enrolled, August 25, 1862, at Utica, to serve three years; mustered in as corporal, Co. F, October 10, 1862; promoted sergeant, April 1, 1863; first sergeant, March 26, 1865; mustered in as second lieutenant, Co. E, March 30, 1865; as first lieutenant, Co. I, May 7, 1865; mustered out with company, July 16, 1865, near Washington, D. C.

Commissioned second lieutenant, March 30, 1865, with rank from February 1, 1865, vice G. J. Klock promoted; first lieutenant, June 17, 1865, with rank from February 1, 1865, vice L. Fitzpatrick promoted; brevet captain, by U. S. Government, from March 13, 1865.

JONES, EDWARD T.—Age, 20 years. Enlisted, August 28, 1862, at Remsen, to serve three years; mustered in as private,

Co. I, October 10, 1862; discharged, June 6, 1865, at Washington, D. C.

JONES, EVAN T.—Age, 22 years. Enlisted, August 13, 1862, at Remsen, to serve three years; mustered in as private, Co. I, October 10, 1862; captured in action, May 5, 1864, at the Wilderness, Va.; paroled, no date; wounded in action, no date; discharged for wounds, March 16, 1865, at hospital.

JONES, EZEKIEL.—Age, — years. Enrolled at Rome, to serve three years, and mustered in as captain, Co. I, October 10, 1862; died of typhoid fever, November 11, 1862, at Rome, N. Y.

Commissioned captain, November 3, 1862, with rank from October 7, 1862, original.

JONES, GEORGE W.—Age, 23 years. Enlisted, August 21, 1862, at Remsen, to serve three years; mustered in as private, Co. I, October 10, 1862; promoted corporal, December 6, 1863; sergeant, January 1, 1864; first sergeant, March 1, 1865; mustered out with company, July 16, 1865, near Washington, D. C.

Commissioned, not mustered, second lieutenant, June 17, 1865, with rank from February 1, 1865, vice George Mould not mustered.

JONES, HENRY E.—Age, 24 years. Enrolled, August 18, 1862, at Steuben, to serve three years; mustered in as private, Co. I, October 10, 1862; promoted first sergeant, no date; mustered in as second lieutenant, Co. G, January 7, 1863; as first lieutenant, Co. D, March 1, 1863; as captain, Co. I, September 24, 1863; wounded in action, May 5, 1864, at the Wilderness, Va.; mustered out with company, July 16, 1865, near Washington, D. C.

Commissioned second lieutenant, February 5, 1863, with rank from January 7, 1863, vice S. B. Alden resigned; first lieutenant, July 29, 1863, with rank from March 1, 1863, vice S. J. Truax resigned; captain, November 9, 1863, with rank from September 23, 1863, vice J. J. Armstrong promoted; brevet major by U. S. Government, from March 13, 1865. Died in 1902.

JONES, JAMES D.—Age, 24 years. Enlisted, September 6, 1862, at Remsen, to serve three years; mustered in as private,

Co. I, October 10, 1862; mustered out, May 23, 1865, at Mower Hospital, Philadelphia, Pa.

JONES, JOHN.—Age, 23 years. Enlisted, September 1, 1862, at Rome, to serve three years; mustered in as private, Co. B, October 10, 1862.

JONES, JOHN E.—Age, 36 years. Enlisted, September 2, 1862, at Utica to serve three years; mustered in as private, Co. H, October 10, 1862; promoted corporal, and sergeant, no dates; killed in action, May 5, 1864, at the Wilderness, Va.

JONES, JOHN P.—Age, 18 years. Enlisted, September 5, 1862, at Remsen, to serve three years; mustered in as private, Co. I, October 10, 1862; promoted corporal, no date; died, March 13, 1863, at Division Hospital, near Potomac Creek, Va.

JONES, JOSEPH.—Age, 21 years. Enlisted, September 2, 1862, at Utica to serve three years; mustered in as private, Co. H, October 10, 1862; discharged for disability, May 31, 1865, at hospital, Philadelphia, Pa.

JONES, MERIT.—Age, 18 years. Enlisted, August 26, 1862, at Utica, to serve three years; mustered in as private, Co. A, October 10, 1862.

JONES, ORLO H.—Age, 22 years. Enlisted, August 30, 1862, at Boonville, to serve three years; mustered in as private, Co. D, October 10, 1862; promoted corporal, sergeant, and first sergeant, no dates; wounded and captured in action, June 2, 1864, at Bethesda Church, Va.; died of his wounds, June 20, 1864, at Richmond, Va.

JONES, OWEN.—Age, 28 years. Enlisted, September 22, 1862, at Utica, to serve three years; mustered in as private, Co. H, October 10, 1862; mustered out, May 24, 1865, at Mower Hospital, Philadelphia, Pa.

JONES, ROBERT.—Age, 21 years. Enlisted, August 25, 1862, at Floyd, to serve three years; mustered in as private, Co. B, October 10, 1862; mustered out with company, July 16, 1865, near Washington, D. C.

JONES, ROBERT O.—Age, 21 years. Enlisted, September 2,1862, at Russia, to serve three years; mustered in as private, Co. I, October 10, 1862; promoted corporal, no date.

JONES, R. OWEN.—Age, 22 years. Enlisted, August 30, 1862, at Utica, to serve three years; mustered in as corporal, Co. C, October 10, 1862; promoted sergeant, no date; mustered out, June 5, 1865, at Elmira, N. Y.

Commissioned, not mustered, second lieutenant, March 30, 1865, with rank from February 1, 1865, vice J. B. Seaman promoted.

JONES, THEODORE R.—Age, 19 years. Enlisted, August 20, 1862, at Utica, to serve three years; mustered in as private, Co. C, October 10, 1862; mustered out with company, July 16, 1865, near Washington, D. C. Died in 1902.

JONES, THOMAS.—Age, 26 years. Enlisted, September 3, 1862, at Utica, to serve three years; mustered in as private, Co. K, October 10, 1862; transferred to Co. A, November 3, 1862; captured in action, May 3, 1863, at Chancellorsville, Va.; paroled, no date; again captured in action, May 5, 1864, at the Wilderness, Va.; paroled, no date; died of disease, March 7, 1865, at Utica, N. Y.

JONES, THOMAS.—Age, 38 years. Enlisted, September 3, 1862, at Utica, to serve three years; mustered in as private, Co. H, October 10, 1862; mustered out with company, July 16, 1865, near Washington, D. C.

JONES, THOMAS C.—Age, — years. Enrolled, September 2, 1862, at Rome, to serve three years; mustered in as first lieutenant, Co. A, October 10, 1862; transferred to Co. C, December 22, 1862; discharged, January 7, 1863.

Commissioned first lieutenant, November 3, 1862, with rank from September 2, 1862, original. Died in 1902.

JONES, WILLIAM.—Age, 32 years. Enlisted, September 6, 1862, at Utica, to serve three years; mustered in as private, Co. H, October 10, 1862; wounded in action and died, August 21, 1864, at Weldon Railroad, Va.

JONES, WILLIAM E.—Age, 25 years. Enlisted, September 5, 1862, at Remsen, to serve three years; mustered in as private, Co. I, October 10, 1862; mustered out with company, July 16, 1865, near Washington, D. C.

JOSLIN, JR., JOHN A.—Age, 22 years. Enlisted, August 28, 1862, at Boonville, to serve three years; mustered in as private, Co. D, October 10, 1862; died, no date, at Washington, D. C.

JOSLIN, JOSEPH B.—Age, 23 years. Enlisted, August 28, 1862, at Boonville, to serve three years; mustered in as private, Co. D, December 31, 1862; discharged for disability, May 9, 1863, at Washington, D. C. Died in 1898.

JOY, HENRY L.—Age, 42 years. Enlisted, September 5, 1862, at Remsen, to serve three years; mustered in as private, Co. I, October 10, 1862; promoted sergeant and returned to ranks, no date; mustered out, May 17, 1865, at Davids Island, New York Harbor. Died, May 31, 1910, at Ilion, N. Y.

KEARNS, JAMES P.—Age, 21 years. Enlisted, August 22, 1862, at Utica, to serve three years; mustered in as private, Co. A, October 10, 1862; captured in action, May 3, 1863, at Chancellorsville, Va.; paroled, no date; wounded and captured in action, May 5, 1864, at the Wilderness, Va.; paroled, no date; died of his wounds, December 10, 1864, at Annapolis, Md.

KEATING, MICHAEL.—Age, 31 years. Enlisted, August 30, 1862, at Utica, to serve three years; mustered in as private, Co. A, October 10, 1862; captured in action, May 3, 1863, at Chancellorsville, Va.; paroled, no date; wounded and captured in action, May 5, 1864, at the Wilderness, Va.; died of his wounds, September 12, 1864, at Andersonville, Ga.

KEEGAN, RICHARD.—Age, 18 years. Enlisted, August 28, 1862, at Hawkinsville, to serve three years; mustered in as private, Co. D, October 10, 1862; appointed musician, no date, mustered out with company, July 16, 1865, near Washington, D. C., as Keigan.

KELLAR, JOHN.—Age, 21 years. Enlisted, August 18, 1862, at Verona, to serve three years; mustered in as private, Co. E, October 10, 1862.

KELLEY, ROBERT.—Age, 21 years. Enlisted, September 6, 1862, at Utica, to serve three years; mustered in as private, Co. H, October 10, 1862; mustered out, June 3, 1865, at Washington, D. C.

KELLSY, JOSEPH S.—Age, 26 years. Enlisted, September 5, 1862, at Camden, to serve three years; mustered in as private, Co. E, October 10, 1862; mustered out with company,

July 16, 1865, near Washington, D. C., as Samuel J. Kellsey.

KELLY, PATRICK.—Age, 35 years. Enlisted, August 26, 1862, at Utica, to serve three years; mustered in as private, Co. E, October 10, 1862; captured, no date; died of disease, December 25, 1864, at Salisbury, N. C.; also borne as Kelley.

KEMPF, JOHN.—Age, 18 years. Enlisted, September 1, 1862, at Whitestown, to serve three years; mustered in as private, Co. A, October 10, 1862; captured in action, May 3, 1863, at Chancellorsville, Va.; paroled, no date; again captured in action, May 5, 1864, at the Wilderness, Va.; died of disease, August 10, 1864, at Andersonville, Ga.; also borne as Kemph.

KENNEDY, JOHN.—Age, 25 years. Enlisted, August 26, 1862, at Utica, to serve three years; mustered in as private, Co. E, October 10, 1862; promoted sergeant and first sergeant, no dates; captured in action, May 5, 1864, at the Wilderness, Va.; died of disease, November 15, 1864, at Milan, Ga.

KENT, GEORGE T.—Age, 22 years. Enlisted, August 19, 1862, at Utica, to serve three years; mustered in as sergeant, Co. C, October 10, 1862; returned to ranks, no date.

KENT, JOSEPH H.—Age, 18 years. Enlisted, September 29, 1862, at New Hartford, to serve three years; mustered in as private, Co. C, October 10, 1862; transferred to Veteran Reserve Corps, July 3, 1864. Died in 1903.

KENT, SILAS.—Age, 22 years. Enlisted, August 30, 1862, at Remsen, to serve three years; mustered in as private, Co. I, October 10, 1862; died, November 18, 1862, at hospital, Washington, D. C.

KILBORN, JAY.—Age, 25 years. Enlisted, October 3, 1862, at Whitestown, to serve three years; mustered in as private, Co. D, October 10, 1862; appointed musician, no date; transferred to Veteran Reserve Corps, September 3, 1863,

KILLIPS, JAMES.—Age, 44 years. Enlisted, August 26, 1862, at Camden, to serve three years; mustered in as private, Co. E, October 10, 1862; discharged for disability, January 26, 1863, at Washington, D. C.

KING, ALONZO I.—Age, 23 years. Enrolled, August 29, 1862, at Whitestown, to serve three years; mustered in as private, Co. K, October 10, 1862; promoted sergeant, same date;

returned to ranks, December 17, 1862; promoted sergeant, January 15, 1863; first sergeant, January 30, 1863; mustered in as second lieutenant, Co. C, to date January 8, 1863; wounded in action, May 5, 1864, at the Wilderness, Va.; mustered in as first lieutenant, Co. A, December 1, 1864; as captain, February 1, 1865; mustered out with company, July 16, 1865, near Washington, D. C.

Commissioned second lieutenant, March 27, 1863, with rank from January 7, 1863, vice E. R. Matterson promoted; first lieutenant, December 30, 1864, with rank from December 1, 1864, vice C. K. Dutton promoted; captain, June 17, 1865, with rank from February 1, 1865, vice T. A. Wilson deceased; brevet captain, by U. S. Government, from March 13, 1865.

KING, CHARLES L.—Age, 21 years. Enlisted, September 1, 1862, at Sangerfield, to serve three years; mustered in as private, Co. H, October 10, 1862; promoted corporal, no date; captured in action, May 5, 1864, at the Wilderness, Va.; paroled, February 25, 1865; promoted first sergeant, June 1, 1865; mustered out with company, July 16, 1865, near Washington, D. C.

KING, CURTIS M.—Age, 21 years. Enlisted, September 6, 1862, at Bridgewater, to serve three years; mustered in as private, Co. G, October 10, 1862; mustered out with company, July 16, 1865, near Washington, D. C.

KING, GEORGE.—Age, 25 years. Enlisted, September 3, 1862, at Utica, to serve three years; mustered in as private, Co. C, October 10, 1862; captured in action, May 5, 1864, at the Wilderness, Va.; died of disease, September 18, 1864, at Florence, S. C.

KING, JAMES A.—Age, 31 years. Enlisted, September 29, 1862, at Bridgewater, to serve three years; mustered in as private, Co. G, October 10, 1862; mustered out, June 6, 1865, at Washington, D. C.

KINGSLEY, GEORGE H.—Age, 25 years. Enlisted, August 29, 1862, at Annsville, to serve three years; mustered in as private, Co. F, October 10, 1862; captured in action, May 5, 1864, at the Wilderness, Va.; died of disease, October 28, 1864, at Florence, S. C.

KIRKLAND, RALPH T.—Age, 18 years. Enlisted, September 1, 1862, at Kirkland, to serve three years; mustered in as private, Co. G, October 10, 1862; mustered out, August 14, 1865, at Elmira, N. Y.

KIRKLAND, THOMAS.—Age, 22 years. Enlisted, August 26, 1862, at Utica, to serve three years; mustered in as private, Co. A, October 10, 1862; promoted corporal and returned to ranks, no dates.

KLOCK, GEORGE J.—Age, 26 years. Enrolled, August 29, 1862, at Boonville, to serve three years; mustered in as corporal, Co. D, October 10, 1862; promoted sergeant and first sergeant, no dates; mustered in as second lieutenant, Co. I, January 17, 1865; as first lieutenant, March 30, 1865; wounded in action, March 31, 1865, at White Oak Ridge, Va.; discharged, June 1, 1865; also borne as Clock.

Commissioned second lieutenant, December 30, 1864, with rank from December 1, 1864, vice A. I. King promoted; first lieutenant, March 30, 1865, with rank from February 1, 1865, vice L. H. York promoted; brevet first lieutenant, by U. S. Government, from March 13, 1865.

KLUMBACH, JOHN J.—Age, 22 years. Enlisted, August 30, 1862, at Utica, to serve three years; mustered in as private, Co. F, October 10, 1862; transferred, January 10, 1865, and mustered out as of Co. D, Ninth Regiment, Veteran Reserve Corps, July 20, 1865, at Washington, D. C.

KNIFFEN, DANIEL.—Age, 19 years. Enlisted, August 29, 1862, at Camden, to serve three years; mustered in as corporal, Co. E, October 10, 1862.

KNIGHT, ALBERT.—Age, 18 years. Enlisted, September 5, 1862, at Ava, to serve three years; mustered in as private, Co. F, October 10, 1862; died of typhoid fever, February 22, 1863, in Regimental Hospital, Potomac Creek, Va.

KRATCHBERG, JOHN H.—Age, 18 years. Enlisted, August 27, 1862, at Utica, to serve three years; mustered in as private, Co. C, October 10, 1862; captured in action, May 5, 1864, at the Wilderness, Va.; paroled, no date; mustered out, May 26, 1865, at Albany, N. Y., as Craschbury; also borne as Cratchburgh.

LAKE, MATTHEW.—Age, 42 years. Enlisted, August 27, 1862,

at Trenton, to serve three years; mustered in as private, Co. I, October 10, 1862; died, February 17, 1863, in Regimental Hospital, near Henry House, Va.

LAMBIE, GAVIN A.—Age, 30 years. Enrolled at Rome, to serve three years, and mustered in as captain, Co. E, September 9, 1862; died of disease, February 15, 1863, at Camden, N. Y. Commissioned captain, November 3, 1862, with rank from September 9, 1862, original.

LAMOUR, JOSEPH.—Age, 21 years. Enlisted, August 30, 1862, at Utica, to serve three years; mustered in as private, Co. A, October 10, 1862; captured in action, May 5, 1864, at the Wilderness, Va.; paroled, no date; mustered out with company, July 16, 1865, near Washington, D. C.

LANG, CHRISTIAN P.—Age, 24 years. Enlisted, August 27, 1862, at Utica, to serve three years; mustered in as corporal, Co. F, October 10, 1862; returned to ranks, January 31, 1863; captured in action, August 21, 1864, at Weldon Railroad, Va.; escaped, April 29, 1865; mustered out with company, July 16, 1865, near Washington, D. C.

LANPHIER, VANESS H.—Age, 18 years. Enlisted, August 30, 1862, at Utica, to serve three years; mustered in as private, Co. A, October 10, 1862; died of disease, October 7, 1863, at Harewood Hospital, Washington, D. C.; also borne as Van Ess H. Lamphear.

LANSING, GEORGE H.—Age, 19 years. Enlisted, August 25, 1862, at Utica, to serve three years; mustered in as corporal, Co. F, October 10, 1862.

LARKIN, PATRICK.—Age, 27 years. Enlisted, August 22, 1862, at Utica, to serve three years; mustered in as private, Co. K, October 10, 1862.

LARMAR, TIMOTHY.—Age, 18 years. Enlisted, August 22, 1862, at Utica, to serve three years; mustered in as private, Co. A, October 10, 1862; captured in action, May 1, 1863, at Chancellorsville, Va.; returned to company, July 26, 1863; killed in action, May 5, 1864, at the Wilderness, Va.; also borne as Larmour.

LASHER, CHARLES E.—Age, 25 years. Enrolled, August 21, 1862, at Paris, to serve three years; mustered in as private, Co. K, October 10, 1862; promoted first sergeant, no date;

second lieutenant, Co. C, January 13, 1863; mustered in as first lieutenant, January 31, 1863.

Commissioned second lieutenant, January 22, 1863, with rank from December 23, 1862, vice W. H. Smith resigned; first lieutenant, February 23, 1863, with rank from February 2, 1863, vice James E. Jenkins promoted.

LATHAM, JOHN.—Age, 20 years. Enlisted, August 28, 1862, at Utica, to serve three years; mustered in as private, Co. A, October 10, 1862; captured in action at Chancellorsville, Va., May 1, 1863, paroled, no date.

LA TOUR, JOHN A.—Age, 22 years. Enlisted, September 4, 1862, at Utica, to serve three years; mustered in as private, Co. K, October 10, 1862; mustered out, July 21, 1865, at Syracuse, N. Y.

LAUNING, RICHARD.—Age, 23 years. Enlisted, August 27, 1862, at Floyd, to serve three years; mustered in as private, Co. B, October 10, 1862.

LAWTON, JEROME C.—Age, 35 years. Enlisted, September 6, 1862, at Marshall, to serve three years; mustered in as private, Co. K, October 10, 1862; transferred to Veteran Reserve Corps, December 12, 1863; mustered out as of Fifty-first Company, Second Battalion, September 19, 1865, at West Philadelphia, Pa.

LAWTON, THOMAS.—Age, 28 years. Enlisted, August 30, 1862, at Utica, to serve three years; mustered in as private, Co. C, October 10, 1862.

LEARY, JOHN.—Age, 23 years. Enlisted, August 26, 1862, at Utica, to serve three years; mustered in as private, Co. A, October 10, 1862; promoted sergeant, no date; captured in action, May 1, 1863, at Chancellorsville, Va.; paroled, no date; killed in action, May 5, 1864, at the Wilderness, Va.

LEE, ANDREW J.—Age, 18 years. Enlisted, August 30, 1862, at Utica, to serve three years; mustered in as private, Co. C, October 10, 1862.

LENT, GEORGE S.—Age, 22 years. Enlisted, August 22, 1862, at Utica, to serve three years; mustered in as private, Co. A, October 10, 1862; promoted corporal, no date; captured in action, May 5, 1864, at the Wilderness, Va.; paroled, no date; mustered out with company, July 16, 1865, near Washington, D. C.

LENT, STEPHEN.—Age, 26 years. Enlisted, August 26, 1862, at Utica, to serve three years; mustered in as private, Co. A, October 10, 1862; appointed wagoner, no date; mustered out with company, July 16, 1865, near Washington, D. C.

LEWIS, GEORGE W. M.—Age, 31 years. Enrolled, August 20, 1862, at Utica, to serve three years; mustered in as captain, Co. C, October 10, 1862; discharged, January 7, 1863. Died in 1866.

Commissioned captain, November 3, 1862, with rank from September 3, 1862, original.

The Lewis Oration Prize of Colgate University was established in his memory by his brother, Professor Lewis, in 1867.

LEWIS, GEORGE W.—Age, 22 years. Enlisted, August 26, 1862, at Bridgewater, to serve three years; mustered in as private, Co. G, October 10, 1862; captured in action, May 5, 1864, at the Wilderness, Va.; died of disease, August 8, 1864, at Andersonville, Ga.

LEWIS, WILLIAM I.—Age, 37 years. Enlisted, September 6, 1862, at Trenton, to serve three years; mustered in as private, Co. I, October 10, 1862; promoted corporal, no date; transferred to Veteran Reserve Corps, September 2, 1863; mustered out therefrom as of Co. F, Fourteenth Regiment, July 29, 1865, at Washington, D. C.

LIAHN, JAMES.—Age, 46 years. Enlisted, August 26, 1862, at Utica, to serve three years; mustered in as private, Co. C, October 10, 1862; discharged for disability, March 12, 1863.

LIMEBECK, GEORGE S.—Age, 21 years. Enlisted, August 27, 1862, at Utica, to serve three years; mustered in as private, Co. H, October 10, 1862; also borne as Limeback.

LINCOLN, GEORGE W.—Age, 18 years. Enlisted, August 23, 1862, at Utica, to serve three years; mustered in as private, Co. C, October 10, 1862; discharged for disability, April 3, 1863.

LOCK, DAVID B.—Age, 26 years. Enlisted, September 1, 1862, at Sangerfield, to serve three years; mustered in as private, Co. H, October 10, 1862; absent, sick, in hospital, since July 11, 1863, and at muster-out of company.

LOMIS, WILLIAM.—Age, 42 years. Enlisted, September 29, 1862, at Rome to serve three years; mustered in as private, Co. H, October 10, 1862; captured in action, May 5, 1864, at the Wilderness, Va., as Loomis; no further record.

LONG, PATRICK.—Age, 44 years. Enlisted, September 6, 1862, at Rome, to serve three years; mustered in as private, Co. H, October 10, 1862.

LOOMIS, EDWIN O.—Age, 18 years. Enlisted, August 30, 1862, at Utica, to serve three years; mustered in as private, Co. C, October 10, 1862; discharged for disability, February 13, 1863, at Washington, D. C.

LOOMIS, HENRY.—Age, 23 years. Enrolled, August 30, 1862, at Kirkland, to serve three years; mustered in as sergeant, Co. G, October 10, 1862; promoted first sergeant, December 10, 1862; mustered in as second lieutenant, Co. K, February 1, 1863; transferred to Co. D, July 12, 1864; mustered in as first lieutenant, September 16, 1864; as captain, February 1, 1865; mustered out with company, July 16, 1865, near Washington, D. C.

Commissioned second lieutenant, February 5, 1863, with rank from January 7, 1863, vice L. C. York promoted; first lieutenant, September 16, 1864, with rank from May 17, 1864, vice J. S. Lowery promoted; captain, March 30, 1865, with rank from February 1, 1865, vice I. P. Powell, promoted; brevet captain, by U. S. Government, from March 13, 1865.

LORD, AUSTIN.—Age, 25 years. Enlisted, September 4, 1862, at Kirkland, to serve three years; mustered in as private, Co. G, October 10, 1862; transferred to Veteran Reserve Corps, April 22, 1864; mustered out therefrom as of Co. D, Twenty-fourth Regiment, July 20, 1865, at Washington, D. C.

LORD, JAMES A.—Age, 19 years. Enlisted, August 30, 1862, at Kirkland, to serve three years; mustered in as private, Co. G, October 10, 1862; captured in action, May 1, 1863, at Chancellorsville, Va.; paroled, no date; again captured in action, May 5, 1864, at the Wilderness, Va.; paroled, no date; mustered out, June 1, 1865, at Annapolis, Md.

LOTT, FREDERIC.—Age, 32 years. Enlisted, August 20, 1862,

at Paris, to serve three years; mustered in as private, Co. K, October 10, 1862; promoted corporal, no date; died of disease, December 18, 1863, at Bealton Station, Va.

LOWERY, JOSEPH S.—Age, 21 years. Enrolled, August 29, 1862, at Boonville, to serve three years; mustered in as sergeant, Co. D, October 10, 1862; as second lieutenant, Co. I, January 31, 1863; as first lieutenant, Co. D, October 23, 1863; wounded in action, June 3, 1864, at Cold Harbor, Va.; transferred to Co. A, October 1, 1864; mustered in as captain, to date September 16, 1864; discharged for disability, January 13, 1865.

Commissioned second lieutenant, February 5, 1863, with rank from January 7, 1863, vice T. A. Wilson promoted; first lieutenant, October 6, 1863, with rank from September 13, 1863, vice C. E. Lasher deserted; captain, September 16, 1864, with rank from May 17, 1864, vice J. H. Durkee resigned; brevet major, by U. S. Government, from March 13, 1865; brevet lieutenant-colonel, by New York State Government. Married Celeste Julia Ward, at Whitesboro, February 9, 1870; died at Utica, October 19, 1891.

LUCAS, ALBERT W.—Age, 44 years. Enlisted, September 1, 1862, at Kirkland, to serve three years; mustered in as private, Co. G, October 10, 1862; transferred to Veteran Reserve Corps, September 1, 1863; mustered out therefrom as of Co. D, Thirteenth Regiment, November 9, 1865, at Augusta, Me.

LULL, HENRY C.—Age, 33 years. Enrolled, August 23, 1862, at Utica, to serve three years; mustered in as corporal, Co. C, October 10, 1862; promoted sergeant, February 1, 1863; first sergeant, no date; captured in action, May 5, 1864, at the Wilderness, Va.; paroled, no date; mustered in as second lieutenant, April 18, 1865; mustered out with company, July 16, 1865, near Washington, D. C.

Commissioned second lieutenant, June 17, 1865, with rank from February 1, 1865, vice J. A. Jennison promoted.

LUMBARD, THOMAS.—Age, 35 years. Enlisted, September 3, 1862, at Utica, to serve three years; mustered in as private, Co. C, October 10, 1862; discharged for disability, March 10, 1863, at Washington, D. C.

LYNCH, ROBERT.—Age, 21 years. Enlisted, August 27, 1862, at Rome, to serve three years; mustered in as private, Co. B, October 10, 1862; mustered out with company, July 16, 1865, near Washington, D. C.

MADRIDE, FRANCIS.—Age, 24 years. Enlisted, August 29, 1862, at Boonville, to serve three years; mustered in as private, Co. D, October 10, 1862; absent, sick, since December 25, 1864, and at muster-out of company.

MAFFITT, NORMAN.—Age, 22 years. Enlisted, August 28, 1862, at Utica, to serve three years; mustered in as private, Co. A, October 10, 1862.

MAGEE, JOHN R.—Age, 18 years. Enlisted, August 19, 1862, at Utica, to serve three years; mustered in as private, Co. H, October 10, 1862; also borne as McGee.

MAHAN, CHARLES P.—Age, 18 years. Enlisted, August 30, 1862, at Kirkland, to serve three years; mustered in as private, Co. G, October 10, 1862; promoted corporal, June 1, 1865; mustered out with company, July 16, 1865, near Washington, D. C.

MAHONEY, MAURICE.—Age, 18 years. Enlisted, August 28, 1862, at Rome, to serve three years; mustered in as private, Co. K, October 10, 1862; wounded in action and died of his wounds, May 5, 1864, at the Wilderness, Va.; also borne as Morris MacHarney.

MAHONEY, MICHAEL.—Age, 24 years. Enlisted, August 28, 1862, at Westmoreland, to serve three years; mustered in as private, Co. I, October 10, 1862; appointed wagoner, no date; mustered out with company, July 16, 1865, near Washington, D. C.

MAHONY, MARTIN.—Age, 36 years. Enlisted, August 25, 1862, at Rome, to serve three years; mustered in as private, Co. K, October 10, 1862; mustered out with company, July 16, 1865, near Washington, D. C.; also borne as Mac-Harney.

MARKELL, RICHARD.—Age, 23 years. Enlisted, August 26, 1862, at Vernon, to serve three years; mustered in as private, Co. B, October 10, 1862; absent, sick, since June 4, 1863, and at muster-out of company; also borne as Markulf. Died, May 9, 1910.

MARKHAM, HERBERT.—Age, 21 years. Enlisted, September 3, 1862, at Rome, to serve three years; mustered in as private, Co. F, October 10, 1862; killed in action, May 5, 1864, at the Wilderness, Va.

MARTEMS, HIENRICH.—Age, 45 years. Enlisted, September 2, 1862, at Remsen, to serve three years; mustered in as private, Co. I, October 10, 1862; discharged for disability, July 31, 1863, at Washington, D. C.

MARTIN, GILBERT.—Age, 18 years. Enlisted, August 22, 1862, at Vernon, to serve three years; mustered in as private, Co. B, October 10, 1862; discharged for disability, March 11, 1863, at camp near Falmouth, Va.; also borne as James E. Martin.

MARTIN, JACOB.—Age, 25 years. Enlisted, August 27, 1862, at Utica, to serve three years; mustered in as private, Co. F, October 10, 1862; captured, September 8, 1864; escaped, April 29, 1865; mustered out with company, July 16, 1865, near Washington, D. C.

MARTIN, JAMES.—Age, 18 years. Enlisted, September 5, 1862, at Remsen, to serve three years; mustered in as private, Co. I, October 10, 1862; wounded, no date; died of his wounds, July 16, 1863, at Williamsport, Md.

MARTIN, JOHN.—Age, 18 years. Enlisted, August 26, 1862, at Utica, to serve three years; mustered in as private, Co. A, October 10, 1862.

MARTIN, LEANDER.—Age, 26 years. Enlisted, September 6, 1862, at Trenton, to serve three years; mustered in as private, Co. I, October 10, 1862; promoted corporal, no date; sergeant, March 1, 1865; mustered out with company, July 16, 1865, near Washington, D. C.

MARTIN, LEWIS.—Age, 24 years. Enlisted, August 26, 1862, at Utica, to serve three years; mustered in as private, Co. A, October 10, 1862; captured in action, May 5, 1864, at the Wilderness, Va.; paroled, December 5, 1864; mustered out, August 8, 1865, at Elmira, N. Y. Died in 1895.

MATHER, JAMES L.—Age, 44 years. Enlisted, August 29, 1862, at Boonville, to serve three years; mustered in as private, Co. D, October 10, 1862; discharged for disability, April 18, 1863, at camp near Falmouth, Va. Died, January 22, 1899.

MATHER, WELLS.—Age, 20 years. Enlisted, August 29, 1862, at Boonville, to serve three years; mustered in as private, Co. D, October 10, 1862; died, January 17, 1863, at Aquia Creek, Va.

MATHEWS, ALBERT.—Age, 19 years. Enlisted, August 29, 1862, at Utica, to serve three years; mustered in as private, Co. H, October 10, 1862; discharged for disability, April 25, 1863, at hospital, Washington, D. C.

MATTERSON, EUGENE R.—Age, 23 years. Enrolled, September 5, 1862, at Rome, to serve three years; mustered in as first sergeant, Co. E, October 10, 1862; promoted second lieutenant, Co. A, December 27, 1862; mustered in as first lieutenant, January 7, 1863; captured in action, May 1, 1863, at Chancellorsville, Va.; returned, July 26, 1863; discharged, June 11, 1864,

Commissioned second lieutenant, December 10, 1862, with rank from November 25, 1862, vice J. Rodenhurst promoted; first lieutenant, February 5, 1863, with rank from January 7, 1863, vice T.C. Jones resigned.

MAY, JOSEPH.—Age, 21 years. Enlisted, October 2, 1862, at Rome, to serve three years; mustered in as private, Co. H, October 10, 1862; mustered out with company, July 16, 1865, near Washington, D. C.

MAYNE, ARTHUR.—Age, 18 years. Enlisted, October 2, 1862, at Rome, to serve three years; mustered in as private, Co. H, October 10, 1862; captured in action, May 5, 1864, at the Wilderness, Va.; no further record.

McCABE, PETER.—Age, 25 years. Enlisted, September 30, 1862, at Rome, to serve three years; mustered in as private, Co. E, October 10, 1862; promoted corporal, June 3, 1865; sergeant, July 1, 1865; mustered out with company, July 16, 1865, near Washington, D. C., as McCabi.

McCANN, MICHAEL.—Age, 29 years. Enlisted, August 28, 1862, at Utica, to serve three years; mustered in as private, Co. K, October 10, 1862.

McCLERNAN, GEORGE.—Age, 21 years. Enlisted, August 28, 1862, at Boonville, to serve three years; mustered in as private, Co. D, October 10, 1862; killed in action, August 19, 1864, at Weldon Railroad, Va.

McCraith, Francis C.—Age, 26 years. Enlisted, August 22, 1862, at Utica, to serve three years; mustered in as sergeant, Co. C, October 10, 1862; returned to ranks, no date; transferred, January 20, 1865, and mustered out as of Co. C, Eighteenth Regiment, Veteran Reserve Corps, July 31, 1865, at Washington, D. C.

McCrehn, William.—Age, 19 years. Enlisted, August 28, 1862, at Rome, to serve three years; mustered in as private, Co. B, October 10, 1862; captured in action, May 5, 1864, at the Wilderness, Va.; died of rheumatism, January 20, 1865, at Florence, S. C.

McDonald, Burton.—Age, 21 years. Enlisted, September 11, 1862, at Utica, to serve three years; mustered in as private, Co. C, October 10, 1862; discharged for disability, January 25, 1863, at Washington, D. C.

McDonall, John.—Age, 30 years. Enlisted, August 22, 1862, at Rome, to serve three years; mustered in as private, Co. K, October 10, 1862; discharged for disability, July 8, 1863, at Washington, D. C.; also borne as McDonald.

McEntee, Hiram K.—Age, 21 years. Enlisted, September 18, 1862, at Boonville, to serve three years; mustered in as private, Co. D, October 10, 1862; appointed musician, no date; discharged for disability, April 10, 1863, at Philadelphia, Pa.; also borne as McIntee.

McGuire, John.—Age, 36 years. Enlisted, September 22, 1862, at Utica, to serve three years; mustered in as private, Co. A, October 10, 1862; promoted sergeant, no date; died of disease, November 28, 1862, at hospital, Washington, D. C.

McGurk, William.—Age, 21 years. Enlisted, September 6, 1862, at Bridgewater, to serve three years; mustered in as corporal, Co. G, October 10, 1862; wounded in action, July 1 to 3, 1863, at Gettysburg, Pa.; promoted sergeant, June 1, 1865; mustered out with company, July 16, 1865, near Washington, D. C.

McKenzie, Walter R.—Age, 18 years. Enlisted, August 19, 1862, at Utica, to serve three years; mustered in as private, Co. A, October 10, 1862; discharged for disability, March 12, 1863, near Falmouth, Va.

McKINNEY, HENRY.—Age, 24 years. Enlisted, August 18, 1862, at Utica, to serve three years; mustered in as private, Co. A, October 10, 1862; captured in action, May, 1863, at Chancellorsville, Va.; paroled, no date; mustered out, May 31, 1865, at Washington, D. C., as Henry L. McKinney. Died in 1900.

McLEAN, JOHN.—Age, 21 years. Enlisted, September 6, 1862, at Utica, to serve three years; mustered in as private, Co. H, October 10, 1862; promoted corporal, no date; captured in action, May 5, 1864, at the Wilderness, Va.; no further record; also borne as McClane.

MEGERT, JOHN.—Age, 22 years. Enlisted, August 22, 1862, at Rome, to serve three years; mustered in as private, Co. B, October 10, 1862; captured in action, May 5, 1864, at the Wilderness, Va.; no further record; also borne as Mygert.

MEISS, CHRISTIAN.—Age, 35 years. Enlisted, August 27, 1862, at Rome, to serve three years; mustered in as private, Co. B, October 10, 1862; died of disease, August 19, 1863, at Washington, D. C.; also borne as Muss.

MERCER, JAMES H.—Age, 39 years. Enlisted, October 8, 1862, at Westmoreland, to serve three years; mustered in as private, Co. B, October 10, 1862; absent, sick, since March 25, 1863, and at muster-out of company.

MERCER, JOSEPH D.—Age, 25 years. Enlisted, September 3, 1862, at Utica, to serve three years; mustered in as private, Co. C, October 10, 1862; promoted corporal, no date; returned to ranks, May 1, 1865; mustered out with company, July 16, 1865, near Washington, D. C.

MICHAELS, THOMAS R.—Age, 33 years. Enlisted, September 6, 1862, at Russia, to serve three years; mustered in as private, Co. I, October 10, 1862; promoted corporal and returned to ranks, no dates; mustered out with company, July 16, 1865, near Washington, D. C.

MILLER, ADAM K.—Age, 25 years. Enlisted, August 21, 1862, at Utica, to serve three years; mustered in as corporal, Co. C, October 10, 1862; returned to ranks, no date; killed in action, May 5, 1864, at the Wilderness, Va.

MILLER, CHARLES.—Age, 23 years. Enlisted, August 29, 1862, at Annsville, to serve three years; mustered in as private,

Co. F, October 10, 1862; discharged for disability, April 1, 1863, at hospital, Philadelphia, Pa.

MILLER, DAVID.—Age, 26 years. Enlisted, August 25, 1862, at Kirkland, to serve three years; mustered in as sergeant, Co. G, October 10, 1862; returned to ranks, March 3, 1863; discharged for disability, March 22, 1864, at Washington, D. C.

MILLER, ELI B.—Age, 21 years. Enlisted, September 4, 1862, at Boonville, to serve three years; mustered in as private, Co. D, October 10, 1862; wounded in action, April 1, 1865, at Five Forks, Va.; absent since, and at muster-out of company.

MILLER, FRANCIS.—Age, 18 years. Enlisted, August 25, 1862, at Kirkland, to serve three years; mustered in as private, Co. G, October 10, 1862; captured in action, May 3, 1863, at Chancellorsville, Va.; and May 5, 1864, at the Wilderness, Va.; paroled, no dates; mustered out with company, July 16, 1865, near Washington, D. C. Died, November 19, 1906.

MILLER, HORACE.—Age, 27 years. Enlisted, August 29, 1862, at Annsville, to serve three years; mustered in as private, Co. F, October 10, 1862; mustered out with company, July 16, 1865, near Washington, D. C.

MILLER, JOHN.—Age, 33 years. Enlisted, August 29, 1862, at Annsville, to serve three years; mustered in as private, Co. F, October 10, 1862; discharged for disability, same date, at Rome, N. Y.

MILLER, LEWIS.—Age, 44 years. Enlisted, August 29, 1862, at Boonville, to serve three years; mustered in as private, Co. D, October 10, 1862; died, January 14, 1863, near Falmouth, Va.

MILLER, JR., LEWIS.—Age, 21 years. Enlisted, September 4, 1862, at Rome, to serve three years; mustered in as private, Co. D, October 10, 1862; mustered out with company, July 16, 1865, near Washington, D. C.

MOLZ, GEORGE.—Age, 21 years. Enlisted, August 29, 1862, at Rome, to serve three years; mustered in as private, Co. F, October 10, 1862; killed in action, June 18, 1864, at Petersburg, Va.; also borne as Moltz.

MOON, GEORGE W.—Age, 34 years. Enlisted, August 29, 1862, at Boonville, to serve three years; mustered in as private, Co. D, October 10, 1862; discharged for disability, January 16, 1863, near Falmouth, Va.

MOORE, HENRY B.—Age, 18 years. Enlisted, August 27, 1862, at Utica, to serve three years; mustered in as private, Co. C, October 10, 1862; died, December 17, 1862, near Falmouth, Va.

MORE, AMASA.—Age, 21 years. Enlisted in Co. F, September 5, 1862, at Western, to serve three years; mustered in as private, Co. I, October 10, 1862; also borne as Moore.

MORENUS, JERRY.—Age, 18 years. Enlisted, August 13, 1862, at Annsville, to serve three years; mustered in as private, Co. B, October 10, 1862; captured in action, May 5, 1864, at the Wilderness, Va.; released, April 16, 1865; mustered out with company, July 16, 1865, near Washington, D. C.

MORENUS, PETER.—Age, 44 years. Enlisted, August 26, 1862, at Annsville, to serve three years; mustered in as corporal, Co. B, October 10, 1862; returned to ranks, no date; discharged for disability, April 25, 1863, at Washington, D. C.

MORGAN, DAVID.—Age, 44 years. Enlisted, August 22, 1862, at Utica, to serve three years; mustered in as private, Co. H, October 10, 1862; mustered out with company, July 16, 1865, near Washington, D. C.

MORRIS, EDWARD.—Age, 30 years. Enlisted, August 29, 1862, at Sangerfield, to serve three years; mustered in as private, Co. H, October 10, 1862; captured, August 19, 1864, at Weldon Railroad, Va.; died, January, 1865, at Salisbury, N. C. Married Sarah A. Penner, of Sangerfield, June 18, 1855, at North Brookfield.

MORRIS, JOHN R.—Age, 23 years. Enlisted, August 30, 1862, at Boonville, to serve three years; mustered in as private, Co. D, October 10, 1862; mustered out with company, July 16, 1865, near Washington, D. C.

MORSE, EDWARD.—Age, 28 years. Enlisted, August 30, 1862, at Camden, to serve three years; mustered in as private, Co. E, October 10, 1862; discharged for disability, December, 1862; also borne as Mors.

MORSE, THOMAS J.—Age, 27 years. Enlisted, August 27, 1862, at Annsville, to serve three years; mustered in as private, Co. B, October 10, 1862; promoted corporal, November 22, 1862; died of disease, October 2, 1863, at Washingtqn, D. C.

MORSS, JOHN F.—Age, 24 years. Enlisted, August 26, 1862, at Camden, to serve three years; mustered in as private, Co. E, October 10, 1862; discharged for disability, December 23, 1862, near Potomac Creek, Va.; also borne as Morse.

MOSES, LEWIS.—Age, 35 years. Enlisted, August 28, 1862, at Florence, to serve three years; mustered in as private, Co. E, October 10, 1862; transferred to Veteran Reserve Corps, November 11, 1864. Died at Florence, N. Y., in 1898.

MOTT, WALLACE M.—Enrolled at Rome, to serve three years, and mustered in as second lieutenant, Co. K, October 10, 1862; discharged, December 28, 1862.

Commissioned second lieutenant, November 3, 1862, with rank from October 8, 1862, original.

MOULD, GEORGE.—Age, 30 years. Enrolled, August 29, 1862, at Paris, to serve three years; mustered in as private, Co. H, October 10, 1862; promoted sergeant and first sergeant, no dates; captured in action, May 5, 1864, at the Wilderness, Va.; paroled, no date; mustered in as second lieutenant, to date October 8, 1864; discharged, June 1, 1865, at Annapolis, Md.

Commissioned second lieutenant, June 6, 1864, with rank from April 28, 1864, vice L. Fitzpatrick promoted.

MOWERS, EZRA.—Age, 34 years. Enlisted, September 6, 1862, at Western, to serve three years; mustered in as private, Co. F, October 10, 1862; killed in action, May 5, 1864, at the Wilderness, Va.

MOYER, DAVID.—Age, 38 years. Enlisted, August 26, 1862, at Annsville, to serve three years; mustered in as private, Co. B, October 10, 1862; wounded in action, May 10, 1864, at Laurel Hill, Va.; mustered out with company, July 16, 1865, near Washington, D. C.

MOYER, LORENZO.—Age, 18 years. Enlisted, August 27, 1862, at Rome, to serve three years; mustered in as private, Co. B, October 10, 1862; mustered out with company, July 16, 1865, near Washington, D. C.

MUENCH, ANDREAS.—Age, 32 years. Enlisted, September 2, 1862, at Deerfield, to serve three years; mustered in as private, Co. F, October 10, 1862.

MULCAHY, JR., RICHARD.—Age, 18 years. Enlisted, August 23, 1862, at Florence, to serve three years; mustered in as private, Co. F, October 10, 1862; killed in action, May 5, 1864, at the Wilderness, Va.; also borne as Mulchey.

MULLEN, EDWARD.—Age, 21 years. Enlisted, August 29, 1862, at Utica, to serve three years; mustered in as private, Co. A, October 10, 1862; transferred to Veteran Reserve Corps, March 5, 1864.

MULLOY, JOHN.—Age, 40 years. Enlisted, August 30, 1862, at Utica, to serve three years; mustered in as private, Co. A, October 10, 1862; transferred to Thirty-third Company, Second Battalion, Veteran Reserve Corps, March 13, 1865, from which mustered out, September 4, 1865, at Washington, D. C.

MURPHY, JAMES.—Age, 27 years. Enlisted, August 28, 1862, at Boonville, to serve three years; mustered in as private, Co. D, October 10, 1862; transferred to Veteran Reserve Corps, January 20, 1864.

MURPHY, JOHN.—Age, 26 years. Enlisted, September 3, 1862, at Annsville, to serve three years; mustered in as private, Co. B, October 10, 1862; promoted corporal, February 21, 1863; killed in action, May 5, 1864, at the Wilderness, Va.

MURRAY, ALONZO.—Age, 22 years. Enlisted, September 24, 1862, at Rome, to serve three years; mustered in as private, Co. A, October 10, 1862; captured in action, May, 1863, at Chancellorsville, Va.; paroled, no date; transferred to United States Navy, May 3, 1864.

MURREY, ALEXANDER.—Age, 28 years. Enlisted, August 28, 1862, at Boonville, to serve three years; mustered in as private, Co. D, October 10, 1862.

NEARKERN, GEORGE.—Age, 24 years. Enlisted, August 28, 1862, at Paris, to serve three years; mustered in as private, Co. K, October 10, 1862; transferred to Veteran Reserve Corps, October 29, 1864; also borne as Noirkern. Died June 10, 1899.

NEEMAN, WILLIAM W.—Age, 22 years. Enlisted, October 2,

1862, at Rome, to serve three years; mustered in as private, Co. D, October 10, 1862; absent, sick, since December, 1862; no further record.

NEISS, ADAM.—Age, 42 years. Enlisted, August 29, 1862, at Boonville, to serve three years; mustered in as private, Co. D, October 10, 1862; promoted sergeant, no date; wounded in action at Gettysburg, Pa., July 3, 1863; returned to ranks and transferred, no date, and mustered out as of Co. F, Twenty-fourth Regiment, Veteran Reserve Corps, July 29, 1865, at Washington, D. C., as Neice.

NELSON, CHRISTOPHER.—Age, 21 years. Enlisted, September 6, 1862, at Remsen, to serve three years; mustered in as private, Co. I, October 10, 1862; mustered out with company, July 16, 1865, near Washington, D. C.

NESKERN, NICHOLAS.—Age, 37 years. Enlisted, August 28, 1862, at Paris, to serve three years; mustered in as private, Co. K, October 10, 1862; discharged for disability, May 20, 1863, at Washington, D. C.

NEUMULLER, JOHN.—Age, 42 years. Enlisted, August 20, 1862, at Kirkland, to serve three years; mustered in as private, Co. G, October 10, 1862; transferred to Veteran Reserve Corps, December 2, 1864; also borne as John Miller.

NEUSHLER, CONRAD.—Age, 25 years. Enlisted, August 29, 1862, at Westmoreland, to serve three years; mustered in as private, Co. I, October 10, 1862; promoted corporal, no.date; captured in action, May 5, 1864, at the Wilderness, Va.; paroled, March 25, 1865; mustered out with company, July 16, 1865, near Washington, D. C.

NEWLOVE, WILLIAM.—Age, 29 years. Enlisted, August 28, 1862, at Utica, to serve three years; mustered in as private, Co. A, October 10, 1862; promoted corporal and returned to ranks, no date; captured in action, May 5, 1864, at the Wilderness, Va.; paroled, no date; discharged, June 2, 1865, at Camp Parole, Annapolis, Md. Died, September 15, 1909.

NEWMAN, MORRIS.—Age, 44 years. Enlisted, August 29, 1862, at Boonville, to serve three years; mustered in as private, Co. D, October 10, 1862; died of disease, March 7, 1863, near Falmouth, Va.

NICHOLLS, EDWARD.—Age, 43 years. Enlisted, August 20,

1862, at Paris, to serve three years; mustered in as private, Co. K, October 10, 1862; promoted corporal, no date.

NICHOLOS, JOHN.—Age, 21 years. Enlisted, August 28, 1862, at Utica, to serve three years; mustered in as private, Co. E, October 10, 1862.

NISBET, BYRON.—Age, 19 years. Enlisted, August 26, 1862, at Lee, to serve three years; mustered in as private, Co. F, October 10, 1862; died of disease, December 18, 1862, in Division Hospital, near Falmouth, Va.

NOLAN, JOHN.—Age, 21 years. Enlisted, August 30, 1862, at Utica, to serve three years; mustered in as private, Co. A, October 10, 1862; wounded, no date.

NORTHUP, JOSEPH A.—Age, 18 years. Enlisted, September 3, 1862, at Marshall, to serve three years; mustered in as private, Co. E, October 10, 1862; died of disease, December 27, 1862, at Henry House, Va.; also borne as Northrop.

O'BRIEN, DENNIS.—Age, 30 years. Enlisted, August 20, 1862, at Rome, to serve three years; mustered in as private, Co. I, October 10, 1862; discharged for disability, July 31, 1863, at Washington, D. C.

O'BRIEN, RICHARD.—Age, 18 years. Enlisted, August 22, 1862, at Utica, to serve three years; mustered in as private, Co. H, October 10, 1862; promoted corporal, June 1, 1864; mustered out with company, July 16, 1865, near Washington, D. C., as O'Brian; also borne as O'Bryan.

ODELL, WILLIAM.—Age, 19 years. Enlisted, September 5, 1862, at Camden, to serve three years; mustered in as private, Co. E, October 10, 1862.

O'LEARY, PATRICK.—Age, 24 years. Enlisted, August 29, 1862, at Boonville, to serve three years; mustered in as private, Co. D, October 10, 1862; discharged for disability, January 29, 1865, near Petersburg, Va.

OLIN, JR., GEORGE.—Age, 32 years. Enrolled, August 30, 1862, at Boonville, to serve three years; mustered in as private, Co. D, December 15, 1862; promoted corporal, no date; mustered in as second lieutenant, Co. F, March 1, 1865; mustered out with company, July 16, 1865, near Washington, D. C.

Commissioned second lieutenant, December 30, 1864,

with rank from December 1, 1864, vice H. Chalmers killed in action; first lieutenant, not mustered, August 31, 1865, with rank from June 1, 1865, vice G. J. Klock discharged.

OSBORN, TRUMAN H.—Age, 20 years. Enlisted, August 29, 1862, at Florence, to serve three years; mustered in as private, Co. F, October 10, 1862.

OTIS, AMOS.—Age, 34 years. Enlisted, August 29, 1862, at Utica, to serve three years; mustered in as private, Co. K, October 10, 1862; absent, sick, since June 13, 1863, and at muster-out of company.

OWENS, JACOB.—Age, 18 years. Enlisted, August 26, 1862, at Utica, to serve three years; mustered in as private, Co. C, October 10, 1862.

OWENS, JAMES.—Age, 38 years. Enlisted, August 28, 1862, at Camden, to serve three years; mustered in as private, Co. K, October 10, 1862; discharged for disability, December 23, 1863, at Washington, D. C.

PAGON, JAMES H.—Age, 18 years. Enlisted, August 28, 1862, at Utica, to serve three years; mustered in as private, Co. E, October 10, 1862.

PAINE, EDWARD B.—Age, 27 years. Enlisted, August 30, 1862, at Utica, to serve three years; mustered in as private, Co. C, October 10, 1862; mustered out with company, July 16, 1865, near Washington, D. C.; also borne as Payne.

PALMER, ALFRED H.—Age, 18 years. Enlisted, August 27, 1862, at Utica, to serve three years; mustered in as corporal, Co. C, October 10, 1862; appointed musician, no date; mustered out with company, July 16, 1865, near Washington, D. C. Born in Warwickshire, England; came to America with his parents when ten years old; lived in the South for a number of years and then moved to Nebraska; died at Omaha, Neb., February 14, 1908.

PALMER, GEORGE H.—Age, 22 years. Enlisted, August 27, 1862, at Utica, to serve three years; mustered in as private, Co. C, October 10, 1862; promoted corporal, no date; mustered out, June 2, 1865, at Washington, D. C.

PALMER, HENRY F.—Age, 41 years. Enlisted, August 22, 1862, at Paris, to serve three years; mustered in as private, Co. K, October 10, 1862.

PALMER, HOMER W.—Age, 34 years. Enlisted, August 29, 1862, at Paris, to serve three years; mustered in as private, Co. K, October 10, 1862; mustered out with company, July 16, 1865, near Washington, D. C.

PALMER, JAMES.—Age, 20 years. Enlisted, August 20, 1862, at Boonville, to serve three years; mustered in as private, Co. D, October 10, 1862; wounded in action, July 3, 1863, at Gettysburg, Pa.; died, July 22, 1863, in hospital at Gettysburg, Pa.

PALMER, WILLIAM.—Age, 28 years. Enlisted, August 29, 1862, at Lee, to serve three years; mustered in as private, Co. F, October 10, 1862; absent, sick, since July 12, 1863, and at muster-out of company. Died in 1896.

PALMER, WILLIAM A.—Age, 30 years. Enlisted, August 28, 1862, at Utica, to serve three years; mustered in as private, Co. A, October 10, 1862; captured in action at Chancellorsville, Va., May 3, 1863, and paroled, no date; absent, sick, since May 9, 1864, and at muster-out of company. Died at Hubbardsville, N. Y., in 1896.

PALMER, WILLIAM E.—Age, 21 years. Enlisted, August 22, 1862, at Bridgewater, to serve three years; mustered in as corporal, Co. G, October 10, 1862; returned to ranks, no date; discharged, July 22, 1864, for promotion to first lieutenant, Forty-third Infantry, U. S. Colored Troops.

PANGBURN, DAVID K.—Age, 22 years. Enlisted, August 20, 1862, at Utica, to serve three years; mustered in as private, Co. A, October 10, 1862; discharged for disability, March 12, 1863, at Falmouth, Va.

PARKE, WILLIAM S.—Age, 40 years. Enlisted, August 29, 1862, at Camden, to serve three years; mustered in as corporal, Co. E, October 10, 1862; killed in action, May 10, 1864, at Laurel Hill, Va.; also borne as Parks.

PARKER, CHARLES.—Age, 18 years. Enlisted, August 30, 1862, at Utica, to serve three years; mustered in as private, Co. C, October 10, 1862; promoted corporal and sergeant, no dates; returned to ranks, March 1, 1865; mustered out with company, July 16, 1865, near Washington, D. C. Died at Rochester, N. Y., in 1898.

PARKER, CHARLES E.—Age, 18 years. Enlisted, August 28,

1862, at Whitestown, to serve three years; mustered in as
private, Co. A, October 10, 1862; transferred to Veteran
Reserve Corps, no date; retransferred to Co. A, March 26,
1864; killed in action, May 5, 1864, at the Wilderness, Va.

PARKER, EDWARD B.—Age, 26 years. Enlisted, August 29,
1862, at Utica, to serve three years; mustered in as private,
Co. C, October 10, 1862; mustered out with company, July
16, 1865, near Washington, D. C.   Died in 1903.

PARKER, ISAAC J.—Age, 35 years. Enlisted, August 30, 1862,
at Utica, to serve three years; mustered in as private, Co.
A, October 10, 1862; captured in action, May 1, 1863, at
Chancellorsville, Va.; paroled, August 4, 1863; captured in
action, May 5, 1864, at the Wilderness, Va.; paroled, no
date; mustered out, June 14, 1865, at Annapolis, Md.

PARKS, ABRAM.—Age, 22 years. Enlisted, August 30, 1862, at
Utica, to serve three years; mustered in as private, Co. A,
October 10, 1862; promoted corporal and returned to ranks,
no dates; captured in action, May 1, 1863, at Chancellorsville, Va.; paroled, no date.

PARKS, THEODORE.—Age, 34 years. Enlisted, September 13,
1862, at Utica, to serve three years; mustered in as private,
Co. K, October 10, 1862; mustered out with company, July
16, 1865, near Washington, D. C.

PARMELEE, JUDSON.—Age, 31 years. Enlisted, September 3,
1862, at Verona, to serve three years; mustered in as private,
Co. K, October 10, 1862; died of disease, January 16, 1863,
at Washington, D. C.

PARSONS, CHARLES.—Age, 30 years. Enlisted, September 2,
1862, at Boonville, to serve three years; mustered in as
private, Co. D, October 10, 1862; transferred to Veteran
Reserve Corps, September 12, 1863.

PATCHIN, DANIEL N.—Age, 34 years. Enlisted, August 27,
1862, at Camden, to serve three years; mustered in as
private, Co. E, October 10, 1862; discharged for disability,
April 19, 1864, at Washington, D. C.; also borne as Patchen.

PENNAR, JOSEPH.—Age, 41 years. Enlisted, August 29, 1862,
at Sangerfield, to serve three years; mustered in as private,
Co. H, October 10, 1862; captured in action, May 5, 1864,
at the Wilderness, Va.; no further record.

PERKINS, DAVID.—Age, 30 years. Enlisted, September 3, 1862, at Marshall, to serve three years; mustered in as private, Co. K, October 10, 1862; transferred to Veteran Reserve Corps, September 1, 1863; also borne as Purkins.

PERRY, FREEMAN H.—Age, 18 years. Enlisted, August 29, 1862, at Lee, to serve three years; mustered in as private, Co. F, October 10, 1862; wounded in action, May 11, 1864, at Spottsylvania, Va.; absent since, and at muster-out of company.

PERRY, GEORGE H.—Age, 43 years. Enrolled at Rome, to serve three years, and mustered in as first lieutenant, Co. F, September 10, 1862; discharged, January 10, 1863, near Falmouth, Va.

Commissioned first lieutenant, November 3, 1862, with rank from September 10, 1862, original.

PETTEE, WILLIAM E.—Age, 18 years. Enlisted, August 22, 1862, at Paris, to serve three years; mustered in as private, Co. K, October 10, 1862; promoted corporal and sergeant, no dates; killed in action, May 5, 1864, at the Wilderness, Va.

PHELPS, FORDIS.—Age, 44 years. Enlisted, August 22, 1862, at Utica, to serve three years; mustered in as private, Co. K, October 10, 1862; discharged for disability, March 12, 1863, at hospital.

PHILLIPS, CHARLES.—Age, 27 years. Enlisted, October 4, 1862, at Verona, to serve three years; mustered in as private, Co. I, October 10, 1862; mustered out with company, July 16, 1865, near Washington, D. C.

PHILLIPS, WHITMAN.—Age, 21 years. Enlisted, August 28, 1862, at Marcy, to serve three years; mustered in as private, Co. K, October 10, 1862; mustered out with company, July 16, 1865, near Washington, D. C.

PICKETT, PATRICK.—Age, 38 years. Enlisted, August 22, 1862, at Utica, to serve three years; mustered in as private, Co. C, October 10, 1862; transferred to Veteran Reserve Corps, August 17, 1863.

PIERCE, CHARLES E.—Age, 19 years. Enlisted, August 22, 1862, at Floyd, to serve three years; mustered in as private, Co. I, October 10, 1862; captured in action, May 5,

1864, at the Wilderness, Va.; paroled, no date; mustered out, May 3, 1865, at Annapolis, Md. Died, July 6, 1907.

PILKINGTON, WILLIAM.—Age, 22 years. Enlisted, August 30, 1862, at Camden, to serve three years; mustered in as private, Co. E, October 10, 1862.

PITCHER, JAMES P.—Age, 18 years. Enrolled, August 29, 1862, at Boonville, to serve three years; mustered in as corporal, Co. D, October 10, 1862; promoted sergeant, no date; quartermaster-sergeant, January 1, 1864; mustered in as second lieutenant, Co. D, October 19, 1864; as first lieutenant, Co. I, January 19, 1865; as adjutant, to date December 1, 1864; mustered out with regiment, July 16, 1865, near Washington, D. C.

Commissioned second lieutenant, September 16, 1864, with rank from June 11, 1864, vice A. E. Brownell promoted; first lieutenant, December 30, 1864, with rank from December 1, 1864, vice Wm. Fowler promoted; adjutant, February 18, 1865, with rank from December 1, 1864, vice Wm. Wright discharged; captain (not mustered), August 31, 1865, with rank from May 15, 1865, vice J. Stewart discharged; brevet captain, by U. S. Government, from March 13, 1865.

PITTENGER, STEPHEN M.—Age, 42 years. Enlisted, August 21, 1862, at Utica, to serve three years; mustered in as wagoner, Co. C, October 10, 1862; discharged for disability, March 12, 1863; also borne as Stephen H. Pittinger.

PITTS, JAMES.—Age, 34 years. Enlisted, August 20, 1862, at Paris, to serve three years; mustered in as private, Co. K, October 10, 1862; discharged for disability, August 28, 1863, at Washington, D. C.

PLETTER, JOHN H.—Age, 26 years. Enlisted, August 26, 1862, at Utica, to serve three years; mustered in as private, Co. H, October 10, 1862; captured in action, May 5, 1864, at the Wilderness, Va.; paroled, no date; died of starvation, December 28, 1864, on board U. S. transport; also borne as Platter.

PLUNKETT, JOHN.—Age, 18 years. Enlisted, August 26, 1862, at Utica, to serve three years; mustered in as private, Co. A, October 10, 1862; captured in action, May, 1863, at

Chancellorsville, Va.; returned to company, July 26, 1863; wounded and captured in action, May 5, 1864, at the Wilderness, Va.; died of his wounds, September 11, 1864, at Andersonville, Ga.

PLUNKETT, THOMAS.—Age, 25 years. Enlisted, August 28, 1862, at Utica, to serve three years; mustered in as private, Co. A, October 10, 1862.

POOLE, ROBERT B.—Age, — years. Enrolled at Rome, to serve three years, and mustered in as captain, Co. H, October 10, 1862.

Commissioned captain, November 3, 1862, with rank from October 6, 1862, original. Died, May 8, 1913, at Utica, N. Y.

PORTER, BENJAMIN.—Age, 42 years. Enlisted, August 22, 1862, at Rome, to serve three years; mustered in as private, Co. K, October 10, 1862.

POWELL, ISAAC P.—Age, 24 years. Enrolled at Rome, to serve three years, and mustered in as captain, Co. G, September 10, 1862; captured in action, May 5, 1864, at the Wilderness, Va.; paroled prior to December 19, 1864; mustered in as major, March 30, 1865; mustered out with regiment, July 16, 1865, near Washington, D. C.

Commissioned captain, November 3, 1862, with rank from September 17, 1862, original; major, March 30, 1865, with rank from February 1, 1865, vice Peter C. Claesgens promoted; brevet major by U. S. Government, March 13, 1865. Died in 1903.

PRATT, BENJAMIN.—Age, 19 years. Enlisted, August 30, 1862, at Kirkland, to serve three years; mustered in as private, Co. G, October 10, 1862; captured in action, May 5, 1864, at the Wilderness, Va.; died of disease, August 18, 1864, at Andersonville, Ga.

PRATT, PETER.—Age, 35 years. Enlisted, August 30, 1862, at Boonville, to serve three years; mustered in as sergeant, Co. D, October 10, 1862; returned to ranks, no date; discharged for disability, December 23, 1862, at Potomac Creek, Va.

PRICHARD, WILLIAM. — Age, 20 years. Enlisted, August 30, 1862, at Remsen, to serve three years; mustered in as private, Co. I, October 10, 1862; also borne as William W. Prichard.

15

PROVOSE, ISAAC.—Age, 30 years. Enlisted, August 28, 1862, at Boonville, to serve three years; mustered in as private, Co. D, October 10, 1862.

PUGH, JOHN R.—Age, 21 years. Enlisted, August 28, 1862, at Marcy, to serve three years; mustered in as private, Co. F, October 10, 1862; transferred to Veteran Reserve Corps, March 26, 1864; promoted sergeant, no date; mustered out therefrom as of Company I, Ninth Regiment, August 3, 1865, at Washington, D. C. Died March 27, 1907.

PUGH, WILLIAM H.—Age, 28 years. Enlisted, August 28, 1862, at Marcy, to serve three years; mustered in as private, Co. F, October 10, 1862; discharged for disability, October 23, 1863, at Washington, D. C.

PURDY, WILLIAM H.—Age, 44 years. Enlisted, August 31, 1862, at Westmoreland, to serve three years; mustered in as private, Co. K, October 10, 1862; discharged for disability, February 15, 1863, at Washington, D. C.

PUTMAN, EDWARD.—Age, 18 years. Enlisted, September 26, 1862, at Utica, to serve three years; mustered in as private, Co. C, October 10, 1862; discharged, October 17, 1863; also borne as Putnam. Died at Soldiers' Home, Los Angeles, Cal., December 30, 1896.

QUACKENBUSH, JAMES.—Age, 26 years. Enlisted, August 23, 1862, at Rome, to serve three years; mustered in as sergeant, Co. B, October 10, 1862; returned to ranks, no date; discharged for disability, April 13, 1863, at camp near Potomac Creek, Va.

QUINN, EDWARD.—Age, 22 years. Enlisted, August 30, 1862, at Kirkland, to serve three years; mustered in as private, Co. G, October 10, 1862; promoted corporal, March 1, 1865; mustered out with company, July 16, 1865, near Washington, D. C. Died in 1897.

QUINN, JAMES M.—Age, 27 years. Enlisted, August 23, 1862, at Westmoreland, to serve three years; mustered in as private, Co. I, October 10, 1862; wounded in action, no date; discharged for wounds, November 10, 1863, at Washington, D. C.

QUINN, PATRICK.—Age, 25 years. Enlisted, September 6, 1862, at Marshall, to serve three years; mustered in as private, Co.

K, October 10, 1862. Died, October 2, 1908, at Washington Mills, N. Y.

RANDAL, JOHN S.—Age, 42 years. Enlisted, August 28, 1862, at Utica, to serve three years; mustered in as private, Co. C, October 10, 1862; discharged for disability, August 26, 1863, at Washington, D. C.

RAY, GEORGE.—Age, 36 years. Enlisted, September 6, 1862, at Bridgewater, to serve three years; mustered in as private, Co. G, October 10, 1862; discharged for disability, June 30, 1863, from hospital at Washington, D. C.

RAYMOND, SAMUEL W.—Age, 20 years. Enlisted, August 23, 1862, at Kirkland, to serve three years; mustered in as sergeant, Co. G, October 10, 1862; discharged for disability, February 26, 1863, from hospital at Washington, D. C. Died, March 30, 1914, at Clinton, N. Y.

REEKARD, JOHN.—Age, 38 years. Enlisted, September 3, 1862, at Sangerfield, to serve three years; mustered in as private, Co. H, October 10, 1862; wounded in action, May 5, 1864, at the Wilderness, Va.; died of his wounds, May 20, 1864.

REES, DAVID.—Age, 25 years. Enlisted, August 22, 1862, at Utica, to serve three years; mustered in as private, Co. C, October 10, 1862; captured in action, May 5, 1864, at the Wilderness, Va.; paroled, no date; promoted corporal, June 1, 1865; mustered out with company, July 16, 1865, near Washington, D. C. Born in South Wales, married at New Hartford, November 18, 1858, to Miss Jane Jones; died, at New York Mills, August 8, 1912.

REES, DAVID G.—Age, 40 years. Enlisted, August 29, 1862, at Kirkland, to serve three years; mustered in as private, Co. F, October 10, 1862; discharged for disability, November 20, 1863, at Kelly's Ford, Va.

REHM, FREDERICK.—Age, 35 years. Enlisted, August 21, 1862, at Utica, to serve three years; mustered in as private, Co. K, October 10, 1862; discharged for disability, April 14, 1863.

REMINGTON, CLARK.—Age, 18 years. Enlisted, September 3, 1862, at Rome, to serve three years; mustered in as private, Co. F, October 10, 1862; discharged for disability, March 9, 1863, at hospital, Washington, D. C.

REYNOLDS, HENRY.—Age, 31 years. Enlisted, September 2,

1862, at Marshall, to serve three years; mustered in as private, Co. K, October 10, 1862; discharged for disability, August 28, 1863, at Washington, D. C.   Died in 1896.

RICE, JOHN.—Age, 21 years.   Enlisted, September 1, 1862, at Utica, to serve three years; mustered in as private, Co. H, October 10, 1862; died of fever, March 13, 1863, near Potomac Creek, Va.

RICHARDS, JOB.—Age, 22 years.   Enlisted, September 2, 1862, at Utica, to serve three years; mustered in as private, Co. C, October 10, 1862; transferred to Veteran Reserve Corps, September 2, 1863; mustered out therefrom as of Co. F, Fourteenth Regiment, July 29, 1865, at Washington, D. C.

RICHARDS, NEWTON J.—Age, 18 years.   Enlisted, August 26, 1862, at Utica, to serve three years; mustered in as corporal, Co. C, October 10, 1862; promoted sergeant, no date; captured in action, May 5, 1864, at the Wilderness, Va.; died of disease, August 31, 1864, at Andersonville, Ga.

RICHARDSON, EDWIN.—Age, 18 years.   Enlisted, August 25, 1862, at Kirkland, to serve three years; mustered in as private, Co. G, October 10, 1862; captured in action, May 5, 1864, at the Wilderness, Va.; paroled, no date; promoted corporal, June 1, 1865; mustered out with company, July 16, 1865, near Washington, D. C.

RICHMOND, JAMES M.—Age, 34 years.   Enlisted, August 22, 1862, at Utica, to serve three years; mustered in as private, Co. C, October 10, 1862.

RIDER, ELI.—Age, 39 years.   Enlisted, September 6, 1862, at Utica, to serve three years; mustered in as private, Co. G, October 10, 1862; mustered out, September 30, 1865, at Elmira, N. Y.

RIMSHOSS, HENRY.—Age, 26 years.   Enlisted, August 30, 1862, at Deerfield, to serve three years; mustered in as private, Co. F, October 10, 1862; also borne as Reimshoss.

RISLEY, CHARLES.—Age, 31 years.   Enlisted, August 29, 1862, at Sangerfield, to serve three years; mustered in as private, Co. H, October 10, 1862; wounded in action, June 19, 1864, at Petersburg, Va.; died of his wounds, July 7, 1864, near Petersburg, Va.

ROBB, JAMES.—Age, 18 years. Enlisted, August 30, 1862, at Utica, to serve three years; mustered in as private, Co. C, October 10, 1862; also borne as Roff.

ROBBINS, THOMAS F.—Age, 24 years. Enlisted, August 28, 1862, at Utica, to serve three years; mustered in as private, Co. A, October 10, 1862; discharged, October 20, 1862, for promotion in First New Jersey Cavalry.

ROBERTS, RICHARD M.—Age, 21 years. Enlisted, August 23, 1862, at Vernon, to serve three years; mustered in as private, Co. B, October 10, 1862; discharged for disability, December 25, 1864, at Morrisville, N. Y.

ROBERTS, ROBERT.—Age, 36 years. Enlisted, August 22, 1862, at Utica, to serve three years; mustered in as private, Co. A, October 10, 1862; mustered out, July 25, 1865, at Syracuse, N. Y.

ROBERTS, THOMAS.—Age, 26 years. Enlisted, September 1, 1862, at Camden, to serve three years; mustered in as private, Co. E, October 10, 1862; mustered out with company, July 16, 1865, near Washington, D. C. Died April 17, 1909, at Sherrill, N. Y.

ROBERTS, WILLIAM B.—Age, 21 years. Enlisted, September 5, 1862, at Rome, to serve three years; mustered in as private, Co. E, October 10, 1862; transferred to Co. A, October 1, 1863; promoted corporal, no date; wounded and captured in action, May 5, 1864, at the Wilderness, Va.; died of his wounds, October 14, 1864, at Andersonville, Ga.

ROBERTS, WILLIAM F.—Age, 23 years. Enlisted, September 5, 1862, at Camden, to serve three years; mustered in as private, Co. E, October 10, 1862; promoted corporal, December, 1863; returned to ranks, April 9, 1864; promoted corporal, July 1, 1865; mustered out with company, July 16, 1865, near Washington, D. C. Died, June 8, 1910, at Camden, N. Y.

ROBINSON, EDWARD.—Age, 27 years. Enlisted, September 1, 1862, at Utica, to serve three years; mustered in as private, Co. C, October 10, 1862.

ROBINSON, JR., JOHN.—Age, 18 years. Enlisted, August 23, 1862, at Western, to serve three years; mustered in as private, Co. B, October 10, 1862; captured in action, August 18,

1864, at Weldon Railroad, Va.; paroled, no date; absent, at Hart's Island, at muster-out of company.

ROBINSON, JOSEPH.—Age, 22 years. Enlisted, September 1, 1862, at Utica, to serve three years; mustered in as private, Co. C, October 10, 1862; captured in action, June 18, 1864, at Petersburg, Va.; no further record.

RODENHURST, JAMES.—Age, — years. Enrolled at Rome, to serve three years, and mustered in as second lieutenant, Co. I, October 10, 1862; promoted first lieutenant, no date; discharged, April 23, 1863.

Commissioned second lieutenant, November 3, 1862, with rank from October 7, 1862, original; first lieutenant, December 10, 1862, with rank from November 25, 1862, vice J. Wicks resigned.

RODGERS, EDWIN B.—Age, 18 years. Enlisted, August 27, 1862, at Utica, to serve three years; mustered in as private, Co. A, October 10, 1862; transferred to Veteran Reserve Corps, no date; mustered out therefrom as of Co. F, Twenty-second Regiment, July 27, 1865, at Camp Chase, Ohio.

ROGERS, HENRY F.—Age, 38 years. Enlisted, August 29, 1862, at Camden, to serve three years; mustered in as sergeant, Co. E, October 10, 1862; promoted first sergeant and returned to ranks, no dates; discharged for disability, September 3, 1863.

ROLLING, CHARLES B.—Age, 22 years. Enlisted, August 29, 1862, at Utica, to serve three years; mustered in as private, Co. A, October 10, 1862; promoted corporal, no date; sergeant, May 1, 1865; mustered out with company, July 16, 1865, near Washington, D. C. Died, at Utica, N. Y., in 1898.

ROOT, ELIAKIM.—Age, 43 years. Enlisted, August 23, 1862, at Vernon, to serve three years; mustered in as corporal, Co. B, October 10, 1862; promoted sergeant, no date; quartermaster-sergeant, October 9, 1863; commissary sergeant, January 1, 1864; mustered out with regiment, July 16, 1865, near Washington, D. C.

ROSEVELT, JACOB.—Age, 43 years. Enlisted, August 29, 1862, at Utica, to serve three years; mustered in as private, Co. H, October 10, 1862; captured and paroled, no date; mustered out, June 28, 1865, at Jarvis Hospital, Baltimore, Md., as Rossevelt.

RUDY, DAVID M.—Age, 32 years. Enrolled, August 26, 1862, at Annsville, to serve three years; mustered in as sergeant, Co. B, October 10, 1862; promoted first sergeant, November 22, 1862; returned to sergeant, May 9, 1863; mustered in as second lieutenant, Co. A, January 16, 1865; wounded in action, March 31, 1865, at White Oak Ridge, Va.; mustered out with company, July 16, 1865.

Commissioned second lieutenant, January 31, 1865, with rank from January 2, 1865, vice D. Timmirman discharged; brevet first lieutenant, by U. S. Government, from March 13, 1865.

RUSCO, EDWIN.—Age, 36 years. Enlisted, August 28, 1862, at Camden, to serve three years; mustered in as private, Co. E, October 10, 1862; transferred to Veteran Reserve Corps, September 5, 1863; mustered out therefrom as of Co. F, Fourteenth Regiment, with detachment, July 29, 1865, at Washington, D. C., as Roscoe; also borne as Ruscoe. Died in 1903.

RUSSELL, EDGAR.—Age, 22 years. Enlisted, September 30, 1862, at Whitestown, to serve three years; mustered in as private, Co. F, October 10, 1862; died of disease, December 28, 1862, at Division Hospital, near Potomac Creek, Va.

RUSSELL, FRANKLIN.—Age, 18 years. Enlisted, September 13, 1862, at Vienna, to serve three years; mustered in as private, Co. B, October 10, 1862; captured in action, August 19, 1864, at Weldon Railroad, Va.; released, May 15, 1865; mustered out, June 22, 1865, at Camp Chase, O.

RUSSELL, WILMOT M.—Age, 44 years. Enlisted, August 20, 1862, at Rome, to serve three years; mustered in as private, Co. B, October 10, 1862; absent, sick, since June 12, 1863, and at muster-out of company.

SADLER, STEPHEN.—Age, 18 years. Enlisted, August 30, 1862, at Westmoreland, to serve three years; mustered in as private, Co. I, October 10, 1862; killed in action, May 5, 1864, at the Wilderness, Va.

SATTERLY, WILLIAM H.—Age, 24 years. Enlisted, August 23, 1862, at Western, to serve three years; mustered in as private, Co. B, October 10, 1862; discharged for disability, April 3, 1863, at camp near Falmouth, Va.; also borne as Sutterly. Died, July 7, 1899.

SAUNDERS, STEPHEN.—Age, 23 years. Enlisted, September 2, 1862, at Annsville, to serve three years; mustered in as private, Co. H, October 10, 1862; captured in action, May 5, 1864, at the Wilderness, Va.; no further record.

SAYER, THOMAS H.—Age, 24 years. Enlisted, August 30, 1862, at Kirkland, to serve three years; mustered in as private, Co. G, October 10, 1862; captured in action, May 3, 1863, at Chancellorsville, Va.; paroled, no date; again captured, May 5, 1864, at the Wilderness, Va.; no further record.

SCHNEEBACHER, JOSEPH.—Age, 43 years. Enlisted, August 30, 1862, at Utica, to serve three years; mustered in as private, Co. F, October 10, 1862; killed in action, July 2, 1863, at Gettysburg, Pa.; also borne as Schneebacker, Shneebacher, and Sneebacker.

SCHOOLCRAFT, GEORGE.—Age, 31 years. Enlisted, September 1, 1862, at Boonville, to serve three years; mustered in as private, Co. D, October 10, 1862; captured, no date; died of disease, January 5, 1865, at Salisbury, N. C.

SCHOTT, HENRY.—Age, 33 years. Enlisted, August 28, 1862, at Utica, to serve three years; mustered in as private, Co. A, October 10, 1862; captured in action, May 5, 1864, at the Wilderness, Va.; no further record.

SCOBIE, FREDERICK.—Age, 21 years. Enlisted, September 3, 1862, at Vienna, to serve three years; mustered in as private, Co. E, October 10, 1862.

SCOFIELD, SHADRACK.—Age, 44 years. Enlisted, August 31, 1862, at Camden, to serve three years; mustered in as private, Co. E, October 10, 1862; discharged for disability, January 15, 1863, at camp near Potomac Creek, Va.; also borne as Schofield.

SCOUTEN, HARVEY.—Age, 31 years. Enlisted, August 30, 1862, at Boonville, to serve three years; mustered in as private, Co. D, October 10, 1862; wounded at the Wilderness, Va., May 5, 1864; promoted corporal, July 27, 1864; sergeant, March 1, 1865; first sergeant, June 8, 1865; mustered out with company, July 16, 1865, near Washington, D. C. Died in 1901.

SCOVILLE, ALBERT.—Age, 21 years. Enlisted, September 6, 1862, at Camden, to serve three years; mustered in as private, Co. E, October 10, 1862; captured, no date; died of disease, October 10, 1864, at Florence, S. C.

SCRANTON, ANDREW J.—Age, 18 years. Enlisted, September 3, 1862, at Remsen, to serve three years; mustered in as private, Co. I, October 10, 1862; killed in action, May 5, 1864, at the Wilderness, Va.

SEAMAN, JEROME B.—Age, 18 years. Enrolled, August 30, 1862, at Kirkland, to serve three years; mustered in as private, Co. G, October 10, 1862; promoted sergeant and first sergeant, no dates; mustered in as second lieutenant, Co. G, December 1, 1864; as first lieutenant, May 30, 1865; mustered out with company, July 16, 1865, near Washington, D. C.

Commissioned second lieutenant, December 30, 1864, with rank from December 1, 1864, vice J. P. Pitcher, promoted; first lieutenant, March 30, 1865, with rank from February 1, 1865, vice R. P. Warren promoted. Died, April 12, 1909, at New Hartford, N. Y.

SEAMAN, LOREN D.—Age, 34 years. Enlisted, August 25, 1862, at Kirkland, to serve three years; mustered in as private, Co. G, October 10, 1862; died, February 15, 1863, in hospital.

SECOR, FRANCIS.—Age, 36 years. Enlisted, August 30, 1862, at Camden, to serve three years; mustered in as private, Co. E, October 10, 1862; killed in action, May 5, 1864, at the Wilderness, Va.

SECOR, JAMES.—Age, 24 years. Enlisted, August 27, 1862, at Camden, to serve three years; mustered in as private, Co. E, October 10, 1862; promoted sergeant, no date; wounded in action, May, 1863, at Chancellorsville, Va.; discharged for wounds, September 10, 1863, at Washington, D. C. Died in 1906.

SHARDIN, JOHN.—Age, 31 years. Enlisted, August 29, 1862, at Boonville, to serve three years; mustered in as private, Co. D, October 10, 1862; promoted corporal, no date; principal musician, August 29, 1864; discharged, June 26, 1865, at Washington, D. C.; also borne as Sheridan, Sharder, and Shardon; brevet first lieutenant, by New York State Government.

SHARP, EUGENE A.—Age, 18 years. Enlisted, August 27, 1862, at Paris, to serve three years; mustered in as private, Co. K, October 10, 1862; appointed musician, no date; discharged for disability, June 24, 1863, at Washington, D. C.; subsequent service in Sixteenth Artillery.

SHAW, JAMES.—Age, 16 years. Enlisted, August 27, 1862, at Utica, to serve three years; mustered in as musician, Co. C, October 10, 1862; mustered out with company, July 16, 1865, near Washington, D. C.

SHEPARD, NORTON.—Age, 21 years. Enlisted, August 28, 1862, at Rome, to serve three years; mustered in as private, Co. B, October 10, 1862; promoted corporal, November 1, 1863; wounded and captured in action, May 5, 1864, at the Wilderness, Va.; paroled, no date; discharged for wounds, October 25, 1865, at Washington, D. C.

SHIPMAN, CHARLES D.—Age, 23 years. Enlisted, September 6, 1862, at Bridgewater, to serve three years; mustered in as private, Co. G, October 10, 1862; discharged for disability, March 18, 1863, near Falmouth, Va.

SHONHAMER, WILLIAM.—Age, 19 years. Enlisted, August 29, 1862, at Boonville, to serve three years; mustered in as private, Co. D, October 10, 1862; wounded in action, May 5, 1864, at the Wilderness, Va.; died of his wounds, June 12, 1864, at Washington, D. C.

SHOTT, GEORGE.—Age, 19 years. Enlisted, August 19, 1862, at Utica, to serve three years; mustered in as private, Co. A, October 10, 1862; captured in action, May 5, 1864, at the Wilderness, Va.; paroled, no date; promoted sergeant, May 1, 1865; mustered out with company, July 16, 1865, near Washington, D. C., as George H. Shott.

SHUCK, JOSEPH.—Age, 35 years. Enlisted, August 30, 1862, at Utica, to serve three years; mustered in as private, Co. C, October 10, 1862.

SHUCKER, JOHN S.—Age, 26 years. Enlisted, August 28, 1862, at Ava, to serve three years; mustered in as private, Co. F, October 10, 1862; captured in action, May 5, 1864, at the Wilderness, Va.; died of disease, November 9, 1864, at Florence, S. C.

SIMMONS, IRA A.—Age, 19 years. Enlisted, August 29, 1862,

at Annsville, to serve three years; mustered in as private, Co. F, October 10, 1862; killed in action, June 18, 1864, at Petersburg, Va.

SIMPKINS, DAVID.—Age, 24 years. Enlisted, August 30, 1862, at Rome, to serve three years; mustered in as private, Co. F, October 10, 1862; mustered out, June 21, 1865, at Washington, D. C.

SIMPKINS, STEPHEN.—Age, 21 years. Enlisted, August 30, 1862, at Rome, to serve three years; mustered in as private, Co. F, October 10, 1862; transferred to Co. I, March 28, 1863; mustered out with company, July 16, 1865, near Washington, D. C.; also borne as Stephen Simpkins, Jr.

SISBAR, JOHN.—Age, 21 years. Enlisted, August 18, 1862, at Verona, to serve three years; mustered in as private, Co. K, October 10, 1862; transferred to Co. I, October 31, 1862; captured in action, May 5, 1864, at the Wilderness, Va.; paroled, March 25, 1865; mustered out with company, July 16, 1865, near Washington, D. C.

SITTIG, FREDERICK.—Age, 22 years. Enlisted, August 30, 1862, at Utica, to serve three years; mustered in as private, Co. H, October 10, 1862; promoted corporal, no date; sergeant, March 28, 1863; wounded on skirmish line, August 18, 1864, at Weldon Railroad, Va.; died of his wounds, September 6, 1864, at City Point, Va.

SKINNER, ALVAH.—Age, 36 years. Enlisted, September 2, 1862, at Camden, to serve three years; mustered in as private, Co. E, October 10, 1862; also borne as Alva Skinner.

SKINNER, EDWIN.—Age, 22 years. Enlisted, September 2, 1862, at Lee, to serve three years; mustered in as private, Co. F, October 10, 1862; promoted corporal, no date; mustered out, October 20, 1865, at Elmira, N. Y.

SKINNER, JOHN.—Age, 32 years. Enlisted, August 26, 1862, at Lee, to serve three years; mustered in as sergeant, Co. F, October 10, 1862; returned to ranks, no date; wounded in action, May 10, 1864, at Laurel Hill, Va.; died of his wounds, May 31, 1864, at Washington, D. C.

SKINNER, LUTHER.—Age, 38 years. Enlisted, September 2, 1862, at Camden, to serve three years; mustered in as private, Co. E, October 10, 1862.

SKINNER, ROBERT.—Age, 24 years. Enlisted, September 2, 1862, at Lee, to serve three years; mustered in as sergeant, Co. F, October 10, 1862; returned to ranks, no date; discharged for disability, April 23, 1863, at Utica, N. Y.

SLIKER, PEMO.—Age, 26 years. Enlisted, September 6, 1862. at Rome, to serve three years; mustered in as private, Co. H, October 10, 1862; mustered out with company, July 16, 1865, near Washington, D. C., as Primo Sliker. Died in 1895.

SMITH, ABLE.—Age, 20 years. Enlisted, August 31, 1862, at Camden, to serve three years; mustered in as private, Co. E, October 10, 1862.

SMITH, ANDREW.—Age, 18 years. Enlisted, August 25, 1862, at Utica, to serve three years; mustered in as private, Co. A, October 10, 1862; captured in action, May 3, 1863, at Chancellorsville, Va.; paroled, June 26, 1863; again captured, May 4, 1864, at the Wilderness, Va.; paroled, no date; mustered out with company, July 16, 1865, near Washington, D. C.

SMITH, CHANCY B.—Age, 30 years. Enlisted, August 30, 1862, at Utica, to serve three years; mustered in as private, Co. H, December 31, 1862; promoted sergeant, no date; captured in action, May 5, 1864, at the Wilderness, Va.; returned to ranks, no date; no further record.

SMITH, CHARLES B.—Age, 21 years. Enlisted, August 29, 1862, at Westmoreland to serve three years; mustered in as private, Co. I, October 10, 1862; died of disease, January 3, 1864, in hospital, Washington, D. C.

SMITH, CHARLES E.—Age, 18 years. Enlisted, September 1, 1862, at Utica, to serve three years; mustered in as private, Co. A, October 10, 1862.

SMITH, DANIEL W.—Age, 21 years. Enlisted, September 6, 1862, at Utica, to serve three years; mustered in as private, Co. G, October 10, 1862; died of disease, December 25, 1862, in hospital near Potomac Creek, Va.

SMITH, GEORGE.—Age, 34 years. Enlisted, August 21, 1862, at Westmoreland, to serve three years; mustered in as private, Co. I, October 10, 1862; mustered out with company, July 16, 1865, near Washington, D. C.

SMITH, JR., GEORGE.—Age, 23 years. Enlisted, August 22, 1862, at Westmoreland, to serve three years; mustered in as private, Co. I, October 10, 1862; discharged, June 2, 1865, at Washington, D. C. Died in 1896.

SMITH, JAMES J.—Age, 33 years. Enlisted, August 16, 1862, at Utica, to serve three years; mustered in as private, Co. A, October 10, 1862; also borne as James A. Smith.

SMITH, PHILIP.—Age, 18 years. Enlisted, August 26, 1862, at Utica, to serve three years; mustered in as private, Co. A, October 10, 1862; captured in action, May 3, 1863, at Chancellorsville, Va.; returned, July 26, 1863; mustered out, June 9, 1865, at Washington, D. C.

SMITH, SIDNEY H.—Age, 18 years. Enlisted, August 30, 1862, at Utica, to serve three years; mustered in as private, Co. C, October 10, 1862; wounded and captured in action, May 5, 1864, at the Wilderness, Va.; died of his wounds, October 3, 1864, at Gordonsville, Va.

Before enlisting, married Amelia Cary. Mrs. Smith died at Waterville, N. Y., February, 1908.

SMITH, WILLIAM H.—Age, 39 years. Enrolled, September 10, 1862, at Rome, to serve three years; mustered in as second lieutenant, Co. F, October 10, 1862; discharged, January 10, 1863, near Potomac Creek, Va.

Commissioned second lieutenant, November 3, 1862, with rank from September 10, 1862, original.

SMITH, WILLIAM H.—Age, 24 years. Enlisted, August 30, 1862, at Floyd, to serve three years; mustered in as private, Co. B, October 10, 1862; drowned, October 12, 1862, at Port Monmouth, N. J.

SNOW, CHARLES T.—Age, 18 years. Enlisted, August 25, 1862, at Vernon, to serve three years; mustered in as corporal, Co. B, October 10, 1862; discharged for disability, April 15, 1863, at Verona, N. Y.

SNYDER, EDMOND.—Age, 20 years. Enlisted, August 30, 1862, at Utica, to serve three years; mustered in as private, Co. C, October 10, 1862; killed in action, May 5, 1864, at the Wilderness, Va.

SNYDER, WILLIAM L.—Age, 28 years. Enlisted, September 2, 1862, at Lee, to serve three years; mustered in as private,

Co. F, October 10, 1862; promoted corporal, February 1, 1863; captured in action, May 5, 1864, at the Wilderness, Va.; paroled, April 1, 1865; mustered out, July 23, 1865, at Syracuse, N. Y.

SOMERS, ELBERT M.—Age, 35 years. Enrolled at Albany, to serve three years; mustered in as assistant surgeon, September 10, 1862; discharged, December 7, 1862.

Commissioned assistant surgeon, November 3, 1862, with rank from September 4, 1862, original.

SOPER, GEORGE R.—Age, 25 years. Enlisted, September 4, 1862, at Marshall, to serve three years; mustered in as private, Co. K, October 10, 1862; captured and paroled, no dates; promoted corporal, June 3, 1865; mustered out with company, July 16, 1865, near Washington, D. C.

SORN, HENRY.—Age, 23 years. Enlisted, September 4, 1862, at Bridgewater, to serve three years; mustered in as private, Co. G, October 10, 1862; promoted corporal, no date; sergeant, February 1, 1865; sergeant-major, March 1, 1865; mustered out with regiment, July 16, 1865, near Washington, D. C.

Commissioned, not mustered, second lieutenant, August 31, 1865, with rank from August 1, 1865, vice H. C. Lull not mustered.

Born in Saxony, November 26, 1838; came to United States when nine years old; soon after he returned from war married Miss Minnie Marker, of Sauquoit; died, July 18, 1913.

SPINK, ALANSON F.—Age, 17 years. Enlisted, August 29, 1862, at Lee, to serve three years; mustered in as private, Co. F, October 10, 1862; captured in action, May 5, 1864, at the Wilderness, Va.; died of disease, August 6, 1864, at Andersonville, Ga.

STAATS, GARET L.—Age, 43 years. Enlisted, August 30, 1862, at Vienna, to serve three years; mustered in as private, Co. B, October 10, 1862; transferred to Veteran Reserve Corps, September 2, 1863; mustered out therefrom as of Second Battalion, July 21, 1865, at Washington, D. C.

STAHL, CHRISTIAN.—Age, 38 years. Enlisted, August 28, 1862, at Rome, to serve three years; mustered in as private, Co.

F, October 10, 1862; discharged for disability, September 7, 1863, at hospital, Washington, D. C.

STANFORD, WILLIAM J.—Age, — years. Enrolled, September 2, 1862, at Rome, to serve three years; mustered in as second lieutenant, Co. A, October 10, 1862; transferred to Co. H, December 27, 1862; discharged, January 7, 1863, near Falmouth, Va.

Commissioned second lieutenant, November 3, 1862, with rank from September 2, 1862, original.

STANNARD, CHARLES A.—Age, 29 years. Enlisted, August 26, 1862, at Remsen, to serve three years; mustered in as private, Co. I, October 10, 1862; promoted sergeant, no date; captured in action, May 5, 1864, at the Wilderness, Va.; paroled, no date; mustered out, June 26, 1865, at Albany, N. Y.; also borne as Stanard.

STAPLES, JAMES B.—Age, 37 years. Enlisted, August 30, 1862, at Vernon, to serve three years; mustered in as private, Co. B, October 10, 1862; discharged for disability, January 30, 1863, at Washington, D. C.

STARKWEATHER, HENRY W.—Age, 23 years. Enlisted, August 30, 1862, at Camden, to serve three years; mustered in as private, Co. E, October 10, 1862; died of disease, February 7, 1863, at Potomac Creek, Va.

STARKWEATHER, LEVIT.—Age, 30 years. Enlisted, August 30, 1862, at Camden, to serve three years; mustered in as private, Co. E, October 10, 1862; captured, no date; died of disease, December 15, 1864, at Andersonville, Ga.

STARR, EMORY C.—Age, 21 years. Enlisted, August 29, 1862, at Lee, to serve three years; mustered in as corporal, Co. F, October 10, 1862; promoted sergeant, January 1, 1864; captured in action, May 5, 1864, at the Wilderness, Va.; exchanged, March 25, 1865; promoted first sergeant, May 18, 1865; mustered out with company, July 16, 1865, near Washington, D. C.

Commissioned, not mustered, second lieutenant, June 17, 1865, with rank from February 1, 1865, vice H. G. Smith resigned.

START, ROBERT.—Age, 45 years. Enlisted, August 26, 1862, at Marcy, to serve three years; mustered in as private, Co. F,

October 10, 1862; transferred to Veteran Reserve Corps, September 1, 1863.

STEPHENSON, GEORGE.—Age, 33 years. Enlisted, August 26, 1862, at Utica, to serve three years; mustered in as corporal, Co. C, October 10, 1862; captured in action, May 5, 1864, at the Wilderness, Va.; paroled, no date; died of disease, December 25, 1864, at Annapolis, Md.

STEPHENSON, MORRIS.—Age, 21 years. Enlisted, August 26, 1862, at Utica, to serve three years; mustered in as private, Co. H, October 10, 1862; promoted first sergeant and returned to ranks, no date; wounded in action, June 19, 1864, at Petersburg, Va.; died of his wounds, July 10, 1864; also borne as Stevenson.

STEWART, JAMES.—Age, 34 years. Enrolled at Rome, to serve three years, and mustered in as first lieutenant, Co. G, September 17, 1862; as captain, Co. K, January 7, 1863; captured in action, August 18, 1864, at Weldon Railroad, Va.; paroled, no date; discharged, May 15, 1865; also borne as Stuart and Steward.

Commissioned first lieutenant, November 3, 1862, with rank from September 17, 1862, original; captain, February 5, 1863, with rank from January 7, 1863, vice D. A. Dodge resigned; brevet colonel, by U. S. Government, from March 13, 1865.

STOCKBRIDGE, JOSEPH.—Age, 31 years. Enlisted, August 26, 1862, at Kirkland, to serve three years; mustered in as private, Co. G, October 10, 1862; transferred to Veteran Reserve Corps, October 6, 1864; mustered out therefrom as of Seventy-first Company, Second Battalion, October 9, 1865, at Baltimore, Md.

STOCKWELL, LORING P.—Age, 30 years. Enlisted, August 20, 1862, at Kirkland, to serve three years; mustered in as sergeant, Co. G, October 10, 1862; promoted first sergeant, no date; captured in action, May 5, 1864, at the Wilderness, Va.; no further record.

STODDARD, JEROME B.—Age, 41 years. Enlisted, August 30, 1862, at Remsen, to serve three years; mustered in as private, Co. I, October 10, 1862; discharged, March 12, 1863, at camp near Potomac Creek, Va.

STOFFORD, JR., THOMAS.—Age, 18 years. Enlisted, September 6, 1862, at Utica, to serve three years; mustered in as private, Co. H, October 10, 1862; mustered out with company, July 16, 1865, near Washington, D. C., as Stafford.

STRONG, GEORGE W.—Age, 18 years. Enlisted, August 25, 1862, at Kirkland, to serve three years; mustered in as private, Co. G, October 10, 1862; captured in action, May 3, 1863, at Chancellorsville, Va.; paroled, no date; mustered out with company, July 16, 1865, near Washington, D. C. Died June 11, 1908.

STROUP, JOSEPH.—Age, 18 years. Enlisted, August 22, 1862, at Steuben, to serve three years; mustered in as private, Co. I, October 10, 1862; transferred to Veteran Reserve Corps, December 25, 1864.

SULLIVAN, ORIN.—Age, 21 years. Enlisted, August 27, 1862, at Camden, to serve three years; mustered in as private, Co. E, October 10, 1862.

SWANSON, JAMES.—Age, 25 years. Enlisted, August 29, 1862, at Camden, to serve three years; mustered in as corporal, Co. E, October 10, 1862; promoted sergeant, September 14, 1863; returned to ranks, February 22, 1864; killed in action, May 5, 1864, at the Wilderness, Va.

SWANSON, JOHN.—Age, 28 years. Enlisted, August 30, 1862, at Camden, to serve three years; mustered in as private, Co. E, October 10, 1862; promoted sergeant, no date; captured in action, June 2, 1864, at Cold Harbor, Va.; paroled, February 26, 1865, at Wilmington, N. C.; mustered out, June 7, 1865, at Albany, N. Y.

SWEET, W. H. SEWARD.—Age, 24 years. Enrolled, September 6, 1862, at Marcy, to serve three years; mustered in as first sergeant, Co. F, October 10, 1862; as first lieutenant, Co. B, January 10, 1863; transferred to Co. F, January 25, 1864; captured in action, May 5, 1864, at the Wilderness, Va.; returned May 6, 1865; mustered out with company, July 16, 1865, near Washington, D. C.

Commissioned first lieutenant, February 5, 1863, with rank from January 7, 1863, vice E. V. Jewell promoted; brevet captain, by U. S. Government, from March 13, 1865.

SWERTFAGER, CHARLES C.—Age, 31 years. Enlisted, August

25, 1862, at Utica, to serve three years; mustered in as private, Co. C, October 10, 1862; discharged for disability, March 1, 1864, at Washington, D. C.   Died in 1905.

SWERTFAGER, HENRY.—Age, 18 years. Enlisted, August 25, 1862, at Utica, to serve three years; mustered in as private, Co. F, October 10, 1862; discharged for disability, October 30, 1863, at Convalescent Camp, Va.; also borne as Shwartfager and Swertfinger.

TALLMAN, PERRY.—Age, 27 years. Enlisted, August 30, 1862, at Utica, to serve three years; mustered in as private, Co. E, October 10, 1862; discharged for disability, September 10, 1863, at Washington, D. C.

TALLMAN, WILLIAM A.—Age, 27 years. Enlisted, August 26, 1862, at Utica, to serve three years; mustered in as private, Co. E, October 10, 1862; discharged for disability, August 18, 1863, at Annapolis, Md.   Died in 1895.

TANNAR, ROSELLE E.—Age, 18 years. Enlisted, September 29, 1862, at Trenton, to serve three years; mustered in as private, Co. I, October 10, 1862; died of disease, December 25, 1862, in Regimental Hospital, Henry House, Va.

TAYLOR, WILLIAM T.—Age, 23 years. Enlisted, September 15, 1862, at Kirkland, to serve three years; mustered in as private, Co. G, October 10, 1862; promoted corporal, no date; captured in action and paroled, no dates; promoted sergeant, March 1, 1865; first sergeant, June 1, 1865; mustered out with company, July 16, 1865, near Washington, D. C.

TEACHOUT, GEORGE.—Age, 39 years. Enlisted, August 30, 1862, at Utica, to serve three years; mustered in as private, Co. H, October 10, 1862; transferred to Veteran Reserve Corps, July 12, 1864; mustered out therefrom as of Co. D, Third Regiment, August 3, 1865, at Hartford, Conn.

TEFFT, JOHN A.—Age, 21 years. Enlisted, September 3, 1862, at Remsen, to serve three years; mustered in as private, Co. I, October 10, 1862; transferred to Co. G, March 27, 1864; retransferred to Co. I, June 28, 1864; promoted corporal and wounded, no dates; died of his wounds, May 25, 1865, at Lincoln Hospital, Washington, D. C.

TEMPLETON, SYLVESTER.—Age, 18 years. Enlisted, August 25,

1862, at Florence, to serve three years; mustered in as private, Co. F, October 10, 1862.

THICKENS, THOMAS.—Age, 31 years. Enlisted, August 26, 1862, at Utica, to serve three years; mustered in as private, Co. A, October 10, 1862; transferred to Veteran Reserve Corps, November 19, 1863.

THOMAS, EDWIN.—Age, 27 years. Enlisted, August 22, 1862, at Remsen, to serve three years; mustered in as private, Co. I, October 10, 1862.

THOMAS, HUGH.—Age, 28 years. Enlisted, August 29, 1862, at Rome, to serve three years; mustered in as private, Co. B, October 10, 1862; mustered out with company, July 16, 1865, near Washington, D. C.

THOMAS, JESSE.—Age, 24 years. Enlisted, August 28, 1862, at Marcy, to serve three years; mustered in as private, Co. E, October 10, 1862; killed in action, June 2, 1864, at Bethesda Church, Va.

THOMAS, NEWTON.—Age, 27 years. Enlisted, September 3, 1862, at Steuben, to serve three years; mustered in as private, Co. I, October 10, 1862.

THOMAS, PATRICK H.—Age, 27 years. Enlisted, September 6, 1862, at Utica, to serve three years; mustered in as private, Co. K, October 10, 1862; promoted hospital steward, same date; returned to Co. K, as private, August 1, 1863; discharged for disability, September 15, 1863, at New York City.

THOMPSON, AARON B.—Age, 31 years. Enlisted, August 22, 1862, at Utica, to serve three years; mustered in as private, Co. A, October 10, 1862; wounded and captured in action, May 5, 1864, at the Wilderness, Va.; died of his wounds, August 24, 1864, at Andersonville, Ga.

THOMPSON, BURTON.—Age, 31 years. Enlisted, August 28, 1862, at Ava, to serve three years; mustered in as private, Co. F, October 10, 1862; promoted corporal, October 1, 1864; sergeant, November 25, 1864; mustered out with company, July 16, 1865, near Washington, D. C. Died in 1902.

THOMPSON, RICHARD.—Age, 31 years. Enlisted, August 22, 1862, at Utica, to serve three years; mustered in as private, Co. H, October 10, 1862; mustered out, June 16, 1865, at Albany, N. Y.

THREADGOLD, JOHN.—Age, 26 years. Enlisted at Rochester, to serve three years, and mustered in as private, Co. K, August 6, 1863; discharged for disability, November 7, 1863, at Kelly's Ford, Va.

TIBBITS, GEORGE O.—Age, 21 years. Enlisted, August 26, 1862, at Rome, to serve three years; mustered in as sergeant, Co. B, October 10, 1862; returned to ranks, November 21, 1862; promoted corporal, October 10, 1864; sergeant, February 4, 1865; mustered out with company, July 16, 1865, near Washington, D. C. Born at Rome, N. Y., April 4, 1841; died at Rome, N. Y., March 7, 1913.

TIMERMAN, DAVID.—Age, 27 years. Enrolled, August 27, 1862, at Deerfield, to serve three years; mustered in as sergeant, Co. F, October 10, 1862; promoted first sergeant, February 21, 1863; mustered in as second lieutenant, Co. E, November 17, 1863; transferred to Co. D, January 25, 1864; wounded in action, May 12, 1864, at Spotsylvania, Va.; transferred to Co. K, July 12, 1864; discharged for disability, August 10, 1864.

Commissioned second lieutenant, October 6, 1863, with rank from September 23, 1863, vice W. A. Walker promoted.

TIMORSON, JOHN A.—Age, 21 years. Enlisted, August 21, 1862, at Paris, to serve three years; mustered in as private, Co. K, October 10, 1862; transferred to Veteran Reserve Corps, January 1, 1865; mustered out therefrom as of Eighty-sixth Company, Second Battalion, August 21, 1865, at Washington, D. C.; also borne as Tymerson.

TOMPKINS, JOHN.—Age, 44 years. Enlisted, September 15, 1862, at Oriskany, to serve three years; mustered in as private, Co. K., October 10, 1862; transferred to Veteran Reserve Corps, September 1, 1863.

TOMPKINS, NATHANIEL H.—Age, 20 years. Enlisted, September 6, 1862, at Bridgewater, to serve three years; mustered in as corporal, Co. G, October 10, 1862; returned to ranks, no date; mustered out with company, July 16, 1865, near Washington, D. C. Died November 29, 1909, at Whitesboro, N. Y.

TOOLY, LUCIUS S.—Age, 28 years. Enlisted, September 5, 1862, at Sangerfield, to serve three years; mustered in as private, Co. H, October 10, 1862; promoted sergeant, no date; returned to ranks, March 24, 1863; promoted corporal, no date; wounded in action, May 5, 1864, at the Wilderness, Va.; died of his wounds, June 10, 1864, at Locust Grove, Va.

TOWNSLEY, A. DEVOMEY.—Age, 26 years. Enrolled, September 3, 1862, at Rome, to serve three years; mustered in as second lieutenant, Co. B, October 10, 1862; discharged, December 25, 1862, near Potomac Creek, Va.

Commissioned second lieutenant, November 3, 1862, with rank from September 3, 1862, original.

TRACY, HENRY C.—Age, 18 years. Enlisted, August 25, 1862, at Vernon, to serve three years; mustered in as private, Co. B, October 10, 1862; discharged for disability, January 18, 1863, at Washington, D. C.

TRACY, JOHN J.—Age, 18 years. Enlisted, August 28, 1862, at Utica, to serve three years; mustered in as private, Co. H, October 10, 1862; mustered out with company, July 16, 1865, near Washington, D. C.; also borne as Tracey.

TRASK, FRANCIS W.—Age, 21 years. Enlisted, August 26, 1862, at Camden, to serve three years; mustered in as corporal, Co. E, October 10, 1862; returned to ranks, no date; discharged for disability, March 27, 1863.

TRIPP, CHARLES A.—Age, 26 years. Enlisted, September 6, 1862, at Lee, to serve three years; mustered in as private, Co. F, October 10, 1862; died of typhoid fever, July 8, 1863, at Frederick City, Md.

TROXEL, HENRY.—Age, 23 years. Enlisted, August 29, 1862, at Boonville, to serve three years; mustered in as private, Co. D, October 10, 1862; died of disease, December 25, 1862, near Falmouth, Va.

TRUAX, SILAS J.—Age, 23 years. Enrolled, August 30, 1862, at Utica, to serve three years; mustered in as first lieutenant, Co. C, October 10, 1862; discharged, November 30, 1862, near Potomac Creek, Va.

Commissioned first lieutenant, November 3, 1862, with rank from September 3, 1862, original.

TURRELL, STIMPSON.—Age, 27 years. Enlisted, September 30, 1862, at Paris, to serve three years; mustered in as private, Co. K, October 10, 1862; promoted corporal, no date; sergeant, January 31, 1863; sergeant-major, June 25, 1863; wounded in action, May 8, 1864, at Spotsylvania, Va.; died of his wounds, May 20, 1864, in hospital, at Alexandria, Va.; also borne as Terrell.

VAIL, DANIEL.—Age, 28 years. Enlisted, August 26, 1862, at Utica, to serve three years; mustered in as private, Co. A, October 10, 1862; transferred to Co. K, October 29, 1862; discharged for disability, January 16, 1864, at Warrenton Junction, Va.

VANDERHOFF, NATHANIEL P.—Age, 20 years. Enlisted, August 25, 1862, at Floyd, to serve three years; mustered in as corporal, Co. B, October 10, 1862; wounded in action, May 1, 1863, at Chancellorsville, Va.; died of his wounds, May 16, 1863, in Division Hospital.

VAN LOUVAN, JONS.—Age, 32 years. Enlisted, August 28, 1862, at Paris, to serve three years; mustered in as private, Co. K, October 10, 1862; mustered out with company, July 16, 1865, near Washington, D. C.

VAN VALKENBURG, HENRY.—Age, 44 years. Enlisted, August 28, 1862, at Westmoreland, to serve three years; mustered in as private, Co. I, October 10, 1862; transferred to Veteran Reserve Corps, November 25, 1863.

VAN VLECK, CHARLES.—Age, 27 years. Enlisted, August 25, 1862, at Utica, to serve three years; mustered in as corporal, Co. C, October 10, 1862; returned to ranks, no date; mustered out with company, July 16, 1865, near Washington, D. C.

VAN ZANDT, HENRY P.—Age, 41 years. Enlisted, August 30, 1862, at Rome, to serve three years; mustered in as private, Co. B, October 10, 1862; discharged for disability, June 30, 1863, at Washington, D. C.

VARLEY, ABRAHAM.—Age, 24 years. Enlisted, August 29, 1862, at Paris, to serve three years; mustered in as private, Co. H, October 10, 1862; transferred to the Navy, May 2, 1864.

VOORHEES, ALBERT H.—Age, 19 years. Enlisted, August 29, 1862, at Camden, to serve three years; mustered in as corporal, Co. E, October 10, 1862; returned to ranks, November 3, 1862; killed in action, May 5, 1864, at the Wilderness, Va.

WAELIAND, MICHAEL.—Age, 32 years. Enlisted, August 29,

1862, at Boonville, to serve three years; mustered in as private, Co. D, October 10, 1862; mustered out with company, July 16, 1865, near Washington, D. C.

WAIT, FRANCIS H.—Age, 27 years. Enlisted, August 18, 1862, at Rome, to serve three years; mustered in as private, Co. I, October 10, 1862; discharged for disability, March 11, 1863, at camp near Potomac Creek, Va.

WALDRON, NELSON.—Age, 22 years. Enlisted, August 28, 1862, at Paris, to serve three years; mustered in as private, Co. K, October 10, 1862; captured in action, May 5, 1864, at the Wilderness, Va.; died of disease, August 27, 1864, at Andersonville, Ga.

WALKER, WILLIAM A.—Age, 21 years. Enrolled, August 22, 1862, at Rome, to serve three years; mustered in as first sergeant, Co. B, October 10, 1862; returned to ranks, November 22, 1862; promoted corporal, January 10, 1863; sergeant, February 1, 1863; mustered in as second lieutenant, Co. D, March 1, 1863; transferred to Co. E, August 20, 1863; mustered in as first lieutenant, Co. C, October 23, 1863; wounded and captured in action, May 5, 1864, at the Wilderness, Va.; returned January 9, 1865; mustered in as captain, April 1, 1865; mustered out with company, July 16, 1865, near Washington, D. C.

Commissioned second lieutenant, February 23, 1863, with rank from February 2, 1863, vice C. E. Lasher promoted; first lieutenant, October 6, 1863, with rank from September 28, 1863, vice J. B. Cushman promoted; captain, February 18, 1865, with rank from January 1, 1865, vice P. Claesgens promoted; brevet major by U. S. Government, from March 13, 1865.

WALTER, HORATIO A.—Age, 19 years. Enlisted, August 19, 1862, at Rome, to serve three years; mustered in as private, Co. B, October 10, 1862; promoted corporal, November 22, 1862; returned to ranks, February 1, 1863; promoted corporal, May 1, 1863; sergeant, April 30, 1864; killed in action, June 18, 1864, at Petersburg, Va.

WARD, JAMES.—Age, 21 years. Enlisted, August 28, 1862, at Utica, to serve three years; mustered in as private, Co. A, October 10, 1862; captured in action, May 1, 1863, at Chancellorsville, Va.; returned, July 26, 1863; again captured in action, May 5, 1864, at the Wilderness, Va.; no further record.

WARD, LORENZO.—Age, 42 years. Enlisted, August 29, 1862, at Annsville, to serve three years; mustered in as private, Co. K, October 10, 1862; promoted sergeant, Co. F, same date; returned to ranks, no date; transferred to Veteran Reserve Corps, April 1, 1865; mustered out therefrom as of unassigned, First Battalion, July 19, 1865, at Washington, D. C.

WARREN, W. FRANK.—Age, 22 years. Enlisted, September 3, 1862, at Trenton, to serve three years; mustered in as private, Co. I, October 10, 1862; discharged for disability, January 1, 1864, at Washington, D. C.

WASHBURN, ADELBERT A.—Age, 18 years. Enlisted, September 13, 1862, at Plainfield, to serve three years; mustered in as private, Co. G, October 10, 1862; died of disease, October 24, 1862, in hospital, Washington, D. C.

WATCHES, ALLEN.—Age, 18 years. Enlisted, August 29, 1862, at Utica, to serve three years; mustered in as private, Co. C, October 10, 1862; captured in action, May 5, 1864, at the Wilderness, Va.; paroled, no date; promoted corporal, June 3, 1865; mustered out with company, July 16, 1865, near Washington, D. C. Died October 6, 1910, at Utica.

WEBB, JOHN.—Age, 23 years. Enlisted, August 28, 1862, at Utica, to serve three years; mustered in as private, Co. A, October 10, 1862; captured in action, May 1, 1863, at Chancellorsville, Va.; returned, August 4, 1863; transferred to Co. I, Fourteenth Regiment, Veteran Reserve Corps, June 13, 1865; mustered out, August 1, 1865, at Washington. D. C. Died, Feb. 17, 1908, at Utica.

WELCH, CHARLES.—Age, 25 years. Enlisted, September 6, 1862, at Bridgewater, to serve three years; mustered in as private, Co. G, October 10, 1862.

WELCH, LAWRENCE.—Age, 24 years. Enlisted, September 3, 1862, at Rome, to serve three years; mustered in as private, Co. B, October 10, 1862; captured in action, May 5, 1864, at the Wilderness, Va.; died of chronic diarrhea, June 22, 1864, at Andersonville, Ga.

WELCH, MICHAEL.—Age, 40 years. Enlisted, August 30, 1862, at Utica, to serve three years; mustered in as private, Co. C, October 10, 1862; captured in action, May 5, 1864, at the Wilderness, Va.; died of disease, November 15, 1864, at Florence, S. C.

WELLER, AARON.—Age, 38 years. Enlisted, September 1, 1862, at Westmoreland, to serve three years; mustered in as private, Co. K, October 10, 1862; captured in action, June 3, 1864, at Cold Harbor, Va.; no further record.

WELLS, ROBERT.—Age, 45 years. Enlisted, August 28, 1862, at Rome, to serve three years; mustered in as private, Co. B, October 10, 1862; discharged for disability, August 19, 1863, at Washington, D. C.

WENTWORTH, NELSON.—Age, 33 years. Enlisted, August 30, 1862, at Lee, to serve three years; mustered in as private, Co. F, October 10, 1862.

WESTCOTT, EDWARD.—Age, 25 years. Enlisted, September 3, 1862, at Trenton, to serve three years; mustered in as private, Co. I, October 10, 1862; mustered out with company, July 16, 1865, near Washington, D. C. Born at Trenton, N. Y., 1836; married in 1862 to Emma F. Smith of Gravesville; died at Utica, Nov. 29, 1911.

WESTCOTT, RIAL J.—Age, 19 years. Enlisted, September 1, 1862, at Camden, to serve three years; mustered in as private, Co. E, October 10, 1862; discharged for disability, August 13, 1863, at Washington, D. C.

WETMORE, LYNDE G.—Age, 18 years. Enlisted, September 29, 1862, at Whitestown, to serve three years; mustered in as private, Co. G, October 10, 1862; promoted corporal and returned to ranks, no dates; promoted quartermaster-sergeant, September 30, 1864; mustered out with regiment, July 16, 1865, near Washington, D. C.

WHALEN, JOSEPH.—Age, 21 years. Enlisted, August 30, 1862, at Sangerfield, to serve three years; mustered in as private, Co. H, October 10, 1862; captured in action, May 5, 1864, at the Wilderness, Va.; confined at Andersonville, Ga.; no further record.

WHEELER, GEORGE.—Age, 20 years. Enlisted, August 25, 1862, at Utica, to serve three years; mustered in as private, Co.

A, October 10, 1862; captured and paroled, no dates; transferred to Veteran Reserve Corps, August 12, 1864; mustered out therefrom as of Co. B, Nineteenth Regiment, July 13, 1865, at Elmira, N. Y. Died in 1902.

WHEELER, GEORGE W.—Age, 21 years. Enlisted, August 28, 1862, at Trenton, to serve three years; mustered in as private, Co. I, October 10, 1862; promoted sergeant and first sergeant, no dates; captured in action, May 5, 1864, at the Wilderness, Va.; returned to ranks, no date; paroled, March 25, 1865; promoted sergeant, no date; mustered out with company, July 16, 1865, near Washington, D. C.

WHEELER, JOSEPH.—Age, 44 years. Enlisted, August 25, 1862, at Camden, to serve three years; mustered in as private, Co. E, October 10, 1862; discharged for disability, April 4, 1863.

WHEELER, NORMAN.—Age, 18 years. Enlisted, September 30, 1862, at Rome, to serve three years; mustered in as private, Co. K, October 10, 1862; no further record.

WHEELER, NORMAN.—Age, 22 years. Enlisted, August 29, 1862, at Trenton, to serve three years; mustered in as private, Co. I, October 10, 1862; discharged for disability, May 20, 1865, at hospital, York, Pa. Died in 1906.

WHEELER, THOMAS.—Age, 18 years. Enrolled, September 30, 1862, at Utica, to serve three years; mustered in as private, Co. A, October 10, 1862; promoted sergeant, no date; first sergeant, May 1, 1865; mustered out with company, July 16, 1865, near Washington, D. C.

Commissioned, not mustered, second lieutenant, March 30, 1865, with rank from February 1, 1865, vice Charles T. Jones not mustered.

WHEELER, WILLIAM W.—Age, 23 years. Enlisted, August 29, 1862, at Boonville, to serve three years; mustered in as private, Co. D, October 10, 1862; discharged for disability, December 22, 1862, at Philadelphia, Pa.

WHITE, ALBERT A.—Age, 36 years. Enlisted, September 6, 1862, at Bridgewater, to serve three years; mustered in as private, Co. G, October 10, 1862; mustered out with company, July 16, 1865, near Washington, D. C. Died at Bridgewater in 1904.

WHITE, ARTHUR.—Age, 19 years. Enlisted, August 19, 1862,

at Utica, to serve three years; mustered in as private, Co. C, October 10, 1862; wounded, no date; discharged for disability, November 9, 1863, at Washington, D. C.

WHITE, CHARLES F.—Age, 24 years. Enlisted, August 27, 1862, at Paris, to serve three years; mustered in as private, Co. K, October 10, 1862; discharged for disability, March 9, 1863, at Washington, D. C.

WHITE, FREDERICK.—Age, 18 years. Enlisted, September 13, 1862, at Utica, to serve three years; mustered in as musician, Co. A, October 10, 1862; mustered out with company, July 16, 1865, near Washington, D. C.

WHITE, JOHN T.—Age, 21 years. Enlisted, August 19, 1862, at Utica, to serve three years; mustered in as private, Co. H, October 10, 1862; promoted sergeant and returned to ranks, no dates; killed in action, May 5, 1864, at the Wilderness, Va.

WHITE, SAMUEL.—Age, 19 years. Enlisted, August 19, 1862, at Utica, to serve three years; mustered in as private, Co. H, October 10, 1862; appointed musician and returned to company, as private, no dates; mustered out with company, July 16, 1865, near Washington, D. C.

WHITFORD, ALMANSON.—Age, 30 years. Enlisted, August 30, 1862, at Florence, to serve three years; mustered in as private, Co. F, October 10, 1862; transferred to Co. E, March 28, 1863; mustered out with company, July 16, 1865, near Washington, D. C.

WHITFORD, CORNELIUS H.—Age, 44 years. Enlisted, August 29, 1862, at Florence, to serve three years; mustered in as private, Co. F, October 10, 1862; transferred to Co. E, March 28, 1863; died of disease, December 9, 1863, at Washington, D. C.

WHITFORD, WESLEY.—Age, 37 years. Enlisted, August 30, 1862, at Florence, to serve three years; mustered in as private, Co. F, October 10, 1862; transferred to Co. E, March 28, 1863; mustered out with company, July 16, 1865, near Washington, D. C.

WHOLAHAN, MICHAEL.—Age, 32 years. Enlisted, August 25, 1862, at Kirkland, to serve three years; mustered in as private, Co. G, October 10, 1862; captured in action, May 1,

1863, at Chancellorsville, Va.; paroled, no date; mustered out, June 3, 1865, at Washington, D. C.

WICKS, JACOB.—Age, — years. Enrolled at Rome, to serve three years, and mustered in as first lieutenant, Co. I, October 10, 1862; discharged, November 25, 1862.

Commissioned first lieutenant, November 3, 1862, with rank from October 7, 1862, original.

WIDRIG, CLARK.—Age, 33 years. Enlisted, August 28, 1862, at Rome, to serve three years; mustered in as private, Co. F, October 10, 1862; died of typhoid fever, January 24, 1863, in Division Hospital, at Aquia Creek, Va.

WIDRIG, MICHAEL.—Age, 24 years. Enlisted, August 30, 1862, at Rome, to serve three years; mustered in as private, Co. I, October 10, 1862; died of disease, January 25, 1863, in hospital at Windmill Point, Va.; also borne as Wedrig.

WIHER, JOHN P.—Age, 28 years. Enlisted, August 29, 1862, at Rome, to serve three years; mustered in as private, Co. B, October 10, 1862; discharged for disability, April 1, 1863.

WILDS, CHARLES B.—Age, 21 years. Enlisted, August 19, 1862, at Rome, to serve three years; mustered in as private, Co. B, October 10, 1862; wounded in action, May 5, 1864, at the Wilderness, Va.; discharged for wounds, July 10, 1864. Died in 1895.

WILE, JOHN.—Age, 34 years. Enlisted, August 29, 1862, at Annsville, to serve three years; mustered in as private, Co. B, October 10, 1862; captured in action, May 5, 1864, at the Wilderness, Va.; died of scorbutis, November 20, 1864, at Andersonville, Ga.; also borne as Wilds.

WILLARD, BURTON.—Age, 23 years. Enlisted, August 26, 1862, at Vernon, to serve three years; mustered in as private, Co. B, October 10, 1862; promoted sergeant, November 22, 1862; discharged for disability, June 3, 1863.

WILLARD, CHARLES W.—Age, 18 years. Enlisted, August 30, 1862, at Kirkland, to serve three years; mustered in as musician, Co. G, October 10, 1862; returned to company as private, no date; transferred to Veteran Reserve Corps, September 26, 1863; mustered out therefrom as of Co. G, Seventh Regiment, June 28, 1865, at Washington, D. C.

WILLIAMS, GEORGE W.—Age, 21 years. Enlisted, September

2, 1862, at Camden, to serve three years; mustered in as private, Co. E, October 10, 1862.

WILLIAMS, GRIFFITH.—Age, 23 years. Enlisted, September 2, 1862, at Remsen, to serve three years; mustered in as private, Co. I, October 31, 1862; absent, sick, in hospital, since May 5, 1864, and at muster-out of company.

WILLIAMS, HORATIO P.—Age, 25 years. Enlisted, August 21, 1862, at Utica, to serve three years; mustered in as private, Co. H, October 10, 1862; captured in action, May 5, 1864, at the Wilderness, Va.; paroled, December 16, 1864, at Charleston, S. C.; mustered out, June 28, 1865, at Annapolis, Md.; also borne as Horatio N. Williams.

WILLIAMS, JR., JOHN.—Age, 25 years. Enlisted, September 6, 1862, at Bridgewater, to serve three years; mustered in as private, Co. G, October 10, 1862; discharged for disability, April 4, 1863, near Falmouth, Va.

WILLIAMS, PETER.—Age, 21 years. Enlisted, September 1, 1862, at Steuben, to serve three years; mustered in as private, Co. I, October 10, 1862; captured in action, May 5, 1864, at the Wilderness, Va.; paroled, no date; mustered out, June 13, 1865, at Annapolis, Md.

WILLIAMS, RICHARD T.—Age, 18 years. Enlisted, September 13, 1862, at Plainfield, to serve three years; mustered in as private, Co. G, October 10, 1862; captured and paroled, no date; mustered out with company, July 16, 1865, near Washington, D. C.

WILLIAMS, ROBERT.—Age, 36 years. Enlisted, August 28, 1862, at Rome, to serve three years; mustered in as private, Co. B, October 10, 1862; transferred to Veteran Reserve Corps, December 4, 1863.

WILLIAMS, WILLIAM.—Age, 33 years. Enlisted, August 24, 1862, at Utica, to serve three years; mustered in as corporal, Co. C, October 10, 1862; returned to ranks, no date; discharged for disability, October 23, 1863, at Washington, D. C. Died June 10, 1910.

WILSON, ANDREW J.—Enrolled at Rome, to serve three years, and mustered in as first lieutenant, Co. H, October 10, 1862; transferred to Co. A, December 2, 1862; discharged, January 7, 1863, near Falmouth, Va.

Commissioned first lieutenant, November 3, 1862, with rank from October 6, 1862, original.

WILSON, EDWARD F.—Age, 39 years. Enlisted, August 29, 1862, at Whitestone, to serve three years; mustered in as private, Co. K, October 10, 1862; discharged for disability, February 17, 1863, at Washington, D. C.

WILSON, THOMAS.—Age, 21 years. Enlisted, September 6, 1862, at Bridgewater, to serve three years; mustered in as private, Co. G, October 10, 1862; mustered out with company, July 16, 1865, near Washington, D. C.

WILSON, THOMAS A.—Age, 40 years. Enrolled, August 25, 1862, at Kirkland, to serve three years; mustered in as first sergeant, Co. G, October 10, 1862; promoted second lieutenant, Co. E, December 27, 1862; mustered in as first lieutenant, January 15, 1863; promoted captain, Co. B, December 4, 1863; wounded in action, April 1, 1865, at Five Forks, Va.; died of his wounds, April 25, 1865, in hospital, at City Point, Va.

Commissioned second lieutenant, December 10, 1862, with rank from November 29, 1862, vice C. K. Dutton promoted; first lieutenant, February 5, 1863, with rank from January 7, 1863, vice A. J. Wilson resigned; captain, October 7, 1864, with rank from July 23, 1863, vice H. H. Curran promoted; brevet lieutenant-colonel by U. S. Government, from April 1, 1865.

WILSON, WILLIAM.—Age, 32 years. Enlisted, August 26, 1862, at Boonville, to serve three years; mustered in as private, Co. I, October 10, 1862; captured, August 19, 1864, at Weldon Railroad, Va.; paroled, March 2, 1865, at North East Bridge, N. C.; mustered out, June 26, 1865, at Rochester, N. Y.

WING, IRA.—Age, 32 years. Enlisted, August 29, 1862, at Sangerfield, to serve three years; mustered in as private, Co. H, October 10, 1862; discharged for disability, March 2, 1863, at hospital at Philadelphia, Pa.

WINIGAR, JOSEPH.—Age, 28 years. Enlisted, August 25, 1862, at Utica, to serve three years; mustered in as private, Co. K, October 10, 1862; also borne as Winegar.

WISER, DAVID B.—Age, 35 years. Enlisted, September 13,

1862, at Trenton, to serve three years; mustered in as private, Co. I, October 10, 1862; died, March 30, 1863, near Henry House, Va.; also borne as Niser.

WITTEN, GEORGE.—Age, 21 years. Enlisted, August 29, 1862, at Utica, to serve three years; mustered in as private, Co. A, October 10, 1862; killed in action, May 5, 1864, at the Wilderness, Va., as Whitten.

WOLCOTT, GEORGE W.—Age, 19 years. Enlisted, September 3, 1862, at Rome, to serve three years; mustered in as private, Co. B, October 10, 1862; captured and paroled, no date; mustered out with company, July 16, 1865, near Washington, D. C.; also borne as George H. Wollcott. Died at Kenesaw, Neb., September, 17, 1911.

WOLCOTT, PROCTOR.—Age, 45 years. Enlisted, August 26, 1862, at Rome, to serve three years; mustered in as private, Co. B, October 10, 1862; died of disease, December 2, 1862, near Potomac Creek, Va.

WOLFE, HENRY B.—Age, 19 years. Enlisted, August 28, 1862, at Boonville, to serve three years; mustered in as private, Co. D, October 10, 1862; discharged for disability, January 23, 1864, at Washington, D. C.

WOOD, ADELBERT S.—Age, 25 years. Enlisted, September 1, 1862, at Kirkland, to serve three years; mustered in as private, Co. G, October 10, 1862; transferred to Veteran Reserve Corps, September 26, 1863; mustered out therefrom as of Co. C, Sixteenth Regiment, July 27, 1865, at Washington, D. C. Died March 10, 1913, at Deansboro, N. Y.

WOOD, FERNANDO D.—Age, 19 years. Enlisted, September 15, 1862, at Trenton, to serve three years; mustered in as private, Co. I, October 10, 1862; discharged for disability, January 15, 1863, at Potomac Creek, Va.

WOOD, HENRY H.—Age, 18 years. Enlisted, August 28, 1862, at Utica, to serve three years; mustered in as private, Co. C, October 10, 1862; wounded in action, March 31, 1865, at White Oak Ridge, Va.; died of his wounds, April 25, 1865.

WOOD, ORSON C.—Age, 30 years. Enlisted, August 29, 1862, at Camden, to serve three years; mustered in as wagoner, Co. E, October 10, 1862; mustered out with company, July 16, 1865, near Washington, D. C.

WORDEN, ANDREW.—Age, 44 years. Enlisted, September 5, 1862, at Verona, to serve three years; mustered in as private, Co. K, October 10, 1862; discharged for disability, March 1, 1863, at Philadelphia, Pa.

WORTH, GEORGE.—Age, 18 years. Enlisted, September 1, 1862, at Rome, to serve three years; mustered in as private, Co. B, October 10, 1862; wounded in action, May 5, 1864, at the Wilderness, Va.; discharged for wounds, June 6, 1865. Died in 1902.

WRIGHT, B. FRANKLIN.—Age, 22 years. Enrolled, September 3, 1862, at Paris, to serve three years; mustered in as private, Co. K, October 10, 1862; promoted sergeant-major, same date; mustered in as second lieutenant, Co. E, December 27, 1862; transferred to Co. D, January 7, 1863; mustered in as captain, Co. E, March 1, 1863; captured in action, May 5, 1864, at the Wilderness, Va.; returned, May 6, 1865; mustered out with company, July 16, 1865, near Washington, D. C.

Commissioned second lieutenant, November 24, 1862, with rank from November 6, 1862, vice Joseph H. Durkee promoted; captain, March 27, 1863, with rank from February 15, 1863, vice G. A. Lambis deceased.

WRIGHT, GEORGE W.—Age, 21 years. Enlisted, August 27, 1862, at Sangerfield, to serve three years; mustered in as private, Co. H, October 10, 1862; wounded in action, no date; discharged for disability, November 26, 1864, at hospital.

WRIGHT, RENSSELAER.—Age, 31 years. Enlisted, August 30, 1862, at Sangerfield, to serve three years; mustered in as private, Co. H, October 10, 1862; mustered out with company, July 16, 1865, near Washington, D. C.

WRIGHT, WILLIAM.—Age, 23 years. Enrolled, September 3, 1862, at Paris, to serve three years; mustered in as private, Co. K, October 10, 1862; promoted corporal, no date; sergeant-major, January 31, 1863; mustered in as second lieutenant, Co. E, April 26, 1863; transferred to Co. G, August 14, 1863; mustered in as first lieutenant, Co. E, October 27, 1863; as adjutant, April 28, 1864; wounded in action, May 5, 1864, at the Wilderness, Va.; discharged for wounds, September 28, 1864.

Commissioned second lieutenant, April 10, 1863, with rank from February 15, 1863, vice B. F. Wright promoted; first lieutenant, February 17, 1864, with rank from October 27, 1863, vice M. Egleston promoted; adjutant, June 6, 1864, with rank from April 28, 1864, vice E. Comstock transferred; brevet captain by U. S. Government, from Mar. 13, 1865.

YEOMANS, WARNER.—Age, 26 years. Enlisted, August 29, 1862, at Boonville, to serve three years; mustered in as private, Co. D, October 10, 1862; transferred to Veteran Reserve Corps, March 13, 1865; mustered out therefrom as of Co. C, Tenth Regiment, at Washington, D. C.

YEOMANS, WILLIAM C.—Age, 28 years. Enlisted, August 29, 1862, at Boonville, to serve three years; mustered in as private, Co. D, October 10, 1862; promoted corporal, March 1, 1865; sergeant, June 7, 1865; mustered out, July 26, 1865, at Syracuse, N. Y.

YOOS, JOHN.—Age, 44 years. Enlisted, August 23, 1862, at Vernon, to serve three years; mustered in as private, Co. K, October 10, 1862; transferred to Co. B, no date; promoted corporal, December 16, 1864; sergeant, May 5, 1865; mustered out with company, July 16, 1865, near Washington, D. C.

YORDAN, JOHN H.—Age, 18 years. Enlisted, August 28, 1862, at Boonville, to serve three years; mustered in as private, Co. D, October 10, 1862; promoted corporal and sergeant, no dates; mustered out, June 7, 1863, at Campbell Hospital, Washington, D. C., as Yourdan.

YORK, LEVI H.—Age, 35 years. Enrolled at Rome, to serve three years, and mustered in as second lieutenant, Co. G, September 17, 1862; as first lieutenant, February 17, 1863; as captain, April 1, 1865; mustered out with company, July 16, 1865, near Washington, D. C.

Commissioned second lieutenant, November 3, 1862, with rank from September 17, 1862, original; first lieutenant, February 5, 1863, with rank from January 7, 1863, vice J. Stewart promoted; captain, March 30, 1865, with rank from February 1, 1865, vice W. A. Walker promoted. Died March 25, 1897, at Washington, D. C.

YOUNG, CHARLES.—Age, 24 years. Enlisted, September 1,

1862, at Whitesboro, to serve three years; mustered in as private, Co. K, October 10, 1862; mustered out with company, July 16, 1865, near Washington, D. C.

YOUNG, PETER.—Age, 31 years. Enlisted, August 23, 1862, at Utica, to serve three years; mustered in as private, Co. K, October 10, 1862; absent, sick, since August 1, 1863, and at muster-out of company.

ZIMMERMAN, FREDRICK.—Age, 33 years. Enlisted, September 23, 1862, at Utica, to serve three years; mustered in as private, Co. H, October 10, 1862; transferred to Veteran Reserve Corps, no date; retransferred to Co. H, December 31, 1864; promoted corporal and captured and paroled, no dates; mustered out, June 1, 1865, at Annapolis, Md.; also borne as Timmerman.

ZINN, HENRY.—Age, 34 years. Enlisted, October 3, 1862, at Utica, to serve three years; mustered in as private, Co. K, October 10, 1862; transferred to Co. F, no date; killed in action, May 5, 1864, at the Wilderness, Va.

ASSIGNED DURING PERIOD OF SERVICE

ACKLEY, SAMUEL.—Age, 25 years. Enlisted at Elmira, to serve three years, and mustered in as private, Co. F, September 19, 1863; captured in action, May 5, 1864, at the Wilderness, Va.; exchanged, March 4, 1865; mustered out, August 22, 1865, at Elmira, N. Y.

ALEXANDER, WILLIAM.—Age, 34 years. Enlisted at Great Valley, to serve three years, and mustered in as private, Co. F, August 21, 1863; discharged for disability, February 3, 1864, at Warrenton Junction, Va.

ANDREWS, JOHN H.—Age, 29 years. Enlisted at Norwich, to serve three years, and mustered in as private, Co. D, September 9, 1863; captured and paroled, no dates; died of disease, March 24, 1865, at Wilmington, N. C.

ASHLEY, CHARLES B.—Age, 18 years. Enlisted at Rome, to serve three years, and mustered in as private, Co. B, August 29, 1864; mustered out with company, July 16, 1865, near Washington, D. C.

ATWOOD, JAMES H.—Age, 27 years. Enlisted at Syracuse, to serve three years, and mustered in as private, Co. H, August 19, 1863; died of disease, January 2, 1864, at Warrenton Junction, Va.

BACKLEY, JUDSON.—Age, 21 years. Enlisted at Norwich, to serve three years, and mustered in as private, Co. D, October 1, 1863; transferred to Veteran Reserve Corps, September 18, 1864.

BACON, GEORGE.—Age, 30 years. Enlisted at Stockton, to serve three years, and mustered in as private, Co. G, August 18, 1863; promoted corporal and returned to ranks, no date; mustered out with company, July 16, 1865, near Washington, D. C.

BAILEY, MYRON C.—Age, 20 years. Enlisted at Middleburg,

to serve three years, and mustered in as private, Co K., July 30, 1863; mustered out, June 21, 1865, at Elmira, N. Y.

BAIN, TILLMAN.—Age, 19 years. Enlisted at Half Moon, to serve three years, and mustered in as private, unassigned, February 24, 1864; no further record.

BARBER, HIRAM.—Age, 31 years. Enlisted at Norwich, to serve three years, and mustered in as private, Co. D, September 8, 1863; mustered out with company, July 16, 1865, near Washington, D. C.

BARHALTER, JOSEPH.—Age, 34 years. Enlisted at Rome, to serve three years, and mustered in as private, Co. B, July 20, 1863.

BARNARD, FRANCIS W.—Age, 36 years. Enlisted, August 24, 1864, at Boonville, to serve one year; mustered in as private unassigned, August 25, 1864; no further record.

BARNES, BENTON C.—Age, 19 years. Enlisted at Elmira, to serve three years, and mustered in as private, Co. C, September 16, 1863; wounded, no date; discharged for wounds, January 26, 1865, at hospital.

BARNES, DAVID.—Age, 19 years. Enlisted at Syracuse, to serve three years, and mustered in as private, Co. G, August 19, 1863; captured and paroled, no dates; discharged for disability, January 6, 1864, at Washington, D. C.

BARTON, HORACE.—Age, 20 years. Enlisted at Carolton, to serve three years, and mustered in as private, Co. E, August 22, 1863; died of disease, December 25, 1863, at Bealton Station, Va.

BEACH, HUBBARD.—Age, 31 years. Enlisted at Norwich, to serve three years; mustered in as private, Co. F, September 24, 1863; wounded in action, March 31, 1865, at White Oak Road, Va.; died of his wounds, April 3, 1865, at City Point, Va.

BECKWITH, LEVI D.—Enlisted in Jefferson County, to serve three years, and mustered in as private, Co. B, August 25, 1863; transferred to Veteran Reserve Corps, June 22, 1864; mustered out therefrom as of Sixteenth Company, Second Battalion, August 23, 1865, at Washington, D. C.

BEERS, JOHN B.—Age, 27 years. Enlisted at Carolton, to serve three years, and mustered in as private, Co. E, August 22,

1863; promoted corporal, no date; wounded, no date; discharged for wounds, March 23, 1865, at Washington, D. C.

BEMUS, CHARLES R.—Age, 26 years. Enlisted at Ashforth, to serve three years, and mustered in as private, Co. B, August 29, 1863; died of disease, November 26, 1863, at Washington, D. C.; also borne as Charles B. Bemus.

BENTON, ORVILLE A.—Age, 19 years. Enlisted at Norwich, to serve three years, and mustered in as private, Co. D, October 1, 1863; discharged for disability, April 7, 1865, at hospital, Washington, D. C.

BLISS, HEZEKIAH.—Age, 40 years. Enlisted at Norwich, to serve three years, and mustered in as private, Co. D, September 5, 1863; absent, sick, since September 5, 1864; no further record.

BODY, ALBERT.—Age, 31 years. Enlisted at Arkwright, to serve three years, and mustered in as private, Co. E, August 18, 1863; discharged for disability, May 16, 1865, at hospital.

BOWMAN, JOHN.—Age, 28 years. Enlisted at Syracuse, to serve three years, and mustered in as private, Co. C, August 20, 1863; captured, May 5, 1864, at the Wilderness, Va.; died of disease, October 22, 1864, at Florence, S. C.

BRADISH, JAMES S.—Age, 36 years. Enrolled, January 22, 1863, at New York, to serve three years; mustered in as assistant surgeon, February 10, 1863.

Commissioned assistant surgeon, February 2, 1863, with rank from January 23, 1863, vice E. M. Somers resigned.

BROWN, CHARLES.—Age, 24 years. Enlisted at Honesdale, to serve three years, and mustered in as private, Co. C, August 21, 1863.

BROWNELL, GEORGE.—Age, 18 years. Enlisted at Utica, to serve three years, and mustered in as private, Co. B, September 16, 1864; appointed musician, no date; mustered out, June 6, 1865, at Washington, D. C.

BRYANT, ALBERT.—Age, 21 years. Enlisted at Lockport, to serve three years, and mustered in as private, Co. B, July 28, 1863; captured in action, May 5, 1864, at the Wilderness, Va.; died of chronic diarrhea, September, 1864, at Andersonville, Ga.

BUCKINGHAM, CHARLES L.—Age, 22 years. Enrolled at New

Baltimore, Va., to serve three years, and mustered in as second lieutenant, Co. I, October 17, 1863; wounded in action, May 5, 1864, at the Wilderness, Va.; mustered in as first lieutenant, July 1, 1864; transferred to Co. B, September 2, 1864; killed same date, at Weldon Railroad, Va.

Commissioned second lieutenant, October 6, 1863, with rank from September 13, 1863, vice J. S. Lowery promoted; first lieutenant, May 18, 1864, with rank from April 4, 1864, vice W. H. S. Sweet promoted.

BUCKLEY, BEMAS.—Age, 22 years. Enlisted at Wert, to serve three years, and mustered in as private, Co. K, July 10, 1865; mustered out with company, July 16, 1865, near Washington, D. C.

BUCKLEY, JUDSON.—Age, 21 years. Enlisted in Nineteenth Congressional District, to serve three years, and mustered in, as private, Co. D, October 16, 1863; transferred to Veteran Reserve Corps, October 18, 1864; mustered out therefrom as of Co. G, Tenth Regiment, July 29, 1865, at Washington D. C.

BUGBY, WILLIAM.—Age, 18 years. Enlisted at Augusta, to serve three years, and mustered in as private, unassigned, December 25, 1863; no further record.

BURGESS, EDMOND.—Age, 22 years. Enlisted in Orange County, to serve three years, and mustered in as private, Co. B, August 21, 1863; captured in action, May 5, 1864, at the Wilderness, Va.; died of chronic diarrhea, October 15, 1864, at Andersonville, Ga.

BURK, JAMES.—Age, 19 years. Enlisted at Rome, to serve three years, and mustered in as private, unassigned, August 24, 1864; no further record.

BYRON, ALBERT D.—Age, 24 years. Enlisted at Buffalo, to serve three years, and mustered in as private, Co. C, August 14, 1863.

CAIN, JOHN.—Age, 24 years. Enlisted at Rome, to serve three years, and mustered in as private, unassigned, August 26, 1864; no further record.

CALHOUN, BENJAMIN.—Age, 32 years. Enlisted at Norwich, to serve three years, and mustered in as private, Co. D, September 5, 1863; captured and paroled, no date; mustered out, June 19, 1865, at Annapolis, Md.

CAMERON, JOHN.—Age, 26 years. Enlisted at Buffalo, to serve three years, and mustered in as private, Co. C, August 5, 1863.

CAMPBELL, JOHN.—Age, 19 years. Enlisted at Robertson, to serve three years, and mustered in as private, Co. G, August 8, 1863; mustered out with company, July 16, 1865, near Washington, D. C.

CARCO, JOHN.—Age, 29 years. Enlisted at Dunkirk, and mustered in as private, Co. H, August 27, 1863, to serve three years.

CARYAL, SAMUEL A.—Age, 30 years. Enlisted at Buffalo, to serve three years, and mustered in as private, Co. A, August 13, 1863; discharged for disability.

CASTOR, ADAM.—Age, 23 years. Enlisted at Leon, to serve three years, and mustered in as private, Co. E, August 21, 1863; captured, no date; died of disease, June 14, 1864, at Andersonville, Ga.; also borne as Carter.

CAVENAUGH, JOHN.—Age, 22 years. Enlisted at Leon, to serve three years, and mustered in as private, Co. H, August 21, 1863; captured, no date; died of disease, June 1, 1864, at Andersonville, Ga.

CELDERED, EDWARD.—Age, 28 years. Enlisted at Watertown, to serve three years, and mustered in as private, Co. A, October 13, 1863; transferred to U. S. Navy, May 2, 1864; borne as Celderd and Pildred.

CHESBORO, STEPHEN.—Age, 27 years. Enlisted at Norwich, to serve three years, and mustered in as private, Co. D, September 10, 1863; captured in action, June 2, 1864, at Cold Harbor, Va.; released, April 25, 1865; mustered out with company, July 16, 1865, near Washington, D. C.

CHILSON, CASSUS V.—Age, 18 years. Enlisted, December 17, 1863, at Farmington, to serve three years; mustered in as private, Co. B, January 5, 1864; mustered out, June 29, 1865, at Washington, D. C.

CLANCY, JOSEPH.—Age, 18 years. Enlisted at Elmira, to serve one year, and mustered in as private, Co. H, March 29, 1865; mustered out with company, July 16, 1865, near Washington, D. C.

CLAPP, BENJAMIN.—Age, 34 years. Enlisted at Norwich, to

serve three years, and mustered in as private, Co. D, September 10, 1863; discharged for disability, February 4, 1864, at Warrenton Junction, Va.

CLARK, JOHN.—Age, 22 years. Enlisted at Hinsdale, to serve three years, and mustered in as private, Co. C, August 21, 1863.

CLARKE, FRANK.—Age, 18 years. Enlisted at Malone, to serve three years, and mustered in as private, Co. I, date not stated; captured in action, May 5, 1864, at the Wilderness, Va.; no further record.

COFFIN, FRANKLIN.—Age, 23 years. Enlisted at Auburn, to serve three years, and mustered in as private, Co. B, July 24, 1863; captured in action, June 2, 1864, at Cold Harbor, Va.; paroled, no date; died of chronic diarrhea, December 3, 1864, on U. S. transport *Baltic*.

COLLAR, ERI S.—Age, 29 years. Enlisted at Norwich, to serve three years, and mustered in as private, Co. D, September 9, 1863; captured and paroled, no dates; discharged for disability, April 3, 1865, from Hospital A, Philadelphia, Pa. Died December 22, 1898.

COLTON, BENJAMIN.—Age, 38 years. Enlisted at Norwich, to serve three years, and mustered in as private, Co. D, October 16, 1863; mustered out with company, July 16, 1865, near Washington, D. C.

CONNELLY, JAMES.—Age, 30 years. Enlisted, August 13, 1862, at New York, to serve three years; mustered in as private, Co. I, November 19, 1862; mustered out, July 2, 1865, at McDougall Hospital, New York Harbor.

CONSTABLE, PETER.—Age, 38 years. Enlisted at Norwich, to serve three years, and mustered in as private, Co. D, October 2, 1863; absent, sick, since April 30, 1864; no further record.

COON, THEODORE D.—Age, 21 years. Enlisted at Utica, to serve three years, and mustered in as private, Co. H, August 27, 1863; promoted corporal, no date; discharged, June 22, 1865, at Carver Hospital, Washington, D. C.

CORREVAN, EMIL.—Age, 25 years. Enlisted at Elmira, to serve three years, and mustered in as private, Co. H, April 1, 1865; mustered out, July 12, 1865, at Washington, D. C.

COSTAR, WILLIAM.—Age, 22 years. Enlisted at Ischua, to serve three years, and mustered in as private, Co. K, August 21, 1863.

CROCKER, GEORGE W.—Age, 21 years. Enlisted, December 17, 1863, at Farmington, to serve three years; mustered in as private, Co. B, January 5, 1864; captured in action, May 5, 1864, at the Wilderness, Va.; no further record.

CROCKER, SMITH H.—Age, 19 years. Enlisted at Canandaigua, to serve three years, and mustered in as private, Co. B, September 19, 1863; captured in action, May 5, 1864, at the Wilderness, Va.; paroled, no date; promoted corporal, February 1, 1865; sergeant, June 3, 1865; mustered out with company, July 16, 1865, near Washington, D. C.

CRUPPER, JOSIAH.—Age, 31 years. Enlisted at Auburn, to serve three years, and mustered in as private, Co. G, July 24, 1863; captured in action, May 5, 1864, at the Wilderness, Va.; also borne as Crippen; no further record.

CUNNINGHAM, JOHN.—Age, 23 years. Enlisted at Watertown, to serve three years, and mustered in as private, Co. A, August 13, 1863.

CUNNINGHAM, JOHN.—Age, 28 years. Enlisted at Leon, to serve three years, and mustered in as private, Co. D, August 21, 1863.

DALTON, GEORGE.—Age, 19 years. Enlisted at Salamanca, to serve three years, and mustered in as private, Co. E, August 24, 1863.

DAVIS, BENJAMIN.—Age, 36 years. Enlisted at Auburn, to serve three years, and mustered in as private, Co. G, July 25, 1863; discharged, June 27, 1864, for promotion to second lieutenant, Sixteenth Artillery.

DAVIS, GEORGE E.—Age, 18 years. Enlisted at Utica, to serve three years, and mustered in as private, Co. A, November 21, 1864; mustered out, June 3, 1865, at Washington, D. C.

DAVIS, G. WILLIAM.—Age, 24 years. Enlisted at Rome, to serve three years, and mustered in as private, unassigned, August 27, 1864; no further record.

DAVIS, JOHN.—Age, 31 years. Enlisted at Buffalo, to serve three years, and mustered in as private, Co. G, August 14, 1863; discharged for disability, January 6, 1864, at Washington, D. C.

DAVIS, ROBERT W.—Age, 40 years.   Enlisted at Utica, to serve three years, and mustered in as private, Co. B, August 22, 1863; discharged, April 23, 1865.

DAY, PATRICK.—Age, 22 years.   Enlisted at New Hartford, to serve one year, and mustered in as private, unassigned, August 30, 1864; no further record.

DILLON, WILLIAM H.—Age, 25 years.   Enlisted at Farmington, to serve three years, and mustered in as private, Co. B, February 15, 1864; captured in action, May 5, 1864, at the Wilderness, Va.; died, January 12, 1865, at Salisbury, N. C., of diarrhea.

DODGE, CHARLES.—Age, 19 years.   Enlisted at Cold Spring, to serve three years, and mustered in as private, Co. F, August 27, 1863.

DOLPH, JOSEPH.—Age, 32 years.   Enlisted at Canandaigua, to serve three years, and mustered in as private, Co. B, August 21, 1863; captured in action, May 5, 1864, at the Wilderness, Va.; paroled, no date; absent at Annapolis, Md., at muster-out of company.

DOWNING, THOMAS.—Age, 19 years.   Enlisted at Norwich, to serve three years, and mustered in as private, Co. A, October 11, 1863; killed in action, May 5, 1864, at the Wilderness, Va.

DRAKE, CHARLES.—Age, 25 years.   Enlisted, August 21, 1863, at Ischua, to serve three years; mustered in as private, Co. B, August 29, 1863; absent, sick, since August 15, 1864, at Emory Square Hospital, Washington, D. C., at muster-out of company.

DROWN, SANFORD.—Age, 33 years.   Enlisted at Auburn, to serve three years, and mustered in as private, Co. G, July 28, 1863; mustered out with company, July 16, 1865, near Washington, D. C.

DUNN, CHARLES.—Age, 18 years.   Enlisted at Utica, to serve one year, and mustered in as musician, Co. F, August 29, 1864; mustered out, June 3, 1865, at camp near Alexandria, Va.

DUNN, DAVID.—Age, 30 years.   Enlisted at Little Valley, to serve three years, and mustered in as private, Co. E, August 21, 1863; killed in action, May 5, 1864, at the Wilderness, Va.; also borne as Daniel Dunn.

EVANS, OSCAR C.—Age, 18 years. Enlisted at Buffalo, to serve three years, and mustered in as private, Co. C, August 14, 1863; discharged for disability, November 7, 1863, at Three Mile Station, Va.

FARRAR, MARTIN V.—Age, 24 years. Enlisted in Thirty-first Congressional District, to serve three years, and mustered in as private, Co. B, August 29, 1863; absent, sick, since October 23, 1863; no further record.

FARRELL, JOHN.—Age, 18 years. Enlisted at New York City, to serve three years, and mustered in as private, Co. B, September 1, 1864; mustered out with company, July 16, 1865, near Washington, D. C.

FARRELL, JOHN F.—Age, 34 years. Enlisted at New York City, to serve three years, and mustered in as private, Co. E, December 29, 1863; transferred to Co. C, February 15, 1864; promoted corporal, June 1, 1865; mustered out with company, July 16, 1865, near Washington, D. C.; prior service, Co. F, Fifth Infantry.

FARRELL, MARTIN.—Age, 39 years. Enlisted at Randolph, to serve three years, and mustered in as private, Co. F, August 22, 1863; discharged for disability, November 7, 1863, at Three Mile Station, Va.

FENWICK, ROBERT.—Age, 44 years. Enrolled at Beverly Ford, Va., to serve three years, and mustered in as assistant surgeon, June 7, 1863; wounded in action, May 6, 1864, at the Wilderness, Va.; mustered out with regiment, July 16, 1865, near Washington, D. C.

    Commissioned assistant surgeon, May 26, 1863, with rank from May 7, 1863, vice J. S. Bradish discharged.

FINCH, DAVID.—Age, 31 years. Enlisted at Norwich, to serve three years, and mustered in as private, Co. D, September 9, 1863; mustered out with company, July 16, 1865, near Washington, D. C.

FITCH, ISAAC H.—Age, 28 years. Enlisted at Norwood, to serve three years, and mustered in as private, Co. D, September 15, 1863; wounded and captured in action, June 2, 1864, at Cold Harbor, Va.; died July 14, 1864, at Richmond, Va.

FITZGERALD, JAMES B.—Enlisted at Randolph, to serve three years, and mustered in as private, Co. A, August 22, 1863.

FITZPATRICK, JAMES.—Age, 24 years. Enlisted at Conewango, to serve three years, and mustered in as private, Co. A, August 23, 1863; absent, sick, since May 5, 1864, and at muster-out of company.

FLOOD, MARCUS.—Age, 21 years. Enlisted at Buffalo, to serve three years, and mustered in as private, Co. B, August 14, 1863; mustered out with company, July 16, 1865, near Washington, D. C.

FOOTE, CHARLES A.—Age, 23 years. Enlisted at Rome, to serve three years, and mustered in as private, Co. B, August 30, 1864; mustered out with company, July 16, 1865, near Washington, D. C.

FOSSARD, GEORGE H.—Enrolled at Culpeper Court House, Va., to serve three years, and mustered in as assistant surgeon, September 22, 1863; discharged, October 17, 1864, for promotion to surgeon, Fifty-sixth Infantry.

Commissioned assistant surgeon, September 14, 1863, with rank from September 10, 1863, vice E. C. Bass resigned.

FRANCIS, DAVID P.—Age, 37 years. Enlisted at Utica, to serve three years, and mustered in as private, Co. F, September 7, 1864; killed in action, March 31, 1865, at White Oak Ridge, Va.

FRANCIS, RICHARD T.—Age, 44 years. Enlisted at Utica, to serve three years, and mustered in as private, Co. K, July 12, 1863; promoted hospital steward, March 1, 1865; mustered out, July 24, 1865, at Syracuse, N. Y.

FRELINGHOUSE, EDWARD D.—Age, 30 years. Enlisted at Rochester, to serve three years, and mustered in as private, Co. B, August 28, 1863; promoted corporal, May 5, 1865; mustered out with company, July 16, 1865, near Washington, D. C.

FRENCH, OTIS.—Age, 23 years. Enlisted, August 5, 1863, at Buffalo, to serve three years; mustered in as private, Co. C, August 15, 1863; mustered out, June 15, 1865, at Whitehall Hospital, Philadelphia, Pa.

GALLAGHER, WILLIAM.—Age, 19 years. Enlisted at Wolcott, to serve one year, and mustered in as a private, unassigned, September 5, 1864; no further record.

GALT, WILLIAM D.—Age, 24 years. Enlisted at Norwich, to

serve three years, and mustered in as private, Co. F, September 3, 1863; mustered out with company, July 16, 1865, near Washington, D. C., as Gallt.

GAULT, ARCHIBALD.—Age, 26 years. Enlisted at Buffalo, to serve three years, and mustered in as private, Co. A, August 14, 1863.

GOODNOUGH, CURTIS.—Age, 22 years. Enlisted at Rochester, to serve three years, and mustered in as private, Co. K, September 30, 1863; captured in action, August 19, 1864, near Petersburg, Va.; no further record.

GORDON, MICHAEL.—Age, 25 years. Enlisted at Auburn, to serve three years, and mustered in as private, Co. K, July 14, 1863; captured in action, May 5, 1864, at the Wilderness, Va.; paroled, no date; mustered out, May 22, 1865, at Elmira, N. Y.

GRAHAM, HUGH.—Age, 24 years. Enlisted at Portville, to serve three years, and mustered in as private, Co. D, August 22, 1863; transferred to United States Navy, May 3, 1864.

GRANT, CHARLES A.—Age, 28 years. Enlisted at Norwich, to serve three years, and mustered in as private, Co. F, September 30, 1863; captured in action, May 5, 1864; at the Wilderness, Va.; paroled, December 16, 1864; died of disease, June 1, 1865, at Syracuse, N. Y.

GRAVES, ROBERT.—Age, 21 years. Enlisted at Norwich, to serve three years, and mustered in as private, Co. F, September 4, 1863; killed in action, May 5, 1864, at the Wilderness, Va.

HADSELL, JOSIAH.—Age, 25 years. Enlisted at Canandaigua, to serve three years, and mustered in as private, Co. B, October 2, 1863; captured in action, May 5, 1864, at the Wilderness, Va.; no further record.

HALEY, THOMAS.—Age, 25 years. Enlisted at Watertown, to serve three years, and mustered in as private, Co. A, October 17, 1863; captured in action, May 5, 1864, at the Wilderness, Va.; paroled, no date; mustered out, June 13, 1865, from Mower Hospital, Philadelphia, Pa.

HARMON, WILLIAM.—Age, 22 years. Enlisted at Buffalo, to serve three years, and mustered in as private, Co. K, August

14, 1863; captured in action, May 5, 1864, at the Wilderness, Va.; no further record.

HARRIS, WILLIAM.—Age, 38 years. Enlisted at New Albion, to serve three years, and mustered in as private, Co. H, August 22, 1863; discharged for disability, November 10, 1863, at Three Mile Station, Va.

HART, ROBERT.—Enrolled at New Falmouth, Va., to serve three years, and mustered in as second lieutenant, Co. F, March 1, 1863.

Commissioned second lieutenant, February 10, 1863, with rank from February 1,1863, vice F. V. Graves discharged.

HARTY, THOMAS.—Age, 19 years. Enlisted at Yorkshire, to serve three years, and mustered in as private, Co. H, August 20, 1863; killed, May 11, 1864, on skirmish line.

HASKINS, GEORGE.—Age, 34 years. Enlisted at Carolton, to serve three years, and mustered in as private, Co. F, August 20, 1863; captured in action, May 5, 1864, at the Wilderness, Va.; paroled, no date; mustered out, May 25, 1865, at Elmira, N. Y.

HAWLEY, ASA.—Age, 40 years. Enlisted, August 26, 1862, at Rome, to serve three years; mustered in as private, Co. F, October 10, 1863; absent, sick, since January 7, 1864, and at muster-out of company.

HEATH, NATHANIEL.—Age, 21 years. Enlisted at Cherry Creek, to serve three years, and mustered in as private, Co. H, August 7, 1863; mustered out with company, July 16, 1865, near Washington, D. C.

HEIMMEL, MICHAEL.—Age, 39 years. Enlisted at Rome, to serve one year, and mustered in as private, Co. F, August 30, 1864; mustered out, June 3, 1865, at camp near Alexandria, Va.

HEWLETT, JAMES.—Age, 42 years. Enlisted at Syracuse, to serve three years, and mustered in as private, Co. F, August 20, 1863; discharged for disability, November 7, 1863, at Three Mile Station, Va.

HILLGER, FRANCIS C.—Age, 18 years. Enlisted, September 2, 1864, at Augusta, to serve three years; mustered in as private, unassigned, September 3, 1864; no further record.

HOLDEN, RICHARD.—Age, 20 years. Enlisted at Utica, to serve

three years, and mustered in as private, Co. H, August 26, 1863; captured and paroled, no dates; mustered out, June 1, 1865, at Annapolis, Md.

HOLLAND, JEREMIAH.—Age, 26 years. Enlisted at Canandaigua, to serve three years, and mustered in as private, Co. B, September 15, 1863; discharged for disability, April 7, 1864, at Washington, D. C.

HOLLOWAY, JOSEPH H.—Age, 20 years. Enlisted at Norwich, to serve three years, and mustered in as private, Co. D, October 16, 1863; captured, June 2, 1864, at Bethesda Church, Va.; died of disease, August 3, 1864, at Andersonville, Ga.

HUFF, REUBEN T.—Age, 29 years. Enlisted, July 28, 1863, at Victor, to serve three years; mustered in as private, Co. C, September 1, 1863; mustered out, May 3, 1865, at Elmira, N. Y.

HUGHES, WILLIAM.—Age, 35 years. Enlisted at Deerfield, to serve one year, and mustered in as private, Co. B, September 2, 1864; mustered out, June 3, 1865, near Alexandria, Va.

HUNT, JOHN C.—Age, 23 years. Enlisted at Rome, to serve three years, and mustered in as private, unassigned, August 26, 1864; no further record.

JACK, JAMES H.—Age, 29 years. Enlisted at Bath, to serve three years, and mustered in as private, Co. K, July 26, 1863; wounded in action, May 5, 1864, at the Wilderness, Va.; died of his wounds, July 12, 1864, in hospital.

JACKSON, JAMES.—Age, 22 years. Enlisted at Conewango, to serve three years, and mustered in as private, Co. F, August 21, 1863.

JOHNSON, WILLIAM.—Age, 20 years. Enlisted at Farnsworth, to serve three years, and mustered in as private, Co. I, August 21, 1863; captured in action, October 14, 1863, at Bristoe Station, Va.; paroled, February, 1865; mustered out, August 3, 1865, at Washington, D. C.

JONES, ARTHUR.—Age, 25 years. Enlisted at New Albion, to serve three years, and mustered in as private, Co. H, August 21, 1863.

JUDSON, HERMAN W.—Age, 37 years. Enlisted at Utica, to serve one year, and mustered in as private, Co. E, September 10, 1864; mustered out, June 3, 1865, near Alexandria, Va.

KELL, MICHAEL.—Age, — years. Enlisted at Utica, to serve three years, and mustered in as private, unassigned, August 23, 1864; no further record.

KELLEY, JOHN.—Age, 30 years. Enlisted at Rome, to serve three years, and mustered in as private, unassigned, August 26, 1863; no further record.

KELLY, JAMES.—Age, 18 years. Enlisted at Portville, to serve three years, and mustered in as private, Co. K, August 22, 1863; captured in action, June 2, 1864, at Bethesda Church, Va.; died of disease, August 11, 1864, at Andersonville, Ga.

KELLY, JAMES.—Age, 29 years. Enlisted at Syracuse, to serve three years, and mustered in as private, Co. G, August 9, 1863; mustered out with company, July 16, 1865, near Washington, D. C.

KEMP, PETER.—Age, 48 years. Enlisted, December 25, 1863 at Augusta, to serve three years; mustered in as private, Co. A, December 29, 1863; discharged for disability, April 22, 1865, in the field; also borne as Kemph.

KESSLER, JOHN A.—Age, 18 years. Enlisted at Buffalo, to serve three years, and mustered in as private, Co. B, August 15, 1863; captured in action, May 5, 1864, at the Wilderness, Va., paroled, no date; mustered out, October 11, 1865, at Buffalo, N. Y.

KING, EDGAR A.—Age, 34 years. Enlisted at Ashforth, to serve three years, and mustered in as private, Co. B, August 20, 1863; discharged for disability, December 25, 1863, at hospital, Washington, D. C.

KING, GIDEON.—Age, 20 years. Enlisted at Rochester, to serve three years, and mustered in as private, Co. H, August 28, 1863; killed in action, May 5, 1864, at the Wilderness, Va.

LACHELL, GEORGE W.—Age, 29 years. Enlisted at Canandaigua, to serve three years, and mustered in as private, Co. H, September 25, 1863; captured in action, May 5, 1864, at the Wilderness, Va.; no further record.

LACY, STEPHEN S.—Age, 22 years. Enlisted at Dansville, to serve three years, and mustered in as private, unassigned, August 3, 1863; died of pneumonia, March 10, 1864, at Washington, D. C.

LAKE, WILLIAM H.—Age, 28 years. Enlisted at Camden, to

serve three years, and mustered in as private, Co. K, July 30, 1863; captured in action, June 2, 1864, at Cold Harbor, Va.; died of disease, November 26, 1864, at Andersonville, Ga.

LATHROP, AARON.—Age, 23 years. Enlisted at Norwich, to serve three years, and mustered in as private, Co. H, August 13, 1863; absent, detached to Battery B, Fourth U. S. Artillery, at muster-out of company.

LAWLER, WILLIAM.—Age, 23 years. Enlisted at Olean, to serve three years, and mustered in as private, Co. K, August 23, 1863; transferred to Army of the Northwest, March 12, 1864.

LENHART, CONRAD.—Age, 23 years. Enlisted at Buffalo, to serve three years, and mustered in as private, Co. K, August 15, 1863; mustered out, June 19, 1865, at Buffalo, N. Y.

MAEBETT, JOSEPH.—Age, 32 years. Enlisted at Ellicottsville, to serve three years, and mustered in as private, Co. I, August 21, 1863; mustered out with company, July 16, 1865, near Washington, D. C., as Marbett.

MAHN, V. P.—Age, 27 years. Enlisted at Great Valley, to serve three years, and mustered in as private, Co. G, August 21, 1863; mustered out with company, July 16, 1865, near Washington, D. C., as Patrick McMahan.

MAPES, JOSIAH.—Age, 21 years. Enlisted at Kirkland, to serve three years, and mustered in as private, Co. A, August 25, 1864.

McCABE, JAMES.—Age, 23 years. Enlisted in Thirteenth Congressional District, to serve three years, and mustered in as private, Co. I, no date; discharged for disability, March 1, 1864, at Warrenton Junction, Va.

McCANN, PATRICK.—Age, 42 years. Enlisted at Buffalo, to serve three years, and mustered in as private, Co. C, August 8, 1863; discharged, July 27, 1864, at Washington, D. C.

McCARTHY, JOHN.—Age, 18 years. Enlisted in Thirtieth Congressional District, to serve three years, and mustered in as private, Co. D, August 8, 1863; promoted corporal, June 3, 1865; mustered out with company, July 16, 1865, near Washington, D. C., as John Baker.

McCARTY, GEORGE.—Age, 21 years. Enlisted at Randolph,

to serve three years, and mustered in as private, Co. C, August 22, 1863.

McCORMICK, JOHN.—Age, 21 years. Enlisted, August 19, 1863, at Syracuse, to serve three years; mustered in as private, Co. A, October 19, 1863; transferred to United States Navy, May 3, 1864.

McCULLOUGH, JAMES.—Age, 20 years. Enlisted at Littleville, to serve three years; mustered in as private, Co. K, August 21, 1863; transferred to Army of the Northwest, March 12, 1864; also borne as McCuloch.

McDERMOTT, CHARLES.—Age, 21 years. Enlisted at Rome, to serve three years, and mustered in as private, unassigned, August 24, 1864; no further record.

McDONALD, HENRY.—Age, 27 years. Enlisted at Utica, to serve three years, and mustered in as private, Co. E, August 12, 1863; transferred to United States Navy, May 3, 1864.

McDONALD, HUGH.—Age, 43 years. Enlisted at Syracuse, to serve three years, and mustered in as private, Co. C, August 20, 1863; mustered out with company, July 16, 1865, near Washington, D. C.

McINTYRE, LEVI.—Age, 24 years. Enlisted at Norwich, to serve three years, and mustered in as private, Co. K, September 8, 1863.

McKNIGHT, GEORGE W.—Age, 34 years. Enlisted at Canandaigua, to serve three years; mustered in as private, Co. C, October 8, 1863; mustered out with company, July 16, 1865, near Washington, D. C.

McLANE, MICHAEL.—Age, 34 years. Enlisted at Farnsworth, to serve three years, and mustered in as private, Co. H, August 18, 1863; absent, sick, since October 20, 1863, and at muster-out of company.

McMANUS, JAMES.—Age, 27 years. Enlisted at Buffalo, to serve three years, and mustered in as private, Co. A, August 14, 1863.

McMILLEN, EUGENE B.—Age, 31 years. Enlisted at Syracuse, to serve three years, and mustered in as private, Co. F, August 17, 1863; captured in action, May 5, 1864, at the Wilderness, Va.; paroled, December 12, 1864; mustered out, August 1, 1865, at Syracuse, N. Y.

McTIGHE, JAMES.—Age, 22 years. Enlisted at Remsen, to serve three years, and mustered in as private, Co. C, January 26, 1865; mustered out with company, July 16, 1865, near Washington, D. C.

MEHAN, PATRICK.—Age, 24 years. Enlisted at Napoli, to serve three years, and mustered in as private, Co. G, August 21, 1863; discharged for disability, February 22, 1864, at Washington, D. C.

MERCHANT, CHARLES.—Age, 23 years. Enlisted in Thirteenth Congressional District, to serve three years, and mustered in as private, Co. I, no date; discharged for disability, December 27, 1864, at hospital.

MILLER, WILLIAM W.—Age, 24 years. Enlisted, November 17, 1862, at Utica, to serve three years; mustered in as private, Co. I, November 30, 1862; no record subsequent to April, 1865.

MOLITOR, CHRISTOPHER.—Age, 21 years. Enlisted at New York City, to serve three years, and mustered in as private, Co. H, February 28, 1865; absent, sick, since March 31, 1865, in hospital at Washington, D. C., and at muster-out of company.

MONROE, JOHN.—Age, 28 years. Enlisted at Canandaigua, to serve three years, and mustered in as private, Co. F, August 28, 1863; discharged for disability, November 7, 1863, at Three Mile Station, Va.

MOORE, JOHN.—Age, 19 years. Enlisted at Hanover, to serve three years, and mustered in as private, Co. D, August 8, 1863; discharged, August 28, 1864.

MOORE, STEPHEN.—Age, 35 years. Enlisted at Olean, to serve three years, and mustered in as private, Co. A, August 22, 1863.

MOREY, GEORGE L.—Age, 30 years. Enlisted at Syracuse, to serve three years, and mustered in as private, Co. C, August 12, 1863.

MORGAN, CHARLES P.—Age, 23 years. Enlisted at Partello, to serve three years, and mustered in as private, Co. F, August 22, 1863; discharged, July 2, 1865.

MORIETY, JOHN.—Age, 30 years. Enlisted at Utica, to serve three years, and mustered in as private, Co. K, October 4,

1863; killed in action, May 5, 1864, at the Wilderness, Va.

MORRIS, WILLIAM H. H.—Age, 25 years. Enrolled, January 13, 1865, at Albany, to serve three years; mustered in as assistant surgeon, February 3, 1865; mustered out with regiment, July 16, 1865, near Washington, D. C.

Commissioned assistant surgeon, January 13, 1865, with rank from January 10, 1865, vice M. A. Sanford never reported.

MORRISON, JOHN.—Age, 22 years. Enlisted in Twenty-first Congressional District, to serve three years, and mustered in as private, Co. E, August 21, 1863; captured, no date; died of disease, September 10, 1864, at Andersonville, Ga.

MYERS, PATRICK.—Age, 26 years. Enlisted at Utica, to serve three years, and mustered in as private, Co. K, October 14, 1863; discharged for disability, November 7, 1863, at Kelly's Ford, Va.

NEAR, ANDREW.—Age, 27 years. Enlisted in Twenty-first Congressional District, to serve three years, and mustered in as private, Co. C, September 16, 1863; absent, sick, since January 21, 1864, and at muster-out of company.

NORRIS, FRANK.—Age, 28 years. Enlisted at Randolph, to serve three years, and mustered in as private, Co. D, August 22, 1863; transferred to the Navy, May 3, 1864.

O'BRIEN, DANIEL.—Age, 18 years. Enlisted, November 17, 1862, at Utica, to serve three years; mustered in as private, Co. I, November 30, 1862; died of disease, January 25, 1863, in hospital at Aquia Creek, Va.

O'KEIF, CHARLES.—Age, 22 years. Enlisted at Buffalo, to serve three years, and mustered in as private, Co. F, August 8, 1863; captured in action, May 5, 1864, at the Wilderness, Va.; died of disease, September 25, 1864, at Andersonville, Ga.

OLIVER, BENDRO.—Age, 26 years. Enlisted at West Union, to serve one year, and mustered in as private, unassigned, November 3, 1864; no further record.

O'NEILL, CHARLES.—Age, 21 years. Enlisted at Stuyvesant, to serve three years, and mustered in as private, unassigned, January 14, 1865; no further record.

ORCUTT, ROBERT C.—Age, 21 years. Enlisted, November 17, 1862, at Utica, to serve three years; mustered in as private, Co. I, November 30, 1862; mustered out with company, July 16, 1865, near Washington, D. C.

ORNO, THEOPHILUS.—Age, 18 years. Enlisted at Utica, to serve three years, and mustered in as private, Co. F, September 5, 1864; mustered out with company, July 16, 1865, near Washington, D. C.

PAGE, OZIAS D.—Age, 33 years. Enlisted at Triangle, to serve three years, and mustered in as private, Co. F, July 17, 1863; captured in action, May 5, 1864, at the Wilderness, Va.; died of disease, September 20, 1864, at Andersonville, Ga.

PALMER, FRANKLIN L.—Age, 36 years. Enlisted at Enfield, to serve three years, and mustered in as private, Co. C, July 25, 1863; discharged for disability, November 7, 1864, at Washington, D. C.

PALMER, HENRY.—Age, 27 years. Enlisted at Norwich, to serve three years, and mustered in as private, Co. E, September 5, 1863; wounded, no date; died of his wounds, June 8, 1864, at Washington, D. C.

PALMETER, MAGINNIS.—Age, 22 years. Enlisted at Norwich, to serve three years, and mustered in as private, Co. F, September 3, 1863; absent, sick, since April 1, 1865, and at muster-out of company.

PARRISH, DELBERT.—Age, 21 years. Enlisted in Thirty-first Congressional District, to serve three years, and mustered in as private, Co. E, August 19, 1863; captured in action, no date; died of disease, August 15, 1864, at Andersonville, Ga.

PAUL, NELSON.—Age, 42 years. Enlisted, December 25, 1863, at Bridgewater, to serve three years; mustered in as private, Co. G, December 29, 1863; no further record.

PAYSON, EDWARD P.—Age, 23 years. Enrolled at Catlett's Station, Va.; to serve three years; mustered in as chaplain, March 12, 1864; mustered out with regiment, July 16, 1865, near Washington, D. C.

Commissioned chaplain, March 15, 1864, with rank from March 5, 1864, vice A. Erdman resigned.

PEMBERTON, BOYD.—Age, 24 years. Enlisted at Little Valley, to serve three years, and mustered in as private, Co. E,

August 22, 1863; promoted corporal, July 1, 1865; mustered out with company, July 16, 1865, near Washington, D. C.

PHILLIPS, WILLIAM.—Age, 32 years. Enlisted at Utica, to serve three years, and mustered in as private, Co. B, August 27, 1863; died of disease, January 19, 1864, in hospital at Washington, D. C.

POGAN, ROBERT.—Age, 21 years. Enlisted at Norwich, to serve three years, and mustered in as private, Co. A, October 2, 1863; wounded and captured in action, May 5, 1864, at the Wilderness, Va.; died of his wounds, July 11, 1864, at Lynchburg, Va.; also borne as Ponge.

POWERS, PATRICK.—Age, 28 years. Enlisted at Canandaigua, to serve three years, and mustered in as private, Co. K, August 21, 1863; mustered out, May 10, 1865, at Fort Snelling, Minn.

PUGH, JOHN.—Age, 33 years. Enlisted at Utica, to serve one year, and mustered in as private, Co. C, August 25, 1864; captured in action, March 31, 1865, at White Oak Ridge, Va.; paroled, no date; mustered out, May 31, 1865, at Annapolis, Md.

REEVES, CHRISTOPHER.—Age, 21 years. Enlisted at Hinsdale' to serve three years, and mustered in as private, Co. K, August 21, 1863; absent, sick, since November 23, 1863, and at muster-out of company.

REID, WILLIAM D.—Age, 33 years. Enlisted at Norwich to serve three years, and mustered in as private, Co. H, September 4, 1863; captured in action, May 5, 1864, at the Wilderness, Va.; died of disease, August 18, 1864, at Andersonville, Ga.

REITZHEIMER, LAWRENCE.—First sergeant, U. S. Army; mustered in as second lieutenant, Co. B, this regiment, April 25, 1863.

Commissioned second lieutenant, March 27, 1863, with rank from March 26, 1863, vice M. Egleston promoted.

RIFFENBERG, DAVID.—Age, 26 years. Enlisted at Norwich, to serve three years, and mustered in as private, Co. K, September 8, 1863; killed in action, May 5, 1864, at the Wilderness, Va.

RILA, THOMAS.—Age, 33 years. Enlisted at Altoon, to serve

three years, and mustered in as private, Co. C, August 22, 1863.

ROBACK, CHARLES V.—Age, 22 years. Enlisted at Deerfield, to serve one year, and mustered in as private, Co. F, August 26, 1864; mustered out, June 3, 1865, at camp near Alexandria, Va.

ROBERTS, GEORGE.—Age, 33 years. Enlisted, August 22, 1863, at Randolph, to serve three years; mustered in as private, Co. A, August 23, 1863; absent, sick, since May 8, 1864, and at muster-out of company.

ROONEY, THOMAS.—Age, 34 years. Enlisted at Rochester, to serve three years, and mustered in as private, Co. H, August 18, 1863.

ROOT, JAY E.—Age, 19 years. Enlisted, August 4, 1864, at Lenox, to serve three years; mustered in as private, Co. B, August 7, 1864; promoted corporal, February 22, 1865; mustered out, May 29, 1865, from Satterly Hospital, Philadelphia, Pa.

ROTHENBECK, JOHN.—Age, 36 years. Enlisted at Perrysburg, to serve three years, and mustered in as private, Co. I, August 20, 1863; discharged for disability, November 7, 1863, at Three Mile Station, Va.

ROWELL, THOMAS.—Age, 39 years. Enlisted at Buffalo, to serve three years, and mustered in as private, Co. C, August 14, 1863; promoted corporal, no date; sergeant, February 1, 1865; mustered out with company, July 16, 1865, near Washington, D. C.

RUNYON, GEORGE H.—Age, 22 years. Enlisted at Binghamton, to serve three years, and mustered in as private, Co. C, July 17, 1863; discharged for disability, January 17, 1864, at Warrenton Junction, Va.

RUSSELL, JOHN.—Age, 38 years. Enlisted at New York City, to serve three years, and mustered in as private, Co. E, February 15, 1865; mustered out with company, July 16, 1865, near Washington, D. C.

RYAN, GEORGE.—Age, 32 years. Enlisted at Rome, to serve three years, and mustered in as private, unassigned, August 24, 1864; no further record.

SCHIRMER, ENGLEBERT.—Age, 37 years. Enlisted at Rome,

to serve three years, and mustered in as private, Co. F, August 30, 1864; mustered out, June 12, 1865, at Albany, N. Y.

SCUDDER, JAMES.—Age, 30 years. Enlisted at Norwich to serve three years, and mustered in as private, Co. H, September 4, 1863; died of disease, March 3, 1865, at Armory Square Hospital, Washington, D. C.

SELL, JONAS.—Age, 37 years. Enlisted at Auburn, to serve three years, and mustered in as private, Co. G, July 24, 1863; captured in action, May 5, 1864, at the Wilderness, Va.; no further record.

SEYMOUR, EUGENE.—Age, 25 years. Enlisted at Auburn, to serve three years, and mustered in as private, Co. G, July 25, 1863; captured in action, May 5, 1864, at the Wilderness, Va.; paroled, no date; discharged for disability, May 3, 1865.

SHAVER, HENRY.—Age, 25 years. Enlisted at Norwich, to serve three years, and mustered in as private, Co. F, September 4, 1863; mustered out with company, July 16, 1865, near Washington, D. C.

SHAW, AMOS.—Age, 45 years. Enlisted at Norwich, to serve three years, and mustered in as private, Co. F, September 4, 1863; discharged for disability, November 17, 1863, at Three Mile Station, Va.

SHAW, WALTER P.—Age, — years. Enlisted at Buffalo, to serve three years, and mustered in as private, Co. K, August 15, 1863; promoted corporal, March 1, 1865; sergeant, May 1, 1865; mustered out with company, July 16, 1865, near Washington, D. C.

SHEDD, JAMES B.—Age, 21 years. Enlisted at Canandaigua, to serve three years, and mustered in as musician, Co. K, September 13, 1863; transferred to Co. E, April 19, 1864; returned to company as private, no date; died of disease, August 10, 1864, at City Point, Va.

SHERMAN, WILLIAM.—Age, 24 years. Enlisted at Canandaigua, to serve three years, and mustered in as private, Co. B, September 9, 1863; captured in action, August 20, 1864, at Weldon Railroad, Va.; died of starvation, January 10, 1865, at Salisbury, N. C.

SHORT, JAMES.—Age, 25 years. Enlisted at Rome, to serve three years, and mustered in as private, unassigned, August 25, 1864; no further record.

SIMMONS, BENJAMIN.—Age, 33 years. Enlisted at Canandaigua, to serve three years, and mustered in as private, Co. C, September 19, 1864; wounded, no date; died of his wounds, November 6, 1864, at hospital, Washington, D. C.

SITTERLEY, WILLIAM J.—Age, 28 years. Enlisted at Utica, to serve three years, and mustered in as private, Co. H, October 7, 1863; discharged for disability, November 10, 1863, at Three Mile Station, Va. Died September 10, 1910, at Utica.

SLACK, DANIEL.—Age, 30 years. Enlisted at Norwich, to serve three years, and mustered in as private, Co. A, September 30, 1863; wounded and captured in action, May 5, 1864, at the Wilderness, Va.; died of his wounds, August 18, 1864, at Andersonville, Ga.

SLADE, HENRY.—Age, 21 years. Enlisted at Randolph, to serve three years, and mustered in as private, Co. K, August 22, 1863; captured in action, May 5, 1864, at the Wilderness, Va.; no further record.

SLOAT, WILLIAM A.—Age, 24 years. Enlisted in Nineteenth Congressional District, to serve three years, and mustered in as private, Co. E, August 22, 1863; captured, no date; died of disease, November 20, 1864, at Andersonville, Ga.

SMITH, CHARLES.—Age, 26 years. Enlisted at Rome, to serve three years, and mustered in as private, Co. B, August 30, 1864; mustered out, July 25, 1865, at Syracuse, N. Y.

SMITH, EDWARD.—Age, 20 years. Enlisted at Auburn, to serve three years, and mustered in as private, Co. G, July 23, 1863; captured and paroled, no dates; mustered out, July 25, 1865, at Syracuse, N. Y.

SMITH, JAMES.—Age, — years. Enlisted at Napoli, to serve three years, and mustered in as private, Co. E, August 21, 1863; discharged for disability, November 7, 1863, at Three Mile Station, Va.

SMITH, JOHN 1st.—Age, 24 years. Enlisted at Randolph, to serve three years, and mustered in as private, Co. H, August 22, 1863.

SMITH, JOHN, 2d.—Age, 35 years. Enlisted at Buffalo, to serve three years, and mustered in as private, Co. H, August 15, 1863.

SMITH, THOMAS.—Age, 18 years. Enlisted at Troy, to serve one year, and mustered in as private, Co. F, September 12, 1864; wounded in action, April 1, 1865, at Five Forks, Va.; died of his wounds, April 3, 1865, at City Point, Va.

SMITH, WILLIAM.—Age, 22 years. Enlisted at Pomfret, to serve three years, and mustered in as private, Co. I, August 21, 1863; mustered out with company, July 16, 1865, near Washington, D. C.

SOUTHWICK, JEREMIAH.—Age, 33 years. Enlisted at Humphries, to serve three years, and mustered in as private, Co. E, August 31, 1863.

SPENCER, WILLIAM.—Age, 28 years. Enlisted at Ellicottville, to serve three years, and mustered in as private, Co. F, August 18, 1863.

STACK, PATRICK.—Age, 30 years. Enlisted at Binghamton, to serve three years, and mustered in as private, Co. C, July 17, 1863; discharged for disability, November 7, 1863, at Three Mile Station, Va.

STICKLE, WILLIAM.—Age, 31 years. Enlisted at Norwich, to serve three years, and mustered in as private, Co. E, September 15, 1863; captured in action, May 5, 1864, at the Wilderness, Va.; died of disease, November 10, 1864, at Florence, S. C.

STONE, ARTHUR.—Age, 19 years. Enlisted at Orleans, to serve three years, and mustered in as private, Co. I, August 22, 1863; captured in action, May 5, 1864, at the Wilderness, Va.; paroled, no date; absent, sick, in hospital, since October, 1864, and at muster-out of company.

SULLIVAN, DANIEL.—Age, 20 years. Enlisted, January 10, 1865, at New York City, to serve three years; mustered in as private, unassigned, January 14, 1865; no further record.

SULLIVAN, DENNIS.—Age, 23 years. Enlisted at Rome, to serve three years, and mustered in as private, unassigned, August 24, 1864; no further record.

SULLIVAN, JEREMIAH.—Age, 32 years. Enlisted at Auburn, to serve three years, and mustered in as private, Co. G, July

23, 1863; mustered out with company, July 16, 1865, near Washington, D. C.

SULLIVAN, JOHN.—Age, 27 years. Enlisted at New Albion, to serve three years, and mustered in as private, Co. K, August 20, 1863; transferred to Army of the Northwest, March 12, 1864.

SWEENEY, PATRICK.—Age, 19 years. Enlisted at Mansfield, to serve three years, and mustered in as private, Co. K, August 21, 1863; mustered out with company, July 16, 1865, near Washington, D. C.

SWINDLEHURST, THOMAS.—Age, 19 years. Enlisted at Buffalo, to serve three years, and mustered in as private, Co. I, August 14, 1863; captured in action, May 5, 1864, at the Wilderness, Va.; paroled, no date; mustered out, June 5, 1865, at Washington, D. C.

TEED, ALONZO.—Age, 20 years. Enlisted at Norwich, to serve three years, and mustered in as private, Co. F, September 4, 1863; transferred to Veteran Reserve Corps, January 18, 1865.

TEFFT, JAMES.—Age, 25 years. Enlisted at Buffalo, to serve three years, and mustered in as private, Co. C, August 19, 1863; mustered out, June 7, 1865, at Satterlee Hospital, Philadelphia, Pa., as Tiffts.

THOMAS, HENRY.—Age, 19 years. Enlisted at Rome, to serve three years, and mustered in as private, unassigned, November 12, 1864; no further record.

TOMPKINS, SAMUEL D.—Age, 40 years. Enlisted at Elmira, to serve three years, and mustered in as private, Co. F, October 7, 1863; wounded in action, May 5, 1864, at the Wilderness, Va.; mustered out, June 6, 1865, at Washington, D. C.

TOY, JOHN.—Age, 35 years. Enlisted at Syracuse, to serve three years, and mustered in as private, Co. G, August 19, 1863; discharged for disability, November 10, 1863, at Three Mile Station, Va.

TREMBLY, ALEXANDER.—Age, 28 years. Enlisted at Syracuse, to serve three years, and mustered in as private, Co. C, August 21, 1863; killed in action, May 5, 1864, at the Wilderness, Va.

TROTTER, GEORGE.—Age, 23 years. Enlisted at Syracuse, to

serve three years, and mustered in as private, Co. A, August 9, 1863; transferred to Co. K, April 12, 1864; absent, sick, since May 12, 1864, and at muster-out of company.

TUTTLE, JAY A.—Age, 20 years. Enlisted at Buffalo to serve three years, and mustered in as private, Co. C, August 29, 1863; mustered out, May 9, 1865, at Washington, D. C.

TWAHY, TIMOTHY.—Age, 24 years. Enlisted at Syracuse to serve three years; mustered in as private, Co. G, August 19, 1863; mustered out with company, July 16, 1865, near Washington, D. C.

VAN AIKEN, WILLIAM D.—Age, 34 years. Enlisted at Norwich, to serve three years, and mustered in as private, Co. D, September 13, 1863; mustered out, June 14, 1865, at Elmira, N. Y.

VANDENBURGH, SYLVESTER C.—Age, 18 years. Enlisted at Albany, to serve three years, and mustered in as private, Co. F, August 30, 1864; wounded and captured, March 31, 1865, at White Oak Ridge, Va.; released, April 2, 1865; mustered out, June 26, 1865, at Annapolis, Md.; also borne as Peter McCabe.

VAN HAZEN, JOHN.—Age, 35 years. Enlisted at Syracuse, to serve three years, and mustered in as private, Co. C, September 29, 1863; mustered out, June 2, 1865, at Washington, D. C., as Vanhusen.

VAN HOUGHTON, MAURICE.—Age, 25 years. Enlisted at Norwich, to serve three years, and mustered in as private, Co. E, September 4, 1863; wounded in action, no date; died of his wounds, July 22, 1864, at Washington, D. C.; also borne as H. Van Houghton.

WAKEMAN, STEPHEN.—Age, 27 years. Enlisted at Norwich, to serve three years, and mustered in as private, Co. D, September 15, 1863; mustered out with company, July 16, 1865, near Washington, D. C.

WALLEY, MARK N.—Age, 37 years. Enlisted at Norwich, to serve three years, and mustered in as private, Co. D, October 2, 1863; wounded in action, May 5, 1864, at the Wilderness, Va.; discharged for wounds, in hospital, December 25, 1864.

WALLY, DAVID.—Age, 27 years. Enlisted at Norwich, to serve three years, and mustered in as private, Co. D, October 2,

1863; mustered out with company, July 16, 1865, near Washington, D. C.

WARREN, ROBERT P.—Age, 18 years. Enrolled, May 30, 1863, to serve three years; mustered in as second lieutenant, Co. H, August 14, 1863; promoted first lieutenant, Co. K, November 20, 1863; mustered in as captain, Co. H, April 1, 1865; mustered out with company, July 16, 1865, near Washington, D. C.; prior service, private, Co. F, Seventh Militia; subsequent service as first lieutenant, Twenty-fourth U. S. Infantry.

Commissioned second lieutenant, July 29, 1863, with rank from May 30, 1863; first lieutenant, November 9, 1863, with rank from September 23, 1863, vice H. E. Jones promoted; captain, March 30, 1865, with rank from February 1, 1865, vice Charles K. Dutton resigned. Brevet major by U. S. Government from March 13, 1865.

WATSON, WILLIAM.—Age, 30 years. Enlisted at Utica, to serve one year, and mustered in as private, unassigned, August 23, 1864; no further record.

WELDEN, PETER.—Age, 31 years. Enlisted at Norwich, to serve three years, and mustered in as private, Co. E, September 5, 1863; discharged for disability, January 12, 1864, at Washington, D. C.

WEST, CHARLES E.—Age, 24 years. Enlisted at Oswego to serve three years, and mustered in as private, Co. F, August 14, 1863; transferred to Veteran Reserve Corps, no date; mustered out therefrom as of Sixteenth Company, Second Battalion, August 23, 1865, at Washington, D. C.

WHIPPLE, JOB P.—Age, 39 years. Enlisted at Vienna, to serve three years, and mustered in as private, Co. A, December 2, 1864; mustered out with company, July 16, 1865, near Washington, D. C.

WHITE, ISAAC.—Age, 26 years. Enlisted at Canandaigua, to serve three years, and mustered in as private, Co. A, August 19, 1863; captured and paroled, no dates; mustered out, May 24, 1865, at Elmira, N. Y.

WHITE, JOSEPH.—Age, 25 years. Enlisted at Utica, to serve one year, and mustered in as private, Co. B, September 7, 1864; mustered out, June 3, 1865, near Alexandria, Va.

WHITE, LAFAYETTE.—Age, 33 years. Enlisted at Canandaigua, to serve three years, and mustered in as private, Co. F, July 28, 1863; captured in action, May 5, 1864, at the Wilderness Va.; died of disease, September 20, 1864, at Florence, S. C.

WHITE, MYRON P.—Age, 22 years. Enrolled at Auburn, to serve three years, and mustered in as private, Co. I, July 24, 1863; appointed musician and returned to company as private, no dates; mustered out, July 25, 1865, at Syracuse, N. Y. Commissioned, not mustered, second lieutenant, August 31, 1865, with rank from August 1, 1865, vice H. Gifford not mustered.

WHITE, ROBERT.—Age, 23 years. Enlisted at Cherry Creek, to serve three years, and mustered in as private, Co. H, August 19, 1863; captured in action, May 5, 1864, at the Wilderness, Va.; no further record.

WHITNEY, LEONARD.—Age, 22 years. Enlisted at Auburn, to serve three years, and mustered in as private, Co. F, August 25, 1863.

WILDS, PATRICK.—Age, 18 years. Enlisted at Portello; to serve three years, and mustered in as private, Co. K, August 22, 1863; absent, sick, since April 21, 1864, and at muster-out of company.

WILLIAMS, GEORGE.—Age, 44 years. Enlisted at Syracuse, to serve three years, and mustered in as private, Co. E, August 11, 1863; mustered out, May 31, 1865, at Washington, D. C.

WILLIAMS, JOHN.—Age, 18 years. Enlisted at Randolph, to serve three years, and mustered in as private, Co. K, August 22, 1863; transferred to Army of the Northwest, March 12, 1864.

WILLIAMS, JOHN.—Age, 23 years. Enlisted at Cold Spring, to serve three years, and mustered in as private, Co. D, August 21, 1863; died of disease, August 10, 1864, at City Point, Va.

WILLIAMS, JOHN.—Age, 32 years. Enlisted at Norwich, to serve three years, and mustered in as private, Co. I, September 5, 1863; absent, sick, in hospital, since December 31, 1863, and at muster-out of company.

WILLIAMS, LORENZO.—Age, 24 years. Enlisted at Rochester,

to serve three years, and mustered in as private, Co. K, August 17, 1863; mustered out with company, July 16, 1865, near Washington, D. C.

WILLIS, LAFAYETTE C.—Age, 28 years. Enlisted at Canandaigua, to serve three years, and mustered in as private, Co. C, August 28, 1863; mustered out, June 7, 1865, at Satterlee Hospital, Philadelphia, Pa.

WING, IRA.—Age, 34 years. Enlisted, August 22, 1864, at Norwich, to serve three years; mustered in as private, Co. H, August 29, 1864; killed in action, March 31, 1865, at White Oak Ridge, Va.

WINTER, GEORGE.—Age, 27 years. Enlisted at Cold Spring, to serve three years, and mustered in as private, Co. I, August 22, 1863; captured in action, May 5, 1864, at the Wilderness, Va.; paroled, March 25, 1865; mustered out with company, July 16, 1865, near Washington, D. C.

WINTER, HENRY.—Age, 30 years. Enlisted at Leon, to serve three years, and mustered in as private, Co. I, August 21, 1863; mustered out with company, July 16, 1865, near Washington, D. C.

WOOD, WILLIAM.—Age, 25 years. Enlisted at Buffalo, to serve three years, and mustered in as private, Co. A, August 14, 1863.

WRIGHT, GEORGE M.—Age, 18 years. Enlisted at Utica, to serve three years, and mustered in as private, unassigned, February 16, 1865; died, April 17, 1865, near City Point, Va.

YAPLE, DAVID R.—Age, 26 years. Enlisted at Ripley, to serve three years, and mustered in as private, Co. K, August 18, 1863; captured in action, May 5, 1864, at the Wilderness, Va.; paroled, December 27, 1864, at Charleston, S. C.; mustered out, June 17, 1865, at Annapolis, Md.

ZELLER, MAX.—Age, 19 years. Enlisted in Fifth Congressional District, N. Y., to serve three years, and mustered in as private, unassigned, March 3, 1865; no further record.

TRANSFERRED FROM OTHER ORGANIZATIONS

FIFTH NEW YORK INFANTRY

ADLEMAN, RICHARD C.—Private, Co. G, Fifth Infantry; transferred to Co. H, this regiment, May 4, 1863; promoted corporal, no date; discharged, May 19, 1865, at hospital, West Philadelphia, Pa.

ALLEN, DAVID W.—Private, Co. A, Fifth Infantry; transferred to Co. E, this regiment, May 4, 1863; mustered out, June 3, 1865, near Alexandria, Va.

ALLEN, THOMAS W.—Private, Co. E, Fifth Infantry; transferred to Co. E, this regiment, May 4, 1863; discharged for disability, March 10, 1864, at Washington, D. C.

ALVERSON, JAMES.—Private, Co. I, Fifth Infantry; transferred to Co. G, this regiment, May 4, 1863; captured in action, May 5, 1864, at the Wilderness, Va.; paroled, no date; mustered out, June 6, 1865, at York, Pa.

BACKUS, ADAM.—Private, Co. E, Fifth Infantry; transferred to Co. D, this regiment, May 4, 1863; promoted corporal, captured in action, paroled and returned to ranks, no dates; mustered out, June 3, 1865, at camp near Alexandria, Va.

BAKER, GEORGE M.—Private, Co. C, Fifth Infantry; transferred to Co. G, this regiment, May 4, 1863; wounded in action, May 5, 1864, at the Wilderness, Va.; died of his wounds, June 4, 1864, in hospital, at Alexandria, Va.

BALL, JESSE.—Private, Co. K, Fifth Infantry; transferred to Co. G, this regiment, May 4, 1863; discharged, July 22, 1864, at Petersburg, Va.

BARNARD, CHARLES U.—Private, Co. C, Fifth Infantry; transferred to Co. B, this regiment, May 4, 1863; promoted corporal, June 25, 1863; mustered out, May 18, 1865, at Arlington Heights, Va.

BAXTER, GEORGE R.—Private, Co. F, Fifth Infantry; transferred to Co. C, this regiment, May 4, 1863, and to Veteran Reserve Corps, August 11, 1864.

BENNETT, CHARLES.—Private, Co. D, Fifth Infantry; transferred to this regiment, unassigned, May 4, 1863; no further record.

BENNETT, JOHN J.—Private, Co. H, Fifth Infantry; transferred to Co. I, this regiment, May 4, 1863; mustered out, June 3, 1865, at camp near Alexandria, Va.

BERTELL, MARTIN.—Private, Co. A, Fifth Infantry; transferred to Co. E, this regiment, May 4, 1863; absent, sick, since June 4, 1863; no further record.

BERTINE, GEORGE F.—Private, Co. K, Fifth Infantry; transferred to Co. K, this regiment, May 4, 1863; captured in action, June 2, 1864, at Cold Harbor, Va.; paroled, no date; mustered out, June 3, 1865, at camp near Alexandria, Va.

BLACK, WILLIAM S.—Private, Co. C, Fifth Infantry; transferred to Co. F, this regiment, May 4, 1863.

BLACKWOOD, ALBERT.—Private, Co. B, Fifth Infantry; transferred to Co. G, this regiment, May 4, 1863; captured and paroled, no date; mustered out, June 3, 1865, at camp near Alexandria, Va.

BLATZ, CHARLES.—Private, Co. I, Fifth Infantry; transferred to Co. A, this regiment, May 4, 1863; mustered out, July 18, 1864, at Petersburg, Va.

BODEN, JAMES S.—Private, Co. E, Fifth Infantry; transferred to Co. D, this regiment, May 4, 1863; discharged, July 1, 1864, near Petersburg, Va., for promotion in organization not stated.

BODEY, HENRY.—Private, Co. F, Fifth Infantry; transferred to Co. C, this regiment, May 4, 1863; promoted corporal, no date; killed in action, May 5, 1864, at the Wilderness, Va.

BOWNE, CHARLES B.—Private, Co. H, Fifth Infantry; transferred to Co. H, this regiment, May 4, 1863; captured, May 5, 1864, at the Wilderness, Va.; no further record.

BRANDAGE, CHARLES.—Private, Co. I, Fifth Infantry; transferred to Co. A, this regiment, May 4, 1863; captured in action, May 5, 1864, at the Wilderness, Va.; paroled, no date; discharged, January 11, 1865, at hospital.

29

BRAYNARD, HENRY A.—Private, Co. C, Fifth Infantry; transferred to Co. B, this regiment, May 4, 1863; mustered out, June 5, 1865, at Philadelphia, Pa.

BRENNAN, JOHN.—Private, Co. E, Fifth Infantry; transferred to Co. H, this regiment, May 4, 1863; promoted sergeant, no date; discharged, July 7, 1864, at Petersburg, Va.

BROGAN, JOHN C.—First sergeant, Co. I, Fifth Infantry; transferred to Co. K, this regiment, May 4, 1863; returned to ranks, no date.

BURDICK, PERRIN.—Age, — years. Quartermaster sergeant, Fifth Infantry; transferred to this regiment, May 4, 1863.

CAMERON, WILLIAM.—Private, Co. A, Fifth Infantry; transferred to Co. A, this regiment, May 4, 1863; mustered out, June 3, 1865, near Alexandria, Va.

CAMPBELL, GEORGE W.—Private, Co. G, Fifth Infantry; transferred to Co. H, this regiment, May 4, 1863; promoted corporal and returned to ranks, no dates; absent, sick, since May 5, 1864, and at muster-out of company.

CAMPBELL, WILLIAM.—Private, Co. B, Fifth Infantry; transferred to Co. G, this regiment, May 4, 1863; promoted corporal, no date; mustered out, June 3, 1865, at camp near Alexandria, Va.

CARGON, SILAS.—Private, Co. B, Fifth Infantry; transferred to Co. G, this regiment, May 4, 1863; captured in action, May 5, 1864, at the Wilderness, Va.; paroled, no date; absent, detached service, at Camp Parole, Md., at muster-out of company.

CARLOW, ALBERT F.—Private, Co. B, Fifth Infantry; transferred to Co. F, this regiment, May 4, 1863; transferred to Veteran Reserve Corps, October 15, 1864; mustered out therefrom as of Ninety-fifth Company, Second Battalion, August 17, 1865, at Hick's Hospital, Baltimore, Md.

CARSON, WILLIAM M.—Private, Co. G, Fifth Infantry; transferred to Co. E, this regiment, May 4, 1863; discharged, December 23, 1863, by civil authority, at New York.

CHALMERS, HUGH.—First sergeant, Co. H, Fifth Infantry; transferred to Co. E, this regiment, May 4, 1863; mustered in as second lieutenant, Co. H, November 20, 1863; transferred to Co. E, January 25, 1864; wounded and captured in action, June 3, 1864, at Cold Harbor, Va.; died of his wounds, June 9, 1864, at Richmond, Va.

Commissioned second lieutenant, November 9, 1863, with rank from September 23, 1863, vice R. P. Warren promoted.

CLARK, JOHN.—Private, Co. G, Fifth Infantry; transferred to Co. E, this regiment, May 4, 1863; discharged for disability, May 31, 1865.

CLAVIN, PATRICK.—Private, Co. E, Fifth Infantry; transferred to Co. D, this regiment, May 4, 1863; discharged, July 3, 1864, at Petersburg, Va.

CLAYTON, EDWARD J.—Corporal, Co. K, Fifth Infantry; transferred to Co. K, this regiment, May 4, 1863; discharged, October 12, 1864, at Weldon Railroad, Va.

CODY, JAMES.—Private, Co. E, Fifth Infantry; transferred to Co. D, this regiment, May 4, 1863; promoted first sergeant, no date; mustered out, June 3, 1865, near Alexandria, Va.

CODY, THOMAS.—Private, Co. K, Fifth Infantry; transferred to Co. K, this regiment, May 4, 1863; wounded in action, no date, at Jericho Ford, Va.; died of his wounds, May 25, 1864.

COLE, GEORGE A.—Private, Co. F, Fifth Infantry; transferred to Co. C, this regiment, May 4, 1863.

COLE, JOHN J.—Private, Co. F, Fifth Infantry; transferred to Co. C, this regiment, May 4, 1863.

COLE, WILLIAM.—Private, Co. G, Fifth Infantry; transferred to this regiment, unassigned, May 4, 1863; no further record.

COLEMAN, JOHN J.—Private, Co. B, Fifth Infantry; transferred to this regiment, unassigned, May 4, 1863; no further record.

COLEMAN, THEODORE.—Private, Co. I, Fifth Infantry; transferred to Co. K, this regiment, May 4, 1863.

COON, DAVID.—Private, Co. E, Fifth Infantry; transferred to Co. D, this regiment, May 4, 1863; captured and paroled, no dates; died of disease, February 25, 1865, at Wilmington, N. C.

CORNELL, ROBERT H.—Private, Co. E, Fifth Infantry; transferred to Co. E, this regiment, May 4, 1863; promoted sergeant and wounded in action, no dates; discharged for wounds, December 14, 1864.

CRAMER, EUGENE H.—Private, Co. I, Fifth Infantry; transferred to Co. A, this regiment, May 4, 1863; discharged for disability, June 18, 1863, at Baltimore, Md.

CRAWFORD, JAMES P.—Private, Co. I, Fifth Infantry; transferred to Co. A, this regiment, May 4, 1863; mustered out, July 10, 1865, at Satterlee Hospital, Philadelphia, Pa.

CROLINS, WILLIAM A.—Private, Co. G, Fifth Infantry; transferred to this regiment, unassigned, May 4, 1863; no further record.

CUNNINGHAM, ALEXANDER.—Private, Co. B, Fifth Infantry; transferred to Co. F, this regiment, May 4, 1863; mustered out, June 3, 1865, near Alexandria, Va.

CURTIS, HENRY B.—Private, Co. H, Fifth Infantry; transferred to Co. I, this regiment, May 4, 1863; killed, May 5, 1864, at the Wilderness, Va.

CURTIS, WILLIAM H.—Private, Co. H, Fifth Infantry; trans, ferred to Co. I, this regiment, May 4, 1863; killed, May 5-1864, at the Wilderness, Va.

DALEY, GEORGE.—Private, Co. D, Fifth Infantry; transferred to Co. I, this regiment, May 4, 1863; transferred to Veteran Reserve Corps, September 2, 1863; mustered out as of Company F, Fourteenth Regiment, Veteran Reserve Corps, June 26, 1865, at Washington, D. C., as George W. Daley.

DALY, ENOS.—Private, Co. G, Fifth Infantry; transferred to this regiment, unassigned, May 4, 1863; no further record.

DARNEY, MORRIS.—Private, Co. G, Fifth Infantry; transferred to this regiment, unassigned, May 4, 1863; no further record.

DAVIDSON, GEORGE.—Private, Co. K, Fifth Infantry; transferred to Co. K, this regiment, May 4, 1863; absent, sick, since May 24, 1864; no further record; also borne as William Davidson.

DAVIS, WILLIAM H.—Private, Co. C, Fifth Infantry; transferred to Co. B, this regiment, May 4, 1863; promoted corporal, November 1, 1863; captured in action, May 5, 1864, at the Wilderness, Va.; paroled, no date; discharged for disability, June 12, 1865.

DAWSON, CHARLES H.—Private, Co. I, Fifth Infantry; transferred to this regiment, unassigned, May 4, 1863; no further record.

DEERY, GEORGE.—Private, Co. B, Fifth Infantry; transferred

to Co. G, this regiment, May 4, 1863; mustered out, June 3, 1865, at camp near Alexandria, Va.

DELMEGE, HENRY A.—Private, Co. B, Fifth Infantry; transferred to Co. C, this regiment, May 4, 1863; mustered out, June 3, 1865, near Alexandria, Va.; also borne as Delmandge.

DE MARARVILLE, GEORGE.—Private, Co. I, Fifth Infantry; transferred to Co. D, this regiment, May 4, 1863, and to Co. A, June 25, 1863; also borne as De Manderville.

DENNIS, FRANK M.—Private, Co. E, Fifth Infantry; transferred to Co. D, this regiment, May 4, 1863; killed in action, July 3, 1863, at Gettysburg, Pa.; also borne as Frank W. Dennis.

DENTON, JAMES L.—Private, Co. E, Fifth Infantry; transferred to Co. A, this regiment, May 4, 1863; mustered out, June 3, 1865, near Alexandria, Va.

DETMER, CHARLES.—Private, Co. I, Fifth Infantry; transferred to Co. A, this regiment, May 4, 1863.

DICKSON, NATHANIEL.—Private, Co. D, Fifth Infantry; transferred to Co. I, this regiment, May 4, 1863; died of disease, December 9, 1863, at Bealton Station, Va.

DIDIER, FRANK.—Private, Co. D, Fifth Infantry; transferred to Co. K, this regiment, May 4, 1863; promoted corporal, no date; mustered out, June 3, 1865, at camp near Alexandria, Va.

DIXON, ROBERT.—Private, Co. B, Fifth Infantry; transferred to this regiment, unassigned, May 4, 1863; no further record.

DOLAN, HENRY.—Private, Co. K, Fifth Infantry; transferred to Co. K, this regiment, May 4, 1863.

DONNELLY, JOHN.—Private, Co. B, Fifth Infantry; transferred to Co. G, this regiment, May 4, 1863; captured in action, May 5, 1864, at the Wilderness, Va.; no further record.

DOOLEY, GEORGE.—Private, Co. F, Fifth Infantry; transferred to Co. C, this regiment, May 4, 1863.

DOREMUS, DAVID M.—Private, Co. A, Fifth Infantry; transferred to Co. E, this regiment, May 4, 1863; mustered out, July 18, 1865, at New York City.

DRUMMOND, GEORGE.—Private, Co. E, Fifth Infantry; transferred to Co. H, this regiment, May 4, 1863· discharged, July 6, 1864, at Petersburg, Va.

DUCKWORTH, JOHN.—Corporal, Co. D, Fifth Infantry; transferred to Co. I, this regiment, May 4, 1863; discharged, July 20, 1864, at Petersburg, Va.

DUFF, JAMES F.—Corporal, Co. E, Fifth Infantry; transferred to Co. C, this regiment, May 4, 1863; killed in action, May 5, 1864, at the Wilderness, Va.

ESTER, WILLIAM H.—Private, Co. C, Fifth Infantry; transferred to Co. B, this regiment, May 4, 1863; also borne as Esler.

EVERETT, JAMES H.—Private, Co. E, Fifth Infantry; transferred to Co. D, this regiment, May 4, 1863; promoted sergeant, no date; wounded in action, May 10, 1864, at Laurel Hill, Va.; died of his wounds, June 3, 1864, at Alexandria, Va.

FARLEY, GEORGE.—Private, Co. E, Fifth Infantry; transferred to Co. D, this regiment, May 4, 1863; discharged, July 6, 1864, at hospital, Washington, D. C.

FARQUHARSON, JOHN N.—Private, Co. A, Fifth Infantry; transferred to Co. E, this regiment, May 4, 1863; promoted corporal and returned to ranks, no dates; transferred to Veteran Reserve Corps, February 25, 1864; also borne as Ferguson.

FARRELL, JOHN.—Private, Co. I, Fifth Infantry; transferred to Co. F, this regiment, May 4, 1863.

FARRELL, MICHAEL.—Private, Co. B, Fifth Infantry; transferred to Co. F, this regiment, May 4, 1863; discharged, June 17, 1864, near Petersburg, Va.

FERRY, SYLVESTER.—Private, Co. H, Fifth Infantry; transferred to Co. I, this regiment, May 4, 1863; promoted corporal, same date; captured in action, May 5, 1864, at the Wilderness, Va.; paroled, December 16, 1864, at Charleston, S. C.; mustered out, June 21, 1865, at Annapolis, Md.

FISHBOURNE, WILLIAM.—Private, Co. C, Fifth Infantry; transferred to Co. B, this regiment, May 4, 1863; wounded in action, May 23, 1864, at North Anna River, Va.; absent, wounded, at muster-out of company.

FISHER, WILLIAM H.—Private, Co. F, Fifth Infantry; transferred to Co. H, this regiment, May 4, 1863.

FISKE, JAMES B.—Private, Co. K, Fifth Infantry; transferred to Co. K, this regiment, May 4, 1863; mustered out, June 3, 1865, near Alexandria, Va.

FITZPATRICK, LAWRENCE.—First sergeant, Co. B, Fifth Infantry; transferred to Co. B, this regiment, May 4, 1863; mustered in as second lieutenant, October 29, 1863; captured in action, May 5, 1864, at the Wilderness, Va.; paroled, no date; mustered in as first lieutenant, May 5, 1865; as captain, June 21, 1865; mustered out with company, July 16, 1865, near Washington, D. C.

FOWELL, EDWARD.—Private, Co. F, Fifth Infantry; transferred to this regiment, unassigned, May 4, 1863; no further record.

FOX, RICHARD.—Private, Co. D, Fifth Infantry; transferred to this regiment, unassigned, May 4, 1863; no further record.

FRANKLIN, JAMES H.—Private, Co. F, Fifth Infantry; transferred to Co. A, this regiment, May 4, 1863; discharged, October 19, 1864, at Weldon Railroad, Va.

FREELAND, CHARLES.—Private, Co. K, Fifth Infantry; transferred to this regiment, unassigned, May 4, 1863; no further record.

FRICHETTE, ACHILLE.—Private, Co. B, Fifth Infantry; transferred to Co. G, this regiment, May 4, 1863.

FRITZ, JOSEPH.—Private, Co. I, Fifth Infantry; transferred to this regiment, unassigned, May 4, 1863; no further record.

FROELIGH, PETER D.—First sergeant, Co. E, Fifth Infantry; transferred to Co. C, this regiment, May 4, 1863; mustered in as second lieutenant, Co. D, August 18, 1863; transferred to Co. H, January 25, 1864; killed in action, May 5, 1864, at the Wilderness, Va.

Commissioned second lieutenant, July 29, 1863, with rank from March 1, 1863, vice H. E. Jones promoted.

FUCHS, ANDREW.—Private, Co. A, Fifth Infantry; transferred to Co. E, this regiment, May 4, 1863; wounded in action, May 10, 1864, at Spottsylvania, Va.; mustered out, May 24, 1865, at Mower Hospital, Philadelphia, Pa.

GALOT, EDWARD.—Private, Fifth Infantry; transferred to Co. E, this regiment, May 4, 1863; captured, no date; absent, sick, since September, 1864; no further record; also borne as Gallott.

GARNEY, BERNARD.—Corporal, Co. C, Fifth Infantry; transferred to Co. A, this regiment, May 4, 1863; discharged, July 18, 1864, at Washington, D. C.

GEARY, LAWRENCE.—Private, Co. C, Fifth Infantry, transferred to Co. A, this regiment, May 4, 1863.

GEROW, THEODORE B.—Musician, Co. G, Fifth Infantry; transferred to Co. B, this regiment, May 4, 1863; discharged, December 14, 1864, near Petersburg, Va.

GILMORE, ARCHIBALD.—Private, Co. D, Fifth Infantry; transferred to Co. I, this regiment, May 4, 1863; mustered out, June 3, 1865, at camp near Alexandria, Va.

GISKING, WILLIAM.—Private, Co. B, Fifth Infantry; transferred to this regiment, unassigned, May 4, 1863; no further record.

GOBLE, ADOLPHUS.—Private, Co. C, Fifth Infantry; transferred to Co. A, this regiment, May 4, 1863.

GREEN, CHARLES.—Sergeant, Co. H, Fifth Infantry; transferred to Co. E, this regiment, May 4, 1863; promoted principal musician, April 21, 1864; discharged, July 17, 1864, near Petersburg, Va.; also borne as Charles C. Green.

GREEN, MORTIMORE.—Private, Co. A, Fifth Infantry; transferred to this regiment, unassigned, May 4, 1863; no further record.

GREGORY, GILBERT.—Private, Co. D, Fifth Infantry; transferred to Co. K, this regiment, May 4, 1863; mustered out, June 3, 1865, at camp near Alexandria, Va.

GRESHAM, GEORGE D.—Private, Co. A, Fifth Infantry; transferred to Co. E, this regiment, May 4, 1863; to Veteran Reserve Corps, February 6, 1864.

GRIFFIN, JEREMIAH.—Private, Co. D, Fifth Infantry; transferred to Co. K, this regiment, May 4, 1863; to Veteran Reserve Corps, September 1, 1863; mustered out therefrom as of Co. F, Twenty-fourth Regiment, June 28, 1865, at Washington, D. C.

GUTHRIE, JOHN A.—Private, Co. B, Fifth Infantry; transferred to Co. G, this regiment, May 4, 1863; absent, sick, in hospital since August 18, 1863; no further record.

HAGERTY, MARK.—Private, Co. G, Fifth Infantry; transferred to Co. G, this regiment, May 4, 1863; discharged, April 15, 1864, for promotion, organization not stated, at Warrenton Junction, Va.

HALEY, THOMAS.—Private, Co. F, Fifth Infantry; transferred

to Co. C, this regiment, May 4, 1863; captured in action, May 5, 1864, at the Wilderness, Va.; no further record.

HALL, WILLIAM H.—Private, Co. H, Fifth Infantry; transferred to Co. I, this regiment, May 4, 1863; captured in action, May 5, 1864, at the Wilderness, Va.; paroled, no date; discharged, March 25, 1865.

HALLETT, JR., GEORGE.—Private, Co. D, Fifth Infantry; transferred to Co. I, this regiment, May 4, 1863; mustered out, June 3, 1865, near Alexandria, Va.

HALSEY, WILLIAM.—Private, Co. F, Fifth Infantry; transferred to Co. C, this regiment, May 4, 1863; mustered out, June 3, 1865, near Alexandria, Va.

HARRINGTON, JOHN H. — Private, Co. H, Fifth Infantry; transferred to Co. I, this regiment, May 4, 1863; captured in action, May 5, 1864, at the Wilderness, Va.; paroled, no date; mustered out, June 3, 1865, near Alexandria, Va.

HART, SAMUEL.—Private, Co. C, Fifth Infantry; transferred to Co. B, this regiment, May 4, 1863; promoted corporal, October 1, 1863; captured in action, May 5, 1864, at the Wilderness, Va.; died of disease, September 10, 1864, at Andersonville, Ga.

HAUSMAN, NICHOLAS V.—Private, Co. F, Fifth Infantry; transferred to this regiment, unassigned, May 4, 1863; no further record.

HAYES, JOHN.—Private, unassigned, Fifth Infantry; transferred to Co. E, this regiment, May 4, 1863; captured, June 2, 1864, at Cold Harbor, Va.; released, April 21, 1865; mustered out, June 27, 1865, at New York City.

HAYWOOD, GEORGE W.—Private, Co. B, Fifth Infantry; transferred to Co. K, this regiment, May 4, 1863; transferred to Veteran Reserve Corps, no date; mustered out therefrom as of Third Company, Second Battalion, August 14, 1864, at Washington, D. C.

HENDERICK, CHARLES A.—Private, Co. I, Fifth Infantry; transferred to Co. E, this regiment, May 4, 1863.

HENDRICKS, ARTHUR.—Private, Co. G, Fifth Infantry; transferred to Co. G, this regiment, May 4, 1863, to Veteran Reserve Corps, September 30, 1863; mustered out therefrom as of Sixty-fifth Company, Second Battalion, July 22, 1865, at Washington, D. C.

HENDRICKSON, WILLIAM.—Private, Co. K, Fifth Infantry; transferred to Co. K, this regiment, May 4, 1863; mustered out, June 3, 1865, at camp near Alexandria, Va.

HERBST, JOHN G. L.—Private, Co. D, Fifth Infantry; transferred to Co. I, this regiment, May 4, 1863, to the Veteran Reserve Corps, February 23, 1864; mustered out therefrom as of One Hundred and Thirty-second Company, Second Battalion, August 7, 1865, at Frederick, Md.

HESS, JACOB.—Private, Co. I, Fifth Infantry; transferred to Co. A, this regiment, May 4, 1863; absent, sick, since June 4, 1863; no further record.

HEWLETT, HOSEA D.—Private, Co. C, Fifth Infantry; transferred to Co. B, this regiment, May 4, 1863; discharged, August 14, 1863, to accept promotion as second lieutenant of the Seventy-first Infantry, at Beverly Ford, Va.

HILTON, FREDERICK.—Private, Co. A, Fifth Infantry; transferred to this regiment, unassigned, May 4, 1863; no further record.

HINCHMAN, JOHN.—Private, Co. A, Fifth Infantry; transferred to Co. E, this regiment, May 4, 1863; promoted corporal, no date; discharged, July 19, 1864, at Petersburg, Va.

HINES, SHERWOOD C.—Private, Co. E, Fifth Infantry; transferred to Co. D, this regiment, May 4, 1863; reënlisted as a veteran, March 21, 1864; mustered out, July 21, 1865, at Washington, D. C.

HODGE, WILLIAM M.—Private, Co. A, Fifth Infantry; transferred to Co. E, this regiment, May 4, 1863; promoted corporal, no date; captured in action, May 5, 1864, at the Wilderness, Va.; paroled, no date; discharged, June 13, 1865.

HOEY, JAMES.—Private, Co. I, Fifth Infantry; transferred to this regiment, unassigned, May 4, 1863; no further record.

HOLLAND, EDWARD.—Musician, unassigned, Fifth Infantry; transferred to this regiment, unassigned, May 4, 1863; no further record.

HOPKINS, EGBERT D.—Commissary sergeant, Fifth Infantry; transferred as private, Co. G, this regiment, May 4, 1863; discharged, July 4, 1864, at Petersburg, Va.

HOPKINS, WILLIAM.—Private, Co. A, Fifth Infantry; transferred to Co. D, this regiment, May 4, 1863; promoted corporal, no date; reënlisted as a veteran, March 21, 1864; discharged August 11, 1864, for promotion to captain, Thirteenth U. S. Colored Heavy Artillery.

HORAN, JOHN.—Private, Co. E, Fifth Infantry; transferred to this regiment, unassigned, May 4, 1863; no further record.

HORGAN, JOHN.—Private, Co. K, Fifth Infantry; transferred to Co. K, this regiment, May 4, 1863.

HORN, MATHEW A.—Private, Co. E, Fifth Infantry; transferred to Co. A, this regiment, May 4, 1863; promoted sergeant-major, May 21, 1864; discharged, December 18, 1864, near Petersburg, Va.

HORTON, WILLIAM H.—Private, Co. E, Fifth Infantry; transferred to this regiment, unassigned, May 4, 1863; to Sixth Regiment, Veteran Reserve Corps, no date; mustered out, July 5, 1865, at Cincinnati, Ohio.

HOWE, CHARLES A.—Private, Co. C, Fifth Infantry; transferred to Co. E, this regiment, May 4, 1863; discharged, December 17, 1864, near Petersburg, Va.

HULSE, CHAUNCEY W.—Private, Co. I, Fifth Infantry; transferred to Co. A, this regiment, May 4, 1863.

HYDE, FREDERICK C.—Private, Co. F, Fifth Infantry; transferred to Co. C, this regiment, May 4, 1863.

HYDE, JR., JAMES K.—Private, Co. A, Fifth Infantry; transferred to Co. E, this regiment, May 4, 1863; mustered out, July 3, 1865, near Alexandria, Va.

INNIS, ALEXANDER.—Private, Co. G, Fifth Infantry; transferred to Co. E, this regiment, May 4, 1863.

JENKS, NATHANIEL F.—Musician, Co. E, Fifth Infantry; transferred to Co. H, this regiment, May 4, 1863.

JOHNSON, CHARLES G.—Private, Co. H, Fifth Infantry: transferred to Co. G, this regiment, May 4, 1863; discharged, July 5, 1864, at Petersburg, Va.

JOHNSON, JESSE C.—Private, Co. F, Fifth Infantry; transferred to Co. C, this regiment, May 4, 1863; to Co. A, May 24, 1863; captured in action, May 5, 1864, at the Wilderness, Va; died of diarrhea, January 28, 1865, at Salisbury, N. C.

JOHNSON, JR., JESSE.—Private, Co. F, Fifth Infantry; transferred to Co. A, this regiment, May 4, 1863; wounded and captured in action, May 5, 1864, at the Wilderness, Va.; died of his wounds, January 28, 1865, at Andersonville, Ga.

JONES, CHARLES T.—Corporal, Co. I, Fifth Infantry; transferred to Co. A, this regiment, May 4, 1863; promoted sergeant, no date; captured in action, May 5, 1864, at the Wilderness, Va.; paroled, no date; mustered in as second lieutenant, to date May 19, 1864; discharged, February 6, 1865.

Commissioned second lieutenant, May 18, 1864, with rank from May 10, 1864, vice C. P. Buckingham promoted.

KANE, JOHN.—Private, Co. C, Fifth Infantry; transferred to this regiment, unassigned, May 4, 1863; no further record.

KEEFE, MICHAEL F.—Private, Co. K, Fifth Infantry; transferred to Co. K, this regiment, May 4, 1863; promoted corporal, no date; discharged for disability, June 25, 1865.

KELLINGER, THOMAS.—Private, Fifth Infantry; transferred to Co. F, this regiment, May 4, 1863.

KENNEDY, JAMES.—Private, Co. C, Fifth Infantry; transferred to Co. B, this regiment, May 4, 1863; captured in action, August 18, 1864, at Weldon Railroad, Va.; released, May 15, 1865; promoted corporal, May 21, 1865; mustered out, June 3, 1865, near Alexandria, Va.

KENNEY, JOHN.—Private, Co. B, Fifth Infantry; transferred to Co. E, this regiment, May 4, 1863.

KEOGH, HENRY W.—Private, Co. D, Fifth Infantry: transferred to Co. K, this regiment, May 4, 1863; mustered out, June 3, 1865, at camp near Alexandria, Va.

KERR, JOHN.—Private, Co. A, Fifth Infantry; transferred to this regiment, unassigned, May 4, 1863; no further record.

KINGSBURY, WILLIAM J.—Private, Co. I, Fifth Infantry; transferred to this regiment, unassigned, May 4, 1863; no further record.

KIRCHNER, PHILIP.—Private, Co. E, Fifth Infantry; transferred to Co. D, this regiment, May 4, 1863; captured, no date; died of disease, October 25, 1864, at Milan, Ga.

KIRRIGAN, MICHAEL.—Private, Fifth Infantry; transferred to Co. D, this regiment, May 4, 1863; absent, wounded, since May 5, 1864; no further record.

KNIFFEN, WILLIAM H.—Private, Co. H, Fifth Infantry; transferred to Co. H, this regiment, May 4, 1863; wounded in action, May 5, 1864, at the Wilderness, Va.; died of his wounds, July 17, 1864, at hospital.

KNOWLES, ROBERT J.—Private, Co. A, Fifth Infantry; transferred to Co. E, this regiment, May 4, 1863; mustered out, June 3, 1865, near Alexandria, Va.

KREIG, MICHAEL.—Corporal, Co. D, Fifth Infantry; transferred to Co. H, this regiment, May 4, 1863; discharged, July 19, 1864, at Petersburg, Va.

KRETZLER, HENRY B.—Corporal, Co. C, Fifth Infantry; transferred to Co. A, this regiment, May 4, 1863; promoted quartermaster sergeant, no date.

LABAUGH, JOHN E.—Private, Co. C, Fifth Infantry; transferred to Co. E, this regiment, May 4, 1863; discharged for disability, September 3, 1863; also borne as John S. La Bough.

LANE, CORNELIUS.—Private, Co. A, Fifth Infantry; transferred to Co. E, this regiment, May 4, 1863; captured in action, May 5, 1864, at the Wilderness, Va.; died of disease, December 3, 1864, at Andersonville, Ga.

LANGWORTH, JOHN N.—Private, Co. A, Fifth Infantry; transferred to Co. E, this regiment, May 4, 1863; killed in action, May 5, 1864, at the Wilderness, Va.

LATHROP, ALONZO.—Private, Co. I, Fifth Infantry; transferred to Co. A, this regiment, May 4, 1863; promoted corporal, no date; captured in action, August 19, 1864, at Weldon Railroad, Va.; paroled, no date; mustered out, July 11, 1865, at hospital, at York, Pa.

LAUGHLIN, JOHN C.—Private, Co. K, Fifth Infantry; transferred to Co. K, this regiment, May 4, 1863.

LEACH, WILLIAM C.—Private, Co. E, Fifth Infantry; transferred to Co. D, this regiment, May 4, 1863; discharged, July 2, 1864, at Petersburg, Va.

LEAHY, JOSEPH.—Private, Co. E, Fifth Infantry; transferred to Co. D, this regiment, May 4, 1863; discharged, July 23, 1864, at Petersburg, Va.

LEWIS, FREDERICK.—Private, Co. B, Fifth Infantry; transferred to this regiment, unassigned, May 4, 1863; no further record.

LIKE, WILLIAM H.—Private, Co. C, Fifth Infantry; transferred to Co. A, this regiment, May 4, 1863.

LING, GEORGE W.—Musician, Co. A, Fifth Infantry; transferred to Co. K, this regiment, May 4, 1863; discharged, July 12, 1864, at Petersburg, Va.

LITTLE, ROBERT.—Private, Co. K, Fifth Infantry; transferred to Co. K, this regiment, May 4, 1863; captured in action, June 2, 1864, at Cold Harbor, Va.; paroled, no date; mustered out, June 3, 1865, at camp near Alexandria, Va.

LUCKERT, JOHN.—Private, Co. K, Fifth Infantry; transferred to Co. K, this regiment, May 4, 1863; reënlisted as a veteran, February 15, 1864; absent, sick, since October 27, 1864, and at muster-out of company.

LUDLOW, SAMUEL H.—Private, Co. D, Fifth Infantry; transferred to Co. I, this regiment, May 4, 1863; captured in action, May 5, 1864, at the Wilderness, Va.; paroled, no date; mustered out, June 3, 1865, from camp near Alexandria, Va.

LUTZ, FRANCIS.—Private, Co. B, Fifth Infantry; transferred to Co. B, this regiment, May 4, 1863; absent, sick, since June 4, 1863, and at muster-out of company.

LUVOILETTE, THOMAS L.—Private, Co. C, Fifth Infantry; transferred to Co. A, this regiment, May 4, 1863.

LUYSTER, WILLIAM.—Private, Co. B, Fifth Infantry; transferred to Co. B, this regiment, May 4, 1863; promoted corporal, April 1, 1864; sergeant, July 1, 1864; first sergeant, September 1, 1864; mustered out with company, July 16, 1865, near Washington, D. C.

Commissioned, not mustered, second lieutenant, June 17, 1865, with rank from February 1, 1865, vice E. O. Jones promoted.

LYNCH, JAMES.—Private, Co. B, Fifth Infantry; transferred to Co. K, this regiment, May 4, 1863; promoted corporal, no date; wounded, June 10, 1864, at Cold Harbor, Va.; died of his wounds, July 1, 1864, in hospital.

MACE, ALONZO.—Private, Co. I, Fifth Infantry; transferred to this regiment, unassigned, May 4, 1863; no further record.

MAGNER, ROBERT.—Private, Co. H, Fifth Infantry; transferred

to this regiment, unassigned, May 4, 1863; no record subsequent to November 4, 1863.

MARGRAF, PHILIP.—Private, Co. F, Fifth Infantry; transferred to this regiment, unassigned, May 4, 1863; mustered out, July 1, 1865, at Fort Delaware, Del.

McCARTHY, EUGENE.—Corporal, Co. B, Fifth Infantry; transferred to Co. B, this regiment, May 4, 1863; promoted first sergeant, no date; captured in action, May 5, 1864, at the Wilderness, Va.; paroled, no date; returned to sergeant, September 1, 1864; mustered out, May 30, 1865, at New York City.

McCARTHY, DANIEL.—Private, Co. G, Fifth Infantry; transferred to Co. H, this regiment, May 4, 1863; mustered out, June 3, 1865, at camp near Alexandria, Va.

McCLOSKEY, JAMES.—Private, Co. F, Fifth Infantry; transferred to Co. C, this regiment, May 4, 1863; discharged, October 31, 1864, at Weldon Railroad, Va.

McCORMICK, ROBERT.—Private, Co. C, Fifth Infantry; transferred to Co. B, this regiment, May 4, 1863; captured in action, May 5, 1864, at the Wilderness, Va.; paroled, no date; mustered out, June 3, 1865, near Alexandria, Va.

McDONOUGH, WILLIAM.—Private, Co. K, Fifth Infantry; transferred to Co. K, this regiment, May 4, 1863.

McELROY, WILLIAM.—Private, Co. H, Fifth Infantry; transferred to Co. I, this regiment, May 4, 1863.

McEWEN, JAMES.—Private, Co. H, Fifth Infantry; transferred to Co. I, this regiment, May 4, 1863.

McGEEHAN, JOHN.—Private, Co. B, Fifth Infantry; transferred to Co. C, this regiment, May 4, 1863; mustered in as second lieutenant, Co. F, August 17, 1863; captured in action, May 5, 1864, at the Wilderness, Va.; paroled, no date; transferred to Co. C, April 28, 1865; mustered in as first lieutenant, to date December 30, 1864; mustered out with company, July 16, 1865, near Washington, D. C.

Commissioned second lieutenant, June 29, 1863, with rank from same date; first lieutenant, December 30, 1864, with rank from December 1, 1864, vice E. Comstock resigned; brevet captain by U. S. Government, from March 13, 1865.

McGLOGHLIN, JOHN.—Private, Co. A, Fifth Infantry; transferred to Co. E, this regiment, May 4, 1863; captured and paroled, no dates; promoted corporal, April 1, 1865; mustered out, June 3, 1865, near Alexandria, Va.

McGRATH, CHARLES F.—Private, Co. E, Fifth Infantry; transferred to Co. E, this regiment, May 4, 1863; mustered out, June 3, 1865, near Alexandria, Va.

McGUIRE, JOHN.—Private, Co. E, Fifth Infantry; transferred to this regiment, unassigned, May 4, 1863; no further record.

McKEEVER, WASHINGTON.—Musician, Co. D, Fifth Infantry; transferred to Co. K, this regiment, May 4, 1863; promoted principal musician, October 9, 1864; re-transferred to Co. K, as musician, April 21, 1864.

McLANE, CHARLES.—Musician, Co. H, Fifth Infantry; transferred to Co. A, this regiment, May 4, 1863; also borne as McLean.

McLEAN, WILLIAM.—Private, unassigned, Fifth Infantry; transferred to Co. A, this regiment, May 4, 1863.

McNEIL, JOSEPH.—Private, Co. K, Fifth Infantry; transferred to Co. G, this regiment, May 4, 1863; mustered out, June 3, 1865, near Alexandria, Va.

McREA, FRANK.—Private, Co. F, Fifth Infantry; transferred to Co. C, this regiment, May 4, 1863; no record subsequent to June, 1863.

MEAGHER, PATRICK.—Private, Co. C, Fifth Infantry; transferred to Co. B, this regiment, May 4, 1863.

MERRITT, CHARLES F.—Private, Co. K, Fifth Infantry; transferred to Co. K, this regiment, May 4, 1863; mustered out, May 13, 1865, at Baltimore, Md.

MILLARD, LENOX.—Private, Co. G, Fifth Infantry; transferred to Co. H, this regiment, May 4, 1863; captured in action, May 5, 1864, at the Wilderness, Va.; no further record.

MILLER, FREDERICK.—Private, Co. E, Fifth Infantry; transferred to Co. D, this regiment, May 4, 1863; wounded in action, July 3, 1863, and died of his wounds, October 30, 1863, at Gettysburg, Pa.

MONROE, RICHARD.—First sergeant, Co. I, Fifth Infantry; transferred to Co. A, this regiment, May 4, 1863; returned to ranks, no date; discharged, August 12, 1864, at Washington, D. C.

MOONEY, DANIEL H.—Private, Co. H, Fifth Infantry; transferred to this regiment, unassigned, May 4, 1863; no further record.

MOREY, DAVID E. S.—Private, Co. B, Fifth Infantry; transferred to Co. F, this regiment, May 4, 1863; absent, sick, since July 6, 1863, and at muster-out of company.

MUCKRIDGE, AARON P.—Private, Co. A, Fifth Infantry; transferred to Co. E, this regiment, May 4, 1863; promoted corporal, no date; wounded in action, May 10, 1864, at Laurel Hill, Va.; died of his wounds, May 12, 1864.

MULCAHY, BARTHOLOMEW.—Private, Co. H, Fifth Infantry; transferred to this regiment, unassigned, May 4, 1863; no further record.

MULLIN, CHRISTOPHER F.—Private, Co. D, Fifth Infantry; transferred to Co. I, this regiment, May 4, 1863.

MURPHY, THOMAS J.—Private, Co. B, Fifth Infantry; transferred to Co. G, this regiment, May 4, 1863; promoted first sergeant, no date; mustered out, June 3, 1865, at camp near Alexandria, Va. Awarded medal of honor for capture of flag at Five Forks, April 1, 1865.

MURRAY, JOHN.—Private, Co. C, Fifth Infantry; transferred to Co. H, this regiment, May 4, 1863; appointed musician, no date; discharged, February 14, 1865, in the field.

MYERS, ALFRED J.—Private, Co. H, Fifth Infantry; transferred to Co. H, this regiment, May 4, 1863.

MYERS, GEORGE H.—Private, Co. G, Fifth Infantry; transferred to Co. H, this regiment, May 4, 1863; discharged for disability, June 29, 1863, at hospital, Washington, D. C.

MYERS, JOSEPH D.—Private, Co. A, Fifth Infantry; transferred to this regiment, unassigned, May 4, 1863; no further record.

NEIBUHR, George A.—Private, Co. A, Fifth Infantry; transferred to Co. E, this regiment, May 4, 1863; promoted corporal, no date.

NEUBER, CHRISTIAN.—Private, Co. F, Fifth Infantry; transferred to Co. C, this regiment, May 4, 1863; discharged, October 31, 1864, at Weldon Railroad, Va.

NEWCOMB, DAVID T.—Private, Co. C, Fifth Infantry; transferred to Co. A, this regiment, May 4, 1863; wounded and captured in action, May 5, 1864, at the Wilderness, Va.;

30

died of his wounds, August 18, 1864, at Andersonville, Ga.

NEWMAN, JOHN E.—Private, Co. D, Fifth Infantry; transferred to Co. A, this regiment, May 4, 1863; promoted corporal, no date; discharged, July 18, 1864, near Petersburg, Va.

O'CONNOR, MATHEW.—Private, Co. C, Fifth Infantry; transferred to Co. A, this regiment, May 4, 1863; promoted corporal and returned to ranks, captured and paroled, no dates; mustered out, June 3, 1865, near Alexandria, Va.

O'CONNOR, WILLIAM.—Private, Co. D, Fifth Infantry; transferred to this regiment, unassigned, May 4, 1863; no further record.

ODLUM, THOMAS J.—Private, Co. I, Fifth Infantry; transferred to Co. A, this regiment, May 4, 1863; captured in action, May 5, 1864, at the Wilderness, Va.; released, April 6, 1865, at Big Black River, Mississippi; mustered out, June 26, 1865, at Annapolis, Md.

OTT, ADAM F.—Private, Co. D, Fifth Infantry; transferred to Co. I, this regiment, May 4, 1863; absent, sick, since June 4, 1863, and at muster-out of company.

PABOR, MARTIN B.—Private, Co. D, Fifth Infantry; transferred to this regiment, unassigned, May 4, 1863; no further record.

PAGE, TRUXTON.—Private, Co. C, Fifth Infantry; transferred to Co. A, this regiment, May 4, 1863; mustered out, June 3, 1865, near Alexandria, Va.

PECK, EDWARD L.—Private, Co. A, Fifth Infantry; transferred to Co. E, this regiment, May 4, 1863; discharged for disability, April 13, 1864, at New York City.

PENDERGAST, JOHN.—Private, Co. H, Fifth Infantry; transferred to Co. H, this regiment, May 4, 1863; absent, sick, in hospital, since June 2, 1863, and at muster-out of company.

PETTIT, ALONZO.—Private, Co. K, Fifth Infantry; transferred to Co. D, this regiment, May 4, 1863; discharged, December 17, 1864, near Petersburg, Va.

PLATT, WILLIAM H.—Private, Co. H, Fifth Infantry; transferred to Co. I, this regiment, May 4, 1863; captured and paroled, no dates; mustered out, June 3, 1865, at camp near Alexandria, Va.

PLEITCH, PETER.—Private, Co. F, Fifth Infantry; transferred

to Co. C, this regiment, May 4, 1863; captured in action, May 5, 1864, at the Wilderness, Va.; paroled, no date; mustered out, June 3, 1865, near Alexandria, Va., as Pletesh.

POLEX, LOUIS.—Private, Co. D, Fifth Infantry; transferrd to Co. K, this regiment, May 4, 1863; killed in action, June 18, 1864, at Petersburg, Va.

POLLOCK, ROBERT A.—Private, Co. F, Fifth Infantry; transferred to Co. C, this regiment, May 4, 1863; mustered out, May 23, 1865, at Mower Hospital, Philadelphia, Pa.

POTTER, THADDUS.—Private, Co. C, Fifth Infantry; transferred to Co. B, this regiment, May 4, 1863; died of disease, December 23, 1863, in hospital at Washington, D. C.

POWELL, ALONZO.—Private, Co. C, Fifth Infantry; transferred to Co. B, this regiment, May 4, 1863; discharged, July 14, 1864, near Petersburg, Va.

PRICE, FREDERICK A.—Private, Co. B, Fifth Infantry; transferred to Co. F, this regiment, May 4, 1863; died, November 13, 1864, in hospital, at Washington, D. C.

PRIMROSE, JAMES M.—Private, Co. K, Fifth Infantry; transferred to Co. C, this regiment, May 4, 1863; wounded in action, May 5, 1864, at the Wilderness, Va.; absent since, and at muster-out of company.

PURDY, JAMES L.—Private, Co. I, Fifth Infantry; transferred to Co. K, this regiment, May 4, 1863; also borne as Purdee.

QUINN, CHARLES E.—Private, Co. B, Fifth Infantry; transferred to Co. G, this regiment, May 4, 1863; mustered out, June 3, 1865, at camp near Alexandria, Va.

QUINN, JOHN.—Private, Co. K, Fifth Infantry; transferred to this regiment, unassigned, May 4, 1863; no further record.

REARDON, JEREMIAH.—Private, Co. K, Fifth Infantry; transferred to Co. K, this regiment, May 4, 1863; captured in action, May 5, 1864, at the Wilderness, Va.; paroled, no date; mustered out, June 3, 1865, at camp near Alexandria, Va.

REDDY, JOHN.—Private, Co. G, Fifth Infantry; transferred to Co. H, this regiment, May 4, 1863; to Co. E, October 1, 1863; captured and paroled, no date; mustered out, June 3, 1865, near Alexandria, Va., as Ready.

REED, JAMES W.—Private, Co. F, Fifth Infantry; transferred

to Co. C, this regiment, May 4, 1863; mustered out, June 3, 1865, near Alexandria, Va.

REYNOLDS, BENJAMIN.—Private, Co. B, Fifth Infantry; transferred to Co. G, this regiment, May 4, 1863; mustered out, June 5, 1865, at Elmira, N. Y., as Benjamin F. Reynolds.

RILEY, HENRY H.—Private, Co. E, Fifth Infantry; transferred to Co. D, this regiment, May 4, 1863.

RILEY, JOHN.—Corporal, Co. C, Fifth Infantry; transferred to Co. A, this regiment, May 4, 1863; returned to ranks, no date.

RISHTON, THOMAS.—Private, Co. E, Fifth Infantry; transferred to Co. A, this regiment, May 4, 1863; transferred to Veteran Reserve Corps, May 1, 1865; mustered out therefrom, November 1, 1865, as of One Hundred and Twelfth Company, Second Battalion, at Washington, D. C.

ROBERTS, WILLIAM S.—Private, Co. D, Fifth Infantry; transferred to Co. K, this regiment, May 4, 1863; transferred to Veteran Reserve Corps, May 13, 1864; mustered out therefrom, June 27, 1865, as of One Hundred and Sixty-sixth Company, Second Battalion, at Point Lookout, Md.

ROBERTSON, JAMES C.—Private, Co. B, Fifth Infantry; transferred to Co. G, this regiment, May 4, 1863; absent, sick, in hospital, since July 3, 1863, and at muster-out of company.

ROBINSON, THOMAS.—Private, Co. H, Fifth Infantry; transferred to Co. I, this regiment, May 4, 1863; discharged, May 11, 1863.

ROCK, PATRICK H.—Private, Co. C, Fifth Infantry; transferred to Co. A, this regiment, May 4, 1863.

ROCKWELL, JAMES.—Musician, Co. I, Fifth Infantry; transferred to Co. A, this regiment, May 4, 1863; discharged for disability, May 18, 1863, at camp, Potomac Creek, Va.

RODMAN, JAMES.—Private, Co. G, Fifth Infantry; transferred to Co. H, this regiment, May 4, 1863; captured in action, May 5, 1864, at the Wilderness, Va.; died, no date, at Millen, Ga.; grave No. 147.

RODMAN, WILLIAM.—Corporal, Co. K, Fifth Infantry; transferred to Co. K, this regiment, May 4, 1863; reënlisted as a veteran, February 15, 1864; promoted sergeant and returned to ranks, no dates; mustered out with company, July 16, 1865, near Washington, D. C.

ROGERS, EDWARD A.—Private, Co. C, Fifth Infantry; transferred to Co. B, this regiment, May 4, 1863.

ROGERS, OLIVER.—Private, Co. B, Fifth Infantry; transferred to this regiment, unassigned, May 4, 1863; no further record.

ROGERS, WILLIAM H.—Corporal, Co. I, Fifth Infantry; transferred to Co. A, this regiment, May 4, 1863; captured and paroled, no dates; discharged, January 18, 1865, from hospital.

ROGGENSTEIN, WILLIAM.—Private, Co. H, Fifth Infantry; transferred to this regiment, unassigned, May 4, 1863; promoted sergeant, no date; transferred to Veteran Reserve Corps, March 23, 1864; mustered out therefrom as of Twenty-second Company, Second Battalion, July 27, 1865, at Washington, D. C.

ROSS, ALBERT.—Private, Co. A, Fifth Infantry; transferred to Co. K, this regiment, May 4, 1863; mustered out, June 3, 1865, at camp near Alexandria, Va.

ROSS, SAMUEL C.—Musician, Co. H, Fifth Infantry; transferred to Co. E, this regiment, May 4, 1863; absent without leave since May 28, 1863, and at muster-out of company.

ROSSMAN, AUGUSTUS.—Private, Co. K, Fifth Infantry; transferred to this regiment, unassigned, May 4, 1863; no further record.

RUDMAN, JOHN.—Private, Co. E, Fifth Infantry; transferred to Co. D, this regiment, May 4, 1863; mustered out, June 5, 1865, at Elmira, N. Y.

RYAN, JOHN.—Private, Co. D, Fifth Infantry; transferred to Co. K, this regiment, May 4, 1863.

SAPHER, WILLIAM.—Private, Co. B, Fifth Infantry; transferred to Co. F, this regiment, May 4, 1863; promoted corporal and returned to ranks, no dates; discharged, October 13, 1864, at Weldon Railroad, Va.; also borne as Sepher.

SAVOIE, CHARLES H.—Private, Co. D, Fifth Infantry; transferred to Co. I, this regiment, May 4, 1863, and to Veteran Reserve Corps, June 15, 1865; mustered out therefrom as of Seventh Company, Second Battalion, June 29, 1865, at Washington, D. C.; also borne as Savoye.

SCHAPPERT, JACOB.—Private, Co. K, Fifth Infantry; transferred to Co. A, this regiment, May 4, 1863.

SCHILLING, SAMUEL.—Private, Co. F, Fifth Infantry; transferred to Co. C, this regiment, May 4, 1863; killed in action, May 5, 1864, at the Wilderness, Va.

SCOTT, WILLIAM J.—Private, Co. E, Fifth Infantry; transferred to Co. D, this regiment, May 4, 1863; captured and paroled, no dates; mustered out, June 3, 1865, at camp near Alexandria, Va.

SCOUTTEN, ISAAC.—Private, Co. C, Fifth Infantry; transferred to Co. K, this regiment, May 4, 1863; discharged for disability, March 29, 1865, at hospital, Washington, D. C.

SEAMAN, RICHARD E.—Corporal, Co. D, Fifth Infantry; transferred to Co. I, this regiment, May 4, 1863; captured in action, May 5, 1864, at the Wilderness, Va.; paroled and returned to ranks, no dates; mustered out, June 3, 1865, at camp near Alexandria, Va.

SEAMAN, WILLIAM A. C.—Private, Co. D, Fifth Infantry; transferred to this regiment, unassigned, May 4, 1863; no further record.

SELKIRK, ROBERT.—Private, Co. E, Fifth Infantry; transferred to Co. D, this regiment, May 4, 1863; reënlisted as a veteran, March 21, 1864; mustered out, July 26, 1865, at Syracuse, N. Y.

SIMON, HENRY.—Private, Co. I, Fifth Infantry; transferred to Co. E, this regiment, May 4, 1863, and to Co. B, June 27, 1863; captured in action, May 5, 1864, at the Wilderness, Va.; died of chronic diarrhea, November 10, 1864, at Andersonville, Ga.

SINGER, JOHN A.—Private, Co. B, Fifth Infantry; transferred to Co. D, this regiment, May 4, 1863; to Veteran Reserve Corps, September 3, 1863.

SMITH, HENRY.—Private, Co. A, Fifth Infantry; transferred to Co. E, this regiment, May 4, 1863; discharged, July 12, 1864.

SMITH, ROBERT C.—Private, Co. K, Fifth Infantry; transferred to Co. K, this regiment, May 4, 1863.

SNYDER, JACOB.—Private, Co. D, Fifth Infantry; transferred to this regiment, unassigned, May 4, 1863; no further record.

SOUTHERN, ABRAHAM.—Private, Co. K, Fifth Infantry; transferred to Co. K, this regiment, May 4, 1863; captured in action, May 5, 1864, at the Wilderness, Va.; paroled, no date; mustered out, June 3, 1865, at camp near Alexandria, Va.

SPADONE, JULIUS H.—Private, Co. B, Fifth Infantry; transferred to Co. G, this regiment, May 4, 1863; promoted sergeant, no date; mustered out, June 3, 1865, at camp near Alexandria, Va.

STAPLETON, WILLIAM A.—Corporal, Co. F, Fifth Infantry; transferred to Co. C, this regiment, May 4, 1863; returned to ranks, no date.

STEARNS, WILLIAM R.—Corporal, Co. K, Fifth Infantry; transferred to Co. K, this regiment, May 4, 1863; mustered out, May 24, 1865, at Ladies' Home Hospital, New York City.

STODDARD, WILLIAM W.—Private, Co. D, Fifth Infantry; transferred to Co. I, this regiment, May 4, 1863; transferred to Veteran Reserve Corps, February 16, 1865.

SULLIVAN, MAURICE F.—Musician, Co. I, Fifth Infantry; transferred to Co. C, this regiment, May 4, 1863; Co. E, May 25, 1863; captured, paroled, and returned to ranks, no dates; discharged, November 1, 1864.

SWIFT, CHARLES N.—Private, Co. F, Fifth Infantry; transferred to Co. A, this regiment, May 4, 1863; to Co. C, May 17, 1863; discharged, March 1, 1864, to accept commission as captain in Thirtieth Infantry, U. S. Colored Troops.

SWIFT, JOHN.—Private, Co. F, Fifth Infantry; transferred to Co. A, this regiment, May 4, 1863; died of disease, September 7, 1864, at City Point, Va.

SWIFT, THOMAS.—Private, Co. A, Fifth Infantry; transferred to Co. E, this regiment, May 4, 1863; promoted corporal, April 9, 1865; mustered out, June 3, 1865, at Alexandria, Va.

TAYLOR, HENRY G.—Corporal, Co. D, Fifth Infantry; transferred to Co. K, this regiment, May 4, 1863; promoted first sergeant, no date; mustered in as second lieutenant, Co. H, October 8, 1864; as first lieutenant, February 1, 1865; mustered out with company, July 16, 1865, near Washington, D. C.

Commissioned second lieutenant, November 30, 1864, with

rank from October 1, 1864, vice P. D. Froeligh killed in action; first lieutenant, March 30, 1865, with rank from February 1, 1865, vice H. Loomis promoted; brevet captain by U. S. Government from March 13, 1865.

THOMAS, JOHN.—Private, Co. D, Fifth Infantry; transferred to this regiment, unassigned, May 4, 1863; no further record.

THOMPSON, JOHN H.—Private, Co. H, Fifth Infantry; transferred to Co. I, this regiment, May 4, 1863; mustered out, June 3, 1865, near Alexandria, Va.

TIBBETTS, GUSTAVUS H.—Private, Co. G, Fifth Infantry; transferred to Co. F, this regiment, May 4, 1863; mustered out, June 3, 1865, near Alexandria, Va.

TILLMAN, RICHARD.—Private, Co. I, Fifth Infantry; transferred to Co. F, this regiment, May 4, 1863; mustered out, June 3, 1865, near Alexandria, Va.

TOELLNER, FERDINAND J.—Private, Co. D, Fifth Infantry; transferred to this regiment, unassigned, May 4, 1863; no further record.

TOMPKINS, EWIN C.—Private, Co. D, Fifth Infantry; transferred to Co. I, this regiment, May 4, 1863; mustered out, June 3, 1865, near Alexandria, Va.

TREGASKIS, JOHN.—Private, Co. K, Fifth Infantry; transferred to Co. K, this regiment, May 4, 1863; mustered out, June 27, 1865, at Baltimore, Md.

TUTTLE, DANIEL.—Private, Co. A, Fifth Infantry; transferred to this regiment, unassigned, May 4, 1863; no further record.

UNDERHILL, OLIVER S.—Private, Co. G, Fifth Infantry; transferred to Co. G, this regiment, May 4, 1863; to Veteran Reserve Corps, August 10, 1864; mustered out therefrom as of Co. B, Nineteenth Regiment, August 2, 1865, at Elmira, N. Y.

VAN BRAMER, PETER.—Private, Co. B, Fifth Infantry; transferred to Co. E, this regiment, May 4, 1863; captured and paroled, no date; mustered out, June 3, 1865, near Alexandria, Va.; also borne as Van Bromer.

VANDEROEF, ARNEST.—Private, Co. E, Fifth Infantry; transferred to Co. C, this regiment, May 4, 1863; promoted corporal, June 1, 1865; mustered out with company, July 16, 1865, near Washington, D. C.

VAN KUSKEY, CHARLES.—Private, Co. I, Fifth Infantry; transferred to Co. A, this regiment, May 4, 1863.

VAN VOOHIS, HENRY.—Private, Co. G, Fifth Infantry; transferred to Co. H, this regiment, May 4, 1863; captured in action, no date; died of disease, November 23, 1864, at Salisbury, N. C.

VELSOR, WILLIAM.—Private, Co. A, Fifth Infantry; transferred to Co. C, this regiment, May 4, 1863; promoted sergeant and returned to ranks, no date; captured in action, May 5, 1864, at the Wilderness, Va.; paroled, no date; transferred to Veteran Reserve Corps, November 9, 1864; mustered out therefrom as of Co. G, Twelfth Regiment, June 29, 1865, at Washington, D. C.

VITTALY, JOSEPH L.—Private, Co. K, Fifth Infantry; transferred to this regiment, unassigned, May 4, 1863.

VIZARD, WILLIAM.—Private, Co. I, Fifth Infantry; transferred to Co. A, this regiment, May 4, 1863; to Veteran Reserve Corps, no date; mustered out therefrom as of Seventy-fifth Company, Second Battalion, June 28, 1865, at Washington, D. C.

VREDENBURGH, WILLIAM H.—Private, Co. B, Fifth Infantry; transferred to Co. D, this regiment, May 4, 1863; appointed musician, no date; transferred to Co. I, August 19, 1863; discharged, July 20, 1864, at Petersburg, Va.

WALLER, WILLIAM E.—Private, Co. B, Fifth Infantry; transferred to this regiment, unassigned, May 4, 1863; no further record.

WALTERS, WILLIAM.—Private, Co. D, Fifth Infantry; transferred to Co. I, this regiment, May 4, 1863; mustered out, June 3, 1865, near Alexandria, Va.

WALTERS, WILLIAM H.—Private, Co. E, Fifth Infantry; transferred to Co. E, this regiment, May 4, 1863.

WANAMAKER, GILES S.—Private, Co. F, Fifth Infantry; transferred to Co. C, this regiment, May 4, 1863; also borne as Wannamaker.

WARD, JOHN.—Private, Co. K, Fifth Infantry; transferred to Co. E, this regiment, May 4, 1863.

WARD, PETER.—Private, Co. K, Fifth Infantry; transferred to Co. K, this regiment, May 4, 1863.

WARNER, HENRY W.—Private, Co. C, Fifth Infantry; transferred
to Co. A, this regiment, May 4, 1863; absent, sick, since June
4, 1864, and at muster-out of company.

WEBB, JAMES.—Private, Co. F, Fifth Infantry; transferred to
Co. C, this regiment, May 4, 1863; discharged, July 27, 1864,
near Petersburg, Va.

WEBB, THOMAS.—Private, Co. K, Fifth Infantry; transferred
to Co. K, this regiment, May 4, 1863; absent, sick, since
September 28, 1864, and at muster-out of company.

WELLS, CHARLES E.—Private, Co. D, Fifth Infantry; transferred
to Co. I, this regiment, May 4, 1863; mustered out, June
3, 1865, near Alexandria, Va.

WEST, JAMES T.—Private, Co. D, Fifth Infantry; transferred to
Co. I, this regiment, May 4, 1863; mustered out, May 18,
1865, at West Buildings Hospital, Baltimore, Md.

WESTERLEY, STEPHEN M.—Private, Co. F, Fifth Infantry; transferred to Co. C, this regiment, May 4, 1863.

WHITING, CHARLES J.—Private, Co. C, Fifth Infantry; transferred to Co. F, this regiment, May 4, 1863; absent, sick,
at Washington, D. C., since August 31, 1863, and at
muster-out of company.

WILKINS, STEPHEN H.—Private, Co. B, Fifth Infantry; transferred to Co. I, this regiment, May 4, 1863; mustered out,
June 3, 1865, at camp near Alexandria, Va.; prior service,
in Co. G, Fifty-third Infantry.

WILLIAMS, GEORGE F.—Corporal, Co. B, Fifth Infantry; transferred to Co. G, this regiment, May 4, 1863; to Co. B, June
25, 1863; promoted sergeant, no date; principal musician,
January 15, 1864; wounded and captured in action, May 5,
1864, at the Wilderness, Va.; discharged, August 3, 1864,
near Petersburg, Va.

WILLIAMS, THOMAS.—Drummer, Co. G, Fifth Infantry; transferred to Co. B, this regiment, May 4, 1863; discharged on
expiration of term of service.

WILLIAMS, WILLIAM.—Private, Co. D, Fifth Infantry; transferred to Co. I, this regiment, May 4, 1863; promoted corporal, no date; captured in action, May 5, 1864, at the
Wilderness, Va.; paroled, no date; mustered out, June 3,
1865, at camp near Alexandria, Va.

WILSON, GEORGE F.—Private, Co. G, Fifth Infantry; transferred to Co. G, this regiment, May 4, 1863; to Veteran Reserve Corps, October 4, 1864.

WILSON, WILLIAM J.—Private, Co. G, Fifth Infantry; transferred to this regiment, unassigned, May 4, 1863; to Veteran Reserve Corps, April 1, 1865; mustered out therefrom as of Co. I, Fourteenth Regiment, August 1, 1865, at Washington, D. C.

WING, GEORGE T.—Private, Co. C, Fifth Infantry; transferred to Co. B, this regiment, May 4, 1863; promoted corporal, June 12, 1863; killed in action, May 5, 1864, at the Wilderness, Va.

WINMER, MICHAEL.—Private, Co. F, Fifth Infantry; transferred to Co. I, this regiment, May 4, 1863; discharged, October 28, 1864, at the Weldon Railroad, Va.

WINSLOW, GORDON.—Private, Co. E, Fifth Infantry; transferred to this regiment, unassigned, May 4, 1863; no further record.

WISE, HENRY.—Private, Co. K, Fifth Infantry; transferred to Co. K, this regiment, May 4, 1863; promoted corporal, no date; mustered out, June 3, 1865, at camp near Alexandria, Va.

WOOD, GEORGE P.—Private, Co. B, Fifth Infantry; transferred to Co. F, this regiment, May 4, 1863.

WOOD, ISAAC H.—Private, Co. H, Fifth Infantry; transferred to Co. F, this regiment, May 4, 1863; to Veteran Reserve Corps, February 23, 1864.

WOOD, ROBERT L.—Corporal, Co. B, Fifth Infantry; transferred to Co. G, this regiment, May 4, 1863; to Veteran Reserve Corps, no date; mustered out therefrom as of Co. C, Sixteenth Regiment, July 28, 1863, at Harrisburg, Pa.

YEOMANS, GEORGE H.—Private, Co. C, Fifth Infantry; transferred to Co. F, this regiment, May 4, 1863; to Veteran Reserve Corps, March 26, 1864; promoted corporal, no date; mustered out as of One Hundred and Thirty-first Company, Second Battalion, Veteran Reserve Corps, at Washington, D. C.

YOUNG, HERMAN H.—Private, Co. H, Fifth Infantry; transferred to Co. I, this regiment, May 4, 1863; promoted corporal, no date; mustered out, June 3, 1865, at camp near Alexandria, Va.

YOUNG, WASHINGTON.—Private, Co. I, Fifth Infantry; transferred to Co. A, this regiment, May 4, 1863.

ZIMMERMAN, JOHN.—Private, Co. A, Fifth Infantry; transferred to Co. H, this regiment, May 4, 1863; mustered out, June 3, 1865, at camp near Alexandria, Va.

ZITTLE, JOHN.—Private, Co. I, Fifth Infantry; transferred to Co. A, this regiment, May 4, 1863.

FORTY-FOURTH NEW YORK INFANTRY

ANGERBINE, JAMES P.—Private, Co. B, Forty-fourth Infantry; transferred to Co. B, this regiment, October 11, 1864; mustered out, June 3, 1865, near Alexandria, Va., as James F. Angervine.

ASELTINE, THOMAS.—Private, Co. B, Forty-fourth Infantry; transferred to Co. D, this regiment, October 11, 1864; mustered out with company, July 16, 1865, near Washington, D. C.

BACKMAN, BARNEY.—Private, Co. B, Forty-fourth Infantry; transferred to Co. E, this regiment, October 11, 1864; mustered out, June 3, 1865, near Alexandria, Va.; also borne as Beekman.

BAKER, ANTHONY.—Private, Co. A, Forty-fourth Infantry; transferred to Co. E, this regiment, October 11, 1864; promoted corporal, returned to ranks and transferred to Veteran Reserve Corps, no dates; discharged for disability therefrom as of One Hundred and Fourth Co., Second Battalion, July 13, 1865, at Alexandria, Va.; also borne as Anthony J. Baker.

BALLARD, HENRY B.—Private, Co. B, Forty-fourth Infantry; transferred to Co. B, this regiment, October 11, 1864; mustered out, June 3, 1865, near Alexandria, Va.

BANCROFT, JOEL B.—Private, Co. A, Forty-fourth Infantry; transferred to Co. G, this regiment, October 11, 1864; mustered out with company, July 16, 1865, near Washington, D. C.

BANNER, DANIEL.—Private, Co. B, Forty-fourth Infantry;

transferred to Co. D, this regiment, October 11, 1864; mustered out with company, July 16, 1865, near Washington, D. C.

BARBEE, JOHN.—Private, Co. A, Forty-fourth Infantry; transferred to Co. E, this regiment, October 11, 1864.

BEMISTER, ALFRED.—Private, Co. A, Forty-fourth Infantry; transferred to Co. H, this regiment, October 11, 1864; discharged, October 23, 1864, at Petersburg, Va.

BENDON, JAMES.—Private, Co. B, Forty-fourth Infantry; transferred to Co. D, this regiment, October 11, 1864; wounded in action, April 1, 1865, at Five Forks, Va.; died of his wounds, April 6, 1865, at City Point, Va.

BENNETT, EDWARD.—First lieutenant, Co. A, Forty-fourth Infantry; transferred to Co. D, this regiment, October 11, 1864; mustered out with company, July 16, 1865, near Washington, D. C.

BENNETT, EDWARD S.—Private, Co. A, Forty-fourth Infantry; transferred to Co. C, this regiment, October 11, 1864.

BERLEE, CHRISTIAN.—Private, Co. B, Forty-fourth Infantry; transferred to Co. E, this regiment, October 11, 1864; mustered out, June 3, 1865, near Alexandria as Burlee.

BLANCHARD, WILLIAM H.—Private, Co. A, Forty-fourth Infantry; transferred to Co. K, this regiment, October 11, 1864; mustered out, June 3, 1865, at camp, near Alexandria, Va.

BOGLE, CLAUSE.—Private, Co. A, Forty-fourth Infantry; transferred to this regiment, unassigned, October 11, 1864; no further record.

BOWER, JACOB.—Private, Co. B, Forty-fourth Infantry; transferred to Co. E, this regiment, October 11, 1864; discharged, May 29, 1865; also borne as Bowers.

BOWERS, HERMAN.—Private, Co. A, Forty-fourth Infantry; transferred to Co. H, this regiment, October 11, 1864; captured and paroled, no dates; mustered out, June 5, 1865, at Albany, N. Y.

BOYD, CLARENCE.—Private, Co. A, Forty-fourth Infantry; transferred to Co. F, this regiment, October 11, 1864.

BRIDGEFORD, WILLIAM W.—Musician, Co. A, Forty-fourth Infantry; transferred to Co. I, this regiment, October 11,

1864; mustered out, June 3, 1865, at camp near Alexandria, Va.

BRIER, CASPER.—Private, Co. B, Forty-fourth Infantry; transferred to, unassigned, this regiment, October 11, 1864; no further record.

BROWN, JAMES.—Private, Co. B, Forty-fourth Infantry; transferred to Co. E, this regiment, October 11, 1864; mustered out, June 3, 1865, near Alexandria, Va.

BURCH, WILLIAM C.—Private, Co. B, Forty-fourth Infantry; transferred to Co. E, this regiment, October 11, 1864; captured and paroled, no dates; mustered out, June 3, 1865, near Alexandria, Va.

BURNS, JOHN.—Private, Co. B., Forty-fourth Infantry; transferred to Co. E, this regiment, October 11, 1864; mustered out, June 3, 1865, near Alexandria, Va.

CADDEN, OWEN.—Private, Co. A, Forty-fourth Infantry; transferred, unassigned, this regiment, October 11, 1864; no further record.

CALLAHAN, JOHN.—Private, Co. A, Forty-fourth Infantry, transferred to Co. C, this regiment, October 11, 1864; mustered out with company, July 16, 1865, near Washington, D. C.

CAREY, RICHARD A.—Private, Co. A, Forty-fourth Infantry; transferred to Co. H, this regiment, October 11, 1864; discharged, March 2, 1865, at Hatcher's Run, Va.

CARLOW, FRANKLIN.—Sergeant, Co. B, Forty-fourth Infantry; transferred to Co. D, this regiment, October 11, 1864; returned to ranks, no date; discharged for disability, January 15, 1865, near Petersburg, Va.

CARRUTH, VIRGIL.—Private, Co. B, Forty-fourth Infantry; transferred to Co. D, this regiment, October 11, 1864; promoted corporal, February 1, 1865; mustered out with company, July 16, 1865, near Washington, D. C.

CASE, EDWARD C.—Private, Co. A, Forty-fourth Infantry; transferred to Co. C, this regiment, October 11, 1864; promoted corporal, February 1, 1865; sergeant, March 1, 1865; mustered out, June 3, 1865, near Alexandria, Va.

CASSIDY, PHILIP.—Private, Co. A, Forty-fourth Infantry; transferred to Co. K, this regiment, October 11, 1864;

mustered out with company, July 16, 1865, near Washington, D. C.

CLEMMER, WILLIAM.—Corporal, Co. A, Forty-fourth Infantry; transferred to Co. H, this regiment, October 11, 1864; mustered out, June 3, 1865, near Alexandria, Va.

COBURN, JAMES M.—Private, Co. B, Forty-fourth Infantry; transferred to Co. D, this regiment, October 11, 1864; mustered out, July 26, 1865, at Syracuse, N. Y.

COMSTOCK, ALBERT.—Corporal, Co. A, Forty-fourth Infantry; transferred to Co. H, this regiment, October 11, 1864; discharged, April 25, 1865, at Washington, D. C.

CONLON, PATRICK.—Private, Co. B, Forty-fourth Infantry; transferred to Co. D, this regiment, October 11, 1864; promoted corporal, no date; mustered out, June 3, 1865, near Alexandria, Va.

COOK, HOBERT.—Private, Co. A, Forty-fourth Infantry; transferred to Co. G, this regiment, October 11, 1864; no further record.

CORCORAN, TIMOTHY.—Private, Co. A, Forty-fourth Infantry; transferred to Co. C, this regiment, October 11, 1864; mustered out, June 3, 1865, near Alexandria, Va.

COSTELLO, PATRICK.—Private, Co. A, Forty-fourth Infantry; transferred to Co. E, this regiment, October 11, 1864; promoted sergeant and returned to ranks, no dates; discharged for disability, May 31, 1865.

COZINE, GEORGE M.—Corporal, Co. A, Forty-fourth Infantry; transferred to Co. E, this regiment, October 11, 1864; mustered out with company, July 16, 1865, near Washington, D. C.

CURETON, JOHN B.—Private, Co. A, Forty-fourth Infantry; transferred to Co. K, this regiment, October 11, 1864; mustered out, May 29, 1865, at Washington, D. C.

DEARING, SYLVESTER.—Private, Co. B, Forty-fourth Infantry; transferred to Co. K, this regiment, October 11, 1864; mustered out with company, July 16, 1865, near Washington, D. C.

DEFREEST, LEWELLEN.—Private, Co. A, Forty-fourth Infantry; transferred to Co. K, this regiment, October 11, 1864; mustered out with company, July 16, 1865, near Washington, D. C.

DOWNS, HENRY.—Private, Co. A, Forty-fourth Infantry; transferred to Co. C, this regiment, October 11, 1864; absent, sick since October 13, 1864; no further record.

DOYLE, WILLIAM M.—Private, Co. B, Forty-fourth Infantry; transferred to Co. D, this regiment, October 11, 1864; mustered out, June 3, 1865, at camp near Alexandria, Va.

DUNCAN, IRVINE.—Private, Co. A, Forty-fourth Infantry; transferred to Co. E, this regiment, October 11, 1864; wounded in action, June 2, 1864, at Cold Harbor, Va.; absent at muster-out of company.

EDDY, CURTIS.—Private, Co. I, Forty-fourth Infantry; transferred to Co. A, this regiment, October 11, 1864; discharged, no date.

ERWIN, WILLIAM H.—Private, Co. B, Forty-fourth Infantry; transferred to Co. D, this regiment, October 11, 1864; mustered out, May 31, 1865, at Washington, D. C.

FERRIS, LANSON.—First sergeant, Co. B, Forty-fourth Infantry; transferred to Co. E, this regiment, October 11, 1864; discharged, November 3, 1864, at Weldon Railroad, Va.; also borne as Lansing L. Ferris.

FISH, SAMUEL.—Private, Co. A, Forty-fourth Infantry, transferred to Co. A, this regiment, October 11, 1864; died of disease, March 5, 1865, in Division Hospital.

FITZGENREIDER, IGNATZ.—Private, Co. A, Forty-fourth Infantry; transferred to Co. C, this regiment, October 11, 1864; mustered out, June 19, 1865, at Washington, D. C., as Fritzenrider; also borne as Fitzgerald.

FLANSBURG, ALFRED.—Private, Co. K, Forty-fourth Infantry; transferred to Co. C, this regiment, October 11, 1864; mustered out, July 15, 1865, at Washington, D. C.

FRINDER, CHRISTIAN.—Private, Co. A, Forty-fourth Infantry; transferred to Co. A, this regiment, October 11, 1864; mustered out, June 3, 1865, near Alexandria, Va.

FRY, JACOB.—Private, Co. B, Forty-fourth Infantry; transferred to Co. E, this regiment, October 11, 1864; mustered out, June 3, 1865, near Alexandria, Va.

FURGUSON, JOHN.—Private, Co. A, Forty-fourth Infantry; transferred to Co. K, this regiment, October 11, 1864.

GAMMEL, WILLIAM W.—Private, Co. A, Forty-fourth Infantry;

transferred to Co. H, this regiment, October 11, 1864; killed in action, March 31, 1865, at White Oak Road, Va.

GONYON, JOHN.—Private, Co. A, Forty-fourth Infantry, transferred to Co. A, this regiment, October 11, 1864; discharged, April 23, 1865, in the field.

GORTON, SIMON A.—Private, Co. A, Forty-fourth Infantry; transferred to Co. H, this regiment, October 11, 1864; mustered out, June 3, 1865, at camp, near Alexandria, Va.

GOULD, THEODORE B.—Private, Co. A, Forty-fourth Infantry; transferred to Co. E, this regiment, October 11, 1864; absent, sick, since October 6, 1864; no further record.

GRAHAM, JOSEPH.—Private, Co. I, Forty-fourth Infantry; transferred to Co. K, this regiment, October 11, 1864; mustered out with company, July 16, 1865, near Washington, D. C.

GRANT, IRA A.—Private, Co. E, Forty-fourth Infantry; transferred to Co. K, this regiment, October 11, 1864; mustered out, June 3, 1865, at camp near Alexandria, Va.

GREEN, SAMUEL R.—Corporal, Co. A, Forty-fourth Infantry; transferred to Co. H, this regiment, October 11, 1864; wounded in action, March 31, 1865, at White Oak Road, Va.; died of his wounds, May 11, 1865, at Lincoln Hospital, Washington, D. C.

GRUNWELL, NICHOLAS B.—Private, Co. B, Forty-fourth Infantry; transferred to Co. D, this regiment, October 11, 1864; mustered out with company, July 16, 1865, near Washington, D. C.

HAMMOND, FRANCIS.—Private, Co. A, Forty-fourth Infantry, transferred to Co. A, this regiment, October 11, 1864; wounded, no date; absent since and at muster-out of company.

HENDRICKSON, ABRAM.—Private, Co. A, Forty-fourth Infantry; transferred to Co. H, this regiment, October 11, 1864; absent sick, since September 30, 1864, and at muster-out of company.

HERKENHAM, CHARLES.—Private, Co. A, Forty-fourth Infantry; transferred to Co. C, this regiment, October 11, 1864; discharged, February 2, 1865.

HEWLETT, JOHN P.—Private, Co. A, Forty-fourth Infantry;

transferred to Co. A, this regiment, October 11, 1864; died of disease, April 20, 1865, at Notaway Court House, Va.

HINCH, WILLIAM H.—Private, Co. A, Forty-fourth Infantry; transferred to Co. A, this regiment, October 11, 1864; mustered out, June 7, 1865, at Washington, D. C.

HINES, PATRICK. — Private, Co. A, Forty-fourth Infantry, transferred to Co. A, this regiment, October 11, 1864; mustered out, June 3, 1865, near Alexandria, Va. Died in 1902.

HOLLENBACK, EDWARD.—Private, Co. B, Forty-fourth Infantry, transferred to Co. B, this regiment, October 11, 1864; mustered out, June 3, 1865, near Alexandria, Va.

HOLLENBECK, CLARK.—Private, Co. A, Forty-fourth Infantry, transferred to Co. D, this regiment, October 11, 1864; discharged, October 12, 1864, near Petersburg, Va.

HOLT, JOHN B.—Private, Co. B, Forty-fourth Infantry, transferred to Co. D, this regiment, October 11, 1864; mustered out, with company, July 16, 1865, near Washington, D. C.

HOSFORD, HOADLY.—Private, Co. A, Forty-fourth Infantry; transferred to Co. G, this regiment, October 11, 1864; promoted sergeant, no date; transferred to Co. H, November 2, 1864; mustered out with company, July 16, 1865, near Washington, D. C., as Hadley Hosford.

HOWLAND, WILLIAM R.—Private, Co. B, Forty-fourth Infantry; transferred to Co. D, this regiment, October 11, 1864; mustered out with company, July 16, 1865, near Washington, D. C.

HUNT, ELI.—Private, Co. A, Forty-fourth Infantry; transferred to Co. A, this regiment, October 11, 1864; discharged, October 24, 1864, at Weldon Railroad, Va.

HYERS, JOHN.—Private, Co. A, Forty-fourth Infantry; transferred to Co. H, this regiment, October 11, 1864; mustered out, June 3, 1865, at camp near Alexandria, Va.

JOHNSON, THOMAS.—Private, Co. B, Forty-fourth Infantry, transferred to Co. D, this regiment, October 11, 1864; mustered out with company, July 16, 1865, near Washington, D. C.

JOHNSON, WILLIAM R.—Private, Co. B, Forty-fourth Infantry; transferred to Co. D, this regiment, October 11, 1864; promoted corporal, March 1, 1865; wounded in action, March 31, 1865, at Dabney's Farm, Va.; mustered out, August 10, 1865, at Elmira, N. Y.

JONES, FRANKLIN.—Private, Co. A, Forty-fourth Infantry; transferred to Co. C, this regiment, October 11, 1864; absent, wounded, since December 13, 1862; no record subsequent to February 29, 1864.

JONES, FREDERICK.—Private, Co. A, Forty-fourth Infantry; transferred to Co. A, this regiment, October 11, 1864; mustered out, June 3, 1865, near Alexandria, Va.

JOSLYN, JOHN.—Private, Co. B, Forty-fourth Infantry; transferred to Co. D, this regiment, October 11, 1864; absent, sick, since October 24, 1864; no further record; also borne as John M. Joslyn.

JUBILIUS, JOHN.—Private, Co. A, Forty-fourth Infantry; transferred to Co. H, this regiment, October 11, 1864; mustered out, June 3, 1865, at camp near Alexandria, Va.

KALDEN, OWEN.—Private, Co. I, Forty-fourth Infantry; transferred to Co. A, this regiment, October 11, 1864; died of disease, November 25, 1864; at Washington, D. C.; also borne as Kaelden.

KEARNEY, PATRICK.—Private, Co. A, Forty-fourth Infantry; transferred to Co. K, this regiment, October 11, 1864; mustered out with company, July 16, 1865, near Washington, D. C., as Karney.

KEMP, PETER H.—Private, Co. A, Forty-fourth Infantry, transferred to Co. E, this regiment, October 11, 1864; mustered out, June 9, 1865, near Alexandria, Va.

KEMPF, JAMES.—Private, Forty-fourth Infantry, transferred to Co. D, this regiment, October 11, 1864; no further record.

KENNY, JAMES N.—Private, Co. B, Forty-fourth Infantry, transferred to Co. D, this regiment, October 11, 1864; promoted corporal, April 9, 1865; mustered out with company, July 16, 1865, near Washington, D. C.

KENVILLE, WILLIAM.—Private, Co. A, Forty-fourth Infantry, transferred to Co. G, this regiment, October 11, 1864; mustered out, June 20, 1865.

KLEMSER, FREDERICK.—Private, Co. A, Forty-fourth Infantry; transferred to Co. H, this regiment, October 11, 1864; to

Forty-second Company, Second Battalion, Veteran Reserve Corps, no date; mustered out, August 24, 1865, at Washington, D. C.

KRENNINGER, ALEXANDER.—Private, Co. A, Forty-fourth Infantry; transferred to Co. A, this regiment, October 11, 1864; mustered out, July 11, 1865, at Washington, D. C., as Kruminger.

KRUSE, HENRY.—Private, Co. A, Forty-fourth Infantry; transferred to Co. F, this regiment, October 11, 1864; mustered out, June 3, 1865, at camp near Washington, D. C.

KUSTEREN, ERNST.—Private, Co. B, Forty-fourth Infantry; transferred to Co. B, this regiment, October 11, 1864; mustered out with company, July 16, 1865, near Washington, D. C.

LABARGE, RONALD.—Private, Co. A, Forty-fourth Infantry; transferred to Co. A, this regiment, October 11, 1864; mustered out, June 3, 1865, near Alexandria, Va.

LA BRACK, PETER.—Private, Co. A, Forty-fourth Infantry; transferred to Co. C, this regiment, October 11, 1864; mustered out with company, July 16, 1865, near Washington, D. C.

LATOV, JAMES.—Private, Co. A, Forty-fourth Infantry; transferred to Co. A, this regiment, October 11, 1864; mustered out, June 13, 1865, at Washington, D. C., as Lato.

LAUFER, HENRY.—Private, Co. D, Forty-fourth Infantry; transferred to Co. A, this regiment, October 11, 1864.

LAVANE, MOSES.—Private, Co. A, Forty-fourth Infantry; transferred to Co. C, this regiment, October 11, 1864; mustered out, June 19, 1865, at Washington, D. C., as Levine.

LEE, ENOCH H.—Corporal, Co. B, Forty-fourth Infantry; transferred to Co. D, this regiment, October 11, 1864; transferred to Co. E, October 31, 1864; wounded, no date; died of his wounds, April 1, 1865, at City Point, Va.

LEWIS, ALLEN.—Private, Co. A, Forty-fourth Infantry; transferred to Co. A, this regiment, October 11, 1864; discharged, October 26, 1864, at Weldon Railroad, Va.

LINTENER, MORRIS.—Private, Co. B, Forty-fourth Infantry; transferred to Co. B, this regiment, October 11, 1864; mustered out, June 3, 1865, near Alexandria, Va.

LUBKE, WILLIAM L.—Private, Co. A, Forty-fourth Infantry; transferred to Co. F, this regiment, October 11, 1864; mustered out, June 16, 1865, at Washington, D. C.

MANSFIELD, CYRUS.—Private, Co. A, Forty-fourth Infantry; transferred to Co. A, this regiment, October 11, 1864; mustered out with company, July 16, 1865, near Washington, D. C.

MAYNARD, RICHARD.—Private, Co. A, Forty-fourth Infantry; transferred to Co. C, this regiment, October 11, 1864; captured in action, March 31, 1865, at White Oak Road, Va.; paroled, no date; mustered out, May 31, 1865, at Annapolis, Md.

McBRIDE, THOMAS.—Private, Co. B, Forty-fourth Infantry; transferred to Co. E, this regiment, October 11, 1864.

McCLEAR, JOHN.—Private, unassigned, Forty-fourth Infantry; transferred to Co. K, this regiment, October 11, 1864; mustered out, June 3, 1865, at camp, near Alexandria, Va.

McCOON, HENRY H.—Private, Co. E, Forty-fourth Infantry; transferred to Co. D, this regiment, October 11, 1864; no further record.

McCORMICK, DAVID.—Private, Co. F, Forty-fourth Infantry; transferred to Co. C, this regiment, October 11, 1864; wounded in action, October 28, 1864, at Hatcher's Run, Va.; mustered out, June 6, 1865, at Albany, N. Y.

McCREARY, JULIAN.—Private, Co. B, Forty-fourth Infantry; transferred to Co. B, this regiment, October 11, 1864; mustered out, June 3, 1865, near Alexandria, Va.

McDONALD, JESSE.—Private, Co. A, Forty-fourth Infantry; transferred to Co. C, this regiment, October 11, 1864; mustered out, June 3, 1865, near Alexandria, Va.

McGOUGH, JOHN.—Private, Co. A, Forty-fourth Infantry; transferred to Co. C, this regiment, October 11, 1864; mustered out, June 3, 1865, near Alexandria, Va.

McKOWN, JOHN.—Private, Co. B, Forty-fourth Infantry; transferred to Co. D, this regiment, October 11, 1864; promoted corporal, no date; returned to ranks, April 9, 1865; mustered out with company, July 16, 1865, near Washington, D. C., as McKowan.

McMANUS, JOHN.—Private, Co. B, Forty-fourth Infantry;

transferred to Co. D, this regiment, October 11, 1864; mustered out with company, July 16, 1865, near Washington, D. C.

MCNEIL, LUKE.—Private, Co. A, Forty-fourth Infantry; transferred to Co. C, this regiment, October 11, 1864.

MEEKER, WILLIAM B.—Private, Co. A, Forty-fourth Infantry; transferred to Co. C, this regiment, October 11, 1864; mustered out with company, July 16, 1865, near Washington, D. C.

MEIER, HENRY.—Private, Co. A, Forty-fourth Infantry; transferred to Co. F, this regiment, October 11, 1864; captured in action, April 1, 1865, at Five Forks, Va.; released, April 30, 1865; mustered out, May 30, 1865, at Annapolis, Md., as Meyer; also borne as Meyers.

MERENESS, DAVID A.—Private, Co. A, Forty-fourth Infantry; transferred to Co. C, this regiment, October 11, 1864; discharged, January 22, 1865, at hospital, Washington, D. C.; also borne as Meriness.

MICKLER, JOHN.—Private, Co. A, Forty-fourth Infantry; transferred to Co. K, this regiment, October 11, 1864; no further record.

MINDERMAN, CHRISTIAN.—Private, Co. A, Forty-fourth Infantry; transferred to Co. F, this regiment, October 11, 1864; mustered out, June 3, 1865, at camp near Alexandria, Va.

MINK, ALBERT G.—Private, Co. B, Forty-fourth Infantry; transferred to Co. D, this regiment, October 11, 1864; discharged, November 19, 1864, near Petersburg, Va.

MONROE, CHARLES J.—Private, Co. A, Forty-fourth Infantry; transferred to Co. I, this regiment, October 11, 1864; captured in action, no date; mustered out, May 30, 1865, at Annapolis, Md.

MORELAND, JOHN J.—Private, Co. A, Forty-fourth Infantry; transferred to Co. E, this regiment, October 11, 1864; absent, sick, since October, 1864, and at muster-out of company.

NELLIGAN, THEOBOLD.—Private, Co. A, Forty-fourth Infantry; transferred to Co. F, this regiment, October 11, 1864; discharged, October 21, 1864, at Weldon Railroad, Va.

O'HORO, WILLIAM.—Private, Co. B, Forty-fourth Infantry;

transferred to Co. D, this regiment, October 11, 1864; mustered out with company, July 16, 1865, near Washington, D. C.

OSSEKER, CHARLES.—Private, Co. A, Forty-fourth Infantry; transferred to Co. F, this regiment, October 11, 1864; mustered out, June 3, 1865, near Alexandria, Va.

OTTERSON, SAMUEL.—Private, Co. C, Forty-fourth Infantry; transferred to Co. K, this regiment, October 11, 1864; mustered out, June 3, 1865, near Alexandria, Va., as Ottison.

OVERTON, CHARLES G.—Private, Co. A, Forty-fourth Infantry; transferred to Co. C, this regiment, October 11, 1864; promoted corporal, no date; wounded in action, March 31, 1865, at White Oak Ridge, Va.; absent since, and at muster-out of company.

PARKER, CHARLES.—Private, Co. A, Forty-fourth Infantry; transferred to Co. G, this regiment, October 11, 1864; mustered out, June 3, 1865, near Alexandria, Va.

PARROW, MICHAEL.—Private, Co. A, Forty-fourth Infantry; transferred to Co. C, this regiment, October 11, 1864; mustered out, June 3, 1865, near Alexandria, Va., as Mitchell Parow.

PETEZOLDT, WILLIAM.—Private, Co. A, Forty-fourth Infantry; transferred to Co. F, this regiment, October 11, 1864; discharged, October 17, 1864, at Weldon Railroad, Va.; also borne as Petzhold.

PHILLIPS, HENRY.—Private, Co. A, Forty-fourth Infantry; transferred to Co. I, this regiment, October 11, 1864; wounded, no date; died of his wounds, April 21, 1865, in hospital.

PHILLIPS, JAMES A.—Private, Co. A, Forty-fourth Infantry; transferred to Co. C, this regiment, October 11, 1864; mustered out, June 3, 1865, near Alexandria, Va.

PHILLIPS, WILLIAM H.—Private, Co. B, Forty-fourth Infantry; transferred to Co. D, this regiment, October 11, 1864; discharged, March 15, 1865, near Petersburg, Va.

PRESTON, WILLIAM.—Private, Co. A, Forty-fourth Infantry; transferred to Co. G, this regiment, October 11, 1864; captured and paroled, no dates; mustered out, June 1, 1865, at Annapolis, Md.

PRICE, JOHN.—Private, Co. A, Forty-fourth Infantry; transferred to Co. F, this regiment, October 11, 1864; absent, sick, since October 31, 1864, and at muster-out of company.

PROVOST, ALFRED.—Private, Co. B, Forty-fourth Infantry; transferred to Co. B, this regiment, October 11, 1864; mustered out, June 3, 1865, near Alexandria, Va.

QUIN, JR., JOHN.—Private, Co. B, Forty-fourth Infantry; transferred to Co. B, this regiment, October 11, 1864; discharged, January 13, 1865, in the field; also borne as Thomas Mack.

RADCLIFFE, CHARLES.—Private, Co. A, Forty-fourth Infantry; transferred to Co. G, this regiment, October 11, 1864; captured in action, March 31, 1865, at White Oak Ridge, Va.; no further record.

RANKIN, AMI D.—Private, Co. A, Forty-fourth Infantry; transferred to Co. F, this regiment, October 11, 1864; discharged, October 21, 1864, at Weldon Railroad, Va.

RANKIN, WILLIAM.—Private, Co. B, Forty-fourth Infantry; transferred to Co. B, this regiment, October 11, 1864; mustered out, June 2, 1865, at Washington, D. C.

REED, WILLIAM.—Private, Co. A, Forty-fourth Infantry; transferred to Co. G, this regiment, October 11, 1864; mustered out with company, July 16, 1865, near Washington, D. C.

REINOLD, WILLIAM.—Private, Co. A, Forty-fourth Infantry; transferred to Co. G, this regiment, October 11, 1864; promoted corporal and returned to ranks, no dates; mustered out with company, July 16, 1865, near Washington, D. C.

RICHMON, CHRISTIAN.—Private, Co. A, Forty-fourth Infantry; transferred to Co. F, this regiment, October 11, 1864; mustered out, June 9, 1865, at Columbia Hospital, Washington, D. C., as Richman.

ROBINSON, JOHN.—Private, Co. B, Forty-fourth Infantry; transferred to Co. B, this regiment, October 11, 1864; captured and paroled, no date; mustered out, June 3, 1865, near Alexandria, Va., as Robertson.

ROCK, FRANCIS.—Private, Co. A, Forty-fourth Infantry; transferred to Co. G, this regiment, October 11, 1864; mustered out, June 3, 1865, at camp near Alexandria, Va.

ROCK, PETER.—Private, unassigned, Forty-fourth Infantry; transferred to Co. G, this regiment, October 11, 1864;

captured in action, March 31, 1865, at White Oak Ridge, Va.; paroled, no date; mustered out, June 8, 1865, at Annapolis, Md.

RUSSELL, ROBERT.—Private, Co. A, Forty-fourth Infantry; transferred to Co. K, this regiment, October 11, 1864; mustered out, June 3, 1865, at camp near Alexandria, Va.

SAUTER, ELIAS.—Private, Co. B, Forty-fourth Infantry; transferred to Co. B, this regiment, October 11, 1864; mustered out, July 17, 1865, at Washington, D. C., as Souter.

SAWYER, JAMES M.—Private, Co. A, Forty-fourth Infantry; transferred to Co. H, this regiment, October 11, 1864; mustered out, June 3, 1865, at camp near Alexandria, Va.

SCHMIDT, JOHN.—Private, Co. A, Forty-fourth Infantry; transferred to Co. I, this regiment, October 11, 1864.

SCHUBERT, GEORGE.—Private, Co. B, Forty-fourth Infantry; transferred to Co. B, this regiment, October 11, 1864.

SCHWERKART, SIGMUND.—Sergeant, Co. A, Forty-fourth Infantry; transferred to Co. G, this regiment, October 11, 1864, and to Co. K, November 2, 1864; mustered out with company, July 16, 1865, near Washington, D. C.

SCOTT, ADDISON.—Private, Co. B, Forty-fourth Infantry; transferred to Co. E, this regiment, October 11, 1864; mustered out, June 3, 1865, at Washington, D. C.; also borne as Scutt.

SCOTT, THOMAS.—Private, Co. A, Forty-fourth Infantry; transferred to Co. E, this regiment, October 11, 1864, while detached to Battery B, Fourth United States Artillery; mustered out, June 9, 1865, near Alexandria, Va.

SCOVILLE, EDWARD.—Private, Co. A, Forty-fourth Infantry; transferred to Co. I, this regiment, October 11, 1864; captured in action, March 31, 1865, at White Oak Ridge, Va.; paroled, no date; mustered out, August 31, 1865, at Elmira, N. Y.

SCRAFFORD, CHRISTOPHER.—Private, Co. A, Forty-fourth Infantry; transferred to Co. H, this regiment, October 11, 1864; mustered out, June 3, 1865, at camp near Alexandria, Va.

SEELEY, WILLIAM S.—Sergeant, Co. B, Forty-fourth Infantry;

transferred to Co. E, this regiment, October 11, 1864, and to Co. B, November 2, 1864; mustered out with company, July 16, 1865, near Washington, D. C.

SENN, ANSON.—Private, Co. A, Forty-fourth Infantry; transferred to Co. I, this regiment, October 11, 1864; killed in action, March 31, 1865, at White Oak Ridge, Va.

SHAW, CHRISTOPHER.—Private, Co. B, Forty-fourth Infantry; transferred to Co. B, this regiment, October 11, 1864; mustered out, June 3, 1865, near Alexandria, Va.

SHAW, OLBOSON.—Private, Co. B, Forty-fourth Infantry; transferred to Co. B, this regiment, October 11, 1864; wounded in action, April 1, 1865, at Five Forks, Va.; mustered out, July 6, 1865, at Washington, D. C.

SHEHAN, JEREMIAH.—Private, Co. A, Forty-fourth Infantry; transferred to Co. A, this regiment, October 11, 1864; discharged for disability, June 7, 1865; also borne as Jerry Schehen.

SHOEFELT, SAMUEL.—Private, Co. A, Forty-fourth Infantry; transferred to Co. I, this regiment, October 11, 1864; mustered out with company, July 16, 1865, near Washington, D. C.

SHUTTER, WILLIAM.—Private, Co. A, Forty-fourth Infantry; transferred to Co. F, this regiment, October 11, 1864; discharged, October 19, 1864, at Weldon Railroad, Va.

SIMPSON, LEWIS.—Private, Co. A, Forty-fourth Infantry; transferred to Co. A, this regiment, October 11, 1864; discharged, no date, on expiration of term of service.

SMITH, FRANCIS.—Private, Co. B, Forty-fourth Infantry; transferred to Co. A, this regiment, October 11, 1864; mustered out, June 3, 1865, near Alexandria, Va.

SMITH, HENRY G.—Corporal, Co. B, Forty-fourth Infantry; transferred to Co. D, this regiment, October 11, 1864; returned to ranks, no date; mustered in as second lieutenant, Co. G, April 27, 1865; discharged, May 26, 1865.

Commissioned second lieutenant, March 30, 1865, with rank from February 1, 1865, vice H. G. Taylor promoted.

SMITH, JAMES.—Private, Co. A, Forty-fourth Infantry; transferred to Co. G, this regiment, October 11, 1864; discharged for disability, June 7, 1865.

SMITH, SAMUEL.—Private, Co. A, Forty-fourth Infantry; transferred to Co. I, this regiment, October 11, 1864; mustered out, June 3, 1865, at camp near Alexandria, Va.

SMITH, WILLIAM.—Private, Co. A, Forty-fourth Infantry; transferred to Co. H, this regiment, October 11, 1864.

STARKINS, JOHN.—Private, Co. A, Forty-fourth Infantry; transferred to Co. H, this regiment, October 11, 1864; promoted corporal, June 1, 1865; mustered out with company, July 16 1865, near Washington, D. C., as Starkings.

SULLIVAN, THOMAS.—Private, Co. B, Forty-fourth Infantry; transferred to Co. B, this regiment, October 11, 1864; mustered out, June 3, 1865, near Alexandria, Va.

TAYLOR, HIRAM P.—Private, Co. A, Forty-fourth Infantry, transferred to Co. E, this regiment, October 11, 1864; discharged, June 3, 1865.

TAYLOR, RICHARD.—Private, Co. A, Forty-fourth Infantry, transferred to Co. I, this regiment, October 11, 1864; to Veteran Reserve Corps, October 18, 1864.

TENEYCK, HENRY.—Private, Co. A, Forty-fourth Infantry, transferred to Co. A, this regiment, October 11, 1864; discharged, June 13, 1865.

TEUFEL, GODLEIPH.—Private, Co. A, Forty-fourth Infantry; transferred to Co. F, this regiment, October 11, 1864; mustered out with company, July 16, 1865, near Washington, D. C., also borne as Sufelt.

THRESHER, NELSON.—Private, Co. A, Forty-fourth Infantry; transferred to Co. H, this regiment, October 11, 1864; mustered out, June 3, 1865, near Alexandria, Va.

TIFF, CHARLES.—Private, Co. A, Forty-fourth Infantry; transferred to Co. G, this regiment, October 11, 1864; discharged for disability, October 12, 1864, at hospital.

TURNER, ANDREW J.—Private, Co. B, Forty-fourth Infantry; transferred to Co. K, this regiment, October 11, 1864; mustered out, June 3, 1865, near Alexandria, Va.

VAN ALSTYNE, THOMAS.—Private, Co. K, Forty-fourth Infantry; transferred to Co. I, this regiment, October 11, 1864; mustered out with company, July 16, 1865, near Washington, D. C.

VAN VALKENBERG, MICHAEL.—Private, Co. K, Forty-fourth

Infantry; transferred to Co. I, this regiment, October 11, 1864; discharged, May 30, 1865, at Campbell Hospital, Washington, D. C.

VISCHER, JOHN V. S.—Sergeant, Co. A, Forty-fourth Infantry; transferred to Co. F, this regiment, October 11, 1864.

WAGONER, MARTIN V. B.—Sergeant, Co. A, Forty-fourth Infantry; transferred to Co. E, this regiment, October 11, 1864; to Co. F, November 1, 1864; absent, on detached service at Brownsburg, Ky., at muster-out of company.

WALSH, WILLIAM P.—Private, Co. A, Forty-fourth Infantry; transferred to Co. E, this regiment, October 11, 1864; mustered out, June 3, 1865, near Alexandria, Va.

WATSON, JAMES.—Private, Co. A, Forty-fourth Infantry; transferred to Co. I, this regiment, October 11, 1864; mustered out with company, July 16, 1865, near Washington, D. C.

WESTFALL, CARL.—Private, Co. B, Forty-fourth Infantry; transferred to Co. K, this regiment, October 11, 1864; mustered out with company, July 16, 1865, near Washington, D. C.

WHEELER, WILLIAM H.—Private, Co. B, Forty-fourth Infantry; transferred to Co. D, this regiment, October 11, 1864; mustered out, June 3, 1865, near Alexandria, Va.

WHITE, JAMES W.—Private, Co. B, Forty-fourth Infantry; transferred to Co. D, this regiment, October 11, 1864; promoted corporal, no date; discharged, May 15, 1865, in the field.

WHITE, TITUS.—Private, Co. A, Forty-fourth Infantry; transferred to Co. C, this regiment, October 11, 1864; mustered out with company, July 16, 1865, near Washington, D. C.

WILLIAMS, ANDREW J.—Private, unassigned, Forty-fourth Infantry; transferred to Co. K, this regiment, October 11, 1864; mustered out with company, July 16, 1865, near Washington, D. C.

WILLIAMS, JOHN A.—Private, Co. A, Forty-fourth Infantry; transferred to Co. I, this regiment, October 11, 1864; killed in action, March 31, 1865, at White Oak Ridge, Va.

WILLIAMS, JOHN P.—Private, Co. A, Forty-fourth Infantry; transferred to Co. I, this regiment, October 11, 1864; mustered out, June 3, 1865, at camp near Alexandria, Va.

WILQUET, MICHAEL.—Private, Co. A, Forty-fourth Infantry; transferred to Co. E, this regiment, October 11, 1864; also borne as Nicholas Wilque.

WINSLOW, CHARLES.—Private, unassigned, Forty-fourth Infantry; transferred to Co. I, this regiment, October 11, 1864; died of disease, November 17, 1864, at Washington, D. C.

WINSTON, JOHN.—Private, Co. A, Forty-fourth Infantry; transferred to Co. I, this regiment, October 11, 1864; no further record.

WISEMAN, WILLIAM.—Private, Co. A, Forty-fourth Infantry, transferred to Co. F, this regiment, October 11, 1864.

WOODWORTH, JUDSON N.—First sergeant, Co. A, Forty-fourth Infantry; transferred to Co, I, this regiment, October 11, 1864; discharged, November 25, 1864, at Weldon Railroad, Va.

WORDEN, WILLIAM.—Private, Co. A, Forty-fourth Infantry; transferred to Co. G, this regiment, October 11, 1864; mustered out, June 3, 1865, at camp near Alexandria, Va.

WYGANT, HENRY C.—Corporal, Co. A, Forty-fourth Infantry; transferred to Co. F, this regiment, October 11, 1864; discharged, October 18, 1864, at Weldon Railroad, Va.

ZACKER, JOHN.—Private, Co. A, Forty-fourth Infantry; transferred to Co. F, this regiment, October 11, 1864; promoted corporal, November 1, 1864; mustered out with company, July 16, 1865, near Washington, D. C.

SEVENTEENTH NEW YORK INFANTRY

AYERS, CLARKSON D.—Private, Co. H, Seventeenth Infantry; transferred to Co. K, this regiment, June 25, 1863; discharged, September 18, 1864, at Weldon Railroad, Va.

BELAIR, LOUIS.—Private, Co. G, Seventeenth Infantry, transferred to Co. F, this regiment, June 25, 1863; captured, May 5, 1864, at the Wilderness, Va.; paroled, no date; discharged, April 25, 1865, at New York City.

BENNETT, LYMAN S.—Private, Co. I, Seventeenth Infantry; transferred to Co. I, this regiment, June 25, 1863.

BERGEN, JOHN.—Private, Co. G, Seventeenth Infantry; transferred to Co. C, this regiment, June 25, 1863.

BROWN, ANSON B.—Private, Seventeenth Infantry; transferred to Co. F, this regiment, June 25, 1863; reënlisted as a veteran, February 21, 1864; promoted corporal, no date; captured in action, May 5, 1864, at the Wilderness, Va.; paroled, February 28, 1865, at North East Bridge, N. C.; mustered out, June 17, 1865, at Annapolis, Md.

BROWN, HENRY C.—Private, Co. I, Seventeenth Infantry; transferred to Co. B, this regiment, June 25, 1863; discharged, June 25, 1865.

BROWN, JOHN.—Private, Co. G, Seventeenth Infantry; transferred to Co. D, this regiment, June 25, 1863; discharged, September 6, 1864, near Petersburg, Va.

BROWN, JOHN.—Private, Co. G, Seventeenth Infantry; transferred to Co. F, this regiment, June 25, 1863; transferred to Veteran Reserve Corps, January 8, 1864.

BROWN, JOSEPH.—Private, Co. G, Seventeenth Infantry; transferred to Co. G, this regiment, June 25, 1863; reënlisted as a veteran, February 20, 1864; captured, May 5, 1864, at the Wilderness, Va.; no further record.

CHAMBERLAIN, HENRY F.—Corporal, Co. I, Seventeenth Infantry; transferred to Co. I, this regiment, June 25, 1863; reënlisted as a veteran, February 20, 1864; captured and paroled, no dates; mustered out with company, July 16, 1865, near Washington, D. C.

CLANCEY, MARTIN.—Sergeant, Co. H, Seventeenth Infantry; transferred to Co. K, this regiment, June 25, 1863; promoted first sergeant, no date; mustered out with company, July 16, 1865, near Washington, D. C.

Commissioned (not mustered) second lieutenant, June 17, 1865, with rank from February 1, 1865, vice L. Empey not mustered. Died at Cedar Rapids, Ia., in 1898.

COMBS, RUFUS.—Private, Co. H, Seventeenth Infantry; transferred to Co. K, this regiment, June 25, 1863; reënlisted as a veteran, February 20, 1864; promoted corporal and returned to ranks, no dates; absent on furlough at muster-out of company.

CRANDELL, CHARLES G.—Private, Co. I, Seventeenth Infantry;

transferred to Co. I, this regiment, June 25, 1863; reënlisted as a veteran, February 20, 1864; died of disease, October 21, 1864, at Wayne County, N. Y.

CURRY, JOHN.—Private, Co. G, Seventeenth Infantry; transferred to Co. B, this regiment, June 25, 1863; captured in action, May 5, 1864; died of chronic diarrhea, July 20, 1864, at Andersonville, Ga.

DARTH, GEORGE.—Private, Co. G, Seventeenth Infantry; transferred to Co. F, this regiment, June 25, 1863.

FAVREAU, JOSEPH.—Private, Co. G, Seventeenth Infantry; transferred to Co. B, this regiment, January 25, 1863; promoted corporal, August 17, 1863; sergeant, November 1, 1863; reënlisted as a veteran, February 20, 1864; wounded in action, May 5, 1864, at the Wilderness, Va.; discharged for disability, September 8, 1864, at Washington, D. C.

FIELDS, JOHN C.—Private, Co. I, Seventeenth Infantry; transferred to Co. I, this regiment, June 25, 1863; promoted corporal, no date; reënlisted as a veteran, February 20, 1864; killed in action, May 5, 1864, at the Wilderness, Va.

FISHER, MICHAEL A.—Private, Co. G, Seventeenth Infantry; transferred to Co. D, this regiment, June 25, 1863; discharged at hospital, date unknown.

HALEY, THOMAS.—Private, Co. C, Seventeenth Infantry, transferred to Co. A, this regiment, December 5, 1863.

HAND, SAMUEL.—Private, Co. G, Seventeenth Infantry, transferred to Co. D, this regiment, June 25, 1863; promoted corporal, no date; discharged, October 14, 1864, near Petersburg, Va.

HESS, WILLIAM.—Private, Co. G, Seventeenth Infantry; transferred to Co. D, this regiment, June 25, 1863; captured and paroled, no dates; discharged, no date, at Annapolis, Md.

HILL, JOHN.—Private, Co. C, Seventeenth Infantry; transferred to Co. C, this regiment, December 30, 1863; mustered out, July 19, 1865, at Philadelphia, Pa.

HOLBORN, W.—Age — years. Private, unassigned, Seventeenth Infantry, transferred to Co. I, this regiment, June 25, 1863; no further record.

ISABELL, ADELBERT.—Private, Co. K, Seventeenth Infantry, transferred to Co. K, this regiment, June 25, 1863; promoted

corporal, no date; discharged, September 18, 1865, at Weldon
Railroad, Va.

KELLOGG, MILES B.—Sergeant, Co. I, Seventeenth Infantry;
transferred to Co. I, this regiment, June 25, 1863; reënlisted
as a veteran, February 20, 1864; captured in action, May 5,
1864, at the Wilderness, Va.; paroled, March 25, 1865;
mustered out with company, July 16, 1865, near Washington,
D. C., as Milo B. Kellogg.

KELLY, WILLIAM.—Private, Co. G, Seventeenth Infantry;
transferred to Co. C, this regiment, June 25, 1863.

LANDRY, GEORGE.—Private, Co. G, Seventeenth Infantry;
transferred to Co. B, this regiment, June 25, 1863; discharged, September 5, 1864, at Weldon Railroad, Va.

LAPOINT, JOSEPH.—Private, Co. G, Seventeenth Infantry; transferred to Co. D, this regiment, June 25, 1863; captured in action, May 5, 1864, at the Wilderness, Va.; paroled, no date;
discharged from hospital on expiration of term of service.

LEGGIN, FRANK.—Private, Co. G, Seventeenth Infantry; transferred to Co. D, this regiment, June 25, 1863; discharged, no
date, from hospital.

LYONS, THEODORE.—Private, Co. G, Seventeenth Infantry;
transferred to Co. D, this regiment, June 25, 1863; discharged, September 24, 1864, near Petersburg, Va.

MACK, JOHN.—Private, Co. K, Seventeenth Infantry; transferred to Co. K, this regiment, June 25, 1863; absent, sick,
since April 21, 1864, and at muster-out of company.

MARTH, DESIRI.—Private, Co. G, Seventeenth Infantry; transferred to Co. F, this regiment, June 25, 1863; discharged,
October 13, 1864, at Weldon Railroad, Va.

McAVOY, JEFFERY.—Private, Co. G, Seventeenth Infantry;
transferred to Co. B, this regiment, June 25, 1863; discharged
October 14, 1864, at Weldon Railroad, Va.

McCARTHY, JOHN B.—Private, Co. G, Seventeenth Infantry;
transferred to Co. F, this regiment, June 25, 1863; killed in
action, May 5, 1864, at the Wilderness, Va.

McGINNIS, ROBERT A.—Private, Co. G, Seventeenth Infantry;
transferred to Co. F, this regiment, June 25, 1863; reënlisted
as a veteran, February 21, 1864; captured in action, September 7, 1864, at Weldon Railroad, Va.; exchanged,

October, 1864; mustered out with company, July 16, 1865, near Washington, D. C.

McGowen, Stephen.—Private, Co. G, Seventeenth Infantry; transferred to Co. F, this regiment, June 25, 1863; promoted corporal, no date; reënlisted as a veteran, February 21, 1864; captured in action, May 5, 1864, at the Wilderness, Va.; paroled, no date; discharged for disability, June 1, 1865, at camp near Alexandria, Va.

Moore, Charles A.—Private, Co. G, Seventeenth Infantry; transferred to Co. F, this regiment, June 25, 1863; discharged October 13, 1864, at Weldon Railroad, Va.

Moore, Milton H.—Private, Co. I, Seventeenth Infantry; transferred to Co. I, this regiment, May 13, 1863; discharged, September 19, 1864.

Mulkern, James.—Private, Co. F, Seventeenth Infantry; transferred to Co. G, this regiment, June 25, 1863; reënlisted as a veteran, February 20, 1864; captured in action, May 5, 1864, at the Wilderness, Va.; no further record.

Murphy, William.—Private, Co. A, Seventeenth Infantry; transferred to Co. G, this regiment, June 25, 1863.

Nodine, Frederick A.—Private, Co. A, Seventeenth Infantry; transferred to Co. G, this regiment, June 25, 1863; captured in action, May 5, 1864, at the Wilderness, Va.; no further record.

Owens, William.—Private, Co. G, Seventeenth Infantry; transferred to Co. F, this regiment, December 20, 1863; discharged, October 13, 1864, at Weldon Railroad, Va.

Owens, William H.—Private, Co. G, Seventeenth Infantry; transferred to Co. F, this regiment, June 25, 1863; mustered out, September 4, 1864, at New York City.

Parkhill, Eugene.—Private, Co. I, Seventeenth Infantry; transferred to Co. I, this regiment, June 25, 1863; reënlisted as a veteran, February 20, 1864; captured in action, August 25, 1864, at Weldon Railroad, Va.; paroled, March 2, 1865, at North East Bridge, N. C.; mustered out, August 5, 1865, at Rochester, N. Y.

Perrot, Joseph.—Private, Co. G, Seventeenth Infantry; transferred to Co. D, this regiment, June 25, 1863; discharged, September 27, 1864, near Petersburg, Va.

RAWLINGS, ROBERT A.—Private, unassigned, Seventeenth Infantry; transferred to Co. I, this regiment, June 25, 1863; captured in action, May 5, 1864, at the Wilderness, Va.; paroled, no date; died, January 9, 1865, at Annapolis, Md.

ROBERTSON, JOSEPH.—Private, Co. G, Seventeenth Infantry; transferred to Co. F, this regiment, June 25, 1863; appointed musician, no date; discharged, October 15, 1864, at Weldon Railroad, Va.

ROBINSON, JAMES H.—Private, Co. I, Seventeenth Infantry; transferred to Co. I, this regiment, June 25, 1863; captured in action, May 5, 1864, at the Wilderness, Va.; paroled, no date; discharged, March 25, 1865.

RUSSELL, DARIUS F.—Private, Co. I, Seventeenth Infantry; transferred to Co. I, this regiment, June 25, 1863; mustered out, October 23, 1864, at Weldon Railroad, Va.

SANDERS, HENRY B.—Private, Co. G, Seventeenth Infantry; transferred to Co. F, this regiment, June 25, 1863; promoted sergeant, no date; reënlisted as a veteran, February 21, 1864; killed in action, June 3, 1864, at Cold Harbor, Va.

SLINOT, JOSEPH.—Private, Co. G, Seventeenth Infantry; transferred to Co. D, this regiment, June 25, 1863; captured in action and paroled, no dates; discharged, no date, on expiration of term of service at hospital; also borne as Solenot.

SOUZER, JOHN.—Private, Co. G, Seventeenth Infantry; transferred to Co. G, this regiment, June 26, 1863; discharged, September 17, 1864, at Weldon Railroad, Va.

TAYLOR, ROBERT.—Private, Co. G, Seventeenth Infantry; transferred to Co. F, this regiment, June 25, 1863; killed in action, May 5, 1864, at the Wilderness, Va.

TERRILL, TIMOTHY.—Private, Co. K, Seventeenth Infantry; transferred to Co. G, this regiment, June 25, 1863; reënlisted as a veteran, February 20, 1864; captured in action, May 5, 1864, at the Wilderness, Va.; paroled, no date; mustered out with company, July 16, 1865, near Washington, D. C.

THOMPSON, JOHN L.—Private, Co. G, Seventeenth Infantry; transferred to Co. D, this regiment, June 25, 1863.

TOWNLEY, WILLIAM F.—Private, Co. G, Seventeenth Infantry; transferred to Co. F, this regiment, June 25, 1863; to

Veteran Reserve Corps, May 3, 1864; mustered out therefrom as of Co. K, Sixth Regiment, October 26, 1864, at Johnson's Island, O.

TREMPER, GEORGE.—Private, Co. F, Seventeenth Infantry; transferred to Co. G, this regiment, June 25, 1863; died of disease, November 12, 1863, at Washington, D. C.

VAN ORDEN, ALFRED.—Private, Co. A, Seventeenth Infantry; transferred to Co. G, this regiment, June 26, 1863; discharged, October 7, 1864, at Weldon Railroad, Va.

WALDRON, CARROLL S.—Private, Co. F, Seventeenth Infantry; transferred to Co. G, this regiment, June 25, 1863; captured in action, May 5, 1864, at the Wilderness, Va.; paroled, no date; mustered out, June 9, 1865, at New York City.

WARD, HALE.—Private, Co. G, Seventeenth Infantry; transferred to Co. D, this regiment, June 25, 1863.

WEAVER, STEPHEN.—Private, Co. G, Seventeenth Infantry; transferred to Co. B, this regiment, June 25, 1863; reënlisted as a veteran, February 20, 1864; captured, June 21, 1864; released, April 16, 1865; promoted corporal, May 5, 1865; mustered out with company, July 16, 1865, near Washington, D. C.

WEEKS, HENRY.—Private, Co. C, Seventeenth Infantry; transferred to Co. I, this regiment, June 25, 1863; reënlisted as a veteran, February 20, 1864; mustered out with company, July 16, 1865, near Washington, D. C.

WENZEL, ADOLPHUS.—Private, Co. G. Seventeenth Infantry; transferred to Co. C, this regiment, June 25, 1863; mustered out, June 19, 1865, at Albany, N. Y.

MISCELLANEOUS

ALLEN, EGBERT D.—Private, Co. E, Thirtieth Infantry; transferred to this regiment, January 14, 1864.

BADGE, WILLIAM.—Private, Thirty-fourth Infantry; transferred to Co. E, this regiment, February 10, 1864.

BOWEN, ROBERT.—Age, date, place of enlistment, term and muster-in as private, Co. A, not stated; wounded and captured, no dates; died, July 11, 1864, at Lynchburg, Va.

BRIMM, JOHN.—Private, Co. G, Second Infantry; transferred to Co. E, this regiment, no date; discharged, December 28, 1864, near Petersburg, Va.

BUNTING, ARTHUR.—Age, date, place of enlistment, term of service and muster-in as private, Co. A, not stated; absent, sick since February 16, 1864, at Washington, D. C.; no further record.

COOK, GEORGE A.—Age, date, place, term and muster-in as private, unassigned, not stated; enlisted in Co. B, Eighty-first Infantry, November 29, 1862; sent to this regiment, December 11, 1862.

DOUSEY, RICHARD H.—Private, Co. D, Sixteenth Infantry; transferred to Co. F, this regiment, January 14, 1864; killed in action, May 5, 1864, at the Wilderness, Va.; also borne as Dowsey.

EZLER, J.—Age, date, place, term of enlistment and muster-in as private, Co. B, not stated.

FOWLER, WILLIAM.—Second lieutenant, One Hundred and Seventy-third Infantry; mustered in as first lieutenant, Co. I, this regiment, November 11, 1863; as captain, Co. C, December 22, 1864; discharged, February 22, 1865, for promotion to captain and A. A. G., U. S. Vols.

Commissioned first lieutenant, July 29, 1863, with rank

500

from April 23, 1863, vice J. Rodenhurst resigned; captain, November 30, 1864, with rank from September 28, 1864, vice J. E. Jenkins discharged. Brevet major by U. S. Gov't, from March 29, 1865.

GRAHAM, JOSEPH.—Age, date, place of enlistment, term and muster-in as private, Co. K, not stated; no further record.

HILL, JOHN.—Age, date, place, term and muster-in as private, Co. B, not stated; captured in action, no date; no further record.

HOGAN, MARTIN.—Private, Co. E, Thirteenth Infantry, transferred to Co. E, this regiment, January 14, 1864; captured in action, May 5, 1864, at the Wilderness, Va.; paroled, and discharged, no dates.

JENKINS, JAMES E.—First lieutenant, Oneida Independent Cavalry Company; mustered in as captain, Co. H, this regiment, March 1, 1863; wounded in action, July 3, 1863, at Gettysburg, Pa.; discharged, September 30, 1864.

Commissioned, not mustered, first lieutenant, January 22, 1863, with rank from January 20, 1863, vice W. Ballou resigned; captain, February 23, 1863, with rank from February 2, 1863. Brevet major by U. S. Gov't from March 13, 1865.

JOHNSON, CHARLES E.—Private, Co. G, Ninth Infantry, transferred to Co. G, this regiment, April 4, 1864; mustered out, September 4, 1865, at New York.

KELLY, ABRAHAM G.—Private, Co. I, Thirty-eighth Infantry; transferred to Co. C, this regiment, August, 1863; discharged for disability, August 15, 1864, at Washington, D. C.; also borne as Abram G. Kelly.

KUHN, FREDERICK.—Private, Co. A, Twentieth Infantry; transferred to Co. C, this regiment, June 7, 1864; captured, no date, died of disease, December 23, 1864, at Salisbury, S. C.

KUHN, JOHN A.—Age, date, place of enlistment, term of service and muster-in as private, Co. B, not stated; joined company, October 29, 1863; no further record.

LITTLE, W.—Age, date, place, term of enlistment and muster-in as private, Co. H, not stated; no record subsequent to October 26, 1863.

Lung, P.—Age, date, place of enlistment and muster-in as private, Co. K, not stated; no record subsequent to October 12, 1863.

Myers, George F.—Private, Co. D, Eighty-fourth Infantry; transferred to Co. C, this regiment, August 28, 1863; mustered out, June 3, 1865, near Alexandria, Va.

Reeves, A.—Age, place, date of enlistment and muster-in as private, Co. K, not stated; no record subsequent to February, 1864.

Simpson, James A.—Private, One Hundred and Sixty-sixth Infantry; transferred to Co. K, this regiment, April 23, 1864; captured in action, May 5, 1864, at the Wilderness, Va.; no further record.

Stone, Adam.—Private, Co. I, Thirty-seventh Infantry; transferred to Co. G, this regiment, January 14, 1864; to Co. E, no date.

Stowell, Henry W.—Private, Co. K, Thirty-fourth Infantry; transferred to Co. E, this regiment, January, 1864; captured in action, June 2, 1864, at Cold Harbor, Va.; released, April 21, 1865; discharged, July 11, 1865, at New York City.

Van Kuren, William H.—Private, Co. G, Eighteenth Infantry; transferred to Co. F, this regiment, no date; discharged for disability, March 16, 1865, at Washington, D. C.

Wilson, Joseph.—Private, One Hundred and Sixty-eighth Infantry; transferred to Co. K, this regiment, March 12, 1864; captured and paroled, no dates; died of disease, October 4, 1864, at Annapolis, Md.

RECAPITULATION

Original Enrollment	837
Subsequent Enrollment	278
By Transfer	
Fifth Infantry	325
Forty-fourth Infantry	196
Seventeenth Infantry	63
Miscellaneous	26
Total	1725

COMPLETE ROSTER OF OFFICERS, 146TH REGIMENT NEW YORK VOLUNTEERS[1]

GARRARD, KENNER.—Colonel, October 10, 1862; promoted brigadier-general of Volunteers, July 25, 1863; brevet major-general, December 15, 1864.

JENKINS, DAVID T.—Lieutenant-colonel, October 10, 1862; colonel, July 25, 1863; killed in action, May 5, 1864, at the Wilderness, Va.

GRINDLAY, JAMES G.—Captain, Co. D, October 10, 1862; major, June 8, 1864; lieutenant-colonel, January 1, 1865; colonel, March 1, 1865; brevet brigadier-general, March 13, 1865.

CURRAN, HENRY H.—First lieutenant, Co. E, October 10, 1862; captain, Co. I, December 10, 1862; Co. B, November 1, 1863; major, same date; killed in action, May 5, 1864, at the Wilderness, Va.

CLAESGENS, PETER C.—Captain, Co. F, October 10, 1862; major, January 1, 1865; lieutenant-colonel, April 1, 1865; brevet colonel, March 13, 1865.

POWELL, ISAAC P.—Captain, Co. G, October 10, 1862; major, March 30, 1865; brevet major, March 13, 1865.

ARMSTRONG, JESSE J.—Captain, Co. B, October 10, 1862; lieutenant-colonel, October 23, 1863; discharged, April 1, 1864.

CORNING, WILLIAM S.—Major, October 11, 1862; lieutenant-colonel, August 28, 1863; discharged, September 23, 1863.

FLANDRAU, THOMAS M.—Surgeon, August 25, 1862; brevet lieutenant-colonel, March 13, 1865; brevet colonel, by New York State Government.

[1] Unless otherwise noted, officer was mustered out with regiment, July 16, 1865.

FENWICK, ROBERT.—Assistant surgeon, June 7, 1863.

ERDMAN, ALBERT.—Chaplain, October 10, 1862; discharged, August 3, 1863.

PAYSON, EDWARD P.—Chaplain, March 12, 1864.

CASE, A. PIERSON.—First lieutenant and quartermaster, October 10, 1862; discharged for disability, October 27, 1863; brevet major by New York State Government.

COMSTOCK, EDWARD.—First lieutenant and adjutant, October 10, 1862; transferred as first lieutenant to Co. E, April 24, 1864; discharged, August 28, 1864; brevet major, March 13, 1865.

WRIGHT, WILLIAM.—Private, Co. K, October 10, 1862; sergeant-major, January 31, 1863; second lieutenant, Co. E, April 26, 1863; Co. G, August 14, 1863; first lieutenant, Co. E, October 27, 1863; adjutant, April 28, 1864; discharged for wounds, September 28, 1864; brevet captain, March 13, 1865.

EGLESTON, MARVIN.—First sergeant, Co. D, October 10, 1862; second lieutenant, Co. B, January 1, 1863; quartermaster, November 19, 1863; brevet captain, March 13, 1865.

PITCHER, JAMES P.—Corporal, Co. D, October 10, 1862; quarter-master sergeant, January 1, 1864; second lieutenant, Co. D, October 19, 1864; first lieutenant, Co. I, January 19, 1865; adjutant, to date, December 1, 1864; brevet captain, March 13, 1865.

KING, ALONZO I.—Private, Co. K, October 10, 1862; sergeant, same date; returned to ranks, December 17, 1862; sergeant, January 15, 1863; second lieutenant, Co. C, to date January 8, 1863; first lieutenant, Co. A, December 1, 1864; captain, February 1, 1865; brevet captain, April 1, 1865.

FITZPATRICK, LAWRENCE.—First sergeant, Co. B, Fifth Infantry; transferred to Co. B, this regiment, May 4, 1863; second lieutenant, October 29, 1863; first lieutenant, May 5, 1865; captain, June 21, 1865; brevet captain, March 13, 1865.

WALKER, WILLIAM A.—First sergeant, Co. B, October 10, 1862; returned to ranks, November 22, 1862; corporal, January 10, 1863; sergeant, February 1, 1863; second lieutenant, Co. D, March 1, 1863; transferred to Co. E, August 20, 1863; first lieutenant, Co. C, October 23, 1863; captain, April 1, 1865; brevet major, March 13, 1865.

LOOMIS, HENRY.—Sergeant, Co. G, October 10, 1862; first sergeant, December 10, 1862; second lieutenant, Co. K, February 1, 1863; transferred to Co. D, July 12, 1864; first lieutenant, September 16, 1864; captain, February 1, 1865; brevet captain, March 13, 1865.

WRIGHT, B. FRANKLIN.—Private, Co. K, October 10, 1862; sergeant-major, same date; second lieutenant, Co. E, December 27, 1862; transferred to Co. D, January 7, 1863; captain, Co. E, March 1, 1863.

SWEET, W. H. SEWARD.—First sergeant, Co. F, October 10, 1862; first lieutenant, Co. B, January 10, 1863; transferred to Co. F, January 25, 1864; captain, to date May 5, 1865.

YORK, LEVI H.—Second lieutenant, Co. G, October 10, 1862; first lieutenant, February 17, 1863; captain, April 1, 1865.

WARREN, ROBERT P.—Second lieutenant, Co. H, August 14, 1863; first lieutenant, Co. K, November 20, 1863; captain Co. H, April 1, 1865; brevet major, March 13, 1865.

JONES, HENRY E.—Private, Co. I, October 10, 1862; first sergeant, no date; second lieutenant, Co. G, January 7, 1863; first lieutenant, Co. D, March 1, 1863; captain, Co. I, September 24, 1863; brevet major, March 13, 1865.

WILSON, THOMAS A.—First sergeant, Co. G, October 10, 1862; second lieutenant, Co. E, December 27, 1862; first lieutenant, January 15, 1863; captain, Co. B, December 4, 1863; died of wounds, April 25, 1865.

DURKEE, JOSEPH H.—Second lieutenant, Co. E, October 10, 1862; first lieutenant, December 10, 1862; captain, Co. A, December 27, 1862; discharged, May 12, 1864.

DUTTON, CHARLES K.—Second lieutenant, Co. H, November 1, 1862; first lieutenant, December 26, 1862; captain, September 20, 1864; discharged, March 13, 1865; brevet major, March 13, 1865.

CUSHMAN, JOSEPH B.—First lieutenant, Co. K, October 10, 1862; captain, Co. C, October 29, 1863; discharged for disability, June 1, 1864.

FOWLER, WILLIAM.—Second lieutenant, 173rd Infantry; first lieutenant, Co. I, this regiment, November 11, 1863; captain, Co. C, December 22, 1864; discharged, February 22, 1865, for promotion to captain and A. A. G. U. S. Volunteers.

JONES, EZEKIEL.—Captain, Co. I, October 10, 1862; died of disease, November 11, 1862.

JENKINS, JAMES E.—First lieutenant, Oneida Independent Cavalry Company; captain, Co. H, this regiment, March 1, 1863; discharged, September 30, 1864; brevet major, March 13, 1865.

LAMBIE, GAVIN A.—Captain, Co. E, October 10, 1862; died of disease, February 15, 1863.

LOWERY, JOSEPH S.—Sergeant, Co. D, October 10, 1862; second lieutenant, Co. I, January 31, 1863; first lieutenant, Co. D, October 23, 1863; transferred to Co. A, October 1, 1864; captain, to date September 16, 1864; discharged for disability, January 13, 1865; brevet major, March 13, 1865; brevet lieutenant-colonel, by New York State Gov't.

STEWART, JAMES.—First lieutenant, Co. G, October 10, 1862; captain, Co. K, January 7, 1863; discharged, May 15, 1865; brevet major, March 13, 1865.

JENNISON, J. ALBERT.—Private, Co. C, October 10, 1862; sergeant and first sergeant, no dates; second lieutenant, Co. K, January 17, 1864; first lieutenant, February 1, 1865; brevet captain, April 1, 1865.

HANDWRIGHT, JR., JAMES.—Private, Co. A, October 10, 1862; first sergeant, no date, first lieutenant, Co. B, June 25, 1865; brevet captain, March 13, 1865.

McGEEHAN, JOHN.—Private, Co. B, Fifth Infantry; transferred to Co. C, this regiment, May 4, 1863; second lieutenant, Co. F, August 17, 1863; transferred to Co. C, April 28, 1865; first lieutenant, to date December 30, 1864; brevet captain, March 13, 1865.

BENNETT, EDWARD.—First lieutenant, Co. A, 44th Infantry; transferred to Co. D, this regiment, October 11, 1864.

DAVIS, EDWARD J.—Private, Co. D, October 10, 1862; Hospital Steward, August 1, 1863; first lieutenant, Co. E, March 3, 1865; brevet captain, April 1, 1865.

JONES, EDWARD O.—Corporal, Co. F, October 10, 1862; sergeant, April 1, 1863; first sergeant, March 26, 1865; second lieutenant, Co. E, March 30, 1865; first lieutenant, Co. I, May 7, 1865; brevet captain, March 13, 1865.

SEAMAN, JEROME B.—Private, Co. G, October 10, 1862; sergeant and first sergeant, no dates; second lieutenant, Co. G, December 1, 1864; first lieutenant, May 30, 1865.

TAYLOR, HENRY G.—Corporal, Co. D, Fifth Infantry; transferred to Co. K, this regiment, May 4, 1863; first sergeant, no date; second lieutenant, Co. H, October 8, 1864; first lieutenant, February 1, 1865; brevet captain, April 1, 1865.

BUCKINGHAM, CHARLES L.—Second lieutenant, Co. I, October 17, 1863; first lieutenant, July 1, 1864; Co. B, September 2, 1864; killed between lines, September 2, 1864.

KLOCK, GEORGE J.—Corporal, Co. D, October 10, 1862; sergeant and first sergeant, no dates; second lieutenant, Co. I, January 17, 1865; first lieutenant, March 30, 1865; discharged, June 1, 1865; brevet first lieutenant, April 1, 1865.

MATTERSON, EUGENE R.—First sergeant, Co. E, October 10, 1862; second lieutenant, Co. A, December 27, 1862; first lieutenant, January 7, 1863; discharged, June 11, 1864.

RUDY, DAVID M.—Sergeant, Co. B, October 10, 1862; first sergeant, November 22, 1862; returned to sergeant, May 9, 1863; second lieutenant, Co. A, January 16, 1865; brevet first lieutenant, April 1, 1865.

OLIN, GEORGE, JR.—Private, Co. D, December 15, 1862; corporal, no date; second lieutenant, Co. F, March 1, 1865.

BROWNELL, ALBERT E.—Private, Co. K, October 10, 1862; sergeant-major, December 27, 1862; second lieutenant, Co. A, January 30, 1863; discharged, November 25, 1864.

CHALMERS, HUGH.—First sergeant, Co. H, Fifth Infantry; transferred to Co. E, this regiment, May 4, 1863; second lieutenant, Co. H, November 20, 1863; transferred to Co. E, January 25, 1864; died of wounds, June 9, 1864.

COAN, ARTHUR V.—Corporal, Co. G, October 10, 1862; promoted first sergeant, March 9, 1863; second lieutenant, Co. G, March 1, 1864; died of wounds, September 30, 1864.

EMPEY, LAFAYETTE.—Sergeant, Co. E, October 10, 1862; second lieutenant, to date November 19, 1864; mustered out, June 20, 1865, at Annapolis, Md.

FROELIGH, PETER D.—First sergeant, Co. E, Fifth Infantry; transferred to Co. C, this regiment, May 4, 1863; second lieutenant, Co. D, August 18, 1863; transferred to Co. H,

January 25, 1864; killed in action, May 5, 1864, at the Wilderness, Va.

JONES, CHARLES T.—Corporal, Co. I, Fifth Infantry; transferred to Co. A, this regiment, May 4, 1863; sergeant, no date; second lieutenant, to date, May 19, 1864; discharged, February 6, 1865.

LULL, HENRY C.—Corporal, Co. C, October 10, 1862; sergeant, February 1, 1863; first sergeant, no date; second lieutenant, April 18, 1865.

MOULD, GEORGE.—Private, Co. H, October 10, 1862; sergeant and first sergeant, no dates; second lieutenant, to date October 8, 1864; discharged, June 1, 1865, at Annapolis, Md.

TIMERMAN, DAVID.—Sergeant, Co. F, October 10, 1862; first sergeant, February 21, 1863; second lieutenant, Co. E, November 17, 1863; transferred to Co. D, January 25, 1864; Co. K, July 12, 1864; discharged for disability, August 10, 1864.

BASS, EDGAR C.—Assistant surgeon, October 10, 1862; discharged, August 17, 1863.

FOSSARD, GEORGE H.—Assistant surgeon, September 22, 1863; discharged, October 17, 1864.

MORRIS, WILLIAM H. H.—Assistant surgeon, February 3, 1865.

SOMER, ELBERT M.—Assistant surgeon, October 10, 1862; discharged, December 7, 1862.

BRADISH, JAMES S.—Assistant surgeon, February 10, 1863.

ALDEN, SPENCER B.—Second lieutenant, Co. C, October 10, 1862; discharged, January 10, 1863.

BALLOU, WALTER.—First lieutenant, Co. D, October 10, 1862; discharged, December 28, 1862.

CONE, GEORGE W.—Captain, Co. A, October 10, 1862; discharged, November 29, 1862.

DANIELS, JAMES A.—Private, Co. A, October 10, 1862; first sergeant, no date; second lieutenant, Co. H, January 31, 1863.

DODGE, DON A.—Captain, Co. K, October 10, 1862; discharged, January 7, 1863.

GRAVES, FERDINAND V.—Second lieutenant, Co. D, October 10, 1862; discharged, January 10, 1863.

HART, ROBERT.—Second lieutenant, Co. F, March 1, 1863.

JEWELL, E. VERN.—First lieutenant, Co. B, October 10, 1862; captain, Co. C, December 25, 1862; discharged, September 23, 1863.

JONES, THOMAS C.—First lieutenant, Co. A, October 10, 1862; Co. C, December 22, 1862; discharged, January 7, 1863.

LASHER, CHARLES E.—Private, Co. K, October 10, 1862; first sergeant, no date; second lieutenant, Co. C, January 13, 1863; first lieutenant, January 31, 1863.

LEWIS, GEORGE W. M.—Captain, Co. C, October 10, 1862; discharged, January 7, 1863.

MOTT, WALLACE M.—Second lieutenant, Co. K, October 10, 1862; discharged, December 28, 1862.

PERRY, GEORGE H.—First lieutenant, Co. F, October 10, 1862; discharged, January 10, 1863.

POOLE, ROBERT B.—Captain, Co. H, October 10, 1862.

REITZHEIMER, LAWRENCE.—First sergeant, U. S. Army; second lieutenant, Co. B, this regiment, April 25, 1863.

RODENHURST, JAMES.—Second lieutenant, Co. I, October 10, 1862; first lieutenant, no date; discharged, April 23, 1863.

SMITH, HENRY G.—Corporal, Co. B, Forty-fourth Infantry; transferred to Co. D, this regiment, October 11, 1864; returned to ranks, no date; second lieutenant, Co. G, April 27, 1865; discharged, May 26, 1865.

SMITH, WILLIAM H.—Second lieutenant, Co. F, October 10, 1862; discharged, January 10, 1863.

STANFORD, WILLIAM J.—Second lieutenant, Co. A, October 10, 1862; transferred to Co. H, December 27, 1862; discharged, January 7, 1863.

TOWNSLEY, A. DEVOMEY.—Second lieutenant, Co. B, October 10, 1862; discharged, December 25, 1862.

WICKS, JACOB.—First lieutenant, Co. I, October 10, 1862; discharged, November 25, 1862.

WILSON, ANDREW J.—First lieutenant, Co. H, October 10, 1862; transferred to Co. A, December 2, 1862; discharged, January 7, 1863.

TRUAX, SILAS J.—First lieutenant, Co. C, October 10, 1862; discharged, November 30, 1862.

OFFICERS OF THE 146TH REGIMENT WHO RECEIVED BREVETS[1]

Under Act of Congress approved March 3, 1863, certain officers of Volunteers were "Brevetted" for "gallant action or meritorious conduct during the war," by the President, with the consent of the Senate of the United States. This honor was bestowed upon thirty (30) officers of the 146th Regiment. No other infantry regiment from New York State received so many such awards and the number is equalled only by the 4th Artillery.

The list of officers of the 146th who were "brevetted" is as follows:

As *Major-General*

Brigadier-General Kenner Garrard, promoted from Colonel.

As *Brigadier-General*

Colonel James G. Grindlay, promoted from Captain.

As *Colonel*

Lieutenant-Colonel Peter C. Claesgens, promoted from Captain.
Captain James Stewart, promoted from First Lieutenant.

As *Lieutenant-Colonel*

Surgeon Thomas M. Flandrau.
Captain Thomas A. Wilson, promoted from Sergeant.

As *Major*

Major Isaac P. Powell, promoted from Captain.
First Lieutenant and Adjutant Edward Comstock.

[1] List compiled from official records in *New York in the War of the Rebellion.*

Captain William A. Walker, promoted from Sergeant.
Captain Robert P. Warren, promoted from Second Lieutenant.
Captain Henry E. Jones, promoted from Private.
Captain Charles K. Dutton, promoted from Second Lieutenant.
Captain James E. Jenkins.
Captain Joseph S. Lowery, promoted from Sergeant.
Captain William Fowler, promoted from First Lieutenant.

As *Captain*

Adjutant William Wright, promoted from Private.
Quartermaster Marvin Egleston, promoted from Sergeant.
Adjutant James P. Pitcher, promoted from Corporal.
Captain Alonzo I. King, promoted from Private.
Captain Lawrence Fitzpatrick, promoted from Sergeant.
Captain W. H. Seward Sweet, promoted from Sergeant.
Captain Henry Loomis, promoted from Sergeant.
First Lieutenant J. Albert Jennison, promoted from Private.
First Lieutenant James Handwright, Jr., promoted from Private.
First Lieutenant John McGeehan, promoted from Private.
First Lieutenant Edward J. Davis, promoted from Private.
First Lieutenant Edward O. Jones, promoted from Corporal.
First Lieutenant Henry G. Taylor, promoted from Corporal.

As *First Lieutenant*

First Lieutenant George J. Klock, promoted from Corporal.
Second Lieutenant David M. Rudy, promoted from Sergeant.

Similarly, brevets were conferred by the New York State Government, under concurrent resolutions of the Legislature of April 24 and 28, 1865. The following officers of the 146th Regiment received such brevets:

As *Colonel*

Surgeon Thomas M. Flandrau.

As *Lieutenant-Colonel*

Captain Joseph S. Lowery.

As *Major*

First Lieutenant and Quartermaster A. Pierson Case.

As *First Lieutenant*

Corporal John Shardin, Color-bearer.

MEDALS OF HONOR

Sixteen medals of honor were awarded to men of the Fifth Corps for distinguished services, under Resolution of Congress approved July 12, 1863, and Section 6 of Act of Congress, approved March 3, 1863. Of the men to receive this distinction, three were members of the One Hundred and Forty-sixth Regiment, this number being the highest of any single regiment of the corps. The members of the 146th to receive the awards were:

James G. Grindlay, Colonel, for conspicuous bravery in the battle of Five Forks, Va., April 1, 1865.

Thomas G. Murphy, First Sergeant, Co. G., for the capture of a flag at Five Forks, Va., April 1, 1865.

David Edwards, Private, Co. H, for the capture of a flag at Five Forks, Va., April 1, 1865.

RECORD OF SERVICE, 146TH REGIMENT N. Y. VOLUNTEERS

Casey's Division, Defenses of Washington, from October 1862 to November 1862.

Third Brigade, Second Division, Fifth Corps, from November 1862.

Second Brigade, Second Division, Fifth Corps, from October, 1863.

First Brigade, First Division, Fifth Corps, from March, 1864.

First Brigade, Second Division, Fifth Corps, from June, 1864.

Duty in Defenses of Washington, October 12 to November 5, 1862.

Moved to near Falmouth, Va., November 6 to 21, 1862.

Battle of Fredericksburg, December 11 to 15, 1862.

Duty near Potomac Creek, from December 17, 1862 to April 27, 1863.

Mud March, January 20 to 23, 1863.

Chancellorsville Campaign, April 27 to May 6, 1863.

Battle of Chancellorsville, May 1 to 3, 1863.

Pennsylvania Campaign, June 13 to July 31, 1863.

Battle of Gettysburg, July 1 to 3, 1863.

Action at Williamsport, Maryland, July 14, 1863.

Duty near Warrenton, Beverly Ford and Culpeper, Virginia, to October 9, 1863.

Bristoe Campaign, October 9 to 22, 1863.

Action at Bristoe Station, October 14, 1863.

Action near Rappahannock Station, October 21, 1863.

Battle of Rappahannock Station, November 7, 1863.

Mine Run Campaign, November 26 to December 2, 1863.

Duty on the Orange and Alexandria Railroad, December, 1863 to May, 1864.

Campaign from Rapidan to Petersburg, May 4 to June 16, 1864.

Battle of the Wilderness, May 5 to 7, 1864.

Battle of Spottsylvania Court House, May 8 to 21, 1864.

Piney Branch Church, May 8, 1864.

Laurel Hill, May 10, 1864.

Gayle's House, May 14, 1864.

Battles of the North Anna River, May 22 to 26, 1864.

Jericho Ford, May 22 to 24, 1864.

Totopotomoy Creek, May 27 to 31, 1864.

Battles of Bethesda Church and Magnolia Swamp, June 1 to 4, 1864.

Battle of Cold Harbor, June 4 to 12, 1864.

Action at White Oak Swamp, June 13, 1864.

Siege of Petersburg, from June 16, 1864 to April 2, 1865.

Assault on Petersburg, June 17 to 19, 1864.

Moved to support of Ninth Corps, in reserve during the explosion of the mine, and Battle of the Crater, July 30, 1864.

Descent on Weldon Railroad, August 18 to 21, 1864.

Action near the Yellow House, August 18 to 20, 1864.

Action near Davis House, August 19, 1864.

Battle of Poplar Spring Church, September 30 to October 2, 1864.

Action at the Davis House, October 8, 1864.

Battle of Hatcher's Run or Boydton Plank Road, October 27 and 28, 1864.

Raid on Weldon Railroad, December 7 to 12, 1864.

Operations at Hatcher's Run, Rowanty Creek, Vaughn Road and Dabney's Mills, February 5 to 7, 1865.

Moved to support the Ninth Corps at Fort Stedman, March 25, 1865.

Appomattox Campaign, from March 29 to April 9, 1865.

Battle of White Oak Ridge, March 29 to 31, 1865.

Battle of Five Forks, April 1, 1865.

Fall of Petersburg, April 2, 1865.

Appamattox Campaign—*Continued*
  Surrender of Army of Northern Virginia, Appomattox
    Court House, April 9, 1865.
March to Washington, D. C., May 1 to 12, 1865.
Grand Review in Washington, May 23, 1865.
Mustered out, July 16, 1865, near Washington.

ROSTER OF 146TH REGIMENT WHEN MUSTERED OUT OF SERVICE, JULY 16, 1865

FIELD AND STAFF

Colonel, James G. Grindlay.
Lieutenant-Colonel, Peter C. Claesgens.
Major, Isaac P. Powell.
Adjutant, James P. Pitcher.
Surgeon, Thomas M. Flandrau.
Assistant Surgeons: Robert Fenwick, William H. H. Morris.
Chaplain, Edward P. Payson.
Quartermaster, Marvin Egleston.
Quartermaster-Sergeant, Lynde G. Wetmore.
Commissary Sergeant, Eliakim Root.
Sergeant-Major, Henry Sorn.
Principal Musician, W. Beriah Chandler.

COMPANY A

Captain, Alonzo I. King.
Second Lieutenant, David M. Rudy.
Sergeants: First, Thomas Wheeler; Second, William Bright; Third, Charles B. Rolling; Fourth, George Shott.
Corporals: First, George S. Lent.
Musicians: Frederick White.
Privates: Richard Bell, Edward Burbridge, Orlando Coster, Joseph Corragan, William Hinkstone, Jr., Sebastian Hamberger, Joseph Lamour, Stephen Lent, Cyrus Mansfield, Andrew Smith, Job P. Whipple, Philip Freas.

COMPANY B

Captain, Lawrence Fitzpatrick.
First Lieutenant, James Handwright, Jr.

Sergeants: First, William Luyster; Second, Daniel Coppersmith; Third, George O. Tibbits; Fourth, William S. Seeley; Fifth, John Yoos; Sixth, Smith H. Crocker.

Corporals: First, Stephen Weaver; Second, Edward D. Frelinghouse; Third, Othello H. Amidon.

Musicians: Charles Hecox.

Privates: Charles B. Ashley, James Conley, Charles A. Foote, Marcus Flood, John Farrell, Robert Jones, Ernst Kusteren, Robert Lynch, Lorenzo Moyer, David Moyer, Jerry Morenus, George W. Wolcott, Hugh Thomas.

COMPANY C

Captain, William A. Walker.
First Lieutenant, John McGeehan.
Second Lieutenant, Henry C. Lull.
Sergeants: First, Thomas Rowell; Second, Edwin Glover.
Corporals: First, David Rees; Second, John F. Farrell; Third, Arnest Vanderoef; Fourth, Frederick Ernst; Fifth, Allen Watches.
Musicians: James Shaw, Alfred H. Palmer.
Privates: Francis Bowers, John Connan, John Callahan, Maurice Godfrey, Cornelius Haley, William Haynes, Theodore R. Jones, Peter LaBrack, Joseph D. Mercer, William B. Meeker, Hugh McDonald, James McTighe, George W. McKnight, Edward B. Parker, Charles Parker, Edward B. Paine, Charles Van Vleck, Titus White.

COMPANY D

Captain, Henry Loomis.
First Lieutenant, Edward Bennett.
Sergeants: First, Harvey Scouten; Second, Alvah Grey.
Corporals: First, Virgil Carruth; Second, James N. Kenney; Third, Chester Bates; Fourth, John McCarthy.
Musicians: Richard Keegan.
Privates: Thomas Aseltine, Daniel Banner, Hiram Barber, Norman Bates, Benjamin Colton, Stephen Chesboro, David Finch, Nicholas B. Grunwell, William R. Howland,

John B. Holt, Thomas Johnson, Lewis Miller, Jr., John R. Morris, John McManus, John McKown, William O'Horo, Stephen Wakeman, David Wally, Michael Waeliand.

COMPANY E

Captain, B. Franklin Wright.

First Lieutenant, Edward J. Davis.

Sergeants: First, Peter Blake, Jr.; Second, Horace M. Case; Third, Thomas Brown; Fourth, Alonzo S. Gibson; Fifth, Peter McCabe.

Corporals: First, George M. Cozine; Second, William F. Roberts; Third, William R. Faulkner; Fourth, Boyd Pemberton.

Privates: George F. Crawford, Henry W. Evans, Joseph S. Kellsy, Thomas Roberts, John Russell, Almanson Whitford, Wesley Whitford, Orson C. Wood.

COMPANY F

Captain, W. H. Seward Sweet.

Second Lieutenant, George Olin, Jr.

Sergeants: First, Emory C. Starr; Second, Burton Thompson; Third, Abram Bergee.

Corporals: First, John Zacker.

Musicians: James C. Eames.

Privates: James Edie, William D. Galt, Augustus Hahn, Christian P. Lang, Jacob Martin, Robert A. McGinnis, Horace Miller, Theophilus Orno, Godleiph Teufel, Henry Shaver.

COMPANY G

Captain, Levi H. York.

First Lieutenant, Jerome B. Seaman.

Sergeants: First, William T. Taylor; Second, William McGurk; Third, John Coogan.

Corporals: First, Anson H. Burlingame; Second, Edward Quinn; Third, Edwin Richardson; Fourth, Charles P. Mahan.

Privates: William Aitken, George Bacon, Daniel Blanchard, Joel B. Bancroft, John Campbell, Henry Clark, Sanford Drown, James Dean, Godfrey Frederick, John Goodfellow, Henry B. Hook, James Kelly, Curtis M. King, V. Patrick

Mahn, Francis Miller, William Reinold, William Reed, George W. Strong, Jeremiah Sullivan, Timothy Terrill, Timothy Twahy, Nathaniel H. Tompkins, Thomas Wilson, Richard T. Williams, Albert A. White.

COMPANY H

Captain, Robert P. Warren.

First Lieutenant, Henry G. Taylor.

Sergeants: First, Charles L. King; Second, John H. Bailey; Third, Hoadly Hosford; Fourth, William Bromily.

Corporals: First, David Edwards; Second, Richard O'Brien; Third, John Starkins.

Musicians: James H. Dagan.

Privates: John Baker, Joseph Clancy, Nathaniel Heath, Thomas Jones, Edward Jones, Joseph May, David Morgan, Thomas Stofford, Jr., Pemo Sliker, Rensselaer Wright, Samuel White, John J. Tracy.

COMPANY I

Captain, Henry E. Jones.

First Lieutenant, Edward O. Jones.

Sergeants: First, George W. Jones; Second, George W. Wheeler; Third, Miles B. Kellogg; Fourth, Leander Martin; Fifth, Jacob P. Fulmer.

Corporals: First, Conrad Neuschler; Second, Henry F. Chamberlain.

Privates: Lysander C. Ball, John Harter, William E. Jones, Michael Mahoney, Joseph Maebett, Christopher Nelson, Robert C. Orcutt, Charles Phillips, Stephen Simpkins, John Sisbar, Samuel Shoefelt, George Smith, William Smith, Thomas Van Alstyne, James Watson, Edward Westcott, George Winter, Henry Winter, Henry Weeks, Thomas R. Michaels.

COMPANY K

First Lieutenant, J. Albert Jennison.

Sergeants: First, Martin Clancey; Second, Michael Doherty; Third, Sigmund Schwerkart; Fourth, Harvey Gifford; Fifth, Walter P. Shaw.

Corporals: First, John Edwards; Second, George R. Soper.

Privates: George W. Bates, Bemas Buckley, Oscar L. Cady, Philip Cassidy, Sylvester Dearing, Lewellen DeFreest, Joseph Graham, Patrick Kearney, Martin Mahoney, Homer W. Palmer, Theodore Parks, Whitman Phillips, William Rodman, Patrick Sweeney, Jons Van Louvan, Lorenzo Williams, Andrew J. Williams, Carl Westfall, Charles Young.

RECAPITULATION

Field and Staff	13
Company A	20
B	25
C	30
D	28
E	19
F	17
G	34
H	22
I	29
K	27
Total	264

BATTLES, ENGAGEMENTS, SKIRMISHES, ETC., IN WHICH THE 146TH REGIMENT PARTICIPATED

The following chronological list of the engagements in which the 146th Regiment participated is taken from the official records embodied in the book, *New York in the War of the Rebellion.* A decision of the War Department is to this effect: Troops on the ground (battle-field), though not engaged, are entitled to be credited with the engagement. Engagements of any duration, as for instance, "Spottsylvania," "Cold Harbor," etc., have been subdivided into the more important actions of which they consisted.

1862

December 11–15. Battle of Fredericksburg, Va.

Brigade 3, Warren; Division 2, Sykes; Corps 5, Butterfield; Commanding Officer, Col. Kenner Garrard. Casualties—1 enlisted man wounded; 17 enlisted men captured or missing. Aggregate, 18.

1863

May 1–3. Battle of Chancellorsville, Va.

Brigade 3, O'Rorke; Division 2, Sykes; Corps 5, Meade; Commanding Officer, Col. Kenner Garrard. Casualties. —2 enlisted men killed; 1 officer, 16 enlisted men wounded; 2 officers, 29 enlisted men captured and missing. Aggregate, 50.

July 1–3. Battle of Gettysburg, Pa.

Brigade 3, Weed (k), O'Rorke (k), Garrard; Division 2, Ayres; Corps 5, Sykes; Commanding Officer, Col. Kenner Garrard (c), Lt.-Col. David T. Jenkins. Casualties.—

4 enlisted men killed; 2 officers, 22 enlisted men wounded. Aggregate, 28.

July 14. Skirmish at Williamsport, Md.

Oct. 14. Skirmish at Bristoe Station, Va.

November 7. Engagement at Rappahannock Station, Va.

November 26–December 2. Mine Run Campaign, Va.

Brigade 3, Garrard; Division 2, Ayres; Corps 5, Sykes; Commanding Officer, Col. David T. Jenkins. Casualties.— 1 enlisted man captured.

1864

May 5–7. Battle of the Wilderness, Va.

Brigade 1, Ayres; Division 1, Griffin; Corps 5, Warren; Commanding Officer, Col. David T. Jenkins (k), Lt.-Col. Henry H. Curran (k), Maj. James G. Grindlay. Casualties. —3 officers, 17 enlisted men killed; 5 officers, 62 enlisted men wounded; 6 officers, 219 enlisted men captured and missing. Aggregate, 312.

May 8–21. Battle of Spottsylvania Court House, Va.

Brigade 1, Ayres; Division 1, Griffin; Corps 5, Warren; Commanding Officer, Maj. James G. Grindlay. Casualties. —3 enlisted men killed; 1 officer, 12 enlisted men wounded. Aggregate, 16.

May 8. Engagement at Piney Branch Church, Va.

May 10. Actions at Alsop's Farm and Laurel Hill, Va.

May 14. Engagement at Gayle's House, Va.

May 22–26. Battle of North Anna, Va.

May 27–31. Battle of Totopotomoy, Va. (Also Bethesda Church, June 1.)

Brigade 1, Ayres; Division 1, Griffin; Corps 5, Warren; Commanding Officer, Maj. James G. Grindlay. Casualties. —1 enlisted man killed; 9 enlisted men wounded. Aggregate, 10.

May 31–June 12. Battle of Cold Harbor, Va.

Brigade 1, Ayres; Division 1, Griffin; Corps 5, Warren; Commanding Officer, Maj. James G. Grindlay. Casualties. —3 enlisted men killed; 2 officers, 3 enlisted men wounded; 47 enlisted men captured and missing. Aggregate, 55.

June 2. Engagement at Bethesda Church, Va.

June 13–14. Skirmish at White Oak Swamp, Va. (Losses included in Cold Harbor.)

June 15, 1864 to April 2, 1865. Before Petersburg and Richmond.

June 15–19. Assault of Petersburg.

Brigade 1, Gregory; Division 2, Ayres; Corps 5, Warren. Commanding Officer, Major James G. Grindlay. Casualties.—4 enlisted men killed; 13 enlisted men wounded. Aggregate, 17.

August 18–21. Battle of Weldon Railroad, Va. (Vaughn Road, Globe Tavern, Yellow House.)

Brigade 1, Hayes; Division 2, Ayres; Corps 5, Warren. Commanding Officer, Maj. James G. Grindlay. Casualties. —2 enlisted men killed; 1 officer, 6 enlisted men wounded; 1 officer, 36 enlisted men captured and missing. Aggregate, 46.

September 29–October 2. Battle of Poplar Springs Church, Va.

Brigade 1, Otis (w), Grindlay; Division 2, Ayres; Corps 5, Warren; Commanding Officer, Maj. James G. Grindlay (c), Capt. Thomas A. Wilson. Casualties.—3 enlisted men wounded.

October 27–28. Battle of Boydton Plank Road, or Hatcher's Run, Va.

Brigade 1, Winthrop; Division 2, Ayres; Corps 5, Warren; Commanding Officer, Major James G. Grindlay.

December 6–11. Raid on Weldon Railroad to Hicksford, Va.

1865

February 5–8. Engagement at Hatcher's Run, Va.

Brigade 1, Winthrop; Division 2, Ayres; Corps 5, Warren; Commanding Officer, Lt.-Col. James G. Grindlay.

March 28–April 9. Appomattox Campaign, Va.

Brigade 1, Winthrop (k), Grindlay; Division 2, Ayres; Commanding Officer, Colonel James G. Grindlay (c), Lieut. Henry Loomis, Col. Grindlay. Casualties.—5 enlisted men killed; 4 officers, 34 enlisted men wounded; 22 enlisted men captured and missing. Aggregate, 65.

March 29–31. Battle of White Oak Ridge.

April 1. Battle of Five Forks.

April 2. Fall of Petersburg and Evacuation of Richmond.

April 11. Appomattox Court House, Va. Surrender of Gen. Robert E. Lee.

CASUALTIES, 146TH REGIMENT N. Y. VOLUNTEERS

During its service the regiment lost by death, killed in action, 3 officers, 81 enlisted men; of wounds received in action, 4 officers, 46 enlisted men; of disease and other causes, 2 officers, 187 enlisted men; total, 9 officers, 314 enlisted men. The total aggregate losses of the regiment in killed, wounded, and missing during their term of service being 654 men; of whom 1 officer, 87 enlisted men died in the hands of the enemy.

The casualties of the regiment in the various engagements in which it participated are as follows:[1]

PLACE	Date	Killed		Wounded — Died		Wounded — Reco.		Missing		Aggregate
		Officers	En. men	Officers	En. men	Officers	En. men	Officers	En. men	
Fredericksburg, Va.	1862 Dec. 11–15	..	..	..	1	..	...	...	17	18
Chancellorsville, Va.	1863 May 1–3	..	2	..	3	1	13	2	29	50
Gettysburg, Pa.	July 1–3	..	4	..	3	2	19	..	...	28
Williamsport, Md.	14	..	1	..	..	..	...	..	...	1
Bristoe Station, Va.	Oct. 14	..	..	..	..	..	...	..	...	...
Rappahannock Station, Va.	21	..	..	..	..	..	...	..	...	...
Rappahannock Station, Va.	Nov. 7	..	..	..	..	..	...	..	...	...
Mine Run campaign, Va.	Nov. 26–Dec. 2	..	1	..	..	..	...	..	...	1
Wilderness, Va.	1864 May 5–7	3	52	..	10	5	52	6	184	312
Spottsylvania C. H., Va.	8–21	..	..	..	..					
Piney Branch Church	8	..	..	..	3	1	8	..	...	16
Laurel Hill	10	..	3	..	1					
Gayle's House	14	..	..	..	..					

[1] From *New York in the War of the Rebellion*, p. 488.

PLACE	Date	Killed		Wounded				Missing		Aggregate
				Died		Reco.				
		Officers	En. men	Officers	En. men	Officers	En. men	Officers	En. men	
North Anna, Va.	22–26	..	1	..	1 ⎫		7	..	...	10
Totopotomoy, Va.	27–31	..	..	..	1 ⎬					
Cold Harbor, Va	June 1–12	..	..	..	1 ⎫	1	1	..	46	55
Bethesda Church.	2	..	4	1	1 ⎭					
White Oak Swamp, Va.	13	..	..	..	..	..	...	..	...	...
Before Petersburg, Va	June 16–Apr. 2, 1865	..	..	..	4	..	28	..	...	32
Assault of Petersburg, Va...	J'e 16–19	..	4	..	4	..	9	..	...	17
Weldon Railroad, Va.	Aug. 18–21	..	3	2	2	..	4	..	35	46
Poplar Spring Church, Va...	Sept. 30–Oct. 2	..	..	..	..	..	3	..	...	3
Hatcher's Run, Va.	Oct 27–28	..	..	..	..	..	...	..	...	...
Hicksford Raid, Va.	Dec. 6–11	..	..	..	..	..	...	..	...	...
Hatcher's Run, Va.	1865 Feb. 5–7	..	..	..	..	..	...			...
Appomattox campaign, Va.	Mch. 28–Apr. 9	..	..	..	..					
White Oak Ridge.	Mch. 29–31	..	5	..	8 ⎫	3	23	..	21	65
Five Forks	April 1	..	1	1	3 ⎬					
Fall of Petersburg.	2	..	..	..	.. ⎪					
Appomattox C. H.	9	..	..	..	.. ⎭					
Total loss.	....	3	81	4	46	13	167	8	332	654

The following list of men who were killed, wounded, captured or missing in the various battles and engagements in which the 146th Regiment participated is as complete as possible. It is compiled from the Report of the Adjutant General of the State of New York, which contains the individual record of each member of the regiment. In many cases, however, the record is not complete, and in others dates are missing which would indicate the battle in which the man was killed, wounded or captured, as the case may be.

FREDERICKSBURG.—Wounded: Chester Hall, Co. D.

CHANCELLORSVILLE.—Killed: Sergeant William P. Burnham, Co. E; John Garlock, Co. B; Menzo S. Gibbs, Co. A.   Wounded: Captain Joseph H. Durkee, Co. A; John Bright, Co. A; William Colwell, Co. A; Frederick Ernst, Co. C; William W. Givens, Co. A; Patrick Hiland, Co. B; James Secor, Co. E; Nathaniel P. Vanderhoff, Co. B.   Captured: Captain Joseph H. Durkee, Co. A; 1st Lieut. Eugene R. Matterson, Co. A; Sergeant Peter L. Dumont, Co. A; Peter Cary, Co. B; James Corey, Co. E; James Corragan, Co. A; James Dean, Co. G; Fletcher W. Dimbleby, Co. A; Harrison W. Elmer, Co. G; Frederick Ernst, Co. C; Thomas Jones, Co. A; James P. Kearns, Co. A; Michael Keating, Co. A; John Kempf, Co. A; Timothy Larmar, Co. A; John Latham, Co. A; John Leary, Co. A; James A. Lord, Co. G; Henry McKinney, Co. A; Francis Miller, Co. G; Alonzo Murray, Co. A; William A. Palmer, Co. A; Isaac J. Parker, Co. A; Abram Parks, Co. A; John Plunkett, Co. A; Thomas Sayer, Co. G; Andrew Smith, Co. A; Philip Smith, Co. A; George W. Strong, Co. G; James Ward, Co. A; John Webb, Co. A; Michael Wholahan, Co. G.

GETTYSBURG.—Killed: Sergeant Robert W. England, Co. K; Frank M. Dennis, Co. D; Ezra J. Hyde, Co. B; Joseph Schneebacher, Co. F.   Wounded: Captain James E. Jenkins, Co. H; Sergeant James P. Pitcher, Co. D; George W. Cook, Co. C; Frederick Ernst, Co. C; Samuel Gibbs, Co. D; Maurice Godfrey, Co. C; William McGurk, Co. G; Frederick Miller, Co. D; Adam Neiss, Co. D; James Palmer, Co. D.

BRISTOE STATION.—Captured: William Johnson, Co. I.

MINE RUN.—Captured: Charles G. Ashley, Co. G; Frederick Baker, Co. H.

WILDERNESS.—Killed: Colonel David T. Jenkins; Lieut.-Colonel Henry H. Curran; 2nd Lieut. Peter Froeligh, Co. H; Sergeant Peter L. Dumont, Co. A; Sergeant Christian Hart, Co. F; Frederick J. Agne, Co. F; George G. Ashforth, Co. B; Henry Bodey, Co. C; Henry B. Curtis, Co. I; William H. Curtis, Co. I; Richard H. Dousey, Co. F; Thomas Downing, Co. A; James F. Duff, Co. C; David Dunn, Co. E; John C. Fields, Co. I; Robert Graves, Co. F; Henry J. Jennison, Co. C; John E. Jones, Co. H; Gideon King, Co. H; John N. Langworth, Co. E; Timothy Larmar, Co. A; John Leary, Co. A; Herbert Markham, Co. F;

John B. McCarthy, Co. F; Adam K. Miller, Co. C; John Moriety, Co. K; Ezra Mowers, Co. F; Richard Mulcahy, Jr., Co. F; John Murphy, Co. B; William E. Pettee, Co. K; David Riffenberg, Co. K; Stephen Sadler, Co. I; Samuel Schilling, Co. C; Andrew J. Scranton, Co. I; Francis Secor, Co. E; Edmond Snyder, Co. C; James Swanson, Co. E; Robert Taylor, Co. F; Alexander Trembly, Co. C; Albert H. Voorhees, Co. E; John T. White, Co. H; George T. Wing, Co. B; George Witten, Co. A; Henry Zinn, Co. K. Wounded: Asst. Surgeon Robert Fenwick; Captain Henry E. Jones, Co. I; 1st Lieut. William A. Walker, Co. C; 2nd Lieut. Alonzo I. King, Co. C; 2nd Lieut. Charles L. Buckingham, Co. I; Adjutant William Wright; Sergeant Joseph Favreau, Co. B; Othello H. Amidon, Co. B; George M. Baker, Co. G; James Gibson, Co. H; Orville J. Barker, Co. G; James H. Jack, Co. K; William H. Kniffen, Co. H; Henry Laufer, Co. A; Maurice Mahoney, Co. K; James M. Primrose, Co. C; John Reekard, Co. H; William Shonhamer, Co. D; Samuel D. Tompkins, Co. F; Mark N. Walley, Co. D; Charles B. Wild, Co. B; George Worth, Co. B. Captured: Captain B. Franklin Wright, Co. E; Captain Isaac P. Powell, Co. G; 1st Lieut. William A. Walker, Co. C; 1st Lieut. William H. S. Sweet, Co. F; 2nd Lieut. Lawrence Fitzpatrick, Co. B; 2nd Lieut. John McGeehan, Co. F; Sergeant George H. Allen, Co. G; Sergeant Louis Dugal, Co. F; Sergeant Edward Dunning, Co.C; Sergeant John W. Goff, Co. G; Sergeant Charles T. Jones, Co. A; Sergeant Eugene McCarthy, Co. B; Sergeant George Mould, Co. H; Sergeant Chancy B. Smith, Co. H; Sergeant Charles A. Stannard, Co. I; Sergeant Emory C. Starr, Co. F; Sergeant Loring P. Stockwell, Co. G; Sergeant George W. Wheeler, Co. I; Samuel Ackley, Co. F; James Alverson, Co. G; Henry W. Baker, Co. F; Orville J. Barker, Co. G; Louis Belair, Co. F; John H. Berry, Jr., Co. I; Peter Blake, Jr., Co. E.; Daniel Blanchard, Co. G; John Bowman, Co. C; Charles B. Bowne, Co. H; Charles Brandage, Co. A; Lorenzo Brower, Co. F; Anson B. Brown, Co. F; Joseph Brown, Co. G; Thomas Brown, Co. E; Albert Bryant, Co. B; Edmond Burgess, Co. B; William Capron, Co. I; Silas Cargon, Co. G; Edward Claghorn, Co. H; Frank Clarke, Co. I; John Coogan, Co. G; George W. Crocker, Co. B; Smith H. Crocker, Co. B; Josiah Crupper, Co. G; John Curry, Co. B; James Dailey,

Co. F; William H. Davis, Co. B; Addison Dillenbeck, Co. I; William H. Dillon, Co. B; Joseph Dolph, Co. B; John Donnelly, Co. G; Alvin B. Dunbar, Co. F; Adam Eipence, Co. H; Anson D. Ellis, Co. I; Sylvester Ferry, Co. I; John Fisher, Co. F; Isaac M. Foster, Co. H; Ephraim French, Co. G; Reuben O. Gates, Co. A; John Gerhard, Co. B; Orville Gibbs, Co. H; Edwin Glover, Co. C; Michael Gordon, Co. K; Hugh Gough, Co. B; Charles A. Grant, Co. F; Josiah Hadsell, Co. B; Augustus Hahn, Co. F; Thomas Haley, Co. A; Thomas Haley, Co. C; William H. Hall, Co. I; Le Roy Hammond, Co. G; James Handwright, Co. A; William Harmon, Co. K; John H. Harrington, Co. I; Samuel Hart, Co. B; George Haskins, Co. F; John Hess, Co. H; Ralph Hinkley, Co. F; William M. Hodge, Co. E; Martin Hogan, Co. E; Henry B. Hook, Co. G; Edward Hughes, Co. E; John J. Hughes, Co. I; Farrar Jackson, Co. G; George W. Johnson, Co. F; Jesse C. Johnson, Co. A; Jesse Johnson, Jr., Co. A; Evan T. Jones, Co. I; Thomas Jones, Co. A; Joseph P. Kearns, Co. A; Michael Keating, Co. A; Miles B. Kellogg, Co. I; John Kempf, Co. A; John Kennedy, Co. E; John A. Kessler, Co. B; Charles L. King, Co. H; George King, Co. C; George H. Kingsley, Co. F; John H. Kratchberg, Co. C; George W. Lachell, Co. H; Joseph Lamour, Co. A; Cornelius Lane, Co. A; Joseph Lapoint, Co. D; George S. Lent, Co. A; George W. Lewis, Co. G; William Lomis, Co. H; James A. Lord, Co. G; Samuel H. Ludlow, Co. I; Henry C. Lull, Co. C; Lewis Martin, Co. A; Arthur Mayne, Co. H; Robert McCormick, Co. B; William McCrehn, Co. B; Stephen McGowen, Co. F; John McLean, Co. H; Eugene B. McMillen, Co. F; John Megert, Co. B; Lenox Millard, Co. H; Francis M. Miller, Co. G; Jerry Morenus, Co. B; James Mulkern, Co. G; Conrad Neuschler, Co. I; David T. Newcomb, Co. A; William Newlove, Co. A; Frederick A. Nodine, Co. G; Thomas J. Odlum, Co. A; Charles O'Keif, Co. F; Ozias D. Page, Co. F; Isaac J. Parker, Co. A; Joseph Pennar, Co. H; Charles E. Pierce, Co. I; Peter Pleitch, Co. C; John H. Pletter, Co. H; John Plunkett, Co. A; Robert Pogan, Co. A; Benjamin Pratt, Co. G; Robert A. Rawlings, Co. I; Jeremiah Reardon, Co. K; David Rees, Co. C; William D. Reid, Co. H; Newton J. Richards, Co. C; Edwin Richardson, Co. G; William B. Roberts, Co. E; James H. Robinson, Co. I; James Rodman, Co. H; Stephen

Saunders, Co. H; Thomas H. Sayer, Co. G; Henry Schott, Co. A; Richard E. Seaman, Co. I; Jonas Sell, Co. G; Eugene Seymour, Co. G; Norton Shepard, Co. B; George Schott, Co. A; John S. Shucker, Co. F; Henry Simon, Co. B; James A. Simpson, Co. K; John Sisbar, Co. K; Daniel Slack, Co. A; Henry Slade, Co. K; Andrew Smith, Co. A; Sidney H. Smith, Co. C; William L. Snyder, Co. F; Abraham Southern, Co. K; Alanson F. Spink, Co. F; George Stephenson, Co. C; William Stickle, Co. E; Arthur Stone, Co. I; Thomas Swindlehurst, Co. I; Timothy Terrill, Co. G; Aaron B. Thompson, Co. A; Lucius S. Tooly, Co. H; William Velsor, Co. C; Carroll S. Waldron, Co. G; Nelson Waldron, Co. K; James Ward, Co. A; Allen Watches, Co. C; Lawrence Welch, Co. B; Michael Welch, Co. C; Joseph Whalen, Co. H; Lafayette White, Co. F; Robert White, Co. H; John Wile, Co. B; George F. Williams, Co. B; Horatio P. Williams, Co. H; Peter Williams, Co. I; William Williams, Co. I; George Winter, Co. I; David R. Yaple, Co. K.

SPOTTSYLVANIA[1].—Killed: John A. Harter, Co. G; Thomas Harty, Co. H; William S. Parke, Co. E. Wounded: 2nd Lieut. David Timerman, Co. D; Sergeant James H. Everett, Co. D; Sergeant Stimpson Turrell, Co. K; Andrew Fuchs, Co. E; David Moyer, Co. B; Aaron P. Muckridge, Co. E; Freeman H. Perry, Co. F; John Skinner, Co. F.

NORTH ANNA RIVER.[2]—Killed: Owen Cavanough, Co. D. Wounded: Edward S. Bennett, Co. C; William Fishbourne, Co. B; John Franklin, Jr., Co. F.

COLD HARBOR AND BETHESDA CHURCH.—Killed: Zadock P. Hoagland, Co. D; Henry B. Sanders, Co. F; Jesse Thomas, Co. E. Wounded: 1st Lieut. Joseph S. Lowery, Co. D; 2nd Lieut. Hugh Chalmers, Co. E; Irvine Duncan, Co. E; Eri Z. Farnsworth, Co. E; James Lynch, Co. K. Captured: 2nd Lieut. Hugh Chalmers, Co. E; Sergeant Orlo H. Jones, Co. D; Sergeant Lafayette Empey, Co. E; John Avery, Co. D; George F. Bertine, Co. K; Stephen Chesboro, Co. D; Franklin Coffin, Co. B; Isaac H. Fitch, Co. D; Alonzo S. Gibson, Co. E; Joseph H. Holloway,

---

[1] Includes engagements known as Laurel Hill, Piney Branch Church, Gayle's House, etc.

[2] Includes Totopotomoy Creek.

Co. D; Samuel Hyde, Co. G; James Kelly, Co. K; William H. Lake, Co. K; Robert Little, Co. K; Henry W. Stowell, Co. E; John Swanson, Co. E; Aaron Weller, Co. K.

PETERSBURG.—Killed: Sergeant Horatio A. Walter, Co. B; Joseph R. Davis, Co. K; Michael Flynn, Co. F; George Molz, Co. F; Louis Polex, Co. K; Ira A. Simmons, Co. F. Wounded: Claude Charmville, Co. B; Charles Risley, Co. H; Morris Stephenson, Co. H. Captured: Curtis Goodnough, Co. K; Jacob Martin, Co. F; Joseph Robinson, Co. C; Stephen Weaver, Co. B.

WELDON RAILROAD[1].—Killed: 1st. Lieut. Charles L. Buckingham, Co. B; Martin Dean, Co. B; William Jones, Co. H; George McClernan, Co. D. Wounded: 2nd Lieut. Arthur V. Coan, Co. G; David McCormick, Co. C; Frederick Sittig, Co. H. Captured: Captain James Stewart, Co. K; Edward Jones, Co. H; James Kennedy, Co. B; Christian P. Lang, Co. F; Alonzo Lathrop, Co. A; Robert A. McGinnis, Co. F; Edward Morris, Co. H; Eugene Parkhill, Co. I; John Robinson, Jr., Co. B; Franklin Russell, Co. B; William Sherman, Co. B; William Wilson, Co. I.

WHITE OAK RIDGE.—Killed: David P. Francis, Co. F; William W. Gammel, Co. H; Anson Senn, Co. I; John A. Williams, Co. I; Ira Wing, Co. H. Wounded: 1st Lieut. Edward J. Davis, Co. E; 1st Lieut. George J. Klock, Co. I; 2nd Lieut. David M. Rudy, Co. A; Adam Cheeseborough, Co. H; Jay Cornwall, Co. F; Samuel R. Green, Co. H; William R. Johnson, Co. D; Charles G. Overton, Co. C; Henry H. Wood, Co. C. Captured: James A. Barnes, Co. G; Hubbard Beach, Co. F; Richard Maynard, Co. C; John Pugh, Co. C; Charles Radcliffe, Co. G; Peter Rock, Co. G; Edward Scoville, Co. I; Sylvester C. Vandenburgh, Co. F.

FIVE FORKS.—Killed: Peter Cary, Co. B. Wounded: Captain Thomas A. Wilson, Co. B; James Bendon, Co. D; Eli B. Miller, Co. D; Olboson Shaw, Co. B; Thomas Smith, Co. F. Captured: Henry Meier, Co. F.

[1] Includes also Yellow House, Davis House, Poplar Spring Church, Hatcher's Run, Boydton Plank Road.

FIFTIETH ANNIVERSARY

1862–1912

146TH REGIMENT N. Y. VOLS. ASSOCIATION

ROME, N. Y.

THURSDAY, OCTOBER 10, 1912

OFFICERS OF THE ASSOCIATION, 1911–12

President.—Alonzo I. King.

Vice-Presidents.—Samuel Raymond, Charles P. Mahan, Horace Miller

Secretary.—Charles L. King.

Treasurer.—James O. Edmonds.

Necrologist.—Lafayette Empey.

Surgeon.—George Mould.

Chaplain.—Francis A. England.

Executive Committee.—Conrad Neuschler, John W. Hughes, Abram Bergee.

Finance Committee.—Leander Martin, Joseph B. Cushman, George O. Tibbits.

Color-bearers.—Edwin Richardson, George W. Johnson.

Advisory Board.—Edward Comstock, W. Beriah Chandler, Henry Hook.

MEMBERS PRESENT

Company A.—John Bright, William Colwell, Thomas Wheeler, Isaac White.

Company B.—John W. Hughes, Norton Shepard.

Company C.—Captain Joseph B. Cushman, Maurice Godfrey, James O. Edmonds, Charles Van Vleck, Frederick Ernst, R. Owen Jones, George W. Lincoln.

534   146th Regiment, New York Vols.

Company D.—W. Beriah Chandler, Alvah Grey, Warner Yeomans, Andrew Dorn.

Company E.—Lieut. Lafayette Empey, Henry W. Stowell.

Company F.—Abram Bergee, William Brown, George W. Johnson, Horace Miller, Jacob Martin, William L. Snyder.

Company G.—Leonard W. Carpenter, Orville J. Barker, Isaac Chapman, Henry B. Hook, William McGurk, Samuel W. Raymond, John Williams, Adelbert S. Wood, Edwin Richardson, Ralph T. Kirkland.

Company H.—Lieut. George Mould, George A. Geer, Owen Jones, Joseph Jones, Charles L. King.

Company I.—Alvah P. Hemstreet, Leander Martin, Conrad Neuschler, George Smith, Francis H. Wait, Peter Williams, Fernando D. Wood.

Company K.—Lieut. J. Albert Jennison, Michael Doherty, Francis A. England, Isaac J. Scoutten.

CONGRATULATORY LETTERS

HEADQUARTERS, THIRD DIVISION, PROVISIONAL CORPS,
July 15, 1865.

COLONEL JAMES GRINDLAY, OFFICERS AND MEN OF THE 146TH
N. Y. VOLUNTEERS:

As our official relations are about to terminate, I take the occasion to express to you my deep regret therefor, though rejoicing in its cause.

During the two years that your regiment has served in my command, and the many battles it has participated in, I have ever felt entire confidence in its discipline and gallantry. I have never called upon it save to see the duty assigned nobly performed.

I believe there is not a more distinguished regiment than yours. Gallantly have you borne those torn and tattered banners. Defiantly have you shaken them in the very jaws of death, and triumphantly waved them on fields of victory.

Well assured that in your reception on returning home will be evinced the deep gratitude of an admiring people, and with my best wishes for your welfare and happiness, I remain,

Sincerely, your friend,

(Signed) R. B. AYRES,
Brevet Major-General, Commanding.

HEADQUARTERS, THIRD BRIGADE, THIRD DIVISION,
PROVISIONAL CORPS, July 15, 1865.

COLONEL JAMES GRINDLAY, Commanding the 146th New York
Volunteers.

COLONEL: In taking leave of you I desire to express to you, and through you, to your officers and men, my high appreciation of your gallant regiment, and of its services in the late war.

Taking the field at an early date, it has participated in the severest campaigns and it has won its reputation where soldiers are best tried, "upon the battlefield."

Associated with many other good regiments and, for a long time, with the infantry regiments of the Regular Army, the 146th yields the palm to none. By the intelligence and ability of its officers, by the discipline, soldierly character and conduct of its men, it has added lustre to the proud name of Volunteer.

After your long and arduous service, having accomplished your work, you return now to enjoy the greetings of your friends and families and the laurels you have so nobly won. Let me assure you, you bear with you the best wishes of your friend and commander.

(Signed)   JAMES HAYES,
Brigadier General, Commanding.

"BALLAD OF THE 146TH REGIMENT"

The following lines, composed by Surgeon Thomas M. Flandrau, were read at the First Reunion of the Regiment, held August 5, 1886, at Rome, N. Y.

Some four and twenty years ago,
　　When fiercely raged the nation's battle,
Our duty bade us seek the foe,
　　Where cannons roar and muskets rattle.

Yes, four and twenty years ago.
　　We marched from Rome, a bold eight hundred;
A roll call now would sadly show
　　How few of them in life are numbered.

We bravely marched, our rifles bright,
　　Drums beating loud and banners flying,
The country joyous in the sight,
　　Our sisters, wives and mothers crying.

But duty calls, though hearts may break,
　　The Union must be eternal,
And who could halt, what hand could shake,
　　When brave Garrard is made our colonel.

A noble, courtly man was he,
　　Rigid in rule, but kindly ever,
He sought the soldier's friend to be,
　　To win high fame by bold endeavor.

Soon faced we grim St. Mary's heights,
　　O'er Fredericksburg, shell-rent and gory,
And first beheld war's awful sights,
　　Unsoftened by the sheen of glory.

537

And then we fought at Chancellorsville,
  And were indeed "baptised with fire";
Through the wood shrieked the deadly shell,
  The rifle rang in volleys dire.

Here Gibbs, our first slain, met his doom,
  Stretched on the sod with face upturned,
He lay like marble knight on tomb,
  Dim the bright eye where courage burned.

Three long days raged the fearful fight;
  Night heard the cannons loudly thunder;
The moon looked on with silv'ry light
  When Stonewall cut our lines asunder.

Who can grim Chancellorsville forget,
  Or Jackson's charge with forces serried?
Not Durkee, nor Secor, I'll bet,
  Whose arm and leg are left there buried.

At Gettysburg fair victory smiled;
  With columns close Lee tried our center,
Thrice charged they where the dead lay piled,
  But failed that line of steel to enter.

From Round Top's lofty rock-ribbed wall
  Our tattered flag was gaily flying;
Beneath its folds the tear drops fall,
  As Weed and Hazlett lay there dying.

Thy choicest gifts, ah! cruel war,
  Peace, freedom, victory and glory,
Are blood-stained all.   Thy lurid star
  Illumes the darkest page of story.

Then Williamsport and Wapping Heights,
  Bristoe, Mine Run and Rappahannock
Soon followed and were pretty fights,
  With deeds of courage and of panic.

The winter speeds at Warrenton
  In ways less purely military,
With sutlers, furloughs, friends and fun,
  And our best friend, the Commissary.

May blooms again and brings us Grant,
  Destined to fill the highest station;
A warrior whom no foe can daunt,
  Mighty to save the struggling nation.

He led us to the Wilderness,
  And here befell our greatest sorrow;
We were four hundred men the less
  After that crushing day of horror.

A line of blue across the plain,
  Advanced the charge, when fierce, infernal,
Burst from the wood a leaden rain,
  And Jenkins fell, our gallant colonel.

By him lay Curran—gifted, brave—
  And Froeligh, young, but hero-hearted;
They died, their native land to save,
  That north and south should not be parted.

Then redder bloomed the flowers of spring,
  Where hundreds bled that day of peril;
Wright, Walker, Chalmers, Jones and King
  Were hit. Here fell bold Sergeant Turrell.

But why prolong this sanguine song?
  War's path is strewn with black disaster.
The right must struggle with the wrong,
  Though thousands die to make it master.

And we must fight another year,
  Till Grant has crushed out every rebel,
And still war's diapason hear,
  The cannon's bass, the rifle's treble.

Through Spottsylvania, Laurel Hill,
  Bethesda Church, the sharp North Anna,
The Weldon Road, where young Coan fell,
  Was borne our regimental banner.

Cold Harbor genial Lowery thought
  Than any fray was rather sadder;
It left his leg a little short,
  May nought decrease his generous shadow.

Then comes the last, the crowning stroke,
  For all war's toils, the longed-for guerdon,
When at Five Forks, the rebels broke
  Before the charge of gallant Sheridan.

Grindlay commands our third brigade,
  And valiant on the foemen rushes;
To tell how flashed his trenchant blade,
  Perhaps may raise his modest blushes.

But ramparts, rebels, flags and guns
  Are captured, as he onward dashes;
Along the line a wild cheer runs,
  While Victory from each proud eye flashes.

Extinguished then the Stars and Bars,
  The fatal blow to treason given,
O'er Freedom floats the Stripes and Stars,
  And slavery's last sad chain is riven.

Richmond is captured, Lee has fled.
  At Appomattox he surrenders:
From their last battle homeward tread
  The Union's valorous defenders.

Here we in pride and grief recall,
  Dear names which fame should make immortal;
Tom Wilson, Buckingham and all
  The noble host which crowd Death's portal.

But time forbids of each to tell,
 Who dreamless lies 'neath southern flowers;
For hundreds of our bravest fell,
 And died to save that flag of ours.

And now we meet after long years,
 So changed that one scarce knows the other;
But soon the eye of memory clears
 And sees in each the friend and brother.

Grandly above us all appear
 The heroic dead, a solemn vision,
Methinks I hear their voices clear
 Salute us from the fields Elysian.

Comrades, oft may we meet as here,
 In festive hall, with song and story,
And the whole regiment be near,
 When the last bugle calls to glory.

BIBLIOGRAPHY

The following books and documents were used in the compilation of the History of the 146th Regiment, New York Volunteers:

BOOKS

War of the Rebellion Records.
The Fifth Army Corps, by WILLIAM H. POWELL.
Personal Memoirs of U. S. Grant, Volume II.
Under the Maltese Cross. (A History of the 155th Pennsylvania Volunteers.)
History of the Army of the Potomac, by J. H. STINE.
Report of the Adjutant General, State of New York, Serial Number 38.
New York in the War of the Rebellion, by FREDERICK PHISTERER.
History of the 117th New York Volunteers. (The Fourth Oneida.)
The Battle of the Wilderness, by MORRIS SCHAFF.
History of the Civil War in America, COMTE DE PARIS.
A History of the War of Secession, by ROSSITER JOHNSON.
The Virginia Campaign of 1864 and 1865, GEN. A. A. HUMPHREYS.
James S. Wadsworth of Geneseo, by HENRY G. PEARSON.

DOCUMENTS

Letters and Diary of James P. Pitcher.
Letters of David T. Jenkins.
Letters of Henry H. Curran.
Letters of James E. Jenkins.
Letters of Alonzo I. King.
Letters of A. Pierson Case.
Letters of W. H. Seward Sweet.
Diary of Orville J. Barker.
Diary of Frederick Ernst.
Diary of William Wright.
Lectures of John W. Goff.
News Items from Utica *Morning Herald,* 1862–1865.
News Items from Rome *Sentinel,* 1865.

PHOTOGRAPHIC INTRODUCTION

The principal addition to this book is the inclusion of over 150 photographs of soldiers who served in the 146th New York. By getting a look at these men, the reader is able to put names with the faces, adding to our empathy with them and what they endured. Biographical information about each soldier comes from compiled service records and pension files at the National Archives in Washington, DC. Additional documentation for some photos came from letters and diary accounts. Most of the portraits are identified, and perhaps in the case of those that are not, a reader will recognize the individual. For the biographical sketches, all towns and cities are in New York and all units are infantry unless otherwise noted. The 146th New York was a highly photographed regiment, and their splendid Zouave uniforms add to the uniqueness of the images. Any additional information or photos concerning soldiers in this unit should be sent to the publisher for future projects concerning this regiment.

A striking albumen photograph showing four members of the 146th New York Zouaves taken in the fall of 1863 at Elmira, where all four men were assigned to duty at the conscript depot. The image was hand tinted at the time. From left to right are David W. Allen, Chauncey B. Smith, Jesse C. Johnson, and John Duckworth. Of these, only Allen and Duckworth survived the war. Smith was shot and killed by a guard while a prisoner of war, and Johnson succumbed to chronic diarrhea. Allen, Johnson, and Duckworth, were all transferred "three-year" men from the 5th New York Infantry, Duryée's Zouaves. The men wear turbans and red shirts. Several interesting things to note in regards to this photograph are that all four men served in different companies, and Smith is armed with a Sharps rifle that was never issued to the 146th, but had been distributed to companies E and I of the 5th. (Hendrick Hudson Chapter, Daughters of the American Revolution, Collection)

David W. Allen enlisted in the 5th New York on Aug. 7, 1862, in New York City. He was a 21-year-old, 5'10", carpenter, with hazel eyes, brown hair, dark complexion, and was born at Morristown, NJ. On May 4, 1863, Allen and 325 of his comrades were transferred to the 146th New York. Allen was assigned to Co. A. He did duty from July to Nov. 1863 at the conscript depot in Elmira. He was treated for syphilis on Dec. 15, 1863, and again from Mar. 26 to May 5, 1864, at Carver Hospital, Washington, DC. Allen was transferred to McClellan Hospital in Philadelphia and treated for secondary syphilis from May 6 to Sept. 11, 1864. He was appointed corporal on Sept. 1, and sergeant on Dec. 9, 1864. During the Appomattox Campaign he suffered a rupture of the right side, and mustered out near Alexandria, VA, on June 3, 1865. After the war he was employed as a draughtsman and married Mary Schenck, who died Feb. 9, 1874. Allen married again on Aug. 26, 1877, in Elizabeth, NJ, this time to a widower named Helena Pennington Lawrence. He died on Apr. 8, 1902, and is buried at Cypress Hills Cemetery.

Chauncey B. Smith enlisted as a private in Co. H at Utica on Aug. 30, 1862. He was 30 years old, 5'10", with a light complexion, gray eyes, brown hair, was employed as a millwright, and had been born in Massachusetts. Smith was made sergeant upon muster in on Oct. 10, 1862. He was present at the battles of Fredericksburg, Chancellorsville, and Gettysburg, before being assigned duty at the conscript depot in Elmira, from July 20, to Nov. 1863. Smith was promoted first sergeant and color sergeant, no dates. He was captured at the Battle of the Wilderness on May 5, 1864, and sent to prisoner of war camp at Andersonville, GA, and then Florence, SC, then to Wilmington, NC. While in the process of moving by rail to Salisbury prison camp, a Confederate guard at the door fired recklessly into the car of crowded and unarmed prisoners. The bullet penetrated Smith's chest, killing him instantly. The guard "supposed they were going to try to escape."

Jesse C. Johnson, who had been born in New Haven, CT, was 33 years old, stood 5'6", with a dark complexion, hazel eyes, dark hair, and was a printer when he enlisted in Co. B of the 5th New York on July 29, 1862. He was one of the recruits that had joined just prior to the Battle of Second Bull Run, where the regiment lost 330 men in ten minutes. During the battle, Johnson was wounded and captured. He was paroled at Centreville, VA, on Sept. 6, 1862, and was treated at Casparis Hospital, Washington, DC, from Sept. to Oct. 1862. He was transferred to an Alexandria hospital in Nov. 1862 and thence to Camp Parole at Annapolis, MD. From there he rejoined the regiment. He transferred to Co. C of the 146th New York on May 4, 1863. Johnson was again transferred on May 9 to Co. G, and promoted corporal. He was assigned detached service at the conscript depot at Elmira from July 20 until Nov. 1863. Captured for a second time at the Battle of the Wilderness on May 5, 1864, Johnson succumbed to chronic diarrhea on Jan. 28, 1865, while a prisoner of war at Salisbury, NC.

John Duckworth enlisted in Co. D of the 5th New York on July 20, 1861, in New York City. He was a 22-year-old machinist, that stood 5'11/2", with a light complexion, gray eyes, brown hair, and had been born in Manchester, England. He was present for every engagement in which the 5th New York participated and was made corporal on Sept. 10, 1862. Duckworth was transferred to Co. I of the 146th New York on May 4, 1863. He was assigned to duty at the conscript depot at Elmira, from July 20 until rejoining the regiment on Dec. 7, 1863. While on this duty, he became sick and was in the General Hospital at Elmira until Nov. 5, 1863. He survived the Wilderness and the assaults on Petersburg to muster out on July 20, 1864, at Petersburg. But Duckworth's military service was not over. On May 29, 1865, he enlisted in Co. G of the 4th US Cavalry and mustered out Nov. 1, 1868. He re-enlisted in Co. B of the 44th US Infantry on June 1, 1869 and transferred to the 17th Infantry on Nov. 2, 1871. Serving through the Indian Wars, Duckworth mustered out for good on May 25, 1885. By 1889, he was a resident at the Soldiers' Home in Washington, DC. Duckworth died Apr. 26, 1892.

JAMES COMFORT ALVERSON

Alverson was born at Poughkeepsie in 1841. He enlisted as a corporal in Co. I of the 5th New York on Apr. 25, 1861, at age 21. Alverson was 5'41/2" with blue eyes, black hair, light complexion, and worked a silversmith with his uncle, Joseph Cornish in Newburgh. He received promotion to third sergeant on May 9, 1861. In the first battle of the war at Big Bethel, VA, on June 10, 1861, he was slightly wounded by a piece of shell striking his right leg. Alverson was reduced to a private in Nov. 1861, and then deserted on Dec. 16, 1861, at Baltimore. He joined the US Navy under the alias James Melvine, and served on the *US Sumter* for one year, then returned to Poughkeepsie and worked as a grocer until being arrested for desertion on Nov. 20, 1863. Alverson was sent under guard to Riker's Island, and then was forwarded to Co. G of the 146th to serve out his time. He was captured at the Battle of the Wilderness on May 5, 1864, and then held at the prisons of Andersonville and Florence. He escaped from Florence but recaptured by dogs after 8 days. Finally paroled at Goldsboro, NC, March 1, 1865, he began this recovery at Newton Hospital in Baltimore, ten days later. Alverson mustered out at York, PA, June 6, 1865— he had lost all his hair, had diarrhea, and rheumatism and according to one neighbor he "was more dead than alive and a complete wreck." After the War he worked as a silversmith for Tiffany & Co. until failing eyesight prompted his return to Poughkeepsie where he worked in the merchant tailoring business for a time. In 1875 operated a root beer factory with his brother in Poughkeepsie. Later, he was a florist (by 1887), a picture-frame maker, and a realtor at the time of his death. He married Caroline Williamson on Nov. 2, 1865, and had five children. Alverson died of a heart attack while at the doctor's office on March 5, 1906, and was buried at the Poughkeepsie Rural Cemetery. This photo was taken at Baltimore in Oct. 1861. (Adriance Memorial Library Collection)

EDWARD BENNETT

First Lieutenant Bennett transferred from Co. A of the 44th New York to Co. D of the 146th on Oct. 11, 1864, but did not join the unit for duty until June 6, 1865. He served with the regiment until the muster out on July 16, 1865, near Washington, DC. Bennett had enlisted in Aug. 1861 and re-enlisted as a veteran volunteer in Dec. 1863. While serving with the 44th, he was captured on May 8, 1864, at the engagement of Laurel Hill during the Spotsylvania Campaign. Bennett was among the 378 men recaptured by Brig. Gen. George Armstrong Custer's Michigan Brigade at Beaver Dam Station the next day. Rejoining his unit, he was wounded at the engagement of Poplar Springs Church on Sept. 30, 1864, during the siege of Petersburg. He died in Oct. 1898. (Department of Military & Naval Affairs, New York State Adjutant Generals Office, Albany, NY)

JAMES SHERMAN BRADISH

Governor Horatio Seymour appointed this 36-year-old Lowville native the regimental assistant surgeon on Jan. 22, 1863. Bradish, born July 31, 1826, attended the Lowville Academy (1842-46) then studied medicine and surgery at Oberlin College, married Harriet E. Shepherd in 1850 and worked at the trade of watchmaker until 1855 when he received certification as a medical doctor. Nicknamed the *Little Philosopher* and a skilled ventriloquist, he joined the regiment in the field on Feb. 15, 1863. As the regiment advanced with the army to Chancellorsville, Bradish was sick and was left behind at Stoneman's Switch, but soon fell to the task of caring for the wounded. In "poor health" and unable to continue with the regiment, he requested to be reassigned to a general hospital, but the 5th Corps medical director described him as "worthless" and "incompetent." Bradish was dismissed from service by special orders on May 6, 1863. He apparently continued to minister to the sick and wounded in the hospitals in Washington, but was "unable to continue in <u>field</u> service." However, by 1865, he was once again in the field, but not on the army pay roll, this time looking after soldiers at Beaufort, SC. Returning North with a group of sick former prisoners of war, he fell ill with yellow fever and died Aug. 3, 1865, in a hospital at Hilton Head, SC, where he was buried. (David Bruinix Collection)

CHARLES BRANDEGEE

Brandegee was born Dec. 12, 1844, at Berlin, CT, the son of a physician. This photograph shows the blue-eyed brown-haired Brandegee at age 17 in his 5th New York uniform, taken in Mar. 1862 while the regiment was stationed at Fort Federal Hill in Baltimore. Transferred to Co. A of the 146th on May 4, 1863, he performed efficiently as the company clerk, the former occupation of this 5'5 1/2", gray eyed soldier. He served faithfully with the 5th and 146th until captured at the Battle of the Wilderness on May 5, 1864. His tent mate, Alonzo Lathrop, wrote Brandegee's parents that their son was amongst the prisoners taken and not among those that escaped the Rebel noose. (Charles Brandegee Livingstone Collection)

CHARLES BRANDEGEE

After being taken prisoner at the Wilderness, Brandegee was confined at Andersonville Prison, GA, and Florence Stockade, SC. Paroled at Aiken's Landing, VA, on Feb. 24, 1865, he was suffering from typhoid fever, diarrhea, and general debility. Unable to return to service, he obtained his discharge on May 5, 1865. This photo, taken in 1925, shows "Charlie" at age 81, the Town Clerk and Registrar of Farmington, CT. He died Sept. 22, 1927, at Somerville, MA. Charles Brandegee's letters are printed in the book *Charlie's Civil War: A Privates' Trial by Fire in the 5th New York Volunteers – Duryée's Zouaves and 146th New York Volunteer Infantry* edited by Charles Brandegee Livingstone. (Charles Brandegee Livingstone Collection)

ALBERT E. BROWNELL

Only 22 years old when he enrolled on Sept. 3, 1862, at Utica, this hazel eyed, brown haired banker was born in Sauquoit and resided in Paris when he mustered in as a private in Co. K on Oct. 10, 1862. On Dec. 27, 1863, he was promoted to sergeant major of the regiment and was commissioned a second lieutenant in Co. A on Jan. 30, 1863, while incapacitated with a severe case of typhoid fever. "Broken down" during the march to Gettysburg, Brownell recuperated in a Georgetown hospital and rejoined the regiment on July 14, 1863. Sick with diabetes in Mar. 1864, he took command of Co. A upon his return in Apr. until a spine injury necessitated his absence in Sept. 1864. He was away from the regiment for over two months unable to return. Arrested by the Provost Marshal for being absent without leave and unable to travel to the army, he resigned his commission on Nov. 25, 1864, on account of "general debility." (Donald Wisnoski Collection)

WILLIAM CAMPBELL

Campbell was born on Sept. 23, 1832, at Blaigawine, Scotland. He migrated to the United States in 1861. This 29-year-old blacksmith, stood 5'11", with hazel eyes, dark hair, and a dark complexion, and enlisted Sept. 1, 1862, at Clinton (also given as Kirkland). He was mustered in as a corporal in Co. G on Oct. 10, 1862, and promoted sergeant Mar. 9, 1863. Campbell was present at the battles of Fredericksburg, Chancellorsville, and Gettysburg. He suffered a laceration of the left ankle and transferred to Co. E of the 6th Regiment Veteran Reserve Corps on Sept. 2, 1863, with the notation that his character with the regiment was "good." Campbell died May 22, 1911, at Westmoreland. (Donald Wisnoski Collection)

SILAS CARGON

Shown here in his 5th New York, Duryée Zouave, uniform, with a large pair of jambiéres on his legs and a turban wrapped around his fez. Cargon joined the United States Navy as a fireman on Oct. 22, 1859. He served on the USS Mohican off the coast of Africa, and participated in the expedition that captured Port Royal, SC, in Nov. of 1861. He was discharged at Philadelphia, PA, on July 15, 1862. He took up a rifle on Aug. 21, 1862, when he enlisted as a private in Co. B of the 5th at New York City, giving his age as 23, with hazel eyes, brown hair and a sandy complexion. He stood 5'11". Among the transferred men to the 146th New York on May 4, 1863, Cargon was one of many unhappy with the transfer and was under arrest from May 16, 1863, until tried by a general court martial. His sentence was remitted and he joined the ranks of Co. G of the 146th. (United States Army Military History Institute)

SILAS CARGON

Cargon was captured after suffering a gunshot wound in the right arm at the Wilderness on May 5, 1864. His arm was amputated at the middle third by a rebel surgeon while on the battlefield the next day. While a prisoner of war the wound became gangrenous and was re-amputated. He was paroled on Sept. 12, 1864, and discharged at Camp Parole near Annapolis, MD, on Jan. 20, 1865. The photograph shows the one-armed Cargon with a woman that is believed to be his first wife, Adelaide L. Burnside, who he married on Sept. 23, 1874, at Upper Marlborough, NY. Adelaide died Mar. 4, 1880. (Michael J. McAfee Collection)

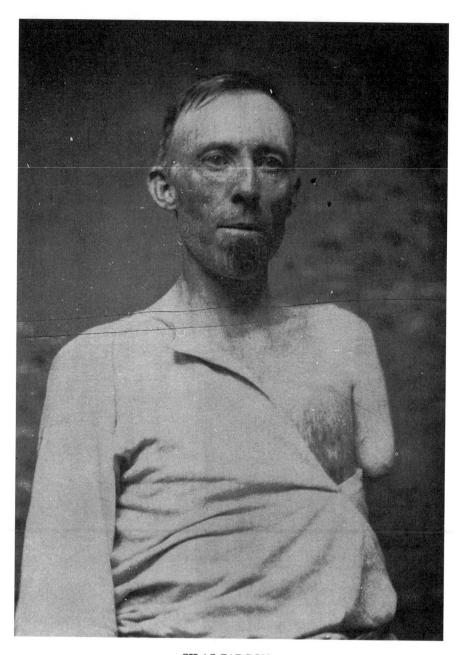

SILAS CARGON

The stump of Cargon's amputated arm troubled him for the rest of his life. This photograph, taken in Albany, is from a tintype of Cargon. It is a reversed image that makes his right arm appear to be his left. Tenderness and pain in the stump prevented Cargon from using an artificial limb. He re-married Nov. 7, 1883, in Albany, to Sarah Peacock. Cargon drew an army pension as compensation for his wound starting in 1866 at $8.00 per month. By the time of his death on June 21, 1922, the pension had increased to $72.00 per month. (National Archives)

A. PIERSON CASE

At 44 years old, the gray bearded Case was one of the eldest officers with the regiment, being mustered in as a first lieutenant and regimental quartermaster on Aug. 30, 1862. The firing of Hazlett's battery over the heads of the regiment during the Battle of Gettysburg on July 3, 1863, led Case to comment that it seemed "as if the end of the world had come." On Oct. 25, 1863, he tendered his resignation on account of "physical infirmities" (diarrhea and severe gastric complications) limiting the performance of his duties. Colonel Jenkins and Brig. Gen. Garrard, regretted the loss of this officer, but endorsed his resignation. It was accepted two days later. Case was of rather distinguished personage. Born in Vernon on Mar. 22, 1818, he had married Lovina W. Coburn of Homer on May 30, 1839. Case served a term in the New York State Legislature in 1852. He was appointed Cashier of the Bank of Vernon in 1879 and in 1893 became the bank's president. Case died Sept. 15, 1900, at Vernon. (Dept. of Mil. & Naval Affairs, NY State Adjt. Gen. Office, Albany, NY)

HUGH CHALMERS

Chalmers joined Co. H of the 5th New York in New York City on July 6, 1861, when he was 22 years old. He stood 5'6¾", had gray eyes, brown hair, a light complexion, listed his occupation as a tinsmith, and was born in Scotland. Absent without leave from Jan. 29 to Feb. 4, 1862, and sentenced to forfeit 20 days pay. He was wounded in the right breast at the Battle of Gaines' Mill on June 27, 1862, and was promoted corporal in Sept. and made sergeant in Nov. of that same year. Transferred to Co. E of the 146th New York on May 4, 1863. Chalmers was again promoted on Nov. 20, 1863, to second lieutenant of Co. H, and made first lieutenant of Co. E on Jan. 25, 1864. He was severely wounded and captured at the Battle of Bethesda Church on June 2, 1864. Perhaps the explosion of an artillery shell disabled him as records list him at Libby Prison "with both thighs fractured" and "both eyes shot out." He died in Richmond on June 7, 1864. He was buried at Richmond National Cemetery, but his body may have been exhumed and re-interred at Rosedale Cemetery in Orange, NJ. His wife, Martha A. Lee, whom he married on Sept. 23, 1860, died in Jan. 1913 at East Orange, NJ. The couple had two daughters Eliza Udora born June 16, 1861, and Anna Margaret Virginia, born Sept. 19, 1864, and died Aug. 16, 1865. (Gordon E. Johnson Collection)

STEPHEN CHESBORO

This 27-year-old farmer from Norwich was drafted and mustered in on Sept. 9, 1863, being assigned to Co. D. He stood 5'8" with brown hair, blue eyes, a fair complexion, and joined the regiment on Oct. 26, 1863. Records show him absent sick at Chestnut Hill Hospital in Philadelphia starting Apr. 30, 1864. He deserted from hospital on June 14, 1864, and was arrested in the 19th District of New York on July 12, 1864. After rejoining the regiment he was captured at the Battle of Weldon Railroad on Aug. 19, 1864, and confined at Salisbury Prison, NC, on Oct. 9, 1864. Chesboro escaped from the enemy and re-entered Union lines on Apr. 25, 1865. He was mustered out with the regiment on July 16, 1865, near Washington, DC. (Donald Wisnoski Collection)

557

PETER C. CLAESGENS

Claesgens is shown here as a captain with extremely elaborate cuff trim on his jacket. Born in Prussia, Claesgens always had a fondness for the military. Before the war in Utica, he was a member of the LaFayette Rifles. He enrolled Sept. 10, 1862 at Rome and mustered in Oct. 10, 1862, as captain of Co. F, he was 36 years old. He suffered from sunstroke during the Gettysburg campaign. Claesgens began doing detached service at Elmira Prison, from Jan. 14 to June 10, 1864. Cited for "gallant and meritorious services at the battles before Petersburg and on the Weldon Railroad"—where he commanded the regiment, and was promoted major on Jan. 1, 1865. Claesgens was absent with leave from Mar. 17 to Apr. 16, 1865, to attend to one of his children that was dangerously ill, and came down with a case of pneumonia himself. While away, he was promoted lieutenant colonel on Apr. 1. Claesgens mustered out with regiment July 16, 1865, near Washington, DC. He was made a brevet colonel July 16, 1867, for "gallant and meritorious services during the war." After the war, Claesgens operated the Railroad Hotel in Deerfield, until 1881, and was twice married. He was an avid hunter, fisher, and storyteller as well, plus a member of Cowan and McQuade posts, Grand Army of the Republic. Claesgens died in the summer of 1882, at age 56, from dropsy. (Donald Wisnoski Collection)

ARTHUR V. COAN

Although only 18 years old at the time of his enlistment at Kirkland on Aug. 29, 1862, Coan rose rapidly through the ranks. He was born at Carthage, and at the time of his enrollment as a corporal in Co. G he was listed as 5'5", with a sandy complexion and hair, blue eyes, and was employed as a clerk. He was promoted first sergeant on Mar. 9, 1863, and second lieutenant on Mar. 1, 1864—still a mere 20 years old. Coan was wounded Aug. 18, 1864, at the Battle of Weldon Railroad. He died of his wounds in a US general hospital on Sept. 30, 1864. (Michael J. McAfee Collection)

559

JAMES COLLEDGE

A heavily mustached Colledge taken years after the war, subsequent to his move from Utica to Redfield, SD. Born in England, he was 31 years old when he enlisted, being described as 5'4" with blue eyes, dark hair, and employed as a furnace man. He was present in the ranks from his enlistment on Aug. 31, 1862, until being seriously wounded in the left foot on Aug. 18, 1864, at the Battle of Weldon Railroad. He was admitted on Aug. 24, 1864, to White Hall General Hospital, Philadelphia. Attended by his parents and taken back to New York on furlough. He received his discharge for disability May 30, 1865. Colledge had two brothers that also served during the war. His older brother enlisted in the 6th Minnesota and served for about one week before being killed in an attack by Indians near Fort Ridgley, MN, on Sept. 3, 1862. His other brother was discharged for disability and crippled by his injuries. Sometime after the war, Colledge moved to Readfield, SD, where he lived until 1903, when he moved to San Diego, CA. Colledge died Feb. 13, 1912. He was also borne on the rolls as Collidge and College. (Patrick A. Schroeder Collection)

WILLIAM COLWELL

Colwell was a 25-year-old farmer with brown eyes, a light complexion, and auburn hair. He had immigrated from Westmeath, Ireland, when he was 15. He stood 5'7" when he enlisted as a private in Co. A, on Aug. 23, 1862, at Utica. Colwell sustained a wound in the right arm at the Battle of Chancellorsville on May 1, 1863. This occurred when Co. A, was nearly surrounded and many of its members were captured. Colwell was one of those to escape, but when he "was retreating . . . the ball entered the posterior surface of the right arm a little above the insertion of the deltoid muscle, comminuted (pulverized) the upper end of the shaft of the humerus and lodged in the shoulder joint. The operation of resection was performed by Dr. Howard, Surg. of [the] 1st Ohio Battery who removed the head of the bone and about three inches of the upper end of the shaft [on] the day of the injury." The next day, he was sent to the division hospital at Brooke's Station, and from there to Lincoln Hospital, Washington, DC, where the arm was placed in splints, bandages, and later adhesive plaster. By June 20, 1863, the wound had entirely healed and new bone was forming slowly. Although his disability was listed as ¾, it was noted that he "will probably have a useful arm"—with a limited range of motion. He received his discharge from the hospital on July 4, and mustered out on account of disability on Aug. 5, 1863. Colwell returned to New York and as an "honest, upright citizen" farmed in New Hartford. He had married Mary E. Quillman of New Hartford in 1858, and they had twelve children. After the death of his first wife, Colwell married Ellen Dulan, of Kingston, Canada. He was a member of St. John's Church in New Hartford. He died at age 77 on June 13, 1915, at New Hartford (Capron). (Dianne Stebbins Collection)

HOBART P. COOK

This is an early wartime picture of Cook in civilian clothes. He served as a drummer in the 44th New York, enlisting when he was 19 years old. While acting as a hospital attendant at Gettysburg, he was accidentally wounded on July 2, 1863. Transferred from Co. A of the 44th to Co. G of the 146th in Oct. 1864. Cook was absent sick and away from the regiment at the time of the transfer until discharged and mustered out from the hospital at Albany, on May 31, 1865. When he enlisted in the 44th New York on Aug. 11, 1862, Cook was listed as a clerk with gray eyes, brown hair, and a light complexion. He was born at Albany. (Dept. of Military & Naval Affairs, New York State Adjt. Gen. Office, Albany, NY)

SYLVESTER O. COOK

Cook was a 28-year-old tinner from Boonville, with gray eyes, dark hair, and a light complexion, and auburn hair. He was born at Townsend, VT. Cook was an avid smoker, and proponent of outspoken New York *Tribune* editor, Horace Greeley. He stood 5'8" when he enlisted as a private in Co. D, on Sept. 5, 1862, at Rome. Promoted first sergeant on Feb. 1, 1863. Cook was participated in the battles of Fredericksburg, Chancellorsville, and Gettysburg, and was present from his enlistment until his discharge on Feb. 14, 1864, at Warrenton Junction, VA. He left the 146th, being commissioned a second lieutenant in Co. B, 16th New York Heavy Artillery. While serving with that regiment he was wounded on Oct. 7, 1864, in fighting along the Darbytown Road in front of Richmond, VA. Cook was discharged for his wounds on Jan. 23, 1865, while home in Boonville. Cook died March 11, 1900. (Donald Wisnoski Collection)

HENRY H. CURRAN

Perhaps the most dashing and promising soldier in the regiment, only 21 years old, Curran left his studies at Hamilton College and was enrolled as first lieutenant of Co. E on Sept. 9, 1862, at Rome. He was quickly promoted to captain of Co. I on Dec. 10, 1862, and transferred to Co. B on Nov. 1, 1863. He was on detached service at Elmira Prison Camp from July 22 to Dec. 5, 1863. Curran was granted leave in Mar. 1864 and present with the regiment in Apr. as acting major. He was killed instantly May 5, 1864, at the Battle of the Wilderness. During the engagement the regiment had already suffered many casualties and was pushing through the underbrush and trees in front of the Confederate works. Lieutenant Alonzo King shouted to Curran: "This is awful!" Turning to Curran he questioned: "Where are all our men?" Curran responded: "Dead." Then a bullet struck Curran in the head. He was left on the field. Confederates rifled his body, and believed by the elaborate manner of Curran's dress that they had killed a general. His corpse was never recovered. A memorial marker was erected for him at Forest Hill Cemetery in Utica. This is the only individual photograph of Curran known and was taken by W. C. North in Utica. (Patrick A. Schroeder Collection)

CHARLES K. DUTTON

A dandy view of Dutton in his Zouave officer's jacket. He was commissioned as second lieutenant by the Governor of New York to date from Oct. 6, 1862, and joined Co. H for duty on Nov. 1, 1862, at Washington, DC. Promoted first lieutenant on Dec. 26, 1862, and captain on Sept. 16, 1864. He performed detached duty at Elmira Prison Camp from Jan. 13 to May 1, 1864. On Jan. 18, 1865, while doing duty as the Brigade Inspector, he applied for a 20-day-leave "for the purpose of fulfilling a matrimonial engagement at Chicago, Illinois on the 30th ult. This ceremony has twice been postponed by reason of Army movements." The request was approved through the army chain of command "owing to the peculiar circumstances of this case." Discharged Mar. 13, 1865, being commissioned captain of Co. M, 24th New York Cavalry. Brevetted a major to date from Mar. 13, 1865, "for gallant and meritorious services at the battles of the Wilderness, Spotsylvania and Bethesda Church, Va." He died in 1897 at New York City. (Michael J. McAfee Collection)

565

JAMES C. ELGER

Elger was a 22-year-old, 5'10", mechanic from Vernon with blue eyes, light hair and light complexion. He enlisted as a private in Co. C, on Aug. 25, 1862. He was appointed a corporal on Nov. 22, 1862, and died of apoplexy (stroke) in camp near Potomac Creek, VA, on Jan. 6, 1863. Remarks on his service record cards note: "Was with the Regt. at Fredericksburg but was not able to carry a gun." Through a Special Act by the Department of the Interior, his sister, Frances J., was able to draw a $12 per month pension on her deceased brother commencing on June 21, 1890. She lived at Vernon in Oneida County and died Nov. 12, 1914. No reason is given for this unusual circumstance. Elger, also borne on the rolls as Elgar and Elgor, is shown wearing the first uniform of the regiment, with the distinctive breast pocket and shoulder tabs. (Harold Akers Collection)

FRANCIS ALONZO ENGLAND

Only 18 years old when he enrolled in Co. K in Clinton. He was a farmer with blue eyes, light hair and light complexion. England stood 5'7" and was born in Utica. He enlisted as a private in Co. G, on Sept. 1, 1862, and then transferred to Co. K. England was sick in hospital at Washington in Nov. and Dec. 1862. At Gettysburg, Frank's brother, Robert, was the first casualty in the regiment, struck by an artillery shell that severed his neck arteries. He died in Frank's arms. One account lists Frank as being wounded in the foot later in the afternoon of July 2. Promoted corporal on Sept. 13, 1863. Sick (nature of disability described as "decided feebleness of constitution") with typhoid fever in Lincoln Hospital at Alexandria, VA, from Nov. 4, 1863, England was transferred to the Veteran Reserve Corps on Apr. 1, 1865, where he served as company clerk and mustered out from the 18th Regiment, Veteran Reserve Corps, on June 29, 1865, at Washington, DC. He had the solemn distinction to be assigned as a guard in the rotunda of the capitol while President Lincoln's body was lying in state. Assigned as part of the honor guard to travel with Lincoln's body to Illinois, but illness prevented him from fulfilling the duty. England appears opposite page 52 in a post-war Zouave uniform of a local militia company. He died Apr. 30, 1925, and buried at Oakwood Cemetery in Syracuse. (Patrick A. Schroeder Collection)

567

ROBERT W. ENGLAND

Like his brother, he was also 18 years old when he enlisted in Co. G in Clinton. He was a clerk with blue eyes, brown hair and a light complexion. He stood 5'8" and was born in Utica. England mustered in as a private in Rome, on Oct. 10, 1862, and transferred to Co. K. He was appointed to the rank of sergeant on Jan. 31, 1863, then to first sergeant Apr. 20, 1863. At Gettysburg, on July 2, 1863, Robert was the first casualty sustained by the regiment, being hit by an artillery shell that cut his neck arteries. He died in his brother Frank's arms. (Gordon E. Johnson Collection)

JOSEPH H. ENTWHISTLE

A mere 18 years old when he enlisted at Utica on Aug. 25, 1862, in Co. H. Entwhistle was born at Providence, RI (one source says England), and was a 5'4 1/2" tall brick maker, with light complexion, light hair, and blue eyes. He was promoted corporal in Mar./Apr. 1864, and sergeant on Oct. 20, 1864. Entwhistle received a furlough on Feb. 27, 1865. He rejoined the regiment and was captured at the Battle of White Oak Road on Mar. 31, 1865. Paroled at Aiken's Landing, VA, on Apr. 4, and reported at Camp Parole, MD, on Apr. 6, 1865. Discharged June 1, 1865, at Annapolis, MD. He died Oct. 12, 1886, at New Hartford from "Acute Softening of the Stomach." He was 42 years old and a hotelkeeper at the time of his death. (Michael J. McAfee Collection)

LAWRENCE FITZPATRICK

Fitzpatrick was born in Ireland and enlisted in the 5th New York, Duryée's Zouaves, on July 17, 1861, at the age of 20. Joined as a private in Co. B, this 5'8", blue eyed, brown haired former sailor was promoted corporal in Sept. of 1862 and then assigned to the color guard, and made color sergeant on Nov. 13, 1862. He was transferred to Co. B of the 146th New York on May 4, 1863, and received promotion to second lieutenant on Oct. 29, 1863. Fitzpatrick was captured at the Wilderness on May 5, 1864. Confined in Camp Asylum at Columbia, SC, he was paroled Mar. 1, 1865 at Northeast Ferry, NC. (Donald Wisnoski Collection)

LAWRENCE FITZPATRICK

Fitzpatrick returned to duty with the regiment on May 2, 1865, and was mustered as a first lieutenant on May 5. He mustered out with the regiment near Washington on July 16, 1865. At the grand celebration welcoming the regiment back to Utica, "Larry" Fitzpatrick had the honor to command the unit's final bayonet drill to the delight of the crowd. After the war he enlisted in the 27th US Infantry at New York City on Sept. 10, 1866, and was promoted first sergeant of Co. K. He was court martialed at Fort Sedgwick for assaulting, while drunk, two enlisted men. Fitzpatrick was found guilty, but the court recommended clemency "in view of the long service and uniform good conduct of the accused." He was sentenced to be reduced to the rank of private, forfeit his pay, and be confined under charge of a guard for three months. He mustered out in 1871. No other information is known about Fitzpatrick after that date. (USAMHI)

GEORGE H. FOSSARD

Fossard had previously served with the 42nd New York Infantry as the regiment's assistant surgeon from May 3, 1861, until he was dismissed on Jan. 23, 1863. At age 24, he was mustered in as assistant surgeon of the 146th New York on Sept. 22, 1863, at Culpeper Court House, VA, for three years' service. Surgeon General Hammond had appointed him to the post on Sept. 22, 1863. From Nov. through Dec. 1863, he was on detached service at the Division Hospital at Catlett's Station, VA, and then rejoined the unit in the field on Feb. 17, 1864. In March he was on extra duty with the 1st Ohio Battery, and from Apr. to Sept., was on special duty with the 14th US Infantry. Given a twenty-day furlough on Sept. 12, being afflicted with "Gravel"—kidney stones. Fossard was discharged on Oct. 16, 1864, for promotion to surgeon of the 56th New York Infantry. He served that unit from Nov. 5, 1864, until it mustered out on July 5, 1865. Fossard wears a 5th Corps badge in this post-war photograph. (Donald Wisnoski Collection)

WILLIAM FOWLER

A Utica native, Fowler previously served as a second lieutenant of the 173rd New York before being promoted to first lieutenant of Co. I of the 146th, and joining the company on Nov. 11, 1863. He received appointment to serve on Maj. Gen. Silas Casey's staff in Sept. 1864, at the headquarters of the Provisional Brigades around Washington, where he served as the general's aide-de-camp and ordnance officer. He returned to the regiment for promotion to captain of Co. C on Dec. 22, 1864, and was posted on detached duty as aide-de-camp to Maj. Gen. Charles Griffin at the 1st Division headquarters of the 5th Corps, which he did until Feb. 22, 1865, when he was discharged for promotion to captain and assistant adjutant general of US Volunteers. This photo of Fowler has an Alexander Gardner back mark. (Rome Historical Society Collection)

PHILIP FREAS

Upon hearing a speech given by Colonel James A. Mulligan in Utica regarding the Battle of Lexington, KY, Freas, and his chums, Alfred H. Palmer, and Henry Herbert Wood, all determined to sign up with the 146th New York. Enlisting on Aug. 25, 1862, Freas was only 18 years old, with a dark complexion, black eyes and hair, and stood 5'4 1/2". This New Hartford born cabinetmaker turned soldier also had a flare for music and was appointed a musician, shortly after mustering in on Oct. 10, 1862. From Dec. 1862 through Mar. 1863, Freas was detailed as an orderly at brigade headquarters, and was regularly posted to this duty throughout his service. On Aug. 20, 1863, he transferred to Co. A from Co. C. He mustered out with the regiment on July 16, 1865 near Washington, DC. Freas died Sept. 28, 1904. (Patrick A. Schroeder Collection)

PETER D. FROELIGH

Nattily dressed in his Zouave officer's uniform, Froeligh was accustomed to wearing Zouave dress since joining the 5th New York on July 6, 1861. At that time, he was a 21-year-old mason with blue eyes, brown hair, and a fair complexion. One of six children, his father died in 1860 and his mother passed away in 1862. This New York City native stood 5'7" had attained the rank of first sergeant by the time of the 5th New York's transfer to the 146th on May 4, 1863. Froeligh was mustered in as second lieutenant of Co. D, and transferred to Co. H on Jan. 25, 1864. He served with the brigade provost guard in Dec. 1863. He captained one of the regiments' baseball teams. Apparently Froeligh had a premonition of his own death, asking the regimental barber to trim his hair as he expected to be shot in the head during the next engagement and it would allow the surgeon to get a better look at the wound. He was killed in action several days later at the Battle of the Wilderness on May 5, 1864, and buried on the battlefield. He was later re-interred at the Fredericksburg National Cemetery. (Rome Historical Society Collection)

JACOB P. FULMER

Fulmer wears the first issue jacket of the regiment, distinct with a breast pocket and shoulder tabs. Fulmer was 18 years old when he enlisted at Stuben on Sept. 6, 1862, and he was mustered in as a private in Co. I, on Oct. 10, 1862. He stood 5'7", with black eyes, dark hair, a light complexion, and had been a farmer. Promoted corporal in Jan. 1863, Fulmer was always present with the regiment, except for when he was sick at the division hospital from late Apr. through July 1863, until wounded in the right arm at the Battle of the Wilderness on May 5, 1864. Listed as a flesh wound, he recovered at Lincoln Hospital in Washington, DC, and was later transferred to Patterson Park Hospital in Baltimore. He recovered in time to rejoin the regiment and fight for the Weldon Railroad at Petersburg in mid-Aug. 1864. He was present for the rest of the campaigns. He received promotion to sergeant on July 1, 1865, and mustered out with the unit on the 16th of that month. Fulmer died Dec. 21, 1927, San Jose, CA. (Seward Osborne Collection)

KENNER GARRARD

Born in Kentucky in 1827, Garrard attended Harvard for a year before leaving to enter West Point where he graduated eighth in the class of 1851. Captured by Texas insurgents on Apr. 12, 1861, and paroled. He served as commandant at West Point until appointed colonel of the 146th. Garrard brought discipline and military efficiency to the regiment. Garrard led the regiment at Fredericksburg, Chancellorsville, and Gettysburg. There, upon the death of Brig. Gen. Stephen H. Weed, he succeeded to command of the brigade. He was promoted July 23, 1863, to brigadier general of volunteers. He commanded the brigade along the Rappahannock River, until put in charge of the cavalry bureau in Washington, DC. Garrard led a division of cavalry during the Atlanta Campaign, then a division of infantry in the 16th Corps during the Battle of Nashville. He took a major role in the capture of Mobile on Mar. 13, 1865, and received the brevet rank of brigadier and major general in the Regular Army. He resigned his commission on Nov. 9, 1866. Garrard died May 15, 1879, and was buried at Spring Grove Cemetery in Cincinnati, OH. Alfred Palmer wrote of his former commander: "to him much is due for the discipline and efficiency [of the regiment] . . . . He was a thorough soldier. A gallant officer, loyal, fearless & true and beloved by all his men." (Donald Wisnoski Collection)

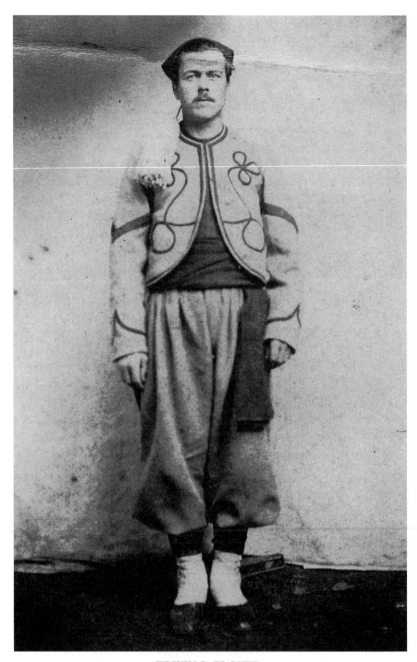

EDWIN J. GLOVER

Glover is shown in full Zouave regalia after his promotion to corporal early in 1865. He had enlisted in Utica on Sept. 3, 1862, and was mustered in as a private in Co. A on Oct. 10, 1862. He was 23 years old at the time. Glover stood 5'8", with blue eyes, dark hair and a light complexion. He had been born in England and was a farmer before enlisting. Records show that he was a reliable soldier, present from his enlistment until being captured at the Battle of the Wilderness on May 5, 1864. (Patrick A Schroeder Collection)

EDWIN J. GLOVER

Glover survived the horrors of Andersonville and was paroled at Charleston, SC, on Dec. 11, 1864. He arrived at Camp Parole, MD, on Dec. 18, 1864, suffering from "Chills & Fever and Camp Diarrhea brought on by ill treatment while a prisoner at Andersonville." He was furloughed home to recover, starting on Dec. 25, 1864. While away, he was promoted corporal in Jan./Feb. 1865. Glover returned to the hospital at Annapolis, MD, on Mar. 3, 1865, and rejoined the regiment on Apr. 1. Promoted to sergeant on June 1, 1865, he was present with the regiment for the muster out on July 16 near Washington, DC. Glover was born in Audley, near Newcastle, Staffordshire, England on Mar. 1, 1840. He worked as a farmer in England until he was eighteen when he immigrated to the United States. After the war he returned to Utica and was employed by Downer and Kellog at the Forest Hill Cemetery, and later in the Mohawk Valley Scotch Cap Factory. In 1865 he married Eliza E. Palmer (shown above), who was the sister of his comrades Alfred and George Palmer of the 146th. Glover's last years were spent in the florist business. He was a member of Plymouth Church and also of the Bacon Post, Grand Army of the Republic. He died Dec. 16, 1902. His wife survived him as well as five children: Mrs. J. R. Pflanz of New Hartford; Mrs. S. C. Ackerman, of Little Falls; and Frank A. Glover, Mrs. Frank Beecraft and Albert E. Glover, all of Utica. There were also 11 grandchildren at the time of his death. (Patrick A Schroeder Collection)

579

JAMES G. GRINDLAY

He was born in Edinburgh, Scotland, and immigrated to the United States while young and began work as bookkeeper at a tannery in Boonville. He was enrolled and mustered in as the captain of Co. D on Sept. 8, 1862. He was sick with fever in mid-Jan. 1863, and was furloughed home to recover his health. Grindlay took command of the regiment after the Battle of the Wilderness. Promoted to major on May 18, 1864. In Sept. 1864 he commanded the 1st Brigade of the 2nd Division of the 5th Corps, while Brevet Brig. Gen. Frederic Winthrop was on leave. Given a furlough on Sept. 26, 1864, to visit his brother who had arrived from Scotland, in Niagara, NY, to transact important private business "being absent from my home in Scotland for the last eight (8) years rendering it very necessary." This photo shows a chubby cheeked Grindlay early in the war, probably with the rank of captain. (Michael J. McAfee Collection)

JAMES G. GRINDLAY

In this photo of Grindlay as colonel of the 146th, taken in Utica during the spring of 1865, he appears to have thinned somewhat since his 1862 photo. He was commissioned colonel on Feb. 1, 1865, with rank to date from Dec. 1, 1864. On Jan. 30, 1865, Maj. Gen. Gouverneur K. Warren approved a ten-day leave for Grindlay to go to Albany to look into the colonelcy of the regiment, to which Warren noted that in the matter "all his superior officers feel much concerned." Promoted colonel on Feb. 15, 1865, and made a brevet brigadier general to date from Mar. 13, 1865. He was given brevet ranks for gallant and meritorious service in at the battles of Spotsylvania, North Anna, and services during the war. On June 29, 1865, he obtained a three-day leave to visit a sick brother in New York City. He moved to Utica after the war and became active in politics. He was a prominent member of the Loyal Legion and served as president of the 5th Corps Veteran Association. His first wife was Miss Anderson of Boonville, and his second wife was Mary Peckham of Utica. In 1892 he began serving at the State Controller's Office in Albany. In Troy, on Oct. 19, 1907, Grindlay was struck and killed by an automobile. (Rome Historical Society Collection)

CHARLES HECOX

A dapper looking Charles Hecox in complete Zouave uniform and sporting a lengthy watch chain. He enlisted as a musician in Co. B at Kirkland when he was 16 years old. At that time he was 5'3", with black eyes, light hair, and a fair complexion. He had been born in New Hartford, and was a farmer before enlisting. Somewhere along the way he learned to play the fife. His July 16, 1865, muster out card reads "Fifer ever since enlistment." He was present with the regiment except on two occasions. In Nov./Dec. 1862 he was sick in quarters, and it is noted that he fell out on the march to Chancellorsville, but had participated at Fredericksburg, and was present from Gettysburg to Appomattox. This picture of Hecox was taken by Baker in Utica. He died Jan. 20, 1931, at Saginaw, MI. (Rome Historical Society Collection)

ARTHUR HENDRICKS

Born on May 12, 1845, near Saugerties, in Ulster County, where he grew up on a farm. Hendricks attended the preparatory branch of the College of New York City when he was thirteen. Later, he resigned to go to work for the Eighth Avenue Railroad Company. At age 17, he joined the 5th New York Infantry in Aug. 1862 and transferred as a private to Co. G of the 146th. A clerk by trade, he was tall, 5'11 1/2", with blue eyes, light brown hair, and a light complexion. He suffered a right inguinal hernia when he fell crossing a ditch on the march from Chancellorsville to the United States Ford on May 6, 1863, just after his transfer. He is listed at Harewood Hospital in Washington, DC, on July 8, 1863. Hendricks was transferred to the Invalid Corps on Sept. 30, 1863. He took part in the Battle of Fort Steven's, July 11-12, 1864, helping repulse Confederate Gen. Jubal Early's raid on Washington. He mustered out from the 56th Company, Second Battalion, Veteran Reserve Corps, on July 20, 1865, at Washington. After the war, in 1866, he married Ida Virginia Moore. He studied law at Columbian Law College (George Washington University), receiving his law degree in June 1872 and was admitted to the bar of the Supreme Court of the District of Columbia in Sept. 1872. He worked in the Register's Office of the Treasury Department and rose to chief of the division, and then served as a law clerk in several offices including the interior department. A member of the 5th New York Veteran Association and became commander of Burnside Post, No.8, Grand Army of the Republic in 1892. He was very active in organizing parades, served on many committees, and was the Grand Army of the Republic assistant adjutant general in 1892. He died Mar. 18, 1917, in Kensington, MD, and was buried at Arlington National Cemetery. (Keith Hendricks Collection)

JOHN HESS

This painting shows Hess in his Zouave uniform. The original is nicely tinted illustrating the light blue of the uniform, the yellow trim, burgundy sash, white shirt, and turban wrapped around his fez. Hess has yellowish blond hair and piercing blue eyes. Born in Albany on Feb. 10, 1841, at age 21, he was 5'9", with a light complexion, was a laborer, and living in Utica. He enrolled in Rome as a private in Co. H, on Oct. 2, 1862. Hess participated in the battles of Fredericksburg, Chancellorsville, and Gettysburg, before being captured at the Wilderness on May 5, 1864. He was held as a prisoner of war at Andersonville, GA, and Florence, SC, until paroled Feb. 26, 1865, at Northeast Ferry, NC. Exchanged Mar. 3, 1865, from Wilmington, NC, to Annapolis, MD. Hess convalesced from typhoid fever at Patterson Park, then Hicks General Hospitals, both in Baltimore. He was discharged June 22, 1865, from the hospital. He returned home and on July 24, 1865, married Anna Elizabeth Baker, and fathered five children. Hess became an active Democratic politician in the Second Ward, and worked as janitor of the City Hall from 1874 to 1876, then served as Assessor of the Second Ward from 1883 to 1887. He belonged to Fire Company No. 7, and was a member of the Association of ex-Prisoners of War. Hess died in Utica on June 19, 1890, and was interred at Forest Hill Cemetery. At the time of his death, he ran a grocery on Hope Street. (Millicent Rader-Harris Collection)

FREDERICK C. HYDE

This photograph, taken at Fort Federal Hill in Baltimore, shows Hyde sporting a borrowed Sharp's rifle. Hyde served with Co. F of the 5th New York and only companies E and I of the regiment were issued that type of weapon. He enlisted in the 5th on July 12, 1861. Hyde, from Hartford, NY, was 18 years old, stood 5'6 1/2", with brown eyes, dark hair, a dark complexion, and gave his occupation as a mechanic. On May 4, 1863, he was one of the 325 three-year men from the 5th assigned to the 146th. Hyde deserted his new regiment on May 14, 1863, at Henry House, near Falmouth, VA. Although a note on his service records credits him participating in the Siege of Yorktown and the battles of Gaines' Mill, Second Bull Run, and Chancellorsville; a secondary inscription states: "This man was never in any engagement." He sometimes went by the alias Charles A. Ames, and died Jan. 2, 1922, at San Antonio, TX. (Michael J. McAfee Collection)

DAVID TUTTLE JENKINS

After assisting to raise the 117th New York Infantry (Fourth Oneida), Jenkins was mustered in as a first lieutenant and regimental adjutant of the 146th on Aug. 26, 1862. Born May 4, 1836, the tall and slender 26-year-old had attended Rensselaer Polytechnic Institute in Troy, and was practicing law in Vernon at the commencement of the war. A competent soldier and skilled engineer, Jenkins was promoted major on Sept. 17, 1862, then to lieutenant colonel on July 23, 1863. On May 5, 1864, he was in command of the division pickets, but learning that an attack was to be made, he asked to be returned to his regiment to lead it into battle. At the head of the regiment he led his men in the charge across Saunders Field in support of the 140th New York. The last time he was seen by members of the unit, he had his back against a tree and was leaning on his sword. He had been wounded at least twice—once in the head and another shot through the body, yet he encouraged his men to "go on." Hopes that Jenkins had been captured faded as time passed. His body was never recovered. Major A. Pierson Case of the regiment remembered: "In a time of heroes, he too was a hero—he was ours, and we ought to be proud of him." This photo was taken by Brady in New York City. (Ann Ford Collection)

586

JAMES EDGAR JENKINS

Born in Vernon on June 22, 1842, Jenkins was a student at Hamilton College at the commencement of the war. He left school along with Henry H. Curran and Charles K. Dutton, who both later served in the 146th, and helped his friends recruit 150 men at their own expense and traveled to New York City with the contingent. Unable to merge the group with another organization, the volunteers disbanded. Jenkins then assisted in raising an independent company that became known as the Oneida Cavalry. This unit had the distinguished honor of being posted to the headquarters of the Army of the Potomac, where it provided couriers and performed escort and guard duty. Jenkins enrolled as first lieutenant on Aug. 17, 1861, and mustered in Sept. 4, 1861, second in command to Capt. Daniel P. Mann. He was discharged from the outfit on Mar. 1, 1863, for promotion to captain in his brother's regiment—the 146th. (Ann H. Ford Collection)

587

JAMES EDGAR JENKINS

Mustered in as captain of Co. H on Mar. 1, 1863, Jenkins may have soon regretted the change. Being in the thick of the fighting at Gettysburg's Little Round Top on July 2, 1863, he was twice wounded. Near the spot where Gen. Weed, Col. O'Rorke, and Gen. Warren were wounded, Jenkins was shot through the neck, most likely by a sharpshooter's bullet. The missile passed through the back of his neck at an upward angle and exited from his mouth. Simultaneously with the bullet wound, an artillery shell exploded nearby tearing a gash in the back of the young captain. His men gathered some pillows from a nearby farmhouse and put them in the bottom of the ambulance that took him to the hospital in Baltimore. The regimental chaplain, Albert Erdman, accompanied him in the journey. The chaplain sent Jenkins' mother a telegram notifying her of Jenkins injuries. She journeyed to Baltimore and brought him home to Vernon, NY, to recuperate. Upon recovering from his injuries, he rejoined the regiment. Jenkins fought gallantly at the battles of the Wilderness, Spotsylvania, Bethesda Church, and at Petersburg, receiving the brevet rank of major in 1867 for his faithful and meritorious services. He continued with the regiment until the expiration of his term of service on Sept. 30, 1864. He was later brevetted a major for faithful and meritorious service in the 146th, to date from Mar. 13, 1865. This image was made at W. J. Baker's Studio in Utica in the spring of 1865. (Ann H. Ford Collection)

588

JAMES EDGAR JENKINS

Jenkins re-enlisted as captain of the Oneida Cavalry on Jan. 18, 1865, and mustered out with that company near Washington, DC, on June 13, 1865. After a short stay in Vernon, Jenkins removed to Worcester, MA, where he engaged in business. There, in 1870, he married Elizabeth Pierce. The next year, they moved to New York City and resided there about ten years. Plagued by exposure and old war wounds, Jenkins' was affected with consumption. In 1881, he gave up business and seeking to restore his health, he moved to Florida, but it did little good. He and his family, now consisting of five children, then moved to Brule County, SD. The climate suited Jenkins much better, though he would have brief relapses. There he was elected the Treasurer of Brule County in 1883 and again in 1886. In 1887, Jenkins was appointed the Adjutant General of Dakota, and thus became known as "General Jenkins." The severe winter of 1888 proved fatal. Though weak, he desired to see his old home. Jenkins traveled to Vernon, NY, in 1888, where he died shortly after arriving. This photograph was taken at Claflin's Studio in Worcester, MA, on Feb. 17, 1869. (Ann H. Ford Collection)

JAMES ALBERT JENNISON

This 5'5", Utica born machinist, is shown wearing a frock coat. Typically cited on records as J. Albert Jennison, he had hazel eyes, brown hair, a medium complexion, and was 21 years old when he enrolled at Utica, along with his brothers Charles and Henry, Aug. 21, 1862. Born on July 18, 1841, after attending public school and completing "Mrs. Platt's school and later the Advanced School", he learned the trade of a brass finisher. The Jennison brothers were all mustered in as privates in Co. C on Aug. 10, 1862. Albert was quickly promoted corporal on Nov. 6, 1862, then sergeant on Jan. 31, 1863. Although, while in Fredericksburg, he had tried to make a batch of pancakes with what turned out to be plaster of Paris, "his record as a fighter was unsurpassed. He was absolutely fearless, and many brave deeds were placed to his credit." He became the hero of the regiment at the Battle of the Wilderness. (Patrick A. Schroeder Collection)

JAMES ALBERT JENNISON

On May 5, 1864, after the regiment had charged across Saunders Field and into the woods, the ground in their wake was strewn with casualties, one being Henry Jennison. Albert was attending to his older brother, but he had to leave him as the regiment fell back. Two color bearers had already fallen, when the only member of the color guard, Cpl. Conrad Neuschler made off with the colors, until he stumbled into a gully and was wounded. Jennison hurriedly scooped the flag up in front of the on rushing Confederates. He continued to the rear despite rebel calls for him to surrender and eluded a fusillade of bullets by dashing side to side as he ran. He made it to the Federal lines despite several encounters with rebel troops and numerous tumbles during his flight. Comrade Thomas Wheeler described the escapade: "The little fellow fell three times when he was coming back with the colors, and each time we thought he had been killed. But he was up again each time, and finally brought the colors in. It was the most daring thing I had ever seen, and it was so daring that he was cheered not only by our own men, but the rebels as well." Promoted second lieutenant and assigned to Co. K, Jan. 17, 1865, and made a first lieutenant on June 27, that same year. He mustered out with the regiment on July 16, 1865, near Washington, DC. Jennison was brevetted a captain on June 22, 1867, to date from Apr. 1, 1865, for gallant and meritorious service at the Battle of Five Forks. His brother Henry died of his wounds in the Wilderness, and Charles mustered out in July 1865, but had been severely wounded at the Battle of North Anna. Upon returning to Utica, Jennison continued his employ as a brass finisher then worked for the postal service. He married Mary Spindler and was a staunch member of the First Church of Christ, Scientist. One day, on the way home for work, he performed another act of bravery and heroism when he rescued a drowning child from the canal. Jennison died on March 7, 1923, at Utica. (Donald Wisnoski Collection)

591

E. VERN JEWEL

At age 23, he was mustered in as the first lieutenant of Co. B on Oct. 10, 1862, and was appointed captain of Co. C on Jan. 7, 1863, "by commission from the Governor of the State Of New York." He was absent with leave from Feb. 19 until Mar. 3, 1863. Jewel was absent again from June 15 to Sept. 23, 1863, suffering from sunstroke affecting his "nervous system and brain" and malarial fever. He was discharged by special order of the War Department on the later date for disability. This photo of Jewel was taken in Rome. He died Aug. 11, 1917, at Chicago, IL. (Rome Historical Society Collection)

EDWARD O. JONES

This photo taken in Utica shows Jones as a corporal. He is decked out in full Zouave regalia, with a checkered shirt, tie, and a paper collar to boot. He also wears a 5th Corps badge and a fully tasseled fez. Company F's descriptive book depicts Jones as 21 years old, 5'6", with a light complexion, blue eyes and light hair, noting that he was born in Newtown, England, and listed his occupation as a bookbinder. He enlisted Aug. 25, 1862, at Utica. Jones was appointed corporal prior to his muster in on Oct. 10, 1862. Promoted sergeant to date from Apr. 1, 1863, and to first sergeant Mar. 26, 1865. He quickly was jumped to second lieutenant of Co. E, on Mar. 30, 1865, and promoted again to second lieutenant of Co. I on May 7, and mustered out July 16, 1865. He was brevetted a captain on July 16, 1867, for faithful and meritorious services to date from Mar. 13, 1865. Jones was with the regiment the entire time it was in service except for the two times he received a furlough in Mar./Apr. 1864 and Feb./Mar. 1865. (Rome Historical Society Collection)

EZEKIEL JONES

Mustered in as captain of Co. I on Oct. 10, 1862, Jones was unable to take the field with the regiment. Jones was commissioned captain, Nov. 3, 1862, with rank from Oct. 7. He died of typhoid fever at his home in Rome on Nov. 11, 1862. (USAMHI)

HENRY E. JONES

Enrolled as a private at age 24 at Steuben on Aug. 18, 1862. He mustered in as first sergeant of Co. I, on Oct. 10, 1862. Jones stood 5'7", had dark eyes, dark hair, was a farmer, and had been born in Steuben. Promoted to second lieutenant of Co. G on Jan. 7, 1863, and mustered in with that rank on Feb. 1. Acting first lieutenant since Mar. 1. Jones requested a furlough on Apr. 6, 1863, having "recently been promoted and am entirely destitute of an outfit necessary for an officer and also desire to visit a sick Brother." The leave was approved by Gen. George Sykes on Apr. 7. Jones was quickly promoted to first lieutenant and transferred to Co. D on July 20, 1863. He reported sick on July 29, 1863, and sent to Washington, DC, for treatment by R. O. Abbottt, "Medical Director of that city." Jones was transferred to Co. G on Aug. 18, 1863. He commanded Co. I since Sept. 17, 1863. He received promotion to the rank of captain of Co. I on Oct. 31, 1863. Jones obtained a furlough home for ten days on Feb. 28, 1864, "for the purpose of visiting my friends in Utica." Jones suffered a bullet wound in the right leg May 5, 1864, at the Battle of the Wilderness. He was furloughed home to recover from his wound in June 1864. (Michael J. McAfee Collection)

HENRY E. JONES

Jones was in the "Officers U. S. A. Hospital" at Annapolis, MD, starting July 9 until he returned to duty on Aug. 12, 1864. Assigned to permanent party at the draft rendezvous at Hart's Island, in New York Harbor and shown as present from Aug. 15, 1864 through May 20, 1865, when he was relieved from duty and rejoined the regiment on June 1. Jones mustered out with the regiment on July 16, 1865, near Washington DC. Brevetted major July 16, 1867, for faithful and meritorious service to date from Mar. 13, 1865. Jones died Nov. 19, 1918, at Portland, OR. (Rome Historical Society Collection)

ORLO H. JONES

Here Jones, as a corporal, poses in full Zouave regalia, adorned with white turban and corps badge; he holds a Sharps rifle. He was 22 years old when he enlisted on Aug. 30, 1862, at his native Boonville. Jones was a laborer, and stood 5'7", with brown eyes, dark hair, and a light complexion when he mustered in as a private in Co. D on Oct. 10, 1862. He was promoted corporal in Jan./Feb. 1863, and appointed sergeant Sept. 22, 1863. Jones was at home and forwarded on the list of "stragglers" to the regiment from Utica on Dec. 30, 1863, and charged $9.78 for transportation. He was appointed first sergeant on Feb. 14, 1864. Jones was last paid Feb. 29, 1864. (Daniel Miller Collection)

ORLO H. JONES

Here Corporal Orlo Jones poses with his older brother, Adelbert Jones, of Co. B of the 97th New York Infantry "Third Oneida"—which also served in the 5th Corps. Adelbert was wounded at the Battle of Second Bull Run on Aug. 30, 1862, at Gettysburg on July 3, 1863, then again at Laurel Hill, VA, on May 8, 1864. He rose from the ranks to the grade of captain before mustering out on Dec. 1, 1864. Orlo survived the horrors of the Wilderness only to be wounded in the ankle and captured at the Battle of Bethesda Church on June 2, 1864. Jones was admitted to General Hospital 21 in Richmond, VA. He died while a prisoner of war in Richmond, on June 30, 1864. Even as late as Sept. 15, 1864, the family had no idea of Jones' fate as a letter was written at that time inquiring of his whereabouts. (Daniel Miller Collection)

HENRY LIVINGSTON JOY
One of the older soldiers in the regiment, Joy enlisted as a private at age 42 on Sept. 5, 1862, in Remsen. He mustered in as fourth sergeant of Co. I on Oct. 10, 1862. Joy stood 5'9", and had gray eyes, brown hair, a light complexion, was employed as a cooper, and had been born in Hampshire County, MA. Joy sustained a slight wound on July 2, 1863, at Gettysburg. He became sick (primarily suffering from chronic rheumatism), and on Sept. 16, 1863, was sent to DeCamp General Hospital at David's Island in New York Harbor. He received a 15-day furlough on Oct. 31, 1863. After his return he did hospital duty as a nurse until mustering out at David's Island on May 17, 1865. After the war, Joy lived in Ilion. He was a member of the Chismore Post, Grand Army of the Republic. Joy died in Ilion on May 31, 1910. (Monica Knight Collection)

IS A FORTY-NINER

Henry L. Joy Recalls His Experiences.

HE WAS AMONG THE FIRST GOLD SEEKERS TO ARRIVE IN CALIFORNIA.

Within a Few Weeks He Will Start From His Ilion Home to Revisit His Old Haunts on the Pacific Coast.

ILION, April 7.—Henry L. Joy, Ilion's oldest citizen, will in a few weeks make a trip to his sons in Chicago and Omaha. He will also go to the Pacific coast. Mr. Joy was one of the old forty-niners, and crossed the plains and the great desert in a prairie schooner, and of the five men in his party, as far as he knows, he of all reached the Pacific coast. His story of his trip, hairbreadth escapes and experiences is entertaining. Mr. Joy carries his 82 years well. His elastic step and quick action is wonderful after the hardship and exposure he went through.

Last evening Mr. Joy sat in his library, and being asked to relate a few incidents of his eventful trip across the continent and his life among the thousands who rushed to California soon after Marshall found the nugget of gold in Suiter's raceway and made California the Mecca of fortune hunters. He said:

"I was born in Hampshire county, Mass., on March 27th, 1819. In 1848 I was running a store in St. Louis. My nearest neighbor was Thomas H. Benton, father-in-law of John C. Fremont. At the time of which I speak, Fremont was in St. Louis, and the government was fitting out an expedition for him to search out a southern trail to the Pacific. Among his followers were 'Kit' Carson, Fitzgerald and other noted scouts, and my association with them ripened into warm friendship. They were all enthusiastic in the project which Fremont was desirous of carrying out. The expedition started out, and it was not long before I too had the fever, and finally decided that I would cross the trackless plain."

"I organized a company of five men. We had a prairie schooner, five yoke of oxen, two horses and a mule, and on the 18th of March, 1848, we drove through the streets of St. Louis out onto the plains and resolutely turned our teams and our faces westward. For a while our spirits were high. Day after day we traveled on night after night we tethered our animals, and with one as sentinel the rest slept. As weeks and months went by dissatisfaction arose among the men and they questioned the course I had taken. The Indians were troublesome and dogged us over hills and through valleys, stopped when we stopped and when we resumed our weary march they followed us."

A Companion Scalped.

"One night one of our men went to attend to the animals who were tethered a short distance away. It was not long before we heard the dreaded Indian war whoop and knew something was wrong. We grabbed our rifles and rushed to the spot where the animals were. A sickening sight met our gaze. Lying upon the ground was our comrade covered with blood and scalped. We carried him to the corral and washed the

600

blood from him and applied restoratives. He recovered slowly, and so far as I know, recovered fully. We greased his head with tallow and made him a skull cap out of some cloth we had brought along. He was the only man I ever saw scalped and live to tell his experience."

"We went to Connell Bluff, crossed the river and struck out into the Indian territory. We reached the Platte river at Larrame forks and entered the Black Hills. We passed the Garden of the Gods and many wonders of nature, but to us then they were but obstacles which we must encounter. We suffered untold hardships when crossing the great desert. We kept a westerly course. We nearly died from thirst and exposure. We were lured off from our course by the seductive mirage, but at last reached the green country after many days of untold suffering."

Party Separates

"We went down into the great Salt lake basin, but went around Salt Lake City, as the sect of Mormons called Donhites were troublesome and we thought it policy to avoid them. Dissensions arose in the party and it was decided that every man must shift for himself. The men took their property and the horses. Some went on alone and I stayed with the cattle. Day after day I wandered on, seeing no human being, now and then from the high ground where I stood I would see bands of Indians, but avoided them. Winter came on as I neared the Nevada mountains, and one morning I woke up to find my faithful animals frozen to death during the night. I sat down by my wagon and wished I was back in the States, but it was useless to think of turning back, so making a pack of the most necessary articles and with my rifle in my hand I started to cross the Nevadas, and all the suffering which I had experienced on the trip so far was concentrated in that which I went through before I crossed to the Pacific. My provisions gave out and I subsisted on game until my ammunition gave out, and to keep my gun from the Indians I broke it over a log. Now and then I caught a crow. I have eaten crow before and since that time with much less relish. When the game gave out I lived on nuts and roots. I finally reached the Sacramento river, and building a raft, floated down the stream. How long I was going down I shall never know, as I lost all record of time. One night I camped on the side of the river and the water rose in the night and compelled me to move, so I climbed up a tree and roosted until morning."

"As I was up in the tree a man came by, the first I had seen since parting with my comrades. I asked him what time of year it was and with much apparent surprise he told me it was New Years, 1849. He doubted my veracity when I told him I had crossed the Nevadas in the winter, as he said no man could survive the journey. I finally reached the coast and began to look for work. It was about this time that gold was discovered and I went to the mines and gold diggings and worked there for two years. I found gold and secured considerable, but was robbed repeatedly. After saving up quite a number of nuggets I started for San Francisco. I was followed by men who wanted to rob me but I managed to keep from a personal encounter with them. They tracked me about the city, so I got aboard of a brig which was ready to sail for South America. I was put off at Panama and walked nearly across the Isthmus about a month, when a vessel, the Crescent City, hove to and took me aboard. I had contracted the yellow fever and was delirious during most of the trip. At last I reached New York city, and after a few weeks in a hospital was well again, but not desirous of repeating the trip."

[HENRY L. JOY OBITUARY]
HENRY L. JOY

In the New York Advocate of April 21st, there appeared an article with the caption
"An Argonaut of 1849." The "Argonaut" entered upon the possession of the heavenly
treasure on the 31st day of May, after ninety-two years of an earthly pilgrimage.
Henry Linvingstone [sic] Joy was born in Plainfield, Mass., March 27th, 1819. His
father, Cyrus Joy, was a lawyer and also a member of the Massachusetts legislature.
When a young man, Henry went west as far as St. Louis and engaged in mercantile
pursuits. He had been there only a few years when the news of the discovery of gold
in California started many a fateful caravan westward in the hope of crossing prairie,
plain and mountain, and reaching the new Eldorado. Brother Joy became infected
with the fever, and five years after setting in St. Louis, he turned his business over to
his partner, kissed his wife and children goodbye, and in company with three
companions, set out with their caravan to cross the continent to California. After
privations and sufferings indescribable, he was the only one to reach the coast.
Staking out a claim he succeeded in finding gold in some quantities, but only to have it
stolen by the lawless element that infected the region at that time. Succeeding in
saving a little he started for the east on board a sailing vessel bound for Bedford, Mass.
Arriving in New York he soon joined his family in Russia, Herkimer county, N. Y.,
where they gone to be with his sister during his absence. In 1862 he enlisted in the
146th New York Volunteers and became sergeant of Company I. He took part in the
battles of Fredericksburg, Chancellorsville, Manassas Gap and Gettysburg. At the
battle of Gettysburg he was wounded and sent to David's Island, where after he
recovered he did hospital duty till the close of the war. When he returned home he
took up his residence in the village of Ilion, and remained here for the rest of his life.
He was a member of Chismore Post G.A.R., and attended memorial service with his
comrades at the Presbyterian Church two days before his death. Brother Joy had been
a member of the Ilion Methodist Episcopal Church for forty-five years, and for forty-
two years had been a class leader. He had a rich Christian experience and his
testimonials and prayers were inspiring. He was zealous in seeking out the
unconverted and in praying with and comforting the sick, particularly after his
retirement from active pursuits. Brother Joy was married in 1843 to Miss Harriet
Brown, of Vermont, who died a few years later. In 1857 he married Miss Mary Payne,
of Massachusetts, who died in 1893. He leaves eight sons, two of whom were by his
first wife, viz.: Frank L. Joy, of Chicago, Ill., and Arthur C. Joy, of Ilion, N.Y. The
sons by his second wife are the Rev. Eugene F. Joy*, of Oswego, N.Y., Charles Joy, of
Boise City, Idaho, Dr. Milton Joy, of Cazenovia, N.Y., Henry L. Joy, of Ilion, N.Y.,
Dr. Fred Joy, of Omaha, Nebraska, and Dr. Louis Joy, of Fulton, N.Y. Besides his
sons he is survived by one half-sister and two half-brothers, viz.: Mrs. Adelaine Farr,
of Philadelphia, Pa. Edwin M. Joy, of Iowa City, Ia., and Charles Joy, of Philadelphia,
Pa.

The funeral services were conducted at the home and afterward at the church Friday
June 3d, by his pastor, the undersigned, assisted by the Rev. D.F. Pierce, D.D.,
Superintendent of the Mohawk District, and the Rev. H.W. Bennett, D.D., of Ilion,
two of his former pastors. Interment was in Armory Hill cemetery—Samuel J.
Greenfield.

* Rev. Eugene Joy's middle initial was "H," not "F."

MILO B. KELLOGG

Shown here as a sergeant of Co. I, 17th New York Infantry, he transferred to Co. I of the 146th New York on June 25, 1863. He had enlisted at age 18. Kellog was born in Marion, stood 5'7", with a fair complexion, dark eyes, light hair, and was a blacksmith. He participated in the engagements of Yorktown, Gaines' Mill, Malvern Hill, Fredericksburg, and Chancellorsville, before joining the 146th. Kellogg re-enlisted as a veteran volunteer on Feb. 20, 1864, and given veterans' furlough beginning on Feb. 28. He was captured at the Battle of the Wilderness on May 5, 1864. He was paroled on Feb. 26, 1865, at Northeast Ferry, NC, and reported at Camp Parole, MD, on Mar. 7. Kellogg was furloughed Mar. 10, 1865, and was at Palmyra, NY, on Apr. 12, 1865, and sent to the regiment on May 2. He mustered out with the regiment near Washington, DC, on July 16, 1865. Kellogg died on Oct. 7, 1918, at Orting, WA. (USAMHI)

ALONZO I. KING

King was born in Sangerfield, and was 5'4", with blue eyes, light hair, a light complexion, and made his living as a landlord when he enrolled as a private on Aug. 22, 1862, at Utica (also given as Aug. 29 at Whitestown). He mustered in as a sergeant in Co. K on Oct. 10, 1862. King was reduced to the ranks on Dec. 17, 1862, however, he was reappointed to the rank of sergeant on Jan. 15, 1863, and on the 31st was made first sergeant of the company. He was again promoted on Mar. 28, 1863, to the rank of second lieutenant in Co. C to date from Jan. 7, 1863, and mustered in with that rank on Apr. 19. He fell ill on June 4, 1863, and was absent at Seminary Hospital in Georgetown, DC, until July 29, 1863, when he returned and took command of Co. C. (Rome Historical Society Collection)

ALONZO I. KING

King, shown wearing his Zouave officer's jacket again became sick with a severe attack of intermittent fever in Oct. and secured a furlough starting on Nov. 4, 1863. The attack developed into "chronic inflammation of the lungs & debility" which was complicated by the effects of typhoid fever and diarrhea. He rejoined the regiment on Jan. 4, 1864, when he took his post with Co. A—having been recently transferred. King was wounded by a bullet in the right arm on May 5, 1864, at the Battle of the Wilderness. He took command of the detachment acting as Provost Guard at Camp Parole, Annapolis, MD, starting on July 5, 1864, and was ordered to rejoin the regiment on Sept. 19, 1864. He was promoted to first lieutenant of Co. A on Dec. 1, 1864, and also acted as the commander of Co. G, (in actuality he had been commanding both companies since his return on Oct. 1). Absent with a fifteen-day leave starting Jan. 15, 1865: "to visit my home at Oriskany, NY. My father died recently . . . . The family looks to me to settle the estate. I being the eldest and my only brother being in the Army." King was promoted captain of Co. A (vice Thomas Wilson killed at Five Forks), which he had been acting commander of from Jan. 1, 1865, on June 17 and he mustered in six days later. He was made captain by brevet to date from Apr. 1, 1865, for gallant and meritorious service at the Battle of Five Forks. King mustered out with the regiment on July 16, 1865, near Washington, DC. This photo of King was taken in Washington. He was active in persuading Mrs. Brainard to write the regimental history. King died on Nov. 14, 1921, at Waterville. (Michael J. McAfee Collection)

605

HENRY E. LOOMIS

Loomis appears wearing a Zouave officer's jacket and a 5th Corps badge. He was 23 years old when he enrolled on Aug. 30, 1862, at Kirkland (also given as Rome) and mustered in as a sergeant in Co. G on Oct. 10, 1862. Born in Burlington, at the time of his enlistment, Loomis was a student. He stood 6 feet tall with a light complexion, blue eyes, dark hair, and was promoted first sergeant on Dec. 10, 1862. Promoted again, to second lieutenant, and transferred to Co. K, on Feb. 1, 1863 (to rank from Jan. 7, 1863). Absent on detached service at General Hospital at Gettysburg, PA, since July 5, 1863. Loomis rejoined the regiment and transferred to Co. D on July 12, 1863, and acted as commander of Co. A from Mar. 3 to Apr. 1, 1864. He obtained a ten-day leave in Jan. 1864 "to visit Onondaga Co." Loomis was wounded May 5, 1864, at the Battle of the Wilderness, then promoted to first lieutenant on Sept. 16, 1864 (which he had been doing duty as such since Aug. 31), and then to captain on Mar. 28, 1865 (to date from Feb. 1). Absent with leave from Jan. 15-25 and June 9-28 (to see his sick sister in Schenectady Co., NY), 1865. He mustered out with the regiment on July 16, 1865, near Washington, DC. Brevetted captain for gallant and meritorious services at the battles of Spotsylvania, Petersburg, and the Weldon Railroad on June 22, 1867, and to date from Mar. 13, 1865. Loomis died on Aug. 27, 1920, at Yokahoma, Japan. (Donald Wisnoski Collection)

JOSEPH STUART LOWERY

Lowery, shown here as a first lieutenant, was 21 years old when he enrolled on Aug. 29, 1862, at Boonville and mustered in as a sergeant in Co. D on Oct. 10, 1862. Lowery was born in Oriskany County, stood 5'5 1/2, had a light complexion, gray eyes, light hair, and was employed as a clerk. He was promoted second lieutenant of Co. I, on Jan. 31, 1863. From July 20 to Aug. 20, 1863, he was in command of Co. I. At the end of Aug. and in Sept. 1863, Lowery was on detached service as Provost Marshal for the 3rd Brigade, 2nd Division, 5th Corps. He received promotion to first lieutenant of Co. D on Oct. 23, 1863. Transferred from Co. I to D on Oct. 30, 1863. Lowery commanded the Provost Guard for the 3rd Brigade, 2nd Division, 5th Corps in Oct. and Nov. 1863. He obtained a ten-day furlough to visit his home at Boonville on Dec. 14, 1863, and again for ten days starting Mar. 25, 1864. Lowery played a conspicuous part at the Battle of Spotsylvania Court House, where he commanded a portion of the regiment. He advanced his men "in a handsome manner as skirmishers clear up to the rebel fortifications, and ascertaining their position and force, for which daring feat Captain Lowery was brevetted and highly complimented in general orders." (Rome Historical Society Collection)

607

JOSEPH STUART LOWERY

Lowery was wounded "while leading his men" June 2, 1864, at the Battle of Bethesda Church (Cold Harbor), the bullet fractured the top of his right thigh. He was admitted to Armory Square General Hospital on June 7. While away from the regiment, Lowery was mustered in as captain to date from Sept. 16, and transferred to Co. A on Oct. 16, 1864. He was furloughed home from the hospital on Sept. 20, 1864, but was unable thereafter to rejoin the regiment owing to the effects of his wound. Lowery was discharged for disability on Jan. 13, 1865. He was brevetted a major on June 22, 1867, for gallant and meritorious services at the battles of the Wilderness, Spotsylvania and Bethesda Church, to date from Mar. 13, 1865. This photo shows Lowery wearing a 5th Corps badge and captains' bars on his shoulder straps. The image was made at Baker's studio in Utica with a tax stamp cancelled "1865," so once he received news of his appointment, Lowery apparently while home on his furlough went out and had the likeness made. (Donald Wisnoski Collection)

JOHN CHRISTOPHER LUCKERT

This photo of Luckert was taken circa 1912. He was born at Pativet, French Parish, in Pottsville, PA, Feb. 10, 1842; however, some sources give his birthplace as Paris, France. At age 19, he enlisted on July 19, 1861, as a private in Co. K of the 5th New York, Duryée's Zouaves. Luckert was 5'8"; with brown eyes, black hair, a dark complexion, and was employed as a clerk. At the time of his enlistment he resided at Stapleton, Staten Island, NY. Luckert went down sick with rheumatism at Savage Station, VA, on June 27, 1862, and was sent to recover at Fort Monroe. He was next sent to Camden St. Hospital, in Baltimore, MD, and was there from Sept. 1862 to June 1863, much of the time he was detailed as nurse and cook. Transferred to Co. K, 146th New York on May 4, 1863. Luckert re-enlisted as a veteran volunteer, Feb. 1, 1864, and mustered in two days later. He received a 35-day-veterans' furlough from which he returned on March 25. Luckert is shown as absent sick at Broad and Cherry Streets Hospital in Philadelphia, since May 5, 1864, and he returned to duty Sept. 14, 1864. He took sick again or may have been wounded on Oct. 27, 1864, being sent to hospital at City Point, VA, then to Washington, DC, where he deserted while on 15-day furlough from Harewood Hospital, Nov. 30, 1864. Luckert was absent at the muster out of his company in June 1865. Under the name John C. Lockert, he subsequently served in Co. K, 18th US Infantry from July 17, 1866, to March 27, 1869; then in Co. D, 27th US Infantry; then as a sergeant with Co. G, 9th US Infantry from June 21, 1869, to July 17, 1869. Luckert finished out his military career in Co. H of the 6th US Cavalry from Nov. 25, 1873, to Nov. 25, 1878, when he was discharged as private. He married Julia Witt Dannert, a native of Passau, Germany. Luckert died at Bloomfield, NE, on Nov. 4, 1923. Sometimes on the rolls his name was carried as Lucket and Louckert. (Paul T. Kuhlman Collection)

JOHN McGEEHAN

A dapper and young looking McGeehan is photographed as a second lieutenant. McGeehan was born Oct. 14, 1841, in Derry, Ireland, and came to the United States in 1847. He was 20 years old and working as a clerk when he and his brother George joined Co. B of the 5th New York, Duryée's Zouaves, on July 14, 1861. McGeehan was 5'8" with a light complexion, light hair, and blue eyes. On Oct. 23, 1861, he requested a transfer to Col. Serrell's Engineer Regiment, "having studied more in that branch of the service," but his request was not granted. In Feb. 1862, he began clerking for regimental Chaplain Gordon Winslow. McGeehan was slightly wounded in the foot at the Battle of Gaines' Mill on June 27, 1862. From Aug. to Oct. 1862, he was on detached service in the Adjutant's Office, and detailed as a clerk at Brigade Headquarters on Nov. 14, 1862. While on these duties, McGeehan came down with remittent fever and could not ride in an ambulance that "produces with him severe headache & general pain throughout his whole system." He was ordered to proceed to Washington and report to Surgeon R. O. Abbott. McGeehan was transferred along with the rest of the three-year men of the 5th New York to the 146th on May 4, 1863, being assigned to Co. C. For May, June, and July, he was on detached duty at Brigade Headquarters. McGeehan was commissioned a second lieutenant on June 29, and mustered in at that rank on Aug. 17, 1863, and was assigned to Co. F. (Donald Wisnoski Collection)

JOHN McGEEHAN

A bust view of McGeehan as a second lieutenant. He was sick with remittent fever from Sept. 17 to Oct. 16, 1863. "Employed and subsisted a soldier as servant from Feb. 29/64." Absent with leave from Mar. 25 to Apr. 4, 1864, to visit his home in Brooklyn. Slightly wounded and captured at the Battle of the Wilderness on May 5, 1864, McGeehan was confined for a time at Camp Asylum in Columbia, SC. He was paroled on Mar. 1, 1865, at Northeast Ferry, NC, reported at Camp Parole, MD, on Mar. 6, and was given a 30-day leave of absence starting on Mar. 12, 1865. He rejoined the regiment on May 2, 1865. Promoted while prisoner of war to first lieutenant on Dec. 30, 1864 (to rank from Dec. 1). He was transferred to Co. C on Apr. 28, 1865. McGeehan began special duty commanding Co. I on May 5, 1865. Sick with remittent fever, May 22-24, 1865. Assigned the special duty of acting as the regimental quartermaster starting on June 1, 1865. He mustered out with the regiment near Washington, DC, on July 16, 1865. On June 22, 1867, made a brevet captain to date from Mar. 13, 1865, for gallant and meritorious services during the war. After the war McGeehan married Elizabeth Howe and had two children. He died Sept. 25, 1893, and was buried at Cypress Hills Cemetery. (Rome Historical Society Collection)

611

JOHN McGOUGH

This image shows McGough in civilian attire after the war. He enlisted in Rochester on July 7, 1862, at age 35, and mustered in on Aug. 10, 1862. He joined Co. F of the 25th New York Infantry, described as 5'5" with a sandy complexion, blue eyes, brown hair, born in Ireland, and employed as a laborer. He was transferred to Co. K of the 44th New York on Oct. 10, 1863. In that regiment, he was transferred to Co. A on Sept. 24, 1864, then transferred to the 146th New York on Oct. 11, 1864, and assigned to Co. C. He was absent at that time being wounded in battle, but at what engagement is not known. McGough joined the regiment in Jan. 1865 and was present until June 3, 1865, when he mustered out of service near Alexandria, VA. He died Oct. 9, 1895. (USAMHI)

WILLIAM McGURK

McGurk, in full Zouave attire, wears a white turban, which with a white background, gives the illusion that there is no cap on his head and that the tassel simply appears to set on his shoulder. McGurk enlisted as a private in Co. G at Bridgewater in Oneida County on Sept. 6, 1862, at age 21 and was working as a teamster. He was 5'6", with a dark complexion, black hair, and blue eyes. McGurk was born in Ireland on June 14, 1841, and came to the United States in 1847. He was appointed corporal on Sept. 17, 1862. Returned to the rank of private by Jan. 1863. McGurk was present at the battles of Fredericksburg, Chancellorsville, and at Gettysburg, where he was seriously wounded in the hand by a shell fragment on July 3, 1863, and was sent to Satterlee Hospital. There, with cold-water dressings and a full diet, he quickly recovered—his general health was noted as "good." He was sent to rejoin the regiment on Aug. 20, 1863. McGurk was present with the regiment for the remainder of the war with the exception of May 1864 when he was absent sick, and Jan. 1865 when he was absent with leave. He was promoted corporal on Feb.1, then to sergeant on June 1, 1865. McGurk mustered out with the regiment on July 16, 1865, near Washington, DC. After the war, he farmed in the Bridgewater area, married twice—fathering children—and died in his sleep on Oct. 27, 1931, at Sauquoit. McGurk was 91. (Jack McGurk Collection)

613

HORACE N. MILLER

The original image of Miller is nicely tinted. He was born Aug. 8, 1835, in Oneida County. He was 27 years old and made a living farming when he enrolled in Co. F at Annsville on Aug. 29, 1862. Miller was 5'3", with a light complexion, brown hair, and brown eyes. He mustered in as a private at Rome on Oct. 10, 1862. On June 1, 1863, he began doing extra duty as Capt. Peter Claesgens' servant, for which the captain provided additional pay and subsistence. Starting in May 1864, he was employed by Lt. John McGeehan as a servant while Claesgens was on duty in Elmira. Miller was present with the regiment continuously until Feb. 1865, when he was absent with leave, then returned and served Capt. Claesgens again. He mustered out with the regiment on July 16, 1865, near Washington, DC. (Leo G. Seaton Collection)

HORACE N. MILLER

Miller is shown in a bust view in civilian attire. Although a successful farmer, he was also widely known as a skilled carpenter. Miller helped build St. Ann's Church in Glenmore and the Methodist Church at Empeysville (now Florence). Miller married Abigail Hanney, and they had seven children. One child was named Ellsworth, probably in honor of Elmer Ellsworth, the "father" of Zouaves in the United States. Miller most likely witnessed Ellsworth and his United States Zouave Cadets when they drilled in Utica in July 1860. Miller was an active member of the Ballard Post, Grand Army of the Republic. Miller wrote his wife on July 5, 1863, to describe her the battle of Gettysburg: "I thought I would write you a few lines to let you know that I am alive & not hurt, yet we have been in battle three days. Men have been kild in our company. Have not heard from Theron since he went to the hospital. Alfred Sheman is kild, George is wounded. The rest of the boys are all rite. The battle has lasted 4 days. We held the 4th the third. Thare is no use to describe the battle that day for it can't be done. the rebs run like sheep. Our line of battle is advancing while I write. I must stop writing or I can't send this." Miller's brother-in-law, Theron Hannay of Co. F, died July 2, 1863, at Frederick, MD. (Leo G. Seaton Collection)

615

HORACE N. MILLER

Miller would occasionally don his old Zouave uniform for veteran reunions and special occasions. Later in life, Miller recited the "Gettysburg Address" at the Taberg Methodist Church every Memorial Day as long as he was able. At age 78, Miller seemed in good health when, while working in his home, he suffered a stroke. After that, his health deteriorated rapidly. Miller died on Dec. 10, 1913, and is buried with his wife at Stanford Cemetery at Annsville. "Mr. Miller was a brave soldier, a loving husband and father and a good citizen, one whose death is despaired by all who knew him." (Leo G. Seaton Collection)

CHARLES J. MONROE

A curious photo of Monroe shows him in the uniform of the 146th New York inexplicably without any tape or trim on the uniform. He had formerly served in Co. B of the 30th New York Infantry. At age 32, he enlisted in Troy as a substitute in Co. A of the 44th New York Infantry for one year on Aug. 15, 1864. Monroe stood 5'10½", was dark complected, with black eyes, black hair, was born in Scotland, and was employed as a molder. He was transferred to Co I of the 146th New York on Oct. 8, 1864. Munroe was captured at the Battle of White Oak Road near Petersburg, on Mar. 31, 1865. He was paroled Apr. 2, 1865, at Aiken's Landing, VA, and reported at Camp Parole, MD, on Apr. 6. Monroe was officially discharged on May 30, he mustered out June 2, 1865, at Annapolis, MD. Also borne on the rolls as Munro. (Michael J. McAfee Collection)

GEORGE MOULD

Shown in the first uniform issued to the regiment, the gentlemanly looking Mould was a 30-year-old miller from the town of Paris. Born in England, Mould had gray eyes, sandy hair, a light complexion, and was six foot tall. He enlisted in as a private in Co. H on Aug. 29. On Oct. 10, 1862, he was mustered in as the third sergeant of the company, at which rank he is shown in this photo. He was promoted first sergeant on June 30, 1863, and was always present with the regiment until captured on May 5, 1864, at the Battle of the Wilderness. Initially reported as killed, Mould, in fact, was on his way south as a prisoner of war (see pages 256-57 for a description of Mould's capture at the Wilderness). After being held at Andersonville, GA, for several months, approximately 6,000 prisoners were transferred to the prisoner of war camp at Florence, SC. (Robert L. Mould Collection)

GEORGE MOULD

Here, Mould poses as first sergeant in full Zouave uniform while seated upon a trunk. Shortly after their arrival at Florence, SC, Mould and 20 other prisoners made their escape. Unfortunately, Mould and three other men were recaptured and returned to prison (see pages 266-67 for a description of this escapade). They remained at Florence until Feb. 17, 1865, when they were marched to Wilmington, NC. As Federal troops approached, the prisoners were again going to be moved, this time to Goldsboro, NC. Mould, Isaac Foster, and Charles L. King from Oriskany Falls (all belonging to the 146th) made a get away on Feb. 25, 1865 (see page 269). (Town of Paris Historical Society Collection)

GEORGE MOULD

Mould shown as a civilian later in life. After Mould, King, and Foster, eluded their captives, the trio hid in the woods with little to eat for three days, when on the fourth day they saw a colored man and inquired as to who had possession of Wilmington. The negro replied: "The Lincoln men." They crossed into Federal lines—Union forces had recently taken Fort Fisher and the city. Mould wrote his wife Louise a letter that day: "Thank God I am once more under the Stars and Stripes having made my escape from the Johnny Rebs on the night of the 21st of Feb. between Wilmington and North Eastern River and entered our lines the 25th of Feb., a day long to be remembered by this individual. Probably I shall be on my way north in a few days, then I will write you more. Excuse me for being so brief at the present. I am in Arthur Knights tent and the boys are talking so I'm scarcely able to think. My respects to your Father and Mother also Gardiner." Mould was staying with friends in the 117th NY from Oneida County who had taken part in the assault on Fort Fisher, south of Wilmington. Mould arrived at Camp Parole, MD, on Mar. 7, 1865, where he was mustered with the "escaped prisoners of 2nd Battalion Paroled Prisoners," and furloughed from Mar. 10 to May 12, 1865. He was honorably discharged on June 1, 1865, at Annapolis, MD. He was promoted a second lieutenant to date from Oct. 8, 1864. (Town of Paris Historical Society Collection)

GEORGE MOULD

After the war, Mould returned home and operated a gristmill in Sauquoit (on Sauquoit Creek) with his brothers and father—who died in 1894. After his brothers died, in Nov. 1900, he established the firm "G. Mould & Son—Dealers in flour, feed and grain." This was his son, Fred L., he also had a daughter, Agnes Mae. Mould died on Dec. 14, 1915, at Sauquoit.

At age 21, in 1853, George Mould decided to go to California to find gold, but he had to borrow money and run away to do so, as his father did not consent. He obtained a $150 loan from a man, agreeing to split all the gold he found. "I went to New York and on the 5th of May 1853 I left for Chagras, isthmus of Panama on the steamer *Pacific*, an eight day journey. There were 1500 passengers in three steamers all going to California via South America. Two of the vessels were to take them from the isthmus to San Francisco. We went from Chagras to Barbados by rail, the terminus of the road. We took small boats when we reached Carzona, going twelve in a boat. Upon runners that ran along the sides of the boat, stood men who pushed it along by using poles."

"From Carzona we walked to Crusus. Six of us stayed one night in a small hut. When we were within twelve miles of Panama we tried to hire mules to carry us but they wanted 25 dollars, so we walked. In my valise besides my clothes I had 25 lbs. of dried beef, Sam Hill it was warm. In Panama I went to the Ewopa House, kept by an American. We were disappointed when we found there was only one steamer *The Golden Gate* waiting to take 1500 passengers. It was so crowded we almost stepped on each other. Steamers were not as large as now. We reached San Francisco on the 25th of May."

"I got acquainted on the steamer with a young fellow by the name of Clemmons, he and I boarded a steamer for Sacramento, a stage coach to Auburn and the next day we walked to Yankee Jim's. We came upon a man working a claim alone in Devil's Gulch. His name was Peter Moulton. He wanted to sell us 1/2 his claim for 50 dollars. He said 'you come down about 4 o'clock and I will show you what I get today.' We went down and he showed us a pan worth 11 dollars. We worked three weeks and couldn't earn our board. A man wanted half of the claim so I sold it for fifty dollars. I was about strapped at that time, wrote home for some travel money and came back." This was told by Mould on Feb. 1, 1914, when he was 81 years and 10 months old. (Robert L. Mould Collection)

WILLIAM NEWLOVE

Born Apr. 24, 1833, in Canada, Newlove was 29 years old when he enrolled at Utica as a private on Aug. 28, 1862. He lived in Utica since boyhood. Newlove was 5'8, with blue eyes, light hair, light complexion, and working as a painter when he mustered into Co. A as a private. Being promoted to corporal in Jan./Feb. 1864, he was present with the regiment and in every battle until May 5, 1864, when he was captured at the Battle of the Wilderness. (Mark Schultz Collection)

622

WILLIAM NEWLOVE

After his capture, Newlove was sent to prison camp at Andersonville, GA, and transferred to Florence, SC. He survived to be paroled at Northeast Ferry, NC, on Feb. 27, 1865. He reported at Camp Parole, Annapolis, MD, on Mar. 12, 1865. Newlove was honorably discharged at Camp Parole on June 2, 1865. After the war, he continued his trade as a painter and decorator in the employ of Homer Townsend. At Utica's Calvary Episcopal Church and with Reverend William A. Matson performing the ceremony, Newlove married Priscilla Stafford on June 30, 1857. They had six children and resided at 188 Neilson Street in Utica. By age 58, he was unable to earn support by manual labor owing to piles, rheumatism, general debility, and heart disease. He died of a cerebral hemorrhage and acute gastro enteritis on Sept. 15, 1909, at his 506 Neilson Street home at age 76. New love was buried at Forest Hill Cemetery in Utica. Priscilla died on Jan. 2, 1926. (Mark Schultz Collection)

JOHN EDWIN NEWMAN

Curiously, in this photograph, Newman has no leggings, only socks under his jambiéres. He originally enlisted as a corporal in Co. D of the 5th New York Infantry on July 8, 1861. Newman was 29 years old, stood 5'9", had a dark complexion, gray eyes, fair hair, was employed as a carpenter and had been born at Stamford, CT. He was reduced to the ranks for disobedience to orders, then was detailed at his trade of carpenter. Newman was wounded at the Battle of Second Manassas, VA, on Aug. 30, 1862. He deserted from the hospital, but returned to the ranks in Apr. 1863. Transferred with the other 234 three-year men present in the field on May 9, 1863, Newman joined Co. A of the 146th. Promoted corporal in Nov./Dec. 1863. Newman took sick on May 5, 1864. He rejoined the regiment in time to be wounded in the right foot during the June 18, 1864, assault on Petersburg. The bullet struck his foot cutting the skin "under the planta perdis and making its exit in a horizontal line without injuring the bone." Sent to the Second Division Hospital in Alexandria and admitted there on July 4. Newman was discharged from the hospital for the expiration of his term of service on July 18, 1864. He returned to New York City, and in 1870 was living on 3rd Avenue. (Brian C. Pohanka Collection)

BYRON NISBET

Nisbet, also spelled Nesbit, is shown in the first uniform of the regiment sporting a New York State jacket with a breast pocket and shoulder tabs. A farmer that was born in Lee, Nisbet enlisted there in Co. F on Aug. 30, 1862. He mustered in as a private on Oct. 10, being described as 5'8", with blue eyes, light hair, a light complexion, and 19 years old. The unfortunate Nisbet was one of the first fatalities in the regiment when he died of disease on Dec. 18, 1862, at the Division Hospital near Falmouth, VA. (Michael J. McAfee Collection)

EDWARD B. PAINE

Paine, shown in complete Zouave garb, was born and raised in Utica. He enlisted at age 27 (also given as 29) in Utica on Aug. 30, 1862. His description lists him as 5'6 1/2", with brown eyes, dark hair, light complexion, and employed as an undertaker. He mustered into Co. C as a private on Oct. 10, 1862. Paine was present with the regiment until wounded at the Battle of the Wilderness on May 5, 1864, and was sent to the Columbian Hospital in Washington, DC. He was furloughed home, and while recovering from his wound, he suffered an attack of "inflammatory rheumatism of the heart." He wrote for an extension of his furlough: "I do not wish to be classified as a deserter to my Country." Upon his recovery, he rejoined to the regiment in Sept./Oct. 1864, and began daily duty as a teamster with the 2nd Division, 5th Corps, Ambulance Corps. He mustered out July 16, 1865, with the regiment near Washington, DC. He returned to Utica and was later buried in the soldier section of Forest Hill Cemetery. (Michael J. McAfee Collection)

ALFRED H. PALMER

When he was 18, Alfred Palmer, along with his brother, George, enlisted in Co. C in Utica, on Aug. 27, 1862. Alfred, at 5'5", was an inch taller than his older brother, and had a light complexion, blue eyes, light hair, was born in Warwickshire, England, came to America with his parents when he was ten years old and was employed as a teamster at the time of his enlistment. Appointed a corporal on Sept. 3, 1862, he mustered in with that rank, but in July/Aug. 1863 he became a musician (drummer). Records show Palmer always present for duty until Feb. 23, 1865, when he was absent with leave. From Mar. to June 1865 he was assigned to daily duty at 1st Brigade, 2nd Division, 5th Corps headquarters. Palmer mustered out with the regiment on July 16, 1865, near Washington, DC. This photo, taken in Utica, clearly illustrates the 146th New York Zouave uniform as well as the distinctive colored cuffs on the musician's jackets. (Edward L. DeSanctis Collection)

ALFRED H. PALMER

Of the several ailments Palmer suffered while in service were chronic diarrhea and piles at Falmouth, VA, from Jan. 18-26, 1863; rheumatism at Chancellorsville in May 1863, and a wound in the right arm just above the wrist at the Battle of Gettysburg—the bullet or piece of shell entered his arm four inches above his wrist, passing upwards and backwards, then exiting two inches above the elbow. He was treated at Stoneman's Switch, VA, and at Gettysburg in the regimental hospital. At the time of Gettysburg, he may have been serving assigned to the headquarters of the Army of the Potomac as a musician for Maj. Gen. George G. Meade. Palmer is shown here in civilian attire. (Patrick A. Schroeder Collection)

ALFRED H. PALMER

By 1867 he had moved to Vicksburg, Mississippi, where he married Emma Elizabeth Brown on June 23, 1873, and they eventually had nine children. Later, he relocated to Omaha, NE, where he was employed as a clerk, an accountant, and ran a store. He died at age 63 in Arapahoe, NE, on Feb. 14, 1908, from "cerebral edema and arterio sclerosis." He was buried in Arapahoe at Forest Lawn Cemetery. Palmer's sister married Edwin Glover, a comrade of the 146th. (Patrick A. Schroeder Collection)

GEORGE H. PALMER

Palmer is splendidly attired in Zouave uniform complete with a turban wrapped around his fez. He and his brother, Alfred, both enlisted in Co. C in Utica, on Aug. 27, 1862. George was 22 years old, stood 5'4", with a light complexion, gray eyes, light hair, had been born in England, and was employed as a teamster. Palmer was promoted corporal May/June 1863. He was present with the regiment until wounded in the right forearm at the Battle of the Wilderness on May 5, 1864, sent to Stanton General Hospital in Washington, DC. He received a furlough from Stanton Hospital to home in Utica on May 17, 1864, for one month, failed to return at expiration of furlough and was listed as a deserter. Reporting to an army hospital, all charges of desertion removed. Upon recovery of his wounds and while waiting at the Rendezvous of Distribution to be sent back to the regiment, Palmer filled the post of Henry Herbert Wood, also of the 146th, as a mounted courier in the quartermaster's department near Washington, DC. While detailed in this work, a severe accident befell Palmer. (Michael J. McAfee Collection)

GEORGE H. PALMER

A post-war photo of George Palmer (seated right) and friends, taken in Utica. On Sept. 18, 1864, Palmer's horse became unmanageable, and galloped out of control and collided with the buggy of Lt. Col. Samuel McKelog—commander of the Rendezvous of Distribution camp near Alexandria, VA. McKelog was unhurt, but Palmer was thrown from his mount. McKelog related: "I came up to him, found that he was bleeding profusely from his side, there being quite a pool of blood on the ground, where he lay. . . . I had him placed in an ambulance belonging to the Commissary Department near long bridge, and taken to hospital at Rendezvous of Distribution." Palmer suffered a severe hernia, and later had to wear a truss. He began his recovery in Augur General Hospital near Alexandria starting Feb. 25, 1865. He mustered out in Washington, DC, on June 2, 1865. Sometime during service he suffered sunstroke. After the war, Palmer was a milkman in Utica and kept a herd of cows. He married Sarah Allen on Dec. 6, 1865. Palmer died at 5 a.m. on Apr. 20, 1886 from a strangulated rupture or stoppage in the bowels. Affidavits in Palmer's pension file attest to his good character, noting that he "drank a glass of beer a day, but did not get intoxicated." Henry Toms recalled: "Though he was not what we would call a temperance man—sometimes he would take a glass of beer or whiskey, but I never saw him drunk . . . he could always go about his business." Palmer was interred at Forest Hill Cemetery in Utica. (Patrick A. Schroeder Collection)

ISAAC P. POWELL

Enrolled at age 24 as captain of Co. G, on Sept. 10, 1862, in Rome and mustered in to date Sept. 17. On May 1, 1863, with his company surrounded in a cornfield at the Battle of Chancellorsville and called to surrender by the enemy, Powell instead rallied his men and made a desperate assault, with much fighting being done hand to hand, and returning the forlorn company to the Federal lines. Powell received a ten-day furlough to visit his family at the end of Jan. 1864. This photo shows Powell wearing an officer's military vest. (Donald Wisnoski Collection)

ISAAC P. POWELL

Powell was captured at the Battle of the Wilderness on May 5, 1864, and confined at prison camp near Columbia, SC. While there, he was given parole promising not to attempt to escape. He was paroled at Charleston, SC, on Dec. 10, 1864, and went to Camp Parole, MD. There, he was ordered to report to Gen. Henry W. Wessells, Commissioner General of Prisoners, in Washington, DC, and granted a furlough home. While at home in Jan. 1865, Powell was diagnosed with chronic diarrhea and a lung infection that he had contracted while a prisoner of war, and his furlough was extended. He returned from furlough on Feb. 4, 1865, and was sent to join the regiment on Apr. 1. Promoted major June 26, 1865, and acting with that rank since Apr. 1, 1865. He joined the regiment on campaign on Apr. 6. On June 26, 1865, Powell requested a 20-day leave to visit his sick mother in Oneida County. Brevetted a major by the War Department on Oct. 14, 1865, for gallant and meritorious services during the war to date from Mar. 13, 1865. Died in 1903. (Gordon E. Johnson Collection)

633

JOHN R. PUGH

This photo was taken of Pugh in New York City; he is wearing the second uniform issued to the regiment. He had enlisted on Aug. 28, 1862, in his hometown of Marcy and mustered into Co. F, as a private, leaving his bride Mary Ida, whom he had recently married on June 4, 1862. Pugh was born in Marcy on Aug. 3, 1841, was 21 when he enlisted, had a light complexion, blue eyes, brown hair, was 5'9", and was employed as a cooper. Pugh participated in the battles of Fredericksburg and Chancellorsville, but came down with chronic diarrhea at Gettysburg on July 2, 1863. He was sent to the hospital in Baltimore on July 10 and he suffered from the ailment for the next six months. He was transferred to McDougal General Hospital at Fort Schuyler (near New York City) and there received a furlough home for late Oct. and early Nov. 1863. Pugh was transferred to Co. I of the 9th Regiment of the Veteran Reserve Corps on Mar. 26, 1864. He was promoted corporal on Sept. 23, 1864, and sergeant on June 28, 1865. He mustered out on Aug. 3, 1865. John and Mary had three children, but all died in infancy. Pugh died Mar. 7, 1907, at Maynard in Oneida County. (Patrick A. Schroeder Collection)

ALBERT ROSS

Here, Ross wears his 5th New York jacket with the pantaloons of the 146th New York. He was born in New York City on July 4, 1843. At age 19 he enlisted in the 5th New York Infantry, and had previously been employed as a steward. Ross had hazel eyes, dark brown hair, a dark complexion, and stood 5'9 3/4". Present at the battle of Chancellorsville. He was transferred from Co. A of the 5th New York to Co. K of the 146th on May 4, 1863. Ross sprained his arm and ankle on June 22, 1863, and never returned to duty with the regiment in the field. In Jan./Feb. 1864 he was posted at the "Rendezvous of Distribution, Va" being detailed in the kitchen. Another accident befell Ross on May 11, 1864, when he toppled from a horse and this time injured his hand and arm. He was discharged June 3, 1865. Ross married Maria Josephine Obider on Nov. 9, 1865. He died at age 82 at 312 Decatur Street in Brooklyn on Aug. 2, 1925. (Brian C. Pohanka Collection)

635

THOMAS ROWELL

Rowell, shown here as a sergeant, wears a shirt vest, a 5th Corps badge, a non-commissioned officer's sash, and has the edge of his fez turned-up. Rowell enrolled as a substitute on Aug. 14, 1863, at Buffalo. He was a laborer who had been born in Northamptonshire, England, and proved a good and reliable soldier, being present from enlistment to muster out. He was 39, with a florid complexion, hazel eyes, brown hair, and was 5'6" tall. He arrived in the field on Oct. 13, 1863. Mustered in as a private in Co. C, he was promoted corporal on Sept. 3, 1864, and to sergeant on Feb. 1, 1865. Rowell mustered out with the regiment near Washington, DC, on July 16, 1865. This picture of Rowell was taken in Buffalo either on furlough or after his return from the war. (Rome Historical Society Collection)

636

HENRY B. SANDERS

Sanders, shown here as a sergeant with three veteran stripes, has a dapper moustache, and is wearing a 5th Corps badge. As a 21-year-old woodcarver, Sanders had served in Co. G of the 17th New York Infantry, before being transferred to Co. F of the 146th, on June 25, 1863. Sanders was on duty at Elmira, from July 22 until Nov. 24, 1863. He was promoted sergeant in Sept./Oct. 1863 and re-enlisted as a veteran volunteer on Feb. 21, 1864, while at Warrenton Junction, VA. He began his veteran's furlough on Feb. 28. Sanders was 23 years old, 5'9", with a light complexion, blue eyes, and brown hair. He had been born in England and listed his occupation as a soldier. Sanders was mortally wounded in the abdomen at the Battle of Bethesda Church (Cold Harbor) on June 2, 1864. He died the next day. He was still owed 375 dollars bounty for re-enlisting. (USAMHI)

637

WILLIAM D. "BUTCH" SAPHAR

One of the true characters of the Civil War. Saphar was born in New York City on Oct. 30, 1840, and served in the United States Navy from Nov. 18, 1856, to Jan. 25, 1861, doing duty on the *USS North Carolina* and *St. Mary's*. When enlisting in Co. B of the 5th New York Infantry on July 8, 1861, Saphar was described as 21 years old, with blue eyes, light brown hair, light complexion, 5'7 1/2", with tattoos on his arms, legs, and chest, and employed as a butcher. While home on furlough in Jan. 1862, he was arrested "on account of a fight he was in March last" in Easton, PA, and he was charged with assault and battery "with intent to kill." He suffered sunstroke during the Peninsula Campaign in 1862. During the Battle of Antietam, Saphar saw General Burnside nearby getting ready to cut a chew from a plug of tobacco. Saphar meandered over to the General to obtain a chew for himself, and came away with the entire plug. He was court martialed for a different transgression in Oct. 1862, and fined $10 a month for two months.

Saphar was transferred to Co. F, 146th New York and promoted corporal in Jan./Feb. 1864. Court martialed on Mar. 29, 1864, for "conduct to the prejudice of good order and military discipline" that on Feb. 27, 1864, Saphar imbibed "so freely of intoxicating liquor as to become drunk." A second charge stemmed from being absent without leave. He pleaded guilty to both charges, except to some of the wording used. Saphar testified "when he got on the train at Warrenton Junction, Va. to bid his friends 'good-bye' that he was carried to Alexandria, and having no pass, was arrested; that he was confined in the Slave Pen, and fed only bread and water; that he immediately wrote his 1st Sergt." First Sergeant Lewis Dugal testified in defense of Saphar: "I received a letter from the prisoner about the 1st of March, which I gave to my commanding officer. It said, 'I am now confined in the Slave Pen.' I have known the prisoner since May last—he has been on duty with the Provost Guard—was always a prompt and attentive soldier." First Lieutenant William Walker, in command of the brigade Provost Guard in which Saphar served then testified: "He has been prompt and attentive to his duties and I have never known of any ill conduct on his part while he has been with the regiment." The testimony did Saphar little good—he was found guilty, reduced to the ranks, and fined ten dollars of his monthly pay for the remainder of his term of service. Saphar had rejoined the regiment from desertion on Mar. 19, 1864. He was wounded by a bullet in the right foot on the skirmish line soon after leaving the trenches at the Battle of Spotsylvania Court House on May 12, 1864. Comrade Alfred Palmer remembered: "the last time I saw him, our Chaplin was taking him off the . . . battlefield (with) part of his heel shot off." He was treated at Lincoln General Hospital in Washington and then sent to Mower Hospital at Chester Hill in Philadelphia.

Upon recovering Saphar was sent to Headquarters 1st Division Rendezvous of Distribution and on July 3, 1864, wrote 5th Corps commander, Maj. Gen. Gouverneur K. Warren: "I have the honor to make application for a pass to travel through your Corps for the purpose of selling Photographs, Photograph Albums, and Medals of different Generals. I am at present at this place waiting for my discharge, my term of service having expired on the 8th of this month. I was formerly a member of your old regiment, the 5th New York Vols. and was transferred to the 146th New York Vols. I was wounded at Spotsylvania May 12th and reached this place a few days ago from the hospital." Sent by Warren to the 5th Corps Provost Marshall, Maj. Henry W. Ryder, to find out if a license was needed, Ryder noted that "no license has been granted to sell photographs or any of the articles mentioned in the within application." Warren forwarded the request to the Army of the Potomac Provost Marshall approved. Saphar was mustered out July 17 to date Aug 22, 1864.

After recovering from his wounds, Saphar married Josephine Augusta Patterson in Baltimore, MD, on Sept. 12, 1864, and they eventually had three children. On Apr. 6, 1865, he joined the 7th US Veteran Volunteer Infantry and served until Dec. 14, 1865. Moving frequently, he became a lecturer, showman, actor, and manager, spending considerable time in Iola, KS, and Oklahoma City, OK, and was widely known as Col. Saphar. His wife died in 1881, and he remarried Emma Louise Orton in 1898. He died of "Septicemia" on Mar. 15, 1918, at the National Soldier Home in Fort Leavenworth, KS, and was buried in the National Cemetery. Part of his obituary read: "The Colonel who possessed a large and powerful physique had lost in strength the last year or two. Col. Saphar was one of the best-known characters in this city for years. . . . He was a typical showman of the age and wore his hair in long locks hanging over his shoulders.' (Patrick A Schroeder Collection)

JEROME B. SEAMAN

A mere 18 years old when he enlisted on Aug. 30, 1862, in Kirkland (also given as Rome), Seaman was 5'9", with a fair complexion, hazel eyes, dark hair, and had been born in Oswego. He mustered in as a private in Co. G, on Oct. 10, 1862. Promoted corporal in May/June 1863, to sergeant in July/Aug. 1864, and first sergeant in Jan. 1865, Seaman was never absent since his enlistment. Promoted second lieutenant on Jan. 16, 1865, he mustered in on Jan. 19, to date from Dec. 1, 1864. He took command of Co. G, being the only officer present at the time. Seaman was again promoted on Apr. 1, 1865, to the rank of 1st lieutenant, to date from Feb. 1. Seaman's only absences from the regiment were early in March 1865. He received leave for 15 days to visit his father who was dangerously ill at New Berlin, in Chenango County, with little hope of recovery. Seaman returned to the regiment and mustered out with it on July 16, 1865, near Washington, DC. This picture of Seaman was taken by Lazier in Syracuse. He died in 1909. (Rome Historical Society Collection)

ROBERT J. SELKIRK

Selkirk was born at Bethleham, NY, in 1832. At age 28, while working as a clerk, he enlisted as a private in Co. E of the 5th New York, Duryée's Zouaves, on July 17, 1861. He was 5'7⁷⁄₈, had a sandy complexion, gray eyes, light hair, and had been employed as a clerk. He was present with the regiment at the battles of Gaines' Mill and Second Bull Run. Selkirk was detailed as Division Postmaster on Dec. 3, 1862; and then was assigned duty as Post Office Agent in Washington, DC, on March 23, 1863, there he was in charge of supervising mail carriers to Aquia Creek; VA, where the Army of the Potomac was encamped. He, along with the three-year men of the 5th New York, was transferred to the 146th New York on May 4, 1863, where he was assigned to Co. D. Selkirk was again appointed Division Postmaster in August 1863. He evidently enjoyed his duties and the service as he re-enlisted as a veteran volunteer on March 21, 1864. Apparently while on his veterans' furlough, Selkirk married Isabella Shick while home in New York City on March 16, 1864. The couple had one son, Robert born on July 17, 1866, and one daughter, Isabel born in July 1870. Selkirk mustered out of service at Syracuse, NY, on July 26, 1865. He died at 1216 5th St., NW, Washington, DC, on May 12, 1875, and was buried at Graceland Cemetery in Washington, DC. His widow, Isabella, died at Martha's Vinyard, MA, on Aug. 16, 1925, and the daughter, Isabel, was living at Oak Bluffs, MA, at the time. (Patrick A. Schroeder Collection)

641

JAMES SHAW

Only 16 years old (or possibly younger) when he enlisted on Aug. 27, 1862, in Utica. Shaw was barely was 5'21/2", but undoubtedly still growing, with a light complexion, black eyes, dark hair, was born in Albany, and employed as a clerk. He mustered in as a musician in Co. C, on Oct. 10, 1862. During the entire service of the regiment, Shaw was never absent, though it is possible that he got a furlough in May/June 1865, as the muster rolls shows that he owed the government $4.10 for transportation. Shaw nearly met his end during the Chancellorsville Campaign. While crossing the Rapidan River at Ely's Ford, the diminutive Shaw, though holding onto two comrades, was swept away by the strong current. Struggling and shouting for help, several men attempted to snag Shaw, but he slipped from their grasps. Shaw stayed afloat by tightly clasping his drum. Colonel Garrard, witnessing the debacle, plunged his horse into the water and intercepted the distraught drummer. He plucked the troubled youth from the stream and carried him to shore. Shaw mustered out with the regiment on July 16, 1865, near Washington, DC. This photo shows Shaw being honored on the 46th Anniversary Reunion Ribbon of the regiment in 1906. (James Hennessey Collection)

JAMES SHAW AND ALFRED PALMER

This picture shows the two young musicians in splendid Zouave dress. Both boys were from Utica, and may have known each other before enlisting. The original image, most likely sent home, was inscribed: "Happy are we." Their records confirm the fact that they did enjoy army life. The image was probably made during the winter encampment of 1863-64. Note the fully buttoned vests and dark jacket cuffs of the musician's jackets. (Michael J. McAfee Collection)

NORTON C. SHEPARD

Shepard is shown wearing full Zouave attire, with a medal on his jacket and toting a Sharp's Rifle, taken during the fall of 1863. He was born in Turin, Lewis County, on Oct. 13, 1844, and although age 17 (he gave it as 21), he enlisted as a private in Co. B of the 146th in Rome on Aug. 28, 1862, making him the fifth brother of ten to join the army, he was the youngest of 11 children. Shepard had blue eyes, dark hair, a fair complexion, was a farmer and also did work as a painter. He was promoted corporal on Nov. 1, 1863, and was present with the regiment until being wounded and captured at the Battle of the Wilderness on May 5, 1864. (Gene Parsons Collection)

644

NORTON C. SHEPARD

After the charge as the regiment was preparing to fall back, a bullet cut through the flesh of Shepard's right shoulder, he raised his rifle to "give one parting shot" when a bullet smashed his right elbow. The missile shattered the joint. Shepard made for his own lines, when another bullet struck him in the side "passing straight through the bowels to the left side, and lodged under the skin of the hip bone." After sometime lying on the ground and making several attempts to get up and move, several Confederate soldiers came by and took his silver corps badge, several articles of clothing (including his new black felt hat) and his haversack. Then they left him by the little stream in Saunders Field to die. Fortunately, another Confederate soldier came by and assisted Shepard to a field hospital by Robertson's Tavern where his wounds were dressed and the bullet by his hip extracted, which he was given as a keepsake. After remaining at this Confederate field hospital for nearly six weeks, the wounded prisoners were recaptured by Federal forces, sent to recover the men. They were taken to Slough Barracks Branch Hospital in Alexandria and treated. A resection of the elbow joint was performed and then treated with cold-water dressings. He was discharged for disability on a Surgeon's Certificate from Augur Hospital in Washington, DC, on Oct. 6, 1864—disability being complete, giving him a pension of eight dollars a month. He stayed in Washington for sometime, and lived in Jamestown, Newark, and Cherry Creek, until settling in Penn Yan, where he engaged in business until ill health forced him to retire. He married in 1868 and had two children. As late as 1921, he was still participating in school programs, telling the children of the occasions he met or saw Abraham Lincoln. On Jan. 11, 1923, at age 78, he passed away and is buried at Lakeview Cemetery, in Penn Yan. Shepard appears at the extreme right of the photo with other members of the J. B. Sloan Post, Grand Army of the Republic. (Gene Parsons Collection)

645

NORTON C. SHEPARD

Although this tintype is not identified and lacking corporal stripes, the soldier bears a very strong resemblance to Shepard, who, in a short memoir about the Battle of the Wilderness writes of having "a good black felt hat" sent from the North. Zouaves, many times had civilian hats for use when not on duty and sometimes wore them in the field as well. (Guy DeMasi Collection)

CHAUNCEY B. SMITH

Smith enlisted as a private in Co. H at Utica on Aug. 30, 1862. He was 30 years old, 5'10", with a light complexion, gray eyes, brown hair, was employed as a millwright, and was born in Massachusetts. He was made sergeant upon muster in on Oct. 10, 1862. Present at the battles of Fredericksburg, Chancellorsville, and Gettysburg, before being assigned to duty at the conscript depot at Elmira from July 20 through Nov. 1863. Smith was promoted first sergeant and color sergeant, no dates. He was captured at the Battle of the Wilderness on May 5, 1864, and sent to prisoner of war camp at Andersonville, GA, then to Florence, SC, and finally to Wilmington, NC. While in the process of moving by rail to Salisbury prison camp, a Confederate guard at the door fired recklessly into the car of crowded and unarmed prisoners. The bullet penetrated Smith's chest, killing him instantly. The guard "supposed they were going to try to escape." Here Color Sergeant Smith is honored on a reunion badge for the 1901 Anniversary of the regiment. (Gordon E. Johnson Collection)

ELBERT M. SOMERS

At age 35, Somers enrolled at Albany to serve three years. He mustered in as second assistant surgeon of the 146th on Sept. 18, 1862, at Utica. Commissioned assistant surgeon on Nov. 3, 1862, with rank from Sept. 4, 1862. On Dec. 2, 1862, Somers offered his resignation: "Having became fully convinced that my health is not sufficient to enable me properly to perform the duties of my office & believing that for a long time to come I must be an encumbrance should I remain." Surgeon Flandreau endorsed the request noting: "I have carefully examined this officer & find that he is now suffering from a severe remittent fever & that in consequence thereof he is unfit for duty." The acting medical director for Sykes' division, W. R. Ramsey, after examining Somers stated: "He is suffering under remittent fever, which now has assumed the typhoid type. He will not be fit for active duty in the field for two months at least . . . ." Somers was discharged on Dec. 7, 1862, at camp near Potomac Creek, VA. (USAMHI)

HENRY SORN

Sorn is shown in this image as a corporal, wears a white turban, and is armed with a Sharp's Rifle--though it might be a photographer's prop. He had been born in Germany (Saxony) on Nov. 26, 1838, and was nine years old when he came to the United States with his parents. At age 23, Sorn enlisted in Co. G at Bridgewater. He was 5'6", with a light complexion, blue eyes, brown hair, and employed as a clerk. Promoted corporal in May/June 1863, Sorn was absent sick at Lincoln Hospital in Washington, DC, from Feb. 2 until Sept./Oct. 1864 and was charged $19.56 for transportation back to the regiment. (Anna E. Pierce Collection)

649

HENRY SORN

This painting is based on the photograph of Sorn. He was promoted sergeant of Co. G on Feb. 1, 1865, then to sergeant major on Mar. 1, 1865. Sorn mustered out with the regiment on July 16, 1865, near Washington, DC. He was later commissioned but not mustered a second lieutenant on Aug. 31, 1865, to date from Aug. 1, 1865. After the war, he married Wilamena Marker of Sauquoit and had four children. Sorn, though a farmer, was also widely known for his knowledge on breeding of horses. He died July 18, 1913. Family tradition has it that during the engagement on Little Round Top at Gettysburg on July 2, 1863, a small bible in Sorn's jacket pocket stopped a bullet and saved his life. (Anna E. Pierce Collection)

WILLIAM RANDOLPH STEARNS

This picture shows Stearns in the uniform of the 53rd New York Zouaves, in which he served in Co. F from Oct. 4, 1861, until Mar. 21, 1862. Known among his comrades as "Billy", Stearns was born in New York City on Oct. 29, 1841, and was 20 years old, 5'41/2", with gray eyes, brown hair, light complexion, and was a draughtsman when he joined the army. He re-enlisted in Co. K of the 5th New York Infantry on Aug. 14, 1862, and was promoted corporal on Nov. 13. Stearns was transferred to Co. K, of the 146th New York on May 4, 1863. He was shot through the right lung at the Battle of the Weldon Railroad on Aug. 18, 1864. The bullet lodged below the left scapula. Surgeon Flandreau left him for dead, but Stearns' comrades saw to it that he was evacuated north on a train. He was treated at White Hall Hospital in Philadelphia, and on Oct. 7 was transferred to DeCamp Hospital at David's Island in New York Harbor. (Charlotte Powell Collection)

WILLIAM RANDOLPH STEARNS

After his recovery Stearns was detailed as a clerk at the Medical Director's Office in the Department of the East where Stearns was praised as: "a young man of good character, steady habits, and faithful in the discharge of his duties." He mustered out at Ladies Home Hospital in New York City on May 24, 1865. The bullet was not removed until Sept. 1866. After the war, he married Julia Lynch and had six children. By 1876, he had moved his family to San Francisco, CA, where his wife died in 1884. In 1911, he was living in Sonoma, CA, and died in San Francisco on June 28, 1927. This photo shows him as he was dressed while clerking for the Medical Director's Office. Stearns wears a double-breasted cavalry overcoat, and apparently a rubberized hat cover. (Charlotte Powell Collection)

JAMES STEWART

This picture of a thickly bearded Stewart shows him in full Zouave officer's regalia, complete with jacket trim, baggy trousers, and sporting a 5th Corps badge. He enrolled at Rome and mustered in as first lieutenant of Co. G on Oct. 10, 1862, to date from Sept. 17. He received promotion to captain of Co. K on Feb. 5, 1863, to date from Jan. 7. Stewart obtained a 10-day leave on Dec. 16, 1863, to go to Clinton, NY, "to visit my wife who has been seriously sick for some time past and also to transact business which demands my personal attention. I have not been absent from the regiment since its organization . . . ." Stewart was captured at the Battle of Weldon Railroad near Petersburg, on Aug. 18, 1864, and sent to Richmond two days later. He was transferred to Salisbury Prison, NC, on Oct. 2, 1864, and remained there until Jan. 30, 1865. On Feb. 8, 1865, Stewart was paroled by the Confederates "for the purpose of distributing supplies of clothing etc." He arrived as a liberated prisoner of war in Richmond, VA, on Apr. 17, 1865, then was sent to Camp Parole, MD, three days later. And was granted a 30-day furlough. Stewart was discharged on June 5, to date from May 15, 1865. For gallant and meritorious services during the war, he was made a brevet major of volunteers on Oct. 14, 1865, and June 22, 1867, and finally to colonel on July 16, 1867, to date from Mar. 13, 1865. Stewart was sometimes borne on the rolls as Stuart and Steward. He died in Scottdale, PA. (Forty Years of Clinton History)

WILLIAM HENRY SEWARD SWEET

Obviously named for the New York politician, later Lincoln's Secretary of State, Sweet was 24 years old when he enrolled on Sept. 6, 1862, at Marcy (also given as Deerfield). Appointed first sergeant on Sept. 10, 1862, he mustered into Co. F a month later. He was 5'9" with black eyes, dark hair, a light complexion, born in Marcy and was a lawyer before joining the army. Sweet was promoted first lieutenant and transferred to Co. B on Jan. 7, 1863. Shortly after that on Jan 20, while in camp at Potomac Creek, Sweet was diagnosed with remittent fever and acute bronchitis, and "unable to march should the regiment move"—he was given a 30-day sick leave. He was still too sick at the time he was due to return with "inflammation and congestion of the lungs," making him absent without leave, but it was noted that he was "known to be sick and unable to join the regiment." In June of 1863, he was signing the returns and commanding Co. A. In an image taken by Brady, he is shown in his Zouave officer's uniform and sword, with a black velvet collar, a badge, and pistol cap box. His cap and cape lie on the chair. (Rome Historical Society Collection)

654

WILLIAM H. SEWARD SWEET

Sweet was transferred back to Co. F on Jan. 23, 1864. He commanded the company from Mar. 20 to Apr. 20. Sweet was absent with leave from Feb. 15-25 (to visit his family in Utica) and Apr. 25-28, 1864, and commanded the company from Feb. 29 to Apr. 30, 1864. He was captured at the Battle of the Wilderness on May 5, 1864. While being taken to the rear, he encountered Confederate Gen. Richard Ewell whose troops they had engaged and was asked by the General: "What makes your boys fight so? Your regiment fought like hell." Sweet was confined at Charleston and Camp Asylum in Columbia, SC, then at Fort Oglethorpe, GA, and finally Goldsboro, NC. He was paroled at Northeast Ferry, NC, on Mar. 1, 1865, and assigned quarters at Camp Parole, MD, on Mar. 9, 1865. He received a 30-day furlough on Mar. 11, which was extended another 30 days "unless sooner exchanged." Sweet was sent to rejoin the regiment on May 2, 1865, and arrived on May 6. Promoted captain, he had been commissioned on Apr. 4, 1864, and mustered in on May 5, 1865, he mustered out with the regiment on July 16, 1865, near Washington, DC. Brevetted captain by the War Department on Oct. 14 for "gallant and meritorious services during the war." This view shows Sweet in an overcoat with the cape thrown back over his right shoulder. (Donald Wisnoski Collection)

655

HENRY "HARRY" GREENWOOD TAYLOR

Taylor, shown here apparently in a pre-war military school uniform, enlisted in Co. D of the 5th New York on Aug. 7, 1862, and was promoted corporal on Dec. 1, 1862. Taylor was 24 years old, with blue eyes, light hair and complexion, employed as a gold-beater, and had been born in London, England. On May 4, 1863, he was transferred to Co. K of the 146th New York. He was promoted first sergeant on July 29, 1863, then made a second lieutenant and assigned to Co. H Oct. 8, 1864. Promoted again on Feb. 1, 1865, to first lieutenant. Taylor commanded Co. H from Jan. 1865 until muster out. Absent with leave from May 25 to June 1, 1865, to go to Baltimore, MD, "to see my brother who is lying dangerously ill." (USAMHI)

HENRY "HARRY" GREENWOOD TAYLOR

Taylor mustered out with the company on July 17, 1865. On Aug. 22, 1865, he was made a brevet captain to date Apr. 1, 1865, "for gallant and meritorious services at the battle of Five Forks, Va." He was one of the founders and active member of the 5th New York Veterans Association, and served as adjutant for the uniformed drill team. He was still living in New York City in 1882, but in 1914 was living in Fitzgerald, GA. He died at Parker, FL, on Aug. 13, 1921. This tintype of Taylor was made in the field while he was first sergeant of Co. K. Another picture of Taylor appears opposite page 52 in this book. (Richard K. Tibbals Collection)

GEORGE O. TIBBETTS

Tibbets appears here in full Zouave uniform with the long tassel of his fez hanging down past his right shoulder. Tibbetts was 21 years old and had blue eyes, black hair, a dark complexion, and was employed as a jeweler when he enrolled on Aug. 26, 1862, at Rome. He had been born in Rome on Apr. 4, 1841. Appointed fourth sergeant of Co. D on Sept. 2, 1862, and mustered in on Oct. 10, 1862. He was reduced to the ranks on Nov. 21, 1862, but for what reason was not specified. Tibbetts was present with the regiment until Jan./Feb. 1865 when he received a furlough, and the picture most likely taken at this time. He had been promoted corporal on Oct. 10, 1864, and then promoted sergeant on Feb. 4, 1865. Tibbetts was present at every battle the regiment was engaged in and emerged from each unscathed. He mustered out with the regiment on July 16, 1865, near Washington, DC. Tibbetts died at Rome, on Mar. 7, 1913. This image of Tibbetts was made in Rome. (Rome Historical Society Collection)

DAVID TIMMERMAN

This photo shows Timmerman in later years, he is the gentleman with the white moustache on the right. When he enrolled on Aug. 27, 1862, at Deerfield, he was 27 years old and had blue eyes, brown hair, a light complexion, stood 5'10", and was employed as a brakeman. Timmerman was appointed sergeant of Co. F on Sept. 10, 1862, and mustered in on Oct. 10, 1862. He was promoted first sergeant on Feb. 1, 1863. Timmerman was absent sick in Baltimore at Newton University Hospital starting on July 18, 1863. While in that hospital it is noted that, on Sept. 12, Timmerman left the hospital and "yesterday came in at dark without pass, attempted to escape from the officer who arrested him." The charge of being absent without leave was later removed. Sent to Patterson Park Convalescent Hospital in Sept./Oct. 1863. Given a furlough from Oct. 4-19, to visit his home in Utica and "purchase there the uniform and equipments of a 2nd Lieutenant to which rank I have" been promoted. He returned to the regiment in Nov. 1863 and on the 17th of that month, after being tested before a board of examining officers, was promoted second lieutenant and transferred to Co. E, then was transferred to Co. D on Jan. 25, 1864. He received a ten-day-leave of absence on Apr. 4, 1864. Timmerman was wounded on May 12, 1864, at the Battle of Spotsylvania Court House, and admitted to Douglas General Hospital in Washington, DC, on May 15, 1864. He was later sent to the hospital at Annapolis, MD. While away from the regiment, on July 12, 1864, he was transferred to Co. K. Timmerman was discharged for disability on Aug. 10, 1864, at Annapolis. He died on Dec. 31, 1921, at Utica. (Mildred Timmerman Collection)

STIMPSON TURRELL

In this bust view, one can just make out the top loops of the braid (tombeau) of Turrell's Zouave jacket. Turrell, born in Orleans, was an unmarried 27-year-old. He had blue eyes, brown hair, a light complexion, was 5'10½", and employed as a bookkeeper when he enrolled on Sept. 3, 1862, at Paris. He was mustered in as a corporal in Co. K on Oct. 10, 1862, and appointed sergeant on Jan. 31, 1863. Turrell received promotion to sergeant major on May 1, 1863. He survived the carnage at the Wilderness, but on May 8, 1864, at the Battle of Spotsylvania Court House, he suffered a gunshot wound in the chest that fractured several ribs and punctured a lung. His last diary entry made on May 6 reads: "Fighting on our right & left A.M. & P.M. Our regt. Numbers only 220 men & 10 officers. There has been heavy fighting all day, result not known, we still hold our own. Pleasant [weather]. Have changed positions several times during the day, rifle works are being thrown up extensively all along our lines." Turrell was sent to the Second Division Hospital in Alexandria, VA, and died of his wounds on May 20, 1864, at St. Paul's Church Branch Hospital. After his death, the hospital auctioned off his greatcoat, uniform coat, shirt, sash, and four blankets for a total of $8.35. He was buried May 27, 1864. This photo of Turrell was taken on April 21, 1864 (as noted in his diary), less than a month before his death. The image was made by Bogardus in New York City, when Turrell was returning from his furlough that began on April 11, 1864. (Rome Historical Society Collection)

660

WILLIAM J. VIZARD

Vizard appears here in his Veteran Reserve Corps uniform. He enlisted in the 5th New York on Aug. 15, 1862, was 19 years old, 5'7", with blue eyes, red hair, had been born in New York City, and was a clock maker. One of the 325 members of Duryée's Zouaves transferred to the 146th, Vizard was only with the regiment on paper as he had taken ill on Aug. 20, 1862—apparently on the way to join the 5th in the field—and was listed at the General Hospital in Washington, DC, from that time. Shown at Ricord Hospital in Washington, DC, when he received a furlough in Oct. and again from Nov. 5-19, 1864, to visit his home in Wales, MA, where this photograph was taken. A notation states that Vizard was "an attendant at the Hospital" and recommended for furlough "on account of faithful service and good conduct." He was again given a furlough on Mar. 1, 1865, "to enable him to proceed with his wife to Milford Conn. for the purpose of attending the funeral of their sister who died Feby. 28th 1865." Vizard was discharged from the 75th Company of the 21st Battalion of the Veteran Reserve Corps on June 28, 1865. (Patrick A. Schroeder Collection)

CARROLL SCOTT WALDRON

Shown here in full Zouave attire complete with a turban, Waldron saw much service before donning this uniform. His father died on Oct. 1, 1861. Ten days later, he and his brother William, left Nyack and joined the 17th New York Infantry, which their two younger brothers had previously enlisted in. Waldron was 24 years old, with a light complexion, blue eyes, brown hair, and stood 5'8 1/2". He was born in Rockland County, and worked as a carriage maker. Unlike his brothers, Waldron made it through the battle unscathed and was transferred as a private to Co. G of the 146th New York on June 26, 1863. He noted that he drew the Zouave uniform of the regiment on Aug. 15, 1863. Waldron was an excellent carpenter and often detailed to work on carpentry projects. Informed that he was detailed as Brigade Carpenter on Mar. 24, 1864, he declined: "I thought some would think that when the spring campaign was likely to begin, I sought a safer place. And I liked the Regt and all the officers, and the men with whom I was in touch and preferred to take my chances with the boys." He should have taken the duty as he was captured at the Battle of the Wilderness on May 5, 1864. Held at Andersonville, GA, then sent to Florence, SC, where he and a comrade escaped for several days but were eventually recaptured and returned to the stockade. He was paroled and exchanged at Northeast Ferry, NC, on Feb. 26, 1865, and reported at Camp Parole, MD, on Mar. 7 and sent to the hospital suffering from fever. His service had expired while in prison, and was sent on Mar. 18 to New York City to be mustered out, which was finally done there on June 9, 1865. Waldron married after the war and had seventeen children. He moved to Nebraska in 1873, and later retired in Los Angles. There he died on Dec. 28, 1921, at age 85. This picture of Waldron was taken at Bealton Station, VA, on Feb. 20, 1864. (Edmond Cocks Collection)

662

WILLIAM A. WALKER

Shown here as a captain, Walker had enrolled on Aug. 22, 1862, was 21 years old, 5'8", with gray eyes, dark hair, was born in Rome and employed as a jeweler (also given as a watchmaker). He mustered in as first sergeant of Co. B, on Oct. 10, 1862, but was returned to the ranks on Nov. 22, 1862. Walker quickly rose in rank once again being made corporal on Jan. 10, 1863, then sergeant on Feb. 1, 1863, then a second lieutenant in Co. D on Mar. 1, 1863. From May-July 1863, Walker was provost marshal for the 3rd Brigade, 2nd Division, 5th Corps and was in charge of the provost guard. Walker was transferred to Co. E on Aug. 20, 1863, then promoted first lieutenant of Co. C on Oct. 23, 1863. Given a ten-day furlough to visit his home on Dec. 12, 1863. He was shot through both arms, and captured at the Battle of the Wilderness on May 5, 1864. Confined at Staunton, VA, until being sent to Richmond on Sept. 8, then was paroled at Varina, VA, on Sept. 12 and arrived at Camp Parole, MD, two days later. Exchanged in Sept. 1864 while a paroled prisoner of war was given a 20-day leave from Camp Parole starting on Sept. 13, which was extended, as his wounds had not healed. Given a two-day furlough to visit Washington, DC, on Dec. 5, 1864, and returned to duty on Jan. 9, 1865. Walker was on special duty as the ambulance officer for the 1st Brigade, 2nd Division, 5th Corps, but returned to command the company in April. He mustered in as captain on Apr. 1, 1865. Granted leave for ten days in June to go to Rome to visit his "aged mother who is dangerously ill and not expected to recover." Walker mustered out with the regiment on July 16, 1865. Walker was made a brevet major on July 16, 1867 for "gallant and meritorious services during the war" to date from Mar. 13, 1865. He died on Dec. 18, 1911. (Patrick A. Schroeder Collection)

ROBERT PARROTT WARREN

Here Warren is shown in the uniform of the 5th New York, Duryée's Zouaves, which his elder brother Gouverneur commanded. He arrived as a recruit for the regiment on Nov. 18, 1861, and was assigned to Co. G. He was absent with leave on Feb. 27, 1862, and discharged on Mar. 23, 1862. He enrolled on May 30, 1863. He mustered in as a second lieutenant in Co. H on Aug. 14, 1863, then was promoted first lieutenant of Co. K on Nov. 20, 1863. (James Hennessey Collection)

ROBERT PARROTT WARREN

Warren was detached as aide-de-camp for his brother at 2nd Corps headquarters starting Dec. 11, 1863, and in March at 5th Corps headquarters, until Aug. 1864, then on duty as aide-de-camp to General Ayres at 2nd Division, 5th Corps headquarters until June 1865. He was appointed captain on Apr. 24, 1865, to date from Apr. 1, and assigned to Co. H. Warren had also served as a private in Co. F of the 7th New York Militia. Brevetted a captain on Oct. 14, 1865, to date from Mar. 13, 1865 for "gallant and meritorious services at the battle of Chapel House, Va." This same general order appears again on June 22, 1867. Brevetted a major on Aug. 22, 1865, to date from Apr. 1, 1865, "for gallant services at the battle of Five Forks, Va." After the war he served as a first lieutenant in the 24th US Infantry. He died Jan. 14, 1876, while serving as a first lieutenant in the 14th United States Infantry. This photo of Warren was made by Brady and is signed "aide-de-camp." (Rome Historical Society Collection)

GEORGE FORRESTER WILLIAMS

Williams' father charged with the Scots Grays at Waterloo. George was born Mar. 21, 1837, on the Rock of Gibraltar, where his father's regiment was stationed. As a child, George saw much of the world and lived for a time in the East and West Indies, the African Gold Coast. The Williams family ended its travels in Canada. While there, his parents died. At age 13, the orphan arrived in the United States with only three dollars on hand and took up the printing trade—setting type for the New York Times. One evening a fire occurred in the city after the editor went home. Williams did a write up of the story and circulated an early morning extra. This caught the attention of the chief editor, Henry J. Raymond, who then made him part of the reportorial and editorial staff. Williams began to make a name for himself. He covered the spring 1861 events of the Virginia Secession Convention, when the state voted to leave the Union. Williams fled North.

On July 21, 1861, Williams enlisted in the 5th New York, Duryée's Zouaves, being assigned to Co. B. At the time of his enlistment, Williams was 24 years old, stood 6'1", had auburn hair and gray eyes. On Jan. 9, 1862, he was promoted corporal. During the siege of Yorktown, Williams took sick with typhoid fever. This incapacitated him from May 9-18, when he recovered enough to command the guard on the Sanitary Commission steamer *Elm City* at White House Landing. Williams longed to rejoin the regiment, and in late June, encountered Col. G. K. Warren, commander of the brigade, and returned to the unit with him. Williams made it back to the red-legs just in time to participate in the Battle of Gaines' Mill on June 27, 1862, where Williams sustained a wound in the right foot.

666

Williams limped along with his regiment. After reaching the James River, he "hobbled" over to the landing and found Dr. Gibbs who was one of the surgeons aboard the *Elm City*. Gibbs operated on the wound, and then ordered Williams to a berth. Williams began his convalescence in Baltimore, then received a furlough home. Upon recovery, he reported to Maj. Harmon Hull who was in charge of recruiting for the 5th in New York and assisted in that duty from July 23 through Jan. 1863. Williams rejoined the regiment in Feb. 1863, and in March he was detailed as company clerk. Following the Battle of Chancellorsville, on May 4, 1863, he was transferred to Co. G of the 146th, but in June was transferred to Co. B. Later in 1863, he was promoted sergeant. On Jan. 15, 1864, he joined the regimental field and staff as principal musician. Perhaps because of his stature, Williams was appointed color sergeant in April. On May 5, 1864, he grasped the regimental colors as the unit charged across Saunders Field at the Battle of the Wilderness. As the Zouaves advanced, three bullets struck Williams in the first Confederate volley, wounding him in both hips. He fell to the ground immobile. Another member of the color guard grasped the flag and the Zouaves pressed on against the Confederate breastworks. Southern soldiers secured Williams as a prisoner and brought him into their own lines. He was soon paroled, and on June 14, 1864, was admitted to the Third Division Hospital in Alexandria, VA.

Williams was again allowed to return to New York to recover from his injuries. While at home, his term expired and on July 13, 1864. He mustered out of service and took up the role of war correspondent for the New York Times. In the fall of 1864, he covered the campaign of Maj. Gen. Philip Sheridan's Federal troops in the Shenandoah Valley. While Williams was in Washington, DC, President Lincoln asked him to recount the details of the victory at Winchester in Sept., which he did to the President's delight. As he prepared to leave, Lincoln "ordered" him to call again when he returned from the front. Williams assumed the President's invitation to be a mere pleasantry. However, a month later, after the battle of Cedar Creek, Williams was again in Washington and was greeted by the President's secretary, John Hay: "Mr. Lincoln saw you on the Avenue today. He is surprised that you have not come to see him." Williams rushed to the White House.

Lincoln greeted the young reporter: "I am always seeking information and you newspaper men are often behind the scenes at the front [and] I am frequently able to get ideas from you which no one else can give." Lincoln listened to several escapades the correspondent had, then broke in: "What do you think of General Sheridan as an army commander?" Williams gave his favorable opinion. Then Lincoln reflected: "General Grant does seem to be able to pick out the right man for the right place at the right time. He is like that trip hammer I saw the other day . . . always certain in his movements, and always the same." Shortly after the meeting with Lincoln, Williams went to Petersburg to cover the grueling siege. General Grant read an article written by Williams for the *Times* concerning Sheridan's Valley Campaign and enjoyed it so much that he invited the reporter to supper.

Williams managed to get away from the field long enough to marry Marie Sophia Van Brunt on Mar. 29, 1865. In 1867, he traveled to Mexico where he served both as a correspondent and as an aide on the staff of President Juarez. He also witnessed the execution of Emperor Maximilian at Queretaro. In 1868, he was appointed Brigadier General and Chief of Artillery in the Army of Guatemala and later served in the Peruvian Army. From 1870-73 he worked as the managing editor of the New York *Times*, and from 1875-76, he was the managing editor of the New York *Herald*. Later, he acted as the night editor of the New York *World* and the *Recorder*. In 1884, Williams completed his novel *Bullet and Shell*. He also edited the *Memorial War Book*. He fathered three daughters— Harriet Susannah, Marie Sophia, and Anne Grace. By 1915, all of his daughters had died and he and his wife resided in West New Brighton on Staten Island. In Nov. 1920, his wife passed away. The next month, Williams fell sick with pneumonia and died on Dec. 31, 1920, at the Staten Island Hospital (also given as Dec. 29, 1920, at West New Brighton). He was buried in the Moravian Cemetery at New Dorp. (Donald Wisnoski Collection)

THOMAS A. WILSON

Being 40 years and three months old when he enrolled in Co. G at Kirkland (also given as Clinton) on Aug. 25, 1863, Wilson was one of the older men in the regiment. Born in Glasgow, Scotland, and employed as a manufacturer, Wilson stood 5'11½" with blue eyes, brown hair, and a light complexion. He was appointed a sergeant on Sept. 17, 1862, and mustered in as first sergeant of the company on Oct. 10, 1862. Wilson was promoted second lieutenant of Co. E on Dec. 27, 1862, and quickly promoted again to first lieutenant on Jan. 7, 1863. This photo of Wilson shows him shortly after his promotion. His hat is adorned with an ostrich feather and has the numerals "146" in the infantry horn. He also wears an officer's frock coat and sports a full, thick beard. (Michael J. McAfee Collection)

THOMAS A. WILSON

Wilson was present with the regiment until being assigned to do conscript duty at Elmira, on July 20, 1863. He returned to the regiment on Dec. 4, 1863. Wilson was once again promoted, to captain of Co. B by command of Col. Jenkins on Dec. 4, 1863. In Oct. 1864, he temporarily commanded Co. K. He received a furlough for fifteen days on Nov. 17, 1864, "for the purpose of visiting his home in Clinton, NY to settle his Father's business, who recently died." Wilson gave more particulars in his request: "My Father has recently died leaving his business and family in an embarrassing situation. Justice to an afflicted, demands my immediate attention." This photo was taken at J.B. Smith at Marble Block in Utica, after June 1863 as he wears a self-styled, Zouave officer's frock coat with elaborately trimmed cuffs. Wilson is a first lieutenant in the photo, holds a kepi, and has grown as moustache as well as thinned out his beard. The young boy next to Wilson decked out in Zouave attire, and holding a tasseled fez, is assumedly his son. (Patrick A. Schroeder Collection)

THOMAS A. WILSON

Shortly after returning to the regiment, Wilson would join his father. He was wounded in the left leg at the Battle of Five Forks, VA, on Apr. 1, 1865. Following an amputation of the leg (and intermittent fever), he died at the 5th Corps Hospital at City Point, VA, on Apr. 25, 1865. Wilson was brevetted a major then lieutenant colonel "for gallant and meritorious services at the battle of Five Forks, Virginia," dated at the War department on Aug. 22, 1865, and again on June 22, 1867. This photo was probably taken on Wilson's trip home upon the death of his father. It was taken at W. J. Baker's Photographic Studio, 12 Tibbitts' Block in Utica, and has a three-cent tax stamp that is cancelled 1864. He is attired a standard captain's uniform, back to his old hat, and wears a 5th Corps badge on his jacket. Another photo of Wilson as a captain is a bust shot that appears opposite page 110 in this book. (Patrick A. Schroeder Collection)

670

HENRY HERBERT WOODS

Here Woods appears shortly after enlistment in the first uniform of the regiment. He enrolled as a private in Co. C in Utica on Aug. 28, 1862, was 18 years old (some sources say 17), 5'6", with blue eyes, light hair, had been born in England, and did not list an occupation. Woods is shown as absent sick in Utica since Mar. 4, 1863, for which he had a ten-day furlough. He over stayed his furlough and was arrested as a deserter and returned to the army. He was in the division hospital from Apr. 26, 1863. Woods was posted to the Quartermaster's Department of Lieutenant Samuels' detailed men, 2nd Division, Rendezvous of Distribution, Virginia, from Sept. 1863 until Aug. 1864, when he entered Augur Hospital, in Alexandria, on Aug. 27. He was furloughed from the hospital on Dec. 9, 1864, for twenty days to visit his family in Utica. He suffered a gunshot wound at the Battle of White Oak Road on Mar. 31, 1865. The bullet passed through the lower third of his left thigh and exited in the rear, it was noted as "flesh severe." Sent from City Point to Emory Hospital in Washington, DC, on Apr. 4, 1865. Treated with cold water dressing, Wood's wound continued to worsen. He died at 11:00 a.m. on Apr. 25, 1865, of "exhaustion." Noted among his effects were a greatcoat, uniform jackets, a pair of trousers, two flannel shirts, a pair of boots, a diary, gold ring, sundries, and $8.60 in notes. His body was shipped home and buried at Forest Hill Cemetery. (Patrick A. Schroeder Collection)

BENJAMIN FRANKLIN WRIGHT

Wright enrolled, with his brother William, as a private on Sept. 3, 1862, at Paris. He was 22 years old, 5'8", with blue eyes, black hair, light complexion, was born in Utica, and a student at the time of his enlistment. He mustered in as sergeant major on Oct. 10, 1862. Promoted second lieutenant of Co. E on Dec. 27, 1862, and transferred to Co. D on Jan. 7, 1863. Wright jumped to the rank of captain of Co. E on Apr. 4, 1863, to date from Mar. 1, 1863. Broken down on the march to Gettysburg, he arrived in Alexandria by railroad from Manassas Junction on June 22, 1863. He apparently rejoined the regiment, but illness continued to plague him. While in camp at Beverly Ford, he applied for a 20-day leave on account of remittent fever. Wright was sick in a Georgetown hospital starting on Aug. 13, 1863, but had returned to duty a month later. Absent with leave from Feb. 28 to Mar. 18, 1864. He was captured while assisting his wounded brother at the Battle of the Wilderness on May 5, 1864. Wright was confined at Camp Asylum, in Columbia, SC, and while there, was on the list of sick and convalescent prisoners for "Fever & Debility." He was paroled at Northeast Ferry, NC, on Mar. 1, 1865, and arrived at Camp Parole, MD, four days later. Wright was given a 30-day leave of absence starting on Mar. 11, 1865. He was on duty at Camp Parole from Apr. 13 to Apr. 30, 1865, when he was officially exchanged and ordered to the regiment. Wright returned to duty on May 6, 1865. On June 30, 1865, he applied for a 15-day leave to visit his brother, William, who was dangerously ill in Utica. Wright mustered out with the regiment on July 16, 1865, near Washington, DC. Brevetted a major on Oct. 14, 1865, to date from Mar. 13, 1865, "for gallant services during the war." Wright died on Feb. 5, 1905, at St. Paul, MN. (Patrick A. Schroeder Collection)

672

WILLIAM WRIGHT

Shown here as a second lieutenant, Wright enrolled as a private on Sept. 3, 1862, at Paris. He was 23 years old, 5'8 1/2", with black eyes, black hair, was born in Utica, and employed as a bookkeeper. He mustered in as a corporal in Co. K, on Oct. 10, 1862. In Dec. 1862 and Jan. 1863, he was on duty as a clerk at regimental headquarters. Wright was appointed sergeant major on Jan. 31, 1863. At this post he served until being promoted second lieutenant of Co. E on Apr. 26, 1863, and transferred to Co. G on Aug. 14. Wright mustered in as the first lieutenant of Co. E on Oct. 27, 1863. He attempted to resign on Nov. 15, 1863, because his widowed mother's health was failing, "she desires my return home to attend to her wants," and his only other brother, Benjamin, was also serving in the regiment. The request was apparently rejected, as "an officer appointed from the ranks is not entitled to the same privileges as one appointed from civil life." This did not sit well with Wright who wrote the Adjutant General: "For the past fifteen mo[nths] I have been engaged in active service with my regiment in the field, and it is my desire to continue with it but matters at home render me extremely anxious to be there and I earnestly hope that my application may meet with your favorable consideration." (Donald Wisnoski Collection)

673

WILLIAM WRIGHT

On Feb. 7, 1864, Wright requested a ten-day leave of absence to visit his family, when this photo was most likely taken by H. W. Oliver, No. 33 Dominick Street, Rome. He is a first lieutenant and has dark Zouave officer braid above his sleeve cuffs. Made the regimental adjutant on Apr. 24, 1864—a duty he had been doing since July 22, 1863. While falling back with the regiment at the Battle of the Wilderness on May 5, 1864, a bullet shattered Wright's left elbow joint. Weakened by his wound, he fell into a small gully as the fighting continued. His brother, Benjamin F.—captain of Co. E—went to his aid, and as Confederates took aim at the wounded adjutant, Benjamin implored them to hold their fire. A Confederate captain came up to the pair and took them prisoner. With many uninjured prisoners on hand, the Southern captain let the wounded adjutant return to Federal lines, but Benjamin was hauled off as a prisoner of war. Wright's arm was amputated above the elbow. He was in the officers' hospital at Annapolis, MD, and was discharged on Dec. 30, 1864. Wright died on June 9, 1925, at Utica. (Patrick A. Schroeder Collection)

JOHN ZACHER

A pre-war tintype of Johann Zacher. He married Catherine Baeder in Buffalo, on July 3, 1853. They eventually had ten children, and by 1861 had moved to New York City. After serving in the 145th New York, Zacher enlisted in Co. A of the 44th New York on Aug. 30, 1864. When enlisting in the 44th, Zacher was described as being born in Prussia about 1830, with dark hair, dark eyes, and dark complexion, standing 5'9 1/2". He first enlisted as third corporal in Co. G of the 145th New York on Sept. 11, 1862, and before mustering out in Oct. 1863, had been promoted sergeant. He was 33 years old at the time and enlisted at Goshen as a substitute. He was transferred to Co. F of the 146th New York on Oct. 6, 1864. Appointed corporal on Nov. 1, 1864, and he was present with the regiment until mustered out July 16, 1865, near Washington, DC. (Allen Zacher Collection)

JOHN ZACHER

In this post war photograph, Zacher has grown a beard. Army comrade Charles V. Roback testified: "I know that John Zacher had Rheumatism, for on the march from Five Forks to Appomattox he complained of it at different times and I also know that on the march back through the City of Richmond he fell down and had to be conveyed back to camp and also that while we were in camp at Alexandria waiting to be mustered out, he complained of rheumatism at different times." On another occasion Roback stated: "I remember that when we were coming through Richmond, Virginia, on our way home that he was overcome by the heat and fell down and he and others were sent down to Alexandria, Virginia, by boat. I recollect seeing him there. He appeared to be all right again so far as the effects of the heat, but while we were there he complained a good deal of rheumatism." After the war, Zacher and his family moved to Peru, La Salle County, IL, where he worked as a mason and bricklayer. Zacher died Feb. 22, 1871, as a result of rheumatism of the legs (with severe swelling) and heart disease. Zacher apparently died while taking a meal, as when the undertaker Louis Lauber arrived, he found Zacher's "limbs in a swollen condition" and "the deceased was still sitting at table." He is buried at City Cemetery in Peru, IL. (Allen Zacher Collection)

676

UNIDENTIFIED
An unidentified private in Co. A of the 146th New York rests against a column with his company letter and regimental number on his cap. He wears a New York State jacket and sky blue trousers, an early issue to the regiment. This fellow bears considerable similarities to the soldier in full Zouave uniform on the next page. (Richard K. Tiballs Collection)

UNIDENTIFIED

Complete with a bow tie, this seated 146th New York sergeant had his picture taken in the town of Oneida. He wears a white maltese cross representing the 2nd Division of the 5th Corps in which the regiment served. The original image is hand tinted in the colors of the uniform—sky blue pants and jacket with gold trim. His sash is purple (possibly may have been burgundy at one time). The issue sash was red with yellow trim. Perhaps the tinter did not have the proper colors, or the sergeant may be wearing a non-commissioned officers sash. Compare this man with the soldier in the last picture. (Richard K. Tiballs Collection)

UNIDENTIFIED

A full-length view of a clean-shaven 146th New Yorker taken at W. J. Baker's Photographic Studio at 12 Tibbits' Block in Utica in 1865. Adorned with an ever-popular checked shirt, bow tie, and watch fob, this Zouave private was apparently fond of having his "likeness" made. He can also be seen in the next picture. (Mark Shultz Collection)

UNIDENTIFIED

The same soldier as on the previous page appears here, seated in a reverse image. Possibly these photos were taken when the regiment returned to Utica in July 1865. (Fred Fabel III Collection)

FIELD MUSIC

A truly remarkable field photograph of the drummers, fifers, and principal musician of the 146th New York, all in Zouave uniform and a 2nd Division, 5th Corps guidon present. The principal musician is George F. Williams (see p. 666), who stands front and center holding the baton. Three other members can be identified. Starting on the right, the first musician with a drum is Alfred H. Palmer (p. 627), then comes his friend James Shaw (p. 642), also holding a drum. The last fifer on the left is Charles Hecox (p. 582). The fifer next to Hecox clearly wears a white 5th Corps badge. A tinted view of this picture shows most of the musicians wearing red shirts. (Rome Historical Society Collection)

681

EDWARD B. KLUNION

This picture is supposedly of Edward B. Klunion, and a female companion. He sports a 146th New York Zouave jacket and regulation non-commissioned officer's trousers, as well as an overcoat. The mystery is that Klunion never served in the regiment, records show him in the 4th New York Heavy Artillery. As the 146th New York was the only regiment issued this distinctive style Zouave uniform, there are several possibilities for Klunion having the jacket. He may have obtained it in a trade—not an uncommon thing among soldiers. Perhaps he received it from a friend or relative who served in the 146th. Or, possibly he served in the 146th under an alias. Most likely he got the jacket from a friend in the 146th as some soldiers in the 4th Heavies came from the same area of New York. Sergeant Major Stimpson Turrell of the 146th noted in his diary on May 4, 1864: "The 4th N.Y. Heavy Arty. is in our rear. I tried to find it after we halted but could not." Klunion enlisted at age 21 in Co. D of the 4th New York Heavy Artillery on Dec. 26, 1861. He re-enlisted as a veteran volunteer on Dec. 28, 1863. Klunion was wounded on May 19, 1864. He was discharged on May 15, 1865 from McClellan Hospital in Philadelphia. His name was also sometimes borne as Kennion and Kenyon. (Michael J. McAfee Collection)

VETERANS ON LITTLE ROUND TOP

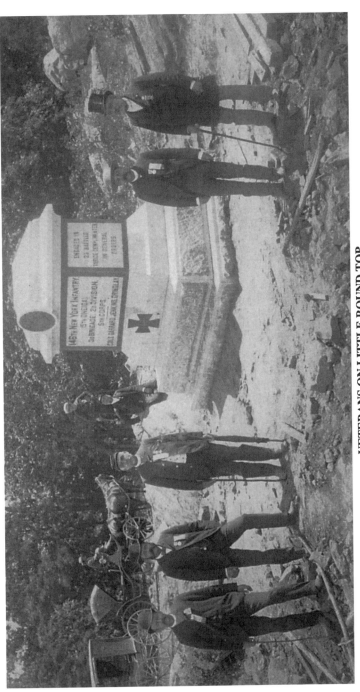

Six veterans of the 146th New York gather around their newly erected monument on Little Round Top at Gettysburg on the ground where the regiment fought on July 2, 1863. This photo was taken by W. H. Tipton, and it shows a carriage waiting in the background and a youth standing on a rock behind an old veteran. On the left is Theodore Dixon (with a cane in his right hand), and next to him is Edward Glover. On the right stands Alva P. Heinstreet (with a cane in his right hand), and next to him is Sylvester O. Cook. The gentleman standing at attention in the center with and umbrella and a cane is believed to be John Comstock, while the fellow behind him sitting on the rock may be William Wilson. Most members of the party wear Grand Army of the Republic ribbons. The photograph was taken circa 1889. (Patrick A. Schroeder Collection)

VETERANS ON LITTLE ROUND TOP

A hazy photo of 146th New York veterans gathered around their monument at Gettysburg. Several of the men are believed to be: Thomas Roberts of Oneida Castle (sitting on the boulder at left); Abram Burgey from Taburg, (standing second from the left, next to the fellow sitting on the boulder); Theodore Dixon from New Hartford (standing fourth on the left with his left leg bowed out. George Mould is the second man to the right of the monument. (Robert L. Mould Collection)

The first reunion of the 146th New York took place on Aug. 5, 1886. One of the topics discussed was erecting a regimental monument at Gettysburg.

Monument at Gettysburg—Beside the permanent organization, one serious purpose was to form plans for the erection of a monument on that part of Little Round Top occupied by the regiment at the battle of Gettysburg. The action of our brigade at this important point, recognized by both Meade and Lee as the key of the critical battle of the war, has been commended by every historian of the fight. That spot will be one of pilgrimage for this and future generations, and it should be commemorated by an enduring monument. The executive committee expected to submit in this pamphlet some definite plan of action for the regiment, and has had one informal meeting for that purpose. Since that meeting they have received an invitation from the New York state board of commissioners on Gettysburg monuments, to co-operate with them so far as this regiment is concerned. So it has been thought best to postpone for a future circular the details which they are unable to give now, and which would delay for some time the publication of these proceedings at the reunion. The whole question of form, situation and cost of a monument, whether the plans of the state committee contemplate a brigade monument, or one for the two New York regiments, or one for each regiment, will, of course, have to govern the conclusions of your committee. Nor have they yet learned what pecuniary aid, if any, can be expected from the state. They do not permit themselves to doubt the cordial and effective action of the regiment upon whatever plan may be approved by it.

684

VETERANS ON LITTLE ROUND TOP

A group of eleven 146th veterans gather around their Gettysburg monument, with the Valley of Death (right) and Devil's Den (left) in the background. Charles Van Vlect is on the far left, with Sylvester O. Cook standing behind him; farthest from the camera stand George Mould (with cane in hand) and seated beside him is most likely Thomas Roberts. The man sitting on the ground to the right of the monument may be Horace N. Miller, while standing next to him is thought to be Amos Phillips of Utica, while Theodore Dixon is probably the second man seated on the rocks to the right. Orvil J. Barker of Oneida may be the gentleman sitting in front of the monument. (Robert L. Mould Collection)

From Alfred Palmer's scrapbook, a newspaper clipping regarding the monument reads, "Oneida county did her share of the fighting at Gettysburg as two splendid regiments fought with the greatest valor on that bloody field—the 97th and the 146th. To-morrow the 97th will unveil their monument on Cemetery Hill and Monday, July 2, the 146th will expose the outlines of the handsome and substantial memorial where the regiment won imperishable renown at Little Round Top. The monument is of the sarcophagus kind, the base of rock-faced granite, the sub-base tool-faced granite, the die polished granite and the cap tool-faced granite. A moulding of cartridges encircles the cap and heightens its appearance. Its elevation is eight feet, its length four feet and width two feet. On the cap is a bronze medallion of the State coat of arms. On the sub-base within a Fifth Corps design is inscribed: '146th, N. Y. Vols.' On other sides are engraved: 'Col. Kenner Girard [sic], Col. David T. Jenkins and Col. James G. Grindley [sic].' 'Here Gen. Weed fell while leading the 3^d Brigade, 2^d Division, 5th Army Corps. From this point Gen. Meade, and his chief-of-staff, Gen. Warren, directed the movements of the Army of the Potomac.' "

"The One Hundred and Forty-sixth Regiment was known as the Fifth Oneida and was recruited in this county in 1862 and left Rome for Washington with 850 men. Col. Kenner Girard [sic] was its first commander, David T. Jenkins succeeded him and James G. Grindley [sic] led it through the Wilderness and took it home. It was one of the best fighting regiments in the Army of the Potomac and suffered severely while endeavoring to occupy Little Round Top. In its jaunty Zouave uniform of light blue it was one of the most conspicuous regiments in the field, and its gallantry in action a familiar theme with the members of the Army of the Potomac. In the terrific fighting in the Wilderness the 146th was very badly cut up."

The actual monument completed in 1889 somewhat differed and reads: **Front**—146th New York Infantry (5th Oneida), 3^d Brigade, 2^d division, 5th Corps, Col.'s Garrard, Jenkins, Grindlay; **Back**—July 2^d and 3^d 1863. Casualties: Killed 4, Wounded 24. **Left side**—From this position Maj. Gen. Meade observed the battle for a time on July 3^d. **Right side**—Engaged in 23 battles, thrice complimented in general orders.

C. A. WILLIAMS, Photo, Gettysburg, Pa.

VETERANS ON LITTLE ROUND TOP

1. John T. Goodfellow, Clinton, N. Y.	9. Horace N. Miller, East Florence, N. Y.	17. George O. Tibbius, Rome, N. Y.	25. George Durant, New Hartford, N. Y.
2. Silas Ervin, Utica, N. Y.	10. Edward Parker, Utica, N. Y.	18. Charles Van Vleet, "	26. Jerome B. Seaman, "
3. Theodore Dixon, New Hartford, N.Y.	11. Alison Dellenbeck, Booneville, N. Y.	19. Amos Phillips, Utica, "	27. James R. Fisk, 317 West 57th St., "
4. Abram Burgey, Taborg, N. Y.	12. Horace Case, Rome, N. Y.	20. William McCormick, Cassville, N. Y.	
5. George Mould, Sauquoit, "	13. S. O. Cook, Booneville, "	21. Daniel Blanchard, Clinton, "	28. George E. Soper, Utica, N. Y.
6. Mrs. Geo. Mould, "	14. Edward Glover, Glenville, "	22. Alva P. Heinstreet, Grant, "	29. Nathaniel Fitch, Boonville, N.Y.
7. Chas. King, Albany Falls, N.Y.	15. William Walker, Sackville, N.Y.	23. Luther Skinner, Camden, "	30. Thomas Roberts, Oneida Castle, N.Y.
8. Orvill J. Barker, Oneida, N. Y.	16. John H. Bailey, Utica, N. Y.	24. Frank J. Miller, Utica, "	31. Isaac Chapman, Westmoreland, "
			32. John Comstock, Plainsburg, N. Y.

Thirty-two veterans of the 146th New York surround their monument on Little Round Top at Gettysburg, possibly during 30th anniversary of the battle. Foliage has grown up around the monument since its erection in 1889. These men garbed in Zouave uniform held this position and helped repulse the assault made by the 4th and 5th Texas advancing towards the crest on July 2, 1863. This photo was taken by C. A. Williams. All the men are numbered and correspondingly identified. (Patrick A. Schroeder Collection)

686

MARY GENEVIE BRAINARD
Mrs. Brainard, in her later years, as she appeared when honored on a reunion ribbon of the 146th New York after completing the book. (Gordon E. Johnson Collection)

INDEX

Gibbs, Capt., 151
Gifford, Harvey, 294
Globe Tavern, 237-38
Glover, Edwin J., **578-79**, 683
Goff, John, 258, 269
Goldsboro, NC, 269, 278
Goose Creek, 129
Gordon's Brigade, 201
Gordon House, 41
Gordonsville, VA, 82, 257, 276
Grace, Harred, 11
Grand Review, 303
Grant, Ulyssess S., 159, 161-65, 168,
172-75, 177, 179-82, 186, 202-3, 205-
7, 213-15, 217-18, 220-21, 232-33,
235-36, 244, 247, 279, 284, 286, 300,
302, 307, 667
Gravelly Run Church, 293
Gray, I. J., 305
Great Dismal Swamp, 222
Great Peedee River, 266, 270, 273
Greeley, Horace, 53
Greensboro, NC, 276
Gregg, David, 144, 250, 279
Gregory, Edgar M., 151, 297
Griffin, Charles, 28, 33-34, 69-70, 73,
77, 86, 161, 179-80, 182, 184, 186,
197, 215-16, 219, 237-38, 240, 244,
246, 250, 280, 282, 288, 293, 296, 302,
573
Grindlay, James, 161, 186, 195, 202,
211, 246, 295, 305-6, 310, **580-81**
Guiney's Station, 208
Gum Spring, 100
Gurley House, 288
Gwyn's Brigade, 280
Hagerstown, MD, 106, 128-29
Hagerstown Road, 107
Hale, Nathan, 264
Halifax Road, 237-38, 250, 254
Hall, Chester, 37
Halleck, Henry W., 6, 15, 25, 47, 244
Hamilton's Crossing, 27, 32
Hammond, Surgeon-General, 61
Hancock, Winfield S., 75, 77, 96, 108-9,
113, 160, 170-71, 173, 177, 180, 207-
8, 212, 217, 232-33, 279
Hanover, PA, 110-11
Hanover Street, 111
Havover Town, 213-14
Harlem, 7
Harper's Ferry, 15, 20, 102
Harrisburg, PA, 102, 104-6, 129
Hartwood Church, 22, 67, 97-99

Hatcher's Run, 247-48, 279, 282, 287-
88, 296
Hayes, Joseph, 183, 219, 238-39, 295
Hazlett, Charles, 112, 119, 555
Hecox, Charles, **582**, 681
Hendricks, Arthur, **583**
Henry, Patrick, 23
Hess, John, **584**
Hicksford, VA, 252, 279
Hill, A. P., 82, 102, 105, 125, 176, 200,
208
Hoffman, J. W., 178
Hood, John B., 284
Hooker, Joseph, 23-24, 27, 32, 34-35,
38, 57, 59, 60, 63, 66, 72-73, 75, 79-
80, 82, 85-86, 96-96, 102, 175
Howard, Oliver O., 30, 60, 80, 96, 108-9
Hubbardsville, NY, *i*
Hubbell, Hon. Alrich, 306, 309
Hudson River Railroad, 9
Humphreys, Andrew, 28, 34-35, 68, 71-
72, 182, 279, 281-82
Humphreys's Division, 35, 77
Hunt, Henry, 168
Hunting Run, 71
Huntington, Honorable B. N., 4
Hyde, Frederick C., **585**
Indiana Units, **19**[th], 107
Irish Brigade, 35
Iron Brigade, 107-8
Jackson, "Stonewall" Thomas, 5, 26, 72,
82-83
Jacob's Mill, 143
James River, 220-21, 223, 225, 232,
236, 242, 287
James Street, 4
Jarratt's Station, 250-51
Jenkins, David T., *i, k*, 3, 32, 40, 74, 80-
81, 87, 93, 119, 124, 132, 135, 139,
141, 150-51, 157, 161-62, 177-83, 185-
86, 190, 196-97, 199, 305, 307, 555,
586
Jenkins, James E., 196-97, 231, **587-89**
Jennison, J. Albert, 39, 194, 243-44,
590-91
Jericho Ford, 207, 210
Jericho Mills, 209, 212
Jerusalem Plank road, 237, 239, 242,
254
Jetersville, 297-98
Jewel, Vern E., **592**
"Johnny Rebs," 16
Johns Street, 306
Johnson, Andrew, 303

694

For a complete book and price list write:

Schroeder Publications
12 Camellia Drive
Daleville, VA 24083
www.civilwar-books.com
e-mail: paspub@rbnet.com

Titles Available:

* **Thirty Myths About Lee's Surrender** by Patrick A. Schroeder
  ISBN 1-889246-05-0

* **More Myths About Lee's Surrender** by Patrick A. Schroeder
  ISBN 1-889246-01-8

* **The Confederate Cemetery at Appomattox** by Patrick A. Schroeder
  ISBN 1-889246-11-5

* **Recollections & Reminiscences of Old Appomattox and Its People**
  by George T. Peers ISBN 1-889246-12-3

* **Tarheels: Five Points in the Record of North Carolina in the Great War
  of 1861-5** by the Committee appointed by the North Carolina literary
  and Historical Society ISBN 1-889246-02-6

* **The Fighting Quakers** by A. J. H. Duganne ISBN 1-889246-03-4

* **A Duryée Zouave** by Thomas P. Southwick ISBN 1-889246-24-7

* **Civil War Soldier Life: In Camp and Battle** by George F. Williams
  ISBN 1-889246-04-2

* **We Came To Fight: The History of the 5th New York Veteran Volunteer
  Infantry, Duryee's Zouaves, (1863-1865)** by Patrick A. Schroeder
  ISBN 1-889246-07-7

* **A Swedish Officer in the American Civil War: The Diary of Axel Leatz of
  the 5th New York Veteran Volunteer Infantry, Duryée's Zouaves,
  (1863-1865)** Edited by Patrick Schroeder ISBN 1-889246-06-9

* **The Bloody 85th: The Letters of Milton McJunkin, A Western Pennsylvania Soldier in the Civil War** Edited by Richard Sauers, Ronn Palm,
  and Patrick A. Schroeder ISBN 1-889246-13-1

* **The Pennsylvania Bucktails: A Photographic Album of the 42nd, 149th &
  150th Pennsylvania Regiments** by Patrick A. Schroeder and Ronn
  Palm ISBN 1-889246-14-X